Passion Is the Gale

On life's vast ocean diversely we sail,
Reason the card, but passion is the gale.
— *Alexander Pope*, An Essay on Man, *Epistle II*

Passion
Is the Gale

Emotion,

Power,

and the

Coming

of the

American

Revolution

NICOLE

EUSTACE

Published for the Omohundro Institute of Early American History and Culture, Williamsburg, Virginia, by the University of North Carolina Press, Chapel Hill

The Omohundro Institute of Early American History and Culture
is sponsored jointly by the College of William and Mary and the
Colonial Williamsburg Foundation. On November 15, 1996, the
Institute adopted the present name in honor of a bequest from
Malvern H. Omohundro, Jr.

Designed by Kimberly Bryant
Set in Arno Pro by Keystone Typesetting, Inc.
Manufactured in the United States of America

Library of Congress Cataloging-in-Publication Data
Eustace, Nicole.
Passion is the gale : emotion, power, and the coming of the
American Revolution / Nicole Eustace.
p. cm.
"Published for the Omohundro Institute of Early American
History and Culture, Williamsburg, Virginia"—T.p. verso.
Includes bibliographical references and index.
ISBN 978-0-8078-3168-7 (cloth : alk. paper)
1. United States—History—Revolution, 1775–1783—Causes.
2. Emotions—Social aspects—United States—History—
18th century.   I. Title.
E210.E96   2008
973.3'11—dc22   2007040049

12 11 10 09 08   5 4 3 2 1

For
James Michael Klancnik, Jr.,
and
James Louis Eustace Klancnik

For
Past, present, and future

Contents

List of Illustrations and Tables

Table

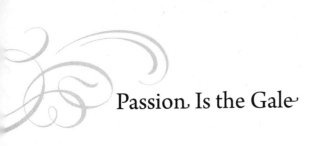

Passion Is the Gale

Introduction

The Rising Tempest

Where should a history of eighteenth-century American emotion begin? We are used to regarding the eighteenth century as the Age of Reason and to seeing the Enlightenment as dependent on the faculty of thought. Indeed, Enlightenment rationalism is generally credited with the defining role in developing theories of natural rights. Reason's conceptual counterpoint, emotion, has seldom garnered the same attention. Though acknowledged as an important element in the Scottish school of moral philosophy, emotion's influence has been thought to reside primarily in the private realm of family, faith, and fiction. So studies of eighteenth-century emotive history have paid close attention to the place of feeling in household functioning, religious awakenings, and literary flowering, but interest has more often waned when the topic has turned to political philosophy or power relations.[1]

Yet, the very man who gave us the catch phrase "the Age of Reason" did so only in 1794, nearly two decades after inciting revolution with a call to "every Man to whom Nature hath given the Power of feeling." That Thomas Paine's 1776 masterpiece *Common Sense* relied explicitly on the notion that the common "passions and feelings of mankind" provided the basis for natural equality and the firmest foundation for natural rights, and that Revolutionary Americans responded so emphatically to this idea, should alert us to a crucial point. Emotion—passion, feeling, sentiment, as it was variously called—contributed as much as reason to the structure of eighteenth-century British-American power and politics.[2]

The conventional view of the dueling nature of reason and emotion—

and of the primacy of the former over the latter—comes to us directly from eighteenth-century commentators. Even essayists in provincial colonial newspapers were apt to declare, as one author did in 1735:

> Reason represents Things to us, not only as they are at present, but as they are in their whole Nature and Tendency. Passion only regards them in the former Light. . . .
>
> Whilst there is a Conflict betwixt . . . Passion and Reason, we must be miserable in Proportion to the Struggle; and when . . . Reason . . . [is] subdued . . . the Happiness we have then, is not the Happiness of our rational Nature, but the Happiness only of the inferior and sensual Part of us.

But focusing too closely on such negative assessments of emotion can blind us to the chance to appreciate how deeply debated such assertions actually were. For every critic of the "sensual," sensate, passionate element of human nature—and of the "inferior" types who allowed themselves to be swayed by such stirrings—we can find adamant defenders of the naturalness and efficacy of emotion.[3]

Consider the views of a young Pennsylvanian named Joseph Shippen who claimed in his commonplace book in 1750:

> All Passions in general are planted in us for excellent Purposes in human Life. Stoical Apathy is not a human Virtue. Agreeable to this Mr. Pope speaks in his Essay on Man, Epist. 2.—viz.
>
> > Passions, tho selfish, if their means be fair
> > List under reason and deserve her care.
> >
> > . . .
> >
> > In lazy apathy let stoics boast,
> > Their virtue fixed, 'tis fixed in a frost,
> > Contracted all, retiring to the breast;
> > But strength of mind is exercise not rest:
> > The rising tempest puts in act the soul,
> > parts it may ravage, but preserves the whole.
> > On life's vast ocean diversely we sail,
> > Reason the card, but passion is the gale.

Shippen regarded the passions as excellent, not inferior, and could turn to the words of the celebrated poet Alexander Pope to support his assertions. He believed that, though reason could provide a "card" (a compass) to steer by, passion alone motivated human actions and drove human decisions. The more we take note of the full range of eighteenth-century commentary on the passions, the more apparent it becomes that positive views abounded. A rising tempest of emotion was sweeping through the Age of Reason.[4]

Assessments of the weight and worth of emotion were fundamental to discussions of human nature and, by extension, to debates about natural equality. Those who derided the passions as inferior to reason often did so in an effort to discredit the emotions of social antagonists. Self-styled members of the elite sought to use emotional critiques to marginalize those they hoped to confine to inferior status. They wished to distinguish their own emotions as refined feelings while deriding the emotions of the lower orders as base passions. Conversely, when commentators like Pope and Paine insisted that the propensity for passion was universal—inevitable, invariable, and even desirable in all people—they paved the way for a new understanding of the fundamental commonalities of human nature, irrespective of artificial social divides. Passion thus mattered as much to politics and political philosophy as it did to domestic life.

Still, a shift toward appreciation of the power implications of eighteenth-century emotion should not distract us from considering the influence of emotion on everyday life. Where scholars have begun to explore the political import of passions, they have too often neglected the evidence of ordinary expression in favor of exclusive examination of the ideas unveiled in cultural productions, from philosophical treatises to poetry and novels. In fact, for every deliberative entry added to a commonplace book, people like Joseph Shippen made countless daily decisions about when, whether, and how to voice their own emotions.[5]

When we turn our gaze from Shippen's literary interests to his living interactions, we find him equally absorbed in the issue of emotion. For example, in a letter to his father at about the same time he was compiling his commonplace quotations, Shippen declared:

> The sincere concern, which I am very sensible you have ever had on my Account, . . . ought to fill me with the highest sense of Gratitude and Esteem . . . Your wholesome Advice . . . I hope I shall enjoy a true Relish of . . . by following it with the readyest Chearfulness.

The modern observer cannot ignore the intensive work of regulation the letter undertakes. Shippen did not so much express feeling for his father as demonstrate a thorough knowledge of the emotions he "ought" to

FIGURE 1. Joseph Shippen.
By Benjamin West. Shippen-
Balch Papers, Historical
Society of Pennsylvania.
*Permission The Historical
Society of Pennsylvania*
*Shippen's claims to social
authority are buttressed by
visual reference to his mastery
of both ancient learning and
modern literature.*

experience and "hope[d]" to act on. Still a student at this letter's writing, Shippen could ill afford to voice anything but grateful esteem and cheerful obedience to the father on whom his life's prospects depended. His careful self-censorship reveals the social stakes of emotional expression; in addressing himself to his father Shippen had to consider the potential of emotion to challenge or affirm his father's authority and thus to define his relative status in their relationship. Thus, the scrutiny of actual emotional exchanges—in addition to the study of abstract philosophical pronouncements—offers an important reminder. If the history of emotion cannot and should not be separated from the analysis of politics and political philosophy, no more should analysis of ordinary expression be divorced from issues of power and authority.[6]

By collapsing distinctions between the personal and the political, by locating the history of emotion in records of daily expression and philosophical speculation alike, this study both provides perspective on the role of emotion in the articulation of eighteenth-century social and political philosophy and offers new insight into how ordinary people tested and contested such theories in the course of their daily lives. Taking the position that expressions of emotion constituted declarations of status, this work analyzes emotional language as a key form of social communication. From fathers and sons to husbands and wives, from magistrates and commoners to masters, servants, and slaves, every exchange of emotion offered implicit commentary on the state of social relations. For example, the master who posted a newspaper ad for a runaway "Irish Servant Woman" named Eleanor Ferrall, by describing her as "red faced . . . very talkative, subject to Passion, and easily offended," surely intended nothing flattering by his depiction. Yet Ferrall herself evidently appreciated the way a display of passion could convey defiance of her master's disrespect. When eighteenth-century actors decided whether to express their emotions as well as how to describe the emotions of others, they either confirmed or contested prevailing assumptions about the terms of social organization. Tracing historical patterns in who expressed what emotions when and to whom, and in how the emotions of various groups of people were conventionally categorized, can both reveal local struggles over status and actually unveil the changing social assumptions of the larger polity.[7]

If the history of colonial British-American emotion challenges traditional divisions between reason and passion as well as between public and private, it also prompts fresh recognition of certain cultural distinctions. To date, European perspectives have dominated the history of emotion in the eighteenth century. Scholars who look to literature for historical evidence of emotion have relied, of necessity, almost entirely on European output (no novels were written on American soil until 1789). As an unintended consequence, it has been difficult to consider particular American emotional streams within broader transatlantic cultural currents. To be sure, as Joseph Shippen's engagement with Alexander Pope indicates, we cannot begin to understand the attitudes toward emotion evinced in colonial British America without reference to European writers—especially English and Scottish. Still, we err just as gravely if we simply assume that the productions of the London stage or the Glasgow lecture hall can be taken to represent *the* ideas and attitudes of denizens of the British Empire on both sides of the Atlantic. On the contrary, even when colonists read European authors, they always did so in the context of their own concerns.

Emotion played a key part in the colonial milieu. Though part of the appeal of colonial settlement lay in its potential to *unsettle* long-standing social, cultural, and political formations, the resulting instability could also cause consternation. Much as colonists throughout British North America appreciated the individual opportunities available to them in fledgling societies, they also faced difficult questions about how to sustain coherent communities. The privileging of personal passion had the potential to promote the expansion of the individual self; but, conversely, sociable feelings might bind people together in a new degree of sensus communis. Exactly because it held such transformative potential, to alternately advance individualism or cement social ties, emotion became an intense focus of personal assertion and political debate alike.

What is more, inhabitants of British America who sought to situate their social position (and implicitly to articulate their political vision) through expressions of emotion found themselves faced with complicated tasks of triangulation. Wish though they might to assert their full membership in the British Empire, colonists frequently found themselves placed at the literal and figurative periphery of British life, their attempts to master the emotional subtleties of British-style gentility ignored or even mocked by those in the metropolis. At the same time, proximity to the challenging presence of autonomous Indian nations augmented anxieties over civility, about the emotional comportment that should characterize the civilized even in the midst of a "savage wilderness." Meanwhile, the stakes of emotion were heightened still further by early associations between the capacity for emotion and the passion for liberty. That is, emotional freedom became symbolically linked to legal standing as a free person, a proposition with significance for everything from the slave system to revolutionary rhetoric.

Such status concerns were endemic to the colonial situation, in which a geographically and socially mobile population of Europeans, Africans, and native Americans, with a variety of languages and from diverse religious traditions, made easy agreement on the meaning and morality of emotion difficult to achieve. As one local observer put it, summing up the state of colonial emotional dilemmas:

> We are a people, thrown together from various Quarters of the World, differing in all Things—Language, Manners, and Sentiment. . . . LIB-ERTY never deigns to dwell but with a prudent, a sensible and a manly People. Our general Character is, I fear, too much the Reverse. We either grovel beneath the true Spirit of *Freedom*; or, if we aim at

Spirit, we are born by a sullen ferocity to the other Extreme. We are
yet too much Strangers to that rational Medium, which is founded on
a more enlarged and refined Turn of Sentiment.

Without denying the transatlantic component of eighteenth-century
American emotional culture, we must remain alert to the special problems of negotiating passion in North America. Balancing the sometimes
opposing emotional qualities associated with gentility, respectability, civility, liberty, and (as this passage hints) masculinity could prove uniquely
challenging in the colonial context.[8]

In order to investigate such issues closely, while drawing meaning-
ful comparisons across public and private realms, this study focuses on
the history of emotion in a single British-American colony: eighteenth-
century Pennsylvania. Though frequently referred to as a "peaceable
kingdom," Pennsylvania actually endured acute social and cultural tensions. As a proprietary colony with a strong tradition of assertive representative assemblies, Pennsylvania offered its inhabitants a combustible
mix of aristocratic and democratic models of society and politics. Quakers had long dominated the colonial Assembly, aided by their alliance
with the colony's many German Pietists. But, by midcentury, the colony's
leading Anglicans had set up a rival camp centered on the proprietors and
their governors, intermittently supported by the colony's growing numbers of Scots-Irish Presbyterians. Coalescing into opposing proprietary
and Assembly-led factions, Pennsylvania colonists enjoyed little consensus regarding the worth of emotion, much less agreement about the kind
of society they hoped to create. Yet, living in and around Philadelphia,
British America's largest and most cosmopolitan port city, they did share
a conviction that their colony was maturing and had earned the right to a
prominent place within the British Empire.[9]

Meanwhile, Pennsylvania colonists' emotional politics were shaped by
contact and conflict with many other groups in their midst. For example,
the traditions of pacifism begun by William Penn brought the European
inhabitants of the colony into closer daily interaction with Indians than in
perhaps any other British-American colony. The resulting familiarity and
accompanying competition made it both more difficult and more culturally urgent for colonists to try to delineate the distinguishing emotions of
civilization. Furthermore, by midcentury, Pennsylvania was rapidly growing into a slave society, with as many as 20 percent of household heads
relying on enslaved labor in the countryside and even higher concen-

trations of enslaved Africans working in urban Philadelphia. Questions about the innate differences—or inherent similarities—in the emotions of the free and the unfree took on added urgency in such a context.[10]

If questions about the problems and possibilities of emotion troubled people on both sides of the Atlantic and up and down the coast of British North America, explicit debates reached a fever pitch in Pennsylvania, where the sheer number and intensity of competing viewpoints pushed the issue to the fore. To illuminate the widest possible range of theoretical debates and actual exchanges, this study draws on a diverse array of sources. Chronologically, it centers on the heart of the century, from the 1740s through the 1770s, when colonial ideas about emotion would be tested and ultimately transformed. Collections of family papers at the Historical Society of Pennsylvania and the Haverford College Quaker Collection yield many hundreds of letters, diaries, and commonplace books, with material on emotion featured in exchanges among family, friends, and business correspondents. Manuscript evidence is then bolstered by research in printed sources, which provide information on the public expression and discussion of emotion. Thus, five decades of the *Pennsylvania Gazette,* from the 1720s through the 1770s, generate examples of the shifting terms of popular conversations about emotion while also allowing a glimpse of the lives of middling and lower colonists (a vantage point often more difficult to find in private papers). Indeed, in the absence of any detailed court records for colonial Pennsylvania, the paper's mix of news reports, popular poems and stories, advertisements, and letters from contributors becomes one of the best-recorded sources of the emotional attitudes and interactions of ordinary folk. Meanwhile, the *Minutes of the Provincial Council of Pennsylvania* for 1754–1776 (that is, from the start of the Seven Years War through the Declaration of Independence) provides insight into the role of emotion in political negotiations, from local governance to transatlantic administration and to diplomatic relations between European and native American nations. Finally, political pamphlets and published sermons printed in midcentury Pennsylvania allow a new appreciation of the role of the rhetoric of emotion in public movements in the critical years at the close of the colonial period.

Having questioned where a history of eighteenth-century Anglo-American emotion should begin, it remains to be asked where such a study might lead. This book opens an interdisciplinary conversation about the sources and methods that can best contribute to scholarly understanding of emotion while also adding to our historical knowledge of colonial British America. In the end, these two aims add up to more than the sum of their parts; setting a study of emotion in the eighteenth century can contribute to our appreciation of emotion as a universal human attribute that nonetheless takes on distinctive meanings in culturally and historically specific contexts. At the same time, the study of emotion, and especially of the ways in which it was defined, discussed, and expressed, can help us to grasp more fully the fundamental social assumptions and daily social negotiations that collectively structured eighteenth-century British America.

The historical approach to scholarship on emotion makes its theoretical contribution by highlighting the interplay of change and stasis in human emotion, for the very kinds of questions about the particularity or universality of emotion that so troubled eighteenth-century observers still bedevil modern scholars. History can intervene in running debates between contemporary scholars of "universalist" and "constructionist" orientations, who have staked out sharply opposing views on the constancy of human emotional capacities across time and space. Theorists who argue for the universality of emotion claim that the experience of emotion is a neurochemical process common to all human beings in every age. By contrast, those who argue from the vantage point of constructionism counter that emotions can be created only through discourse. Feelings must be filtered through language, which is highly culturally specific. A historical approach can eschew such extremes.[11]

One of the first scholars to advance such a hybrid perspective was the historian William Reddy. Reddy asserts that feelings are universal; it is their descriptors that vary across time and culture. There is a space between subjectivity and expressivity, that is, between the initial feeling of emotion and the subsequent application of linguistic descriptors to it. The distinctions between this formulation and the strict constructionist stance are important. For, if all people have the potential to *feel* the same emotions, then patterns in who expresses what and when and to whom assume real political significance. As Reddy so succinctly puts it, "Emotional control is the real site of the exercise of power: politics is just a process of determining who must repress as illegitimate, who must foreground as valuable, the feelings that come up for them in given contexts and relationships." To study emotional expression, then, is necessarily to investigate power relations.[12]

My attention to the historical element of emotion, to the changing

ways in which emotion was subjectively verbalized and socially categorized, highlights the practical and theoretical utility of combining biological and cultural approaches. On the one hand, we are able to analyze
eighteenth-century emotion today only because of the existence of a
shared physiology of feeling that stretches over the centuries. On the other
hand, we cannot simply assume that eighteenth-century emotional expression can now be understood transparently and without translation. In
fact, the very meaning of many terms of emotion changed discernibly
from the eighteenth century to today. (This point is detailed in the discussion of eighteenth-century Anglo-American words for the concept of
"emotion" featured in the Appendix.) Moreover, the conditions in which
emotional exchanges were conducted have also changed dramatically.[13]

The historical perspective especially accords with anthropological approaches when it comes to questions about the shifting nature of the self.
Much of modern psychologically oriented theorizing about emotion pre-
supposes that each party to an emotional exchange brings to the interaction a stable and autonomous identity that can be expressed or repressed, but not fundamentally altered, by the act of emoting. Yet such a
model proves utterly inadequate to understanding how emotion functioned in the eighteenth century. The mid-eighteenth century was a
transitional period in which traditional communal visions of the self as
created through social relations coexisted and competed with modern
individualized notions of the self as autonomous and independent of
social roles. Because eighteenth-century actors could not yet conceive of
a self entirely separate from the social order, their expressions of emotion
could never be entirely personal. Rather, they were inherently relational.
The subject of this study, then, is not the internal *experience* of emotion,
but rather the external *expression* of emotion through language. Refining
William Reddy's analysis, I document that eighteenth-century expressions of emotion inevitably served as the vector for social communication, for the assertion and contestation of status, never simply for the
outer realization of inner consciousness.[14]

At the same time, a historical view of emotion proves equally unsup-
portive of a strict constructionist approach to discourse. No notion of
culture as a closed system, in which social actors are irreducibly constrained by the language with which they seek to articulate feeling, can
stand up to the reality of the eighteenth-century Atlantic world. In British
America, myriad languages and emotional styles mixed and remixed in

innovative and unpredictable ways, producing new opportunities for consciousness as well as for culture. My work shows how emotional competition and contestation among various groups can allow for advances in the political potential of emotion.

Substantively, then, this study focuses on emotional exchanges, revealing emotion's cultural and political significance in eighteenth-century British America through scrutiny of social interactions. In the early decades of the century, Pennsylvanians indeed looked to Europe for their ideas about emotion. Yet, from the very beginning, the works they preferred revealed local peculiarities. In particular, colonists were drawn to the ideas of Alexander Pope, whose singular poem *An Essay on Man* offered a far more emphatically positive view of the passions than nearly any other philosophical work. A preliminary chapter describes the transatlantic context of Pennsylvania's passion debates, focusing on the American reception of Pope's *Essay*, from the 1730s, when it was imported by learned elites, through the 1760s and 1770s, when it was printed locally in inexpensive popular editions. Pope's ideas proved pivotal, over the course of this period, to increasing acceptance of the legitimacy of personal passions and to expanding belief in the universality of human emotional attributes.

Subsequent chapters then explore specific dilemmas of emotional expression and control common to the colonial condition. Unlike other marks of rank associated with eighteenth-century British America (such as those encoded in styles of dress and other forms of consumption), articulations of emotion gave unmatched flexibility and immediacy to moments of social assertion. That is, expressions of emotion not only conveyed information about global status claims in the world at large but also could create and communicate microhierarchies in unfolding dialogues between particular people. Chapters devoted to the explication of central emotions—selected for the notable frequency of their appearance in primary sources—include one each on love, anger, sympathy, and grief. These chapters offer close semantic analysis of the vocabulary of emotion employed by Pennsylvanians and give careful attention to recurring motifs in utterance and attribution. Linguistic decisions, such as whether to express and discuss anger as unbridled "rage" or as measured "resentment," about whether to share feeling in the form of benevolent "mercy" or of judgmental "pity," allowed not just for the imposition of power but also for subtle negotiations, even unmistakable stands of resistance. Pennsylvanians expended considerable effort deciding how to describe their own emotions and those of others according to the social ranks and relations they wished to establish.[15]

At moments of public crisis, the cultural disputes and social confrontations over the expression of emotion that were ever simmering in the colonial context took on heightened strategic significance. Chapters devoted to key political turning points, including the Seven Years War of 1754–1763, the Paxton crisis of 1764, and the revolutionary protest movement from the Stamp Act of 1765 to the Declaration of Independence of 1776, explore the role of emotional rhetoric in civic debates. Emotion served vital political purposes: in contests between Quaker pacifists opposed to anger and proarmament Anglicans and Presbyterians convinced of the crucial links between passion and action during the Seven Years War period; in questions about the connections between inhumanity, insensibility, and cultural or racial proclivities that swirled around Indians, frontier commoners, and elite critics after the Christian Indian massacres at Paxton; and in mass demonstrations of the spirit of liberty that revolutionary protesters claimed as evidence of their natural right to freedom. As a Postlude devoted to describing and documenting the Pennsylvania origins of Thomas Paine's *Common Sense* makes clear, Pennsylvanians' deliberations from the Seven Years War through the Revolution helped shape the emergence of emotional language as the lingua franca of Revolutionary American political culture.

Attention to emotion reveals colonial British America as a society in flux, where individual and communal models of the self overlapped, personal passions and sociable sentiments could have contradictory implications for the growth of individualism or the promotion of communalism, and the universal presence or differential prevalence of human attributes remained open to debate. Elite efforts to discriminate between the sociable feelings of the genteel and the selfish passions of the masses, the better to fix supposedly natural divisions in the social order, foundered in the face of mounting arguments that all emotions were naturally universally pervasive. Because of emotion's eighteenth-century links to developing moral sense philosophy and awakened Christianity, the marking of social divisions on the basis of emotional difference had the seeming potential to cloak social dominance in moral probity. However, elite attempts to lay exclusive claim to refined emotions (while denying a propensity for base ones) could not be sustained in the course of ordinary social interactions.

Instead, emotional exchanges revealed the underlying commonality of human potential across artificial status divides.

The study of emotion thus exposes the centrality of hierarchical notions of rank and authority to eighteenth-century understandings of society while confirming how fragile and contingent such status divisions truly were. Indeed, though members of eighteenth-century colonial elites initially turned to emotion in search of a reliable *mark of exclusivity,* they could not hinder emotion's eventual emergence as a key element of *natural equality.* Thomas Paine's invocation of "the passions and feelings of mankind" announced a new vision of society, in which the natural equality of all would be acknowledged and increased opportunities for personal advancement would augment, not undermine, devotion to the nascent community. Having had numerous occasions to test such ideals in the course of daily emotional exchanges over the preceding decades, Revolutionary Americans were uniquely prepared to embrace Paine's radical stance.

To argue that emotion was central to Paine's revolutionary philosophy is not to say that an emphasis on emotion would always have progressive implications. Indeed, as demonstrated by today's scholarly debates, the question whether emotion is universal has never been finally decided. Moreover, efforts to differentiate between desirable and risible emotions continued to be a potent weapon of social division through the nineteenth century. We cannot forget that even Paine, the man who launched the loudest and best-heard plea for recognition of the passions and feelings common to all mankind, eventually gave up emphasizing emotion in favor of commemorating the eighteenth century as "the Age of Reason." Part of the work of this project, then, is to attempt to understand the limitations as well as the possibilities of emotion as a medium for social and political innovation. Still, if we ignore the prominent place of passion in the eighteenth century, we miss the chance to appreciate the standpoint of the countless colonists like Joseph Shippen, who used the adage, "Passion is the gale," to argue that emotion had a potent part to play in the reordering of Anglo-American life. If Pennsylvania began as a point of reception for the writings of Europeans like Alexander Pope, it emerged by century's end as an original site of production for a new American emotional culture, one with revolutionary—if never fully realized—social and political potential.

Better for Us, perhaps, it might appear,
Were there all harmony, all virtue here;
That never air or ocean felt the wind;
That never passion discompos'd the mind:
But ALL subsists by universal strife;
And Passions are the elements of Life.
—Alexander Pope,
An Essay on Man, Epistle I, 165–170

I

"Passions Rous'd in Virtue's Cause"

Debating the Passions with Alexander Pope, 1735–1776

When a small, select group of Pennsylvanians gathered at the behest of Benjamin Franklin to form the Library Company of Philadelphia in 1731, they believed that much more than personal amusement or even literary advancement was at stake. As they explained to proprietor Thomas Penn, they intended their members-only lending library (the first of its kind in the colonies) to help Philadelphia become the "future Athens of America" while allowing "her Sons [to] arise, qualified with Learning, Virtue, and Politeness for the most important offices of Life!" Enamored of an emerging eighteenth-century transatlantic culture of politeness, Pennsylvania colonists nevertheless remained divided about how best to pursue virtue in the colonial context. Classical conceptions of virtue had called for stoic self-sacrifice in the interest of the common good, but newer philosophical fashions hinted that personal passions might well serve social as well as selfish ends. Among eighteenth-century Pennsylvanians at least as eager to ensconce themselves in "the most important offices of life" as to see their colony accorded a place alongside Athens, pure self-sacrifice was unpalatable. They wanted, instead, to balance the interests of self and society, to pursue personal progress while promoting communal constancy. An innovative means of straddling such extremes was soon to be proposed by Alexander Pope in his 1733 poem, *An Essay on Man*. Not surprisingly, the aspiring members of the Library Company lost little time in importing a copy for their collection.[1]

With his *Essay on Man*, Pope claimed to have arrived at a solution to the question of how to reconcile civic virtue and personal passion. He

17

announced in a preface to prospective readers of the book-length work that "the science of Human Nature" could be "reduced to a *few clear points*." With words that would resound with Pennsylvania readers, he declared, "If I could flatter myself that this Essay has any merit, it is in steering between doctrines seemingly opposite . . . and in forming out of all a *temperate* yet not *inconsistent,* and a *short* yet not *imperfect* system of Ethics." What "doctrines" did Pope's poem promise to steer between? His *Essay* asserted that, while reason could play important functions, passions were "universal" and socially useful "elements of Life." Meanwhile, his claim that "Self-love and Social be the same" offered the enticing prospect that proper emotional modulation could reconcile the competing claims of individual ambition and social cohesion.[2]

Alerted by returning travelers from abroad that a new essay by the illustrious English translator of Homer's *Iliad* and *Odyssey* was the talk of London, members of the Library Company moved quickly to obtain the *Essay on Man,* taking receipt of first-edition copies of the poem by April 1735. Thus began Pennsylvania's engagement with Pope's *Essay,* a passionate interest that would stretch over decades. From that first copy to arrive in Philadelphia to the edition of Pope's collected works offered for sale by Franklin's partner in the printing business, David Hall, in 1774, Pope's *Essay on Man* featured in Pennsylvania importers' advertisements and booksellers' catalogs more than two dozen times in the forty-odd years between the publication of the *Essay* and the onset of the American Revolution. So great was Pennsylvanians' interest in Pope's *Essay* that it was eventually not only imported but also published in the colony itself, going through three editions in thirteen years, one in 1747 and two in 1760. Few other English works could claim such popularity. That fact begs an important question: why did Pennsylvanians respond so emphatically to Pope?[3]

There was something singular about the pull of Pope's *Essay on Man* in the colonies. Of course, part of the *Essay*'s success simply sprang from an ever-growing interest in European literature and philosophy among colonists as well as from the rapid general development of colonial print culture. Pope's work shared shelf space with numerous other eighteenth-century literary giants: moral philosophers like David Hume, Francis Hutcheson, John Locke, the earl of Shaftsbury, and Adam Smith; novelists like Henry Fielding and Samuel Richardson; and satirists and dramatists like Joseph Addison, Richard Steele, and Jonathan Swift. Yet, unlike writers in the Stoic tradition who urged the avoidance of all emotion, or the latest moral philosophers who encouraged emotion only in the service of others, Pope offered people an out. He urged them to embrace their own passions fully, secure in the belief that emotions were as natural and irreducible as the very elements of life.[4]

Pope's emphatic endorsement of the passions spoke strongly to colonists struggling to find a way to advance self and society simultaneously. With a reputation as the "best poor man's country" where people could enjoy unprecedented degrees of religious freedom and democratic government, Pennsylvania promised its inhabitants myriad new social, political, and economic opportunities. What is more, Philadelphia's position as a premier colonial port city gave it access to the constant transatlantic transportation of people, goods, and ideas, which gave Pennsylvania colonists an expansive sense of possibility and mobility. Reflecting such hopes, Library Company members declared to Penn their conviction that the colony's moment had arrived. Though well aware that "when Colonies are in their Infancy, the Refinements of Life . . . cannot be much attended to," members believed that Pennsylvania was at last ready for refinement.[5]

Yet fluidity could also foster an atmosphere of uncertainty. Founded by Quakers on the principle of religious liberty, the colony's very openness provided wide doorways for divisiveness. By the middle of the eighteenth century, restive coteries of Anglicans and Presbyterians began to challenge Quakers' long-standing social and political dominance. The emerging elite of all religious persuasions remained eager to have their social position validated by their British peers. Meanwhile, of course, the ranks of the would-be colonial elite remained ever indistinct, vulnerable to repeated challenges and incursions. People could never be sure precisely where they stood vis-à-vis their fellow colonists or the countrymen they had left behind. At a time that might have been highly conducive to the emergence of individualism, most Pennsylvanians remained preoccupied with establishing communities and defining their position within them.

Ultimately, then, colonists' desires for self-advancement coexisted uneasily with a wish for social stability, since individual shifts in status threatened to create aggregate social flux. In light of this dilemma, emotion had the paradoxical potential to strengthen (or threaten) self and society simultaneously, depending on whether it was turned inward or outward. Pope's *Essay on Man* resonated so strongly with colonists because it seemed to offer a solution to this conundrum.

By declaring self-love and social to be the same, Pope provided an apparent rationale for the pursuit of self-advancement as an avenue to social good. Taken up first by elite members of the Library Company, many of them Anglican and Presbyterian rivals of establishment Quakers, over the ensuing decades the poem touched wider and wider circles of ambitious colonists. Elite Company members wished to consolidate their claims to refinement and their consequent right to fill "important offices"; nevertheless, an ever-expanding range of Pennsylvania readers embraced the poem as their own. In so doing, they evinced their interest in passion and the pursuit of self-love. While Company members had initially imported Pope as part of an effort to assert their mature status as full partners in the British Empire, the reading of Pope in Pennsylvania came in response to uniquely colonial anxieties and opportunities. Passion's volatility meshed well with colonial conditions of social mobility.

The goal of this chapter is to explore the debates on the passions that Pope's poem helped provoke, to chart the ways in which ever-widening circles of Pennsylvanians made use of the poem, and, finally, to sketch how positive views of the passions influenced five tumultuous decades of religious and political upheaval. Positions on passion and the pursuit of self-love helped to define key debates on everything from the morality of slavery to the defensibility of war. Many of these topics are developed in greater depth later in this book. The present chapter offers an overview of issues and events as well as a chance to underscore their transatlantic cultural context. Subsequent chapters deal more broadly with other categories of emotion (including affections, feelings, and sentiments) as well as more specifically with particular varieties of emotion (including love, anger, sympathy, and grief); this chapter focuses on the passions.

Passion, because of its highly particular relation to the self, was the most vexed and contested of all emotional categories. Fundamentally, "passion" could be defined as "a fit or mood marked by stress of feeling or abandonment to emotion; a transport of excited feeling." The sense of abandonment carries with it the idea that passions involved selfish capitulation to the will, a flouting of all social and self-restraint—qualities that had traditionally led to associating passion with sin. Still, passion could also be linked with positive attributes—action, movement, "transport"—and therein lay its dormant attraction for colonial British Americans. Over the course of the eighteenth century, many eventually became enamored of the idea that, because of its intrinsic connection to human will, passion alone, of all varieties of emotion, could confer the socially useful power of action. And many Pennsylvanians adopted Pope as passion's spokesman.[6]

To appreciate the stir Pope's position on passion caused among colonists and to understand the contentious contemporary questions his poem helped them to confront requires investigation of the response of readers to *An Essay on Man*. Fortunately, colonial Pennsylvanians made casual private references to Pope almost as frequently as they published advertisements for his work. At least two dozen references to Pope, from almost as many individuals, survive in the letters, diaries, and other writings of colonial Pennsylvanians, and half of them mention, either directly or implicitly, *An Essay on Man*. Listening in on Pennsylvanians' discussions of Pope, peering over readers' shoulders as they made marginal notes on the poem can allow us to see how colonists called on his promise to steer a virtuous path between extremes, how they sought to use the passions to articulate and negotiate the ideal relationship between self and society. Taken together, the central decades of the eighteenth century might well be called "the era of the passion question," when concerns about the optimal development of personal passions became a matter of the most pressing public importance.[7]

The 1730s: Logan and Franklin on Presumptuous Men and Poison Fruit

Colonial Pennsylvanians could not get enough of Pope. As Benjamin Franklin remarked to one London bookseller, "Everything, good or bad, that makes a noise [in London] . . . has a run" in Philadelphia. Of Pope specifically, he added, "That Poet has many Admirers here, and the Reflection he somewhere casts on the Plantations . . . is injurious." Concerned that an author like Pope would cast reflections on colonials and criticize them for having provincial literary tastes, Franklin declared, "Your authors know but little of the Fame they have on this Side [of] the Ocean." At a moment when the members of an emerging local elite saw their colony as approaching maturation, nothing could prove to a British audience that they had come of age like a sophisticated appreciation of the most up-to-date works of European language and literature.[8]

Regardless of how they sought to position themselves, Pennsylvanians could not escape the distinct coordinates that defined their social, cultural, and political place in the transatlantic system. Their location was marked not only by their distance from London markets, by their central spot on the eastern coast of British North America, and by their proximity to a western hinterland but also by the diverse ethnic and religious origins of the colony's inhabitants. The competing viewpoints various groups brought to questions about emotion and virtue ensured that Pennsylvania debates on the topic would be contentious. Any consensus would have to incorporate diverse influences. Eager though they might have been to demonstrate that they appreciated Pope's work as well as any Englishman living on the other "Side [of] the Ocean," colonists could not but develop distinctive reactions to Pope's teachings on the passions as put forth in *An Essay on Man*.

Try as they might, Pennsylvanians could never read Pope on exactly the same terms as Englishmen did at home. For Pope's praise of passions ran counter to the settled opinions of the colony's traditional Quaker elite. At a time when restive members of rising Anglican and Presbyterian factions had begun to agitate for influence, Pope's teachings appeared simultaneously more dangerous and more desirable than they otherwise would have.

The best way to appreciate what so attracted many Pennsylvanians to Pope's *Essay* may be to consider what made it repulsive to one of its first colonial readers, prominent Philadelphia Quaker James Logan. Mayor of Philadelphia in the 1720s and acting governor of the colony itself in the 1730s, Logan probably read Pope's *Essay* some time shortly after the Library Company's copy arrived on April 18, 1735. In any case, one day that year, perhaps while sitting in the large and comfortable second-floor library of the stone mansion called Stenton that he had built for himself on the outskirts of Philadelphia, Logan penned a poem of his own, "On Reading Pope's Essay on Man, by J.L." In it, he denounced Pope's poem as poison. Dipping quill in ink, he began:

> Illustrious Pope! How Truth triumphant Shines
> In the Strong Periods of thy laboured Lines!
> How just thou shews the active Passions' force
> And by what Culture they each Talent nurse!

These initial couplets sound positive enough. But, as will shortly become clear, Logan's opening salvo belied his true purpose.[9]

Logan's first lines summed up exactly what so many eighteenth-century Pennsylvanians found so captivating about Pope: his open and unequivocal embrace of the passions. While classical philosophy had promoted the virtues of Stoicism and many contemporary moral philosophers were forcefully advocating selfless benevolence, Pope alone took a dramatic stand in favor of personal passions, arguing that they were the active force behind the human will. Such a position would prove enticing, even intoxicating, to colonists of many faiths who, though long schooled to contain their emotions and submerge their sense of self in favor of the greater social good, saw in Pennsylvania the opportunity to pursue personal advancement.[10]

Far from being blind to the traditional notion that selfish and willful emotions were the source of sin, Pope mounted the novel argument that vice could nurture virtue, much, one might say, as manure can be used as fertilizing mulch. Pope himself favored botanical metaphors and explained his position by comparing the relation of virtue and sin, of selfless benevolence and selfish passions, to the relation between a fruit-bearing limb and the ordinary trunk, or stock, onto which it is grafted.

> As fruits ungrateful to the planter's care
> On savage stocks inserted learn to bear;
> The surest Virtues thus from Passions shoot,
> Wild Nature's vigor working at the root.
> What crops of wit and honesty appear
> From spleen, from obstinacy, hate, or fear!
> —Epistle II, 181–186

Pope's contention was, not simply that passionate emotions were not necessarily sinful, but rather that they were an essential element of effective virtue. Just as the support and nourishment provided by the host tree allowed grafted branches to flower, so, Pope argued, attention to self and to selfish passions strengthened social life and maximized the public good. Hating a person could be what motivated someone to take positive action and tell the truth about that person. In other words, Pope argued that vice (such as hate) could strengthen virtue (such as honesty); thus the more one felt for one's self, the more likely one would be able to feel for others.[11]

Logan found this point of view appalling and used the rest of his poem, "On Reading Pope," to counter this logic couplet for couplet. He began with a gibe at Pope's own wit and ended by asserting that, beautiful as Pope's poem—the fruit of his wit—appeared to be, it was deadly for readers to eat. Rejecting the notion that "savage stocks" could ever be made to bear wholesome produce and writing as if to address Pope directly, Logan exclaimed:

> The feeble Cyon [Scion] of thy Wit
> On th' Energetic Stock of Malice hit
> By whose full strength vast Productions Shoot

Infernal *"vigorous working at the root."*
Hence beauteous blooms, hence spangled fruit appear
That charm the astonish'd sense, yet viewed more near
The glittering streaks still their Root's Livery bear
And while th' Ear's ravish'd with thy Sounding Strain
We Spy the Poison creeps through all thy vein.

Though Logan mixed his metaphors, comparing Pope's poem simultaneously to spangled fruit and ravishing strains of music, he made his point about its toxic origins and effects quite clearly. As far as this Quaker grandee was concerned, Pope's poem and the passions it promoted were simply bitter poison.[12]

Logan's concerns over passion's poison grew out of the Quaker conviction that, while inner feelings might open the way to God for individual believers, selfish passions could fatally undermine communal bonds. Quakerism itself rested on an exquisite tension between self and society. As a "Society of Friends," it both encouraged the development of individual faith and insisted on the importance of joining individuals in communal worship. On the one hand, members of Quaker meetings were taught to search their own feelings as a means to receive God's grace and perceive his will. Yet, they were encouraged to share in the feelings of other meeting members in an effort to achieve religious concord, communal agreement on the true direction of divine leadings. In Pennsylvania, these tensions between self and society followed Friends out of the meetinghouse, affecting social and political philosophy as much as theology. Logan worried that Pope's positive position on the passions—his claim that "savage stocks" could be made to bear "beauteous blooms"—might tip the unsteady philosophical and political balance Quakers had strived so long to maintain.

Indeed, Logan was remarkably prescient in his assessment of Pope's potential impact, for, if his reaction to reading Pope's *Essay on Man* was unusual in its perspective, it was typical in its fervor. Benjamin Franklin soon made sure that even many ordinary readers could easily encounter the essential ideas of the poem, by including an *Essay* excerpt in the pages of the 1736 edition of Poor Richard, *An Almanack for . . . 1736*. Published in advance in 1735 (the year the Library Company imported the *Essay*), the *Almanack* introduced Pennsylvania commoners to Pope. Many buyers would have owned few other books, yet, through the *Almanack*'s pages, a growing market of recreational readers could gain access to literary quotations. On page 4, Franklin included a few crucial lines from Pope.

Presumptuous Man! the Reason wouldst thou find
Why form'd so weak, so little, and so blind?
First, if thou canst, the harder reason guess
Why form'd no weaker, blinder, and no less?
Ask of the Mother Earth, why Oaks are made
Taller or stronger than the Weeds they shade?
Or ask of yonder argent Fields above,
Why JOVE's Satellites are less than JOVE?

These verses announce a key argument that runs through Pope's work: God made man only as virtuous as he was supposed to be, in accordance with a divine plan unknowable to mankind. In seeming to lecture people not to question acts of God, Pope could be seen as excusing them from the shame of original sin. Small wonder, then, that the devout James Logan regarded the *Essay* itself as a poisoned apple.[13]

This section of Pope's poem concludes with a direct endorsement of the passions.

. . . In the scale of reas'ning life, 'tis plain
There must be, somewhere, such a rank as Man;
And all the question (wrangle e'er so long)
Is only this, if God has plac'd him wrong?

. . .

When the proud steed shall know why Man restrains
His fiery course, or drives him o'er the plains;

. . .

Then shall Man's pride and dulness comprehend
His actions', passions', being's, use and end;

. . .

Then say not Man's imperfect, Heav'n in fault;
Say rather, Man's as perfect as he ought.
—Epistle I, 47–50, 61–62, 65–66, 69–70

In many ways, then, Franklin's inclusion in the *Almanack* of the Jove excerpt from Pope's *Essay* stands as a rhetorical rebuke to the poem Logan wrote in the same year. Passions might not be perfect, but they were part of God's plan. What the Quaker met with alarm, the civic innovator greeted with complaisance and even approval. Though close associates, they maintained sharply opposing worldviews. Their contradictory reactions neatly summarize the broader debates in which Pennsylvanians would engage in the coming decades.[14]

Try though men like Logan might to hinder Pope's influence, his poem spoke to the concerns of a great number of Pennsylvanians, particularly those growing restive with Quaker rule. To be sure, Franklin himself remained a Quaker ally until the eve of the American Revolution, and some Quakers did join the Library Company. Yet Franklin did not hesitate to oppose Quakers as he saw fit (notably, as we shall see, regarding colonial defense). Meanwhile, many elite families early associated with the Library Company, including the Hopkinsons, the Morgans, and the Chews, would soon emerge in the arena of politics and polemics as Quaker antagonists. The *Essay on Man* offered the ambitious the seductive suggestion that a focus on self-advancement might be not only an expedient response to colonial conditions but also the truest enactment of divine intentions. Radical though the embrace of passion and the virtual elimination of original sin seemed to many, such innovations also held great attraction in this new, enlightened age. Pope was thus ideally poised to become the unofficial poet laureate of eighteenth-century Pennsylvania.

Franklin, for one, did what he could to assure the spread of the *Essay's* popularity. Not only did he publish snippets of the *Essay* in his *Almanack;* he also featured Pope in his newspaper, the *Pennsylvania Gazette.* One especially suggestive entry from this early period comes from a comic poem published in 1736. Purportedly sent to the printer by a fellow colonist who had recently been traveling in London and introduced by an unsigned letter to "Mr. Franklin," it began with the witty observation: "There is nothing more uncertain than the Guesses made at the Author of an anonymous Piece. The Sentiments and the Stile are the only two Things we have to found a Conjecture on, and we are frequently deceiv'd in both." Franklin's correspondent explained:

> In a late Conversation at *London,* upon this Subject, a Gentleman
> chanc'd to say, *he thought any of our modern Poets, might easily be imi-*
> *tated;* which being deny'd by the rest of the Company, he was put
> upon making the Experiment himself; They gave for the Subject To-
> BACCO, and he undertook the Performance; in Imitation of Mr. *Pope.*

In printing this letter, Franklin invited his colonial customers to imagine themselves as citizen-subjects in a transatlantic British community of letters. Though far from London's social whirl, Pennsylvania readers could participate vicariously in the diversions of polite society, so long as they schooled themselves in the literary style of authors like Alexander Pope.[15]

The farcical poem that followed this letter, "TOBACCO, In Imitation of Mr. *Pope*," took as its model none other than Pope's *Essay on Man* and revealed once again the peculiar appeal of that work. Some of its more significant lines ran:

> BLEST Leaf, whose Aromatick Gales dispense,
> To Templars Modesty, to Parsons Sense;
>
> · · ·
>
> Poison that cures—a Vapour that affords,
> Content more solid—than the Smiles of Lords.

Tweaking Pope's lines about sure virtues shooting from savage stocks, in a way that coincidentally echoes Logan's thoughts on poison, this ditty boasted that, like the passions, tobacco could have paradoxically positive effects. Gales of tobacco smoke—like gales of passion—could promote virtue, even impart modesty to the swaggering barristers of the Inner Temple at London's Inns of Court. Perhaps most significant, such gales could promote true social contentment. Only readers already conversant with Pope's *Essay* would be able to appreciate this riff on the celebrated author's popular poem, so the social anxieties it laid bare could be partly assuaged by the satisfaction of being in on the joke. In reprinting the poem for his Pennsylvania audience, Franklin both indicated and expanded the extent of the *Essay*'s colonial popularity.[16]

Pennsylvanians' preoccupation with Pope betrayed a set of problems and concerns growing out of colonial social uncertainty and local political rivalry. Try as they might to use an author like Pope to showcase their readiness for what the Library Company referred to as the "refinements of life," Pennsylvanians' readings of and reactions to Pope hastened the development of a specifically colonial and ultimately American perspective on the passions.

The 1740s: William Bradford, Joseph Shippen, and the Popularization of Pope

Franklin offered Pope's collected works for sale numerous times in the coming years, so those readers left out of the London gentleman's tobacco joke in 1736 had ample opportunity to amend their ignorance. In fact, by 1743, some booksellers had begun importing stand-alone copies of *An Essay on Man*, slim books that were cheaper and thus more accessible than multivolume sets of Pope's complete oeuvre. Still, many ordinary readers of the kind in the market for Franklin's *Gazette* or Poor Richard's *Almanack* would have balked at the cost of purchasing a copy of the poem that was available only through importation. This situation did not change until 1747, when William Bradford, one of Franklin's competitors in the printing business, produced the first-ever edition of *An Essay on Man* to be published in the colonies.[17]

Bradford's determination to publish *An Essay on Man* represented a significant sally into the refined territory staked out by the Library Company in the 1730s. While members of the Library Company might well have intended to keep Pope's justification of the passions largely to themselves, the encouragement that his *Essay* offered to those interested in the pursuit of self-love and self-interest could not be easily contained. Franklin's brief early forays into popularizing Pope smoothed the way for the entire poem to become more widely read and appreciated. Though many among the emergent elite might have liked to confine opportunities for advancement to the ranks of those who had already largely arrived, they simply did not have the ability. The market for Pope and a positive view of the passions expanded apace.

The title page of Bradford's edition pointedly announced that it was a Philadelphia reprint of a London edition ("London, Printed: Philadelphia: Re-printed, and Sold by William Bradford"). Yet the volume Bradford offered differed markedly from the versions of Pope's *Essay* printed in Britain; it was much simplified in content and design. By 1747, two years after the death of Alexander Pope, most British editions of his *Essay* included substantial introductory material and copperplate illustrations. Bradford omitted these extras and thus produced a pamphlet of just fifty-two pages, at a point when bound British versions often numbered at least seventy. Whereas a two-tone title page set off with both red and black ink had become almost standard in London, Bradford printed his Philadelphia edition in basic black. Together, these economies indicate that Bradford intended to position his edition as an inexpensive alternative to imported copies of the *Essay*, to appeal to a broader spectrum of colonial book buyers than had ever before been able to own and read Pope's work.[18]

Yet the Bradford edition simultaneously eliminated many of the intellectual and ornamental details that would have been recognized as important elements of refinement. Once again, then, efforts to increase the inclusiveness of transatlantic culture succeeded only in highlighting the peculiarities of the colonial condition. What led Bradford to think he could succeed in marketing Pope's poem in this way? Given the pitfalls of attempting to broaden the poem's distribution in a colony under the political and cultural sway of Quakers—not to mention the rarity of producing local editions of European books—Bradford was taking a risk. However, as a quick look at local events of 1747 will reveal, the *Essay* might have had particular strategic value in Pennsylvania at this time.

Pope had promised to explain the "being, use, and ends" of "passion" and "action." By 1747, Pennsylvanians were becoming increasingly embroiled in debates about just such questions, especially the relationship between passion and military action. With imperial tensions rising between Britain, France, and Spain, many observers argued that conflict was sure to touch the colony and thus that the government ought to organize for defense. Yet pacifist Quakers staked out a firm antiwar position. Those opposed to armament believed that the best means of avoiding war was by eliminating passion, since, as one pacifist writer bluntly put it, "Passions, and lusts . . . are the Causes of all Wars." The Quaker Yearly Meeting printed and circulated official pronouncements to defend and disseminate this pacifist stance among the public. Thus, Pennsylvanians who favored armament stood to benefit greatly from any popularization of Pope's favorable position on the virtue and utility of the passions.[19]

These local preoccupations governed many of the choices Bradford made as he put together his edition of Pope's *Essay*. A militia supporter himself, he nevertheless needed to be mindful of likely Quaker objections. In this respect, his inclusions were as significant as his omissions. Despite all the increasingly customary front matter that he left out, Bradford did take care to retain significant features that had been absent from the earliest version of the *Essay* imported into Philadelphia in 1735. Most important, Bradford reframed the work by inserting a prefatory "Advertisement" while also featuring a separate concluding poem called "The Universal Prayer." Given his other efforts at economy and brevity, the decision to print these items seems of some consequence. What did they contain?[20]

The same "Advertisement" featured in Bradford's volume also appeared in contemporary London editions of the *Essay*. It was composed by Pope's British editor, William Warburton. Unlike London printers who usually credited Warburton in some way in their title pages, Bradford avoided any mention of the man, leaving less savvy readers free to assume that he himself might have written the "Advertisement," or at the very least that it had been written for a Pennsylvania readership. This fact indicates that it must have had real resonance in the colony.[21]

Warburton had begun the "Advertisement" by reiterating Pope's claim that his poem provided "a perfect System of Ethics," thus highlighting its import and intent as a serious work of moral philosophy, not simply as a diverting or trifling bit of poetry. Even more significant, however, is the concluding paragraph, which attempts to account for the insertion of the additional poem, "The Universal Prayer." Warburton explained:

> Some passages in the *Essay* having been unjustly suspected of a tendency towards Fate and *Naturalism,* the Author composed that Prayer . . . to shew that his system was founded in Free Will and terminated in Piety: That the first Cause was as well the Lord and Governor as the Creator of the Universe and that by Submission to his Will (the great Principle enforced throughout the *Essay*) was not meant the suffering ourselves to be carried along with a blind Determination; but a religious Acquiesence, and Confidence full of Hope and Immortality.

This aspect of the advertisement could not have been better suited to Pennsylvania, for Pope's poem was subject to sustained objections on the basis of piety in the Quaker-dominated colony.[22]

The problem that James Logan had with Pope, and that some other Pennsylvanians perceived as well, was that in many ways the logic of the poem's premises undermined its stated intent. If submission to the divine will constituted the basis of Christian life and was *the* essential element in the avoidance of sin, then the charge to accept as God's will any and every earthly circumstance that occurred—including the human propensity for passion—could challenge the idea of human implication in sin. This problem, commonly called the problem of the freedom of the will, had vexed religious writers for centuries and was certainly not invented by Pope. Christian thinkers had long struggled with the contradiction between the idea of an all-powerful God and the insistence on man's complete culpability for his own corruption. Generally, theologians who addressed this problem confined their efforts to trying to reconcile the apparent opposition between infinite divine authority and absolute mortal accountability, in order to convince mortals that final responsibility for sin could ultimately be laid to no one but themselves. But Pope's formulation pushed this paradox to its logical extreme, implying not simply that God's infinite power excused men from answerability for sin but that it logically precluded the very possibility of sin itself.[23]

Warburton's "Advertisement" explicitly rejected this reading of Pope's *Essay*. Yet, whatever Pope himself intended his poem to say, many eighteenth-century Pennsylvanians interpreted it according to its most permissive implications. Just this kind of position was being parodied in the tobacco poem, which declared the "BLEST Leaf" to be simultaneously a poison and a cure, that is, to be as morally neutral and intrinsically unobjectionable as Pope declared the passions to be. When Benjamin Franklin excerpted in Poor Richard's *Almanack* verses from the *Essay* that chided man as presumptuous for questioning his own imperfections, he had this very component of Pope's poem in mind.[24]

It does seem that Pope himself was taken aback by such understandings of his *Essay*, for his addendum, "The Universal Prayer," openly disavowed the idea that there were no clear differences between good and evil. It likewise opposed the accompanying claim that human beings were therefore at liberty to indulge their own passions without restraint. Early in the poem, Pope addressed himself to God and declared:

> Thou great first cause, least understood,
> Who all my sense confin'd
> To know but this, that thou art good,
> And that myself am blind;
> Yet gave me, in this dark estate,
> To see the good from ill;
> And, binding nature fast in fate,
> Let free the human will.
> What conscience dictates to be done,
> Or warns me not to do,
> This teach me more than hell to shun,
> That more than heav'n pursue.

These lines make clear that Pope did not invariably deny that mankind had freedom of the will, and he did believe that mortals were liable for sin. Despite the many readers, critics and admirers alike, who read Pope's *Essay* as promoting moral relativism in the guise of religiosity, he himself adamantly denied that this was his intent.[25]

In any case, "The Universal Prayer" is also at variance with the main body of *An Essay on Man* in another obvious and important way: its direct advice concerning the regulation of emotion. Where the *Essay* recommended the sanguine acceptance of passions in the expectation that virtue would shoot from even the foulest root, just as wit and honesty could arise from spleen and hate, the "Universal Prayer" far more carefully qualified its explanation of the ideal working of emotion. Pope prayed:

> Teach me to feel another's woe;
> To hide the fault I see:
> That mercy I to others shew,
> That mercy shew to me.

Asking for aid in imagining the feelings of others in order to be able to overlook their faults was a far cry from claiming that hatred of others allowed people to rise to new heights of honesty and wit. The net effect of concluding the *Essay* with "The Universal Prayer" was thus to substantially recast much of the meaning of the central work.[26]

The remaining question, of course, is why William Bradford would seek to soften the message of Pope's *Essay* by including "The Universal Prayer," despite his very evident desire to curtail the length and expense of his edition as much as possible. One obvious possibility is that Pope's work needed to be sanitized if it was to be fully popularized. By including "The Universal Prayer," Bradford preserved the possibility that Pope's *Essay* could be understood as innovative in its teachings on the self and its passions, yet conservative on questions of traditional Christian morality. Such tactics were crucial if the *Essay* was to withstand the critiques of Quakers like Logan and allow positive messages concerning the passions and the rise of the self to gain greater currency.

Indeed, Bradford's decision to print a cheap edition of the *Essay*, including "The Universal Prayer" while omitting much other material, represented a targeted response to pacifist Quaker publications. Not only did the *Essay* as a whole provide an important rationale for the passions, "The Universal Prayer" related directly to details of Quaker objections. It just so happened that in July 1746, mere months before beginning the print run of the *Essay on Man*, Bradford (himself a Presbyterian) had published a copy of the Yearly Meeting *Epistle* of the Society of Friends that spoke out critically on crucial questions of the will. The Quakers' four-page pamphlet (which, as publisher, Bradford almost certainly read) contained numerous "*Cautions* and *Advices*" for New Jersey and Pennsylvania Quakers on the "Practice of a CHRISTIAN LIFE." One central element was the declaration that only when "natural Wills [were] subjected" would

Quakers be "qualify'd to Worship" God "in an acceptable Manner." Significantly, the very definition of *willfulness* is the "disposition to assert one's own will against reason"; every discussion of the selfish will involved inherent comment on the contest between reason and passion. In reminding believers of the importance of subjugating the will, Quakers well might have had the dangerous influence of thinkers like Pope at least partially in mind.[27]

To be sure, these words of warning made no specific mention of Pope's *Essay*. Yet, the matter of the will was just exactly the element of Pope's philosophy that Bradford's insertions aimed to clarify. Furthermore, prominent Quakers who likely attended the 1746 meeting had recently been reading Pope and ruminating on just such issues. The Philadelphian Isaac Norris, one of the more politically active Friends, wrote to Quaker elder Susannah Wright in 1746 and discussed—in a single letter—both the difficulties of raising pious unworldly daughters in a "world that [wa]s newly glittering to their view" *and* his and Wright's readership of Pope. Following a paragraph in which he offered to lend Wright his copy of "Pope's Letters" (the *Essay on Man*, published as four "epistles"), he added another paragraph musing about his duty to "rectify the understanding" of his "little babes." The date of this letter was July 22, 1746, the same month in which the Quaker caution was published.[28]

Thus, when Bradford set out to market Pope's *Essay* just a few months after this, his inclusion of Warburton's and Pope's reassurances concerning the importance of submission to God's will might well have been aimed at mollifying the many Quakers likely to be piqued by unmediated editions of Pope's poem. Indeed, the full contents of the 1746 Yearly Meeting *Epistle* indicate the need for just such philosophical maneuvers, for that pamphlet also made strong comments on the moral indefensibility of war, "entreat[ing] all who profess themselves Members of our Society . . . against *bearing of Arms* and *Fighting*," thus drawing links between the problems of willfulness, passion, violence, and sin.[29]

Subsequent pacifist pamphleteers, who took up the issue repeatedly, stressed the fateful links between willful passion and military action. One such writer was a young Quaker named John Smith, then courting James Logan's daughter Hannah. In an antiarmament essay written in 1748, Smith lamented that "the Simplicity of the Gospel" was being "misconstrued to allow of Violence and Oppression," declaring, "The Design of Gospel Dispensation, was to redeem Man from [his] Deplorable Corruption . . . by . . . rectifying his Will [and] governing his Passions."

Smith, like so many Quakers, believed the passions to be antithetical to pacifism, productive only of unreasoning and selfish destruction.[30]

Bradford's decision to introduce his edition of Pope's *Essay* into this highly fraught atmosphere thus worked in tandem with the efforts of religious leaders from outside the Quaker faith to articulate a religious rationale for the moral defensibility of war. One such preacher, the Presbyterian evangelical Gilbert Tennent, struck a Popian note when he argued in a 1747 sermon, *The Late Association for Defence, Encourag'd,* that "we must love our selves first and most." Echoing Pope's assertion that self-love and social were the same, Tennent explained that self-love should not be opposed, "seeing that *love* to ourselves, is proposed by God as the Standard of our *love* to our Neighbour." For Tennent, it was a short step from justifying self-love to promoting self-defense. Not surprisingly, William Bradford soon rushed Tennent's sermon into print.[31]

As a printer, Bradford openly welcomed any available customer, whether Quaker or Presbyterian; still, his own views were unmistakably proarmament and pro-Pope. In time, Bradford would actually serve in the Pennsylvania militia. Meanwhile, Benjamin Franklin, that other prominent popularizer of Pope, anonymously wrote and published in 1747 a prodefense pamphlet, *Plain Truth; or, Serious Considerations on the Present State of the City of Philadelphia and Province of Pennsylvania,* in which he argued forcefully in favor of arming the colony. He began that pamphlet with a Latin epigram (translated into English in its second printing) that urged: "*To succeed, you must* join salutary Counsels, Vigilance, *and* couragious Actions." To the extent that passions were a prod to action, the prodefense camp had an interest in seeing them promoted. Colonial Pennsylvanians' eagerness to embrace Pope's *Essay* thus stemmed in large part from the poem's promise to explain mankind's "actions', passions', being's, use and end" (I, 66).[32]

Just how well Pope's positive view of the passions accorded with that of proarmament colonists is further suggested by the response of another enthusiastic proponent of his ideas, the young Anglican Joseph Shippen, Jr. In 1750, at the age of eighteen, Shippen had begun a commonplace book in which he copied a passage from Pope's *Essay on Man,* and soon afterward Shippen responded to Franklin's 1747 call by accepting a commission as a major in the service of the British army. Thus, on the brink of choosing the military life and settling himself firmly in the proarmament camp, Shippen turned for guidance to the writings of Alexander Pope.[33]

Shippen's commonplace selections highlighted passages that described and defended the relationship between passion and action. In claiming that "stoical apathy is not a human virtue," for example, Shippen placed special stress on Pope's declaration that "strength of mind is exercise not rest." To argue that "passion is the gale," that passion's tempestuous winds "put in act the soul," was to highlight emotion's role in human motivation. For a young man like Shippen, eager to make his mark on the world and to spring to the defense of his colony, the link between passion and action could not have been more congenial. Meanwhile, in a place where Quakers argued that pacifism was the product of true religion, those in favor of armament gravitated toward the image of a passionate God who, like those created in his image, "mounts the storm, and walks upon the wind."[34]

Bradford's inclusion of "The Universal Prayer" in his 1747 edition of *An Essay on Man* bolstered the contention that passionate action constituted a crucial element of true Christianity. The theological abstractions of Pope's poem came to have important policy implications in the colonial setting. Faced with the Quaker claim that war and the selfish passions that provoked it were the symptoms of original sin, Anglican and Presbyterian advocates of armament could turn to Pope's poem for a counterargument.

The metropolitan sophistication of Pope's poem offered an attractive alternative source of cultural authority against Quaker hegemony. As theoretical debates about passion and action became more urgent with the arrival of armed conflict in Pennsylvania in 1754, Pope's poem only gained greater resonance. As the Seven Years War began, the very same passage from Pope quoted by Joseph Shippen appeared in modified form in the *Pennsylvania Gazette,* in a report on a performance by a "company of COMEDIANS from London" before a "polite audience" of Philadelphians that had included the recitation of the following poem:

TO this new World, from fam'd *Britannia's* Shore,
Thro' boisterous Seas, where foaming Billows roar,
The Muse, who Britons charm'd for many an Age,
New sends her Servants forth to tread the Stage;
Britain's own Race, tho' far remov'd, to show
Patterns of every Virtue they should know.
For gloomy Minds thro' Ignorance may rail;
Yet bold Examples strike, where languid Precepts fail.
    The World's a Stage, where Mankind act their Parts,
The Stage a World, to show their various Arts:

Whilst the Soul touch'd by Nature's tenderest Laws,
Has all her Passions rous'd in Virtue's Cause.
Reason we bear, and coolly may approve;
But all's inactive till the Passions move.
Such is the human Soul, so weak, so frail;
*Reason her Chart; but Passion is the Gale;
Then raise these Gales to waft fair virtue o'er
The Sea of Life; while Reason points the Shore.

*A Line of Mr. *Pope's.*

Read in the context of Pennsylvania's provincial anxieties and wartime uncertainties, the poem takes on very pointed political meaning. It began
with the premise that colonists were morally backward compared with
their brethren in Britain but quickly went on to offer a cure for coarseness
to colonists much concerned with "politeness." The play would teach those
of "Britain's own Race" who lived in the "new World . . . far remov'd" from
the mother country the "Patterns of every virtue they should know." It then
critiqued those with "gloomy Minds" who, "thro' Ignorance," advocated
"languid Precepts." Such sniping at the purportedly dour pacifism of
Quakers, who preferred "languid" inactivity to military action, would have
been well understood by those theatergoers—and newspaper readers—
inclined to Franklin's view of the necessity of attending to defense.[35]

Like Pope, the London players insisted that they maintained a cool
approval of reason but reserved their highest praise for passion. With its
references to nature's tender laws and to the frailty of the human soul, the
poem invoked Pope's position that man's passionate nature was not only
natural (and therefore morally acceptable) but was also intrinsic in God's
design. In so doing, it reemphasized the very elements of Pope's *Essay* that
had already made the clearest mark on the consciousness of colonial
Pennsylvanians. The gales that blew over boisterous seas from London to
Philadelphia carried passion in their wake.

The 1750s: John Woolman and Anthony Benezet on Slavery and the Self

Much as men like Joseph Shippen, Jr., might champion the idea that
selfish passions could take on "virtue's name" so long as they were pursuing noble aims, such views did not hold much weight with pacifists.
Quakers took quite seriously the need to promote an alternative view of

the self and its passions. In fact, in 1754, the same year in which the London players argued in favor of passionate action, Quakers published two important and unequivocal statements attacking the argument that selfish passions could have salutary public effects. They launched their critique from what may at first appear an unrelated platform: the issue of slavery.

Blending arguments against both armament and slavery helped Quakers take a comprehensive philosophical stance against selfish passions. Pennsylvania Quaker publications of the 1750s, including religious elder John Woolman's 1754 treatise, *Some Considerations on the Keeping of Negroes,* the Yearly Meeting's 1754 *Epistle of Caution and Advice concerning the Buying and Keeping of Slaves,* and Anthony Benezet's 1759 *Observations on the Inslaving, Importing, and Purchasing of Negroes* mounted arguments against selfishness in direct opposition to the very elements of Pope's philosophy that many Pennsylvanians sought to spread. While proarmament critics castigated pacifists for their passive lack of passion, for their failure to see that even selfish concerns could have positive social consequences, Quakers countered that passion's promoters lacked the capacity to feel for any but themselves, to imagine either the sufferings inflicted by war or the evils endured by the enslaved.[36]

For Quaker activists, the turmoil of the 1750s, from the onset of war to the burgeoning of the slave trade, evidenced the trouble with passion and demonstrated God's displeasure with colonists who failed to understand that "corrupt Passions and [selfish] Inclinations . . . must be driven out." Anthony Benezet made this point with special clarity. When he bought membership in the Library Company in 1735, just in time to borrow Pope's *Essay on Man,* he might not yet have been convinced of the "absolute Necessity of Self-Denial." Yet, by the time of writing a 1759 pamphlet including this in the title, he was ready to "declare open War against the Kingdom of Self." Benezet linked the issues of war and slavery explicitly in his analysis, going so far as to suggest that colonists captured as prisoners of war and held captive by French-allied Indians were simply reaping the wages of slavery's sins. He demanded to know, Who could doubt "that the Captivity of our People is not to teach us to feel for others, and to induce us to discourage a Trade, by which many Thousands are Yearly captivated?" In fact, the link between war and slavery was more than just rhetorical. Because white servants could be drafted to serve in the war effort but enslaved Africans could not, masters in search of laborers stepped up the importation of enslaved workers dramatically after 1754. Their actions added urgency to the moral problem of the passions that writers like Woolman and Benezet perceived.[37]

Quakers' efforts to demonstrate the nefarious effects of Pope's teachings on the self focused on self-love. In the final lines of Epistle II of the *Essay on Man* (the epistle singled out by both Logan and Shippen), Pope had offered the following conclusion:

> Ev'n mean Self-love becomes, by force divine,
> The scale to measure others wants by thine.
> See! and confess, one comfort still must rise,
> 'Tis this, 'Tho Man's a fool, yet GOD IS WISE.
> —Epistle II, 291–294

Quakers found such reasoning utterly absurd. Far from agreeing that a wise God made even self-love a divine means of advancing virtue, John Woolman argued, "When *Self-love* presides in our Minds, our Opinions are bias'd in our own Favour; in this Condition . . . there's Danger of using ourselves to an undisturbed Partiality, till, by long Custom, the Mind becomes reconciled with it, and the Judgment itself infected." In other words, Woolman feared that self-absorption led toward a self-justification that could ultimately construct a false defense for a wide array of self-serving decisions, from the choice to buy slaves to the resolution to go to war. He denied that, as Pope would have it, love of self ultimately allowed people to expand their love for others.[38]

Pope's contention, "In the scale of reas'ning life, 'tis plain / There must be, somewhere, such a rank as Man," met concerted opposition from his colonial Quaker critics. Woolman did make some concessions to Pope's claim, at the close of Epistle III, that "Self-love and Social be the same" (III, 318). But, the Quaker explained, "to me it appears an Instinct like that which inferior Creatures have; each of them, we see, by the Ties of Nature, love *Self* best; that which is a Part of *Self* they love by the same Tie or Instinct." In other words, Woolman did not wish to see mankind rest content with baser animal instincts. Christian love should encompass more than the animal tendency to "watchfully keep, and orderly feed their helpless Offspring." Social love should transcend—not simply extend—self-love.[39]

Pursuing this point still further, Woolman declared, "Earthly Ties of Relationship, are, comparatively, inconsiderable to such who, thro' a steady Course of Obedience, have come to the happy Experience of the

Spirit of God." In other words, the highest duty of mankind was to love God and in so doing to submerge the self. Compared to this religious duty, all earthly love, whether defined as selfish or social, was inferior, even counterfeit. Woolman asserted finally, "To *love* our children is needful; but except this *Love* proceeds from the true heavenly Principle . . . it will rather be injurious than of any real Advantage to them."[40]

The real issue was whether British-American colonists could or should feel for the suffering of enslaved Africans who lived in the colony under bondage. The point of putting love of God before all else was to ensure that, when love *was* bestowed on fellow mortals, it would be a pure and holy love, not a false or opportunistic love influenced by selfish considerations. When love was not tainted by selfishness, it could be shared with all, not simply with those who could lay claim to a close connection such as the animal tie between parent and child. Woolman addressed the barriers to extending love to those who were enslaved in his second part, *Considerations on Keeping Negroes*:

> To come at a right Feeling of their Condition, requires humble serious Thinking; for in their present Situation, they have but little to engage our natural Affection in their Favour.
>
> Had we a Son or a Daughter involved in the same Case, in which many of them are, it would alarm us, and make us feel their Condition without seeking for it.

In other words, while the "instinct[s]" of "inferior Creatures" ensured love between parents and children, only a higher love that began and ended with God could ensure love to all. The simple shortcut Pope proposed, that love of God and love of man be considered one and the same, allowed the prejudicial effects of self-love to influence decisions about slaveholding. In Woolman's words, "So long as Men are biassed by narrow Self-love, so long an absolute Power over other Men is unfit for them." Statements such as Woolman's would have been most unwelcome to the many slaveholding members of the colony, including both Benjamin Franklin and Joseph Shippen.[41]

Indeed, part of Pope's attractiveness for Pennsylvania's elite must be attributed to the potential social conservatism of his doctrines. While there was something revolutionary about Pope's validation and even valorization of the individual self, his concomitant justification of self-love and selfishness could have profoundly regressive implications. Pope's own intellectual intentions remain ambiguous. Yet the seductive power of his poem lay in its subversive potential to promote two opposing agendas at the same time; the fact that it could be used to encourage conventional morality did not mean that it would be.[42]

In assessing Pope's popularity among colonial Pennsylvanians, it is crucial to recognize his singularity. While many other moral philosophers were also read and admired, Pope's flexibly indeterminate doctrine held special appeal. Unlike Adam Smith, whose *Theory of Moral Sentiments* was soon to be published in Britain (1759) and imported to Pennsylvania, Pope did not argue, "To feel much for others and little for ourselves . . . to restrain our selfish, and to indulge our benevolent, affections, constitutes the perfection of human nature." He argued, instead, that self-love was the natural and necessary foundation of all other kinds of love and, furthermore, that God had already made man "as perfect as he ought." Meanwhile, Pope's assertion of an equivalence between love of God and love of man was also at odds with Adam Smith, who affirmed, "All affections for particular objects ought to be extinguished in our breast [and] one great affection take the place of all the others, the love of the Deity."[43]

In his *Essay on Man,* Pope not only failed to anticipate the views of Adam Smith; he also declined to conscientiously follow the thinking of benevolist philosophers who came before him, including Anthony Ashley Cooper, third earl of Shaftesbury. Where Pope declared that *all* passions were natural and God-given, that even spleen and hate could produce virtue, Shaftesbury had distinguished carefully between "the *good* and *natural,* and . . . the *ill* and *unnatural* Affections." What is more, Shaftesbury's approval of self-love, enunciated in his 1714 *Inquiry concerning Virtue and Merit,* was far less sweeping than Pope's:

> If the Affection towards private or Self-Good, however *selfish* it may
> be esteem'd, is in reality not only consistent with the publick Good,
> but in some measure contributing to it; if it be such . . . 'tis so far from
> being ill or blameable in any sense that it must be acknowledg'd abso-
> lutely necessary to constitute a Creature *Good.*

As Shaftesbury's repeated use of the qualifier "if" indicates, he discouraged the blanket belief that self-love and social love were inevitably the same. On the contrary, he carefully explained that only in cases where selfish affections could be proven to help—not harm—the public good could they escape the charge of being blamable and boding ill. Where Smith would eliminate all self-love in favor of social and Shaftesbury would allow self-love only where it could be proven to promote public good, Pope could be read as claiming that self-love and social were always one and the same.[44]

Ironically, while critics of Quakers championed Pope's position as a means of justifying the morality of taking action and going to war, Quakers themselves viewed Pope's teachings on self-love as dangerous precisely because they could be used to justify *inaction*. Their 1754 *Epistle of Caution and Advice* urged readers to think of people who had been enslaved and "make their Case our own." It demanded that Pennsylvania slaveholders "consider what we should think and how we should feel, were we in their Circumstances." But Quakers wanted their fellow colonists not only to feel for the enslaved but also to take action on their behalf. Leaders of the newly emerging antislavery movement charged Pennsylvanians, "Remember our blessed Redeemer's positive Command, *To do unto others, as we would have them do unto us.*" Pope's position, by contrast, could excuse extreme social conservatism, to justify inaction as deference to God's will, as evidence of a holy acquiescence to the dictates of a divine plan.[45]

The Quaker stance was all the more radical in a colony where many were enamored of the idea that self-love was in itself sufficient to signal submission to God. Consider, in this context, one of Franklin's more lurid arguments in favor of armament back in 1747. He bellowed from the pages of *Plain Truth*, "Who can, without the utmost Horror, conceive the Miseries . . . when your Persons, Fortunes, Wives and Daughters shall be subject to the wanton and unbridled Rage, Rapine and Lust of *Negroes, Molattoes,* and others, the vilest and most abandoned of Mankind." Franklin took for granted that those capable of feeling future suffering would be highly motivated to take up arms when faced with the prospect of enraged *"Negroes, and Molattoes."* Franklin did not contemplate the feelings of those he dismissed as the "vilest and most abandoned of Mankind." For Quakers, Franklin's was by far the more serious failure of imagination. While proarmament critics castigated pacifists for their lack of passion, for their failure to see that even selfish concerns could have positive social consequences, Quakers countered that passion's promoters lacked the capacity to feel for others, to imagine either the sufferings inflicted by war or the evils endured by the enslaved.[46]

Remarkably, in a colony so deeply invested in contemplating the passions, Franklin's outburst is one of the rare instances in which the emotions of the colony's African inhabitants were imagined at all. Not only are there relatively few surviving records of expressions of emotion on the part of either free or enslaved Africans (to be expected given their limited access to literacy), but there are also few instances where Pennsylvanians took the trouble to record any reference to the emotions of the Africans among them. Even criticisms of African emotion, such as Franklin's reference to rage, appear very seldom. Instead, members of the slaveholding class expended considerable effort in denying recognition to black emotion. It was no accident, then, that eighteenth-century Quaker antislavery activists chose emotional identification as a key means of illuminating the plight of the enslaved. This was a strategic move in direct opposition to the traditional practices of slavery's supporters.

The social realities reinforced by the repression of slavery stand out in a 1756 address from the Pennsylvania Assembly to the colonial governor. Legislators were concerned about the loss of indentured laborers to the war effort—and the subsequent turn toward slaves, inalienable property in persons that could not be commandeered by the military. They petitioned the government to disallow indentured servants to break their contracts in order to join British forces. In setting forth their case, the assemblymen predicted ominously, "Thus the Growth of the Country by Increase of white Inhabitants will be prevented [and] the Province weakened rather than strengthened (as every Slave may be reckoned a domestick Enemy)." Like Franklin's offhand and wholly unapologetic reference to *"Negroes, Molattoes"* as "the vilest and most abandoned of Mankind," this forthright acknowledgment that enslaved laborers should be automatically counted as dire enemies now seems shocking in its directness. Such unvarnished racism, such unequivocal acceptance of the raw reality of slavery's physical imposition of power, sits uneasily with images of Enlightenment-era refinement. Yet, these were everyday ways of discussing enslaved people in eighteenth-century Pennsylvania. The paternalistic apologia of nineteenth-century proslavery commentary lay many decades away.[47]

Nineteenth-century slaveholders would perpetuate myths about happy slaves content to live in bondage, but white eighteenth-century Pennsylvanians wasted no time fabricating such fantasies. They rarely deigned to consider African emotion, because to do so could undermine one of the fundamental rationalizations propping up the slave system. British colonists simply assumed, perhaps rightly, that the Africans and African-Americans in their midst were deeply down and dispirited, if not actually seething with rage. Taken as a given, such dangerous emotions were then disregarded as much as possible; they were nothing that the master class cared to criticize, much less regularly contemplate. So low was the standing accorded to Africans in colonial Pennsylvania that it was not necessary to discredit them further by disparaging their emotions. If possible, slaveholders simply preferred to avoid mentioning them at all.[48]

It then becomes clear just how revolutionary was the call that antislavery activist Anthony Benezet issued in 1759 in his *Observations on the Inslaving, Importing, and Purchasing of Negroes*: "While we feel for our own Flesh and Blood, let us extend our Thoughts to others . . . I mean . . . the poor Negroes." In urging them to feel for those who had been enslaved, Benezet asked readers to engage in an act of imagination unlike any most had ever undertaken. Paradoxical as it sounds, Franklin's bare mention of the rage of the so-called vile and abandoned actually represented a hesitant first step on the tortuously long road to abolition. The simple act of attributing emotion—any emotion—to Africans represented a radical departure from the colonial convention of silence. In fact, by century's end, Franklin would become a leading figure in the antislavery movement. Thus, if the regulation of emotion entailed the communication and negotiation of status, then the failure of the master class to comment on African emotion throughout the colonial period indicates their determination to hold Africans to a fixed and uncontestable status as the "vilest . . . of Mankind."[49]

The refusal to discuss African-American emotion must be understood not just as a sign but also as a strategy of oppression. At a time when, by scholarly estimates, Africans and their descendants, both free and enslaved, made up something like 9 percent of the colony's population, this silence speaks volumes. Ironically, Afro-Pennsylvanians, who were denied any recognition of passion or self-assertion, had been assigned a role of such utter selflessness they should have won acknowledgment for their moral superiority. Conveniently, however, the master class had just discovered and embraced an expedient new doctrine that applauded the virtues of self-love. Such issues must be addressed when considering the popularity of Pope.[50]

The 1760s: William Dunlap, Elizabeth Sandwith Drinker, and the Rays of Reason

In 1760, just one year after Benezet's antipassion foray, another Philadelphia printer readied his press and published a new colonial edition of Pope's *Essay on Man*. William Dunlap, an Irish immigrant from County Tyrone, who had initially settled among the Scots-Irish Presbyterians in the Pennsylvania backcountry, had only recently arrived in Philadelphia. A quick consideration of his background provides some clues why he might have been so eager to publish a new edition of Pope.[51]

From backwoods beginnings, Dunlap quickly rose as a printer by positioning himself as a cultural broker in command of the transatlantic print trade. Early in his career, Dunlap worked to transmit debates about passion and action between metropolitan Philadelphia and frontier settlements. While city folk often dominated such discussions, backcountry inhabitants were the ones predominantly affected by them. One of the first such efforts from Dunlap's press was a coproduction with Franklin's shop. They printed and circulated a 1755 anti-Quaker, proarmament sermon that had been preached by an Anglican minister named Thomas Barton in Carlisle, located beyond the Susquehanna River in the colony's western hinterland. Franklin's printing house oversaw sales in Philadelphia, and Dunlap offered a Lancaster edition under his own imprint. Soon after, Dunlap's ambitions brought him to Philadelphia itself, where he began striving to bring the latest ideas from Britain to bear on discussions in the colonial port.[52]

He appears to have been eager to supply Philadelphians with the newest of the new in every respect and to appeal to a customer base interested in cultivating genteel and sophisticated transatlantic tastes. In 1760, for example, Dunlap printed a seven-page catalog entitled "Books and Stationary, Just Imported from London, and to Be Sold by W. Dunlap, at the *Newest-Printing-Office* on the South-Side of the *Jersey*-Market, Philadelphia"; it included (along with the almost standard selection of British authors, including Addison, Locke, Swift, and Shaftesbury as well as Pope) an especially noteworthy entry: "Smith's Sentiments." Adam Smith's *Theory of Moral Sentiments* had only just been published for the first time in London in 1759; Dunlap had added it to his stock very swiftly indeed. He thus made every effort to ensure that he and his readers would keep up with the very latest in British philosophy. His announcement that he could supply the public with up-to-date goods "Just Imported" was no idle boast. Meanwhile, he took considerable pride in positioning himself as the purveyor of only the "the best and genteelest" goods from London.[53]

Thus, when Dunlap produced his own edition of Pope's *Essay on Man*, he did so as part of a larger effort to profit from his self-proclaimed position as an exclusive purveyor of all the best and latest goods. Unlike William Bradford, whose economical edition of Pope's poem took many shortcuts compared to British editions, Dunlap took great pains to try to replicate London imprints in as many respects as possible. At seventy pages, Dunlap's edition included all customary front matter and achieved a completeness that Bradford's had not. Readers of the Dunlap edition would thus have encountered, after perusing the title page crediting William Warburton as the editor, the two-page "Advertisement," followed by six pages of laudatory letters to the author (the same ones that had long appeared in London editions), Pope's preface ("The Design"), and, finally, the detailed table of contents. After the four epistles, the volume closed with "The Universal Prayer." Dunlap did cut a few corners, no doubt in the interest of keeping down costs. His edition employed only black ink and omitted both a portrait of Pope and interior illustrations. Still, it contained a crowning, extravagant touch certain to set it a notch above: a copy of the engraving that Pope himself had created to accompany his poem, shortly before his death in 1744.[54]

At the most basic level, including the engraving must be regarded as a marketing ploy. Dunlap's customers demanded a version of the *Essay* that could replicate the quality of genteel British books yet still lessen their costs. Dunlap's elegant yet less expensive edition of the *Essay* thus exactly conformed to the social ideas and desires of the book's colonial readers. By creating in the colonies a version of the book in close accord with English standards, he bolstered the claims to gentility of colonial elites. At the same time, he also expanded the range of readers who could not only purchase Pope but also obtain a locally produced edition no less "genteel" for being less expensive. By 1760, ambitious colonists believed that they should be able to acquire urbane goods at basic prices. Drawn to the passionate pursuit of self-interest, such readers desired an edition of Pope that added to their new claims to status materially even as it helped reinforce them philosophically.[55]

The engraving itself brings us face-to-face with Pope's own last effort to inform readers' understanding of the social meaning of his poem's praise of the passions. On the eve of his death in 1744, Pope created a sepia drawing illustrating two key lines from the poem, which was then made into an engraving to serve as the frontispiece for the *Essay on Man*. Editions including the engraving were first published by the London press J. and P. Knapton in February 1744, mere months before Pope's death in May. Like his earlier addition of "The Universal Prayer," the lines Pope highlighted were selected to shape readers' response to the work, rendering his final comment on the true meaning and intention behind his highly ambiguous poem. Beneath a scene of crumbling decay—a

FIGURE 2. Frontispiece. Alexander Pope, *An Essay on Man*
(London: J. and P. Knapton, 1751). *Permission Henry W. and Albert A.
Berg Collection of English and American Literature, The New York
Public Library, Astor, Lenox and Tilden Foundations*

broken statue lying in pieces in the foreground, Roman ruins moldering in the background, a senile old man blowing bubbles by a fountain, and a dying tree dripping with cobwebs arching over all—ran the lines: "Here in the rich, the honour'd, fam'd and great, See the false scale of Happiness complete." What was the final message Pope tried to send?[56]

The lines were from Epistle IV of the poem, which largely sets aside the question of the propriety of passion that dominated much of Epistle II, the most-quoted epistle among Pennsylvanians. Instead, it narrows its focus to assessing human happiness. Epistle IV opens: "OH HAPPINESS! our being's end and aim! / Good, Pleasure, Ease, Content! whate'er thy name" (Epistle IV, 1, 2). From optimistically declaring in the best Enlightenment vein that God had created man with the sole aim of ensuring his happiness, the epistle goes on to try to define the true meaning of happiness.

Pope's meandering definition remains subject to myriad interpretations. Early on in the epistle, he proclaimed:

Remember, Man, "the Universal Cause
Acts not by partial, but by gen'ral laws;"
And makes what Happiness we justly call
Subsist not in the good of one, but all.
    —Epistle IV, 35–38

Such lines could easily be read as affirming that selfish interests should be subsumed in pursuit of the common good, that happiness could be justly called such only when it touched all.

Yet, a little farther down, Pope returned to the notion that humans had a duty to accept as God's wisdom any and all earthly circumstances. This idea implied that the truly virtuous would accept without question their God-given lot in life, in the full faith that God had arranged all for the greatest good.

Condition, circumstance is not the thing;
Bliss is the same in subject or in king,

    . . .

If then to all Men Happiness was meant,
God in Externals could not place Content.
    Fortune her gifts may variously dispose,
And these be happy call'd, unhappy those;
But Heav'n's just balance equal will appear,
While those are plac'd in Hope, and these in Fear:

Not present good or ill, the joy or curse,
But future views of better or of worse.
   —Epistle IV, 57–58, 65–72

These lines seem to bolster the socially conservative stance that, since happiness did not consist in material things, no one should bother to contest, or "curse," material inequality. Denying any relationship between external appearance and intrinsic merit *could* have leveling implications. Read in a Christian context, such sentiments could also be interpreted as an inducement to accept earthly inequalities without protest, could encourage the downtrodden to be resigned to their lot, in the belief that all would be made even in heaven.[57]

Given these ambiguities, it becomes easier to understand the potential impact of Pope's engraving. Pope intervened in the interpretation of his poem by depicting a scene of symbols of high culture left to go to rack and ruin and by highlighting the idea that the rich and famous could expect to gain nothing by weighing their lives on a false scale of happiness. In so doing, he seemed to be persuading readers that the true message of the *Essay* lay, not in the promotion of selfishness, but in the promise that self-love would plant the seeds of social harmony. Since true happiness could be attained, not by the ruthless pursuit of self-interest, but only by meritorious striving for virtuous conduct, gentility was of far less lasting value than humility. Indeed, the last lines of the *Essay* make exactly this point about the poem's intended message:

When statesmen, heroes, kings, in dust repose,
Whose sons shall blush their fathers were thy foes,
Shall then this verse to future age pretend
Thou wert my guide, philosopher, and friend?
That urg'd by thee, I turn'd the tuneful art
From sounds to things, from fancy to the heart;
From Wit's false mirror held up Nature's light;
Shew'd erring Pride, WHATEVER IS, IS RIGHT;
That REASON, PASSION, answer one great aim;
That true SELF-LOVE and SOCIAL are the same;
That VIRTUE only makes our Bliss below;
And all our Knowledge is, OURSELVES TO KNOW.
   —Epistle IV, 389–398

The argument that the fullest possible expression of humility acknowledged that human imperfections—and especially the passions—were divinely ordained smacked of the same circular logic that plagued the poem as a whole. In the end, the *Essay*'s underlying ambiguities foiled even Pope's best attempts to fix his poem's implications once and for all.[58]

Dunlap evidently believed that the engraving, like the message it sent, was important enough to warrant its considerable trouble and expense. There was no way Dunlap could reproduce the English engraving exactly; his illustration flipped the original. There is something strangely appropriate in the fact that Dunlap's rendition of the engraving reversed Pope's original image. After all, the ambiguity of the poem itself meant it frequently served as a kind of mirror of the mind of the reader, easily reflecting a wide variety of philosophies. By the 1760s, would-be elites like the founding members of the Library Company were not the only ones interested in the passionate pursuit of self-advancement, nor were they alone in the belief that sentiment should play a key role in shaping society. On the contrary, Dunlap's potential readers came from a wide spectrum of Pennsylvanians, including backwoods commoners, increasingly attracted to the most modern aspects of Pope's poem, particularly his implied belief in natural equality.[59]

Crucial to questions about natural equality, about how to separate a man's worth from his earthly condition, was the figure of the Indian. With moral philosophers like Pope positing that the passions were the basis of all human nature, colonists constantly scrutinized native Americans for signs that they shared or lacked the passionate qualities they debated among themselves. Just as Britain provided one crucial point of reference for Pennsylvanians engaged in collective self-presentation and self-assessment, so native Americans living on the colony's western borders supplied them with another key counterpoint. As will be seen repeatedly throughout this study, Anglo-Americans alternately admired and vilified native Americans as both overly passionate *and* as excessively stoic, all in accordance with their own varying rhetorical needs. For the Philadelphia merchants who drove much of colony policy and for the frontier farmers and traders who began to take exception to their dominance, Indian emotion served as a rhetorically useful point of reference.

In this, as in so much else, colonists were in close accord with Pope, who in the *Essay on Man* alternated between holding native Americans up as a model for the British to follow and putting them down as bad examples the British ought to shun. Mocking the skepticism of those who questioned the propriety of God's allowance of passion, for example, Pope chided:

Lo! the poor Indian, whose untutor'd mind
Sees God in clouds, or hears him in the wind;
His soul proud Science never taught to stray
Far as the solar walk, or milky way;
Yet simple Nature to his hope has giv'n,
Behind the cloud-topt hill, an humbler heav'n;
   . . .
Go, wiser thou! and in thy scale of sense
Weigh thy Opinion against Providence.
     —Epistle I, 99–104, 113–114

Here Pope scorned those learned Christians who could not accept the passions as part of God's will when even "untutor'd" Indians did so gracefully. Yet, later in the poem, lecturing against materialism and once again using native Americans as a point of comparison, Pope urged his readers not to replicate Indians' mistakes by setting too much store on earthly things:

Weak, foolish man! will Heav'n reward us there
With the same trash mad mortals wish for here?
   . . .
Go, like the Indian, in another life
Expect thy dog, thy bottle, and thy wife.
     —Epistle IV, 173–174, 177–178

If Pope's impulse to ridicule native Americans as being more wedded to the world than Europeans were now seems absurd, it is also strangely appropriate. For, in fact, Anglo-Americans' sporadic and inconsistent commentary on native Americans usually reveals far more about European needs than Indian realities.

Significantly, native American emotion, unlike Africans' and African-Americans', was not simply ignored. In the era of the Seven Years War, continual frontier fighting on Pennsylvania's western border made it all too clear to colonists that Indian peoples loved liberty as much as, if not more than, they themselves did. Furthermore, treaty negotiations with native Americans forced Anglo-Americans to engage in elaborate emotional protocols of Indian design. Much as they might try to cast their own emotion as more civilized and advanced than that of Indians, colonists could not afford to ignore indigenous emotion altogether. Because the balance of power between native Americans and Anglo-Americans was subject to much greater shifts than that between master and slave, the importance of the passions was correspondingly increased. As colonists sought to establish their place on contested terrain, they could not turn a blind eye or deaf ear to native American expressions of emotion.

Indeed, frontier settlers came to complain that city elites gave more credence and paid more heed to demands for feeling from native Americans than from lower-ranking Anglo-Pennsylvanians living on the frontiers. The resulting tensions would eventually erupt into the controversy known as the Paxton Crisis of 1763–1764, in which disgruntled frontier folk took the law—and the language of feeling—into their own hands. Meanwhile, pamphlets written in defense of the frontier protest action at Paxton expounded at length upon backcountry settlers' capacity for civilized feeling.

Dunlap's backwoods background might have made him especially aware of the popular appeal Pope's poem could have if presented in its most progressive light, as affirming natural equality across all classes of men. In fact, it seems likely that he took the trouble to create a copy of Pope's engraving for his edition of the *Essay* precisely because the engraving could advance this aim. The best evidence for this surmise comes from certain simple but strategically significant alterations Dunlap deliberately made in the engraving. While some differences between the British and American versions of the illustration must simply be put down to questions of technique, others clearly occurred as the result of intentional modifications.

In one crucial and obvious change, Dunlap omitted all Latin mottoes from the scene's marble figures. He thus removed the one element in the original image that smacked of exclusivity, allowing the engraving to appeal to a wider public. The change might have helped resolve lingering debates about the poem's true meaning by tipping the balance toward greater egalitarianism, a move that would likewise have broadened the poem's marketability. At the same time, by effacing the classical mottoes, Dunlap further advanced the "Americanization of Athens" proposed decades before by the founding members of the Library Company. On both sides of the British Atlantic, preoccupation with Greek and Roman decay served as the proxy for concerns about contemporary decline. For opposition politicians from England to America, stories of Roman decadence and degeneracy served as cautionary tales about the need for vigilant attention to virtue. If Pope himself intended his scene of antiquity in decline to send a note of political caution, Dunlap's decision to make the

Herein the rich, the Honour'd, fam'd, and Great,
See the false Scale of Happiness, compleat.

FIGURE 3. Frontispiece. Alexander Pope, *An Essay on Man* (London Printed, Philadelphia Reprinted: W. Dunlap, 1760). *Permission The Library Company of Philadelphia*

scene more comprehensible to ordinary colonists might have been an early signal of what Revolutionary Americans would come to assert: that people up and down the social scale could be swayed by passion into virtuous action and that Americans themselves were especially suited to the task.[60]

Stressing the egalitarian implications of Pope's poem could also have helped address objections of radical Quakers of Woolman's and Benezet's ilk. Indeed, by the 1760s, many Quakers seem to have softened in their initial opposition to Pope's positions. A number of reports from this period indicate that Quaker admirers had begun to swell the ranks of Pope's appreciators. For example, two well-off single Quaker women in their mid-twenties, Elizabeth Sandwith and Elizabeth Moode, passed many a pleasant hour reading aloud to each other from the *Essay on Man* around 1760. Reminiscing about that time years later, upon being given a set of Pope's collected works, Sandwith would remark that she was once again reading "the 3 first Volls. of the works of Alexander Pope, much of which I have by rote but it revived old feelings as Betsy Moode and myself did read them in times of old together, with pleasure." Since Betsy Moode had married and become Betsy Emlen by 1761 and since the *Essay on Man* often appeared in Volume III of standard editions of Pope's works, it seems a fair inference that Sandwith and Moode enjoyed the *Essay on Man* together in their single days sometime around 1760. Meanwhile, in 1762, another Quaker, Eliza Stedman (who tended to socialize in elite Anglican circles), quoted directly from the closing lines of the *Essay,* remarking casually in a letter to a friend of hers, Elizabeth Graeme, that it was probably "best to conclude with Mr. Pope that whatever is is right." This easy acceptance of what was once one of the more controversial elements of Pope's poem indicates how widely influential his ideas had become after several decades of constant discussion in Pennsylvania.[61]

When Dunlap advertised his wares in 1761, he thought that, in order to make his merchandise "still more extensively useful and acceptable, especially to the Ladies," he would have to "intersperse [other] Articles, most of which are also just arrived from *London,* and may be depended on, as being the best and genteelest of their Kind," including everything from silver teaspoons to jeweled rings. He simply assumed that "the Ladies" would be more interested in baubles than books. Yet, as the remarks of Drinker and Stedman show, Pope's *Essay on Man* held great appeal for many a woman. Indeed, in assessing the implications of Pope's promotion of the self, we must remain aware of just how complicated the repercussions of his philosophy might be. Even as it could be used to justify the self-interested actions of slaveholders, it could also appeal to aspiring commoners on the colony's frontiers or to elite women eager to assert an independent sense of self.[62]

Ultimately, the many ironic implications of Pope's poem actually stemmed from the contradictory effects of a rising emphasis on the self. Though selfishness could create social injustice and undermine traditional communal values, it could also foster independence and allow individual advancement. Cultural fascination centered on the passions because they appeared to offer a way to bridge the gap between communalism and individualism while drawing out the best in both. At the same time, of course, emotion could also be alternately invoked in the service of extremes, from annihilating selflessness to the advancement of utter selfishness. It was the paradoxical nature of the passions that made them the center of such sustained debates.[63]

Pennsylvanians' fascination with Pope's "science of Human Nature" stemmed largely from the hope that he had, somehow, arrived at a perfect system of ethics. Though Pope *could* legitimately be read primarily as a proponent of the passions, and inspire both fierce opposition (as in the case of James Logan) and equally fierce admiration (as in the case of Joseph Shippen), he could also be understood as advancing a far more nuanced view. The resounding penultimate couplet of the *Essay on Man* embraced all of the poem's complexities and contradictions, asserting, "That REASON, PASSION, answer one great aim; / That true SELF-LOVE and SOCIAL are the same." It insisted on obliterating the binaries that so many relied on in trying to define the world, holding that reason and passion were complementary, and self-love and social love were mutually compatible. Despite the dreary imagery of the engraving that described his system of ethics, Pope finally offered readers a profoundly optimistic vision. This was the version of Pope's philosophy that Dunlap's 1760 edition promoted and colonial Pennsylvanians increasingly embraced.[64]

Dunlap made one other key intentional modification to Pope's engraving that indicates once again how highly colonists valued Pope's efforts to reconcile reason and passion. In comparing the London engraving with the Philadelphia one once more, it is clear how much cruder in overall appearance Dunlap's was. His engraving contains a greater number of fussy lines, a distracting degree of visual busyness. Yet the changes had analytic as well as aesthetic impact. The heavily rendered lines in Dunlap's engraving made the sun's rays far more pronounced, and in Pope's poem sunbeams symbolize the rays of reason, which help to give force and focus to passion.[65]

Pope equated reason with the rays of the sun. Speaking of passion in Epistle II, for example, he made the claim, "Reason itself but gives it edge and pow'r; / As Heav'n's blest beam turns vinegar more sowr" (147–148). Strange though this metaphor may now seem, it probably did not strike eighteenth-century readers as odd. It alluded to a treatise by Francis Bacon on how to make a good, strong, and sour vinegar by leaving vessels of wine out in the noon sun. Pope's point, then, was that reason acted to transform passion, giving it a useful edge. Writing in a similar vein in the closing lines of the same epistle, Pope substituted the word "opinion" for reason:

> . . . Opinion gilds with varying rays
> Those painted clouds that beautify our days;
>
> . . .
>
> [Thus] Ev'n mean Self-love becomes, by force divine,
> The scale to measure others wants by thine.
> —Epistle II, 283–284, 291–292

In other words, if passions (or self-love) were clouds with the potential to darken the sky, they could be lit up, gilded, made divine by the rays of reason. In Dunlap's engraving the clouds, like the sun, were etched deeply. Upon closer inspection, it becomes clear that in both versions of the print, one side of the picture is bathed in light, the other cast in the tree's shadow. In his last addition to the *Essay,* Pope offered and Pennsylvanians accepted a philosophy that called for a balanced approach to reason and passion, one designed, as Pope had insisted all along, to steer "between doctrines seemingly opposite."[66]

The 1770s: William Percy and Benjamin Swett on Gales and Tempests

Certain factions within Pennsylvania had been eager from the very start to accept the proposition that passions could and should play a useful part in life. Others had recoiled against an innovation they believed would be conducive only to sin. Yet, as time wore on, Pope's perspective became ever more prevalent. It has been noted that some of the most popular lines from Pope's work were "On life's vast ocean diversely we sail, / Reason the card, but passion is the gale." By the 1770s, these lines had sunk so fully into public consciousness that they began to appear in private papers without attribution—no longer quoted explicitly, but instead integrated seamlessly into individual people's musings on emotion.

Consider the words of the devout Quaker Benjamin Swett, in the midst of an emotional and spiritual crisis in 1771. Like James Logan a generation before him, Swett did not entirely trust the motions of the passions. He confided to a correspondent, "My mind has endured various vicissitudes," complaining of swinging back and forth between "being ready to conclude" that he was journeying "under a prosperous gale" and worrying "at other seasons" that "a Tempestuous wind has driven me back." Yet, he accepted that the winds of passion would blow whether he wanted them to or not. Ruminating over his situation, in terms that might have been taken straight from the pages of Pope, he confessed:

> The sun has hid under a thick cloud wherein darkness alone prevails
> over my mind and thereby rendered it utterly incapable of judging
> whether I am in my course or bordering upon rocks and sands that
> will inevitably be my destruction until from a degree of the dawning
> of Celestial light, I reflect upon past favours (altogether unmerited by
> me) a secret hope again recurs.

Swett's concern that he was not able to accurately chart his emotional course echoes Pope's famous lines, if only faintly. The rest of his commentary makes the allusion still more clear. His chief concern was to balance passion with reason, to not let "darkness" prevail over his mind, nor let the sun to hide "under a thick cloud," but to await the dawn of "Celestial light" that could allow him to sail smoothly in the right direction. Guided by light, passions could indeed provide a "prosperous gale" that might bring weary sojourners closer to heaven. To be sure, where Pope saw light as reason, this Quaker might well have meant to invoke divine guidance, in keeping with Quakers' customary focus on the light of Christ within. Either way, the basic point stands. Where once Pope's praise of passion had seemed pure poison, by 1771 the claim, "Passion is the gale," was widely accepted.[67]

The idea that passions were permissible precisely because they were divinely ordained appealed across a broad religious spectrum. Thus, the Methodist minister William Percy in his commonplace book in 1774 defended evangelicals' emotional preaching style on exactly these grounds:

Formal ministers may steal a sermon and add a little out of their own heads, but a minister of the gospel cannot preach to purpose without the assistance of the spirit of God, no more than a ship can sail without wind. As for a carnal man, he may take his sermon in his pocket and you will find his sermon is always alike; but *spiritual* preachers . . . seldom do. . . . Sometimes they have a full gale and go before the wind and this is all by the assistance of the spirit of God.

Like Swett, Percy never actually mentioned Pope. Yet his discussion of gales and wind, of God's spirit and the spirit of emotion, wholly relied on the ideas advanced in the *Essay on Man*. This positive view of the passions, which had once seemed highly controversial, had become almost commonplace.[68]

Pennsylvanians began their engagement with Pope determined to acquire access to the latest British culture. They imported volumes of Pope's *Essay on Man* as much out of a desire to display genteel taste as to enjoy British literature or absorb innovative philosophy. As they read Pope in a colonial setting, their responses and reactions built, by slow accretion, a highly distinctive understanding of emotion. Where mainstream moral philosophy from Hume and Shaftesbury through to Hutcheson and Smith continued to argue that some emotions were blameworthy, especially those that promoted the self, Pope insisted that all passions were natural and that self-love was the source of social good. Torn between individual and communal models of the self, striving to create and maintain communities yet accommodate the eager impulses of individualism, colonial Pennsylvanians clung to the promises offered in Pope's poetry.

Despite the apparent simplicity of *An Essay on Man*, its promise to deliver complex philosophy in the pithy couplets of poetry, its deeper meaning often seemed elusive. Though ever a proponent of the passions, Pope's endorsements alternated between the forceful and the equivocal. Close to the end of Epistle IV, for example, just before delivering his resounding final lines, Pope himself offered a final hesitation:

And while the Muse now stoops, or now ascends,
To Man's low passions, or their glorious ends,

. . .

Say, shall my little bark attendant sail,
Pursue the triumph and partake the gale?
   —Epistle IV, 375–376, 385–386

Seeming to retreat from the heady claim of Epistle II that man, to be like God, should shun the still calm and mount the storm, Pope questioned one last time the wisdom of sailing his own little ship in passion's gale. Thus, even many of his most emphatic pronouncements could be made to support multiple conflicting interpretations. In Pennsylvania, home of the largest port in the colonies and one of the most religiously and ethnically diverse colonial populations, Pope's readers took many different tacks. Then, as now, the poem's lines could be rigged to many different sails.

If Pope's poem functioned as something of a social mirror, those who peered into it could hope only to see through a glass darkly. Nevertheless, Pope's poem would eventually serve as a lens that helped focus the social philosophy of a revolution. Just as men like Swett and Percy incorporated and extended Pope's ideas in their private ruminations, so his poem would leave its mark on many Revolutionary declarations. Meeting in Philadelphia at the first Continental Congress, Americans would put to use Pennsylvania's long debates on the passions in ways unimaginable to most back in Britain. In eighteenth-century Pennsylvania, self and society seemed continually intertwined. A judicious reliance on reason to direct the driving force of passion thus seemed the only means by which to honor the imperatives both of self-love *and* of social benevolence.

As unrest gave way to revolution, these once-contested principles would come to have decisive and far-reaching political consequences. While most of this project focuses on colonial Pennsylvania from 1745 to 1765—during the years of debate in the heart of the century—it will close by considering the coming of the American Revolution and, with it, the ascendance of self in American society.

The century's core debates could have been conducted in the absence of Pope's *Essay on Man*. Yet the fact remains that Pennsylvanians went to great lengths to import, buy, and read the poem, even going so far as to print copies in the colony itself, an effort expended for very few other literary works. Something in the poem spoke to eighteenth-century Pennsylvanians. Whether in the accessible simplicity of its rhymes or the complex optimism of its philosophy, the *Essay on Man* captivated colonists across a wide social spectrum. While duly pronouncing the importance of sociable feelings, it proposed a laudable purpose for selfish passions as well. Even those who initially opposed its influence could not ignore the poem's cultural sway.

The chapters that follow detail the everyday exchanges among ordinary Pennsylvanians that effectively put Pope's precepts to the test. In analyzing the role of emotion in the mediation of ordinary social inter-actions, it will be helpful to remember that social exchanges in the colony were conducted in the context of (and frequently commented on) a much wider and deeper transatlantic debate. In personal journals and private letters, in business correspondence and government minutes, in public sermons and political pamphlets, across the widest possible array of historical situations and sources, eighteenth-century Pennsylvanians pondered when, whether, and how to "walk upon the wind."

It all began, of course, with that first volume of *An Essay on Man* eagerly imported in 1735 by the fledgling Library Company of Phila-delphia. We know of that fateful purchase order, not because of records created at the time, but rather because of notes "collected, copied, and continued" in 1759 by a young man named Francis Hopkinson. The son of founding member Thomas Hopkinson, Francis Hopkinson began to serve as the Library Company's secretary shortly after taking a bachelor's degree from the College of Philadelphia in 1757. In the very year of his graduation, Hopkinson acquired a fine imported edition of Pope's com-plete works, nicely bound and illustrated. On the title page of each volume he carefully inscribed "F. Hopkinson's, bought 1757." Like the Library Company itself, which aspired to make Philadelphia the "Athens of America," Hopkinson was eager to make his mark on the world, but uncertain of the best means of doing so. If this chapter has emphasized the ultimate ascendancy of the passions, in actuality even passion's heart-iest proponents harbored enduring ambivalence about the moral and social implications of emotion, about the practical and philosophical trade-offs between dedication to self and devotion to society. Let us turn, then, to the story of Francis Hopkinson and the daily debates about power that drove (and derived from) eighteenth-century Pennsylvanians' preoccupation with the passions.[69]

2

The Dominion of the Passions

*Dilemmas of Emotional Expression and Control
in Colonial Pennsylvania*

Francis Hopkinson had much to ponder as he stood among the small band of students gathered for the first-ever commencement ceremonies of the newly established College and Academy of Philadelphia. Just twenty years old on that May day in 1757, he had already achieved his father's dream too late. For his father, Thomas Hopkinson, had spent some of his last days working to establish the school his son was now to graduate from. Dying in 1751, Thomas had left his son Francis, then fourteen, in a perilous position on the cusp of manhood. The young Francis, his mother, and his siblings were all accustomed to the comfortable way of life allowed by Thomas's law practice and his social connections with leading lights of Philadelphia like Benjamin Franklin, printer and all-around civic innovator, and Richard Peters, Anglican preacher and governor's confidant. Yet Francis had not then, at fourteen, chosen a method of earning his living or cemented his ties to the local elite. Now his graduation from the college would help address both of those issues; still, it would be years before Francis could feel that his social place was secure.[1]

In many ways, Francis Hopkinson's concerns mirrored those of the college's founders. For men like Thomas Hopkinson and Benjamin Franklin, both of whom had also helped foster the ambitious Library Company, social rank was never far from mind. With no local college available even for members of Philadelphia's most prominent families, young men of means who desired an education had been forced to travel outside the colony or to shift for themselves. Many of Philadelphia's most successful

FIGURE 4. Francis
Hopkinson. By R. E. Pine.
Phillip B. Wallace Portraits,
Historical Society of
Pennsylvania. *Permission
The Historical Society
of Pennsylvania*

families had found the expense of educating their sons abroad to be
prohibitive, a fact that only added to the embarrassment of their situation.
Thus, the creation of a college presented itself as the solution to two
pressing problems—how to educate local young men and how to further
consolidate the standing of an emerging local elite.[2]

And so Francis Hopkinson, fatherless son and would-be member of
the privileged few, must have listened especially intently to the parting address delivered by a father of Philadelphia's Anglican church and
provost of the College of Philadelphia, the Reverend William Smith.
Smith's address to the nine graduates assembled before him in Academy
Hall—there were eight new bachelors of arts in all plus one student taking
a master's degree—stuck closely to the theme of class advancement up-
permost in the minds of many assembled there. He told the graduates to
"consider [themselves], from this Day, as distinguished above the Vulgar
and called upon to act a more important part in Life," exhorting them to
"strive to shine forth in every Species of *Moral Excellence*." To do so, Smith
told them, they would need to focus their efforts on their emotions.[3]

To all who wished to claim moral excellence and social prominence he
urged, "Let it be your primary and immediate Care, to get the Dominion
of your own Passions." Warming to his theme, he exclaimed, "Thrice
happy you, when by *divine Grace* you shall have obtained this dominion

FIGURE 5. William
Smith. By Joseph Sartain,
after engraving by
Benjamin West. University
Preseidents Portraits,
Historical Society of
Pennsylvania. *Permission
The Historical Society of
Pennsylvania*

over yourselves." Such advice harkened back to classical admiration for Stoicism and adhered to the traditional attitude that unfettered emotions were the hallmark of the unworthy and the uncouth. For those, like Smith, who sought to employ emotion in the service of social distinctions, recognition of the universality of human passions was highly unpalatable. And, yet, the graduates in Smith's audience, who might have read the work of Alexander Pope as a formal part of their curriculum, were well aware of newer cultural currents arguing for a more permissive—and inclusive—view of passion. So Smith could not simply disavow emotion altogether. Instead, he argued for a more nuanced and complicated view of emotion, one that would counter the selfish excesses of a Popian embrace of passion yet allow new forms of feeling to flourish. Attempting to hew to the approach of benevolist philosophers like Shaftesbury, he argued that a "true *Discipline* of the HEART and MANNERS" required his listeners to "disdain a narrow unfeeling Heart, coiled up within its own scanty Orb." By combining advice to "get the Dominion of your own Passions" with an exhortation to "disdain a narrow unfeeling Heart," Smith appeared to offer a workable solution to the dilemma of how to strengthen the emotional bonds that cemented community without allowing the growth of atomizing individual emotions.[4]

No sooner did Smith pronounce his approval of selfless feeling over personal passion than he betrayed the fundamental paradox at the heart of the colonial endeavor: Pennsylvanians could not devote themselves wholly to the promotion of social stability when the very rationale for their society's founding—and the source of their devotion to it—was the creation of new social, cultural, political, and economic opportunities. While members of the emergent elite needed social stasis in order to stabilize their standing, these same people could not do without some social mobility. In other words, the very ascendance of self that the careful modulation of emotion could supposedly cut short was actually the underlying aim of emotional regulation. In reality, members of the elite could no more eschew personal passions than could the lower orders. Smith almost admitted as much when he promised his audience that accomplishing the emotional adjustments he proposed "will give you a Kind of Empire over the human Heart, which you will, no Doubt, exert for the noblest Purposes." Echoing the concerns of Pennsylvania colonists, Smith advocated self-mastery only as a means to achieve social mastery.[5]

Eighteenth-century people—navigating a social system that publicly reified gentility while clandestinely permitting mobility and an emotional system that espoused social feelings but covertly encouraged personal passions—were bound to confront contradiction around every corner. The putative elite's desire for a stable social order based on genuine shared feeling led members to insist on the importance of emotional sincerity. But the centrality of careful emotional regulation for the successful performance of gentility and civility meant that any guarantee of authenticity, emotional or social, was all but impossible. Theoretically, at least, those securely atop the social pyramid could be sincerely devoted exclusively to the kind of social feelings certain to reinforce the standing order. In reality, few if any members of the elite could ever be completely secure in their position and free from personal passions. Meanwhile, the deck was far more dangerously stacked for those further down the ranks. With the exception of those who uncritically accepted their social subordination (doubtless a rare breed indeed), the ideal of emotional sincerity would prove wholly impossible for the "lower sort," be they Euro-American, African American, or native American. Given only the options of faked compliance or genuine complaint, common folk attempting to negotiate the murky rules of emotional regulation had an exceptionally difficult path to tread. All sorts of entanglements ensued from the task that William Smith set his students to and so many other eighteenth-century Anglo-Americans also undertook. Ultimately, even those colonial inhabitants who initially espoused tight emotional regulation would end by claiming residence in the dominion of the passions.

The career of Francis Hopkinson, in the context of comments by numerous fellow colonists, can help to particularize the details and personify the acute dilemmas created by this highly complex system of social and emotional control. For a young man like Francis—ready to make his way in the world, born to membership among the elite, yet uncertain of the security of his class position—mastering the social meaning of emotional expression could prove of great practical importance. Even a decade after leaving college, Francis continued to grapple with the emotional dilemmas William Smith had imposed. Letters he wrote home in this period, during a yearlong trip to Britain in 1766–1767, open a remarkable window onto his efforts to "get the Dominion" of his passions yet disdain an "unfeeling Heart." Far from easily accommodating two opposing approaches to emotion at once, Francis, like so many others, found himself battered painfully back and forth between them as he tried to travel the road toward higher status.

Heaven Has Thy Part Assigned: Social Order and the Self

In the decade after graduation, Francis Hopkinson's career consisted of a series of promising dead ends and disappointing false starts. Shortly after taking his bachelor's degree, Francis took on the post of secretary of the Library Company and began studying for a master's degree. He successfully completed the master's in 1760 and then spent the next year, at least, studying law with Benjamin Chew, a noted local lawyer and member of the governor's commission on Indian affairs, before passing the bar in 1761. So far, so good. In that year, perhaps through the influence of Chew, he was made the secretary at a treaty negotiation with members of local native American nations in the Lehigh Valley. Clearly viewed as an up-and-coming young man, he had some initial successes at winning the kinds of honorary posts that helped to mark a colonial gentleman as a member of the ruling elite.

But then there were setbacks. Francis never managed to get a law practice off the ground, turning instead to commerce and opening an office on Market Street where he hoped to establish himself as a cloth merchant. This venture, too, soon lost its charm. His brief tastes of the perks and pleasures of appointed office—he was also made the official librarian of the Library Company in 1764 and 1765—left him hungry for a more permanent and profitable official post. And so it was that Francis Hopkinson began a yearlong quest to enhance his standing in Pennsylvania by forging connections with the English elite. His plan was to travel to his country of origin to try to ingratiate himself with some highly placed previously unknown family relations, who might have the influence to help him obtain a colonial sinecure.[6]

In his search for a post that would allow him to act an "important part in life," Francis paid careful attention to the emotional prescriptions of William Smith. His earliest letter from abroad, in the first flush of optimism in June 1766, fulfilled the second half of Smith's mandate. He assured his mother, "Now that I am writing to you I feel every tender sensibility revive and the pangs I suffered at parting again throb in my breast." Far from maintaining an unfeeling heart, he declared that *his* sensible organ panged and throbbed in his breast. Still, he would not always find the task of optimal emotional equilibration so easy to achieve. When his journey failed to produce any real job offers, a frustrated Francis would invert his emphasis on emotion, addressing instead the first of Smith's charges, to "get the Dominion" over his passions. Struggling to marshal his feelings about the social and professional disappointments suffered during his sojourn, he would describe the results of his trip to his mother in July 1767: "I do think and am determined to think that . . . I am satisfied." Here, rather than straightforwardly claiming satisfaction—or openly admitting his frustration—Francis instead laid bare the deliberation required to control his emotional expression. In so doing, he purposefully performed an act of self-mastery that should, and he still hoped would, legitimate him as a social leader. Even in the pages of a family letter, then, Francis could not articulate emotion without also offering comment on his social station.[7]

The public social impact of putatively personal expressions of emotion becomes clearer if we pause to note the ways in which ideas about the self were evolving in the early modern period. Consider, in this light, the words *disposition* and *personality*. Today these two words are virtual synonyms; modern concepts credit each individual with having a unique and independent self, a disposition or personality made up of the feelings and opinions a person expresses, the mood a person is habitually in. But, while *disposition* was a word familiar to most in the eighteenth century, *personality* was not. The distinctions between them, their divergent roots and differing time courses, reveal much about the way conceptions of the self have changed over time. *Disposition,* presently defined by *The Oxford English Dictionary* as a "natural tendency or bent of the mind, *esp.* in relation to moral or social qualities; mental constitution or temperament," has held this meaning at least since 1387. *Personality,* on the other hand, in the sense of "traits of character," dates from much later, 1795. While *disposition* and *personality* are near synonyms now, they weren't in the eighteenth century.[8]

The development of the word *personality* was possible only once the idea of the self as an autonomous and free individual had reached full bloom. Intrinsic to *personality* is the idea of *personhood,* autonomous identity, for *personality* denotes not merely "traits of character" but more fully describes "that quality or assemblage of qualities which makes a person what he is, as distinct from other persons; distinctive personal or individual character." *Disposition,* on the other hand, derives from a much different root. It relates to the word *position,* and indeed the first definition of *disposition* refers to "arrangement, order, relative position of the parts or elements of a whole." Fundamental to the word *disposition,* therefore, is the idea that the self exists only in relation to other selves, that one's "bent of mind" reflects, not one's autonomous individuality, but rather one's position vis-à-vis a collective whole. This relational view of the self remained highly prevalent in the heart of the eighteenth century.[9]

The idea of the individual—so closely associated with the Age of Enlightenment—simply did not develop all at once. There was no abrupt break between collective and individualistic visions of the self. On the contrary, the two ideas coincided in the mid-eighteenth century and often competed directly. Even as explorations of emotion in the mid-eighteenth century aided the development of the autonomous self, the expression of emotion continued to have ramifications for the collective communal self.

The complex interconnections between emotion, self, and society had profound implications for the conduct of eighteenth-century social relations. Consider now, by way of example, the emotion cheerfulness. Francis Hopkinson's expression of satisfaction in the face of disappointment grew in part from a deep cultural devotion to the ideal of cheerfulness. In this as in other matters, Francis followed closely the admonitions of William Smith. During his commencement speech, Smith had especially commended cheerfulness as an ideal emotional quality for members of the self-styled elite. He admonished his students: "Preserve a *Chearfulness of Countenance,* never affecting to appear better than you are. . . . 'Tis dishonouring GOD, and discouraging Goodness, to place Virtue in a downcast Look, or in any thing external." With the creation of this maxim, Smith drew explicit links between displays of good cheer and acceptance of social rank. Only those who overemphasized the importance of worldly, external status would betray dissatisfaction with their rank by permitting their cheer to crack. Of course, in promoting cheerfulness, Smith intended to encourage communal feelings and thus prop up the standing social order. But, in regarding expressions of cheer as a kind of social commentary, Smith belied his own claim that personal passions and sociable feelings could ever be disengaged.[10]

In the world of William Smith and Francis Hopkinson, declarations of cheerfulness could communicate contentment with (or at least acceptance of) one's social position as much as they could indicate a satisfactory state of mind. The instruction on the social meanings of cheerfulness that Smith handed down to his students appeared frequently in other instances as well. For example, a 1757 commonplace book begun by a Quaker woman named Mary Flower declared in a poem:

> What heaven has given thee, be therewith content;
> With no success elate, nor loss lament
> That bus'nes Heav'n has to thy part assign'd,
> Pursue in quiet, with a chearful mind;
> Convinced the rank you hold without dispute
> Shall best thy temper and thy talents suit.

Here again the message was clear; cheerfulness signaled contentment with one's rank, an acceptance of the part assigned by heaven. Meanwhile, expressions of loss or lamentation implicitly contested status.[11]

The dictates of the social messages sent by displays of cheerfulness had as much impact on women as on men, if not more, among the elite. An anonymous piece in the manuscript collections of an Anglican family contains advice targeted at young women that bears a startling similarity to the advice recorded by Mary Flower. This especially blunt testimonial in favor of cheerfulness came in the form of a poem written in 1768 by a single woman to her newly engaged friend, "Clemy":

> Small is the province of a wife,
> And narrow is her sphere of life.
> Within that sphere to move aright,
> Should be her principal delight
>   . . .

Heaven gave to man superior sway,
Then heaven and him at once obey.
Let sullen frowns your brows never cloud,
Be always cheerful never loud.
Let trifles never discompose,
Your temper features or repose.

A woman could best be a good wife by demonstrating her acceptance of her subordinate social position. Contentment was a matter not simply of personal peace but of smooth social relations. Sullen frowns could well be interpreted as a sign of disobedience or even of a desire to strain against the confines of woman's narrow sphere, but a cheerful manner signified a wife's acquiescence in her social allotment.[12]

Once the association of cheerfulness and social satisfaction has been acknowledged, seemingly innocuous emotional comments can be evaluated anew on several levels of meaning. For example, when the governor of Pennsylvania instructed one of his military officers, "By all means get the work finished as soon as possible: and the men ought to labor chearfully as their own safety depends greatly upon it," we apprehend that the governor was not merely saying that work should gladden the hearts of laborers but that laborers should willingly follow the benevolent dictates of their superiors whose task it was to protect the common interest. Here, the concept of cheerfulness helped to soften the sharp edges of hierarchy even as it strengthened them; the military men who joined cheerfulness to obedience supposedly did so in the service of their own safety as well as in deference to the governor's command. This is one of the most important features of eighteenth-century rules of emotional expression: they could help to mask continuing inequalities of power even as they maintained them. Such finesse became especially important in the colonial context, where heightened social fluidity both exacted and exacerbated a certain ambiguity in the signaling of hierarchy.[13]

Conversely, a refusal to show cheer could be in its own way a subtle contestation of subordinate status. This was the case, for example, with an army captain who was sent a copy rather than the original of a letter written by a major in the army. He recorded receipt of the letter in his journal, saying, "Rec'd a copy of a letter of the majour . . . I opn'd the same and found it to be a copy from the original . . . with which I could not content myself but went off immediately to Easton to see the majour." The captain's declaration that he could not content himself with a copy was not merely a comment on his feelings but a claim of social worth. By refusing to be content until he received an original, he affirmed that he was a man important enough to compel others not to disturb his emotional equanimity. He would not display cheerfulness, even before the higher-ranking major, unless and until he felt sure his own status was being accorded the proper respect.[14]

The social significance of cheerfulness becomes even more apparent when we consider that exactly the opposite emotional comportment was commonly associated with the lowest-ranking members of colonial society. Few direct records of emotional expression survive for any of the lower sort, and the upper orders rarely commented on the emotions of those they hoped to keep in the most subordinate social positions. Nevertheless, newspaper descriptions of "negroes" and servants provide some important insights into how ideas about cheerfulness and discontent could be incorporated into efforts at social control. For slaveholders chose to deny or deliberately ignore the emotions of the enslaved, not out of uninterest, but rather out of a strategic desire to legitimate their own dominance. In contrast to nineteenth-century stereotypes of happy slaves content to live in bondage, eighteenth-century slaveholders in Pennsylvania depicted the enslaved as chronically lacking in cheer, their emotional dejection the natural corollary of their social subjection.

If elite Philadelphians, like the founding members of the Library Company, spent a good deal of time hoping to make their colony the equal of ancient Athens, it should hardly be surprising that they would also turn to classical precedents when it came to slave emotion. From at least the time of Aristotle, slaveholders had adhered to the idea that enslaved people did not feel the same kinds of emotions as free people. Indeed, Aristotle's *Politics* made the explicit claim that "natural slaves," that is to say people "slavish" by nature, could be recognized by their singular lack of spirit, or *thumos*, that "quality of the soul which begets friendship and enables us to love." "The power of command and the love of freedom are in all men based upon this quality." According to Aristotle, then, slave status was less a legal category than a state of being. While Aristotle also claimed that natural slaves lacked *logos*, that is, logic or intellect, he regarded emotional failings as more fundamental. Thus, those who lacked *thumos*, the emotional capacity to love freedom, could naturally be accounted slaves, but those possessed of the proper spirit, the ability to love their fellows and value their liberty, deserved the reward of self-command.[15]

In accordance with such ideas, slaveholders in colonial Pennsylvania exhibited a remarkable tendency to describe the enslaved as dispirited. For example, one common way of referring to an enslaved person was as a "wretch," that is, a person "sunk in deep distress, sorrow, misfortune, or poverty . . . a vile, sorry, or despicable person of . . . reprehensible character." Consider the enslaved man accused in an unsuccessful arson plot whose execution was reported in the *Gazette* in 1741. The unnamed man "died like an impudent hardened Wretch," his fate "the Effect of his own sottish wicked Heart." The writer betrayed a startling constellation of assumptions in the course of this brief description. The accused was supposedly "hardened," or totally immune to emotion, yet also simultaneously "wretched," or both disconsolate and contemptible. Furthermore, he was also depicted as "sottish," that is to say, "foolish [or] doltish," and as "wicked." Having decided to burn the enslaved man at the stake, his executioners took care to justify their actions by stressing his supposedly slavish nature, characterized by an Aristotelian lack of spirit and logic alike.[16]

Proslavery forces repeatedly emphasized the idea of natural slavery, the notion that the "slavish" nature of American bondmen and -women arose from the innate emotional shortcomings of Africans. Thus a 1759 *Gazette* article recounted the misadventures of a slave ship:

> A Sloop . . . Slaving up the River Gambia, was attacked by a Number of the Natives . . . rather than fall into the Hands of such merciless Wretches, when about 80 Negroes had boarded his Vessel, [the Captain] discharged a Pistol into his Magazine, and blew her up; himself and every Soul on board perished.

The glaring irony that leaps out to the modern reader of this tale, that Africans resisting an English slave ship were derided as "merciless wretches" while the slavers themselves were portrayed as worthy objects of pity, was lost on the writer of the report. Far from being meant as an indictment of the slave trade, the story seems to have been offered as further proof that native Africans were wretched and slavish by nature.[17]

For thousands of Africans less lucky than those living on the Gambia River in 1759, the burden of bondage in colonial Pennsylvania would only have been augmented by such emotional expectations. On the rare occasions when Anglo-Americans considered African-American emotion at all, they simply assumed that slave spirits were always as low as their rank. We can easily see this attitude in the wording of runaway ads appearing in the *Pennsylvania Gazette*, remarkably few of which ever connected the enslaved with good cheer. In fact, in some thirty-five hundred articles pertaining to "Negroes" that appeared in the paper between its inception and the Revolution (from 1728 to 1776), only twice was cheerfulness mentioned in connection with blacks. True, most ads devoted very little space to any description of black emotion, hardly surprising given that transitory emotional states would have been of limited use for the identification of escaped slaves. Still, one remarkable exception to this general trend was the tendency for slaveholders to represent fugitives as having a "down look."[18]

At first glance, the true meaning of this common descriptor is difficult to discern, for the ads themselves are often opaque. For example, when a twenty-one-year-old man known as Joe ran away from a Pennsylvania forge in 1761, his erstwhile master's ad in the *Gazette* described him as "a Negroe man . . . marked with the Small-pox, has a flat Nose, Down-look, about 5 Feet 5 Inches high." Did the claim that Joe bore a "Down-look" refer to the habitual downward cast of his gaze, to a slumping posture, to his down-and-out social and economic status, or even possibly to a down and depressed state of mind? Some evidence supports the notion that such writers had physical posture in mind. This is one way to interpret the intent of the slaveholder who advertised for "A young Molattoe Fellow, named Jacob, about 5 Feet 10 Inches high, stoop shouldered, and has a Down-look" in 1763. On the other hand, the advertiser who sought Robin Cooper, with "a grim Countenance, down look," seems to have thought the enslaved man could be easily recognized by the emotionally dispirited look on his face. Meanwhile, when a twenty-four-year-old runaway called Mark was described as "round shoulder'd, down look, wants one of his foreteeth, and much given to swearing," his "down look" seems to refer equally to his physical bearing and his emotional burdens. Doubtless such vague descriptions did little to actually aid in the apprehension of runaways. Their frequent use, however, worked to uphold slaveholder pretensions about the naturalness of slavery. In depicting runaways as having a "down look," erstwhile owners claimed, essentially, that their slaves could be easily recognized because they looked "slavish."[19]

In the end, it seems clear that physical degradation, social subordination, and emotional depression were inextricably linked in the minds of the master class. William Smith, of course, had warned his elite charges that a "downcast Look" dishonored God and discouraged goodness. If cheerfulness was in a sense the exclusive privilege of the socially dominant, this was all the more reason why people eager to defend pretensions to status might find themselves ready, like Francis Hopkinson or the affianced Clemy, to lay claim to cheerful satisfaction, whether or not genuinely pleased with their social position. How better to dodge the association between downcast looks and downtrodden status? If people aspiring to the highest ranks of society showed cheerfulness to substantiate their status claims while middling sorts like the army major occasionally refused to show cheer as a means of social protest, then, among marginal members of society, displays of cheerfulness could, ironically, subvert the basic notion that they were naturally both emotionally and socially subdued. Indeed, because elite Pennsylvanians insisted that the enslaved felt little beyond a tepid emotional malaise, they made themselves vulnerable to any and every slave assertion of emotion.

With emotional control linked so closely to social control, shows of emotion by the enslaved had the potential to shake the colonial slave system to its very foundations. Tellingly, the rare occasions when African-Americans *were* credited with displaying spirit were always in the context of white alarm over black rebellion. One *Gazette* report of a "horrid Negro plot" to commit mass murder in Antigua in 1737 claimed that the slaves in revolt had "Hearts and Minds capable of conceiving, Heads fit for contriving, and Hands and Courage for executing the deepest and most bloody Crimes." No failure of *thumos* or *logos* in those hearts and heads! Recounting efforts to round up and execute every slave participant, the article emphasized the emotional strength of those involved: "Upon the Execution of the first [men captured], it might have been reasonably thought, that . . . a . . . Stop might have been put to their prosecuting this Bloody Conspiracy; but the Conspirators Spirits seem'd rather to be raised than sunk." Suddenly, the shared etymological root of the words *spirit* and *conspire* takes on tactical significance. Enslaved people who began by bolstering one another's spirits might well end by cooperating in armed insurrections.[20]

Perhaps in reaction to such reports, in 1741, Governor George Thomas of Pennsylvania issued a dire warning to members of the Assembly regarding "the defenceless Condition" of a colony "exposed . . . to the Domestick Insurrections of . . . Negroes spirited up." To be sure, coordinated violent uprisings were fairly rare in the sugar islands and never occurred at all in Pennsylvania. Nevertheless, considered in this light, slaveholders' usual remarks about the down and wretched nature of those they had enslaved begin to sound like so much wishful thinking.[21]

Even something as innocent as the expression of merriment could convey a sense of threat to eighteenth-century slaveholders. When in 1738 "several Negroes . . . appointed a rendezvous for a merry Frolick, in order to which, some provided Fowles, some Bread, others Rum, and others Sugar," only to have an accidental chimney fire spoil their feast, the report in the *Gazette* expressed as much consternation at their daring to engage in merrymaking as at the danger posed by the fire. Noting that the warehouse in which the enslaved people had met could have been burned, the author sniffed: "The whole range of Warehouses [c]ould have been consumed. Nevertheless the Negroes were apprehended, and as we hear, had a Frolick . . . of Fifty Lashes each, well applied." Here the idea that black people would ever try to be merry sets up the punch line of the story, contrasting the "Frolick" they created for themselves in the form of a clandestine feast with the "Frolick" provided by whites in their physical violence. The extremity of the white reaction in this case reveals the importance that the master class attached to maintaining the symbolism of the down and dispirited slave.[22]

With the stakes of black emotion set so high, it becomes all the more clear why whites generally preferred to disregard its existence altogether. First of all, on the rare occasions when they did take notice of the emotional expression of blacks, whites were unlikely to like what they heard and saw. A basic means of undercutting the effectiveness of emotional rebelliousness was to simply ignore it, if possible. Second, there was scant social ambiguity in the stark imposition of slavery; for whites the social niceties of sentiment were scarcely relevant to the relationship. Finally, the early start that antislavery activists gained in Pennsylvania (calling for feeling for the enslaved) gave slaveholders there added incentive to try to blot out evidence of black emotion; slaveholders could hardly be called upon to sympathize with black feeling if it did not exist. As a result, the vast majority of commentary on the emotions of Afro-Pennsylvanians comes only in the context of runaway ads like those just quoted or in reports of defiant action, instances when black emotion was simply too dramatic to be denied.[23]

In sum, when communal and individual models of the self coincided, all expressions of emotion inevitably contained social communication. Declarations of cheerfulness were one of the few expressions of emotion that ordinarily implied little interest in amending the social order. Nearly any other expression of emotion could communicate a desire to change the terms of social relations. The weight such expressions of emotion carried goes far toward explaining both why personal passions were so often discouraged by members of the elite and why they nevertheless continued to be covertly expressed. Only those completely content with their social position could be inevitably and invariably cheerful.

As Francis Hopkinson embarked on a transatlantic effort to cement his membership in the Pennsylvania elite, he placed as much emphasis on his appearing cheerful as on the fine impression created by what he described as his "elegant," "wholesome," and "fine" travel accommodations. Once he reached England, however, his confidence began to crack. His plan was to travel to the home of his cousin, a bishop with ties to the Penn family, in hopes of ingratiating himself and thereby procuring a post. But, before he even reached his destination, he began to be more concerned about the state of his emotions. He explained to his mother, "I was seized with a chilly fit . . . which was succeeded by a smart fever and ended in a total dejection and loss of spirits, greater I think than I ever before experienced." Little wonder that Francis could not keep up his cheerfulness now that he had begun actively and obviously seeking to improve his station! It bothered him to find he had lost the good spirits he enjoyed when setting out on his trip. Fortunately, the episode was short-lived, and he regained both health and spirits promptly: "I thank God I am now as well and hearty as ever I was in my life." He had need of this renewed self-control, for he was soon to arrive at Hartlebury Castle, the home of a cousin neither he nor his mother had ever met.[24]

Betwixt the Devil and the Dragon:
Dilemmas of Emotional Expression and Control

Francis's entrance to Hartlebury Castle was grander than he could possibly have anticipated. He had sent advance word of his approach, hoping that his uncle would do him the honor and courtesy of sending someone to meet him at the inn where the public coach stopped. But a late-evening arrival left him apprehensive that he might be forced to pass the night alone at the inn. Instead, to his surprise, the bishop sent his personal carriage to convey him to Hartlebury with, not one, but two servants to attend him. No sooner did the public coach draw up to the inn than Francis "lept into the chaise and was whirled away in state for Hartlebury." Now concerned that he had "had but little time to shake the dust off from my cloathes and fit myself up a little," he told his mother days later that he "had not yet got over the palpitations I suffered as I came along in the post chaise."[25]

The castle itself impressed Francis greatly, and he wrote breathlessly to his mother of being escorted by servants holding lighted tapers through a "beautiful courtyard" and a "spacious hall" before passing through "a long gallery lined with paintings" and, finally, being conducted back into the private apartments of the bishop's family. Though the bishop and the members of his household received him with cordiality, Francis remained ill at ease. He explained to his mother, "They treat me with great affability and kindness," but added, "The solemnity of my introduction did not a little increase my palpitations." Francis wrote two different letters, dated two days apart, trying to convey the gravity of the situation. Refusing to elaborate on his emotions, he hinted to his mother that they had indeed been intense: "I leave you to imagine the variety of thoughts which suggested themselves and the different agitations I underwent on the road."[26]

Palpitations and agitations: the task of fitting his clothes—and his countenance—for an audience with the bishop was of the utmost importance to Francis. His circumspect account of his emotions was an attempt to bridge the contradictions of his culture's emotional ideals. He did not claim that he felt little; on the contrary, he dwelt on the strength of his sensations in two successive letters. At the same time, he sought to demonstrate that he was sufficiently the master of his passions to become a master of men, and he declined to express to his mother just what his different emotions were.

Francis's contradictory impulses to assure his mother of the depth of his feeling while declining to specify just what he felt stemmed directly from the dilemma posed by Smith and reflected a widespread problem in a society that simultaneously promoted and prohibited emotion. Countervailing ideals for the cultivation of feeling and the suppression of passion made any expression of emotion a risk. Throughout their personal correspondence, men and women alike commented frequently on the pitfalls of uncensored emotional expression.[27]

A Quaker woman named Mary Peasely, for example, congratulated herself in 1751 on the progress she had made in modulating her emotions: "I am, by the favour of heaven, so far mistress of my own will and affections." To control her affections (that is, her emotions) and to control her will were one and the same task for Mary; success indicated an admirable self-control that enhanced her worldly standing even as it confirmed her submission to God. But she was not always this successful, for at the close of the same letter she admitted, "I have just freely scribbled my thoughts as they occurred, and wish thou would burn them when read." Mary regretted her uncensored personal expression as soon as the ink marked the page. Fortunately for us, however, her thoughts were, not burned, but preserved.[28]

People spoke often of the need for vigilance, as though their emotion was a force unto itself that they could only partially contain. The merchant John Swift wrote an apologetic letter to his uncle in 1750: "I am very sorry that anything that has slipped from my pen should give you cause to be offended at me as you seem to be when you wrote this letter. I assure you that I had no intention to give offense, nor did I imagine that anything I said in that letter could have had that effect, but I shall [for the] future endeavor to be more upon my guard." Swift deliberately cast himself as a passive onlooker of his own emotional expression; he apologized, not for what he wrote, but for what had somehow slipped from his pen as if of its own accord. And he resolved, not to alter his emotions, but to keep a better watch over their expression. Significantly, the surviving copy of this letter is a draft version in which Swift tried out several variations on the two sentences quoted above, documenting his efforts at the very watchfulness he promised to his uncle.[29]

In a similar vein, a trader named George Morgan pleaded with a correspondent in 1768 not to reveal his emotions toward a man they both considered an enemy. "I beg you will not let my sentiments be known to your nearest relations unless his impertinence obliges you to it. This I make a point of." Just in case his point was still not clear, he added, "He returns home deeply determined on revenge for some unguarded expressions . . . [in] the contents of some of your letters to me . . . on which he puts the most forced constructions." Morgan echoes Swift's emphasis on the perils of free expression and the need to maintain a constant guard on emotion.[30]

In both these instances, unguarded expression created potential crises in social relations. To show deference to superiors or consideration to peers, people were expected to keep a close watch over the emotions they expressed. Swift was forced into an abject apology to an uncle who was also his mentor and patron, precisely because unguarded expression constituted a breach of deference. Morgan's antagonist sought revenge against unguarded expressions in order to reassert his own social standing; to passively accept those expressions would have been to acquiesce in the dominance of his rivals. Thus polite men, who considered one another equals, would strive to strike a balance between free expression, which asserted their own status, and emotional control, by which they courteously acknowledged the status of their fellow gentlemen. The very ability to modulate emotions at will in this way was itself a mark of gentility.

Although those who aspired to genteel status were required to curtail expressions of emotion with superiors and censor those they shared with equals, they were allowed (if they chose) to express themselves freely before supposed inferiors. Such was the case in a letter from the Reverend Richard Peters—William Smith's fellow minister at commencement—to one of his correspondents. Peters, the highly prestigious secretary to the governor, wrote to one of the colony's most important Indian agents, Conrad Weiser. Weiser was generally well liked and respected by the colony's elite, but his backwoods life, uncertain fortune, informal education, and German origins hardly made him a social equal in the eyes of Peters.[31]

The finer points of their relative status can be seen in the emotion Peters expressed to Weiser and in his comments about that display. After describing a number of recent events that "grieved" him, Peters concluded his letter with a humorous reference to the need to curtail his expression: "But hold, I am too bold, well for you that there is no more paper." His expression of grievance represented boldness, the opposite of cheerful acceptance of his circumstances. As such it asserted his claim to status as a gentleman. But, in a nod to the respectable if somewhat lesser status of his correspondent, he broke off his remarks with a joking admission of his too free expression. The signals of dominance and deference encoded in the regulation of emotional expression were extremely subtle but nonetheless real and recognizable to eighteenth-century actors.[32]

There is an irony at work here. How were lower-ranking people to monitor their emotional expression before those of higher rank? On the one hand, social subordinates who censored their self-expression demonstrated deference. On the other hand, lower-ranked members of society who did express emotion only fulfilled elite expectations that they would always fail at the task of refining their feelings. Either way, their repression or expression of emotion marked them equally as inferior. The double standard ensured that, no matter what members of the lower orders did, they could always be dismissed as incapable of conforming to the genteel ideal.

Of course, lower-ranked members of society could and sometimes did try to use expressions of emotion to further assertions of self, potentially committing subtle breaches in deference through too-ready expressions of emotion—the kind of emotion John Swift was anxious to assure his uncle he had never intended to express. But the elite standard of emotional regulation was neatly designed to forestall the lower orders from defying the conventions of deference and mounting assertions of status simply by displaying their emotions. Elites could dampen the effectiveness of this expression by claiming that such emotional displays—such supposed failures of emotional control—were themselves proof of the inferior status of the person making the emotional challenge.

By asserting that members of the lower sort were naturally subject to passion, leaders could claim that they were also logically subject to subordination. On the rare occasions when whites recorded information on black emotion, they often added discrediting remarks regarding its unchecked nature. Comments that a runaway was "subject to fits especially when cross or vexed" or "very talkative, and subject to laugh" fall into this category. Whether laughter or anger was at issue, the important point was that the enslaved exercised no control over their own emotions. Those subject to passion deserved to be subjected to power.[33]

A key variation on this rhetorical tactic involved accusing blacks of being fools incapable of reason. While Anglo-Pennsylvanians prided themselves for using reason as a compass to guide them as they rode the gales of passion, they denied that blacks could exercise such direction. When the "Spanish Negro" called Mooner ran away from Philadelphia in 1749, his mistress vented her frustration by declaring that he "has a down-look, and has a very foolish laugh." By emphasizing foolishness, by denying that black emotions were at all regulated by reason, whites could write them off as actually unreasonable. When defiant down looks were too dramatic to be ignored, slaveholders could fall back on the claim that emotional rebellion reflected mental as well as social inferiority.[34]

Still, such dilemmas of emotional expression versus control can also be turned around and looked at from the opposite angle. In many respects, elites were the ones in a double bind. Those who sought deference from their subordinates could never find it in perfect form, for inferiors who expressed their emotions showed disrespect for their betters, but those who contained their emotions completely demonstrated a self-control that was in itself a bid for status. A related and very similar phenomenon for the case of all kinds of manners has been identified in colonial New England, where the elite wished to receive polite treatment as a mark of respect from members of the lower orders yet tried to keep the actual rules of polite behavior to themselves as the exclusive preserve of genteel culture.[35]

The full measure of both the elite's dilemma and its ultimate price for commoners is vividly demonstrated by a particularly gruesome crime account that appeared in the *Pennsylvania Gazette*. One Dr. Evan Jones, whose pretensions to high status were evident in his use of a title, employed as a servant a young man who claimed to be interested in joining the Freemasons. Jones and his friends (not themselves Masons) evidently considered the servant's interest in status advancement as threatening as it was absurd and saw in his aspirations a chance to humiliate him.[36]

They told the servant that in order to join the Freemasons, he would have to sign a pact with the devil. They first blindfolded the young man, and then "one of the Company indecently discovered his [own] Posteriors, to which the Lad, under the same Impediment of Sight was led to kiss." Behind the screen provided by the delicacy of eighteenth-century language stands the stark truth that Dr. Jones's accomplice forced the blindfolded would-be Mason to kiss his ass.[37]

They did not stop there. Jones poured a large quantity of rum into an earthenware pan and lit it on fire. At that point:

> Some of the company then diverted themselves at a Play called *snap dragon,* holding their Heads over the Pan, that their Countenances, from the blue Reflection of the Flames, might appear ghastly and hideous; hoping from thence that the Youth, upon taking the Bandage from his Eyes, would imagine he saw the real Servants of the Devil, who was personated by a Fellow dressed in a Cow's Hide with Horns. But the Deceased not expressing that Surprize which was expected, his Master asked him if he was not afraid; He answers, he is not. The Doctor thereupon takes up the Pan in his Hands, and throws the burning Spirits on the Breast of the Youth, who being covered with flames, his master threw himself upon him, and extinguished them. Here the scene of Hell closed, but with a fatal Consequence.

In other words, the servant's success in controlling his emotions and refraining from expressing the surprise and fear expected of him proved the final provocation to men intent on stymying his social aspirations, demonstrating his laughable inferiority, and affirming their own superior status. For the young servant, the cost of breaching class conventions by containing his emotions and regulating their expression was quite literally death.

Jones was tried for murder. The *Gazette* reported that the flesh of the deceased "appeared like the skin of a toasted pig." But Jones was convicted only on a lesser charge of manslaughter. Of the two accomplices tried with him, one was pardoned, and the other found not guilty. If low-ranking members of society could count on being denigrated for expressing their emotions, the consequences of attempting to adhere to upper-class ideals clearly could be even worse. Ironically, then, the lower orders could actually breach the standards of deference by adhering to the conventions of upper-class emotional expression, but elites could sometimes assert their social dominance by flouting those same conventions.

Does this then mean that emotional expression didn't actually matter much for the assertion of status? Not at all. In fact, this kind of doubleness often plagues marks of social distinction. Just as the lesser sort in the seventeenth century could be ridiculed for their rough and rude apparel but slapped with a fine if they dared to dress in finer fashion, so subordinate members in the eighteenth century were expected to be unable to control the very emotions they were required to restrain. What is especially important to take note of here is that, at a time when such overt social discrimination as the use of sumptuary laws was no longer common, a more subtle but no less pervasive set of social signals was conveyed through the regulation of emotional expression.[38]

These complicated status calculations gave rise to an interesting dodge in elite exchanges about emotion. People frequently described themselves in the act of subduing their emotions. Thus one man complained in 1754, "I think my letter . . . deserved a civiler answer, but that to myself." The beauty of this kind of remark was that it allowed the person making it to give free rein to expression even as he confirmed the cultural importance of emotional censorship and his own facility at the same time. Just this strategy was used by the man who told his correspondent, "I won't mention a single syllable of my uneasiness." Another man commented on the new necessity for genteel emotional restriction, "Perhaps these lines may give thee offence for as times go now we must not compl[ain] of wishes private nor publick disappointments no not to one's perticular friends." Here again the writer complained even as he affirmed the necessity of not doing so. In yet another instance, a writer described feeling "deeply plunged in suffering" but then in the same breath prayed, "Keep my tongue, and lips, yea my very heart from repining." In all these cases, people invoked the imperative of guarding their emotions yet simultaneously expressed just what they wished to.[39]

Indeed, what these remarks indicate is that the supposed inability to regulate emotional expression could in fact be turned to strategic purposes. A fine example of this tactic comes in the letter an Anglo-American woman wrote her husband protesting his plan to rent out their country house: "I must check my growing attachments for now and then a melancholy thought of who will succeed me and its being to be let out for a lake house as you sometimes sug[gest] it must be forbids me wishing to make those little improvements I think I could. But of this another time." Here she described her melancholy in the same breath that she confirmed the need to check her attachments and put aside her emotions "for another time." Should her husband remonstrate with her for expressing her emotions, she could plausibly say that she had tried to restrain them. At the same time, she disputed her husband's decision to let out the lake house she loved. In this lay the full potential of emotional expression as a mechanism of power relations. Just as the calculated display of emotion could subtly yet substantially further assertions of dominance, so also could such displays provide subordinates with a covert means of resistance. Given the complexities of the emotional conventions he had to negotiate, it is small wonder that Francis Hopkinson went to great lengths to recount his agitations and palpitations but then retreated, leaving his mother to imagine what they were.[40]

Stabbing in the Dark: Ascertaining Authenticity—Asserting Sincerity

In the real world, decoding the social meanings of emotion was even more difficult because the ideal of emotional modulation, and the resultant strictures on emotional expression, applied to both parties to social exchanges. Just as Francis guarded his expression, so too were his new friends regulating theirs. And so Francis soon faced another task, perhaps even more daunting than the first—attempting to ascertain the actual emotions of his hosts. "His lordship" and "Mrs. Johnson," as Francis called the bishop of Worcester and his sister, embodying the ideal of gentility, could hardly be expected to allow any uncensored emotions to break their careful composure. And so Francis, because his future success depended very much on the way these people felt about him, was forced to spend considerable time trying to determine just what their feelings were.

More than a month into his stay he cautiously reported to his mother: "His Lordship and Mrs. Johnson have taken great liking to me at least I may judge so from their exceeding kindness and affection which [they] are continually showing me. They have both assured me that they only want to be informed in what way they shall exert their interest in my behalf." Was the liking implied by their behavior genuine? Or did their kind treatment of him merely reflect the reflexive politeness of the well-heeled and well-bred?[41]

The longer Francis stayed on in the home of the bishop, the less sanguine his assessments became. In January 1767, by which time he had been a guest at the castle for a good four months, he told his mother:

> I am as much in the dark as ever with respect to any post being procured for me. It is a matter altogether uncertain. I would not therefor by any means have it whispered out of our family that I have any expectations of that sort. The Bishop . . . is a man of few words whatever, therefore, his designs or proceedings with respect to me are, he never divulges them.

Perplexed, Francis assured himself that he was at least a competent judge of the bishop's emotions. "Certain I am, however, that I have the happiness of being very high in his Esteem and have the greatest reason to believe that he will not neglect me as soon as an opportunity shall offer." Francis remained determined to keep as tight a grip as possible on his own self-expression. As he explained to his mother: "You have no idea of the delicacy and caution needed on these occasions. I shall endeavor to conduct myself with all the prudence in my power." But the strain of the effort was beginning to show.[42]

The dual problem Francis faced—one, identifying the emotions his hosts might feel but not express and, two, assessing the sincerity of those emotions they did deign to share—plagued many eighteenth-century Pennsylvanians. The inevitable consequence of a mass preoccupation with the regulation of emotional expression was an equally acute crisis of authenticity. If emotions had to be guarded, how could anyone be confident that emotions that were expressed were genuine? This crisis of sincerity and authenticity was in part a consequence of the fact that Anglo-Americans linked expressions of emotions to assertions of status in an age when social status itself was often uncertain. Colonial interest in social mobility and obsession with assessing sincerity fed off each other precisely because mobility and sincerity were oftentimes mutually incompatible goals. Newly arrived members of the local elite wished to look as though they had hardly exerted themselves in the journey, even if, as with Francis Hopkinson, they had recently made a transatlantic voyage in pursuit of social advancement.[43]

Considering the problem of sincerity from the vantage point of mid-twentieth-century philosophy, Lionel Trilling has argued: "The person who accepts his class situation, whatever it may be, as a given and necessary condition of his life will be sincere beyond question. . . . [But] a weakening of the fabric of personal authenticity might follow from the abandonment of an original class position." In a society in which people of all ranks remained invested in the possibility of social advancement, few could ever truly be cheerful—that is, willing in their social submission and satisfied with their social standing. Yet open and sincere emotional expression was supposed to be the surest authentication of social position. In any given social interaction, the meaning of the emotions expressed (or repressed) had to be weighed even as the rank of the speaker was measured.[44]

Comments like Francis's remark that he was certain of the bishop's feelings toward him occurred with enough frequency to provoke the suspicion that these people did protest too much. Letter writers peppered their missives with assurances of their complete confidence in the sincerity of their correspondents. In 1742, a man thanked his friend for writing to him, saying, "I am obliged to thee for those fresh marks of thy sincere friendship," and a decade later in 1752 a woman assured her friend: "Nor could I ever doubt the sincerity of thy friendship. I think I know thee too well in the holy covenant of life to do so." Should introductions be made on behalf of a new acquaintance, assurances of sincerity were among the essential components of a good reference, as when a man declared of his business associate in 1751, "I look upon him to be a sincere and worthy man."[45]

In such a situation, affirmations of sincerity were among the finest marks of respect that people could be given. John Kinsey, a chief justice in Pennsylvania, would have been pleased could he have heard the eulogy lauding him for exhibiting "an affable and benevolent disposition, a chearful steady conduct and manifestly flowing from a sincere honest heart, which gained him the most universal esteem that ever any one man had in the province." Likewise, Quaker minister William Hunt would doubtless have been gratified to be remembered as one "free from affectation in speech and carriage." To the socially well established came the advantage of ready assumptions of sincerity, or at least the advantage of immunity from overt scrutiny of their authenticity.[46]

Covert scrutiny was another question, however. Emotional sincerity and social authenticity seldom occurred simultaneously. Low status was easy to authenticate, but less likely to be sincerely accepted by the person consigned to such a position. Conversely, claims to elite status were less likely to be legitimate, but high status was more likely to be sincerely and cheerfully enjoyed. Thus, for would-be members of the elite, the slightest public slip in sincerity could have serious social consequences, indicating that one was not what one appeared to be, perhaps even that one was, in Smith's words, "affecting to appear better than you are." And so the charge of insincerity ranked with the worst of slurs. When military man James Read decided to denounce a fellow officer, he asked why anyone should "conceive so high an opinion of an insincere, glor[y]ing, avaricious, deceitful, sling drinking, wh——ring fellow." First in the long list of insults came the implication of insincerity, and along with it an allusion to social ambition in the form of accusations of avarice and vainglory.[47]

At the very same time that testimonials of authenticity abounded, numerous stories circulated about false friends—people who appeared to be sincere in their affections but who in fact worked at cross-purposes to those they ingratiated. Refrains against insincere friends echo through the record. From a woman to her husband: "I am well assured thou hast been deceived in those thou took for thy most sincere friends." From one man to another: "He has been constantly stabbing my reputation in the Dark . . . [but] at the same time he has kept an appearance of friendship." From a merchant to his partner: "I think [I] can discern some who profess friendship to us both to be alarmed at . . . our prospects . . . therefor just hint this to thee that thou may be on thy guard." From a man to a woman: that a certain lady's behavior "did not seem to correspond to the appearance of friendship which had apparently subsisted" between the two. Amid many mutual assurances of sincerity, considerable countervailing commentary on false friends reveals the great extent of anxiety over authenticity.[48]

Meanwhile, withering contempt awaited those who were themselves unable to discern the inauthentic. Members of the local elite had greater reason to fear falling prey to the insincere than did anyone else. In 1755,

Robert Hunter Morris, the governor, became exposed to ridicule of this kind when he provided patronage to men who flattered him rather than to men of merit. An observer analyzed the pitfalls that could befall a would-be patron surrounded by people professing allegiance and attachment: "Now this . . . attachment a man of sense may either really have, or the patron may only think so, and in that case, (as I have before expressed it) he will stumble. . . . A designing knave or obsequious fool will in general stand much the fairest chance of being his favorites." In the face of insincere flattery, the highest-ranked might easily falter. This critique of the governor concluded:

> How unfortunate has he been in the choosing of his favorites. . . .
> Thus has that unfortunate well-meaning gentleman been the instrument of aggrandizing and enriching two men whose behavior of late to him and those he was connected with, I need not describe to you, as you are well acquainted with it. He really has been nursing two snakes at his bosom.

In short, the governor had been duped. The ultimate irony of social subordination through emotional regulation was that, just when high-ranking individuals were most successful in curtailing the open emotional expression of their subordinates, they were most vulnerable to the slow poison of insincerity.[49]

Not surprisingly, then, the sincerity of enslaved African Americans, the lowest-ranked members of colonial society, was regularly called into question. Runaway advertisements warned of fugitives who were "very full of Flattery," who wore "down, designing look[s]," or else who were "smooth-tongued, talkative, and apt to deceive." Such attitudes offered insult to the enslaved even as they also attested to the vulnerability of slaveholders, who up until the moment their slaves broke free had been able to fool themselves that those they enslaved accepted the inevitability of bondage. Ironically, widespread agreement on blacks' inability to control their passions did not prevent whites from also claiming that blacks could successfully counterfeit feelings. Thus, when a Philadelphia man known as Sampson stood trial for arson in 1737, the *Gazette* gave his emotional self-defense nothing but contempt. "He made a long, artful and pathetick Defence, which wanted nothing to make it effectual but good English and Truth." Sampson was found guilty and sentenced to death. For whites, consistency mattered less than mastery, and accusations of insincerity provided an easy means of reinforcing hierarchy.[50]

Attitudes toward European indentured servants were similarly dismissive. When "an Irish Servant Man, named William Carmichael," ran away in Lancaster County in 1745, his erstwhile master described him as "very talkative . . . very much addicted to Lying," adding, "He pretends to know something of several Trades, but knows nothing of any." Likewise, when "an indented German servant man, named Frederick Meyer," broke his bonds in Berks County in 1775, the advertisement for his return warned, "He pretends to a great deal of sincerity, sings hymns, and makes long prayers." While blacks were uniquely burdened by claims about the "natural slavishness" of their emotions, all subordinate members of society bore the brunt of assumptions that they were incapable of factual veracity, emotional sincerity, and social accountability alike.[51]

In this context, an odd little anecdote recorded in the diary of a traveling Quaker preacher begins to make more sense. In 1764, when Benjamin Mifflin was just a few days' journey from Philadelphia, he suddenly "observed a great concourse of people from all parts that appeared as if drawn to a particular centre." The "particular centre" turned out to be a man who claimed a calling as a religious savant. Though most believed the man to be simply out of his mind, the would-be spiritual leader tried to rally people around him by "pretend[ing] to sinless perfection." He claimed as proof of his mystical powers that "he can know a man's heart by looking in his face." How telling of the anxieties of the era that a man boasting of divine attributes offered as proof of his potency an ability to judge the sincerity of others![52]

For every inquiry into the authenticity of the emotions of others that survives, there are two statements in which individuals assert the sincerity of their own emotional expression. With sincerity so important for the authentication of social status, one and all were anxious to appear sincere regardless of their actual emotions or social position. In essence, only those truly content with their class condition could actually and invariably be sincere in their emotional expression.[53]

Not only did people sign their letters with the conventional closing promising sincerity—a closing still in common use today—they sprinkled declarations of sincerity throughout their correspondence. Assurances of sincerity could be over anything from the profound to the mundane. One merchant told a correspondent: "I believe you want no assurances of my friendship. My dear Abram, I have a sincere love and regard for you . . . and I believe you are well convinced of it." With equal earnestness he proclaimed in another letter, "I am sensible . . . the owner of the wines must have expected they would have done better, but can sincerely assure thee I took as much pains to make the most of them as I could have done if they had been my own." And writers took pains to assert their sincerity not only in isolated incidents but in general terms.[54]

Widespread emphasis on the importance of authentic expression resulted in frequent attempts by writers to establish claims to sincerity as a fixed character trait. Thus one man proclaimed that his affection did "not consist merely in ceremony but proceeds from the very soul." A woman boasted, "I have always been used to write my sincere thoughts as they come and hope I always shall." Likewise, two other men echoed each other in claiming, "My soul detests insincerity," and, "I know not what it is to be insincere." As with the countless assurances of unquestioning belief in the authenticity of the emotions expressed by others, these mid-eighteenth-century Pennsylvanians' intense focus on justifications of personal sincerity points to probable tensions at work. Sincerity became the particular preoccupation of would-be members of a still-nascent elite because these people had the most to fear from exposure of their social striving.[55]

Such concerns troubled Francis Hopkinson greatly; much as he wanted to rise in the world, he didn't want to appear to *want* to rise. His anxiety to know whether the apparent affection of his hosts stemmed from real feeling for him or merely from convention grew out of his other anxiety— the possibility that his acquaintances at home might become aware of his social machinations. Trying to guard against the possibility of public ridicule, he warned his mother not to divulge the full reasons behind his English voyage: "I would not have . . . this much talked of out of our family. It will no doubt be supposed that I shall endeavor to make use of so good an opportunity of providing for myself. But no one need know that I actually have anything particular in my view." To be seen to receive an official appointment as the recognition and confirmation of his already high status was one thing. But to be caught attempting to use the acquisition of an office to enhance his formerly insecure standing was something else altogether.[56]

As far as Francis was concerned, everything depended on his ability to present himself as exactly the right kind of person, everything including his own pride in himself. As he confided to his mother: "I cannot help looking on the ensuing twelve months to be the crisis of my fortunes. If I miss this opportunity and should be disappointed in my expectations I shall never more make applications for any Post whatever nor will I accept of any. My pride will be touched and I will determine to set down with patience and render myself independent by some honest and industrious business." Did Francis actually link his own concern to cover his social striving with the issue of his own sincerity? Indeed he did.[57]

He betrayed the full extent of his preoccupation with sincerity in his very next letter home. He assured his mother, and no doubt himself:

> When I return you must not expect to find me much altered. You may perhaps fancy I shall come back greatly improved, a fine gentleman and all that but I have avoided with all possible care every innovation in my sentiments and manners and shall think myself very well if I return with the little stock of virtue and zeal for true religion which I brought with me from home. I am no more of a beau than I was when I left you and I think and feel very much as I did then.

With these lines, Francis staked a claim to personal authenticity explicitly on the grounds of the genuineness of his emotions. After spending six months seeking status advancement in England, he insisted that he thought and felt just as he had before his covert class-climbing adventure began.[58]

Many Treaties but Little Sincerity: Authenticity Anxieties in Colonial Context

Francis Hopkinson's career as a would-be colonial gentleman was shaped in large part by his position as a provincial outsider seeking recognition at the centers of British power. Literally following Francis Hopkinson east as he made his way to England, we have begun to see the ways in which members of a nascent Anglo-American elite relied on emotional expression as part of their efforts to assert their elevated social status and gain social acceptance in the metropole. But to try to explain the emotional culture of colonial British America only with reference to relations with Britain would be to overlook another equally important influence: relations with those to the west, with those whom they colonized.

British Americans generally and elite Pennsylvanians particularly were a people in the process of self-definition. They feared to appear as lowly provincials by contrast to the English aristocracy, yet hoped to appear as models of civilization when compared to the native Americans they lived beside and sometimes fought against. As emotion gained currency as a language of social stratification, its expression took on race and class inflections. Unfortunately, given that the only correspondence from Francis Hopkinson that remains from this period is what his mother happened to save from his visit to Britain, we cannot know exactly what he himself might have had to say about the regulation of emotion in the context of British-American–native American interactions. But we do know that Francis himself, like so many members of Philadelphia's ruling classes, had traveled west to treat with Indians on at least one extended occasion, during his appointment as secretary to the Lehigh negotiations. Enough reports of native American–British-American interactions have survived that we can garner a good idea of the part such exchanges might have played in the development of British-American emotional culture as a whole, if not what Francis Hopkinson thought specifically.

The proximity of native Americans brought added urgency to Pennsylvanians' preoccupation with identifying emotion and evaluating authenticity. Real gaps in language and gulfs in culture between Indians and English prevented the easy evaluation of social relations. Because the balance of power between the two groups remained contested through to the end of the colonial period, the social signals encoded in emotional expression remained significant strategic information. For colonial Pennsylvanians, the ability to assess Indian emotions took on practical importance. During the era of the Seven Years War—Francis Hopkinson graduated when the war was still in its early stages and left for England shortly after it ended—Indian traders, agents, and negotiators sent reports back to the city that continually emphasized the difficulty of determining Indian emotions. Again and again, these writers discussed the way that native Americans had "seemed," judging alternately that they "seem much offended" or "seem well pleased." Always, they wondered how they could perceive whether Indians felt more or less than what met the eye.[59]

One Indian trader, a Quaker named James Kenny who traveled to Pittsburgh to trade for furs in 1759 during a phase of uneasy truce in Pennsylvania, commented on how the "Indians seem" at least eight times in seven pages of diary entries over the course of a month. "The Tawny Indians . . . seemed satisfied." "James Morris a little short Indian seemed very saucy." "Two of the Shawnees from the lower town one of which is called Nantucke Will he talks English well but seems very churlish." "Nanticoke Will seems much better satisfied." "Shawanees warriors being come . . . they seemed very saucy." "The Indians . . . seem very loving." "An

Indian called kaykays . . . seems friendly to us." And finally, "The Indians I think seems to appear pleasant." Kenny had an obvious motive for his interest in the Indians' state of mind; he had set up shop on the frontier in wartime and was vulnerable at any moment to a hostile siege. The fascinating point is how reliant he was on his own ability to judge emotional appearances and weigh sincerity in the absence of more direct sources of information on the state of social relations. Expressions of emotion and negotiations of power blended together in Kenny's record. When Nanticoke Will apparently moved from churlish to satisfied, the state of power relations between him and Kenny changed at least as much as his state of mind.[60]

Not surprisingly, where Indian emotion appeared so open to question, Indian sincerity became subject to serious doubt. If concerns about false friends among themselves troubled Anglo-Americans, worries about the reliability of their sometime enemies and rivals the native Americans plagued them even more. As one man described the situation at the outset of the war, "Those few Indians that profess some friendship to us are mostly watching for an opportunity to ruin us . . . most of the Indians which are so cruel are such as was allmost dayly familiars." Likewise, the Indian agent Conrad Weiser, who communicated often with Richard Peters, the governor's aide, made sincerity the frequent subject of his reports. "It was only their lips that spoke and not their hearts," he warned of the Six Nations of Iroquois in 1746. Being a good judge of sincerity became more than a mere drawing room skill in a volatile frontier.[61]

Yet, Weiser knew of the possibility of insincerity in 1746 only because a trusted contact of his within the Six Nations told him so; the apt native American metaphor for insincerity suggests it was not just Anglo-Americans who cared about this issue. Indians clearly valued emotional authenticity as much as, if not more than, Europeans did, for the influence of emotion was deeply imbedded in Indian ideas about honesty. While in eighteenth-century English, sincerity could refer specifically to genuineness of emotion or more generally to fidelity to fact, the native American conception of integrity seems to have been based inherently in the heart, on a foundation of explicitly emotional openness.[62]

Indeed, on many occasions, Indians expressed great concern about the emotional sincerity of Europeans. Openly critiquing Pennsylvania colonists, the Cayuga chief Tokaaion complained: "When they speak to us they do it with a Shorter Belt or String than that which we spoke to them with. . . . I fear they speak only from their Mouth, and not from their

Heart." Without hesitation, Tokaaion compared colonists' sincerity directly and unfavorably to that of his own countrymen. Equally striking was the irritation of another Indian, from the Nanticoke nation no less, who rejected what he regarded as an ambiguous diplomatic overture: "We think that whatever it is it could not come from the Governor's heart." It is hard to escape the conclusion that Indians worried at least as much about colonists' emotions as colonists did about theirs.[63]

Colonists seldom acknowledged their own lack of emotional credibility, preferring to abrogate native American sincerity rather than admit the existence of any shared cultural concerns. As war drew nearer in 1754, Conrad Weiser wrote of the need for informants who might be able to tell "of the true sentiments of the Indians concerning the French on their undertaking." In that same year, he complained in a similar vein, "I do not know how to act in Indian affairs anymore, they are apostates as to their old natural principal of honesty." Here Weiser acknowledged Indian sincerity only in the breach, in the midst of proclaiming they no longer adhered to their own principles.[64]

The trope of the honest European and the insincere Indian proved popular indeed. It might have reached its height when Governor Morris opened a wartime treaty council in 1756 by telling the assembled Indians, "By this Belt I open your Eyes and Ears, and particularly the Passage from your Heart to your Mouth, that in what you have to say to this Government they may both concur, nor the Mouth utter anything but what is first conceived in the Heart." Never mind that the governor was performing a ritual invocation of sincerity initiated by Indians and articulated in metaphoric terms that they, not he, had originated; the Indians were the ones who had to be sure to prove their emotional authenticity.[65]

Only in 1759, when the native American nations closest to Pennsylvania at last formed an alliance with the English against the French, did many negotiators change their tune and begin trying to confirm rather than challenge the sincerity of Indians. By then the British were trying to regularize their dealings with native Americans by appointing an Indian agent, William Johnson, to coordinate relations throughout the colonies. The journal of treaty negotiations of Johnson's deputy in Pennsylvania, William Trent, sheds considerable light on the question of sincerity in Anglo-native relations. Eager as they were to cement an alliance against the French with members of as many native American nations as possible, Anglo-Americans relaxed their critique of native American sincerity.

Thus, after one early meeting, Trent remarked, "I called all the Indians here together . . . they all seemed well pleased and in my opinion were sincerely so." Indeed, Trent noted a number of instances in which native Americans themselves asserted their own sincerity, including one instance when they swore, "A little time would convince us of their sincerity," and another in which they promised to "convince us of the sincerity of their professions." Even in such cases Anglo-Americans declined to receive native Americans' assertions of sincerity with the same courtesy they regularly accorded to members of their own elite.[66]

Instead, Anglo-Americans devalued native American emotional expression by claiming that for them actions mattered more than attitudes. Trent recorded one exchange in which Anglo-Americans lectured native Americans: "[You say] you are sincere in what you have said but promises without performances is like the wind that blows every way." Native Americans addressed such concerns with promises "that they would convince me of their sincerity by their future conduct." Still, the need for verification remained a frequent point of tension. Five years later, in 1764, Colonel Henry Bouquet would likewise insist, "You may have expressed the true Sentiments of your nations, but we shall judge of your Sincerity, not from your Words, but from your Actions." In part, Anglo-American insistence that native American performances must conform to their promises resulted from the same insecurities about false friendship that underlay their own exchanges. At the same time, their stance exalted Anglo emotion over native emotion and promoted exclusive English claims to facility and familiarity with sincerity. Little merit as they might have had, these assertions confirmed Anglo-Americans in their own sense of themselves as a cultural group with a unique capacity for civilized emotion.[67]

Not only did Indian agents and interpreters make cultural critiques of native American sincerity, but those who came into more casual contact with Indians did so as well. Consider the self-serving comments of Captain Thomas Lloyd, a military man who served under Major James Burd during the Seven Years War. In 1759, at the height of the war, Lloyd sent his superior a letter complaining that, though the Indians he had to deal with were willing to make "many treaties," they were a people of "little sincerity." So common were such generalized disparagements of native American sincerity that this remark alone would provide scant new insight into the problem of cross-cultural authenticity assessments, if not for the cache of correspondence that preceded it. For Lloyd impugned the authenticity of native Americans at a time when his own reputation for sincerity was very much at stake.

Thomas Lloyd had landed himself in hot water by failing to report for duty. In October of 1757, he dodged orders to join Major Burd in camp by citing an illness in his family. He told Burd, "I hope you will do me the justice to believe that no other cause except the regard due to my family would have interfered with my observance of your orders which as soon as I possibly can, I shall obey with the utmost pleasure." Lloyd sought to assure Burd of his sincere and cheerful submission when he asked him to believe that he would always obey with pleasure. Given his appearance of defiance, such expressions were crucial to maintaining social relations. Yet two weeks later, Lloyd still had not obeyed his orders, saying this time, "I hope [you] [w]ill readily believe that I have not [delayed?] lea[ving] here in opposition to your orders . . . that I shall always with pleasure and particularly in the present case endeavour to obey your commands . . . and that I am [yours] with the utmost respect." Again Lloyd pleaded for credence and denied any intent to rebel against orders by insisting on his pleasure in obedience.[68]

Burd remained unconvinced and spread the word about Lloyd to his fellow officers. One wrote Burd in early November, "I am sorry to find that Lloyd has made my words good. . . . I told you that he did nothing to return as he promis'd, I find he has procured orders from your governor to stay recruiting here, but I hope . . . that we shall be able to overset that sche[me] and send him up." Lloyd had tried to work two angles at once, professing his sincere and respectful obedience to Burd while going over Burd's head all the way to the governor in an effort to secure himself a more favorable post. Far from accepting Lloyd's sincerity, his superior officers detected his scheming and vowed not to let his rebellion go unnoticed. By questioning the authenticity of Lloyd's pretensions and by seeking to get the governor's orders reversed, Burd and his fellow officer could reassert their own social status. They affirmed both their military rank and their social standing by refusing to be duped.[69]

In the wake of this episode, as he sought to recoup his own reputation, Lloyd sent Burd the memo of 1759: "As to Indian affairs they don't seem to be at present on the best footing. Many treaties but little sincerity. I believe their Friendship like the rest of the world will attend those who stand least in need of it and that in order to gain it we must first convince them that it can be of no service to us after which per- haps we may obtain it." Knowing of the earlier episode in which Lloyd's own credibility came into question, it is hard not to wonder how much of a coincidence his later condemnation of native Americans on the very same grounds could have been. It seems quite possible that, with his credibility damaged and his social status in doubt, Lloyd found in the disparagement of native American sincerity an enticing way to improve his own image.[70]

Partly through lack of understanding and partly by way of deliberate distortion, Anglo-Americans consistently questioned native American sincerity while taking for granted their own. To do so required them to fly in the face of historical fact, as Anglos—not natives—were generally the first to pawn friendships and break treaties, even in Pennsylvania. But doing so also allowed Anglo-Americans to enhance their confidence in their own cultural superiority and so bolster their claims to gentility. As late as 1764, a Quaker who had long worked to bring peace between Anglo- and native Americans complained that the many Pennsylvanians with party interests opposed to Quakers continually claimed, "The Indians are a treacherous people void of truth keep no engagements and therefore it was in vain to treat with them [so they should] Extirpate them." Indeed, as Pennsylvanians searched for new modes of gentility and novel avenues of advancement open to those not directly linked to the British social system, native Americans came to play an important negative role. The culture at large followed, as it were, the lead of Thomas Lloyd.[71]

William Smith, in his 1757 address, created a striking metaphor for the need to simultaneously encourage and control one's own capacity for feeling that also hints at the importance of the colonial context in the development of attitudes toward emotions. When Smith told Francis Hopkinson and his friends to seek to gain "a Kind of Empire over the human Heart," the Seven Years War was still being fought, a fact that adds new layers of significance to his remark. Get the dominion of your own passions *and* seek an empire over the human heart. Conquer yourself, and you may win the conquest of the world, Smith seemed to say. The dominion of the British Empire was based not only on the seizure of land but also on the claim that the English alone had the cultural capacity for genteel emotional expression and control. Each individual who struggled with the proper modulation of emotion contributed to the idealized vision of civility and gentility that came to characterize Anglo-American culture.[72]

A Quiet Mind and a Heart Alive:
The Personal and Religious Stakes of Emotional Regulation

For Francis Hopkinson, at least, this genteel ideal remained tantalizing but elusive. Though he hoped the connection he had established with the bishop might prove valuable in time, for the moment he had failed to achieve his objective. By late April he was forced to tell his mother, "I would not have you by any means occasion yourself to think that I shall return with any profitable post, much less encourage such a report to prevail; for I assure that I myself see no probability of any such thing coming to pass . . . for the present I have no other prospect but to return to Philadelphia and industriously set up in the Conveyancing Business." With his hopes of obtaining an official position dashed, his control of his own emotions remained an important means of asserting his continued claim to social prominence. In his next and last letter he explained, "I confess that I retained all along some hopes of having one of these commissions, but as it hath turned out otherwise I do think and am determined to think that it is much better for me." Faced with social setback, Hopkinson struggled to keep a further emotional failure from forever hindering his status aspirations. He was, in his own words, "determined" not only to prevent the outward expression of discontent but also to circumvent any inward feeling but cheerful acceptance of his lot. If only he could express nothing but sincere cheerfulness, he might be able to recoup at least some of his lost social capital.[73]

But the effort to both regulate and authenticate his emotions seemed to cost him something. In the late-April letter (where he had also "avoided . . . every innovation in my sentiments"), he reported making the acquaintance of a man who would accompany him on his travels home. In contrast to his previous confident assessments of the emotions of those he met, from his remark that he judged that the bishop and his sister had taken a great liking to him, to his later professed assurance that he held a high place in the bishop's esteem, he now appeared less certain about how to judge emotions. Of his new friend he said, "He has been extremely kind to me and very free and familiar; we ride out together walk out together and seem well pleased with each others company." Most striking in this description is not just the fact that Francis scrutinized his new friend's emotions, but that he also seemed to examine his own. The phrasing "*we . . . seem* well pleased with each others company" extended his doubts all the way to himself. It was as if his long and careful struggle to express only the proper emotions had left him as uncertain about how to discern his own emotions as about how to determine others".[74]

As much as social position mattered in questions of sincerity, more than just class was involved. Sincerity pierced to the core of the complex of individual and communal selves in the eighteenth century. How could people be expected to express only what they genuinely felt when faced with so many strictures concerning what was acceptable to feel? The social importance of emotional sincerity collided with the equally important social imperative of emotional regulation such that the problem of emotional expression became dizzying indeed. How were people to keep a guard over their expression and simultaneously ensure that every emotion they did express was unimpeachably authentic? And, if they did somehow manage to ensure emotional expression that was simultaneously socially acceptable and sincere, at what cost to the self would this success come? The need to censor emotional expression could create a crisis of authenticity not only between people, who could never completely trust the feelings expressed by another, but within each person.

If people sought to ensure the propriety *and* sincerity of their emotional expression by inhibiting any feeling they could not comfortably voice, they could begin to lose the capacity to identify what their feelings actually were. Francis's remark, *"We . . . seem well pleased,"* was echoed a few years later by Ann Graeme, the mother of a close friend of Francis. About herself and a social acquaintance Ann said, "We appeared to have a very easy afternoon, and . . . we parted with great ease, and politeness on all sides." Did she actually have an easy and enjoyable afternoon? Ann Graeme did not seem to know herself. The appearance of her emotions mattered more than the substance; the crucial thing was to conclude a social call with all the boundaries of genteel politeness securely intact.[75]

The stress engendered by the imperative of emotional regulation led to a recurring theme in the writings of many eighteenth-century correspondents: emotions could make people ill. Some people simply likened the experience of emotion to a bout of sickness, as when a young woman told her brother: "I am glad to hear of your bodily health but very sorry to hear of the disease of your mind for that is hard to cure. It is much easier to cure distempers of the body than of the mind." Many people went further still and asserted that unwelcome emotions could actually cause bodily sickness. Thus one young woman wrote home while traveling with her mother: "Poor mama has had several fits of illness which we think was greatly owing to the disappointments . . . she has met with since she has left home." Likewise, Mary Peasely, the woman so pleased when she felt herself to be the mistress of her emotions, reported discouragement on a different occasion: "I am somewhat better in my health than when thou left us, but not fully recovered nor hardly expect to be while this exercise of mind continues, which I cannot for my life get from under." And James Kenny, the diary keeper and Indian trader, believed he had to end a dispute with a man named John Longdale because "Longdale has been so much perplexed in mind about this matter that until this settlement was made he seem'd as if he was sick constantly." Again and again, people linked emotional distress to physical disease.[76]

Faced with the pain of personal passions, many did attempt to empty themselves of all agitations arising from within, the better to make themselves receptive vessels of feelings from without. Religious leaders who claimed that emotion could help believers achieve salvation provided another important impetus for this effort. As emotion became an essential element of conversion in many Protestant denominations, from Quakers to Anglicans, to New Side Presbyterians, believers were encouraged to attempt to eliminate selfish passions in favor of religious affections. Writers remarked repeatedly on their desire to eliminate the personal passions associated with willfulness, selfishness, and servility in favor of the feelings that met with social and religious approval. Doing so would bring them out of themselves and closer to God. In Pennsylvania, where Quakers had long led the way in arguing that feelings were fundamental to faith, such efforts took on special urgency.[77]

Quakers spoke often of the need for emotional receptivity in religious contexts, as when one Quaker wrote to the religious elder John Churchman, "I never found myself in a more hardened state, having no power to come to any stillness within myself at any time but especially in [religious] meetings . . . and quite insensible to any impression from what is said by any ministering friend." This man sought to still his own emotions in order to heighten his sensibility, his emotional openness to the spiritual messages of his fellows. In this process of emotional exchange lay the foundations of the communal consensus so critical to Quaker spirituality. Likewise, Churchman in turn counseled another believer a few years later, "Be still and labour for a quiet mind and . . . desire above all to have a heart alive to the Truth." Once again, this advice to drain the mind in order to open the heart did not involve eliminating all emotion. Rather, Churchman was asking his correspondent to eliminate selfish emotions in order to propagate spiritual ones. Only after stilling their own inner turbulence could believers begin to sound their feelings for the signs of God's will. For Quakers, eliminating personal passions involved more than personal comfort; it was an actual religious requirement.[78]

By the mid-eighteenth century, efforts to quiet emotional turmoil within in order to be more open to emotion from without had spread widely among many religious groups. An Anglican man writing in 1757 spoke longingly to his brother of "that tranquility I live in hopes one time or another to enjoy." No less an emotion expert than Anglican William Smith encouraged all who would listen to his commencement speech to strive to secure "the Serenity of your Temper." Likewise, in 1753 the Presbyterian preacher James Sproat confided to his diary: "Before meeting my thoughts seem'd wonderfully composed and a sweet calm settled upon me. . . . Oh Lord mold my temper into the gospel mold for Christ's sake." For him as for so many others, the religious mold for feeling required a purging of passion in order to achieve what writers called, variously, "peace," "calm," and "stillness."[79]

Few were able to confine questions of emotional regulation to worship alone. Instead, they found themselves grappling with dilemmas of emotional expression and control in all their interactions. Consider the comments of the young Quaker Joseph Norris, who was tormented by the strength of his own emotions. He promised his father, "There is nothing under the sun I so pant for as a few years of calm before I am taken hence, that my mind being in some degree of ease I may endeavour at my duty to God, mankind and myself." For Joseph, the religious, social, and personal imperatives of emotional regulation all ran together, and each added to his almost unbearable sense of pressure. Despite these compulsions, he still struggled to regulate his own emotional expression in socially appropriate ways. Apparently in apology for some verbal transgression, he told his father, "I am conscious of my unaptness to express myself to thee as I can to others [and as] I am sensible is oft my duty and interest to do." Writing this letter while he was still a dependent in his father's household, Joseph knew it was his duty to express himself carefully to his father. While uncensored emotional expression would have carried a certain disrespect, so too would insincere expression have involved a breach of deference. He struggled to prove his emotional sensibility and perform his social duty at the same time.[80]

In fact, mid-eighteenth-century people spent much time teetering between efforts to access and avoid their own emotions. A remarkable dream vision concerning the problems inherent in emotional expression is recorded by Mary Flower, commonplace keeper. The detailed dream narrated in her commonplace book—a dream copied in many other eighteenth-century compilations—suggests that, for Mary, expressing only religiously and socially approved emotion was such a serious exercise it could become actually hellish. The vivid account of a guided tour through heaven and hell dramatizes the real tension involved in emotional expression.[81]

The dreamer described hell and its inhabitants in detail, starting with the gateway to the abyss:

> I beheld a lofty grand arch of great wealth, where we entered into a large room . . . I had just time to take a view of this fine place before a number of persons richly dressed passed us, who smelled so strong of brimstone that I seemed almost suffocated, all of them were talking to themselves and before they came to us looked well, but when they came near there appeared a blackness in every face; those that did not talk loud mov'd their lips and seemed to mutter to themselves, which was also the manner of some who walked at a distance (or alone). I was seized with horror . . . these are miserable forever[.] They were when in the body in tumults and will be so everlastingly.[82]

One of the most remarkable features of this dream is that it portrayed hell as less a matter of physical torture than of emotional torment. The place smelled of brimstone, to be sure, but it was lofty and grand. The dreamer was seized with horror, not by some instance of physical cruelty, but by the sight of well-dressed people muttering miserably to themselves. Hell was a place of sorrow where the principal punishment was the struggle to express an infinite sadness.

The accompanying description of heaven is equally telling, for, on the same journey, the dreamer also caught a glimpse of paradise. Heaven was "a large building, the outside [of which] appeared strongly built with large rough stone." The narrator continued:

> The house . . . seemed white and bright and a large company setting. . . . I looked at the countenances of those I could see . . . there appear'd a sweetness and composure in every countenance far beyond what I had ever seen in any person while in the body. . . . I was filled with admiration; I looked to see if I could distinguish men from women but could not. . . . I followed [on] often halting and admiring the pleasure I saw in every countenance.[83]

Unlike the miserable murmurers of hell, the inhabitants of heaven were perfectly silent and serene. In Mary Flower's imagination, heaven was a place where countenances were completely composed, the task of regulating emotional expression over forever. Perhaps equally tellingly, heaven was without gender, a place where women could not be distinguished from men and every face was filled with sweetness. For those of lower rank or position, negotiating the public impact of so-called private emotions might have been especially burdensome and restrictive.

The dreamer's description of reawakening reinforces the interpretation that anxiety about emotional expression was among the principal concerns behind this dream:

> I awoke. But the horror and distress I felt on my mind, I am not capable of expressing . . . I seemed as if the smell of Brimstone was in my stomach, and I really thought I could not live many hours, nor do I believe I should [have] if the Almighty . . . had not . . . caused that suffocating smell to pass from me . . . and enabled me to vent my sorrows in many tears. After which my tossed mind was favored with a calm.

Here, once again, emotional and physical ailments went together, with mental disturbance and respiratory distress each threatening the well-being of the dreamer. As we might expect, the dreamer sought release from the torments of emotion in the abatement, not elevation, of her spirits.[84]

Ironically, much as Mary Flower (like the dream's author) might have wished to eliminate her own sinful and selfish emotions in order to experience the serene pleasures of heaven, such a covenant would prove impossible to keep. Even in this dream account, the antidote to emotional ailments proved to be, not their repression, but their successful expression. Only after the dreamer expressed her sorrow and vented her tears was her tossed mind freed from emotional tumults. Faced with conflicting requirements to regulate their emotional expression in such a way as to ensure sincerity, social acceptability, and religious approbation, people paid lip service to the socially sanctioned idea that they should rid themselves of selfish passions. In the event, they found this exercise hellish indeed and sought above all to gain relief by releasing their emotions.

Ironically, the people that took this trend the furthest might actually have been those that labored under the tightest emotional constraints. According to the complaints of their masters, at least a few enslaved men eventually turned the emotional system of signification on its head and refused to restrain their emotions at all. By the 1760s, newspaper ads began to fault blacks, not for being innately void of reason and thus subject to passion, but rather for their calculated decisions to express emotion openly. Thus one 1766 ad claimed that a nineteen-year-old called Cato "pretends to be foolish, to obtain his freedom," and another from 1772 asserted that Moses Grimes was a "very artful" man who "pretends to be free . . . and if spoke familiarly to pretends to simplicity and laughs." In these examples, whites paid blacks the backhanded compliment of disbelieving that they were actually simple and foolish, incapable of reasoned emotional restraint. Blacks, meanwhile, turned whites' racist rules against them and laid claim to the free emotional expression usually reserved for only the highest-ranked.[85]

Up and down the social scale then, people found they could empty themselves of personal passion only by venting it through expression. Each time people described their "exercise of mind," their "inability to come to stillness," or their as-yet-unrealized "hopes to live in tranquility," they sounded the very notes they pledged to silence. However much they might try to submerge selfish concerns in favor of social interests, in actuality the elimination of emotion was not only impracticable but also undesirable. So long as religious rules and social conventions alike decreed the importance of being open to emotions from without, people would inevitably become increasingly aware of those from within. Though the social significance attached to emotional expression was explicitly intended to bolster the stability of the communal self, in the end the ascendance of the individual self would prove inexorable. From Francis Hopkinson to Moses Grimes, Pennsylvania colonists used emotional expression as a fundamental sign of self-assertion. Still, inevitable as the rise of personal passion may seem in retrospect, we should not overlook the intense ambivalence that accompanied its emergence.

Night and Day—Sincerity and the Self

When William Smith advocated that the graduates gathered at commencement should "get the Dominion" of their passions while "disdain[ing] a narrow unfeeling Heart," he did not foresee the complexity of the final task he set his students to. Rather than confronting the contradictory nature of his advice, Smith simply tried to separate the two standards for emotional regulation he proposed: one pertained to the question of "how to *live* with YOURSELVES, and your GOD," whereas the other applied to the issue of "how to *live* with the WORLD." Such a division assumed an easy split between private and public selves, the one in control of its passions, the other ready to feel. It was just such a split that was impossible at a time when communalistic and individualistic notions of the self so closely coincided.[86]

The Reverend Mr. Smith was far from alone in making the claim that passions should bear no part in living with the self and that feelings should be reserved for living with others. The emotional paradox he promoted was widely accepted as the ideal. In fact, William Smith's delineation of the difference between passion and feeling in 1757 neatly anticipated Adam Smith's dictum: "To feel much for others and little for ourselves . . . constitutes the perfection of human nature." Yet, as already hinted by the popularity of Alexander Pope's proposal that "SELF-LOVE and SOCIAL are the same," few Pennsylvanians stood ready to embrace the communal self at the expense of the individual self. Both Smiths asked their audiences to perform the impossible, because communal bonds based on shared feeling required the very kind of inward turn most likely to promote development of the individual self. The very act of examining, identifying, and expressing emotion aided the expansion of the autonomous self.[87]

Competition between these two concepts of the self—the self as individual and autonomous versus the self as part of a communal whole—explains the great eighteenth-century preoccupation with sincerity so remarkable in writings from Pennsylvania. For pronounced concern for sincerity arose precisely when the two concepts of the self coexisted, and sincerity could bolster, or threaten, either one. Because expressions of emotion carried social implications, only sanctioned *and* sincere expression could maintain the stability of the communal self. If the emotion to be expressed could not pass public muster, then conflict inevitably ensued. Either sincerity could be sustained, honoring the individual self that gave rise to the socially unacceptable emotion but undermining the community by violating its sanctions, or the problematic emotion could be suppressed and sincerity submerged in favor of social conformity. In that case, social ideals could be upheld only at the expense of the individual *and* at the added cost of introducing inauthenticity into social relations.

The unique dilemmas engendered by eighteenth-century understandings of the self can be further appreciated if we contrast them again with the perspective offered by Lionel Trilling. When Trilling set out to explore sincerity and authenticity, he turned to that traditional figure of the

Western canon, William Shakespeare. Using Shakespeare's line, "To thine own self be true," as a starting point, Trilling defined sincerity in a way that speaks directly to the themes of this chapter: "At a certain point in its history the moral life of Europe added to itself a new element, the state or quality of the self which we call sincerity. The word as we now use it refers primarily to a congruence between avowal and actual feeling." Truth to self undoubtedly was one of the primary concerns behind the rising preoccupation with sincerity, yet this concern could only emerge with the development of the concept of an autonomous self.[88]

There is a second and equally fundamental concern at issue in Shakespeare's lines that Trilling does not address: the impact of sincerity (or the lack thereof) on social relations and especially on power relations. For the full quotation from Shakespeare continues, "thou canst not then be false to any man." When Shakespeare wrote this, the communal self was the dominant model of the self; thus the second concern—to not be false to any—was in fact the primary one. In Shakespeare's time, people were concerned with sincerity not so much out of a desire to create an authentic autonomous self, but because expressions of emotion contained social declarations. Then, by the mid-eighteenth century, overlapping conceptions of self created a severe crisis of sincerity: it was then that social authenticity and personal sincerity became tangled together. In eighteenth-century Anglo-America, emotional expression could create, confirm, or contest *social* status even as it aided the construction of an *individual* self.[89]

Perhaps that is why William Smith, self-appointed professor of the passions, closed his 1757 commencement remarks on emotional regulation with the very lines from Shakespeare singled out by Trilling:

To your *ownselves* be TRUE,
And it must follow, as the Night the Day,
You cannot then be FALSE to *any Man*.

Ultimately, then, Smith closed his case in a Popian vein, acknowledging two realms of self, yet insisting that individual interest could cement communal bonds. In reality, the selves that professors and philosophers insisted were complementary existed in competition. The strain of trying to combine these selves—to simultaneously ensure social sincerity and personal integrity—involved eighteenth-century Philadelphians in a difficult dilemma, one too complex to be readily resolved at the close of a commencement speech.[90]

All of William Smith's facile formulations could not prepare Francis

Hopkinson for the difficulty of navigating the contradictory requirements of his culture's emotional ideals. Like many members of colonial Anglo-American society, Francis had attempted to enhance his social standing even as he denied all interest in status advancement. While cheerfulness, willing submission, and acceptance of rank remained cultural ideals, sincerity would continue to elude most colonists. In a society in which social striving remained an often unacknowledged and largely unaccepted practice, mobility and sincerity would prove mutually incompatible goals. Ironically, the greatest claims to sincerity could be made by the least members of society, such as those few enslaved African Americans who dared to openly express their passionate discontent with bondage. In blacks' occasional open expressions of emotion and admitted desire for improved social position lay the future direction of American society. Yet few would then have guessed this. For the time being, continued emphasis on communal solidarity, and the accompanying need for social stability, made individual assertions of emotion seem as much threatening as promising, particularly to members of the elite.

So long as communal and individual models of the self overlapped, personal expressions of emotion retained serious social implications, and social conventions for emotional expression carried deeply felt personal ramifications. The depth of such connections will be seen in the strategic significance and public consequences of what we might take to be the most intimate of human emotions: love.

3

"A Corner Stone . . . of a Copious Work"

Love and Power in Eighteenth-Century Alliances

When Henry Drinker set sail from Philadelphia to attend to business in England in the winter of 1760, he left behind negotiations of a most important and delicate kind. Until the moment he was called away by demands of trade, Henry Drinker, staunch Quaker and promising merchant, had found his time consumed by the effort to persuade a certain young woman named Betsy Sandwith to become his wife. Forced to continue his courtship by correspondence, he sent frequent letters home. At the close of one such missive, Henry found that his love nearly overflowed his letter and wrote, as he sealed it, "I find that without a Cover there is some danger of losing a word by Wax or Wafer which word may perhaps be as a Corner Stone to my Love-Fabrick, and by losing it Sap the foundation . . . of a copious work." We might well expect that these flirtatious lines about his "Love-Fabrick" were meant for the eyes of his intended, Betsy. In actuality, this epistle (which to the modern reader looks very much like a love letter) was sent, not to Betsy, but to her sister Mary instead. This poses an intriguing question: why would Henry attempt to lay the cornerstone of his love for one sister by writing a letter to the other? Strange as this procedure may seem, it was nothing out of the ordinary in the eighteenth century. In fact, the phenomenon of the public love letter was quite common.[1]

Just two years earlier, in the autumn of 1758, another young man, William Franklin, had followed a similar procedure. Like Henry, his professional ambitions called him to England before his courtship could be brought to closure. And so William, son of Benjamin and aspirant to

FIGURE 6. Elizabeth
Sandwith. Society Portrait
Collection, Historical Society
of Pennsylvania. *Permission
The Historical Society of
Pennsylvania*

colonial office, also relied on correspondence in the long-distance pursuit of his marriage. From his lodgings in London he scrawled off a closely written eight-page letter so personal, it initially appears as if the "dear Madam" he addressed be none other than Elizabeth Graeme, the young lady he was courting. William spoke of his hope that overseas communications could "raise or keep alive some soft emotions in my favor." In fact, the "Madam" in question was, not William's Elizabeth, but one Madam Abercrombie, a married woman and a mutual friend. The stories of these courting couples provide an opening to examine the public expression, social meanings, and political implications of love, an emotion many modern readers might assume to be among the most private of all.[2]

Close attention to the language of love and affection can highlight key intersections of personal feeling and public status in eighteenth-century British America: the peculiar phenomenon of the eighteenth-century public love letter resulted from the continuing overlap of competing notions of self. Well into the eighteenth century (as argued earlier) traditional models of the self as communal and constructed through social relations persisted alongside new models of the self as individual and autonomous. Nothing dramatizes this quite like the public avowals of private feeling common in eighteenth-century romances. Because becoming a

FIGURE 7. Elizabeth
Graeme. Shippen Portraits,
Historical Society of
Pennsylvania. *Permission
The Historical Society of
Pennsylvania*

husband or wife changed social roles as much as it did personal relationships, expressions of love meant as much for community as for identity.[3]

Indeed, because of the intersection of public and private, declarations
of affection commonly appeared not only in the course of courtship
between young men and women but also in the negotiation of associations of many kinds. Most prominently, ceremonial declarations that
cemented bonds between king and subjects, or between colonial governors and their assemblies, relied heavily on the language of love. Another
important instance of the public use of affection came with the creation
of diplomatic alliances, particularly those between Anglo-Americans and
native Americans. Just as marriage was supposed to make husband and
wife one flesh (and, under the system of coverture, one legal person), so
the exchange of affection between ruler and ruled or between two parties
to a pact helped further the fiction that their interests naturally and
entirely coincided. The language of love thus worked to elide distinctions
between self and society, theoretically easing the tensions between communal and individual visions of the self.[4]

Eighteenth-century documents, from private correspondence to public records, quickly reveal the prevalence of loving language in the Enlightenment, but coming to a firm understanding of such language has

long proved elusive. On the one hand, it could be argued that greater emphasis on personal affections implied increased concern for personal fulfillment, a new privileging of the needs of the individual self. This perspective is summed up by the term "affective individualism," a phrase linking the search for love to the realization of self. According to such views, the promotion of love led to the diminution of patriarchy. The problem is that emphasis on affection predated—and by no means presupposed—interest in individualism. As the prevalence of public love letters shows, courtship could be romanticized without being privatized. Likewise, tying the rise of romantic love to the decline of patriarchy ignores the fact that affectionate rhetoric developed within a political system yet dominated by hereditary monarchy and within a social system in which men remained the undisputed heads of household. That loving language increased just as these customary social and political forms came under critique does not prove that love was necessarily emancipating. Despite the causal links many historians draw between the emergence of affection, the rise of individualism, and the decline of patriarchy, romantic rhetoric actually developed in defense of the very institutions it would hasten toward demise.[5]

On the other hand, neither can the evidence fully support the opposite interpretion, that a new emphasis on love served as the basis for an emerging brand of "affectional authoritarianism." Though one might argue, in opposition to "affective individualism," that the language of love arose primarily as a new tool of coercion, as the velvet glove over the iron fist, this model too comes freighted with problems. Tracing patterns in the expression of love reveals eighteenth-century Anglo-Americans engaged simultaneously in the search for personal fulfillment, the effort to assert social status, and the quest to stabilize community. Love's efficacy lay in its mutability.[6]

Eighteenth-century expressions of love served to veil exertions of power, yet not to end them. The metaphor of the veil is crucial; while the image of shrouding suggests that men and women took interest in softening the imposition of power, it also affirms that they continued to credit its importance. In contrast to more fixed kinds of status signifiers, expressions of love and affection could mediate social interactions in creatively complex and even apparently contradictory ways. Such ambiguity had particular strategic advantages in eighteenth-century British America, a time and place in which status remained unstable and social ideals remained in flux. Like clouds that gauze without wholly covering, expressions of love and affection could both reveal and conceal, allowing simultaneously for the contestation, negotiation, and affirmation of power, whether around the tea table, in the statehouse, or at a treaty meeting.[7]

Eighteenth-century claims of love and affection thus comprised crucial statements of social and political alignment as much as personal expressions of enamourment. The public love letters of those courtships reflected and reinforced the continuing social (and economic) stakes of marriage matches even in the face of new romantic ideals. Meanwhile, mutual expressions of devotion remained a key element of Pennsylvanians' struggles for colonial position and affiliation—whether conceived as transatlantic ties, local political links, or frontier alliances. Examining the emotions expressed in manuscript correspondence illuminates the former, and the comments in the published record can spotlight the latter. In combination, such close studies of the language of love and affection, of when, how, and by whom it was employed, can reveal the intimate eighteenth-century connections between the personal and the political, between love and power.

To understand the full implications of expressions of love, we must examine the stories of Henry and Betsy and of William and Elizabeth from first flirtations to final declarations. At the same time, we must also follow William and others like him not only through the rituals of courtship but also amid the affairs of court. For William was eventually to be appointed the last royal governor of colonial New Jersey, a position in which he would have ample occasion to encourage his subjects in their "professions . . . of Duty and Affection" to his administration.[8]

"Social Love Exerts Her Soft Command": Affection, Dominance, and the Submergence of Self

When Henry Drinker told Betsy Sandwith's sister Mary that he intended his love letter to serve as the cornerstone of a copious work, his choice of an architectural metaphor underscored the relationship between love and mastery. Marriage marked an important rite of passage for young people, making young women into wives and young men into household masters. Married men headed households and controlled the labor and property of all household members. Young never-married men, on the other hand, were bound first by law and then by custom to live and work in the households of other men, be they fathers or masters.[9]

Henry's reference to building underscored marriage's role transforming young men into heads of home. So closely connected were marriage, manhood, and mastery that, in practice, many young men would not move into houses of their own until their marriage. Reporting on a friend's marriage, one man noted, "Jemmy Tilghman was marry'd about the 1st instant to Miss Nancy Francis and they are just come down and going to take possession of Mr. Francis's house in Talbott." So long as marriage remained a key measure of maturity, men's efforts to win women's love would remain closely coupled with their efforts to consolidate status.[10]

Young men themselves were acutely aware of the full stakes of courtship. Samuel Allinson devoted an entire section of his commonplace book to quotations on marriage. There he recorded a telling commentary on this anxiety in 1761 when he transcribed a passage from a pseudo-serious history of the ancient world: "By the law for encouraging matrimony, as a penalty upon those who lived bachelors, they were declared incapable of inheriting any legacy by will, so likewise if being married they had no children, they could not claim the full advantages of benefactions of that kind." Young men of marriageable age faced nothing like these restrictions then in Pennsylvania; nevertheless, Samuel's interest here shows his consciousness of the continuing social significance marriage held for men. Much as young men and women might have desired to come to courtship decisions as unfettered individuals, they could not do so in an age in which so-called private decisions had such a profound impact on social station and community formation.[11]

Links based on love were supposed to shore up men's traditional social and familial roles, not to weaken hierarchical forms of social organization. Indeed, outside the romantic realm, few hesitated to link the expression of love with the recognition of authority. Children, of course, were supposed to love and obey their parents. Ministers regularly reminded young people to "honour and love their Fathers and Mothers, to help them as Occasion may require, and to . . . submit themselves, *consistent with what they owe to God and their own Souls,* to all their Governors, *Teachers,* Spiritual Pastors and Masters." As in this advice from George Whitefield, love and submission flowed quite naturally together. Perhaps more surprisingly, love and authority also cropped up side by side in many extra-familial realms. One prime example of this comes with military relationships. Consider the militia captain, "who for his known Courage . . . and for his humane Treatment of his Men, was always both fear'd and lov'd by them." Between militia leaders and their troops, fear mingled with love; command of obedience and command of affection were regarded as one and the same.[12]

So closely linked were invocations of affection with exertions of authority that the king himself was frequently quoted as requiring love and submission together. In one example, from 1753, the *Pennsylvania Gazette* quoted King George II's complaints about colonial "Animosities and Divisions, amongst the different Branches of the Legislature[s]." The danger, in the royal analysis, was that such disputes would "lessen and impair the due Authority which, by Right, belong to us . . . and thereby alienate the Hearts and Affections of our loving Subjects." Alienation of affections and impairment of authority went hand in hand. Meanwhile, the converse proposition—that, where hearts were tendered, authority was acknowledged—also enjoyed widespread currency. The king continued:

> Being determined . . . not to permit our own Authority and Prerogative to be in any Degree violated . . . you are hereby strictly . . . required . . . to use your best Endeavours . . . to quiet the Minds of our loving Subjects, and . . . to signify to them . . . that we do strictly charge and enjoin them for the future, to pay to our said . . . Instructions due Obedience; receding from all unjustifiable Encroachments upon our legal Authority and Prerogative, and demeaning themselves in their respective Stations.

As the king's comments make clear, there was nothing at all antithetical in the expression of love and affection and the imposition of social subordination.[13]

Yet ambiguity about the true nature of love allowed it to perform important functions, enforcing social distinctions with exquisite subtlety. Records of the expression of love and affection stem primarily from situations where power imbalances needed to be finessed. Not only did kings claim affectionate and loving relations with their far-flung colonial subjects, as courting men did with their intended wives, but business partners too could use loving words to smooth over looming conflicts. Consider a Philadelphia cloth merchant who fell into a disagreement with his London supplier about the quality and cost of a shipment of goods. In one letter, the trader told his supplier forthrightly that he was "thoroughly convinced" his own version "of the account was right, because [he could] bring vouchers for every article in it." Any shortfall in cash must have occurred at the wholesale end, he insisted, telling the supplier, "You was ill used by those you bought the [goods] off." Yet, when the supplier took offense at the merchant's accusations—and threatened to cease dealing with him at all—the dependent colonial shopkeeper attempted rapprochement in dramatic emotional terms. Admitting, "I have no money to send you [because] I sold but few goods," the merchant stated his fear: "The remaining part of my life will be attended with very little satisfaction to myself. Your affection upon which was all of my dependence seems to be worn out, so that all the comfort I have to depend on now is in hoping that it will not be long before it ends." In the midst of a serious billing dispute, one large enough to make or break his fortunes, this man tried to shift the focus from economic exchanges to emotional ones. Reliant on his supplier for connections to English manufacturers and credit contacts, the colonial merchant was certainly the lesser member of their partnership. But, by insisting that nothing mattered more than mutual affection, the two men could cease struggling for monetary superiority and instead cultivate emotional parity, which allowed them to continue trading for years after this incident.[14]

Underscoring the point that love and affection mattered only for palliating status discrepancies between higher-ranking people is the fact that Pennsylvania masters never proclaimed love for servants or slaves in either public or private documents. Just once between 1728 and 1776 did an author link an African-American with the word "love" in the pages of the *Gazette*—and then only in the context of a lewd comment about a black man's lust for white women. Only once in the *Gazette* in this period was a black person discussed in terms of affection; in 1760 an unnamed enslaved "Negroe Man, about 28 or 29 Years of Age," characterized as "a good Seaman," was offered for sale and described as "much liked by all Masters of Ships he has sailed with." This is the kind of exception that perfectly proves the rule. In the relatively leveling atmosphere of a sailing ship, in which a captain had to rely on the ready cooperation of his men, there might be room for the articulation of affection between the white master of the ship and a black crewmate. But it was a rare moment in colonial Pennsylvania when power relations between whites and blacks were compatible enough to allow such careful calibration.[15]

Only where status divisions were more mutable did expressions of love play a significant role in mediating social relations. Stressing the familial nature of affection, that is, linking ties of biology and lines of authority, had the effect of naturalizing distinctions that might otherwise have met with protest. Thus, leaders commonly applied the adjectives "maternal" or "paternal" when describing the affection of rulers for subjects. Such conventions formed the basis for the remarks of the Pennsylvania governor who declared, "Britain, our Mother Country, by the vigilant Care and Paternal Affection of the best of Princes . . . fully enjoys the great Blessings of Peace and Plenty." People also routinely referred to affection as "natural" when trying to compare political bonds to familial ties. In 1743, the governor of New York assured assembly members, "His Majesty's . . . natural Affections extend to the Remotest of his Subjects." In such situations, the greater power and status of the ruler might not itself have been in doubt, yet the legitimacy of his authority rested in part on the expression of affection. By implication, if the king's affection for his subjects was natural and even familial, then the relationships of dominance and dependence that affection helped to inaugurate were themselves not only natural but also incontestable.[16]

Indeed, as this discussion of adjectives indicates, one useful way of examining the power implications of affection is to look closely at the vocabulary with which affection was verbalized. Excerpts of speeches featured in the *Gazette* frequently employed the word *affection* in tandem with a complementary word that shaded its meaning in significant ways. A significant example of this came with the tendency to pair affection directly with the word *duty*. Massachusetts governor Jonathan Belcher typified such usage when he urged members of the legislature in 1730 to remember "your Loyalty and Obedience to the King, and your Affection and Duty to his Royal House." Here affection implied duty just as loyalty obliged obedience. Maryland's clergy spoke in much the same vein when they assured Lord Baltimore in 1733, "Both Duty and Affection . . . inviolably attach us to your Lordship." Again and again these speakers suggested that the expression of affection and the acknowledgment of obligation arose from the same set of hierarchical social relations. In fact, next to the word *duty*, the most frequent pair of words for affection was those that communicated deference and respect, such as *regard* and *esteem*, as well as the word *respect* itself. Far from being an automatic harbinger of egalitarianism, expressions of affection could describe and inscribe unequal status relations.[17]

Whether the king came to Parliament to ask for passage of a revenue bill, a colonial governor appeared before the legislature that controlled his salary, or a suitor addressed the woman he courted, in every instance the social superiority of the former over the latter was clearly understood. At the same time, in each case the supposedly superior person was also a supplicant, someone who needed the support as well as the subservience of those he addressed. All parties stood to gain if the naked imposition of subordination, so common between masters and servants, could instead be shielded by loving sentiments. Indeed, because convention demanded that expressions of love should be reciprocal, exchanges of affection could promote notions of social interdependence even in the midst of negotiations over dominance and submission.

Declared mutuality of feeling helped lighten the weight of authority on affection; as a result the official record is rife with the details of affectionate exchanges that, however formulaic, were too socially significant to be omitted from the conduct of power relations. When word reached Philadelphia in late 1730 of the imminent arrival of William Penn's son and heir Thomas, governor and legislature lost no time in lavishing each other with affectionate exchanges on his behalf. Assembly members started things off by assuring Governor Patrick Gordon of their "Duty and Loyalty to His Majesty, Affection and all due Respect to Your Honour, and Fidelity to Our Proprietor." Gordon replied by casting his own affections in with those of his subjects: they should "between Us shew . . . mutual Harmony . . . with Loyalty to his Majesty, Fidelity to Our Proprietors, and with Benevolence and Affection in every Individual towards his Neighbour." A year later, almost as if without interruption, they were at it again. Gordon promised to pass on the Assembly's many dutiful declarations; he would "esteem it a Happiness . . . to represent to our Proprietors that Regard and Affection which the Assemblies of the Government have so frequently expressed for their Honourable Family." The Assembly replied in kind that it rested "fully assured" the governor had "on all Occasions represented the good Affections and Regards of this People to our Honourable Proprietors." The governor then followed with one more acknowledgment that thanks were "due for this your obliging and affectionate Address." A whole new volley began again a month later when Gordon informed the "Representatives of the Freemen" that Penn's sons had not only "succeed[ed] to the Honours and Estate of their much esteemed Father" but would no doubt "imitate his Example in their Affection . . . for this Province." The Assembly assured him that the proprietors, "being Inheritors" of William Penn's "Vertue and Affection to the People," would be "justly entitle[d] . . . to a joyful Welcome." Though modern readers may well begin to glaze over while reading such exchanges, the *Gazette* brims with evidence of such give-and-take. Providing full documentation of the reciprocity of such expressions was too important to skip.[18]

Still, each such exchange of sentiment enacted the terms and conditions of unequal social relations. In the model affectionate exchange, the person of higher rank offered protection or provision (or both) along with affection, promising to watch over subordinates and secure their interests. Conversely, when a person of lower status expressed affection, custom called for declarations of submission along with material demonstrations of support. Ideally, then, speakers would cement the expression of affection with more concrete symbols. As Gordon told the legislature in 1731, "NOT only my Thanks in Words, but likewise in Actions, are due for this your obliging and affectionate Address."[19]

A few examples will suffice to show how protection and provision were traditionally traded for submission and supportive contributions whenever love and affection were exchanged. Shortly after Britain declared war on Spain in 1739, the *Gazette* quoted the king as saying, "The Honour of our Crown . . . call[s] upon us to make use of the Power which God has given us, for vindicating our undoubted Rights, and securing to our loving Subjects the[ir] Privileges." Here the king cast his own role in terms of the obligations of affection, promising to tend to the security of his "loving subjects." In return, he expected that the love of his people would lead them to back his efforts. He concluded by declaring that he would "vigorously prosecute the said War, being assured of the ready Concurrence and assistance of all our loving Subjects." According to the king's formulation, subjects who loved him could best demonstrate their feelings by offering material and practical support for the British cause. Pressing home the point, he told Parliament, "I cannot doubt, from your known Affection to My Person and Government . . . but you will grant Me such effectual Supplies . . . as may . . . enable Me to carry on the War with Vigour." Protection—security—came in exchange for support: "assistance" and "Supplies."[20]

Seen in this light, the frequent linguistic pairing of *duty* with *affection* becomes all the more significant. If the first definition of *duty* was "the action and conduct due a superior," an important related one was "a payment made in recognition of feudal superiority." Mining the meanings of *affection* reveals that buried deep within ideas about love and duty were feudal traditions of dominance and dependence. Pennsylvania's governor picked up on exactly these themes when, just one month after the king's speeches were published in the colony, he issued a proclamation to "earnestly invite His Majesty's Subjects . . . chearfully to inlist in this Service," in recognition of the fact that the king had "engaged in Affection to protect their Persons and secure their Interest." Meanwhile, members of the Virginia assembly followed protocol perfectly when, as quoted in the *Gazette,* they "resolved to give such a Sum of Money, as the Circumstances of this Colony will allow" to support the war effort. Echoing royal phrasing, they explained that they did so because they were "desirous to give the utmost Testimony of their Loialty and Affection to His Majesty's Person and Government." Expressions of love and affection were intended to fortify the links of lord and vassal, not to enfeeble the workings of patriarchy.[21]

At the same time, the expectation of reciprocity meant that people anticipated love and affection would knit them together in communal relations, not sunder society in the name of individualism. An essay appearing in the *Gazette* in 1756 summed up this attitude succinctly. The author began by claiming that "Society is a Sort of Machinery" and that within that machine "every Individual has his Part to act." In this mechanistic model of human relations, individual identity mattered less than common cooperation. This would-be social engineer went on to explain that, in the ideal society: "All Persons will be engaged by Choice to do their Duty with the greatest Chearfulness. All Discord and Party Disputes will for ever cease. The truest and sincerest Love, Esteem and Affection will be encouraged and cultivated, and the Whole will be made happy." This writer's attitude reflected the common eighteenth-century assumption that love's basic purpose was to bring, not contentment to the individual, but happiness to the whole, reinforcing hierarchical relations and community integration alike.[22]

Many regarded the promotion of social love as a religious requirement as well as a moral imperative. Quakers did so, of course (as we saw in the Chapter 1). Evangelicals and others did so as well. As one believer agonized in the pages of the *Gazette* after hearing a sermon of the evangelical preacher John Wesley:

> O CHARITY! Oh whither art thou fled?
> When wilt thou raise again thy drooping Head?
> When wilt thou abject Bigotry remove,
> And every Breast inspire with Social Love?

Such writers tried to impose the judgment that selfish love tinged with individualism was akin to bigotry, a kind of hypocritical intolerance of others. Social love, on the other hand, promised to reinforce the values of community.[23]

Still, writers also betrayed a nagging awareness of other contradictory implications of love and affection. The *Gazette* contains many more anxious testimonials in favor of the socially supportive functions of love than actual reports of its successful employment. Self-styled repairmen who offered fix-it manuals for the social machine tacitly admitted it might be broken. The problem, according to many *Gazette* authors, was that too often true love was mistaken for self-love, a brand of affection tied to the promotion of the individual. Books and pamphlets throughout the mid-eighteenth century offered to teach readers the difference between "Self love and Constant love" or made comment on the connections between "Self Love and Bigotry." Often exhorted, but harder to find, was the kind of love extolled by the social mechanic.[24]

Popular critiques of self-love reveal that emphasis on affection accompanied a rising awareness of individualism. In Pennsylvania, where many people hoped to pursue their own interests and advancement even as they bemoaned the erosion of communal structures, love seemed to offer a solution. If affection could marry personal interest to the public good, then perhaps the impulses of self and society could be made compatible. As yet another poet and moralist put things:

> Where social love exerts her soft command,
> And plays the passions with a tender hand;
> Whence every virtue flows, in rival strife,
> And all the moral harmony of life.

Or: virtue and morality flowed naturally from social love. Once people relinquished their own passions for social satisfactions, the only remaining rivalries would be among competing varieties of virtue. Setting social love against the competing impetus of presumably personal passions, this poet argued that authority promoted harmony. Was the persuasive power of this poem's argument limited by the counterposition, already advanced by Alexander Pope, that self-love and social were one and the same? Perhaps. Then again, perhaps not, for the full implications of Pope's equation of self-love and social love were quite complex. While the meld of self-love with social might allow individuals to pursue personal advancement under the guise of communal goals, it also allowed the opposite kind of elision. People could be pushed to subsume their own interests to those of society, on the grounds that anything conducive to the common good by definition brought benefit to each and every member of the whole. The language of love and affection thus helped to curtain struggles for power.[25]

Within the context of courtship, ardent declarations of affection could no more than partially obscure the real social stakes of marriage. If young men knew that the decision to wed meant nothing less than gaining the right to the title of household master, young women equally well understood the ways in which marriage would alter their status. Agreeing to assume the role of wife involved far more submersion of self than a man's task of donning the mantle of mastery. Among the literate, leisured, and well-to-do, young women began to express dissatisfaction with their subordination to men. Thus, even as courtships were increasingly couched in terms of romantic rhetoric, they continued to carry important implications for gendered divisions of power.[26]

Though relatively few critical commentaries about patriarchy have survived among the writings of young Philadelphia women, several vivid statements do stand out. In one instance, Betsy Sandwith's friend Ann Swett recounted her efforts to stand up for the rights of women. Writing in French she explained: "My Daddy . . . has been letting us know that a husband has a right to correct his wife when she deserves it, that is endeavoring to convince us of it. But we were determined not to be convinced . . . I am determined to plead for the liberties of my sex in every station." Particularly for young women of the elite, the pleasures of courtship could pale in the face of the real-life responsibilities of a new household position. As another friend, Eliza Moode, exclaimed privately to Betsy in French, discussing a man they knew:

> Does he think that women were made for no other purpose than that
> of being slaves to men? . . . Does he think that all the business of our
> lives is only to learn how to make a sausage or roast a joint of meat
> and take care of a House and practice in short Good Economy. All
> That is Necessary, I avow it. But Can't we be that and take charge of
> our spirits at the same time; must we Neglect the most Valuable part
> for fear of offending Our masters? . . . Even the most Mediocre capacity is capable of learning.

For single women who had the leisure and leeway to cultivate their learning and their spirits so long as they remained adult daughters in the homes of their fathers, marriage could mean great sacrifices. While young men might long to take up their rightful place as household heads, young women hesitated long and well over thoughts of the strictures to be endured for the sake of not "offending Our masters."[27]

In another case, a father reported on the views of his daughter. Isaac Norris sent news of Betty to a favorite female relative of the family: "I had heard her sister Hannah and she intended to become Authors, by writing a learned piece, to shew the injustice of men's assuming so great superiority over the women; this is no fiction I assure thee, for I once by accident saw some sheets of the work." Though Norris did not take his daughters' concerns entirely seriously, it is clear that they objected in earnest to the costs that wedding imposed on women. In marriage, the elisions of self-love and social cut two ways, allowing husbands to advance their own interests in the name of the household good while asking wives to subordinate themselves to the same.[28]

For her part, it seems that Elizabeth Graeme was no more eager than Betsy Sandwith to give up the freedoms of girlhood and take on the role of wife and mother. Elizabeth's friend Eliza Stedman joked while surveying the courtship scene: "There is nothing new in the diversion way and as to marriages they ante thought of. Those that are in that state of bondage think fit now and then to increase and multiply in downright compassion as this is a young country and wants peopling." Childbearing was work women did for the good of their communities—not necessarily something they themselves looked forward to. Marriage, meanwhile, could be compared to a state of bondage, a view that did not bode well for young men seeking to become heads of household. Henry Drinker could speak of the fabric of his love while William Franklin implored for soft emotions in his favor, but the women they addressed remained acutely aware that beneath such romantic language lay real considerations of dominance and dependence. However finely tempered, women and men alike recognized the power conferred by love's commands.[29]

Affection Alone Promotes Inseparable Interest: The Useful Fiction of Identity of Interest

Like women, men too might hesitate before deciding to enter the "state of bondage." Many questioned whether the responsibilities of mastery were worth the rewards, not least because of women's own increasing assertiveness. So when Elizabeth Graeme embroidered William Franklin a silk watch chain as a present, he reacted with marked ambivalence.

Eager as he was to court Elizabeth, William also chafed under her yoke. Though he assured her that he would put the gift to good use, claiming, "Immediately upon receipt of the silken chain . . . away flew the steel one" he "before had in possession," he also remonstrated with her: "Not contented with having bound my soul to you with indissoluble Ties, must every moveable about me also wear your fetters?" Clear as the links between watch chains and female fetters appear in this passage alone, William's protest would have been even better understood in the context of a culture that often employed binding metaphors for marriage. As just noted, Elizabeth's friend Eliza Stedman referred to marriage as a "state of bondage," and Elizabeth herself would later compose a poem warning a young man to beware "the dragging chain" of marriage. Even as he avowed that his soul was bound with hers, William rebelled at the thought. He was not completely confident that he and Elizabeth could unite their interests, especially since she herself had not verbally declared her affections. Having confirmed his own attachment, he did not like to be left dangling.[30]

A brief poem submitted to the *Gazette* in 1735 summed up such concerns when it warned young men of the dire outcome that could follow when the wish for marriage was fulfilled:

> Your Wishes crown'd, your Bliss dissolves
> To Cares in Bondage; Curse compleat.
>
> . . .
>
> Let Fools in Life content to wed,
> Submit to MISS's Tyrant Reign,
>
> . . .
>
> To Interest, Friendship, Freedom, lost,
> Dear Purchase for this mighty Boon.

Members of either sex might regard marriage as a kind of bondage in which both lost the ability to preserve and pursue their own separate interests. Tellingly, however, men were quick to reassure one another they had far more to gain than to lose. This poetic alarm, in particular, was quickly countered in a subsequent issue of the *Gazette* by an extended essay that dismissed the poet as "an old He-Maid" and declared, "A Man does not act contrary to his Interest by Marrying; for I and Thousands more know very well we could never thrive till we were married." The promarriage essayist went on to explain: "A Man that has a Wife and Children, is sooner trusted in Business, and can have Credit longer and for larger Sums than if he was single, inasmuch as he is look'd upon to be more firmly settled." If marriage was to a man's economic and social advantage, it was love that could best secure his interest.[31]

The promarriage commentator insisted that, unlike laws or any other artificial means of social regulation, love could naturally and completely unite a man's and a woman's interests. He closed his remarks with a poem of his own:

> But happy they! the happiest of their Kind!
> Whom . . . Stars unite, and in one Fate
> Their Hearts, their Fortunes, and their Beings blend.
>   . . .
> Attuning all their Passions into Love;
> Where Friendship full-exerts his softest Power.

The soft power of love could supposedly blend separate people into a single being. Men, in particular, had nothing to fear from this process. "Every Man that is really a Man is Master of his own Family; and it cannot be Bondage to have another submit to one's Government. If there b[e] any Bondage in the Case, 'tis the Woman enters into it, and not the Man." The common eighteenth-century assumption about the proper role of love in the implementation of power could hardly have been more bluntly put. Love furthered the fiction that competing interests could be made not only compatible but also inseparable, even as all parties also understood that the participants were never actually equal. A wife's interests were to be subsumed within and beneath those of her husband, whereas his were to advance enhanced yet unchanged.[32]

Invocations of affection beyond the romantic realm relied on the same basic assumptions about the workings of love and power. One of the most salient features of this kind of emotion was its supposed ability to unite people with otherwise divergent needs and desires. For example, while Pennsylvania's proprietors frequently found themselves at odds with the populace over taxes and land policy, the Penns still insisted through the 1740s that such conflicts of interest could be surmounted by love. In one typical case, they took care to tell colonists in 1742, "We have a most tender and affectionate Concern for the Welfare of the whole Body of the Inhabitants, and of every Part of them, to all of which we bear so near a Relation." Here the Penns insisted that affection bound every part of the colony so close as to allow its inhabitants to "turn [thei]r Thoughts" only "to the general Good of [thei]r Country." By eliding distinctions between self and society, combining them into the category of the "general good," emotions like love and affection were expected to eliminate the tensions of opposing wills. Yet, as with husbands and wives, affection did little to actually erase the overarching power differential between ruler and ruled.[33]

Leading citizens credited love with great ability to integrate interests. Indeed, they regarded the spread of affection as a key means of involving the lower sort in society. Without much property, members of the lower orders might be thought to have little stake in the common good. Yet, elites proclaimed, love could induce the poor to put loyalty to community ahead of concern for self. The founders of the Pennsylvania Hospital regarded the "poor sick" as being morally and financially deficient as well as physically disabled. A charity hospital would "promote a spirit of religion and virtue amongst the common people . . . by the regularity of manners enjoined to be maintained [t]here." Once the poor had been confined to the hospital and prevented from following "their own way of living," charitable boosters could "hope to secure their affections, soften their passions, reform their manners, and posses them with a sense of their duty to God, and their neighbours." According to this blueprint for social engineering, if the affections of the common people could be secured, such folk would forsake selfish passions in favor of their duties to their neighbors and fellow citizens. Clearly, the notion of shared interest did not preclude the simultaneous assumption of hierarchical strata. On the contrary, the defining element of the fiction of identity of interest was always that subordinate members of society should be first in line to relinquish selfish impulses.[34]

A return to the issue of word usage helps illustrate this point. As we have seen, the *Gazette* evidences that the most common terms associated with affection were those conveying duty and respect. The next largest category of words implied unwavering devotion. Significantly, many regarded these traits as mutually reinforcing. The Pennsylvania governor who declared in 1738 that "Loyalty, Duty and Affection" were all "justly due to his Majesty" certainly thought so. Meanwhile, members of the Pennsylvania Assembly betrayed the same assumption when they declared they were "willing to demonstrate the Fidelity, Loyalty and Affection of the Inhabitants of this Province to our gracious King." The frequency with which terms for faithfulness and for obligation were linked with love and affection underscores the complicated expectations for these emotions. Love and affection were supposed to play important roles in the confirmation of social bonds even as they also helped communicate hierarchical boundaries.[35]

Anglo-Americans expected expressions of love to perform much the same functions in forging alliances with native Americans that they did in furthering relations between courting couples or king and subjects. Again and again, colonial negotiators invoked affection in the course of their interactions with Indians. In fact, in a revealing symbolic coincidence, Anglo-American diplomats often exchanged strings with Indian allies, even as young women did with their suitors. The Pennsylvania governor who told an assembled group of Delaware Indians, "I cannot take my Leave of You without giving You this String as a Token of my Affection," offered along with the wampum an important cross-cultural marker of emotional and practical ties.[36]

Anglo-Americans consistently and deliberately interpreted exchanges of affection with native Americans in their own favor. Affection should encourage respect, affirm esteem, enforce obligations, initiate relations of dominance and dependence, further the fiction of converging interests, and all the while obscure its workings. The Anglo-American view of how love and affection should shape alliances is well summed up in the 1733 translation of a speech by Creek Indians reprinted in the *Gazette*. According to colonial interpreters, the Indians had declared: "We all love your People so well, that with them we will live and die. We . . . desire to be instructed and guided by you." In this example, Indians appeared so willing to subsume their interests within those of colonists that they were literally ready to live and die as the English did. Anglo-Americans enforced the obligations of affection wherever they could, celebrating every perceived instance of success.[37]

Expressions of love inaugurated alliances in which colonists hoped to play the master part, and Indians were to acquiesce in their own submission. Englishmen on both sides of the Atlantic adhered to such models; a 1733 *Gazette* article reprinting a letter from London that in turn purported to report on conditions in colonial Georgia captures the essence of such transatlantic English hopes. An unnamed Indian offered Georgia proprietor James Oglethorpe the gift of "a Buffalo's Skin, painted on the Inside with the Head and Feathers of an Eagle," explaining that "the Feathers of the Eagle were soft, and signified Love; the Buffalo's Skin warm, and signified Protection; therefore he hoped that we would Love and Protect [them]." The English eagerly recorded this diplomatic gesture. For them, the exchange of affection implied agreement to a traditional set of social relations in which Indians would offer fealty to the English (in the form of everything from trade ties and defensive alliances to land cessions) while the English would promise them protection and symbolic gifts of provision.[38]

Providing for the Indians marked the first step in a kind of diplomatic courtship. Though eighteenth-century Anglo-Americans underplayed their own economic investment in the Indian trade, they placed great emphasis on trade's role in the promotion of affection-based alliances. This was never truer than with the outbreak of the Seven Years War in 1754, when diplomatic issues took on heightened strategic importance. In that year, Maryland's governor Horatio Sharpe urged members of his colony's assembly to send "a present to the Indians" gathering in Albany for a war conference, "as a Means of securing the Affections of those People at this critical Juncture, when, their being alienated from the *English* Interest, would threaten us with the most fatal Consequences." In Sharpe's summation, securing Indian affections would automatically align them with Anglo-American interests, irrespective of actual conflicts over resources of land and population. Sharpe and those like him intended the building of affectionate alliances to end with native Americans' agreeing to obey Anglo-American masters and subordinate their interests to Anglo-Americans.[39]

For their part, native Americans of many nations well understood Anglo-American claims that mingled affections would create melded interests. Yet this understanding did not stop them from criticizing colonists who claimed to honor affection while working to undermine Indian objectives. In one example, the Onondaga representative, Saquayanquaraghta, speaking on behalf of the Six Nations at a 1763 conference in Albany, reproached colonists on account of "stolen . . . lands" and urged them, "Take it seriously into your Consideration, how strong our Union used to be formerly, when we were, as it were, united under one Head, and were one Body and Blood, and happily united in our Affections." Saquayanquaraghta seems to have shared the colonists' idea that united affections should provide the basis for a union of interest. However, his expectations for the "one body" model differed markedly from the Christian plan of marriage, which held that man and woman became "one flesh" when the husband covered the wife. Such a notion of the consequences of affection directly contradicted the values and assumptions of the Iroquois's matrilineal society, where husband and wife alike remained autonomous persons, each free to maintain property and to leave the marriage at will. Saquayanquaraghta saw nothing but disappointment and dysfunction in what Anglo-Americans took to be the ideal operation of affection.[40]

Indeed, a closer look reveals that Anglo-Americans seldom bothered to mention *Indian* interests at all, instead focusing on the role of affection in encouraging Indians to further *Anglo-American* aims. When the Cherokee known as Little Carpenter took "twelve Scalps, and three Prisoners" in an expedition against the French in 1758, a *Gazette* update originating in South Carolina reported the actions as "undoubted Proofs of Valour and of his firm Attachment to our Interest." When Little Carpenter then went on a diplomatic mission to the Chickasaw and "gave them two of the Scalps he had taken," colonists claimed he had done so, not out of respect for the Chickasaw, but only as a "Token of his Regard for them as our Friends and hearty Affection for us." According to these South Carolinians, Little Carpenter's hearty affection for the English and devotion to their interests outshone all his other ties and obligations, even when he went to treat with members of a fellow native American nation.[41]

No matter the source of the external conflict, Anglo-Americans invariably viewed internal shows of united affections as a key source of imperial strength. The king set the standard when he declared, at the onset of hostilities with the French in 1744, "The Duty, Affection, and Zeal for me and my Family, which have been so fully and cordially expressed ... ought to have convinced our Enemies, how ill-grounded any Hopes of Success were." According to the classic formulation, united affections led to military invincibility. As conflict continued into the Seven Years War, the rhetoric from London remained the same. A dispatch appearing in the *Gazette* in 1758 declared, "Never did a minister enjoy the love of all people here more than the present—It is thought the harmony and unanimity with which the parliament act, will cast a terror on our enemies." If love could inspire fellowship, it could also be used to inflict fear. Far from being a purely personal passion, love could be the most important feeling to bolster the state.[42]

Colonists responded to royal calls in kind. Members of the New Jersey assembly hastened to assure the king, "We humbly beseech Almighty God ... to frustrate the Councils of Your Majesty's Enemies, and make their wicked Devices subservient to the Establishment of Your Person and Family (if possible) more firmly in the Affections of Your People." Amity's finest hour came only when enmity was present to provoke it. Indeed, failures of affection amounted to the dereliction of patriotic duty, if not something close to treason. So the governor of Massachusetts implied in 1756 when he lectured his legislature on the importance of presenting a united colonial front against the French. Reminding them that "the most perfect Harmony ought to subsist among the Governments, in order to [ensure] Opposi[tion to] the common Enemy of all His Majesty's Colonies," he warned them against taking any actions that might "have a Tendency to alienate the Affections of the several Governments from each other." Enemies abroad only increased the importance of maintaining affections at home.[43]

Indeed, if unions of affection rested on the fiction of identity of interest, the idea that love for country constituted the height of selflessness took this idea to its extreme. National affection supposedly exacted the highest degree of self-sacrifice in the service of common good. In fact, Anglo-Americans consistently claimed that love of country was a sure sign of disinterested virtue. If all exchanges of love and affection required some relinquishment of self-interest, love for country was supposed to represent the summit. When a new governor arrived in New Jersey in 1738, inhabitants there declared that the event "must needs move us, and stir up our Hearts to the faithful Discharge [our] Duties . . . as becomes the Loyal Subjects of so good and great a King." Denying that they would ever put personal interest above public good, they concluded by promising, "We aim at nothing more . . . than to behave ourselves in the Discharge of our respective Duties, like Men fearing God, honouring the King, and loving our Country." Again and again, declarations of affection were made synonymous with assertions of civic loyalty. As explained by a self-styled "Lover of his Country" who published in the *Gazette* in 1754, any claim that people were "void of Love for their country" amounted to an accusation that they were "destitute of Virtue," "abandon'd to Wickedness," "influenced by a Party Spirit," and incapable of impartial devotion to the common good. By contrast, affection's role in policing membership in the polity repeatedly remained unstated. Love exercised its strongest effects by making the imposition of dominant interests appear inevitable and nearly invisible. Declaring love for country, Anglo-Americans shrouded the divisive work of emerging nationalism in the warm folds of love.[44]

At the heart of love's social power lay its conceptual connection to the voluntary. Popular wisdom maintained that, while obedience could be forced, love itself could only be offered freely. To do something "for love" was to act on one's own initiative, to exercise free will. Thus, expressions of affection were often regarded as evidence of consent. When Pennsylvanian Isaac Pearson ran for reelection as county sheriff in 1753, he placed a notice in the *Gazette* telling voters, "I Return you Thanks for your Favour and Affection towards me at our last County Election, and request your Votes and Interest on my Behalf, for the Sheriff's Office at our ensuing Election." Pearson took for granted that affection would garner favor, favor would gain votes, and a vote won indicated a union of interest between governors and the governed.[45]

In theory, love could be courted but never commanded. Thus, when people expressed affection for one another, they entered into a mutually binding relationship most notable for being offered freely. A poem about the biblical characters Saul and Jonathan published in the *Gazette* in 1743 described their service to King David and explained, "No tyrant Duty binds / The Subjects willing Minds; / Love taught the People to obey." Love was supposedly antithetical to tyranny; if exchanged between ruler and subject, the subject's obedience could be assumed to be voluntary.[46]

Arguing in this vein, Isaac Watts, the Calvinist English hymnist whose poetic invocations of the passions were highly popular in Pennsylvania, advised a colonial governor:

Thy Power shall rule by Love;
So reigns our Jesus in his Realms above.
Illustrious Pattern! Let him fix thine Eye,
And guide thy Hand . . . from the Worlds on high.

Watts viewed love and power as intricately interconnected. As these verses explained, those who ruled in the name of love followed the example set by Christ, thus grounding their own dominion in that of the divine. According to this model, exchanges of affection not only confirmed the willingness of a subordinate's submission but also affirmed the legitimacy of a ruler's authority.[47]

Like Isaac Pearson, the candidate for sheriff who asked voters to cast their interest in with his and show their support for his office by their affection for his person, Pennsylvanians in many realms of public life seized on the idea that, where love thrived, obedience would flourish. The editors of the *Gazette* took such connections for granted when they declared in 1758, in the midst of the Seven Years War, "We have the Pleasure to inform our Readers, . . . that there is the greatest Harmony among the Troops, who, we hear, love their Officers, and obey them chearfully." Love and cheer were supposed to work in tandem, performing overlapping social functions. If displays of cheer helped demonstrate willing submission, expressions of love were supposed to authenticate it.[48]

Ultimately, members of the elite sought to establish that vows of affection and declarations of consent were essentially one and the same. William Smith, Anglican minister and college provost, tidily summed up the myriad social subtleties conveyed by the language of love when he declared in 1756 that the king, "as the *royal Protector* and kind *nursing Father of these Colonies,* is entitled to every Return of Duty, Gratitude and Affection, which it is in the Power of *a loyal, a favoured* and *free* People, to express or bestow, by Words or by Actions." In a single sentence, Smith encapsulated nearly all of the political work expressions of love and affection were intended to accomplish. He referred to the role of affection in inaugurating apparently natural, almost familial relationships of dominance and dependence. He described love's part in initiating the kind of exchange in which the protection of the superior was offered in return for the active loyalty of the inferior. He alluded to affection's power to define community membership by distinguishing the favored from the dispossessed. And, perhaps most important, he asserted that affection was a brand of feeling that could be bestowed only by "a free people." The power of love rested on its ability to both authenticate authority and communicate obedience. Yet, if love and affection were truly voluntary offerings, then their bestowal was always contingent. The fatal flaw of affection as a mechanism of coercion lay in the unpredictability of reciprocity. Love offered might or might not be returned. Though love could help establish an apparent identity of interest among those with different degrees of power, such a perfect union between people could never be more than a useful fiction.[49]

In order to advance his cause, a suitor had no choice but to attempt to convince a woman to unite her interests with his own. Yet young men too often had to proceed through courtship without the benefit of loving words from the women they wooed. In the midst of young men's flirtations, women seldom declared their love at all. We know that William's courtship correspondence must have mattered to Elizabeth Graeme, else she would not have kept it all her life and personalized it with her own clipped comments, such as clarifications of dates. And yet, despite William's desire to "provoke soft emotions," we have no evidence she ever offered hers unguardedly during their courting. In one exceptional poem she did allow that there was a "Warm Affection" between them, but she conceded this only in the context of warning him, "There's various Reason to be seen, which make it wrong to join." Accomplished wordsmith though she was, when Elizabeth did wish to signal her regard for William, she did so nonverbally by weaving him a watch chain to carry as a memento. This might have been a common symbol used by young women, for Betsy Sandwith likewise made a "watch string" for Henry Drinker in July 1759. But such gifts stopped far short of communicating women's love, much less their consent to marriage. Long after the watch strings had been handed over, both Betsy and Elizabeth were discussing with their female friends the pros and cons of taking new "masters" and entering a "state of bondage." While men enunciated the strength of their love, women opted to remain strategically mum.[50]

Indeed, one of the most striking patterns in courtship correspondence is the prevalence of men's public expressions of love and the relative absence of any reciprocal declarations from women to their suitors. This tendency cannot be explained away by any assertion that women were simply less expressive. On the contrary, these same women easily and eagerly articulated their love for their female friends. In the midst of their prolific girlhood correspondence, Eliza Moode told Betsy Sandwith, "It is true that we see one another very often, But when two people like each other entirely There is even a pleasure in Thinking of each other." And Elizabeth Graeme devoted one of her first literary attempts to discussing affection between female friends, reserving her praise, not for her suitors, but for "Friendship's Steady Flame." In yet another example, young Peggy Emlen declared herself to her close friend and cousin Sally Logan: "If tis not true love and friendship, what is it I feel for thee? Nothing less I am sure." The prevalence of loving letters between female friends makes clear the singularity of the fact that no similar letters have survived from young women to their suitors. With declarations of love supposed to consolidate relationships and initiate a confluence of interests, silence on the part of women in the midst of courtships could represent resistance to men's ambitions.[51]

"Let Not Our Affections Be Torn": Authority and Alienation

Return now to the problem with which this study began—the puzzle of the public love letter. Like Henry Drinker and William Franklin, many young men saved their most emphatic declarations of love—the very

"Corner Stone to [their] Love-Fabrick"—for the friends and family of the young women they pursued. Betsy Sandwith's friend Eliza Moode wrote with great excitement on the day her father received a letter from a young man abroad whom she fancied. His letter declared, "I take Pen in Hand to show you and the young ladies, your daughters, all imaginable gratitude for your civility and your courteous entertainment." The young man ended his letter with a postscript that read: "P.S. My body is in the Brig But My Heart is in Philadelphia: I will return soon to see you. . . . I conclude with a full heart with these lines." This young man put his body on ship, left his heart in the city, and sent word of his love to the father of his beloved, not to the woman herself.[52]

How did such open assertions of love and sincerity serve men's interests? With social and economic prowess already at stake in courtship negotiations, why would young men add the possibility of exposure for personal romantic failings as well? In fact, such tactics might have lessened, not worsened, men's public insecurity, for public declarations of love could help cloak the negotiations of power that still accompanied courtship. By insisting that love triumphed over all, young people could attempt to paper over the practical calculations that underlay courtship, the very real ramifications marriage held for matters of social status. Consider the comments of William Franklin. His courtship with Elizabeth Graeme ended in an abrupt and dramatic rupture. Only then did William scrawl off the eight-page letter meant for Elizabeth's eyes but addressed to Madam Abercrombie, in which he freely asserted that Elizabeth "must be fully sensible" that *his* "affection was in no wise abated."[53]

He reproached Elizabeth explicitly for failing to return his love and for lacking the kind of "soft emotions" he had so hoped to arouse. Explaining Elizabeth's rejection of him, he invoked the standards of newly popular sentimental literature:

> The Slightness of the foundation I built upon is now fully discover'd. . . . The contemptuous Reception she gave a Small Present I sent her, particularly the Muff . . . must be owing I suppose either to her being anxious to take all opportunities of showing I held not the least remains in her Esteem, or that she thinks it somewhat presumptuous in me to make her any present at all. . . . But I must confess, I had a tender motive for sending her a Muff. As she was often pleased to liken me to Tom Jones, and express herself much delighted with the story of Sophia's muff in that Novel, I could not help flatter-

ing myself that this might, in the same Manner, tend to raise or keep alive some Soft Emotions in my Favour. But now, alas, I see there is no intrinsic Merit in a Muff. It can have no Avail where a Sophia's Breast is wanting.

Strikingly, William employed the same metaphor of foundation building that Henry Drinker used in describing his own courtship. The allusion to building a household implicit in this language underscores young men's awareness of the stakes of courtship. William made clear that a good deal of the pain he suffered at the demise of their relationship was caused by discomfort at being the object of public contempt. Yet he did not reprove himself for any lack of prowess; instead, he attributed the unsuccessful conclusion of his own courtship to a failure of romantic feeling on the part of his intended. Invocations of romantic love allowed men to shift the burden of failure in botched courtship attempts from their own inability to close a bargain to women's incapacity for feeling.[54]

When supposedly dominant members of society found themselves on the losing end of social and political contestations, or when would-be alliance builders could not control diplomatic negotiations, the language of love provided them with one last means to palliate their failures. They could dress down their opponents for absence of affection rather than upbraid themselves for their own lack of effectiveness. In such situations, love worked not so much to soften the imposition of power as to swathe its true fragility.

Within Pennsylvania, public exchanges of affection seldom flowed as smoothly as they were supposed to in theory. When William Penn guaranteed his subjects liberty of conscience in the colony's constitution, he inaugurated a culture of dissent that could not be confined to the religious realm. Ever protective of their property rights and political prerogatives, Pennsylvania colonists and their legislative representatives engaged in spirited contests with members of the Penn family and their appointed governors throughout much of the colonial period. The colony's governors reacted with a mixture of confusion and consternation. Governor George Thomas, whose initial arrival in the colony in 1738 was apparently greeted with the usual emotional formalities, complained shortly after:

IT is now more than Twelve Months, since I was appointed to the Governments of *Pennsylvania* . . . and entertain'd a reasonable Expectation of soon taking upon me the Execution of that Charge: But, notwithstanding no Objection was made, either to my Affection for his Majesty's Person and Government, or to my Character, I met with unexpected Delays.

Thomas professed to believe that when colonists had accepted him as the emissary of royal affections—they offered no opposition to his claim to govern the colony out of love for the king—they had also consented to obey his command. When members of the Assembly instead proved resistant to his every order, Thomas admonished them for failing to live up to the social and political contract supposedly initiated by the invocation of affection. Perhaps he should have taken warning from the fact that the affectionate remarks he set such store by never gained notice in the *Gazette*. Despite Thomas's positive rendition of his early reception, no articles documented the supposedly affectionate ceremonies of his arrival.[55]

Nor were Pennsylvania governors alone in their frustration with the limits of affection. At almost the same time, Governor George Clarke of New York remonstrated with representatives in that colony, "Look up . . . to the great Example of a British Parliament, who express their Duty, their Zeal and Affection to His Majesty, by devoting their first Councils to His Service, in giving him an Honourable Revenue." Clarke hoped, however much in vain, to inspire New Yorkers to meet English standards of civility by offering *him* affection and humility. Like many colonial governors, Clarke found himself with little leverage with which to bargain over the colony's budget, save that conferred by the obligations of affection. As he attempted to induce legislators to raise funds for the colony's treasury, he argued, "Actions, not Words, must be the Measure of your Zeal and Affection to his Majesty's Person and Government," telling them, "You have now an Opportunity to shew that your Zeal and Affection are nothing short of that which former Assemblies have manifested on the like Occasion." Like William Franklin, who chided Elizabeth Graeme for her want of a tender breast, Governor Clarke challenged the New York assembly to meet the colony's financial shortfall through chastising them for their emotional shortcomings.[56]

Meanwhile, the Pennsylvania Assembly's uninterest in affection signaled problems for George Thomas's administration. By the summer of 1740, William Penn's sons and heirs had become so concerned about the governor's impotence that Thomas Penn traveled to the colony himself to try to negotiate with the Assembly directly. Perhaps alarmed by the implications of the visit, the governor sputtered to the legislators in remarks published on August 7: "If you can shew me, that you have contributed in the minutest particular to the Execution of His Majesty's Orders, tho' so pressingly and affectionately recommended to you by His Majesty . . . I will readily acknowledge and publish to the World, the Share of Merit due to you." Belatedly awakening to the importance of publication, the governor rebuked the Assembly for refusing to answer the king's call of affection. Just a week later, on August 14, the *Gazette* reported that Thomas Penn had reiterated the point in still stronger terms:

> I am much concern'd to see an Assembly of this Province seem willing to excuse themselves from assisting the King and Nation . . . notwithstanding his Majesty's Confidence in their Zeal, and the affectionate Manner in which he has been pleased to demand that Assistance; and rather to indulge a Spirit of Contention with a Gentleman, who, through the Whole of his Procedure, has acted such a Part as becomes a good Subject, zealous for the Honour of his King and Country.

Even as he reprimanded colonists for defying the king's will by opposing that "Gentleman" Governor Thomas's orders, Penn reproached them particularly for failing to respond in kind to the affectionate nature of the king's requests. Though the king had offered affection and protection, they had failed to reciprocate and step into the subordinate role associated with such exchanges. Pressing home the point, Penn added, "You . . . by the whole Course of your Proceeding . . . have evinced to the World, that you are satisfied with shewing a very moderate Degree of Duty to your King, and Affection to your Mother Country." Unable to coerce the legislature into raising troops or levying taxes, the colony's administrators resorted to admonishing it for its scanty levels of affection. They attempted to divert attention from their own ineptitude onto the colonists' supposed emotional inadequacies.[57]

Despite the sometimes-obvious impotence of the accusers, allegations of inadequate affection retained appeal because they did help to redefine the moral standing of the parties involved in disputes. Since love was supposed to be one of the most important attributes of Christ, a lack of affection could be seen as a sign of impiety. By extension, any lack of love—and of the supposedly corresponding social submission—could be billed as a sign of sin. Similarly, because moral philosophy had made the promotion of social emotions seem key to the advancement of virtue, those who would not or could not express love risked being cast as uncouth or even uncivilized. As the Seven Years War approached in Pennsylvania, leading to further clashes between governors and the pacifist-dominated Assembly over military funding and policy, charges and countercharges of inadequate affection became ever more common. While demands for affection betrayed a certain hint of desperation, they could also hand adversaries a potent new weapon of moral suasion.

The end result of efforts to use affection as a kind of moral ammunition was often to incite erstwhile lovers to engage in dueling accusations over whose affection had failed first. In practice, charges of inadequate affection could be lobbed by the lesser member of a negotiating pair just as effectively as by the greater. Thus, in the midst of yet another set of disputes over military expenditures, this one with Governor Robert Morris (who took office in 1754), Pennsylvania Assembly members upped affection's ante in exactly this fashion. When Morris told them, "I am sorry to find, that neither the Danger to which this Country stands exposed, nor his Majesty's repeated and affectionate Calls, have had any Weight with you," Assembly members retaliated by hinting that it might be the governor himself who had betrayed a reprehensible lack of love. They informed Morris, "The Danger to which this Country stood exposed, and his Majesty's repeated and affectionate Calls, had great Weight with us, whatever they had with the Governor." Though the substance of the dispute concerned questions about how public revenue should be raised (with the Assembly members attempting to tax the proprietors along with other colonists as well as advocating a paper currency that the governor believed would be dangerously inflationary), love provided the symbolic language for the debate. Invoking issues of affection imbued economic and political disputes with deeper ethical dimensions.[58]

By summer, Assembly members went so far as to claim that, if indeed their affections did come up short, the governor himself was largely to blame. Warning the governor against attempting to usurp any of the Assembly's traditional functions, they exclaimed, "Let not our affections be torn in this Manner from a Family we have long loved and Honoured!" If the governor truly wished to serve the Penn family of proprietors, he would have to begin by securing the affections of its subjects. Morris did his best to dodge this tactic, demanding in return, "Had you really any Tenderness for your bleeding Country, would. . . . you have been deaf to all the affectionate Warnings and Calls of his Majesty, the faithful Guardian of his People's Safety?" Once again, Morris tried to turn the tables: when the king offered affection and protection, then, by definition, his subjects owed him obedience. Yet colonists refused to be cowed. Two years later, they still would not be "terrified" by "the repeated and numerous Threats the Governor" made that he would report their "Conduct to the King's Ministers." On the contrary, they declared, "We are by no Means doubtful, but His Majesty, when he shall be truly acquainted with the Facts, will be convinced of our Loyalty and Affection to his Royal Person, and [of] our Regard for the People we represent." Not only did the assemblymen defend their own affections; they also intimated that they harbored strong doubts about the substance of his.[59]

The problem with relying on affection for the authentication of authority was that it left leaders vulnerable to the fickleness of love. If love could supposedly unite the interests of disparate people, any alteration of affection rendered such ties vulnerable. If exchanges of affection purportedly signaled the voluntary nature of consent, the withdrawal of affection could as easily indicate willful dissent. And, if affection conferred legitimacy on relations of dominance and dependence, due to its supposedly unforced spontaneity, then its absence could call into question the entire basis of social relations.[60]

Perhaps inevitably, then, leaders spent an inordinate amount of time worrying about the possibility of alienation of affection. Governor Morris himself had raised this issue early on in his skirmishes with the Pennsylvania Assembly, telling members in December of 1754:

> It gives me particular Concern, that you should purposely enter into a Dispute [about the issue of proprietary taxation] at a Time like this, when a *French* Army are fortifying themselves in your Country; and I earnestly recommend it to you to consider, whether such [attitudes] may not have a Tendency to alienate the Affections of the People of this Province from his Majesty's Person and Government.

A charge of this kind did more than simply reproach assemblymen for their own lack of affection; it actually cast them in the role of debauchers, accusing them of leading the common people astray.[61]

Members of the Assembly lost little time in working to refute such inflammatory accusations. They retorted that the real issue was neither the people's loyalty to the crown nor their willingness to raise funds for defense, but rather their impatience with proprietary directives instructing the governor not to allow taxes to be imposed on Penn family lands. In a retaliatory message to Morris, they declared:

> It surprizes us, that a Request of this House, respectfully addressed to
> the Governor, that he would be pleased to lay before us those [pro-
> prietary] Instructions . . . in order that we might examine how far
> they interfere with that Allegiance [that] the Proprietaries
> themselves . . . owe to the Crown . . . should be represented by
> our Governor as an Act that have a Tendency to alienate the Affec-
> tions of the People of his Province from his Majesty's Person and
> Government.

In other words, they warned the governor not to switch the subject to failures of affection when they demanded to see his secret instructions regarding Penn family property. If the governor portrayed them as evil tempters out to alienate the affections of the people, they were willing to indict the loyalty of the Penns themselves, to accuse the proprietary family of not doing enough to support the king in his war against the French. The Assembly concluded that alienating the people's affection for the king was "foreign from our thoughts." If the governor's and proprietor's conduct "should have a Tendency to alienate the Affections of the People from being bound by private Proprietary Instructions, the Blame is not with us." With these words, Assembly members served notice that, while they would not stand for being accused of disloyalty to the king—a treasonous offense—they were quite prepared to aid the alienation of the people's affections for the proprietors themselves. Indeed, this symbolic break-down of affection presaged an impending breakdown of proprietary control in the colony. Exactly a decade after this exchange, colonists under the leadership of Benjamin Franklin made good on their threats and began advocating formally for a royal takeover of the Penn family's colony.[62]

However weak Governor Morris's political position, the charge of alienation did in fact strengthen his rhetorical position—hence the strenu-ousness of the Assembly members' denials. Indeed, the phrase "alienation of affection" often implied the existence of a culpable third party whose interference initiated the alienation. Such political seduction amounted to sedition, a charge few could afford to ignore. Thus, in 1763 the *Gazette* would report that a member of Parliament had been arrested on a warrant setting forth that he had "endeavoured to sow Sedition, and alienate the Affections of his Majesty's Subjects." Accusations of alienation provided rulers with a convenient excuse to explain away political discontent as a mere problem of emotional disintegration rather than as the direct result of their maladministration. In this way, the dominant person could cast himself as the injured party, someone who bore no responsibility for deleterious social and political conditions but only the burden of others' iniquity.[63]

Colonial subjects had to defend themselves especially vigorously against charges of political infidelity. Pennsylvanians had always lived under the suspicion that their commitment to the British nation might be less than that of Englishmen living closer to home. Indeed, as far back as the 1740s, Governor George Thomas had mocked members of the Pennsylvania Assembly: "His Majesty's Subjects in Europe, have given Proofs of their Loyalty and Affection to his Person and Government, beyond the Examples of former Ages to the best of their Kings." He chided Pennsylvanians: "An Opportunity is now offer'd to those of North America, to shew, that a Change of Climate has made no Change in theirs." Little patience as Pennsylvanians had with their governors, they did take great pains to defend themselves against the idea that they were emotionally or morally inferior to any of the king's European subjects, much less that they purposefully sought to alienate commoners from the king.[64]

Assertions about the dangers of alienation likewise framed Anglo-American accounts of their diplomatic relations with native Americans. Throughout the mid-eighteenth century, the French figured prominently as potential seducers. Anglo-Americans preferred to characterize Indians as morally vulnerable French targets rather than to recognize them as self-conscious political actors with their own rightful needs and agendas. On this point Pennsylvania governors and assemblies, so often at odds, maintained easy agreement. For example, when members of the legislature warned Governor James Hamilton in August 1750 that the Six Nations Indians weren't of the "most prudent Behaviour" and that "the *French* leave no Means unattempted to alienate their Affection from us," Hamilton replied exactly in kind: "The *Indians* . . . are not of the most prudent Behaviour, and therefore it seems necessary . . . to regulate their Conduct, and keep them firmly attached to the *British* Interest; more especially at a Time when the *French* leave no Means unattempted to alienate their Affection from us." According to these Pennsylvanians, Indian imprudence and French perfidy were the root cause of all conflicts between Anglo-Americans and native Americans, not competition over land and labor resources.[65]

Such comments attempted to assign Indians subordinate symbolic roles as morally weak women, whose flighty affections were easily susceptible to the suggestions of the French. They mirrored the advertisements disaffected husbands often took out in the pages of the *Gazette* to denounce their wayward wives. When Amos Austin gave notice that "Esther, the Wife of Amos Austin, hath alienated her Affections from me her Husband, and hath, for some Time, shewed a Desire to convey my Money, Goods, and Effects, into the Hands of another Man," he not only sought to destroy her public credit but also to rehabilitate his own image. If the alienation of his wife's affections could be traced to the machinations of "another man," then Amos Austin could shrug off some of the opprobrium that attached itself to him as a man unable to maintain his supposedly rightful control of his wife. Indeed, the problem of alienation of affection was always couched in terms of lower-ranking people losing love for their superiors, never vice versa. Just as adultery remained a crime committed by wives against husbands, but never the other way around, so alienation of affection earned a place in the historical record only when a supposedly subordinate person ceased to offer affection to someone of higher rank. Fundamentally, discussions of lost love implied a desire on the part of rulers to reimpose authority by exposing their subordinates' supposed lack of moral probity.[66]

Ironically, then, accusations of "adulterous" alienations of affection revealed the underlying vulnerability of structures of authority. Not surprisingly, as antagonism toward the colony's proprietors increased, the Pennsylvania Assembly seized on the issue of Indian alienation as a further means of undermining their governors. While Governor Hamilton and the Assembly had heartily agreed back in 1750 on the idea that the French were to blame for seducing the affections of the Six Nations, by 1755 the Assembly shifted tactics and began accusing Governor Morris of provoking Indian alienation through his emotional and practical neglect. They demanded of Morris, for example, "whether he knows of any Disgust or Injury the *Delawares* or *Shawanese* have ever received from this Province, and by what Means their Affections can be so alienated as . . . to take up the Hatchet against us." Raising the possibility that the governor and proprietors had taken measures inimical to peace, they reminded Morris how important it was to try, "if possible, to regain their Affections, rather than by any Neglect or Refusal of that Justice we owe to them . . . entail upon ourselves and our Posterity the Calamities of a cruel *Indian War*." Members of the Assembly seemed to imply that the alienation of the Delawares' affections might well have resulted from the same kind of reasonable objections to the governor's rule that they themselves frequently raised. It was no coincidence that their remarks about the Delawares came just a month after Morris accused *them* of working to alienate the affections of the colony's commoners.[67]

If one response to the alienation of affection was to offer forgiveness to the wayward one and make efforts at reconciliation, another was to announce instead a final renunciation of all emotional ties. Faced with the Assembly's defiant intransigence, Morris took just this tack. In a dramatic about-face, he rebuked members of the Assembly for so much as seeking to raise the issue of affection in the midst of war:

> Instead of strengthening my Hands, and providing for the Safety and Defence of the People and Province in this Time of imminent Danger, you have sent me a Message, wherein you talk of regaining the Affections of the *Indians,* now employed in laying waste the Country, and butchering the Inhabitants. . . . Such Language at this Time, and while the Province is in its present Circumstances, seems to me very extraordinary.

Morris once again exposed the limits of the language of affection. Expressions of affection were supplied and solicited only so long as cooperative reciprocal relations of dominance and dependence were sought. Should Morris make offers of affection only to have them be shunned by Indians, he stood to lose stature. Yet, if he chose instead to withdraw his own affections as well, the veil of love would be blown aside by the strength of the ensuing naked struggle for power.[68]

When expressions of affection faltered, the love that had once held the potential to tie people together could instead, by its obvious absence, draw new boundaries between them. Indeed, beneath love's link to amity lay its equally integral connection to enmity. The literal meaning of *alienation* (as defined by the *OED*) is "to convert into an alien or stranger." By turning "away in feelings or affections," alienated people announced that they each belonged to "another person, place, or family," that they were of "foreign nation[s] and allegiance." If a key part of affection's efficacy as a mechanism of control lay in the promotion of seemingly natural and familial connections that implied identity of interest, failures of devotion exposed this fiction for what it was and brought the issue of power out into the open.[69]

Nothing marked a transition to open hostility like the utter absence of affection. Governor Morris, for example, made the tactical decision to claim that there was no love lost between Indians and colonists, knowing that he had the force of considerable public opinion behind him. Not only did many Scots-Irish frontier dwellers within Pennsylvania scorn the idea of affectionate relations with their Delaware Indian neighbors, but many observers back in London also adopted this attitude. As a piece from the *Gentleman's Magazine* reprinted in the *Gazette* back in 1754 had explained, "If we cannot learn the Art of gaining the Affections of our Indian Neighbours, which the French boast of . . . it is incumbent on us to supply this Defect by our Care to put it out of their Power to hurt us." Where the niceties of affection ended, the raw realties of force began.[70]

Significantly, no governor ever delivered any such renunciation of the importance of affection when it came to the far more powerful Iroquois, despite their uncertain allegiances throughout the war. So in 1758 Morris's successor, William Denny, declared:

> It highly behoves us, by every probable Expedient, to confirm the *Indians* on the *Ohio* in their present good Dispositions, and conciliate their Affections to His Majesty. . . . To effect this, . . . we [must] speedily evince to them that a firm Reliance may be had on our Friendship, and that we are able and willing to protect them against the *French*.

The Six Nations retained such military might that the governor continued to frame relations with them in the coded terms of love that allowed him to assert dominance in indirect ways—such as positioning himself as their affectionate protector. With the weaker Delawares, however, governors were willing to explicitly jettison any pretense to affection.[71]

Ultimately, the language of love was called on only to help mediate interactions where the relative standing of negotiating parties could be called into question. If tactical considerations called for the polite diminution of status differences, expressions of affection could do much to smooth over underlying power struggles. On the other hand, when power imbalances were starkly drawn and obedience was to be obtained by open force, few bothered with exchanges of affection and the fiction of consent. Here again, the wholly unequal relationship between master and slave well illustrates the irrelevance of affection in extremis. In places like Pennsylvania, where sheer numerical superiority allowed members of the master class to believe in the certainty of their suzerainty, they seldom bothered to draw on the language of love. Yet, where demographic realities made masters' grasp on power seem somewhat less certain, they eagerly turned to love—and especially to convenient critiques of the alienation of affection—in an effort to belie the brittleness of their regime.

Comparing statements from slaveholders in Maryland and Pennsylvania during the Seven Years War, when leaders in both colonies became concerned that their enslaved populations might be drawn into domestic insurrections, helps highlight the connections between relative social instability and turns toward affection. On the one hand there was Maryland, where the census of 1755 showed that nearly one-third of the population was enslaved while fewer than one-fourth of the white population owned slaves. Outnumbered by those they kept in bondage, members of Maryland's master class sought to shelter themselves behind the issue of affection, pretending that alienation could result only from emotional betrayal. In 1755, slaveholders worried aloud about "the constant and unwearied Application of the Jesuits to proselyte, and consequently to corrupt and alienate, the Affections of our Slaves from us, and to hold themselves in Readiness to arm at a proper Time for our Destruction." These planters made no mention of the possibility that enslaved people might rebel in consequence of a legitimate desire for liberty; instead they described slave resistance as a matter of emotional incontinence. By contrast, slaveholders in Pennsylvania (where only about one-eleventh of the population was then of African descent) wasted no ink claiming to share bonds of affection with those they held in chains. Safe in their majority and sure of their power, the Pennsylvania Assembly declared forthrightly in 1756, "Every Slave may be reckoned a domestick Enemy." Quite literally, there was no love lost between socially secure Pennsylvania slaveholders and those they enslaved.[72]

Likewise, once Britain had secured victory in the Seven Years War and its grasp on power seemed more certain, colonists began to abandon their commitment to maintaining affectionate relations with Indians. By 1764, ensconced as the royal governor of Pennsylvania's neighbor New Jersey, William Franklin would disavow all interest in affectionate relations with Indians in favor of strengthening the bonds of love that united colonists against them. In an address to the New Jersey assembly, he declared that troops from New Jersey were needed because the colony was once again in an "actual State of . . . Indian War," telling the representatives, "His Majesty trusts that the Legislature of this Government, from their Zeal and Affection for His Service, as well as from a just Regard to the Safety and Welfare of the Colony, will readily and chearfully concur in exerting themselves." In a lengthy reply, the legislators stressed that they had long "conciliated their [the Indians'] Affection," but that they now concurred in the need to arm against them. If one response to the alienation of affection was to attempt to win back the beloved, another option was to spurn those who themselves offered only scorn. The New Jersey colonists followed this path, agreeing with Franklin that the Indians' "Perfidy to the neighbouring Governments seems to require Chastisement."[73]

William Franklin's decision not to attempt to conciliate the Indians, but rather to castigate them for their own failures of affection, echoed the attitude he had taken toward Elizabeth Graeme just six years before. In his wide-ranging letter to Madam Abercrombie, William explicitly accused Elizabeth of inconstancy, blaming her for the failure of their love affair. His letter claimed that, though they had concealed their commitment from many, he and Elizabeth had actually agreed to an informal engagement before he left for England. He claimed that he himself had proposed to marry quickly and quietly before his departure, hoping thereby to "guard against all accidents," especially the possibility of an estrangement between them. However, "this . . . was objected to as improper and I was told that it was best to defer everything of that kind till I returned from England." When he "could not help mentioning [his] fears of what might happen," he was assured that he "need be under no Apprehensions that her Regard . . . could by either time or distance be set aside or diminish'd." Yet, William claimed, that was exactly what had happened.[74]

He indicted women generally and Elizabeth specifically for their supposedly shallow and capricious feelings:

> I at length began to please myself with the Thoughts that . . . as I knew her Superior to most of her Sex in many other Respects . . . she might be in this likewise. It is perhaps natural for Persons at her Time of Life to be more susceptible to the tender Passion of Love than those of advanced years; and that very susceptibility may prevent those impressions having any long Duration. . . . I perhaps, altho' but a few years older, may have reach'd that stage which, tho not quite so liable to receive those Impressions, may yet retain them longer when once receiv'd. . . . I am at a Loss otherwise to account for so great an alteration in her and none in myself.

According to William, sincere and lasting love was generally the product of maturity and the purview of men. His condescending comments about women and children sought to take the sting out of his own failure to advance in status by winning a wife. Such statements not only helped hide the full significance of courtship negotiations from public view; expressions of love might also give young suitors added leverage in their quest to be accorded status as men. Their supposedly sincere and open expressions of emotion provided them with an additional point of superiority over women, useful in reestablishing their predominance in the court of public opinion. Indeed, William would soon take a wife in England, Elizabeth Downes, then return to North America in triumph to take up his post as New Jersey's governor.[75]

If men found some measure of comfort and some saving of face by blaming botched courtships on the emotional shortcomings of the women they wooed, women who did acquiesce to marriage proposals finally had reason to reciprocate men's affections. Their suitors would soon move from a position of supplication to one of domination. In the final analysis, women had as vital an interest as men in obscuring the relations of power and negotiations of status that so often accompanied bids for love.

The Veil of Love

Many women commented explicitly on the potential perils of their enhanced status during courtship negotiations, for courtship tipped the scales in women's favor for only a brief period, just until the moment they accepted a man's hand. Women who acquiesced to men's entreaties would effectively place themselves in the power of those they had recently exposed to the possibility of public ridicule. Marriage might be the subject of nervous humor and the occasional feminist-leaning critique, but in practice eighteenth-century women had few other viable options. Though they might put marriage off for a time, in the end it was the fate they had to accept and expect. Even Betsy Sandwith's friend Eliza Moode concluded her spirited rebellion against the mere roasting of meat:

> I'll . . . finish this subject by telling you that which you already know—
> that everything I write On this subject is only for the love of writing
> to you and not because I think economy is a thing beneath the notice
> of you or me, On the contrary I think it is the proper Business of a
> woman and a person who neglects it does not do her duty.

So long as young women did their duty by marrying and taking up the proper business of a wife, they would have small choice but to spend their lives in "fear of offending [their] masters." In such a situation, woe to the woman who had gone too far in offending her would-be master before they wed.[76]

Indeed, as prevalent as men's public declarations of love were women's private discussions of the limits of female power. The final task to be accomplished in successful courtships was a smooth reversal of women's previous steadfast refusals to confide their feelings or commit their hearts. So, when the time came for Betsy herself to make her decision regarding Henry's offer of marriage, Eliza Moode dropped her critique of men's power and instead advised Betsy against abusing her own. "[Do] not take pleasure in shewing thy power, neither stretch it to the limit, for thou knows these things are weakened when carried too far, but grant him what he so earnestly wishes for, and which I hope he will make it his study to deserve." Such a warning testified as much to women's awareness of the limitations of the power courtship brought them as to their consciousness of that power itself. Only by demonstrating their love could young women avoid wounding the breasts of the men who would one day rule them.[77]

In that same decade, another young woman sent her friend a copy of a poem containing remarkably similar advice, describing the ephemeral nature of young women's power directly in the context of courtship. Quaker Sally Logan had apparently lent her friend Peggy Emlen a book of popular fables. Thanking Logan for sending the book, Emlen recopied a favorite passage and commented, "In one of the fables there is this advice and I think I like the most of it":

> Condemn the girlish arts to teaze
> Nor use your power unless to please
>
>   . . .
>
> With caution every look forbear
> That might create one jealous fear
> And lovers ripening hopes confound
> And give the generous breast a wound
>
>   . . .
>
> For fools alone with rigor sway
> When soon or late they must obey.

No more succinct statement of the pitfalls of women's power in courtship could be asked for than the final couplet of this poem: "For fools alone with rigor sway / When soon or late they must obey."[78]

A key element of negotiations of authority couched in the language of love was that they were intended to yield enduring results. In affection-based models of the social contract, consent was to be asked and given only at the outset of the relationship. Authority, once legitimized, was supposed to enjoy finality; just as husbands and wives joined in marriage till death, so sovereigns ruled for life. In a society without easy divorce, as in a polity without regular executive elections, emphasis on affection implied only the slightest mitigation of rigor's sway. Yet the acknowledged possibility of alienation meant that, no matter how great the degree of authority, those in positions of mastery could never entirely escape the exigencies of consent.[79]

Within the realm of courtship, women's power, though fleeting, was real. How could women transform the terms of their courtships and confirm their love for those they had so long declined to favor with their feelings? Emlen's poem contained a final crucial piece of advice to women:

> Reluctant hear the first address
> Think often ere you answer yes
> But once resolved throw of[f] disguise
> And wear your wishes in your eyes.

Though this poem approved of the hesitant and even reluctant attitudes women initially displayed toward courtship, it also underscored the importance of women's eventual capitulations to men's declarations of love. Once a woman had accepted a man's proposal, her early reticence on the subject of love could be attributed to a deferential reluctance to assert herself and her feelings rather than to any deliberate attempt to frustrate and tantalize her suitor. Significantly, Emlen's poem advocated that even engaged women should reveal their love only in looks, not in words. Where women's habit of waiting demurely for men to take the lead and declare their love might irritate men early on, ultimately it helped restore initiative and authority to men.[80]

In the end, Betsy took Eliza's advice, did her "duty," and finally agreed to marry Henry. Her consent came in November 1760, some nine months after Henry himself had sent home the cornerstone of his love to her sister in order to declare himself to Betsy. So far as the record can tell us, Betsy remained mute on the subject of love right through to the end. Even within the confines of her diary she never addressed the topic directly, going only so far as to say: "went to monthly meeting this morning . . . diclar'd my intentions of marriage with my friend HD." Still, Betsy's choice confirmed that the love she did not express aloud was there none-theless for Henry to discern.[81]

Even in the midst of uncertainty, Henry himself claimed that he never had serious doubts about his ultimate success. Through the long months of travel abroad, Henry encouraged himself to persevere in his pursuit of Betsy by thinking of "those sentiments I saw with pleasure rising from the Heart to the Eyes of my dear Girl before I left her." Important as they might have been for cementing romantic ties, women's eventual unspo-ken but unmistakable avowals of love—the wishes they wore in their eyes —also served another vital function. Loving looks lifted the veil that for so long had hidden women's emotions from sight and disguised instead the negotiations of power inherent in exchanges of love and affection.[82]

Taking time to translate the eighteenth-century language of love—to notice when it was spoken, by whom it was voiced, and to whom it was addressed—reveals much about the social meanings of this deceptively simple emotion. In this period, expressions of love oiled the negotiations of power that were endemic to a society in which many relations of dominance and dependence had entered a period of flux. The social and political effects of expressions of love and affection were quite complex. They could strengthen the obligations of allegiance, yet soften the im-position of authority. They could further the fiction of identity of interest even as they advanced efforts at domination. They could define the bounds of amity while drawing lines of enmity. They could legitimate the exercise of power and create the appearance of consent, yet also subtly communicate dissent. When love faltered and alienation ensued, contests to determine who deserved blame for the failure of affection were quick and deadly earnest. Whatever else they did, eighteenth-century expres-sions of affection always raised the moral stakes of discussion.

The prominence of the language of love in courtship correspondence, political parlance, and diplomatic exchanges alike was far more than mere coincidence. It confirmed the notion, recently proposed by John Locke, that affectionate alliances provided the most legitimate basis for the for-mation of social contracts of all kinds. While some scholars have claimed that Locke, in opposing absolute monarchy and Sir Robert Filmer's no-tions of patriarchy, severed all associations between family relations and state formation, his *Two Treatises on Government* can also be read quite differently. In fact, Locke regarded marriage as a model for social con-tracts, stating in the First Treatise that "the Power of a Husband" is "founded on Contract" and reiterating in the Second Treatise that *"Conjugal Society* is made by a voluntary Compact between Man and Woman . . . it draws with it mutual Support, and Assistance, and a Communion of Interest too, as necessary . . . to unite their Care, and Affection." As such statements indicate, Locke subscribed to the soon-to-be-widespread claim that united affections could promote common interests. Even more important, his formulations asserted that exchanges of affection could establish the principle of consent between rulers and the ruled. On the one hand, he took care to draw sharp distinctions between marriage and absolute monarchy: "The *Power of the Husband* [is] so far from that of an absolute Monarch, that the *Wife* has, in many cases, a Liberty to *separate* from him; where natural Right, or their Contract allows it." He likewise affirmed that "as [in] any other voluntary Compacts, there [is] no necessity in the nature" of marriage "that it should always be for Life." On the other hand, he was also explicit in affirming that the marital contract established rather than threatened the power of husbands: "The Husband and Wife . . . will unavoidably sometimes have different wills . . . it therefore being necessary, that the last Determination, *i.e.* the Rule, should be placed somewhere, it naturally falls to the man's Share, as the abler and the stronger." Thus, eighteenth-century emphasis on affection allowed for adherence to the principle of consent even in the face of continued commitments to hierarchical forms of social and political organization. Affection's uneasy place at the heart of eighteenth-century Anglo-Americans' interactions reflected broader ambivalence in Enlightenment attitudes toward authority even as they also responded to the special conditions of colonial insecurity.[83]

Claims that love fostered a new kind of "affective individualism" that promoted individual autonomy while undermining patriarchy or, conversely, that love initiated a new form of "affectional authoritarianism" each advance excessive interpretive extremes. Rather, love helped people come to parley in uncertain social and political circumstances, unrolling a scrim before impotence and authority alike. In the end, the veil of love revealed as much as it concealed; it allowed for the imposition and the refutation, but above all for the negotiation of power. By dint of strategic ambiguity, invocations of love and affection allowed for the sure transmission of coded status signals.

Should ever the veil of love fall away, social strife lay waiting beneath. If alienation was the opposite of affection, anger was in many ways the antithesis of love. While love and affection served to smooth over social contests, expressions of anger could inject assertions of status into exchanges where relative rank was disputed or indeterminate. It is to such overt uses of emotion as social marker that the next chapter, on anger, is addressed.

4 Resolute Resentment versus Indiscrete Heat

Anger, Honor, and Social Status

Benjamin Chew had traveled seven hours on horseback by the time he reached Easton, Pennsylvania—the site of an upcoming treaty negotiation with neighboring Indian nations—and he was hungry for dinner. It was October 7, 1758, about midway through the Seven Years War, though Benjamin of course could not have known how long the war would last. What the attorney general of Pennsylvania did know was that he wanted to find his lodgings before he settled down to work. He and his traveling companions made straight for the governor's house, "as well to pay our compliments to him as to inquire of Mr. Peters [the governor's secretary] where our quarters were."[1]

But their expectations of being welcomed and exchanging a round of genteel compliments were dashed immediately when, "on going into the governors room," they "found him warmly engaged in conversation," that is, in the middle of a dispute. A provincial representative had opposed a war order the governor intended to give. Benjamin reported that "the governor was very angry [and] inveighed bitterly against the province." Benjamin watched in silence until the governor "at last appealed to me for my opinion in the matter," upon which Benjamin equivocated, confirming the governor's jurisdiction in the matter but urging him to moderate his demands. His efforts to intervene were to no avail: "The governor was deaf to everything I could say to him, and seemed more enraged than before, whereupon I went into the next room to sit down to a cold dinner." So begins a diary that Benjamin Chew called simply "Journal of a Journey to Easton."[2]

Benjamin probably thought of his journal as a quasi-public document, a recording of treaty proceedings that could prove a useful reference for evaluating any legal questions arising out of negotiations. Indeed, the subjects he set out to discuss, such as the governor's military instructions, were uniformly public in nature. And, yet, from the very beginning of the diary, many of Benjamin's private musings and personal preoccupations— from his long ride to his cold dinner—wove their way into his narrative. Taken as a whole, the diary reads less as a detailed record of governmental procedure than as an extended meditation on one of Benjamin's most pressing personal concerns: evaluating his own and others' relative social stature.

Anger was the key to Benjamin's ever-changing assessments of himself and his fellow treaty participants. Scarcely a day went by without Benjamin's describing the details of one angry exchange or another, among colonists and Indians alike, complete with commentary regarding the impact of these emotional displays on the status of those who made them. Just as with the governor, whom Benjamin described as veering from warmth to anger to rage over the course of a few short minutes, Benjamin attributed an astounding variety of anger to himself, his opponents, and his allies.[3]

So all-encompassing did anger seem to those in the eighteenth century that the most common word for emotion of any kind—"passion"—could also refer to anger alone. Anger was, quite simply, the most passionate and problematic of all the passions. Its value was multivalent; those who displayed it could be judged according to a wide variety of standards, involving anything from "servile" tantrums, to "savage" aggression, to honorable judgment. Discriminations among the various available words for anger allowed observers not only to comment on the status of the person expressing the anger but also to judge the moral worth of his or her emotions. In the colonial context, in which Anglo-Americans sought to match the strength they admired in Indians even as they fretted about how to maintain their own strategic claims to civility and gentility, the ability to regulate and articulate different strains of anger held considerable social and cultural significance.

Words for anger are among the most charged in the English language. This highly fraught emotion has more synonyms than almost any other kind, each carrying a slightly different connotation, implying not only degrees of intensity but also rank. In some cases, the ways that anger could code for social standing are quite clear. Consider the word *indigna-*

tion, a term for anger inseparable from the idea of status. According to the *Oxford English Dictionary, indignation* began by meaning "the action of counting or treating (a person or thing) as unworthy of regard or notice . . . contemptuous behaviour or treatment." In modern usage, the word denotes "anger at what is regarded as unworthy or wrongful . . . righteous or dignified anger." *Indignation* is a brand of anger that at once *dignifies* its subject and subordinates its object. But, in many cases, the social significance of various kinds of anger is less immediately transparent to the modern reader.[4]

Because Benjamin employed such a complicated array of terms for anger in the pages of his diary, and was himself so preoccupied with questions of social position, his book can function as a kind of primer for learning the anger codes that eighteenth-century people lived by. By supplementing Benjamin's comments on anger, his own and others', with a range of other sources, from correspondence and family papers, to pieces in the *Pennsylvania Gazette,* to Benjamin's own extensive collection of private papers, we can begin to put his comments in context. The varied uses of anger words among Anglo-Americans ultimately defy conclusive categorization; anger standards were hotly contested even as their broad outlines were widely accepted. Still, once the circumstances surrounding Benjamin's remarks about anger are understood, from his personal history to the way attitudes toward anger changed over time and varied from one group to another, his comments will appear complex— but comprehensible. His journal provides an evolving view of anger in action, revealing the central importance that eighteenth-century Anglo-Americans attached to emotional modulation as a mechanism of social regulation as well as cultural definition. Expressions and descriptions of anger provided a key means of negotiating status, of establishing honor and dishonor, in the fluid colonial world.[5]

Furious Sailors and Stammering Servants:
Traditional Associations of Passionate Anger and Servility

The governor was warm, the dinner was cold, and Benjamin Chew was bemused by the turn events had taken. He had approached the governor's house conscious of the latter's dignity and status, wishing only to make the proper acknowledgments. His first impression of the governor's conversation was that the governor was "warm," that his temper had been raised. Next he reported that the governor grew angry and bitter, and finally that he had become actually enraged. While warmth might be compatible with the conduct of a gentleman, Benjamin believed rage was not, and he could hardly help telling the governor so.

As soon as he was finished eating, he went back to have another try with the governor: "Though the governor did not ask my opinion, I could not be silent. . . . I told him with all [the] respect and modesty in my power that he would do well to consider what he was about, that his honour and reputation was greatly at stake in the steps he was about to take." Benjamin rejected the governor's angry orders on legal grounds, but his disapproval touched on moral and emotional grounds as well. Such shows of rage, along with such arbitrary exercise of power, could damage the governor's honor.[6]

The governor understood exactly what Benjamin meant, and the implications did not please him. The attorney general might weigh in with opinions on the law, but not on the governor's conduct: "To this the governor in a very insolent taunting way said, Sir, you give your opinion I suppose as a lawyer and I am very much obliged to you; as for my honour and reputation; it is my business to take care of that, and as to the order I'm determined to give it." The governor rejected Benjamin's judgments on both counts, denying that his reputation was at risk and that his orders were unwise. As far as he was concerned, his show of anger in no way tainted his honor.[7]

Why did Benjamin and William Denny disagree so strongly on what symbolic messages were conveyed by the governor's outburst? How could Denny believe that anger was compatible with honor while Benjamin seemed to think displays of rage could only damage reputations? Of course, the disagreement stemmed in part from the obvious point that the first response of anyone accused of acting inappropriately is often to deny that this is so and to defend the objectionable behavior down to the last detail. But something more complicated was also afoot; each man had chosen to draw on different—coexisting but competing—standards for the expression of anger.

Such ambivalent, if not contradictory, assessments of anger drew on long tradition. From ancient philosophers who abjured anger to medieval clerics who counted it among the seven deadly sins, anger had long carried heavy connotations of moral weakness and social danger. It was often dismissed as the degrading emotion of debased people. In early-eighteenth-century British America, accusations of excessive and passionate anger were an almost standard part of the repertoire of criticisms used to discredit colonial officials. Yet anger was also often heralded as the admirable attribute of knights and kings. In fact, contradictory dictates concerning anger had bedeviled Christian culture throughout the West from the very beginning. The Old and New Testaments present very different views of anger, from the righteous wrath of the Old Testament's Jehovah to Christ's admonishments against anger in his Sermon on the Mount.

Such discrepancies became particularly acute in colonial Pennsylvania, where diverse cultural groups brought very different religious traditions to bear on their social interactions. Early in the century, negative Quaker views, which associated anger with sin, dominated much of public comment on the subject. An essay that appeared in the *Gazette* in 1736 sums up the prevailing negative attitude and yet contains hints of underlying ambivalence. Celebrating the "late wonderful discoveries and improvements of arts and sciences," the essayist declared, "The world but a few ages since was in a very poor condition . . . you have scarce a man eminent in the world for anything before that time, but for a furious, outrageous falling upon his fellow creatures." Dismissing furious anger and the violence that accompanied it as outrageous and even primitive, this author asserted that the limitation of anger represented the advance of civilization. Even this apparent denunciation of anger acknowledges that anger *could* be a source of eminence, albeit of the least elevated kind. Burdened as it was with the taint of sin, anger also brought with it the advantage of strength. The double-sided nature of anger helps account for the remarkable amount of disagreement about its social meanings.[8]

William Denny, Benjamin Chew, and countless other Pennsylvanians had to struggle to define the social meanings of angry expression precisely because so many multivalent interpretations were available. Quakers believed that all people had equal innate propensity for anger—and equal obligation to master it. Yet many members of other religious and cultural groups in Pennsylvania were as willing to differentiate between acceptable and undesirable forms of anger as they were to discriminate between different classes of people. For many among the would-be elite, then, the task became to find a way to appropriate desirable attributes of anger (like strength) for themselves while attributing anger's many negative qualities to members of the lower orders. Gentlemen who cared to take care of their honor and reputations understood that one crucial element of performing their social role involved using reason to maintain tight control over anger. Conversely, a sure way to insult and undermine social competitors was to imply that they were absurdly angry.[9]

The remarks of a leading merchant, Isaac Norris, made back in the 1720s capture widespread early attitudes. Norris commented frequently in his correspondence on shows of anger by others, and always in the most disparaging terms. On one occasion, Norris was drawn into a dispute over the distribution of a deceased man's estate. He became involved simply because he had agreed to act as one of the will's executors, despite having no personal stake himself in the terms of the will. On receiving a letter of complaint from one of the interested parties, he wrote back that he could think of no "excuse for the warm treatment thou art pleased to give the Executors . . . avowedly and ungenerously in a manner we could never have expected from a gentleman, or anybody that could treat the reputation of another as he would desire his own to be handled." As far as Norris was concerned, any show of warmth, of angry or passionate feeling, was simply incompatible with the decorum necessary for those who wished to be accorded status as gentlemen. So certain was he of the negative association between open anger and high status that he closed his letter with another warning of the social risks run by those who allowed themselves to be overcome by angry emotions. Norris declared his hope that his correspondent would "treat us more civilly if not for our sakes yet for thy own, as thou bears the character of a gentleman." For Norris the situation was clear; passionate anger endangered a gentleman's status.[10]

As Norris was certain that high-ranking men should never show heated anger, so he took it for granted that low-ranking members of society would be frequently subject to such fits. Grousing to a fellow gentleman about recent elections to the colonial Assembly, he deplored political aspirants who tried to rally voters by raising their passions. "The common people," Norris explained, "are by the designers inflamed almost to madness." Just as one gentleman should never show warmth to another, commoners were easily inflamed. Likewise, younger men, who were automatically accorded inferior status in this rank-ordered society, might also fall prey to the anger a gentleman should never display. Caught up in yet another legal dispute over the terms of a will in 1727, Norris attempted to dismiss the concerns of the testator's son by declaring, "The resentment of th[is] unthinking youth is below my concern." Whenever faced with legal difficulties or political setbacks, Norris seems to have turned to accusations of anger as an effective means of marginalizing his opponents and establishing himself in a position of dominance. Indeed, his continual references to status in connection with emotional heat, from gentlemen to commoners to those "below" his concern, indicate how closely linked anger and status were—and how widely understood those connections must have been to his correspondents.[11]

The vocabulary Norris used to describe the emotions of those he wished to denigrate through accusations of anger is significant. He chose his words carefully and depicted his opponents' anger as "warm," "inflamed," even tainted with "madness." Unacceptable, ungentlemanly anger was characterized by its passionate nature, by its heated, "unthinking," and even insane qualities. His stance drew on traditional thinking about anger, which distinguished between brands of anger that relied on reasoned judgment and appraisal of wrong and those that resulted from a thoughtless capitulation to passion and willfulness. Though gentlemen might indulge in reasoned forms of anger on rare occasions, commoners were portrayed as incapable of exercising such rational restraint. Thus, the words chosen to describe people's anger carried important information about their purported capacity for making reasoned moral judgments and hence about their social status.[12]

Pennsylvanians started out nearly unanimous in their disapproval of passionate anger and the violence and destruction they assumed would inevitably accompany it. For about the first half of the eighteenth century, *rage* and *fury*—the words for anger that most clearly signaled capitulation to passion—were seldom if ever used to describe the anger of an elite man or woman. In fact, every time the words *rage* or *fury* were used in the *Pennsylvania Gazette*, from its first printing in 1728 through 1754, the first year of the Seven Years War in North America, they were attributed to sources of trouble. In 1731, the paper reported, "The smallpox now violently rages." In 1733 it described the attack of a bear which, "with the utmost Rage and Fierceness, roaring out in the most hideous Manner, plung[ed] into the Seas, sw[am] with an open Mouth to seize and devour . . . with great Noise and Fury" the hunters who found it. An essay published in 1733 spoke of the need to "oppose and vanquish the Rage of Fire." Numerous other examples of inanimate and animal fury could be cited. Naturally, animals and forces of nature could not be said to reason; theirs was the anger of unthinking destruction.[13]

People of the lower ranks accused of anger in the first half of the eighteenth century fared little better than bears or plagues. A 1742 election riot in Philadelphia was blamed on "furious Sailors" who "fell upon the People"; "Confusion and Terror was inexpressible." "Negroes" were another favorite target of such attributions of anger. Though Pennsylvanians preferred to avoid the subject of slave anger when they could, violently angry "Negroes" frequently played central parts in pieces reprinted from the Caribbean colonies. An account in 1734 described a "number of white People destroy'd by Negroes" because they could find no "means to escape their Fury." Likewise, a 1753 letter from Jamaica decried "our intestine Enemies, the rebellious Negroes," and deplored the "Rage of a cruel and intestine Enemy." Marginal members of society, from sailors without fixed residences to enslaved Africans, were indiscriminately denounced as angry, as violent and animalistic.[14]

A key example of this trend comes in a runaway ad placed in the *Gazette* in 1742 for a man who "call[ed] himself Abraham Brick" but whose putative owner, Hannah Pugh, insisted he was really "named Cambridge." Despite trying to saddle her enslaved servant with a name that made reference to one of England's best-known university cities, Pugh denied that the runaway should be regarded as a man capable of reason. Describing his general character, she claimed, "He is subject to fits especially when cross or vexed." The phrase "subject to fits" was telling, implying that Brick's anger and vexation resulted, not from his reasoned appraisal of an unjust situation, but rather from his irrational inability to control his own emotions. By Pugh's way of thinking, Brick, having fallen slave to his own passions, deserved to be enslaved to her as well. Brick, on the other hand, seems to have concluded that running away represented a far more promising option than attempting to reason with one who claimed a right to be his "mistress."[15]

Taking another look at Benjamin Franklin's 1747 comments on "the wanton and unbridled Rage, Rapine and Lust, of *Negroes, Molattoes,* and others, the vilest and most abandoned of Mankind," neatly confirms the contours of this pattern. Franklin did not simply label people of African descent as rageful; he also described their rage as "unbridled," lacking just the sort of shackles that blacks themselves were supposed to require. What is more, he specified that their rage was "wanton"—willful, meaningless, and motiveless—far from the sort of reasoning and reasonable anger to which a self-styled gentleman might admit.[16]

Likewise, the anger ascribed to the lowest-ranking white members of the community, runaway servants and petty thieves, always carried connotations of irrational passion. A 1738 piece advertised for an "English servant . . . named John Rachford, a lusty fellow, pock broken, light grey Eyes, brown curl'd Hair, and stammers and swears much when in a Passion"; another from 1747 asked for information on the whereabouts of "a Irish servant man, named Francis Grachams; he is a short lad, about 21 or 22 years of age . . . short red hair, and talks English short and quick, and passionately, as if angry." In these advertisements John Rachford's and Francis Grachams's propensity for anger was treated as an easily recognizable part of their personhood, as clear a sign of their identity or of their low social station as their economic occupation or the clothes they wore.[17]

Criminals were described in similar terms. One James McDonald, a shoemaker, was jailed in 1753 on suspicion of being a pickpocket. Witnesses "questioned McDonald with Moderation." Confronted, he "flew into a Passion," snatched up a pair of tongs, and "assaulted" his questioner "furiously." Reports of a convicted murderer that same year noted that one Francis Grant "made not the least offer to defend himself but seem'd insensibly resigned to drink the bitter cup which Predominacy of passion, [and] rejection of Reason . . . has brought him near." Likewise, an advertisement for a wanted man in 1759 described "Jockey Jones, a notorious thief," as a man who "talks fast, soon angry if attacked, and of a wild Look." In all of these cases, habitual anger and criminal conduct were treated as twin attributes, one a sure mark of the other.[18]

In the first half of the eighteenth century, people simply assumed that uncontrolled angry outbursts and an inability to reason went hand in hand with low status. Traditional codes that asserted that extreme anger was the attribute of the animalistic, the criminal, or the insane did so in large part to undermine the effectiveness of anger-based assertions of status. Elites sought to ensure their own place in the social order by insisting on interpreting popular displays of anger as evidence of depravity, not opposition to injustice.[19]

However much Norris and others like him might insist that anger served only to unmask the contemptible status of the person whose emotion broke out, the fact remained that expressions of anger did constitute claims to power. The links between anger and destruction were as strong as those between anger and debasement. Norris himself hinted at the importance of anger control for social control when he commented on the failure of a fellow member of the elite to contain the anger of a subordinate. He recounted how an "unprovoked, domineering, threatening rant broke out, which James [Logan] with all his imagined authority with the man or deference from him could not quash or allay." Norris's analysis of Logan's altercation admitted a crucial weakness in the traditional anger code; displays of anger *did* constitute a lack of "deference." Only by finding ways to discriminate between the anger of elites and of the lowly could men of rank even hope to neutralize the subversive power inherent in commoners' anger.[20]

The traditional solution to this dilemma was to insist that the anger displayed by elites was of an entirely different character from that of commoners. Elites claimed, as their own, an anger tempered by reason. This reason-anger alloy resulted in a form of anger—resentment—that was supposedly entirely different from the lowly anger driven by passion. Resentment resulted from a man's rational appraisal that the words or actions of another menaced his honor and social standing. For example, Governor George Thomas in the early 1740s boasted of his capacity for resentment and chided his critics in the colonial Assembly: "If Resentment for imaginary injuries, or even an opposition to your Sentiments, can be justified by your Example; that surely will be an ample Justification of me, where the Injuries were real, and without Provocation. The assembly . . . publickly defamed me." The brand of anger elites admired was clearly viewed as a measured defense against threats to fortune and character, to economic and social reputation. The governor's gibe about "imaginary injuries" underscores the importance attached to reasoned judgment as the basis for gentlemen's resentment. So important was the connection between rational anger and elevated status that on the rare occasions when the anger of a subordinate *was* described with the term "resentment" it was nearly always accompanied by some contradictory pejorative, as when Isaac Norris took care to describe the anger of the young testator as "unthinking" resentment.[21]

The mere display of resentment could in some cases be enough to recoup one's reputation. A man who declared that he resented another laid claim to honor, as when an apologist for the Penn family asserted in 1733, "Now whether [it] be decent Treatment of a Gentleman of the Pro[prieto]r's Character . . . [to] suppose him to want resolution to resent any injury done him by any man . . . I leave the World to judge of." According to this author's reasoning, merely to suspect a high-status man of lacking the capacity for resentment was itself an indecent insult to his honor. He concluded his defense of the proprietor of Pennsylvania by assuring readers of his confidence that any insult to the proprietor or his family "will at one time or other meet with a resentment adequate to the injury done the persons concerned."[22]

Resentment represented a quintessentially masculine form of anger both because of its association with reason (which men also sought to monopolize) and because of its link to honor. Though some forms of honor certainly were open to women, sexual propriety being the most obvious example, honor was more often associated with questions of property and associated exclusively with men. In all of the research in both public and private sources for this project, only one example of a woman's directly expressing resentment surfaced. This single, intriguing instance seems to underscore the connection between resentment and honor based on economic status. The woman in question, Sarah Ashmead, was a widow whose grandson, John, had offered for sale some land she claimed as her own. She took out an ad in the *Gazette* to declare that she had "an indisputable right during life" to the property "by virtue of the last will and testament of [her] late husband." She concluded by explaining, "There is an advertisement published in this paper . . . by John Ashmead for the sale of 10 lots of land . . . the which I take as an affront and insult put upon me and do resent it accordingly." Perhaps so few women were recognized as resentful, or dared to declare that they were, because this emotion was so intimately bound up with the right to property that they could ordinarily lay no claim to it or its accompanying social honor.[23]

Indeed, few people, male or female, ever accused women of being resentful either. In one telling case, a young man engaged in a disagreement with a young woman sat down to write her a letter to reproach her for their differences. In the surviving draft copy, the gentleman informed the lady: "I think I may venture to stand my ground and enquire whether you have yet a mind to quarrel with me. I will answer for you that you have not and that your benevolence and innate goodness have already changed all your resentments." Then, thinking the better of calling her resentful, he crossed out the line "changed all your resentments" and replaced it with the far more conciliatory phrase "made you forgive and forget all my sins and iniquities." It would have been impolite in the extreme for this young man to accuse his genteel correspondent of being resentful. Of course, his correspondent might well have felt resentful. The point is not that women did not *experience* such anger, but rather that social obstacles hindered its *expression*. It seems equally important that the word "resentment" could not be appropriately applied to elite women and that, for them, the emotion itself was simply not recognized as legitimate.[24]

The pattern of omission in records of women's anger was even more dramatic for black women than for white. On the very rare occasions when the emotions of women of African descent were mentioned at all, anger seems not to have figured as a subject of discussion. Indeed, a survey of all mentions of "negroes" in the *Pennsylvania Gazette* between 1728 and 1776 turns up not one instance of feminine anger of any variety. While it is impossible to believe that enslaved women were never angered, members of the master class deliberately avoided taking any notice of such emotion. This silence can be understood in a number of ways. First of all, as the lowest-ranking members of the colony, subordinated by gender and race as well as by bondage, enslaved women would have had little access to honor within white society. Not only were they, like many white women, generally cut off from access to property; they were also frequently denied any claim to sexual honor. Furthermore, their subordination was taken to be so complete as to obviate any risk of social rebellion. While the anger of enslaved men might presage violent opposition, enslaved women were supposed to be too downtrodden for anger and too docile for resistance. On the contrary, they were more likely to be described in advertisements as "good tempered" or "good natured in a family." Given that enslaved women were frequently employed in domestic service in urban Philadelphia—and hence in close daily contact with whites—we have to assume that black women's anger was unthinkable for whites exactly because slaveholders could tolerate neither the idea of female violence nor the awareness of an immediate and intimate threat in their own households. Altogether, then, the lack of expressions of anger attributed to women, black and white, underscores the degree to which the articulation of anger was linked to the assertion of self, a severely restricted activity in eighteenth-century British America.[25]

Not surprisingly, in the rare instances in which men publishing in the *Gazette* deigned to take notice of resentment on the part of lower-ranking members of society, they were quick to portray it as passionate and to dismiss it as ridiculous. In 1740 one Ebenezer Kinnersley, a preacher appalled by what he regarded as the "enthusiastic ravings," "roaring harangues," and "affected nonsense" of evangelical Baptists, stood up during a meeting and ridiculed those who allowed their "passions [to be] work[ed] up to a warm pitch of enthusiasm." The assembled congregation did not welcome Kinnersley's remarks and "shewed their resentments by running out of the place of worship" in what Kinnersley dismissed as "a very disorderly and tumultuous manner." He concluded, "The foremost of the gang . . . was a woman who supports such a character as modesty forbids to mention; and as one fool has often times made many, so in this infamous leader was followed by a multitude of Negroes and other servants . . . not over-burthen'd with discretion." Here again, the anger of lower sorts was denied any association with honor or respectability; women of "bad character" and "Negroes" incapable of reasoned "discretion" were among the targets of Kinnersley's sarcasm.[26]

Did Kinnersley actually believe that his reputation was threatened by the resentment of women, "Negroes," and servants? He must have so believed, or else he would not have bothered to defend his conduct in the *Gazette.* Yet he seems to have been confident that gentlemen of discretion would agree that displays of resentment by the lower orders only marked them out as fools. If showing resentment meant having honor, having a character and fortune to protect, then clearly, elites seemed to argue, the resentment of their inferiors was more ridiculous than ominous. Resentment based, not on a reasoned assessment of a wronged reputation, but on a passionate excess of feeling aroused derision instead of respect.

So closely were displays of resentment linked to claims of authority that gentlemen who wished to defend their standing declined to show resentment to anyone they regarded as inferior. Only an insult from another honorable person could threaten a man of honor and elicit resentment in response. One gentleman confronted with libelous charges against him declared in 1738: "Senseless scribblers should never be noticed. . . . Their scurrility is too *low* and their malice too *dull* . . . to Deserve resentment." So-called senseless folk devoid of reason did not "deserve" to be noticed, much less to be met with reasoned anger. Ironically, then, a gentleman who had been insulted needed to show resentment at the injury to his social position, but in showing such anger he implicitly affirmed the status of the one who evoked it. Thus, elite men generally tried to reserve resentment to themselves as a brand of anger accessible only to those who had honor and were able to reason. They deigned neither to direct resentment toward nor to recognize resentment from those they regarded as inferior.[27]

On the other hand, resentment between two low-ranking men, though only rarely acknowledged or commented upon, does not seem to have been viewed as particularly problematic. A 1749 account of a fatal skirmish between two sailors provides a case in point. "Two seamen . . . being at a tavern, one of them took occasion to boast of his bravery; which the other resenting a little, they agreed to walk out, and take a trial of skill at boxing; which having exercised a while, they were parted, and came in and drank friends, where[upon] the person who boasted of his strength, died in a few minutes after." Clearly the upper-crust writers of the *Gazette* were willing to credit the idea that members of the lower orders had a sense of honor and might fight to defend it among themselves. So long as commoners' resentment remained directed at one another, and not at members of the ruling classes, it posed little social threat to the elite. Yet it does seem remarkable that the *Gazette* contains only one other case of resentment between two male commoners, which also ended with a fatality. This fact may well indicate that elites took satisfaction in noting lower-ranking men's inability to restrain murderous passions and exercise true gentlemanly resentment.[28]

Both Governor William Denny and Attorney General Benjamin Chew agreed that the crucial concern in assessing the expression of anger was to determine its effect on a man's reputation. Though Benjamin portrayed the governor as enraged, Denny might well have seen himself as resentful, a much more respectable kind of anger and one that, it just so happens, Denny had previously praised in public. Just a few months before, Denny had complained to the Assembly about the "remarkable . . . Freedom with which [they were] pleased to treat [his] character" and declared, "I should be unworthy indeed of the Commission I have the honour to bear under his Majesty, tamely to suffer such an Indignity without . . . publickly expressing my . . . just Resentment." Resentment represented the kind of anger that arose in response to insult. It was intimately bound up with the idea of honor, with the ability to make a reasoned appraisal of an injury to one's reputation and to mount an effective response.[29]

When Benjamin reproached Denny for growing enraged, he drew on long-standing conventions, which held that passionate anger made wretched the one who displayed it. However, the two could not agree on what standards of anger and honor should apply to their interactions. Clearly, the negative view of anger that Benjamin chose to draw on was not the only standard by which the governor could be judged, for the governor did not accept the idea that anger inevitably demeaned the one who expressed it. In any case, the governor seems to have taken no further notice of Benjamin's critique, but simply to have renewed his determination to assert his place at the top of Pennsylvania's provincial hierarchy. Contrary to Benjamin's initial hopes and expectations, the governor ordered that the members of his council "should be provided with a table separate from him and that he would have no company with him except such as he thought proper to invite from time to time." Benjamin reported this treatment matter-of-factly, simply noting, "Accordingly we have breakfasted and supped at our lodgings and dined at Scull's, a public house." The simple fact that he recorded these arrangements shows that he noticed the slight to his own status that the governor's standoffishness implied.[30]

Benjamin retaliated privately within his diary by reporting on the governor's anger in less-than-respectful terms. Where the governor seemed satisfied that he could display anger and still take care of his own reputation, Benjamin took solace in making anger the subject of continued ridicule. The day after his arrival he recounted a new story about the governor's temper in terms even more disparaging than before. Apparently, the governor had ordered his secretary "never to let his nephew come into his sight, saying he was not a companion for boys." Perhaps reacting to the fact that he himself had been treated with hardly more respect than a boy, Benjamin exclaimed to himself, "What a strange, peevish, petulant creature it is!" Peevishness and petulance were hardly the marks of a widely respected man of prominence. On the contrary, they were the kinds of angry fits of temper seen only among the infantile and the impotent.[31]

A Daily Cross in Opposition to Wrath: Unqualified Quaker Objection to Anger

At the treaty council at Easton, as in Pennsylvania itself, struggles for social prominence and political dominance were greatly complicated by the sheer number of interest groups competing for influence and power. While Benjamin Chew might struggle to enhance his social standing vis-à-vis the Pennsylvania governor, he also had to contend with numerous alternate powers: the governor of New Jersey, who was also present at the Easton proceedings, the chiefs of the numerous native American nations in attendance—as well as the leaders of a rival Pennsylvania delegation, the Friendly Association for Regaining and Preserving Peace with the Indians by Pacific Measures. The unofficial head of the pacifist Quakers, Israel Pemberton, emerged as Benjamin's personal rival and nemesis.

Their conflict centered on interpreting the control and display of anger and soon overshadowed Benjamin's initial frustrated evaluations of the governor.

Benjamin and Pemberton met at Easton by accident. The official Pennsylvania delegation had spent Monday and Tuesday waiting in vain for an audience with representatives from native American nations, including the Delawares, the Senecas, and the Munsees. Though the governor had prepared a speech to deliver to them on Monday, they had informed his delegation that they would prefer to speak first and would inform the governor and his council when they were prepared to. So the representatives of Pennsylvania were forced to spend two days cooling their heels and waiting. They were thus startled to discover on the morning of the third day that, heedless of the supposed authority of the Pennsylvania governor, the native American chiefs had chosen to meet with members of the Friendly Association instead.[32]

Benjamin was determined to get to the bottom of the matter. He stole over to the Lutheran church, where he "received intelligence that the Quakers were at that time assembled with a number of Indians." He then decided to look in on the meeting.

> I went up first and put my head in a window that stood open. There I
> observed a large assembly of Indians and Quakers sitting some round
> a long table and others on benches behind with great solemnity and
> as much form as is usual in public treaties. Israel Pemberton was on
> one side, about midway [down] the table sitting with a pipe in his
> mouth collected in himself in great state.

The situation appeared to be as bad as Benjamin's worst fears. Not only had the Indians kept the governor and his delegation waiting in order to negotiate with their rivals the Quakers, but also those very rivals had the audacity to set themselves up with the trappings of leadership.[33]

Pemberton quickly invited Benjamin inside or, as Benjamin described it, "accosted me and asked me to walk in and smoke a pipe with them." But Benjamin declined, insisting that he was "only taking the air and did not come to interrupt them." He was appalled to see the number of Indians present, with more than thirty in attendance. Though he "knew very few of them," he did "distinguish Tagashata the Seneca chief and Tom King." The presence of such high-ranking native Americans did nothing to allay his outrage and anxiety. When Pemberton assured him "they were about no harm" and were talking "upon the best subjects in the world, love and friendship," Benjamin was hardly reassured. But he could do no more than offer a lame reply. To his journal he reported, "I told him they were noble subjects and I wish all those success who were sincerely disposed to promote and cultivate them."[34]

What lay behind Benjamin's and Pemberton's veiled discussions of love and friendship? Why did Pemberton emphasize these emotions while Benjamin felt compelled to defend his own appreciation of their worth? Quakers opposed anger unequivocally: from any person, for any reason. In fact, anger avoidance formed one of the fundamental pillars of their faith. Taking their inspiration from Christ's Sermon on the Mount, which commanded believers to love their enemies while admonishing them not to be angry without cause, they sought to model their emotions on New Testament teachings. As the Quaker elder Sophia Hume explained it, "Our communion is in the self-denying life and a daily cross in opposition to sensual lust, vanity, pride, bitterness of spirit, corruption, enmity and wrath." Quakers based their abhorrence of anger on the theory that passion—anger, lust, and willfulness—lay at the root of discord and self-ishness. The brand of love that Pemberton recommended, and for which Quakers are often celebrated, depended explicitly on individual believers' commitment to shunning anger every day. Furthermore, Quakers took the widely accepted association of anger and violence to its logical con-clusion and argued that angry emotions—like "enmity and wrath"—were the ultimate cause of war. So a Pemberton-style peace treaty required a commitment to anger's opposite: love.[35]

The Quakers' stance against passion generally and anger specifically was unequivocal and oftentimes undifferentiated, as exemplified by the disparaging remarks by Quaker elder Susannah Wright toward a public critic of the Quakers. In a letter that circulated widely in the Quaker community, Wright declared that an essay written by an unnamed Quaker opponent was "penned with a degree of anger and malignity more than human" and concluded, "His passion runs away with his judgment." Ma-lignant anger and runaway passions were so often equated in Quaker teachings as to appear indistinguishable; each impeded the operation of reasoned judgment. Where people like Governor Denny had clearly come to believe that some forms of anger could be deemed honorable, Quakers continued to claim that all instances of anger were more than—that is, not at all—human.[36]

Quakers simply could not abide anger in any form. Wright was no more tolerant of resentment than she was of malignant anger. She gave short shrift to the idea that reason could somehow legitimate some forms of anger. In a despairing poem written to a friend who was angry with her, Wright tried to dismantle all justifications for resentment. She began by telling her correspondent that it was a dark day when resentment over-mastered love: "If Resentment, Friendship must outlive / and injur'd Love forbids thee to forgive / [I] who [already] feels the worst, have nothing more to fear." Comparing all mankind to Adam in Eden—"Weak was his Reason, and his Will was strong"—Wright argued that, because humans were incapable of ever attaining the kind of complete and perfect knowledge reserved for God, they could never exercise truly reason-able anger:

> We cannot love or censure as we ought,
> Unless we had a more extensive Thought,
> Of ev'ry Cause the real Merit knew
> Can say that this is false, and this is true.

In other words, Wright repudiated the idea that *any* anger, even resent-ment, could ever really be based on impartial judgment and therefore justified. All anger stemmed from selfish will; she believed human beings were simply incapable of engaging in sufficiently "extensive Thought" to be able to evaluate real merit or truth: "Human nature . . . / has never been impartial." On the contrary, in man's breast "num'rous Passions, num'rous Folly's reign." By these lights, *all* anger was without cause. Wright's poem found its way into Milcah Martha Moore's commonplace book, where it was widely circulated among members of the Society of Friends, another testament to their extensive embrace of anti-anger doctrines.[37]

Quakers adhered to the idea that anger and passion were antithetical to humanity. Even as Christ had linked the commandment, "Thou shalt not kill," to the injunction that the angry were in danger of judgment, Quakers believed that the links between anger and violence could not and should not be ignored. From great questions of war to petty personal confrontations, Quakers always assumed that anger was the chief cause of conflict. For example, when the traveling Quaker minister, Benjamin Mifflin, came upon an unbending opponent of Quaker doctrine during a journey in 1764, he declared that because of the man's "vindictiveness, heat, and violence of temper there is no arguing fairly with him." Physical violence and violence of temper went together in Quaker teaching like chicken and egg, and both were the bane of reasoned and civilized conduct. So when Pemberton chided Benjamin about love and friendship, he questioned his emotional culture, his propensity for violence, and his commitment to peace as well.[38]

Pemberton's remarks resonated with Benjamin for a closely related and highly personal reason: Benjamin's own father was a onetime member of the Society of Friends who had been disowned by his religious fellows for daring to publicly contradict Quaker teachings on war. In 1742, just two years before his death, Samuel Chew underwent a crisis of conscience, which led him to assert that war, when engaged in purely for self-defense, was just, according to the laws of God and man alike.

The elder Chew's break with the Quakers affected him profoundly, hurting his political fortunes and personal relationships alike. An early favorite to represent the county of Kent in the colonial Assembly, Chew found himself faced with united Quaker opposition to his election. Indeed, the chief engineer behind the challenge was his own brother-in-law, a man Chew had long regarded as a friend. He confided to his son, "Your uncle Peter . . . made it his business to ride over the country propagating lies and villainous insinuations about me tho' we have not had a word of difference since you left us." Quaker efforts to secure Chew's defeat were successful, and Samuel informed his son that he and his uncle were "not now on speaking terms." Samuel died only months thereafter, leaving his son a bitter legacy indeed.[39]

Samuel's son, Benjamin, still a student at the time of his father's rupture with the Society of Friends, soon followed his father out of the Quaker Meeting and joined the Anglican Church. Yet many of the younger Chew's attitudes and ideas remained tied to the very Quaker strictures he meant to reject. His lingering reliance on Quaker teachings comes through clearly in his youthful commentary on the passions. Sent to England to study law in July 1743, Benjamin wrote home regularly to his father both to apprise him of his progress and to account for his expenditures. Criticizing "the corruption of the times" and the conduct of his fellow students, Benjamin gossiped to his father that they "seem to glory in making a sacrifice of their understandings, constitutions and estates to their unbridled passions." He hastened to note that he kept a firm reign on his own passions: "I hope you will not doubt my discretion so far as to entertain any fears of my running into the prevailing extravagancies." And he assured him, "I can foresee my ruin would be the infallible consequence of it and you cannot think me so void of reason or common sense as to rush headlong to my destruction with my eyes wide

FIGURE 8. Benjamin Chew. Simpson Portraits, Historical Society of Pennsylvania. *Permission The Historical Society of Pennsylvania.*

Benjamin Chew's beginnings show clearly in this portrait silhouette with distinctive Quaker hat.

FIGURE 9. Benjamin Chew. By Albert Rosenthall. Simpson Plates, Historical Society of Pennsylvania. *Permission The Historical Society of Pennsylvania.*

The Chew family turn from Quakerism to Anglicanism is dramatized by this nineteeth-century etching of Benjamin Chew.

open." Here Benjamin censured passion and championed reason in no uncertain terms. Though it is unlikely he had anger specifically in mind when he made these remarks, his attitude toward the willful emotion branded passion conformed closely to Quaker beliefs.[40]

Samuel Chew might have challenged Quaker teachings by endorsing defensive war, but his son could not quite make the logical leap to espousing the passions as well. Inconsistency on this point lay behind much of Benjamin's profound preoccupation with anger. He wanted above all to confirm his membership in the elite community his father had joined, and yet he remained troubled by the teachings of his youth. At a secondary peace treaty held in the midst of a wider war, Benjamin could hardly help being defensive about his own devotion to love and friendship, and uncertain about embracing the alternative standards of anger he found available.

Benjamin's father's Quaker history might or might not have been on the minds of many of the Anglo-Americans gathered at the Lutheran church that Wednesday morning. But Israel Pemberton, for one, was quick to point out that the deeds of the father did hold significance for the son. When one of Benjamin's companions also refused to enter and join the assembled Quakers, arguing that "they did not know him," Pemberton replied that he was welcome anyway, for "there were many there who know his father." That was the last remark Benjamin allowed Pemberton to make, at least in the pages of his diary; for he noted next that "we came away leaving them behind us." What he could not put so easily behind him was his preoccupation with anger itself.[41]

Fresh Inspiration from Anger: Anger as a Source of Enemy Strength

That very same afternoon, Benjamin reported with some pleasure that Israel himself had been guilty of breaching the principles of love and friendship. Another Quaker, William Logan (a son of the more famous statesman James Logan and not a strict pacifist), told Benjamin "he [Logan] had been very ill-used by I Pemberton in the public street." According to Logan, "on his saying the governor had been ready to meet the Indians from the time of the Quakers meeting them in the morning," Pemberton "told him it was a lye." Logan responded to Pemberton's hostile accusation with violence. "He clenched his fist and told him he had often abused him but to take care of himself for he would bear it no longer and said that the affinity that was between them was the only reason he did not knock him down which he would certainly do if he took the like liberties with him for the future." In this altercation, Logan found Pemberton publicly disrespectful and responded to the assault on his dignity by threatening an attack on Pemberton's person. Benjamin seems to have viewed Logan's talk of violence (so often associated with anger) in a decidedly favorable light and to have concurred with Logan's judgment that such a display would strengthen, not sully, his reputation.[42]

Indeed, Benjamin would soon move from approval of fisticuffs to open admiration of anger itself. When the Pennsylvania delegation finally got down to business with their fellow negotiators from the native American side on the following afternoon, they faced great hostility from the Delaware leader Teedyuscung. According to Benjamin, he "came in very drunk . . . was very troublesome the whole time." To the consternation of the assembled colonists, he "interrupted the conference very much, swearing that he was king of all the nations and of all the world . . . [and that the way] to behave to the English . . . was to make war on them and cut their throats, that he had struck them and would continue to do so as long as he lived." This outburst was a far cry from the docile subservience the Pennsylvania governor and his council would have preferred. But Benjamin comforted himself by observing, "The Indians and even his own people seemed angry and much disgusted with his behavior." Just as he appreciated Logan's threatened violence against his rival, Benjamin approved of anger directed at one who took a menacing, not ingratiating, stance toward his colony. Benjamin might easily have adopted a disdainful attitude toward this show of anger by Indians. The fact that he did not provides a valuable clue to the shifting valuation of anger.[43]

Although rage, fury, and passion were viewed in an unrelentingly negative light throughout the 1730s and 1740s, something did begin to change before 1750. The Quakers never wavered in their opposition to anger, but members of other religious groups began to revise their opinions. A growing interest in the positive moral properties of passion helped to pave the way for new attitudes toward passionate anger. Starting in the mid-1740s, Philadelphia booksellers began to include tracts from Scottish moral philosophers among their wares. Stephen Potts, proprietor of a shop "at the Sign of the Bible and the Crown," on Front Street in Philadelphia, advertised in the *Gazette* that he had copies of Watts's *Doctrines of the Passions* three separate times (April, May, and November 1743). By

FIGURE 10. James
Pemberton. By David
McNeely Stauffer. Stauffer
Collection, Historical Society
of Pennsylvania. *Permission
The Historical Society of
Pennsylvania*

1749, David Hall was selling books out of the post office and advertising that he had both "Hutcheson on the Passions" (in October and December) and "Hutchinson on the Passions" (in May 1751). It is impossible to know for sure just who bought these books, but it is worth noting that by the time William Smith, the College of Philadelphia provost, published an essay describing the college curriculum in 1756, "moral philosophy" was one of the chief subjects studied by second-year students, and third-years were urged to read "Hutcheson's Works" in their free time. Clearly the rising generation of young gentlemen was expected to be conversant with the latest modern thinking on the passions.[44]

The rising popularity of Pope's *Essay on Man* was, of course, but one of the more dramatic manifestations of this development. When Joseph Shippen created a "passion" section in his commonplace book in 1750, he not only quoted from Pope's line, "Passion is the gale," but also included much explicit commentary on anger itself. Far from the traditional view that passions characterized the "poor condition of the world" before the advent of a wonderful modern age, or the Quakers' unvarying determination to bear a daily cross against wrath, the new perspective Joseph Shippen and many other Anglo-Americans began to explore stressed that even angry passions could play a positive role in life. Shippen closed his section on passion with a startling assertion that appears to have been his own. "All anger is by no means sinful, it was made for self-defense and it has many times a design to reclaim and recover the offend.r from sin and danger." Shippen's claim that anger was not necessarily sinful directly confronted older, negative notions of anger. By linking acceptance of anger explicitly to new ideas about passion, Shippen affirmed a radical new conception of passionate anger as the cure for, not the cause of, sin and danger.[45]

What changes inspired this emerging new attitude toward anger? What made Pennsylvanians, who had abjured anger for so long, receptive to the new ideas being promulgated by the likes of Pope? As Shippen's emphasis on the importance of self-defense indicates, a heightened popular perception of danger prefaced the turn toward anger. By the middle to late 1740s, Pennsylvanians were becoming increasingly anxious about military security. Indian raids and intercolonial skirmishes on the Pennsylvania border made clear the difficulty of maintaining peace while refraining from making provisions for defense. Samuel Chew's personal metamorphosis from Quaker pacifist to measured militarist occurred amid widespread public interest in such issues. Confronted with growing threats both real and imagined from the native American neighbors whom they alternately cooperated with and competed against, Pennsylvanians initially seem to have turned to accusations of anger, that old reliable smear tactic, as a way of denigrating their foes.

A remarkable shift in the way that Indian anger was assessed is seen in the *Pennsylvania Gazette* in the years surrounding the outbreak of the Seven Years War. In the 1730s and 1740s, colonists displayed little interest in—or tolerance for—native American anger. Significantly, on the rare occasions when they did comment on it, colonists urged Indians to avoid even so much as resentment. In 1746 the governor of South Carolina reportedly asked representatives of the Catawbas, "Remember, that about two Years ago, when some-of the *Notchees* had in a cruel Manner murdered several of your people, and you were ready to take Revenge . . . I . . . desired you to suspend your Resentment, promising to do my Endeavours to procure you Satisfaction." He reminded them that as a result the Notchees had delivered the murderers to justice, allowing both nations to once again "eat and drink together, and shake Hands, and promise to live like Brothers for the future." Anglo-American leaders clearly recognized the potential for native American anger, yet they avoided acknowledging it as long as they could. Rather than attempting to class native

American anger with the sordid and passionate variety they attributed to lower-ranking members of their own society, elite Anglo-Americans simply tried to ignore native American anger altogether. In the patronage relationship colonists hoped to impose on Indians, all anger, and especially resentment, was to be the exclusive preserve of those who styled themselves masters and protectors. So long as general peace prevailed, Anglo-Americans were free to maintain the fantasy that they alone had the right to act on anger.[46]

But, when faced at last in the 1750s with rising military threats from native American groups they had long sought to control, prodefense inhabitants of Pennsylvania turned to the same tactics that had long worked to marginalize low-ranking members of their own society: they accused Indians of unruly and unreasoning anger. Not surprisingly, the favored brand of anger attributed to native American enemies was fury— the anger most closely associated with wildness, fierceness, and violence. The turn toward accusations of anger against Indians was as swift as it was dramatic. From 1729 through 1750, fury was never once mentioned in connection with native Americans in the pages of the *Gazette*. Fury—the anger of wind and fire and storms at sea—sometimes marked sailors, servants, and people who were enslaved, but never native Americans. Then, beginning in 1751, native Americans all at once became the supreme symbols of fury. From 1751 until 1758, the year of the treaty meeting at Easton, nearly two-thirds of all descriptions of fury targeted native Americans.[47]

Initial descriptions of Indians as furious people were no doubt intended in the most pejorative possible sense. Such propaganda could help vilify those native Americans perceived as threatening and establish them as a deserving enemy. Tellingly, colonists now described the anger of native Americans they regarded as *allies*, not as rage or fury, but as resentment. Thus, Governor Dinwiddie of Virginia was quoted in the *Gazette* in 1753: [Some] friendly Indians . . . seem much surprized at the Conduct of the *French*, and appear full of Resentment; and have assured the commissioners, sent from me, of their sincere Attachment to the *British* Interest." By contrast, a 1751 description of *enemy* Indians recounted the tale of a woman from Dartmouth who "escaped their Fury . . . with one Breast cut off by them." This account emphasized the fact that "a large Party of Indians" had murdered townspeople in their beds, "mangl[ing] [them] in a most surprizing Manner." This description neatly fits the traditional mold of anger accusation as denigration. Likewise, an article recounting native American cruelties "too shocking to be described" had clear political aims. The author concluded that the only way to *"be safe from their Fury"* would be to "build a Sort of Fort in every Parish." Descriptions of surprising and shocking fury were clearly intended to mark out native American enemies as a people apart, a people so given to unreasoning anger they could have nothing in common with the civilized British.[48]

Beneath the self-righteous condemnation of the shocking nature of enemy Indian anger lay a kind of grudging admiration for the military might their fury implied. It required only the shortest of steps to shift from presenting attributions of furious anger as evidence of depravity to viewing that same trait as an indication of strength. The issue of power had long been latent in discussions of anger. But, when the face of anger became united with the face of danger, the valuation of anger began to change. Indeed, by the time the Seven Years War officially began in 1754, the force of native Americans' anger had become a common explanation for their success in battles with the British. A 1754 letter from a Virginia soldier to a friend in Philadelphia, reprinted in the *Gazette,* remarked, "By their furious Attack and superior Numbers, we expected they would storm us at once." In battle, anger was counted as much an asset as superior manpower.[49]

In the early years of the war, in the mid-1750s, colonists began to focus increasingly on detecting the anger of their enemies as a means to predicting possible attacks. In hindsight, commentators on a successful native American ambush at Shamokin, Pennsylvania, believed the British should have predicted the enemy onslaught based on evidence of Indian anger. The report in the *Gazette* explained: "There were at Shamokin about 40 Indians, mostly painted black (which, 'tis said denotes Anger). . . . It is believ'd some of them slipp'd off in the Night to waylay our party . . . as our People were returning from Shamokin, they were fir'd upon unawares." The popular perception of anger among Anglo-Americans was beginning to shift in value, from a trait that tainted the servile to one that braced the strong. It is difficult to know how native Americans themselves viewed angry emotions, or whether indeed they would have agreed that black face paint evidenced anger. Rather, the important point is that Anglo-American rhetoric had cycled back on itself. Colonial elites began to respect, and even covet, the very forms of intense anger they had once rejected as unworthy.[50]

Of course, the transition to more positive assessments of extreme anger did not occur all at once. The following description of French and Indian tactics, which appeared in the *Gazette* in 1756, shows the conflicting attitudes of interest and abhorrence that characterized Anglo-American ideas about anger as the war deepened. The paper purported to be reprinting the translation of "a genuine French Letter," which revealed that "the French, instead of the Humanity they so much boast of to the world, not only delight in Cruelty and Bloodshed themselves, but encourage their Indians to commit the most unheard of Barbarities." The French letter supposedly bragged: "The English upon this Continent are driven to the last extremity. . . . Our Indians are animated against them even to Fury, and are never to be glutted with Scalping." Pennsylvanians would have well understood the implied association between aggressive anger and military prowess, even as they tried to maintain the claim that such an outlook reflected poorly on the French.[51]

If Indian fury was the wellspring of enemy success and strength, how long could it be before Anglo-Americans would be tempted to draw on such sources themselves? By the midpoint of the war, when things had begun to look up for the British and the *Gazette* began printing articles to encourage Anglo-American colonists to fight on to the finish, anger continued to be stressed as a formidable enemy asset. One author exhorted, "The foe staggers [but] . . . if we allow him respite, he recovers his vigour, misconstrues our delays into fears, and renews the attack with double fury; for the most dangerous wounds, unless seasonably prevented, will heal and inspire a man with fresh anger." Anger and attack, fury and inspiration—more and more, anger was associated with desirable traits like success, strength, and power.[52]

For his part, Benjamin Chew continued to make favorable comments about anger when displayed by Indians he regarded as allies. On Friday, the day after he angered his fellows, Teedyuscung's right to represent the views of the native Americans continued to be a central topic of dispute. Perhaps because of his confrontational stance—or perhaps because he was known to be friendly to Quakers—the governor's contingent opposed acknowledging Teedyuscung's leadership. When Nichas, a Mohawk leader, denied that Teedyuscung, a Delaware, had any authority to speak for Indian nations as a whole, Benjamin remarked approvingly that he "spoke for some time with apparent warmth and resolution in his face and manner, turning frequently and pointing to Teedyuscung." Here Benjamin attributed to a native American, not beastly rage or childish peevishness, but rather an admirable warmth that spoke of resolution.[53]

By contrast, Israel Pemberton was troubled by Nichas's apparent anger and "said loud enough to be heard by many round the table" that Nichas's speech "ought not to be interpreted for it would make a difference among the Indians." Certainly Pemberton was concerned that his ally Teedyuscung's credibility was being undermined, but just as surely he was perturbed by the appearance of anger that might well lead to further discord and even bloodshed. Both Benjamin and Pemberton understood the links between anger, conflict, and aggression, but where one saw trouble and strife the other saw only worthy resolve.[54]

Benjamin and the rest of the governor's coterie did their best to ignore Pemberton's perspective and to relegate him instead to the obscure status of an unseemly upstart—this despite the fact that he clearly did enjoy the respect of many native American leaders. For example, during a ceremonial exchange of wampum belts and strings between native Americans and Pennsylvanians that same afternoon, one of the Indians present specifically requested that Israel Pemberton be given a string—a symbolic mark of affection, and a clear reminder of the continuing ties between Indians and Quakers. In response, "the governor said jocosely to those who sat next to him: I hope he will soon be favored with another string which he richly merits." This bit of witty repartee pleased Benjamin so much he included it in his summary of the negotiation proceedings. And something—perhaps delight at the fantasy of seeing Pemberton swing from a noose—would soon embolden Benjamin still further.[55]

Noble Indignation and Virtuous Rage:
The Anglo-American Elite's Appropriation of Extreme Anger

Following the exchange of strings, tensions continued to rise between the governor's council and members of the Friendly Association. Though he had begun by scrutinizing the governor's angry displays and analyzing the social slights he received at his hands, Benjamin now focused all of his rivalrous impulses and social frustrations on Israel Pemberton. After ten days of cataloging the anger and categorizing the status of others—from peevish rage to resolute warmth—Benjamin at last allowed himself to try on anger's mantle. Another chance meeting with Pemberton on the street provided the pretext.

According to Benjamin, Pemberton confronted him with the claim that efforts to discredit Teedyuscung had originated with an Indian trader and go-between named George Croghan, a man Pemberton regarded as both a "rascal and a villain" *and* a tool of the governor. In reply, Benjamin taunted him, saying that Croghan had at least as much right to attend the treaty negotiations as Pemberton himself did. In his own account of what happened next, Benjamin wrote:

> I told him with a great deal of warmth . . . that what he said was false. On this he chuckled meanly and said he . . . did not mean to affront me, why was I so warm. Indeed I only wanted a fair opportunity to hit him a slap in the chops, and he saw it plainly, on which like the pitiful dog he is, he became suave and complaisant.

Both men agreed that Benjamin had grown warm, and at first Pemberton regarded Benjamin's outburst as an opportunity to deride him in turn for his embarrassing lapse of propriety. But Benjamin himself evaluated their exchange in exactly the opposite way. He credited his anger with forcing Pemberton into an abject and subservient position. Implicitly linking his own show of warmth with both Logan's earlier boasts of threatened violence and Nichas's resolute manner, Benjamin portrayed his display of anger as an effective means of demonstrating his own masculine mastery in the face of Pemberton's animal servility.[56]

As dramatic as the rise of accusations of anger (and especially fury) against native Americans was the subsequent appearance—for the first time in the three decades of the *Gazette*'s publication—of positive assessments of rage and fury displayed by elite Anglo-American men. The timeline for this transition was by no means identical for every possible synonym for extreme anger; nevertheless, the overall trend is remarkably clear. Up until 1754, only resentment was ever mentioned in a positive light in the *Gazette*. Then, beginning in exactly the same year as the war— and after five years of attributions to native Americans—all kinds of anger suddenly became acceptable for Anglo-Americans. First to be used was the word *rage*, to which *Gazette* articles gave positive connotations for a brief window in time from 1754 to 1759, the year that British forces scored a decisive victory at Quebec and reached a turning point in the war. Then *fury* gained acceptance in 1758 and 1759. Finally, the actual word *anger* itself came into use among Anglos and lingered until 1763, the final year of the war. Simply charting the timing of this shift makes clear how central the war, the desire for strength, and the crisis over self-defense were in transforming anger into an acceptable and even desirable emotion. But the explicit comments made by colonists laid bare the roots of this change.

Take the 1755 story recounted by Thomas McKee, a militia member and farmer living on the Susquehanna River in Pennsylvania's western hinterland. Hearing a report of a possibly hostile Indian sighted near a distant settler's house, McKee "raised 24 young men and went with them . . . in order to attack if an enemy." Along the way, McKee stopped off at his own plantation, hoping to spend the night at a house he had there. To his surprise, he "discovered an Indian within the dwelling house which I formerly lived in." McKee apprehended him with the hope of interrogating him and was considerably startled to see that he was dressed in European clothes, wearing a shirt bearing a "bullet hole . . . whereby the [previous] owner, as we suppose, was killed." McKee and his company reacted swiftly. As McKee recounted, "seeing the white men's cloaths upon him in such a condition put me in a very great rage and [I] told him he must die for he was a murderer." Though McKee intended to spare the man just long enough to grill him for information, a "young fellow came and shot him" just a few moments later.[57]

McKee's story highlights several important aspects of the colonists' embrace of rage. Passionate anger first became acceptable on the frontier in response to a sense of profound physical and cultural threat. Not only might native Americans kill European settlers; they might move into their houses and dress in their clothes, which themselves represented frontiersmen's tenuous connections to the civility of the metropolis. In response, colonists in Pennsylvania attempted to steal back a source of native American strength, at last appropriating the rage they had long attributed to their enemies. Separated from city Quakers by religion and ethnicity as much as by geography, frontier Scots-Irish Presbyterians, in particular, would turn to new alternatives for passionate anger.[58]

In all aspects, then, it was a long way from the Susquehanna to Philadelphia; new backwoods conventions for emotion were a far cry from the self-consciously genteel codes of expression espoused by urban gentlemen. Indeed, in the same year that McKee reported unabashedly on his own rage, the *Gazette* printed a letter from the Pennsylvania Assembly to the governor reproaching him for the "storm of angry questions" he had posed to the legislature and proffering a "few cool sober questions" in return. Of course, key to this exchange about anger was the fact that the majority of the assemblymen were Quakers and the governor was not; here, writ large, was the personal conflict between Pemberton and Benjamin. Still, as the history already recounted makes clear, at the outset Quakers were far from unique in their disavowals of anger. So what could legitimate the sort of angry displays that colonists, from backcountry commoners to state bureaucrats, had begun to experiment with?[59]

In order for explicitly passionate forms of anger to take on new meaning as desirable, their very nature had to be transformed. Where once rage and fury had been linked to base and servile natures, such associations began to be outweighed by the accompanying attractions of strength. But strength alone was not enough to transform this disreputable emotion; after all, gentlemen could acknowledge among themselves that earlier generations had achieved distinction through fury without wanting to allow such standards to apply in contemporary times. No, anger's alchemists needed to find a way to gild it with virtue as well as strength. Some of the earliest evidence of such attempts comes in a 1754 *Gazette* article describing the performance of a traveling English theater group. In a closing oration reprinted in the *Gazette,* the players took up themes of danger, rage, and virtue that had relevance for a stage much wider than the one they had just performed on. Addressing concerns that the theater was immoral because of its tendency to induce emotions in its audience, the players argued:

> Too oft, we own, the Stage with dangerous Art
> In wanton scenes, has play'd the Syren's Part.
>
> . . .
>
> [Yet] Has she not oft, with awful virtuous Rage,
> Struck home at Vice—and nobly trod the Stage?
>
> . . .
>
> The Play just finish'd, Prejudice apart,
> Let honest Nature speak—How feels the Heart?
> Did it not throb, then tell it to our Foes,
>
> . . .
>
> Whilst . . . a noble Indignation rose?
> If then the Soul in Virtue's Cause we move,
> Why should the Friends of Virtue disapprove?

These lines clearly stated that anger in the guise of "virtuous rage" or "noble indignation" should be met with approbation, not trepidation. Impassioned anger invoked in the cause of virtue was not to be confused with the kind of wanton anger so long avoided among those who counted themselves respectable.[60]

Such advice did not actually explain just what distinguished dangerous anger from the virtuous variety, nor how anyone could guard against the one while exercising the other. A solution to this conundrum was soon presented in another poem appearing in the *Gazette*. Like the poem arguing that theater could promote virtuous varieties of anger, this next one, in 1756, also claimed that the arts were the answer to anger regulation. First the author asserted:

> The ruffled Passions potent to asswage,
> To conquer Fear, and to enervate Rage,
> Was Music's Power, by *Orpheus* first ordain'd
> Fierce Beasts were tam'd, and fiercer Tyrants chain'd.

Readers were assured that music could always counter anger; they need have no fears of giving way to unbridled emotions while they lived in a civilized society. True, anger had long been associated with "fierce beasts" like the raging bear reported years before, but even the anger of such wild creatures could be soothed by music. Having established this cultural safeguard, the poem then went on to encourage readers to cultivate their own capacity for angry emotion:

> Britons attend. . . .
> Dare to invent yourselves, to FAME aspire
> Be justly warm'd with your own native Fire.

Since music could quench the flames of anger's fire, Anglo-American colonists could allow themselves to grow warm without fear that they would grow so irretrievably angry as to transgress the bounds of British respectability. Indeed, this poem seemed to argue that the "native" anger natural to the British people was something altogether different from the wild anger they so often attributed to outsiders.[61]

Such advice must have met with a ready reception in Pennsylvania. Just four years before this poem appeared in the *Gazette*, Joseph Shippen (as we have seen, an early apologist for anger) actually scribbled down one day a few lines of poetry remarkably like those in the *Gazette*. The surviving scrap of paper, dated 1752 and signed by him, contains William Congreve's lines, "Music has Charms to sooth the savage B[ea]st, to soften Rocks or bend the knotted Oak." Here Shippen affirmed the civilizing power of music. While he made no explicit reference to anger here, these lines, together with his known interest in anger, suggest he would have welcomed the view that music could assuage angry passions. Playing with similar themes, Shippen's brother-in-law, James Burd, wrote to his wife, Sally Shippen Burd, in 1758: "200 Indians . . . attacked me on Thursday the 12th . . . at 11 AM with great fury until 3 PM . . . but in return for their most immelodious Indian music, I gave them a number of shells from our mortars which made them retreat soon."[62]

Though the *Indians'* fury made only "immelodious music," many *colonists* believed they could afford to grow angry themselves, secure in the knowledge that European music had potent powers to enervate rage should it ever threaten to burn out of control. Mixed though these metaphors grew in the mouths of various Pennsylvania colonists, an important recurrent theme does emerge. European culture supposedly safeguarded the emotions of European colonists, ensuring that noble indignation would not spill over into beastly rage.[63]

Indeed, so long as they could keep their own anger from being called beastly or savage, Anglo-Americans began to grow more and more comfortable with the idea of extreme yet efficacious anger. For example, a report from Pittsburgh in 1759 claimed, "Indians came here who said they came to see if the English were not angry at them." What a turnabout from the days when Pennsylvanians chided themselves for not noticing the signs of Indian anger, so clearly signaled by blackened faces, to a day when the Indians had to check to see if the English were angry![64]

By the height of the war, Anglo-Americans congratulated themselves frequently on the successes imparted by passionate anger. A 1758 *Gazette* report in praise of a "lower country" officer with the felicitous (and perhaps fictitious) name of Captain Bullet explained, "As the enemy came up to Capt. Bullet, he attacked them very furiously for some Time . . . [and] his attacking them, stopt the[ir] Pursuit." Another article in 1759 described the British victory at Quebec and noted that, in a "very hot Dispute," the British "drove the French out of their Lines . . . [with a] furious Attack." Reporting on the death of General James Wolfe in the wake of that crucial victory, another writer asserted that this "last great Scene, should melt each *Briton's* Heart, / And Rage and Grief alternately impart." Far from being regarded as sinful or servile, rage and fury had come to be seen as an admirable, reliable source of British strength. In contrast to the French, who would ridicule the English for obtaining victory in North America at the cost of civility, British Americans celebrated the newfound force anger added to their claims of masculine mastery.[65]

Colonists' growing confidence in their ability to mete out anger appropriately can also be traced through changes in the use of the word *wrath*. Wrath was perhaps the strongest possible form of anger—certainly greater than resentment, irritation, warmth, or heat and even superseding fury and rage. In fact, the word *wrath* was not applied to British Americans in any context until 1763. Before then, only God could be wrathful with impunity, as when a Caribbean writer said his people "justly feel the wrath of God," or when a synod of Philadelphia ministers warned the townspeople to beware "the deserved Wrath of Heaven." Anyone but God who was described as wrathful was simultaneously derided with epithets like "anti-Christian." By the close of the war, with France in defeat and the jubilant British Americans victorious, they began to feel that they, too, might express anger as unalloyed as actual wrath. As one New Yorker writing from Detroit put it in 1763, we shall take "such Revenge for the Butcheries committed by the Barbarians as shall be a LASTING MONUMENT of the Wrath of INJURED BRITONS, and be sufficient to deter the BEASTS from ever attempting the like hereafter." Victory confirmed power, and power conferred the right to express anger. Of course, the expression of anger itself created a further claim to power. Still, it must be kept in mind that much of the public approbation of anger appearing in the *Gazette* derived from sources outside Pennsylvania. Within the colony, opinion was sharply divided about anger's true impact and importance.[66]

Despite his own apparent satisfaction with what he hoped had been a masterly show of warmth, Benjamin must have been troubled by the knowledge that his anger *could* have been interpreted another way. When Pemberton switched from derisive laughter to a more soothing and placating demeanor, he left Benjamin room to conclude that his anger had in fact created the effect he desired. But Benjamin well knew that he had run a risk in expressing anger, for his very next portrayal of warmth was unequivocally critical.

A few days after Benjamin and Pemberton disputed, a new and greater upheaval disturbed the proceedings of the treaty conference: the governor ordered up sentries to guard the liquor supply. This precaution proved exceptionally unpopular with the assembled men, and "a confounded fracas happened." According to Benjamin, some of the Quaker leaders on hand "interfered with great warmth and indecency" and "made the streets resound with epithets." The Quakers "seemed determined to kick up a riot with what view except to make themselves popular, God knows." Benjamin credited himself with working industriously to suppress the potential riot and congratulated himself with being "happy enough to succeed." Yet he could not but have noticed in the back of his mind that displays of warmth could be as easily smeared with aspersions of indecency as varnished with positive associations of resolve.[67]

Restraint and Resolution: The Reemergence of Resentment and the Nuances of Elite Anger Codes

Following the indecent warmth displayed during the "confounded fracas," Benjamin reverted without explanation to a critical stance on anger. When that afternoon's discussions again grew acrimonious, Benjamin attempted to remain calm and reported on his own behavior with smug satisfaction. At issue were the terms and scope of a land grant negotiated between Pennsylvania colonists and members of the Delaware nation in 1749. Israel Pemberton and the Indians both objected to the smooth excuses and partial explanations proffered by the Pennsylvania governor.

At length Pemberton rose and spoke on behalf of the Friendly Association: "We as free men will not sit patiently by and be witnesses of it [the governor's speech] without bearing our public testimony against it." With gathering intensity he warned his fellow colonists that the governor's "speech would set the Indians together by the ears and it would end in cutting our throats." Benjamin himself retorted that Pemberton "was a mad man and took the ready way to make the Indians cut our throats." He reported scornfully in his diary that Pemberton had "wriggled and twisted about in his seat at a strange rate and muttered," claiming that Pemberton "was crazy and an enemy to the peace of his country." As Benjamin told it, Pemberton then "walked off and left me in a crowd of his creatures who had gathered round us."[68]

Now was Benjamin's chance to try to prove that his own earlier confrontations with Pemberton did not stem from any overriding feelings of anger, but were simply the considered remarks of a naturally masterful man. Again, believing that he had acquitted himself quite admirably, he summed up the outcome:

I then entered coolly into conversation with them, told them their suspicions were unjust and they would own it when I explained the thing to them, which I did explain it as clearly as I could. They were immediately softened down, blamed Israel much for his heat and indiscretion and owned that the measures we had pursued were salutary and for the public good.

Unlike his altercation with Pemberton just three days before, in which he reported with pride on his own display of warmth, Benjamin now claimed that he had remained "cool" while Pemberton had displayed "heat."[69]

How could Benjamin now reproach Pemberton with the very behavior he himself had refused to concede was improper just days before? Benjamin's condemnations of indecent warmth and blameworthy heat served an important function: they helped to establish (in his own mind at least) that his approval of anger was not indiscriminate. On the contrary, Benjamin believed that the careful and measured use of anger conveyed strength and resolution, whereas careless and uncontrolled expressions of anger betrayed a servile and uncivilized nature incapable of exercising discretion. Here Benjamin's frequent use of metaphors of warmth and heat in lieu of direct discussions of anger become significant. In Benjamin's view, anger, like fire, was dangerous only if allowed to burn out of control. Properly regulated, it could prove a useful and potent tool.

Although anger did lose the almost automatic stigma it had carried in the early part of the eighteenth century, it was never accepted without reservation. As the war wore on, leaders in Pennsylvania still offered only an equivocal and qualified acceptance of anger, one that stressed that anger came in many forms and in different strengths, some less objectionable than others. Discussions of anger and passion in the *Gazette* increasingly focused on the importance of effective anger control. Still, such discussions of control implied only a need for the regulation, not the actual elimination, of anger. A poem in the *Gazette* in 1759, shortly after the British victory at Quebec, declared that the task of the Muse of Language was "to rouse each Passion dormant in the Soul, / Point out its Object, or its Rage controul." Passions came in many varieties, all valuable, all deserving to be roused. But rage, once roused, should always remain controlled.[70]

Indeed, one of the most important determinations came to be whether a person was the master or the servant of angry passions. Not surprisingly, such distinctions could be used to legitimate the anger of elites, lending them strength while demeaning and discrediting the anger of lesser members of society. Compare this 1760 description of the celebrated General Wolfe, mastermind of the British victory at Quebec, with a parallel description of a runaway servant. Both pieces appeared in the *Gazette*. Of Wolfe it was said: "With an unusual liveliness, almost to Impetuosity of Temper, he was not subject to Passion . . . [He was] Manly and unreserved, yet gentle . . . in his manners." A leader like Wolfe was expected to display strong emotion, even "impetuosity of temper," yet always to be the master, not the subject, of passion. Unreserved emotions would add to such a figure's manliness because of the safeguard provided by his naturally gentle and temperate modes of expression. By contrast, a runaway ad posted in 1762 noted that the absconded servant was "subject to violent Passions." Just a few years earlier the simple mention of passion was all that was needed to brand a person as subordinate. Now it became necessary to specify not only that people displayed passions but also that they were *subject* to them, that they were incapable of the sort of manly control that characterized the anger of men of the elite.[71]

The very fact that the passions of General Wolfe, one of Anglo-America's most admired men, were the subject of such scrutiny highlights how important emotions had become as a mark of mastery. Anger was never more broadly accepted than at the moment of British triumph. And Wolfe, as much as anyone, had championed the propriety of anger. Facing the fallen people of Quebec, the *Gazette* quoted Wolfe: "The King, my Master, [is] justly irritated against France and resolved to . . . revenge the Insults committed against the Inhabitants of the English Colonies." Still, he assured them that they, the common people, were "not the Objects of the King of Great-Britain's anger: 'Tis not against them this his Arm is lifted." If they would but agree to remain neutral for the war's duration, he promised clemency. If they should take up arms for the French, he warned, "I will not paint to them the Excesses of an enraged Soldier: The Image would be too Shocking." Anger was the attribute of kings and masters, the arm of the British king in his colonies and the substance behind the soldier's threat. Yet, anger and associated passions had to be controlled and carefully aimed.[72]

In the face of dramatic wartime expansions of the acceptable bounds of passionate anger, and in light of its real potential to confer power on the dispossessed, elites were forced to articulate anew an ideal of anger that could apply to gentlemen only. Though the strongest forms of anger

—like rage and fury—enjoyed a brief vogue in the early years of the war, the popularity of the most passionate forms of anger proved short-lived. Following the victory at Quebec, Anglo-Americans did not abandon altogether their appreciation of passionate anger, but they placed a much greater emphasis on the importance of leashing such anger securely so that it might never run out of control. Provost William Smith of the College and Academy of Philadelphia captured the emerging attitude on the importance of anger control in his instructions on the right regulation of the passions. He told his students:

> If on any occasion ... an Abhorrence of Vice and Dissimulation, should oblige you to bear your Testimony against [them] ... you must blame without Anger. . . . 'Tis true, sometimes a strong conviction of important Truth ... will, in the best of Men, produce a seeming Acrimony of Expression ... especially when heated by Opposition. But if, from the general Tenor of your Conduct, you have convinced the World of the *Goodness of your heart,* such Starts of Passion will be forgiven ... or considered only as the Fire from the Flint; "which being smitten, emits its hasty spark and is straightway cool again."

In other words, gentlemen did not give up entirely their right to passionate brands of anger. But elite use of such anger was contingent on the idea that the best of men had flint, not fire, at the core, that they would make virtuous use of passionate anger only occasionally and only against obvious vice.[73]

A poem prepared for the entertainment of commencement-goers at the college in 1763 captures the restricted approval of anger that prevailed by the close of the war.

> As Wrath subsides, and War's loud tumults cease,
>
> . . .
>
> Old Warriors now with Rage shall glow no more.
>
> . . .
>
> Countries oppress'd by War's destructive Rage
> [Will] Again revive to bless a milder Age.

Though this poem acknowledged the association between anger and strength, the glowing rage that had allowed the English victory, it decreed that such anger was appropriate only in wartime and encouraged the emergence of a milder age. The poet urged the commencement audience:

Heart-chearing Mirth, and Plenty ever gay,
With rosy Joy, shall tend thy gentle Sway!
HASTE then, O haste, thy softening pow'r renew,

. . .

And bid Mankind with Anger burn no more.

Elites, even more than commoners, needed to be certain they could soften their passions once the urgent need for anger had passed.[74]

More and more, control became the key to genteel appropriations of the passionate anger once indiscriminately derided as servile. Even resentment, which had previously enjoyed great favor among the elite because of its links to reason, became subject to the same strictures of control. Self-styled gentlemen who now displayed resentment had to be careful to indicate they were not indulging in utterly unbridled passion. At least this seems to have been the approach beleaguered frontier trader George Morgan took when, describing skirmishes with his competitors to business associates back in Philadelphia, he declared, "I would not choose to be actuated altogether by resentment, but I flatter myself you will not let pass unnoticed the many insufferable insults I have received." Careful to claim he was not "altogether actuated" by anger, Morgan nevertheless asserted that resentment was the necessary and proper response to the social threat represented by other men's efforts at intimidation and insult. He evidently believed he had displayed the optimal degree of anger in drawing on restrained resentment to defend his honor and social standing.[75]

Much the same inference about the renewed importance of *restrained* anger can be drawn from the case of another man, one who resorted to too great a degree of anger in response to a personal insult. John McPherson actually took out an advertisement in the *Gazette* to explain that an "unjust Attack upon my good Name, raised my Passions almost to a Degree of Fury." Though he condemned the man who had insulted him for his "cruel and unprovoked Abuses," he felt himself bound to apologize for the fact that "this unhappy Incident drew from me some Expressions, which my Respect to the Publick ought to have restrained." Clearly anger was the proper response to insult; but, where restrained anger could reclaim a man's standing, unmitigated fury might well keep him from "standing well in the opinion of good men."[76]

Similar evidence about the importance of restrained resentment in a gentleman's emotional repertoire comes in comments from a father about the education of his son. Edward Tilghman sent his young son, Neddy, to be educated at the academy in Philadelphia, hoping to eventually apprentice him as a lawyer; obviously he entertained expansive social aspirations for his son. He speculated on the effect that overly severe school discipline might have on him: "He has the quickest sense of injury, though I think not enough of resolution in resenting so that probably it may break out in grief and complaint. To have his failings made subject of derision he never could bear from earliest infancy." Here a father displayed pride in his son's intolerance for derisive treatment and wished only that he might learn to have more resolve in his resentment. Being resolved meant being firm, unyielding, and above all controlled. Tilghman worried that his son's as yet incomplete mastery of his passions might allow them to "break out" in grief, an emotional alternative to anger that was (as will become evident later) most frequently employed by subordinate members of society. Still, with a firm foundation of self-respect, he was confident his son would learn unwavering resentment in time. The positive connection between moderate anger and the maintenance of honor could not be more clear.[77]

Among those men who came to espouse anger as an important component of masculine honor, restraint was key to the social code. Scholars have noted the increasing importance of anger control in Anglo-American culture and concluded that this emphasis on regulation implied a desire for anger's elimination. What I wish to argue, conversely, is that the regulation of anger was intended only to result in its moderation. This new ideal for anger control served important social functions and actually accompanied an increasing acceptance of anger among selected social groups. The successful mastery of anger showed that one was fit to be master of men.[78]

Still, for a sizable segment of this population—that is, for the women— all anger was indeed supposed to be eliminated. In order for controlled anger to be counted a hallmark of honorable manhood, it had to be made absolutely inaccessible to women. In the very same era in which elite men first began to appropriate the rage and fury once attributed only to members of marginal groups, they stepped up advice to women to shun all shows of anger. "A Maiden's Best Adorning, or A Fathers Advice to His Daughter," which the Quaker Mary Flower included in her 1757 commonplace book, contained the following signal instructions:

> Let reason with sweet calmness keep the throne
> Treading fierce wrath and lawless passion down,
> The grace of meekness is the woman's crown.

To be worthy of a throne, women were supposed to work not merely toward the regulation of anger commended to their male counterparts but toward its total elimination. By 1757, anger avoidance was being redefined as a feminine emotional task, the crowning attribute of admirable women.[79]

Indeed, the subject of women's anger represents an instance where historians can look easily at prescription but seldom at practice. No doubt many Anglo-American women felt anger. They might well have expressed anger explicitly in the course of their daily conversations. The survival of a few disparaging comments about women who were accused of anger indicates that they must have done so. But the prohibition against women's anger was strong enough that, so far as I have been able to find, *direct* verbal expressions of anger scarcely ever made their way into the written record in colonial Pennsylvania, either in personal papers or in published outlets. Obviously, the self-assertion inherent in expressions of anger would have been especially unwelcome in the mouths of women. But the effort to eliminate women's anger served another function as well, for women's complete containment of anger was also billed as an essential component of the manly program of civilized anger control.

Feats of masculine mastery of wrath and rage required the ready assistance of women. Another poem on women's anger, this one containing advice on the proper emotional expression for young wives, urged:

> Never in wordy war engage
> Nor ever meet his rage with rage.
> With all our sexes softening art
> Recall lost reason to his heart.
> Thus calm the tempest in his breast
> And sweetly sooth his soul to rest.

In this poem, rage, like war, was acknowledged as an appropriate element of masculine action, and women were warned against imitating such masculine emotion. At the same time, these verses suggested a powerful positive function for women's restraint of rage. By pressing all of their own passions down, Anglo-American women could compensate for their husbands' wrath. By extension, it could be concluded that Anglo-American men who wished to express anger without jeopardizing their culture's claims to civility and humanity needed their wives' assistance to achieve this aim.[80]

Any woman who managed to eliminate all outward traces of her own anger could expect high public praise indeed. Consider the 1773 obituary of Ann Ross, the wife of a Lancaster lawyer, who passed away at the age of forty:

> This amiable woman may truly be said to have possessed those Virtues, that adorn human nature. . . . In the different Stages of *moral, social, relative, and domestic Life,* her conduct was directed by Principles of Goodness, Benevolence and Prudence. . . . Over those rough and tumultuous Passions, which so often rob us of Humanity, she kept the strictest guard, and therefore was seldom, or never, disquieted by the Disorders of ANGER.

Ann Ross was praised for safeguarding the virtues of humanity by guarding against her own anger. Tellingly, this anger avoidance was closely linked to moral and domestic life. To men fell the right to use anger as a tool of war, to women the task of preserving the virtues that adorned human nature according to the values of eighteenth-century Anglo-America. This gendered division of emotional labor allowed men to adopt the anger they had long attributed to alien groups without undue concern that they were undermining the exclusive claims of their own culture and class to humanity and civility.[81]

So important had measured and honorable anger become in the emotional repertoire of men of the elite that even some Quakers grudgingly accepted it. Those who wished to remain in positions of public service were forced to make some accommodation to anger. Perhaps the most striking example of this comes from a Quaker diarist living on the frontier in 1761. James Kenny was a fur trader working out of Pittsburgh who found himself surrounded by other combative and competitive men, from the native Americans who supplied him with furs to rival traders and military men. In this volatile environment, Kenny struggled to reconcile the ideals of his Quaker faith with the realities of the backcountry conditions with which he was faced. The exigencies of his life in the hinterlands led Kenny to bend the Quaker prohibition on anger, underscoring the influence of backwoods interactions on the reformulation of Anglo-American valuations of anger and illustrating the growing appreciation of controlled passions.[82]

From the opening pages of his diary, Kenny reminded himself repeatedly of his obligation to conduct himself according to Quaker principles and thus to serve as a model of piety to all that he encountered. He wrote at the outset "that the [military] officers liked me much the better for standing true to my principles." True to Quaker precepts, Kenny stressed emotional regulation as the hallmark of Quaker practice. He took pride in the fact that "the Indians say that the general report amongst their people is that friends [Quakers] are kinder and better humoured than any others." And he lectured native Americans on the evils of anger. Coming upon an Indian fur trapper whom he suspected of idolatry, he informed the hunter that "the good spirit" watched over all men. "Good men, that was known by him, always loved all men and would not be wrath or angry with any." For Kenny, the essence of Christianity could be boiled down to two central emotional precepts: embrace love, and shun anger. He followed Quaker teachings to the letter.[83]

Yet, Kenny acknowledged that he sometimes departed from these precepts, to the detriment of the good name of Quakerism. In the same breath that he reported others' admiration for his strict adherence to principle, he lamented, "Notwithstanding I have been so foolish in days past as to give cause of reproaching the name I went by . . . and it [ha]s been ever [a] cause of sorrow and repentance to me when I think of my folly." Despite his ideals, Kenny was unable to resist resorting to anger on occasion. Like so many Pennsylvanians, he first embraced anger in the cause of virtue and directed it against native Americans. Confronted with temptations of the flesh, he countered with the weapons of anger. As he recounted in his diary, "It is lamentable and grievous the customs of the heathen. . . . It's very like the Indians never had any law from God or man to forbid em of fornication. . . . Several of their young women has at times endeavour'd to tempt me to this act but I always resented the same with indignation." Despite his keen awareness of the impropriety of anger, Kenny felt justified in opposing it to what he viewed as the still more dangerous threat of sexual improprieties. Significantly, the two kinds of anger that Kenny confessed he had expressed—indignation and resentment—were the very two varieties so often appropriated by elite Anglo-Americans who desired to distinguish *their* emotions from supposedly more servile forms of anger.[84]

Though Kenny followed Quaker orthodoxy in shunning outright anger and wrath, he viewed resentment in an altogether different light. On the one hand he still eschewed passion generally; when another trader challenged him, he ridiculed his rival's anger and boasted of his own composure: "I told him not to be in a passion as I had no intention of affronting him. So I took my leave of him . . . [and] was very well satisfied in mind." On the other hand, he congratulated himself on a dream in which he "looked with resentment at the Devil." While Kenny avoided "anger" and "passion," he freely employed "indignation" and "resentment" in support of virtue.[85]

Faced with the threat of enemy strength, Kenny seemed convinced that a mild and moderate form of anger could provide him and his people with important protection. He complained in his diary in 1763 that native American–Anglo-American go-betweens like George Croghan (the very one Israel Pemberton regarded as a "rascal and a villain") stirred up more trouble than they soothed when they soft-pedaled white objections to Indian actions. In remarks that were prescient in the light of mounting frontier tensions, Kenny explained that if Indian agents did not "spake right or boldly telling them the consequence of their thieving . . . the Indians are not let into the knowledge how much it is resented and may be of dangerous consequence to the public peace." In other words, native Americans should be made aware of how angry Anglo-Americans actually were in time to offer amends; otherwise, Anglo-American anger would spill over into the kind of violence that precluded peace. In his assertion that anger led to war, Kenny could not have been more Quakerly. But, in his assumption that anger first vented in the form of resentment could intimidate Indians without the need for further force, Kenny relied on an entirely different view of anger, one forged on the frontier and then made fashionable throughout the colony.[86]

As far as Benjamin Chew was concerned, Israel Pemberton's "heat and indiscretion" were blameworthy precisely because they betrayed a lack of restraint, whereas his own warmth was advantageous because it had cut short Pemberton's ability to insult and "affront" him. But Benjamin could be confident that the anger he chose to label "warmth" would not meet the same disapproval as Pemberton's "heat" only if he was able to demonstrate that he could remain "cool" when the situation called for such control: hence his detailed recounting of his calm response to the liquor riot and of his measured and moderate reasoning with the "crowd" of Pemberton's "creatures."

The resolution of Benjamin's final confrontation with Israel Pemberton came in a conversation with Pemberton's brother. Meeting James Pemberton later that same afternoon, Benjamin informed him that "his brother was a violent unmannerly brute." In associating Pemberton's anger with brutishness, Benjamin harked back to traditional negative stereotypes of anger and animality. In accordance with current views that stressed moderation, not elimination, he hastened to add, "If he would conquer his passions and become a rational creature, I should have no objections to confer with him." According to Benjamin, then, the problem with Pemberton's anger was in its excess. He presented his own coolness in contrast to Pemberton's heat as evidence that his rival was subject to passion while Benjamin himself had mastered it. Evidently unaware of any potential for irony, Benjamin boasted of telling James, "I was unwilling to trust myself in his [brother's] company because if he took the same liberties with me as he had done with others I should not keep my hands off him." Having proven to his own satisfaction his ability to head off indecent warmth and indiscreet heat alike, Benjamin seemed convinced that he himself could use anger as a source of strength without endangering his claims to honorable status.[87]

The ultimate irony for Israel Pemberton was that James remained true to Quaker principles to the last and denounced his own brother's anger. According to Benjamin, James Pemberton "censured his brother and said that he was of an unhappy temper." Basically, Benjamin contended that he had condemned Pemberton, not because he showed anger, but because he failed to control it. Pemberton and his fellow pacifist Quakers, on the other hand, believed that any show of anger was cause for reproach. As late as 1772, when the Quaker elder William Hunt passed away, an obituary by a fellow member of the Society of Friends praised him for being "easy to forgive injuries" and "not apt to resent personal wrongs." Quakers, who stressed simplicity and eschewed social distinctions, could abide neither the social posturing nor the violent aggression associated with displays of resentment—even by men they recognized as eminent. Their rivals within Pennsylvania, on the other hand, came to claim moderate anger as the exclusive preserve of elite Anglo-American men. James Kenny's backwoods bending of Quaker anger prohibitions truly was the exception that proved the rule.[88]

In fact, Kenny represents less an exception than an example of the pragmatic accommodation to anger that certain other Quakers also felt forced to make. Those who wished to remain in public life in Pennsylvania after the onset of the Seven Years War found that they had to make allowances for the anger they had once pledged to avoid at all costs. Perhaps the most dramatic example of this change occurred in the Norris family. Back in 1727, Isaac Norris, Sr., had dismissed the demonstration of resentment as something "below [his] concern." Like all pacifist Quakers, he abjured anger absolutely, even in its most restrained and genteel incarnation. The same cannot be said of his namesake, Isaac Norris, Jr., speaker of the Pennsylvania Assembly from 1748 to his death in 1764. The younger Norris remained in power long after many Quakers had fled the political stage to pursue their pacifism in private. To do so, he had to bend Quaker teachings on war and on anger as well. Speaking of the plight of Pennsylvanians taken captive during the course of the war, he declared in 1763, "Nothing less than a vigorous Exertion of the united Strength of the Colonies, in offensive Operations against the Enemy and making them sensible of the Weight of our just Resentment for their Perfidy in captivating and cruelly murdering our Inhabitants . . . can procure a Restitution of our Fellow Subjects." The fact that Norris and Kenny felt forced to break with Quaker prohibitions on anger and acquiesce in assertions about the virtue and justice of resentment shows how pressing the connections between anger, power, and status had become.[89]

Considering the Resentment of Inconsiderables

In some sense, little change occurred in the social signals sent by the expression and evaluation of anger during the mid-eighteenth century. Resentment reigned supreme as the most honorable and gentlemanly form of anger before the war, and it continued to reign afterward. In this context, the crisis-driven rage for rage that arose at the height of the war appears to be only an insignificant and temporary anomaly in otherwise unvarying uses of anger. Yet, to draw such a conclusion is to miss subtle but very important shifts in the qualities attributed to resentment that signaled social changes still to come.

Approved resentment in the first half of the century was supposed to be the outcome of reasoned appraisal. It is questionable whether gentlemen would have been comfortable calling such honorable judgments anger at all. Certainly, they would not have conceded that *their* anger had any connection whatever with the reckless, ridiculous passion they were so quick to condemn in the lower orders. By the war's end, however, such thinking had changed considerably. Many who styled themselves gentlemen now admitted that they themselves had much the same passions as those they regarded as social inferiors. Elites even asserted that the passions, once believed sinful, could actually serve virtue. They now drew distinctions, not between those who had passions and those who did not, but between those who were subject to passion and those who had mastered it. Only those who had harnessed their passions could employ them to useful ends. Resentment was what anger looked like once it was reined in. So important had moderate anger become as an emblem of status that Quakers who wished to remain in the ruling elite were forced to accommodate to it.

Widespread embrace of the idea that the same kinds of passions characterized all members of society regardless of rank carried important further consequences. At last, elites made allowance for the possibility that even the most marginal members of society *could* feel resentment. Once in 1755 and again in 1760, the *Gazette* actually reported instances in which low-ranking men displayed "resentment" against men of the elite. In both cases the resentful men were enslaved African-Americans responding to unaccustomed "correction" from their masters. Both accounts linked their resentment to murderous impulses that resulted, not in the deaths of their masters, but in their own. After his "Master . . . had him corrected" for a minor infraction, the first man "resented it so highly" that he killed a child, then claimed to have committed the capital crime deliberately because "he wanted to die." The second, when "threatened with [a] Correction" that he seemed to resent most "viciously," chose to hang himself rather than suffer abuse at his master's hand. In some ways these cases came from the same script as that assigned to angry sailors, whose unrefined resentment was supposed to stem from sinful impulses and always brought fatal consequences. Yet the admission that "Negroes" laid claim to honor and could resent elite attempts to undermine it does represent an important change from the days when resentment by commoners toward elites had been all but unmentionable.[90]

During the war, elites not only appropriated to themselves the kinds of anger they had previously attributed to those of low rank; they also accorded to the "lower sort" the resentment they had once reserved to themselves. Elites came to believe that, just as the resentment of Indian allies could be advantageous to the Anglo-American cause, so the nation as a whole could benefit from resentment on the part of the common people. In the mid-1750s Anglo-Americans of every rank sought to build a firewall of resentment against their common enemies. As members of the New York governor's council demanded in 1754: "Can *Englishmen,* can We who are under so many Ties of Duty and Gratitude; We, who so often have made Profession of Duty and Loyalty to the best of Kings; hesitate one Moment to exert with Indignation, our utmost Efforts of Resentment? Surely not!" Wartime skirmishes over honor, strength, and masculinity thus resulted in a new cultural emphasis on the value and validity of masculine, martial anger. Where once the passions had been derided as necessarily selfish and inherently destructive, they were now beginning to be recast as socially useful and conducive to communal interests.[91]

Though British Americans set aside the rhetorical extremes of wrath and rage when they laid down their arms, emotional aggression had, nonetheless, been newly legitimated as a bulwark of communal solidarity and a key element of British colonial culture. The immediate practical consequences that anger's ascension had for local politics will be explored in the next chapter, which moves beyond the investigation of Quakers' and Anglicans' interpersonal rivalries to examine their competitions for control of the colonial government. The same kinds of concerns about anger and civility that helped establish status in one-on-one interactions had a similar collective impact on the colony's politics.

Anger's full social and political influence on British America would emerge only with revolution. For now it is enough to note that if, resentment was construed as a national trait, and not simply as an elite prerogative, then one crucial mark of social differentiation carried somewhat less force than before. In Pennsylvania none other than Benjamin Chew addressed rank and resentment head-on when he declared on behalf of inhabitants of Delaware, "We are fired with the highest Indignation and Resentment. . . . [Though] inconsiderable in Point of Numbers and Riches . . . we beg Leave to assure you, that we have not less Zeal for His Majesty's Honour and Service." Even those without great riches could at times become indignant. The recognition that common people could be capable of worthy resentment marks a significant shift from earlier attitudes. Such statements helped flatten discriminations between the elites and commoners and would ultimately, as we shall see, pave the way for universal visions of human nature.[92]

At war's end, elites could not entirely eradicate this tentative leveling effect, despite their obvious interest in maintaining social distinctions. Governor William Denny, for one—whose own anger had caused such consternation to Benjamin Chew—was loath to relinquish the right to distinguish his anger from that of his servants. Placing a runaway ad in the *Gazette* in 1766, Denny claimed that his servant, Daniel McClain, was "a half-witted Fellow [who] conducts himself in a furious, passionate, Witless manner, which may easily be seen, if closely examined, by his indiscreet angry Answers." This ad is in every way a throwback to prewar ideas about the social significance of anger. Not for Denny the mincing hairsplitting about the masters and subjects of universal human passions. The very brashness, the almost comical intensity, of Denny's ad underscores the lengths he now felt compelled to go to in order to make a case against his servant. It was not enough to claim McClain did not know how to reason; Denny had to pronounce him "half-witted." Indeed, not merely a half-wit but wholly "Witless." Should readers have forgotten that lack of reason always went along with propensity for passion, Denny specified that McClain was "furious passionate." Just in case his servant's nature was still not clear, Denny concluded by calling him indiscreetly "angry." In a world where slaves resented and warriors had only recently raged, Governor Denny was forced to go to new lengths to demarcate the ways that the anger of his servant differed from his own. One can only wonder what reception his advertisement received.[93]

*With respect to the Commotions and Stirrings of
the Powers of the Earth at this Time . . . we are
desirous that none of us may be moved thereat,
"but repose ourselves in the Munition of that Rock
that all these Shakings shall not move."*
—Society of Friends, 1755

*Men of warmth and zeal, can hardly bear with
[those] . . . who are not so easily, nor so vehemently,
moved against the errors and iniquities of the times,
as they themselves are.*
—Sermon at a Presbyterian Synod, 1758

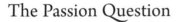

The Passion Question

Religious Politics and Emotional Rhetoric in the Seven Years War

During the Seven Years War in Pennsylvania, emotional movement became a question of great political and military moment. Not only
did emotions like love and anger play crucial roles in the signification of
social status, but they also served key functions in the articulation and
negotiation of political positions. Though discussions about the relationship between the emotional and the martial—and the impact of both on
the civil—were being carried out across the Atlantic world, they had special relevance in North American contests between the English, the Indians, and the French. Such issues rose quickly to the fore in Pennsylvania,
where religiously grounded political rivalries lent force to the debate. The
very kinds of competition that Benjamin Chew and Israel Pemberton
engaged in while participating in the 1758 Indian treaty at Easton reverber-
ated in Pennsylvania at large, where Presbyterian and Anglican upstarts
challenged established Quaker leaders for control of public life against the
backdrop of the military struggles of the Seven Years War.[1]

The focus here is the use of emotional rhetoric in the political contests
that erupted in Pennsylvania at midcentury. Wartime competition over
political leadership forced Quakers, their allies, and their rivals to articulate anew the essential elements of political virtue. Because of the close

correlation between denominational divisions and political loyalties, religious leaders played an especially prominent role as public advocates and agitators in these debates. In an era when "heart religions" of many varieties regarded the cultivation of emotion as essential for the attainment of salvation, invoking emotion could create new kinds of moral leverage for parties on both sides of Pennsylvania's policy divide. Pacifist Quakers who spoke out against "movement" did so in order to declare their unwavering opposition both to war and to the anger that they believed provoked it. Their rivals in other religious camps (who hoped to usurp Quakers' traditional dominant role in colonial government) employed the metaphor of "movement" for exactly the opposite end, to declare their support for defensive war and to chastise Quakers for failing to take action. We cannot wholly understand the competing political stances taken by Quaker pacifists and their prowar opponents unless we consider the intimate interrelationship between emotionalism and militarism reflected in the linguistic links and kinks of the verb *to move*.[2]

What exactly did this word connote? What concerns lay behind debates about movement? In eighteenth-century usage, the verb *to move* encompassed a complicated tangle of associated meanings that, together, linked questions about the moral admissibility of war, the efficacy of emotion, and the advisability of anger. In its most basic sense, the word *move* means to change places, to take oneself or someone else to another location. A related symbolic meaning grows out of that definition; to move people can also mean to change their mental position, to stir them up, excite them, provoke them, evoke emotion in them. *Move* means this today and has meant this as far back as 1377 (*Oxford English Dictionary*). Yet two other important meanings for *move* have since been lost. In eighteenth-century usage, *to move* could mean specifically "to make angry." It could also mean "to stir up . . . [or] commence strife, war, or other turbulent action." So, while growing emotional and going to war may now seem only tangentially related, in the eighteenth century they were closely associated activities.[3]

At the core of debates about the permissibility of war and the desirability of emotional movement were questions about the legitimate leadership and the right regulation of the self. In Pennsylvania, where religious liberty of conscience brought many starkly opposing viewpoints into proximity, Quakers began by insisting that the self should be sublimated to the public good, that anger arose from the demands of the self, and that war was the ultimate public manifestation of personal anger. In place of anger they urged an emphasis on love. Their rivals countered: the pursuit of self-interest would, in the end, promote the public interest, and anger was essential for both the activation of virtue and the administration of justice. At the same time, Quaker opponents also emphasized the importance that anger had assumed as a cross-cultural marker of masculine honor, one they could ill afford to concede to either their French Canadian or their native American opponents. From these antithetical starting points, pacifists and prowar activists eventually arrived at a remarkable consensus that would seek to combine the apparently contradictory values of love and anger.[4]

Efforts to balance anger and love—self-interest and common interest—ultimately promoted a brand of emotion that culled important qualities from each: compassion. Eighteenth-century Pennsylvanians became preoccupied with the issue of emotion precisely because it provided a medium through which to negotiate the relationship between self and society, allowing for the defense of individual interest while affirming the value of civil community. By studying the twining of Quaker love and Anglican and evangelical Protestant anger, we can begin to trace the thread that bound together the values of two ostensibly oppositional political outlooks.[5]

The "Prince of Peace" versus the "Man of War": Emotion in Religion

The debates about military and emotional movements that framed Pennsylvania's political contests during the Seven Years War were decades in the making. Quakers, the founders of Pennsylvania, had maintained a disproportionate degree of control over colonial affairs long after they had ceased to make up the majority of settlers. As their numbers dwindled, a new rival elite composed largely of Anglicans and Presbyterians grew up around them. This aspiring elite, restive and dissatisfied with the Quakers' continued domination of government, remained ever alert for issues that might help to undermine Quaker power and prestige in the colony. The coming of war to Anglo-America in the mid-eighteenth century provided an opening to question the propriety of pacifist leadership in wartime. Partisans on all sides agreed that God should provide the model for earthly governors. However, they disagreed about the nature of God and the emotions he modeled for men, about whether he was best understood as a loving Prince of Peace or an angry God of War.[6]

Beginning in the 1740s, as Britain became embroiled in King George's

War, Quakers began issuing statements of principle that outlined their opposition to war. As yet, Pennsylvania faced little immediate physical threat; still, members of the Society of Friends felt it would be prudent to make their position clear on such potentially divisive issues as defining God's teachings on war, discerning the nature of his emotions, and delimiting the equivocal worth of the self. A Yearly Meeting epistle from 1746 set out the initial Quaker position on the moral inadvisability of war: the Lord's pleasure was to "unite us in Love, not only to one another but to the whole creation of God, by subjecting us to the Government of his Son the Prince of Peace." The epistle then asked that the society's members "be faithful to that ANCIENT TESTIMONY born by us, ever since we were a people, against *Bearing of Arms* and *Fighting,* that . . . we may demonstrate ourselves to be real followers of the MESSIAH." This pronouncement established several crucial elements of Quaker belief and practice: Christ set the example that men should follow, and he could best be characterized as a Prince of Peace whose aim was to spread love. Crucially, the brand of love such Quaker thinkers had in mind was supposed to bear little resemblance to the kind that flowed between particular people; rather, they sought to promote the ideal of universal love, a love so selfless and disinterested as to apply equally to "the whole Creation of God."[7]

The 1746 epistle had one further important point to make: the necessity of subjugating the will, the source of selfishness. Quakers opposed war on the grounds that taking up arms meant raising up the self and selfish concerns. They "exhort[ed] all to [show] . . . Zeal in the performance of Worship to Almighty God . . . whereby our natural Wills being subjected, we shall be qualify'd to Worship him in an acceptable Manner." Though emotion (zeal) was important in worship—this very piece also warned against "Lukewarmness and Indifferency" in matters of religion— Quakers maintained that the loving feelings that could promote connections with God were of an altogether different order from the angry passions that led to assertions of self. Quakers believed that the self-discipline urged in the commandment *"to love our enemies, and to do Good even to them that hate us"* required them to abstain from private fights as from public wars. Involvement in either kind of conflict would promote the pursuit of self-interest at the expense of the common good.[8]

Shortly after the Quakers had put forward this position, a raid by a French privateer in Pennsylvania waters roused considerable public concern both among those who were simply civic-minded and among those who had partisan ambitions to pursue. In December 1747, Gilbert Tennent, a well-known evangelical Presbyterian preacher, took it upon himself to deliver a sermon, *The Lawfulness of Defensive War*. Though Tennent agreed with Quakers on the agenda for discussion, he diverged from Quaker conclusions on every significant point.[9]

Tennent underscored his opposition to the Quaker position most dramatically by beginning his sermon with a quotation from Exodus declaring, "The Lord is a Man of War." While Quakers had declared themselves "real followers of the Messiah," dedicated to following the example of Christ's love, Tennent boldly asserted that he and his constituents were determined to obey the rules of the Father, not simply "the government of his son." Though he accepted the convention that the character of God should provide the model for men, Tennent denied that Christ alone could provide the ideal pattern.

> Now seeing *Jehovah* is the Fountain of Excellency, it must of consequence be the highest Honour our Nature is capable of, to be conformed to him. Let none think it a Disparagement to their Character, to be concerned in War, but on the contrary, their high Honour and Dignity: Forasmuch as it is the *Name and Title* of the great GOD himself to be a *Man of War*.

Here the "Man of War" was set against the "Prince of Peace," Jehovah against Christ, the Old Testament against the New. Tennent took Quakers to task for emphasizing only the newer half of the Bible and complimented himself and his constituents for not forgetting the old.[10]

Expounding on his own conception of God's emotions, he declared: "If the *Almighty* be *a man of War* as well as a *God* of *Love* and *Peace*, why should any imagine that those are inconsistent Characters in Men? Tho' the blessed God loves all his creatures, yet does he not *execute Indignation and Wrath upon those that do evil?*" Where Quakers had claimed that God's primary affect was love, Tennent insisted that God's love was balanced by anger, by indignation and wrath. He argued, in essence, that if an angry God might choose to punish those who did evil, his people might follow his example. If God was a Man of War, then men might be such, too.[11]

Meanwhile, on the subject of the self, Tennent decreed, "Tho' there is a Self-love which is criminal and vicious, *viz.* that which hath no regard to the Honour, Safety, and Interest of our Neighbour; yet there is a Self-love which is rational and excellent, which inclines us primarily to regard our own [interests]." According to this reasoning, self-love was the foundation of all love. Indeed, the adage, "Do unto others as you would be done by," implied that self-love was the standard by which love for others was to be measured. Pushing his argument one step further, Tennent claimed that love for others could best be conveyed by a common commitment to self-defense: "A generous *love* to your *Country* . . . *sublimates* the human *Soul,* and raises it above the incomparably mean *Circle,* of our own private Interests!" Where Quakers had emphasized the need to subjugate the will and subsume the self, Tennent argued that the cultivation of the self would lead to social good, that is, that selflessness was born of selfishness. If this position sounds decidedly Popian, it bears remembering that the proarmament printer William Bradford had published the first-ever colonial edition of the *Essay on Man* in Philadelphia just a year before Tennent made his remarks.[12]

Quakers determined to refute Tennent's polemic point by point. One earnest young merchant named John Smith drafted and published a reply at his own expense within the month. He began by explaining that passion made men less, not more, like God; the design of divine light and truth was to give "Victory over the fallen Passions, and [renew] the Image of God in the Soul of Man." Claims that as God grew angry so could man, Smith denied absolutely: "Whatever Affronts or Provocations you may receive, let it not anger you, or begat any Desire in you to return Injury for Injury." "It will be vain to talk and preach about loving . . . our Enemies unless we shew the world . . . in what high Estimation we hold the . . . holy Example" of Christ. God's love overwhelmed all else. Smith concluded his essay by relating the story of Jacob and Esau. Esau was an "angry Brother" feared by Jacob, but God had the power to soften "his hard and rugged Spirit" and turn his anger "into a quite contrary Temper of Compassion and Brotherly Love." Anger was the very opposite of the essence of God, the antithesis of compassion, the adversary of love.[13]

According to Quakers, then, to be like God was to overcome the passions that drove the human will, *not* to cultivate selfishness in the vain hope that selflessness would somehow grow alongside. Quakers emphasized again and again that "the design of Gospel Dispensation, was to redeem Man from the deplorable Corruption which was the Consequence of his Fall" by "rectifying his Will [and] governing his Passions." As Smith explained the Quaker position, "many . . . passages in the New Testament positively declare (if we [are to] become the children of God) the Necessity of having our Corruptions wholly subdued [and] the

Deeds of the Flesh thoroughly mortified, with the Lusts and Affections thereof." A central aim of Quakerism was to restrain lusts and passions, in order to edge out selfishness. Quakers remained convinced that the loving example of Christ left no room for either anger or war.[14]

At the crux of the argument between Smith and Tennent, between Quaker and evangelical Presbyterian outlooks, was a dispute about the nature of the relationship between emotion and war. As the multiple meanings of the word *movement* suggest, broad agreement existed that military and emotional motions were somehow connected. But there was no consensus about the causal relationship between the two. Quakers insisted that angry emotions were the source of war. As Smith unflinchingly stated, they believed that "Mens Pride, and Passions, and Lusts . . . are the causes of all War and Contentions." Presbyterians, on the other hand, approached the question from exactly the opposite direction and argued, not that the passions instigated war, but rather that they ameliorated the worst of war's effects. As Tennent contended, "the clearest Reason dictates, and the tenderest passion recommends" the necessity of "self-defence." These two conflicting statements encapsulate the fundamental question that would continue to bedevil debates about Pennsylvania's military policies: was passion the appropriate response to—or the proximate cause of—war?[15]

The Quaker-Presbyterian arguments of the 1740s were advanced in an atmosphere far removed from real urgency. The military conflict that occasioned these exchanges, King George's War, scarcely touched the colony and ended uneventfully in 1748. So long as war remained little more than a theoretical consideration, disagreements such as John Smith and Gilbert Tennent's had few practical implications. But with the onset of the Seven Years War, a conflict that jarred the colony directly, philosophical debates quickly acquired political significance.

1755: The Season for Warmth

In the spring and summer of 1755, Pennsylvanians anxiously awaited the onset of war. British regulars massed in the west, and armed conflicts flared in the hinterland. In the midst of these rising tensions, members of the Society of Friends remained determined to stand firmly behind their long-held positions. In April 1755, the epistle of the Philadelphia Meeting declared their unflinching commitment not to be moved by the "Commotions and Stirrings of the Powers of the Earth." Once again, they reasserted their most basic belief, their vision of God as an exemplar of love, affirming that God's "tender Love to his Children exceeds the most warm Affections of natural Parents." Intended as proclamations of religious faith, such official epistles from the meeting nevertheless carried weighty political portents. The epistle of 1755 forcefully reiterated the orthodox Quaker position on pacifism, for the benefit of any wavering Quakers as well as for agitators in other denominations who had begun to call for war.[16]

At this point, members of many groups with little previous interest in the workings of the passions—matters so absorbing to members of emotion-based faiths—became eager to add to debates. Anglicans, Lutherans, and Old Side Presbyterians, all of whom hoped to profit from the Quakers' problematic position as pacifists in wartime, suddenly found a vital interest in these concerns. By aligning themselves with Pennsylvania's proprietors against the Quaker-led Assembly and using the issue of war as a wedge, they hoped to end the Quakers' control of colonial government. Finding moral flaws in the pacifist position appeared to be a likely way of improving their own political fortunes.

The first Anglican to step into the fray was the minister Phillip Reading, who preached a sermon in support of defensive war in June 1755. In the face of the Quaker epistle's emphasis on the image of a loving God, Reading insisted, as Tennent had before him, that God's love in no way precluded his approval of war. In fact, he demanded to know, "May we not . . . look upon it as an Act of God's particular Love . . . when he raises up . . . Instruments to chastise and check Oppression?" All those who felt themselves "inflamed" by "Love of Freedom" should also feel "Indignation" swell in their breasts. But his insistence that love was in fact compatible with anger did little to advance debate beyond the point to which Tennent had brought it.[17]

This rhetorical stalemate might have persisted, had not news arrived in July of the defeat of the British general Edward Braddock at the hands of the French. The resulting alarm injected fresh energy into debates and paved the way for another Anglican to stride onto the stage: the Reverend William Smith. Unbeknownst to most colonists, Smith had already been secretly maneuvering against Quakers for months, having penned and published an anonymous pamphlet against them earlier in the spring. Ever on the alert for ways to create quandaries for Quakers, yet unwilling to reveal his hand totally, he was eager to find other ministers who shared his opinions. He soon identified an ally in fellow Anglican Thomas Barton, who was serving as a minister at Carlisle, Pennsylvania, in the colony's western hinterland. Following Braddock's dramatic defeat, Barton delivered a sweeping sermon on the need for public safety and public spirit. Delighted to learn of the sermon, Smith soon arranged to have it published along with a promotional preface he wrote himself—signed this time.[18]

In their pamphlet, Smith and Barton broached the subject of warmth directly. Smith offered his highest approval of Barton's sermon in favor of war: "I am sensible . . . that your appearing warm in these grand concerns will . . . procure opposition to your ministry." But "surely no Warmth can be unseasonable at a Time all that we account dear or sacred is threatened. . . . In such a Case can we be silent to avoid the Imputation of being thought too warm?" Whatever his philosophical equivocations on passion, Smith's political opinion was obvious: hot rhetoric and angry emotions were not just permissible but vitally important in seasons of war.[19]

Barton himself had given a great deal of thought to the workings of warmth and the problematic place of the passions in politics. First, addressing the Quaker claim that passions were inevitably selfish, he shifted—slightly but significantly—the rationalization that self-love was the source of all love. Instead, he said that love of country was not a component of self-love but was simply a coexisting and competing kind of love. As such, this love of country had the potential to overwhelm self-love. He explained: "Other Passions often center in, and have a principle Regard to, our own Selves. . . . But *love of our country* [is the] brightest ornament of human nature. It checks and regulates the inferior Affections." Thus he argued that, although some inferior passions *were* grounded in the self, other, better ones could exist beyond it.[20]

Acknowledging some truth in the Quaker contention that angry passions were the source of animosity and war, Barton simply inverted their logic. "The glorious Flame of Zeal for the common Cause, which, at the same Time that it warms only and enlivens ourselves, will effectually scorch and consume the Disturbers of our Peace." The passions, like fire, could warm the hearth at home even as they burned out the enemy abroad. Far from being dangerous or undesirable, angry warmth was a positive good. Barton went on to describe just what it meant to warm oneself at passion's hearth: "If I should be warm on the subject [of war] I hope I may be excused." Such warmth simply demonstrated "compassionate Concern, not merely for any private or personal Suffering, but for the general Calamity which roars at our very Doors." With these remarks,

Barton reinvented war, not as a selfish response to passion, but as a compassionate response to suffering.[21]

This represented a substantial advance over the claim that selfishness led to selflessness. For how could fellow feeling exist without feeling? There could be no sympathy without pathos, no compassion without passion. John Smith had claimed for the Quakers that compassion was exactly contrary to anger and war. Barton now retorted that emotional zeal was as much a sign of compassionate concern as a symptom of passionate anger. Sympathy and anger worked together, warming one's fellows even as they scorched one's foes.

William Smith was quick to capitalize on Barton's innovation and expand it to encompass considerations about the nature of God. His political piety soaring, he asked to be allowed to "plead the Example of our blessed Lord and Master, that great *High-Priest* and best *Preacher of Righteousness,* who had a Tear—yes a Heart-Shed Tear—for . . . *civil* Distresses." Thus God took on a new characteristic as the exemplar of compassion. William Smith had succeeded in upping the ante, altering the calculus of God's characteristics to include compassion, a brand of passion associated with war but untainted by selfishness.[22]

Of course, Quakers themselves associated God with compassion; John Smith had closed his reply to Tennent with the story of how Esau's anger was transformed into compassion. But the Quaker view that God could make angry enemies compassionate (thereby obviating the need for any preparation for self-defense) was subtly but substantially different from William Smith's new claims. Where Quakers asserted that the example of God's compassion might commute *Esau's* anger, William Smith's logic implied that compassion would lead God instead to exact vengeance for *Jacob's* plight. In discussing the nature of God, Quaker publications had focused on contrasting anger with love. Though Friends had always valued compassion, they had not thought to emphasize the issue. Prowar pamphleteers were quick to take advantage of this Quaker lapse and seize the issue of compassion for themselves. Those arguing for armament justified violence, and the anger that inspired it, by arguing that passion bred compassion.

Pressing home his point, Smith introduced another key consideration into his propassion argument by making the declaration (quoted in the introduction), "LIBERTY never deigns to dwell but with a prudent, a sensible, and a manly people." Drawing on Anglo-Pennsylvanians' pride in the traditions of English liberty (and painting an implicit negative comparison to Indians and the French), Smith asserted that effective defense of the British way of life required a masculine devotion to feeling and sentiment. If Quakers wished to claim a share of British glory, Smith implied, they would have to prove their sensibility as well as their manhood by going to war. Quakers must have smarted under such critiques, for they responded to Smith's criticism word for word later in the summer of 1775.[23]

Quakers, like their opponents, viewed masculinity and emotionality as mutually compatible traits that were also critical characteristics setting Anglo-Americans apart as a people. This fact became apparent in the midst of debates about military spending conducted in August that year. All along, some Quaker assemblymen had claimed that they were more opposed to approving burdensome new taxes to support the war effort than to war itself. They argued that Pennsylvania's wealthy proprietors ought to be the ones to put up the funds for the colony's defense. Whether this was actually just a pacifist ruse or really a genuine point of democratic principle is now difficult to determine. More interesting is the fact that, in contesting the issue, Quaker Assembly speaker Isaac Norris condemned the governor's calls for new taxes using precisely the same gendered emotional language as William Smith had used.

> How odious must it be to a sensible manly People, to find *him* who ought to be their Father and Protector, taking Advantage of Publick Calamity and Distress, and their Tenderness for their bleeding Country, to force down their Throats Laws of Imposition, abhorrent to common Justice and common Reason!

Along with concurring that manliness and emotional sensibility were connected, Norris also agreed that both were important attributes for those who would be viewed as leaders, as "fathers and protectors."[24]

Although manliness and movement quickly became linked, Quakers remained conflicted about invoking such ideals. As debates passed from the ponderous pages of ministers' sermons and government papers to the crackling sheets of public petitions, Quakers seemed to step back. For example, on November 6, about twenty pacifist Quakers—including Israel Pemberton and John Smith—submitted a petition in which they took care to explain that they favored raising funds to "support such of our fellow subjects who are or may be in distress," yet still insisted that they could only go along with "measures consistent with our peaceable principles." In taking this stance, they failed to capitalize on popular devotion to manly sensibility, to exploit the moral leverage that could come with explicit invocations of emotion. They acknowledged the need to lend support, but not the importance of expressing compassion. Thus, Quakers quickly lost the initiative.[25]

Their rivals would not make the same mistake, and they responded six days later, on November 12, with a petition signed by 150 city inhabitants that asserted, "Upwards of a thousand families, who lately enjoyed peace and comfort in their own habitations, [were] now dispersed over the province, many of them in the most miserable and starving condition." True "fathers and protectors" would not allow such wartime family disruptions to go unaddressed. The petitioners declared, "We should think ourselves greatly wanting in regard for our own personal safety, as well as in compassion for our bleeding and suffering fellow subjects, if we did not publicly request . . . you to pass a law, in order to put the province in a posture of defense." A second, similar petition was submitted two weeks later, on November 25. Then, on November 27, the Quaker-dominated Assembly voted sixty thousand pounds "for the kings use," which clearly would wind up applied toward war. Forced to agree that legitimate leaders who wished to follow the divine example should demonstrate their compassion by coming to the aid of their suffering subjects, the Quaker-dominated assembly bent its antiwar stance enough to allow a military appropriations bill to pass. The prowar faction had just scored its first major political point using the issue of compassion.[26]

1756: Feeling for "Submissive Wives" and "Tender Infants"

The year 1756 brought considerable political and military turmoil to Pennsylvania. The tactics of the Quakers' opponents, elaborated in 1755, became entrenched in 1756 and seemed for a time to be garnering the desired results. Not only did prowar factions in Pennsylvania speak out publicly against Quakers in numerous sermons and political pamphlets; they also sent letters and petitions back to London, hoping to undermine the Quakers' hold on the colonial Assembly from across the Atlantic.

Their efforts met with some success. In February 1756, the Board of Trade in London recommended against allowing Quakers to serve in the Pennsylvania Assembly in wartime on the grounds that their pacifist principles inhibited effective defense. Then, in April, Governor Robert Morris issued a declaration of war against the Delaware Indians. By June

6, Quakers had voluntarily resigned from the Assembly, declining on principle to remain in public office while a war was in progress. By September, when new Assembly elections were held, only sixteen Quakers were offered the office, and four of these declined, with the result that Quakers lost their majority status in the Pennsylvania Assembly for the first time. Quaker resignations were voluntary. Nevertheless, the change appeared to augur well for those who hoped to permanently displace them.[27]

Altogether, 1756 was a year when the Quakers' critics were at their strongest and the Quakers themselves were all but silenced in the public record. Back in the 1740s, Quakers and evangelical Presbyterians had been engaged in largely academic debates about the passions. Yet, once Anglicans entered the discussion in the 1750s, they politicized it irrevocably and radically altered its stakes. The passions became so much the political fashion that even leaders of religious groups like the Lutherans, who had traditionally scorned the use of emotion in religion, began to invoke them in promotion of war.

On February 14, 1756, John Abraham Lidenius, an itinerant missionary to Swedish Lutheran congregations, borrowed a line from Tennent and delivered a sermon, *The Lawfulness of Defensive War,* that once again took up questions of God's love and men's anger. Preaching before the Association for Defense gathered in Chester County, he demanded: "Is it more love to permit the enemy [to go] unrevenged . . . than to hinder him by force? Is it Christian love to let anyone rob, kill or destroy?" He came quite close to an actual endorsement of anger, assuring his listeners, "It is possible to love our enemy while we are defending ourselves against his invasions. . . . God . . . strengthens . . . men under all their trouble, and softens their fury that they do not forget mercy." Though Quakers had argued that anger and compassion were incompatible, Lidenius appeared confident that they were in fact complementary, that one might balance the other. Arguing that angry resolve to do justice resulted naturally from compassionate concern, Lidenius ended on a rousing note: "Hear and listen to the cries and groanings of your exposed fellow-countrymen! . . . Methinks I feel your hearts bleeding and your resolution full with just vengeance! O revenge God of such crimes!" Love required vengeance; mercy could accompany fury; and, perhaps most important of all, real feeling inspired action.[28]

Like Thomas Barton, who preached his sermon in Carlisle and then saw it published in Philadelphia, Lidenius was a frontier preacher whose proximity to armed conflict in the backcountry lent urgency and legitimacy to his rhetoric. Where Philadelphia was a stronghold for Quaker pacifists, the hinterland was the preserve of prowar faction, in part because of the immediacy of the war and in part because of the religious and cultural makeup of the inhabitants there. (Indeed, as seen earlier, embrace of anger came more openly and easily there than in the city.) Thus, those factions in Philadelphia that sought to undermine Quaker power imported the rhetoric of frontier preachers to legitimize their claims, a tactic that was to climax and ultimately backfire with the Paxton riots of the 1760s.

In arguing the importance of pairing anger and love, Lidenius once more raised the issue of men's emotional responsibilities as heads of families. Painting a lurid picture of the disruption of domestic ties imposed by the violence of war, he exclaimed:

> See the flames! Smell the smoak! Look and behold the dear submissive wives, the delight of their husbands . . . now almost dead, and fetching their last sighs in their running blood! See the small babes, the darlings, the recreation of their tired parents, the innocent children, following the murtherers of their protectors, not knowing foe from friend, good from evil, right from left, and calling in the wilderness for bread and milk! Nay, see many of these innocent ones wallowing and crawling in their blood, before the eyes of their tender mothers! O cruelty! O matchless, merciless inhumanity!

Blood and milk, merciless inhumanity and innocent children. Part of what proarmament advocates found so threatening about French and Indian attacks was that they occurred not simply on the battlefield but also in the very households these men regarded as the seats of their own claims to masculine mastery. They feared to lose, not just their lives, but also their "dear submissive wives." When Lidenius exhorted his audience to a sensory awakening, to see the flames, smell the smoke, hear the sighs, and above all feel and act upon mercy—the emotion enemy attackers supposedly lacked—he reinforced the argument that real sensibility and true masculinity went hand in hand.[29]

Such positions had considerable popular resonance, as seen in the anxious imagery that pervaded the private correspondence of a Pennsylvania man that same year:

All ages sex and station have no mercy extended to them. A young man with vigor and activity perhaps with harty steps and filled with raptures of love is going to visit his intended spouse [when he] is unexpectedly pierced by a silent ball shot by distant secreted enemy. His active arms [are] unbraced, his vigorous sinews relaxed, and his body roiled in blood and exposed to the fouls of the air. Our tender infants have their brains dashed out. Our wives big with child have their bellies ript open. . . . The beautiful but modest virg[in ob]tains no more mercy than ouldest and [most] decreped. If they fly into the woods or hide in the hedges the murderers soon find them and plunge their hatchets either into their brest or scull where they are exposed to the inclemency of the weather day and night, their once sweet cheeks and lips now stained with dust and blood and their bosom[s] filled with clotted gore.

In this elaborate and bloody fantasy, the imagined victims were all members of society struck down just at the moment of fulfilling their proper social role: the young man about to marry and become a master himself, the woman about to become a mother, the young girl with virginity in place. Most terrifying of all was the threat that the Anglo-American social order could be overturned and Anglo-American masculinity undermined by enemy incursions.[30]

Urging their followers to subscribe to an alternative construction of Anglo-American society, not the one proposed by pacifists, prowar preachers demanded that Pennsylvanians demonstrate both their manly strength and their own civilized capacity for compassionate feeling by going to war. According to Lidenius:

Our business is to pray, to fight manfully. . . . The Gospel saith that *he that does not provide for his family, has denied the faith, and is worse than an Infidel.* . . . Methinks I see your eyes full of tears! . . . O let not their blood! their misery! gather guilt upon your heads!

This approach to the passions attempted to find a midpoint between so-called Indian cruelty and the Quaker pacifism so often dismissed as insensate and effeminate passivity. While Quakers and native Americans (as well as the French) might be called inhumane, only Quakers were ever called unmanly. In essence, both humanity and masculinity demanded a capacity for family feeling that twined anger and love into active compassion.[31]

Meanwhile, when Gilbert Tennent reemerged on the scene later that same week with a new sermon of his own, he too ratcheted up his rhetoric. In the main, Tennent reiterated the position on passions that he had staked out fully a decade before. Once again he described divine emotions in terms of the "terrible Vengeance of an angry God." Tennent, like Lidenius, relied on the new nexus of passion and compassion to justify anger on the basis of shared feeling: "Every Consideration that ought to influence a human Soul, conspires to incite you . . . to relieve your suffering Brethren, and avenge your country's wrong." The confluence of the words "relieve" and "avenge" in this passage is striking. To feel compassion was to become angered; to go to war was to alleviate suffering. Quakers had once declared that God's mission was to aid man in overcoming mortal passions. But Tennent now insisted that the "melancholy subject" of wartime suffering "deserve[d] to be lamented with the tenderest Passion!" According to this reasoning, passion spurred action. Indeed, love seemed almost incidental to the combustion process that allowed anger to burn through to compassion.[32]

As for the equivocal worth of the self, Tennent now felt confident enough to exploit the issue that had once been his weak point. He claimed that *lack* of self-love, far from being divine, was actually a sign of depravity and even monstrosity: "When we therefor neglect a necessary and seasonable Self-defence, we are without *natural Affection, Self-haters; a rare and strange sort of Monsters in Nature.*" In fact, self-love served a useful purpose. "The Principle of *Self-Love* . . . is implanted in all, and . . . when kept within due Bounds, is good and necessary, and [it is] therefore made by our Lord the Standard of Love to our Neighbour," he explained. Such an unqualified celebration of the self was rather a wild turn for him to take. The lengths to which Tennent was willing to go suggest just how heady he must have found the apparent successes of the prowar faction.[33]

The logic advanced in sermons resonated in secular political pamphlets as well, where good leadership was linked to forceful demonstrations of sympathy with suffering. A ditty about George II declared, for example, "George by force, we must confess, / Has freed his Neighbours from Distress / . . . And set their aching Hearts at Ease." Such pamphlets focused on asserting the importance of compassion for determining who had the right to rule and challenged Quakers to give up their places in the Assembly. The author of the King George poem decreed, for example, that, if Quakers could not follow the compassionate example of their king,

"I think they shou'd, / Have left their Seats to those that wou'd."[34]

Links between the ability to feel for others and the ability to lead others became ever more explicit. Another pamphlet praised the king by saying, "Our gracious sovereign on the *British* throne, touched with a deep sense of these things . . . was pleased to appoint and command a Day of public *Fastings, prayer,* and *supplication.* . . . as the province which we inhabit is at this Time . . . being already laid waste . . . [and] great Numbers of our unhappy Fellow subjects cruelly murdered." Here the king's leadership over his dominions was praised on the basis of his "deep sense" of the sufferings of his "unhappy subjects." Religion, the passions, and the right to rule were becoming more and more intertwined.[35]

If war demonstrated compassion and compassion was required to lead, then it took no great leap of logic to assert that war alone could legitimize leaders. This of course was the original argument of those who sought to drive Quakers from power because of their refusal to fight for Pennsylvania. But by weaving the willingness to wage war into the capacity for compassion, prowar preachers transformed the moral basis of political debates. Just one further step was required to arrive at the conclusion that Quakers were not fit to lead: an assertion that Quakers lacked compassion.

The author of the *George and Lewis* poem hinted as much when he portrayed a Quaker character named Nathan as unwilling to come to the aid even of his own wife. The satire intoned:

Quoth Nathan . . .

. . .

"I'd rather lose my tender Wife,
My fortune, [prop]erty and Life,
Than to resist [the] murd'ring Foe,
And by his Death avert the Blow."
Quoth Simon . . .

. . .

"What! See thy [wife] with all her Charms,
Distress'd and [in a] Ruffian's Arms.
And not thy [best] Assistance give?

. . .

I'm shock't, and beg to hear no more,
Return my Answer—there's the Door."

The poem's author, Nicholas Scull, ridiculed the extremes of pacifism, suggesting that the Quaker Nathan would rather give up his wife and "all her Charms" to another man than stand up and defend her as a husband ought. Unlike the proarmament advocates determined to defend their "dear submissive wives," this Quaker was supposedly content to be made a cuckold. The poem thus implied that Quakers' much-vaunted belief in fellow feeling counted for little if they were unwilling to take action in manly fashion. Reviving critiques of Quaker masculinity along with comments on their supposed insensibility, this poem offered to show Quaker legislators out the door of the Assembly house.[36]

Others eager to tie the demonstration of compassion to military action lost little time improving upon the hint contained in *George and Lewis*. The occasion of a public fast, a ritual observance called for by the governor to mark the colonists' solidarity in the face of a mounting crisis, provided an opportunity to increase criticism of pacifist Quakers. When many of them refused to observe the fast, the prowar side responded with an anonymous *Address to Those Quakers Who Perversely Refused to Pay Any Regard to the Fast,* which evaluated the Quakers' capacity for compassion in most unflattering terms. "Such was the perverseness" of Quakers that they ignored the fast despite the governor's order that it be observed by all who had "COMPASSION for their suffering Brethren, and *Regard* for their own IMMEDIATE SAFETY." By failing to participate in a public fast in support of the war, Quakers had revealed themselves once and for all as wanting in the *"universal Duties . . . of affection . . .* [and] *compassion."* Drawing this line of reasoning out to its fullest, the author demanded:

> Whether Men who thus despise every ordinance of the *Powers that be,* and seem unconcerned at the Sufferings of their Fellow-Citizens, as well as the Visitations of their ALMIGHTY CREATOR, are fit to receive any civil Truth, either as Magistrates, or as our Representatives . . . ?

The pamphlet asserted, in effect, that, if Quakers did not have the emotional capacity to respond to suffering, then they should not be allowed to serve in government as either elected representatives or appointed magistrates.[37]

The author crowned his efforts by taking up the issue of the self. He demanded to know "whether all these things put together do prove that a *Quaker* will be continually the same perverse, self-will'd, deceitful Thing." Far from admitting that it was prowar advocates' favorable beliefs about the passions that promoted self-assertion, this author claimed that Quakers' lack of compassion for others proved them to be the true devotees of the self. Such an assertion may seem extraordinary, given that Quakers had spent more time decrying the influence of the self than nearly anyone else. But, by co-opting instead of contradicting the Quaker position on the self, this pamphlet recast pacifists as the ones who were truly selfish. The passionate emotions that had only recently been closely associated with willfulness were now being redefined as the surest source of selflessness. Finally, then, the religious and political rivals of the Quakers had found a way to promulgate a new view of emotion, one that vindicated the passions by linking them to compassion and that validated their own ambitions by larding them with righteousness.[38]

In maneuvering to secure for themselves the best possible rhetorical position, members of the prowar camp apparently stopped short of accepting the extreme stance on the self that Gilbert Tennent had advanced. While Tennent might continue to exult about the social efficacy of self-love, popular prowar pamphlets preferred to claim that the embrace of compassion allowed selflessness to transcend the potential selfishness of unadorned anger. For the moment, Quakers remained on the outs. But popular reluctance to follow Tennent's formulations without hesitation hinted at the possibility that Quakers might be able to achieve a relatively quick resurgence.

1757: "Unnatural Heats"

The year 1757 brought wild swings of fortune to both combatants in war and contestants in politics. In 1756, the sense of urgency created by wartime emergency had made possible many of the advances accomplished by Quaker rivals. In the early months of 1757, when British military prospects yet looked bleak, Anglicans, evangelicals, and others remained determined to maintain—and, if possible, enhance—their political gains of the previous year. But, as the outlook for Britain began to improve with the appointment of the optimistic William Pitt as the new head of the royal ministry, Quakers began looking for pragmatic ways to reassert themselves in political affairs and public debates. In the Assembly, those Quakers who remained in their seats quietly admitted the need to bend on matters of militarization, leaving strict pacifist pronouncements to the Quaker Meeting to make. Meanwhile, Quakers in and out of office continued publishing position statements and funding treaty negotiations with native Americans. By year's end, the elements were in place for a turn of the tides, and the Quakers' rivals were back on the defensive.

In April 1757, William Smith once again tried to inject fresh energy into debates by preaching a sermon, *The Christian Soldier's Duty,* that reprised the "best" of anti-Quaker rhetoric of the previous few years. Confident now of the moral force conferred by claims of compassion, he dismissed Quakers by saying that if the horrors of war had "not already pierced their stony hearts . . . I am sure any thing I may say farther, would have but little weight." Notwithstanding the uselessness of further discussion, he then went on for another twenty pages. He instructed the soldiers in his audience that "NEXT to religion . . . it will be of the utmost importance to cultivate . . . a noble, manly, and rational *Enthusiasm* in the glorious cause wherein you are engaged; founded on a thorough conviction of its being the cause of Justice, the Protestant-cause, the cause of Virtue and Freedom on earth." With this call for an enthusiasm that was both "noble and manly," Smith not only confirmed his belief in the complete compatibility of masculinity and emotion but also linked both explicitly to other key elements of Anglo-American identity. Again, he tied enthusiasm, that is, emotion, to justice and asserted that it was a peculiarly Protestant trait that enhanced, not endangered, virtue.[39]

One especially vivid passage recalled the themes of family disruption that had been described to such dramatic effect by Lidenius the year before.

> What a sight do I behold? 'Tis odious to the view, and horrible to re-
> late! See . . . a set of human monsters hounded out against us from
> their dark lurking places; brandishing their murderous knives; sparing
> neither age nor sex; neither the hoary Sire, nor the hopeful Son; nei-
> ther the tender virgin, nor the helpless Babe. Ten thousand furies fol-
> low behind and close up the horrid scene! . . . While, in the midst, and
> all around, is heard the voice of Lamentation and Mourning and Woe.

Again and again, prowar agitators stressed the danger native American attacks posed to the Anglo-American family, the foundation of manly authority and indeed, they believed, of civilization itself. Here Smith repeated the refrain that effective fathers and leaders could not but respond emotionally and react forcefully to the "voice of Lamentation and Mourning and Woe" sounded by their dependents. Smith also spoke with casual matter-of-factness on the subject of the "Fire of God's wrath" and seized on the suggestion that anger and compassion were complementary qualities, exhorting his listeners, "Rise Indignation! rise Pity! rise Patri-otism!" all in one breath. Anger and compassion, indignation and pity: the violence of war could be laundered clean with passion.[40]

Contrasting Smith's speech to the soldiers with his exhortation to university graduates like Francis Hopkinson just more than a month later reveals the social assumptions beneath his political pronouncements. In his commencement ceremony advice to "disdain a narrow unfeeling Heart," he might have been lobbing one more blow at Quakers' supposedly unpierceable "stony hearts." Yet, in simultaneously recommending that putative social masters should "get the Dominion" of their own passions, he would depart significantly from the counsel he had so recently offered to the rank and file in the "first Battalion of his Majesty's Royal American Regiment at the Request of their Colonel and Officers." Smith's level of approval for manly passion varied according to the status of the men he addressed, with patriotic indignation in the common soldier apparently far more palatable than corresponding levels of anger in elite gentlemen. With these speeches, Smith veered toward what would be his final position on the passions, one that asserted vital differences between the emotions of elites and commoners, even as it affirmed the positive contributions popular passions could make in select circumstances controlled by members of the upper orders. Such a stance allowed him to take nearly any political position on the passions he desired, depending on his own definition of events, and he reveled in this tactical flexibility.[41]

Still, Smith allowed himself to triumph too soon. The carefully calibrated case for martial passions, presented almost without debate for nearly two years, was about to encounter renewed opposition. In July a fellow Anglican preacher from Delaware named Mathias Harris weighed in. Harris had apparently been observing the controversies in Pennsylvania with a critical eye, for his sermon contained at least as much political commentary as religious reflection. Harris sided with Quaker opponents on the subject of warmth. He asserted that, as he gave his sermon, he felt "zeal warm, and glow in his own breast" and explained that he "endeavoured . . . to communicate and diffuse the same Spirit into his audience" so "that a warm and animated zeal for the honour and safety of his King and Country" might come over every listener. Harris concurred that passion, when it amounted to passion for country and compassion for compatriots, indeed should be counted a positive good. But he stopped far short of condoning anger, warning his listeners to avoid "Contention, heats, divisions and animosities" and congratulating Delaware colonists that *"here* our spirits are not raised, or minds embittered with *unkind* speeches, or *angry* messages." He attributed much of Pennsylvania's military vulnerability to the addition of anger to politics and complimented his own colony by contrast: *"Such then* are the different situations of the two governments . . . if [ours] has not raised the *envy,* it has certainly excited the attention of *theirs."*[42]

This must have been the opening Quakers had been waiting for. Scarcely a week later they, too, reentered the fray, hoping to oppose a countervailing wind to Smith and company's gusty bluster and thereby change the course of debate. They began by summarizing their view of the events of the last two years. "Frequent melancholy Accounts" of the progress of the war had "filled the Minds of People in general with a Spirit of Indignation and Resentment" while creating in Quakers an "earnest Concern" to prevent "impending Desolation" by any means consistent with their peaceable principles. They acknowledged the risk of "impending desolation" in order to counteract implications that they were indifferent to their colony's danger. But they also deliberately contrasted the general "spirit of Indignation and Resentment" evident in the popular reaction with their own calm "earnest Concern," which, they added, they had been given no opportunity to demonstrate. This oblique critique of anger and quiet assertion of Quaker concern was still pretty thin stuff, compared to the rich blend of passion and compassion manufactured by the prowar faction. But the Quakers were not finished.[43]

Just two months later they came back with another public statement that made the same points but in much stronger terms, this one called *An Apology for the People Called Quakers.* In this apology they made a very significant claim, marking an important turn in strategy. They explained that, since the first casualties among their fellow subjects, they had been "affectionately concerned in true Sympathy, freely contributed towards their relief; and [had] been engaged both in publick and private to put up our Supplications to Almighty God on their behalf." For the first time they publicly addressed concern for others in terms that explicitly invoked emotion. In so doing, Quakers confirmed that claims of compassion had the power to confer political legitimacy. By acknowledging the significance of shared feeling, Quakers also accomplished something else; they reappropriated a crucial element of the prowar faction's rhetoric on their own terms. For, though they endorsed sympathy, they denied that it had any basis in anger.[44]

Addressing once again public fasts, which had prompted some of the most virulent printed attacks of the previous year, Quakers renewed their critique of their opponents' anger. Rather than apologize for refusing to participate in the fasting, pacifist Quakers challenged their opponents to participate in a fast of another kind:

> This will be an acceptable Fast to the Lord, to Fast from Pride Strife, Contention, unnatural Heats, Broils, Animosities, Blood . . . then we might have some well grounded reason to hope that the Scourge which hangs over us, will in due time be removed and we again be favour'd with Days of Peace and Tranquility.

Far from conceding that abstaining from the public fast proved their lack of compassion and natural affection, Quakers turned the tables by charging that their rivals were the ones who refused to fast—from unnatural heats. They claimed that the horrors of war were caused, not by their lack of compassion, but by the prowar faction's ungodly indulgence in broils, animosities, and blood. Quakers thus reclaimed the issue of shared feeling for themselves while renewing reproaches of their rivals' propensity for anger and passion.[45]

In response to this Quaker resurgence, Samuel Finley (an evangelical Presbyterian minister and an ally of Gilbert Tennent) set out to attack Quakers where they were most vulnerable—on their vision of the nature of God. Instead of arguing that God was angry as well as loving, Finley now felt forced to focus on dismantling the logic that said a loving God would be invariably opposed to war. Finley declared, "Whoever imagines, that my *Office,* as a minister of CHRIST, confines me to . . . the Publication of Gospel Blessings . . . alone . . . understands it no better than they do the divine *Nature,* who fancy God has no Attributes but Kindness and Love." Finley affirmed, "He is the *God* of *Love.*" But he then went on to qualify that love, asking, "Will not Love direct" "God's subjects . . . to suffer their Foes to kill, or enslave them, rather than *repel Force* by *Force?*" Of course not, Finley assured his listeners: "This would doubtless have been the divine Order, if *Love* had not been tempered with *Justice.*" Such careful requalifications of the meanings of God's love showed how effective Quaker inroads against anger had become. It also marked the first time that anyone had accused the Quakers directly of failing to recognize the true nature of God.[46]

Making a last-ditch effort to explain why Quakers were unfit to lead despite their recent embrace of empathy, he concluded: "These Men . . .

who profess more Love to Peace, than to Justice, Propriety, and Fitness, do, by that very Thing, break the Harmony of divine Attributes, and prove themselves unlike to God." If God set the standards for rulers and Quakers were not like God, then Quakers should not rule. Besides, Finley was not ready to concede that Quakers had proved they actually shared the same capacity for shared feeling their opponents had rhetorically reserved for themselves. Repeating once more that waging war was the only acceptable proof of compassion and that only those capable of such compassion had any claim to lead, Finley demanded:

> Could our *pious* and *valiant Forefathers* rise from their *Graves,* and see the *dastardly, sordid,* and *selfish* Dispositions of many of their *Off-spring;* their *Effeminacy,* luxury, false Notions, *Confinement* to little *Party-Interests,* and absolute *Want of public Spirit,* what would they think? . . . When our *King* (the Darling of every faithful *British* Subject) when our *Country,* our *Wives, Mothers, Sisters,* tender *Infants* and *Children not yet born,* all with one Voice *cry* to us for *Help,* shall we refuse to exert ourselves? Are our *hearts* made of steel or *Adamant,* that they can resist the perswasive *Oratory* of such *Supplicants?* . . . Will nothing but *Destruction* itself make us *sensible?* Then it is high Time we go off the *Stage,* and give Place to others who will act a better Part.

According to Finley, when Quakers "refused to exert" themselves in defense of their colony, they betrayed, along with a lack of public spirit, a lack of masculinity and sensibility alike. He lobbed an astounding assortment of charges against the Quakers, but most telling was his decision to dismiss them as an insensible and effeminate people. In altogether ignoring Quaker sympathy claims, Finley made it painfully clear that the only consistent argument the prowar faction made was in demanding that Quakers abstain from politics.[47]

Finley lapsed fully into incoherence when it came to discussing the self. On the one hand he fell back on the tactic of trying to discredit Quakers by accusing them of being too selfish to share in the suffering of others. He claimed, for example, that anyone "so selfish, or so peaceful, as to decline *War,* when *Deliverance* of their Country requires their *Aid*" should be "blasted with a curse." Yet, just a while later, he returned full circle to claim once again that selfishness nurtured selflessness. "Love and Mercy are false, when partial: We should love and pity our Enemies; but ourselves too . . . For self-defense is our original Law. Wherefore, if an Enemy seeks to kill us, our killing him to save ourselves, is no Violation of the Law of Love, but rather a Fulfilling [of] it." In trying to have it both ways on the self, Finley only revealed how little ammunition remained for the prowar, propassion faction once the Quakers had stated their sympathies. William Smith began the year by reviewing the Quaker rivals' greatest hits; Samuel Finley ended it by grasping at any and every argument ever advanced against the Quakers.[48]

1758: "Dirty Purposes of Party and Passion"

If 1756 was the year when the proponents of war, the champions of passion, and the political opponents of the Quakers held sway, then 1758 was its negative image. A series of British military victories in that year, combined with the signing of a successful Indian treaty at Easton, had the ironic effect of readying Pennsylvanians to turn their attention from the crisis of imperial war back to questions of domestic politics. The year 1756 saw the Quaker withdrawal from the colonial Assembly and the near silencing of the Quakers, who issued not one major pamphlet in that year. In 1758, by contrast, Quakers dominated the debates and called for a reevaluation of the impact of their ouster on the colony. Indeed, as the dust began to settle, it appeared that, despite a strict reduction of their numbers in the legislature and a popular rejection of the extreme pacifist position, overall Quaker influence in the colony remained undiminished.[49]

The political divisiveness that had roiled the colony in the previous couple of years appeared less and less palatable to most Pennsylvanians. Quaker-allied candidates were more successful than ever at the polls, and mouthpieces for many groups began to call for an end to political splintering within the colony. If public opposition to extreme pacifism had complicated Quaker governance in 1755 and 1756, by 1758 Friends wishing to maintain leadership positions had displayed enough flexibility to put themselves on firmer footing with the public. Once the colony was armed for defense, few cared to countenance the overtly partisan polemics men like William Smith had been putting forth. One major factor working in the Quakers' favor was that, following the fall of Fort Louisburg, the Delaware Indians stopped their attacks in Pennsylvania. Pacifist Quakers could and did take some of the credit for laying the diplomatic groundwork for peace with neighboring native American nations. A further aid to Quaker resurgence was the imprisonment of the Reverend William Smith on a charge of libel against the Quaker-influenced Assembly. In the end, the libel charge did not stick. Still, it did take Smith off the scene for a time, allowing for the possibility of rapprochement between Quakers and other Anglicans.[50]

With the imprisonment of Smith, his erstwhile allies like Philip Reading and Thomas Barton seem to have fled the stage as well. A document published that year urged a reconciliation between Anglicans and Quakers and conceded the negative impact of anger obliquely. One Ebenezer Durham (a probable pseudonym, given that the author was also described at the top of the piece as an "unknown gentleman") declared:

> So long as Animosity and Division subsists between the People called *Quakers* and the *Episcopal* Church, so long you will naturally remain in a defenseless and a most ruinous situation. . . . This glorious Country may be preserved to us and our Posterity . . . if we would one and all universally exert ourselves, and contend for it with the same Ardour your unseasonable Divisions have been occasioned.

Recalling, yet contesting, Smith's claim that "no warmth can be unseasonable," such remarks document the lessening of Anglican-Quaker tensions made possible by his removal from prominence. The writer was not himself a pacifist.

> We shall see who will readily take up Arms and who will not, in so glorious a Cause, as the Preservation of so many grand and noble Objects, as is undoubtedly this fine Country, our Religion, Life, Liberty and Property, not to omit our pretty Wives and Sweethearts, etc. who ought to claim a very great Share of our Consideration.

Here, Durham stressed once again the connection between masculinity, emotional ardor, and martial activity. Although he still contended that ardor could play a positive role in war, he conceded that animosity (and by extension anger) was extremely undesirable.[51]

Meanwhile, even many Presbyterians must have decided that Gilbert Tennent had simply gone too far in his efforts to establish a prowar position that was in every way the antithesis of Quaker teachings. Presbyterians across the colonies had come to the conclusion that it was time to heal divisions between Old Side and New Side members of their denomination; in such a situation there was little tolerance for Tennent's kind of politicking, for his uncritical devotion to emotion, or for his unfettered praise of the self. At a synod held in Philadelphia, the Old Side Reverend Francis Alison summed up erstwhile divisions between the evangelical and conservative Presbyterian camps by criticizing those "men of warmth and zeal [who] can hardly bear with their fellow Christians of equal goodness, who are naturally more calm and moderate; who are not so easily, nor so vehemently, moved against the errors and iniquities of the times, as they themselves are." This was a backdoor attack on the passions, which asked, not that passions be eliminated, but that men who chose not to emphasize them should not be dismissed as unbearable.[52]

Despite the limited nature of this critique, Alison's statement had far-reaching political implications. For the word "warmth" was as highly fraught as was the word "movement." "Men of warmth" were about to find that their style of politics had abruptly fallen into deep disfavor. Who and what were men of warmth? To call a man "warm" could indicate that he was good-tempered, affectionate, and loving. Then, again, it might also mean that he was hostile and angry. Alternatively, it could simply signify that he felt vehement about some unspecified emotion, that his passions had grown heated along with his blood. Or, and this is the significant point, it could mean he had become deeply engrossed in party politics. According to the *Oxford English Dictionary,* this meaning for *warm* ("ardent, zealous . . . heated" as in "party-feeling, controversy") was "very common in the seventeenth and eighteenth centuries, though now somewhat *rare*." In fact, *warm* could carry any one of these connotations and oftentimes several together, with love, anger, vehement emotion, and political zeal all coalescing according to the beliefs—the political and religious affiliations—of the person employing the term. In eighteenth-century Pennsylvania, "men of warmth" were those who hoped to establish a new kind of party politics that could effectively challenge Quaker power and who were not averse to using emotional rhetoric to help accomplish this aim. Given Smith's and Barton's open advocacy of warmth, Alison's analysis rebuked politicized Anglicans along with New Side evangelicals like Tennent.[53]

Alison's reproof of "men of warmth" contributed to the gathering disapproval of "animosity and divisions" also signaled by the writer signing himself "Ebenezer Durham." A new sense was emerging that people had begun to grow tired of the politicking of those who had criticized Quakers simply for the sake of their own advancement. The official pacifist stance articulated by the Quaker Meeting had indeed been widely opposed in the colony as a whole. But men like William Smith, who thought that dissatisfaction with strict pacifism could be parlayed into widespread opposition to Quaker rule, had seriously miscalculated the tenor of the times. Once the most unbending pacifists had resigned from the Assembly and the colony had at last assumed a "posture of defense," few had any desire to embrace an entirely novel system of political thought.

Francis Alison's opposition to the ministry of Gilbert Tennent did much to undermine the political potential of evangelical theology. He claimed that the emotion felt by the newly converted was merely a passing phase that reflected the immaturity of their spiritual development, not the authenticity of their awakening. He dismissed such people as young troublemakers:

> Young converts are not only ready to blame and condemn the ignorant, the profane, and the careless; but even to censure men of superior attainments and experience, who enjoy the comforts of religion, without that emotion and transport, which they felt at their first experience of the spiritual life.

Far from espousing the view advanced by Tennent and others that the passions were a central source of religious progress, Alison dismissed them as a detour on the path to spiritual maturity. He continued, "Some, in CHRIST's visible church, are little children, dear to GOD, and members of his family, yet are children in knowledge; noisy, peevish and troublesome, and have every other bad quality of children." Significantly, Alison, like Quakers, linked emotionalism with that most problematic of passions: anger. He branded those who favored a warm approach to religion as "peevish," a class of anger closely associated with childishness. Even more, Alison decried the self along with the passions that promoted it. His sermon was actually subtitled *The Self Disclaimed and Christ Exalted*. A more thorough repudiation of Tennent's formulations can hardly be imagined.[54]

So effective were the numerous aspersions cast on emotion that even Tennent himself softened his stance considerably in 1758. Reporting on a renewal of religious revivalism at the College of New Jersey, he recounted the events in a way that can be described only as defensive on the matter of emotion: "This Religious Concern was not . . . promoted by any alarming Methods. . . . There was little or no Motion of the Passions in the Preachers . . . Only . . . some plain and brief scriptural Exhortations and Directions . . . were delivered." "These things, viewed in connection, manifest the Finger of God." Here Tennent's stance seems to concur with Alison's charge that passions did not prove the authenticity of religious conversion. If anything, Tennent went further than Alison did by arguing that the very absence of passion was convincing proof of sincerity and spontaneity. This eagerness to eschew any association with passion was all the more remarkable coming from a man who had preached in favor of "natural affection" and "tenderest passion" just two years earlier. It shows the depths of the disfavor into which the passions had suddenly sunk.[55]

Even as Anglicans and Presbyterians backed away from the factionalism they had so recently tried to foment and began to call for an end to divisions, Quaker sympathizers jumped in to condemn their opponents' recent activities. Where Anglicans talked abstractly about bringing an end to animosity and Alison obliquely criticized warmth, the pro-Quaker camp called outright for an end to party politicking. Quakers signaled their return to public prominence and their determination to reassert their views on policy and passion alike by allowing the publication of a pamphlet called *Tit for Tat; or, The Score Wip'd Off*. Seldom has a pamphlet been more aptly named.[56]

Written in 1755, *Tit for Tat* had been held back from circulation for fear it would only deepen disputes. By 1758, Quakers were ready to even the score. As an introduction explained, " 'Twas hoped that the violent Rage of Party would have subsided, and every Heart and Hand been employed in promoting an Union." But they found that their rivals had instead used their "silent moderation" against them. "In short, all who cannot blindly approve what is dictated by Party and Passion, are become the Butts of Malice and Resentment." In a parody of those who insisted that war aroused passion for country and not vice versa, the pamphlet urged readers to clothe their "feigned zeal in rage, in fire, in fury." In the process, *Tit for Tat* elaborated views already enunciated in part in 1755: that party politics were prompted by anger *and* that anger and passion aroused national contests as well as war.[57]

This pamphlet was accompanied by another that attacked Smith directly. "Can we ever forget," it asked, "the flagitious and virulent libels, called the B. State and B. View, wrote at the Instance of *him* and his party, *by a certain Parson* equally remarkable for Want of Piety and Want of Truth!" Quakers recast the terms and costs of debate: "The great Contention is,—Whether . . . our Assemblies shall be governed . . . by P[erson]s, residing in *London*, both ignorant of what may be necessary for the Good of the Province, and liable to be imposed [on] by their faithless Servants here; who too often sacrifice their Master's Reputation and Fortune to their dirty Purposes of *Party* and *Passion*." Once again Quakers dismissed political maneuvering as the ill effects of a susceptibility to passion. They lambasted Smith and his allies for sending anti-Quaker petitions to London when they could not win power through the polls at home. Clearly, according to the Quakers, only those who had not succeeded in subjugating their passions would fall prey to the ruinous temptation of party politics. The net effect of public pamphleteering in 1758 was to set the stage for a new era in Pennsylvania politics.[58]

1759 and Beyond: The Right Use of Passion

In 1759, English forces scored a decisive victory over the French with the siege of Quebec. Though the war lingered on for several years more, with a peace treaty not signed in Paris until 1763, the worst of the crisis was over. With the most critical period of wartime emergency behind them, Pennsylvanians of diverse religious groups began to consolidate their positions on the passions. Seemingly chastened, Anglicans generally remained quiet on questions of emotion, but evangelical Presbyterians—led by Gilbert Tennent—reemerged from the shadows to propose revised and somewhat restrained ideas on the self and its passions. Meanwhile, Quakers made further adaptations to their arguments based on the popular position on passion. From their mutual concessions arose a surprising consensus about whether and how the passions could play a useful part in public affairs. Quakers and evangelical Presbyterians, who had initiated the debate, were the two to end it. But the most extreme views of both had been softened through their public skirmishes with Anglicans and others.

Tennent had begun reconciliation in 1758, when he spoke critically of the passions for the first time ever. Quakers followed suit in 1759, offering a significant reinterpretation of the nature of God. In a statement on religious practice (intended for use by members of the Society of Friends, yet published) Quakers warned their brethren that though God was a "tender parent" who "dealt bountifully" with his children, his "anger is now kindled because of our backslidings." Along with a traditional reaffirmation of the love and mercy of God came a new emphasis on God's judgments and anger. This formulation, quite close to the evangelical one, stressed God's anger along with his love and opened the way for renewing dialogue. Despite this accommodation on anger, Quakers remained steadfast in their disapproval of the self, warning their brethren to beware the "Snares that m[ight] more grievously entangle them in that Spirit of Selfishness and Exaltation." Now, as always, the self stood in the way of righteousness.[59]

In a later annual letter published in 1760, Quakers evaluated the passions in far more equivocal terms than they ever had before. Quaker elders were urged to aid members to "subject the creaturely Passions, and convince them of the Nobility of their own Original, and that they are born for higher Purposes, than the Gratification of those Appetites." For the first time, Quakers clarified their critique of the passions, distinguishing between the lowly creaturely passions, which drove selfish appetites, and the original passions, which were endowed by God at Creation and could be trained toward noble ends. Though Quakers might still strive to contain the lustful aspects of passion that could lead to anger or acquisitiveness, their long rhetorical struggle with their rivals had forced them to reiterate another basic belief of Quakerism—that feelings served valuable religious and moral functions. In the end, they confirmed that noble uses for personal passion did exist alongside the destructive impulses they had so long deplored. Furthermore, by affirming that the noblest passions were "original"—that is, endowed by God at Creation, innate in all people, and distinct from those of "creatures" or beasts—the Quaker Meeting departed significantly from the Smith position, that human emotions varied according to social rank, and moved toward the universal view of passion espoused by Pope and ultimately popularized by Thomas Paine.[60]

Tennent reciprocated the Quaker concessions. Delivering and then publishing the sermon *A Persuasive to the Right Use of Passion in Religion*, Tennent concurred with the Quakers' new claim that passions could be good or bad, "true zeal" or "false zeal." False zeal, he characterized as "the Effect of a sprightly *Temperature* of body; which tho' it be not positively Evil, yet has nothing spiritual or saving in it." Among the varieties of true zeal, he most recommended "pious *Zeal,*" defining it as "a devout Fervour or Warmth, wrought in the Affections of a regenerated Person by the holy Spirit" and having "the following *Properties,* viz. *tempered* with *Humility* and *Love,* and attended with *Meekness* [and] *Self-denial.*" Tennent's distinctions between true and false zeal sounded remarkably like Quakers' own descriptions of noble versus creaturely passion. And his assertion that true zeal required self-denial differed dramatically from his many earlier pronouncements on the propriety of self-love. Only on the subject of God's love and anger did he hold fast to his original ideas, reiterating that the "Lord looked on ungrateful Impenitents with *Anger*" and adding, "The *Lord Jesus Christ* proposes . . . *As many as I love, I rebuke and threaten;* be ZEALOUS *therefore and repent.*"[61]

From nearly antithetical starting points, Quakers and evangelical Presbyterians had arrived at very close conclusions about the proper role of
the passions in human affairs. Exhausted by years of political skirmishing,
both sides sought to discourage continuing the conflicts. Not surprisingly,
the Quaker epistle that acknowledged the existence of noble passions
nonetheless admonished against plunging into "Heats and Party-work,
which hath ever been found [to be] of a dangerous Tendency." Less
expected, however, was that prowar agitators, too, had wearied of political
intrigue. No longer were Quakers chided for lacking masculinity or emotional sensitivity. Their own assertion that Anglo-Americans as a whole
were "a sensible manly People" no doubt made this accusation difficult to
sustain once the worst of the military crisis was over. Instead, Pennsylvanians across the religious and political spectrum sought ways to unite as
a single "people." Tennent was more than ready to do his part. Among the
varieties of false zeal he counted *"Factious zeal,"* defined as "when *pride* or
covetousness hath engaged Men in a *Party*." Any emotion that divided "the
people," any passion tainted with a selfish lust for power, was now certain
to meet with censure.[62]

On the contrary, any passion that could be linked to a sociable and
selfless concern for the public good was now counted an incalculable
political asset and crucial to legitimate leadership. Indeed, in a 1764 letter
written in defense of their wartime conduct to the proprietor of Pennsylvania, Quakers were extremely careful to stress, "We are not conscious
that as Englishmen and dutiful Subjects we have ever forfeited our Right
of Electing or being Elected . . . [though] many of us have chosen to
forbear the Exercise of these Rights." Affirming the importance of couch-
ing political involvement in terms of fellow feeling, they stated a few pages
later, "It hath been . . . our Regard to our fellow Subjects on the Frontiers,
and Sympathy with their afflicting Distresses, and a Concern for the
general Welfare of the Province, that engaged our Brethren to raise the
Money they applied to promote a Pacification with the Natives." Far more
important than the remaining differences between Quakers and other
religious groups was the emergence of a unanimous agreement on the
importance of shared feeling in public life.[63]

Emotion and Moral Action

On its face, this common commitment to sympathy and compassion
suggests a united opposition to self-interest as the ruling principle of

public life. The new emphasis on emotional reciprocity was supposed to promote feelings for others, to motivate leaders and followers alike to act in selfless fashion for the common good. Yet this apparent consensus on the need to contain the self was qualified, modified in crucial ways from the most extreme Quaker stance.

Acknowledgment of passion as the root of compassion and acceptance of personal feelings as a positive contribution to public life represented a subtle but significant drift away from the principle of pure self-denial. This allowance had the potential to provide a wedge for the ever-greater promotion of self, but for the moment the emphasis remained on trying to maintain a hard-fought middle ground. Quakers and Presbyterians alike now sought to avoid the fanaticism of 1740s formulations in which Quakers had insisted that earthly leaders should emulate only the love of Christ while evangelicals had emphasized the example of Jehovah's wrath. Instead, spokesmen for both camps now tried to promote an integrated vision of ideal leadership. They sought to balance the divine qualities described in the Old Testament with those advocated in the New by twining anger and love together into the strong cord of compassion. The resulting set of moral guidelines for governance made concessions to the concerns of the prowar camp of the 1750s yet retained a distinctive Quaker cast.[64]

To be sure, the consensus that crystallized around shared feeling did not end disputes between religiously allied political groups. Controversy and factionalism continued to divide Pennsylvania throughout the coming years, from the Paxton uprisings through to the Stamp Act Crisis (events that will be further analyzed below). Still, for all the questions left unsettled in the Pennsylvania pamphlet wars of the 1750s, one issue was resolved definitively: shows of caring for the feelings of constituents were a prerequisite for the exercise of power. Competition for social prominence and political dominance between Quakers and other Protestant groups had led to the articulation of standards for rulers that would have widespread appeal. Acknowledging that *warmth* referred equally to love and to anger, that these key emotions were in some essential way related, allowed for the conceptualization of a brand of feeling that drew on both. Pennsylvanians thus would call for passionate leaders who could act compassionately on behalf of their subjects. The resulting religiously inspired, emotionally inflected political rhetoric would resonate for the remainder of the colonial period, eventually forming the basis for an important strain of Revolutionary thought.[65]

Emphasis on shared feeling in Pennsylvania grew out of a widespread preoccupation with emotion's relation to moral action common to many involved in eighteenth-century imperial wars. However, a unique combination of factors in Pennsylvania encouraged especially explicit discussions there. The synergy between Pennsylvania Anglicanism, evangelical Presbyterianism, and Quaker piety, sparked by the tensions of frontier warfare, ignited intense political disagreements that could be argued only in emotional terms. Pacifists' critiques of vehement movements forced people to consider connections between selfish passion and outward aggression. Meanwhile, armament advocates' emphasis on the links between passion and masculine action pushed recognition of the way emotional agitation could spur manly efforts at communal protection. No matter how fine the resultant balance between self and society, how fragile the acceptance of universal views of human emotion, or how finite the cultural and racial bounds of sympathy's circle, commitment to noble passions was the point upon which Pennsylvania debates came to rest. While the limitations of shared feeling as an avenue for social integration will be explored at length in the next chapter, common agreement on the relevance of passion for the definition of public policy made debates about movement *the* defining element of eighteenth-century Pennsylvania politics.

6

"The Turnings of the Human Heart"

Sympathy, Social Signals, and the Self

In the December darkness of 1762, Elizabeth Graeme remained mired in regret for her failed relationship with William Franklin. William's last letter, back in 1758, had reproached Elizabeth for her fickle feelings, lamenting the flight of "soft emotions" from her breast. In the aftermath of their courtship's demise, Elizabeth, as her mother described it, allowed her "heart [to be] torn to pieces by . . . many different emotions." After four years of watching her daughter languish, Ann Graeme had seen enough. She wrote Elizabeth a letter telling her that she could "know no peace, while you want it" and urging her to forget William's condemnation and accept instead "that most tender and affectionate invitation of our Lord's." She implored Elizabeth, "Cast thy burden upon the Lord," and "Submit your will to his, who is your supreme Lord and Governor." She promised her daughter that God's yoke "lightens every other burden, by pressing down those passions which add weight to every burden." As far as Ann Graeme was concerned, Elizabeth's eventual embrace of her own emotions had merely allowed the unchecked growth of willful passion, opening her up to an excessive and unhealthy focus on the self. She urged her daughter to use her emotions to further her Christian progress rather than to prolong her personal disappointment. For Elizabeth's emotional ills had fostered numerous physical ailments to the point that her parents began to fear for her health.[1]

Elizabeth's father, the Philadelphia physician Thomas Graeme, shared his wife's concern and wrote to Elizabeth to tell her of the "anxiety [he] was under considering the present situation of [he]r mind." Like his wife,

FIGURE 11. Francis Hopkinson and Elizabeth Graeme. By Benjamin West. Society Portrait Collection, Historical Society of Pennsylvania. *Permission The Historical Society of Pennsylvania*

Thomas Graeme counseled his daughter against giving way to passion and urged her to stop mulling over her failed affair. "When reason brings you back to its trust you'll soon discover the insidious paths of a deceiver in every step taken [by William]." But the remedy he proposed did differ somewhat from that of his wife. Where Ann Graeme stressed religion and told their daughter to cast aside selfish passions in favor of spiritual affections, Thomas Graeme emphasized reason and its potential to promote social feelings over personal passions. Believing that the best antidote for Elizabeth's emotional ills was yet another kind of emotion, he told her to stop dwelling so deeply on herself and instead focus her efforts on giving and receiving fellow feeling. "A cure . . . must be left to time, the power your reason has over all your thoughts and inclinations, joined with the sympathy your friends partake with you." Though passions ailed Elizabeth, feelings could be what cured her. The sympathy of Elizabeth's friends could end her illness.[2]

Elizabeth and her friends shared her parents' conviction that her physical decline had been triggered by her emotional suffering. Reflecting on this period much later in life, Elizabeth herself explained, "I had a Violent Nervous fever 20 years ago, And I think My Constitution never Entirely Recovered the Shock." Yet she and her friends were not as quick to accept the need to confine the self. Inquiring about Elizabeth's persisting physical problems at the height of her illness, her close friend, Eliza Stedman, declared, "I was extremely pleased to hear yesterday by Mr. Hopkinson you were so much better." She confided to Elizabeth that she and their mutual friend, Francis Hopkinson, still remained "under some apprehensions" regarding the "delicacy of your constitution" and warned her against too much activity. Tellingly, however, she concluded, "But I will not preach on so disagreeable a subject as self denial and more especially as I cannot set an example." Eliza then ended her letter with the quotation from Alexander Pope's *Essay on Man* (mentioned in Chapter 1); it was "best to conclude with Mr. Pope that whatever is is right." Like Joseph Shippen, Francis Hopkinson, and so many of their Philadelphia contemporaries in the 1750s and 1760s, she found Pope's praise of the passions and implicit acceptance of the self far more congenial than competing advice to tamp emotion down.[3]

The Graeme family's related yet divergent interpretations of the causes of and possible cures for Elizabeth's ailments reflect central strains of thought about emotion and the self in the eighteenth century. Both heart religions and moral sense philosophy encouraged emotion while still calling for curbs on the self. The theologians who shaped the beliefs of people like Ann Graeme preached the value of feelings for the furtherance of faith. They urged believers to seek self-transcendence in the search for God, to lose their will in God's will. Meanwhile, the philosophers who influenced people like the physician Thomas Graeme theorized that feelings for *others* could prove to be the firmest foundation for social life. They proposed the moral sense as an ideal mechanism for advancing social benevolence. Ultimately, these two cultural currents flowed into the same surging stream.

Abstract as debates about passion and feeling, self and society, may seem to the modern reader, the social and political implications of emotional questions loomed large in the eighteenth century. An anonymous essay in the *Gazette* in 1756, for example, took great pains to detail just why the personal passions were a dangerous basis on which to form stable communal bonds. Beginning with a summary of the propassion perspective, the author explained:

> When a Man [has] entirely given himself up to a selfish Disposition, and is, in his own Imagination . . . the Center of all the World about him; he is apt to tell you that Interest governs Mankind, and that very little would be done or attempted . . . if it was not for the Expectation of some private Advantages; that mutual Benefits create mutual Dependencies, and those are necessary Cements of all Society.

Eager to overturn the idea that pursuit of self-interest could ever "cement" social bonds, the author plowed his way against the Popian wave that swept self-love and social love together in its wake. Searching for the flaw in propassion logic, he claimed, "The Fallacy of all this Sort of Discourse will be easily seen, when we consider that Interests are of two Kinds, the Interest of the Whole, and the Interest of the Particular; the one is great and noble, the other may be mean and scandalous; nay, they are often Opposites." Instead, he urged:

> If . . . every one . . . will divest himself in particular of all Pride, Ambition, Passion, Revenge, and other selfish Views, and have no other Emulation than to prove himself a worthy Member of the Community, . . . then . . . Government will appear delightful, and the lowest Station not seem despicable. . . . All Persons will be engaged by Choice to do their Duty with the greatest Chearfulness. . . . The truest and sincerest Love, Esteem and Affection will be encouraged and cultivated, and the Whole will be made happy.

Emphasizing the importance of cheerfulness and affection from those subordinated in the "lowest Station" of life, this advice encapsulated the conventional view of the social dangers of personal passions and advocated only outward, community-focused feelings.[4]

The initial intended effect of an emphasis on emotion had always been self-negation, not self-exaltation. Yet, when seventeenth-century Protestantism promoted introspection as a means of determining individual salvation, it set the stage for an increased emphasis on personal identity that could not easily be contained. The subsequent rise of moral philosophy and heart religions in the eighteenth century served only to continue this trend. To be sure, eighteenth-century promoters of shared feeling believed it might be possible to bypass selfish passion altogether in favor of purified feelings for others. In the event, this era saw at best a temporary slowing of the inexorable rise of individualism.[5]

Many on the receiving end of antipassion prescriptions, such as Elizabeth Graeme and her friends, remained uncertain of the practicality, or even the desirability, of trying to put them into practice. Attempting to deepen emotion while denying the self was a difficult if not impossible task. For every person wary of the atomizing influence of personal passions, there was another who saw in individual emotion, not the potential for social corrosion, but the simple opportunity for self-enhancement. If the early modern Western world was a place where hierarchical social relations were both accepted and expected, where people's unique traits and talents were less important than the social station they were born to occupy, then eighteenth-century Anglo-America was a place where all these old assumptions about communal values and stable social orders came into question. Even as members of nascent colonial elites sought to promote the selfless sharing of feeling as a means of shoring up the communal social order on which the maintenance of hierarchy relied, many of them were simply shrouding their own social maneuvering in the mists of moral sentiments.[6]

Shared feeling emerged as cultural fashion in Pennsylvania in the eighteenth century. Looking specifically at the use of sympathetic language in daily interactions can uncover how such feeling gained conceptual importance as an antidote to the autonomous self, account for the social capital attached to shared feeling, and reveal the differing sympathetic capacities attributed to various groups according to gender, rank, and race. Finally, a close examination of the vocabulary of shared feeling details the differing social intentions and practical interventions signaled by the varied language of emotional exchange. The meanings conveyed by words like *mercy, pity, compassion,* and *sympathy* differed subtly but significantly one from another, and the cultural predominance of each varied over time. As with anger terms, careful attention to the distinct connotations of seemingly synonymous words for shared feeling can reveal anew the hidden stakes of social and political negotiations, from the invocation of sympathy and compassion alternatively by Quakers and their adversaries in electoral contests to the differential ascription of mercy and pity to Indians and Anglo-Americans.

During these crucial years, Elizabeth Graeme, like so many of her fellow British Americans, made only sporadic attempts to press down her personal passions while practicing the art of giving and receiving sympathetic feeling. As a member of the colonial elite, Elizabeth had every reason to make use of shared feeling to help reinforce a communal social order that accorded greater power and privilege to those who could show they belonged among the genteel. As a woman, she could not but hope for just a bit more space in which to carve out an identity of her own. She remained troubled by an attraction to the ideas of Alexander Pope, and it seems that she still half believed that "passion is the gale." Some time after Eliza Stedman broke off her admonishments on the need for self-denial with a nod to Pope, Elizabeth herself confided, in turn: "I cannot help classing my Books like my Friends, they all have their Merits, but I am not equally acquainted with them. . . . Mr. Pope I am a little afraid of, I think he knows so well the turnings of the human Heart." Try as people might to press passion down and beat back individualism, the self died, phoenix-like, only to rise again.[7]

"Nor Sea nor Land Divide": The Bridge of Fellow Feeling

The Graemes decided that the only effective way to take Elizabeth's mind off herself was to send her on a voyage so absorbing that her self-preoccupation would simply subside. Dr. Graeme's ample income as a physician would provide the means; the solicitude of his friend the Reverend Richard Peters, who invited Elizabeth to accompany him on a trip to England, provided the way. After many long months of discussing this plan, the two finally embarked in the spring of 1764. Though Richard took his duties as chaperon seriously, he and Elizabeth were often separated for brief periods. Their resulting correspondence provides a glimpse of the concerns they shared during Elizabeth's convalescence.

Richard inquired unfailingly about Elizabeth's emotional health, often wishing that she might "be favored with a continuance of . . . health and happy flow of spirits." At the same time, he reminded her about the importance of directing her feelings away from herself: "You are too apt to let . . . things enter deeper into your heart than they should do." Throughout their journey, Richard took pains to instruct Elizabeth in her duty to cultivate her capacity for selfless emotion, encouraging her to succor others through sympathy as she herself was being treated. Thus, when Elizabeth was late in writing him a letter, he chided: "Did you but know what pain I have suffered at not hearing anything from you since I came here you would not be so cruel as to do so again. The state of my health . . . will not admit of discomposure. I need say no more to one who can feel for others."[8]

In a society balanced on the brink of change, teetering between communal and individual models of the self, the ideal of fellow feeling proved to be most attractive. It seemed to promise that the very emotions that defined people as isolated individuals would, in the end, pave the way for return to a renewed communalism. As early as 1721, when William Attkinson was worried that his passions were excessive, he declared, "When I am in any trouble or exercise, the revealing of it to my friends doth somewhat mitigate the passion thereof." Such views argued that the very act of expressing emotion could lessen its intensity and thereby dampen its potential to contribute to self-absorption. By 1753 another man, Thomas Wiley, could eloquently sum up the communal impact of fellow feeling by defining "true sympathy" as a bond that "n[either] distance [n]or time can wear out, nor sea nor land divide which instead of diminishing grows stronger and stronger." Wiley told his friend Samuel Neale, to whom he addressed these comments, that it was just this brand of sympathy "which united [us] in a very near and dear manner when I saw thee first." At its best, the expression of feeling—far from drawing strict boundaries around individual subjectivity—could actually build bridges between people.[9]

That the men just quoted were Quakers is far more than mere coincidence. Though moral philosophy and evangelical religions played an important part in spreading the new emphasis on emotional exchange across Anglo-America, in Pennsylvania the tenets of Quakerism provided an additional important vector for cultural change, for shared feeling had long enjoyed a central place in Quaker belief and practice. Though Quakers privileged direct communion with God over written or ritual authority and believed that feelings were the conduit for faith, they did worry about how they could determine whether the spiritual insights they achieved were in fact God-given. Anxiety that those who spoke out during meetings for worship might be answering the prompting of the self or, worse yet, of the devil made many a believer hesitate to express any feelings at all. But shared feeling offered a way out of this difficulty. As Wiley's correspondent, Samuel Neale, himself explained to a friend later that same year: "At our select half-year's meeting the concurrence of friends and unanimous sympathy with them in their concern dispelled the doubts I was under." If the concern felt by one person was shared by others, then this confluence of feeling could serve as confirmation of its divine origins.[10]

Emotional reciprocity thus played a central role in religious observance within the Society of Friends. Time and again, Quakers commented on the importance of sympathy in certifying the righteousness of their religious feelings. In one example, a Quaker elder, Jane Hoskins, recalled that she had felt drawn to serve as a minister despite her lowly earthly station as a servant girl. Initially reluctant to heed this spiritual call, she eventually decided that it would be "dangerous and criminal to withhold the Word of the Lord." Her growing belief that she should take up religious work was confirmed when she met David and Grace Lloyd, a wealthy Quaker couple who hired her as their housekeeper when her indentures were completed. As she later told the story, "I afterwards understood that David Lloyd and his wife fixing their eyes on me felt a near sympathy with me, such as they had never known towards a stranger before, and said in their hearts this young woman is or will be a preacher." Like Neale, Hoskins found the sympathy of fellow Friends to be the crucial factor in ending her anxiety that her intentions stemmed from self-will rather than divine inspiration.[11]

Significantly, Quakers did not limit their appreciation of the power of fellow feeling to religious worship. On the contrary, they believed that shared emotion could enhance all areas of life. William Logan sought sympathy for his wife when she was in distress. He wrote to Quaker minister John Churchman to ask for his aid, explaining: "My dear wife has been very low spirited and much dejected in her mind. . . . She thinks a few consolatory lines from her father Churchman when he finds himself so disposed will be as a cordial to her, which I shall also be much pleased to see." Here sympathy could be the cordial that cured the ills of the mind. In a similar celebration of shared feeling, the young Samuel Allinson cited

Cicero's observation "that friendship improves Happiness and abates misery, by doubling our joy and dividing our grief." Though part of the appeal of fellow feeling was its presumed ability to mitigate the unchecked growth of the self, its value was much more than merely negative. People also appreciated the positive effects of shared feeling on the general experience of living.[12]

Without doubt Quaker influence was important in bringing an emphasis on emotional reciprocity to bear in Pennsylvania. Like William Attkinson, whose 1721 reflections on the importance of emotional exchange predated not only the Great Awakening but the development of a great deal of moral philosophy as well, Quakers were in the forefront of the movement in favor of communal feeling. Yet, by the time the Seven Years War was well under way, declarations of the ability to feel for others became quite common and came from all sides. For example, in 1754 Anglican convert Edward Shippen prefaced a dry report about the condition of his correspondent's property with the declaration, "Grief seized my heart at hearing of your great danger in your late sickness; but the welcome news of your perfect recovery filled me with joy and pleasure." In a similar vein, Presbyterian schoolgirl Tace Bradford assured her brother, "Nothing can give me more pleasure than . . . [what] would give you pleasure and myself so much the more because it would give you so much." Meanwhile, Anglican merchant John Swift reported to a correspondent in 1761 that his son had a toothache, so that, though the weather was fair, "that pleasure is nearly balanced by my son John's . . . pain." Again and again at midcentury, writers of widely different religious affiliations asserted their capacity for shared feeling.[13]

For her part, Elizabeth did take to heart her parents' and Richard Peters's admonishments on the importance of feeling for others. Indeed, she wrote in one letter to Peters, "I Must Envy you a little In So Frequently Being the Instrument of Good to Others." Yet to her close friend, Eliza Stedman, Elizabeth confided continuing doubts. Describing her voyage from Philadelphia to Liverpool, Elizabeth noted, "Whatever way the Ship moved she appeared to be in the centre of a Circle . . . so that our own Eyes form the Horizon, and like Self-Love, we are always placing ourselves in the Middle, where all Things move round us." To an extent, Elizabeth recognized self-centeredness as nothing more than an illusion of self-importance. She acknowledged the need to expose this false impression for what it was and to attempt to center her life on others, not on herself. Unlike the *Gazette* commentator (who claimed that the virtuous could avoid giving themselves "up to a selfish Disposition" and seeing themselves as "the Center of all the World") she seemed to insist that placement of the self at the center of the firmament was natural and inevitable, no more avoidable than the ocean mirage that one's own ship was the point around which the whole horizon circled.[14]

"Such Splendid Weakness": Reconciling Manhood and Requirements for Feeling

The Reverend Richard Peters demonstrated again and again his familiarity with, and appreciation of, the language of feeling. When he praised Elizabeth as one who could feel for others, he demonstrated his own refined appreciation of this quality. Like her father, Richard expressed a strong desire to soothe her emotions with his own, as when writing to her in December 1764:

> I want much to give you all the comfort I can [and] I cannot but be very uneasy at being absent from you in so bad a state of health as you have been in since I left you. . . . Don't you think too much about home? I am apprehensive such thoughts are too much indulged and hurt you. This is one reason why I want to be with you. We can talk about them and these will achieve better than thinking.

For her part, Elizabeth appreciated emotional sensitivity in the men she knew. Of the physician who attended her in England, Dr. John Fothergill, she remarked, "The Company of a Man of Sense, with a good Heart [is] so very pleasing." Yet even as he declared his own desire to share her feelings, Richard Peters revisited the idea that Elizabeth's emotion was excessive, entreating her, "Pray write me by return post how you are," and demanding: "Are your intermittents come again? Are you pensive or low spirited?" Here Elizabeth's emotional difficulties, like menstrual irregularity, seemed to take on the taint of a uniquely feminine disorder.[15]

The gender connotations of eighteenth-century emotional display were complex and contested. Scholars have engaged in a great deal of debate about when and whether the eighteenth-century "cult of feeling" became masculinized or feminized. In most cases such authors have failed to distinguish between displays of feeling for others and more self-centered emotional exhibits. In fact, from the point of view of gendered status, it matters very much not only who showed tears but for whom they shed them.[16]

On the one hand, by the 1750s there was a certain unquestioned association between women, weakness, and weepy emotions. When Anglo-American celebrants wished to underscore the utter defeat of their French rivals at Quebec, they "observed a day of general rejoicing" in part by mounting a public viewing of a painting that depicted "France in tears; represented by a female Figure, wrapped in a Shroud, adorned with Flower de Luces, and sitting on the ground in a dejected Posture, weeping: at her Feet this Inscription, CANADA REDUCED; and over all, a Representation of the Sun, shining in its full Lustre." Such iconography left little room for doubt about either the subordinate social signals sent by such shows of emotion or the assumption that women were far more likely than men to wind up in states of tearful subjection.[17]

Similar evidence that an opponent's tears signaled the triumph of stronger men comes several years later in a *Gazette* account of a successful effort by provincial officials to quash a backwoods rebellion on the Susquehanna. The article reported that "Two Hundred Miscreants, composed of the Dregs of the Colony . . . Horse-stealers, Debtors, and other Runaways . . . came likewise armed into this Province, and built a large Fort, or Block-house, at Wyoming." After establishing this base of operations, "this lawless Gang of *fierce Warriors*" attacked neighboring property owners in an attempt to take over their land. But, when regular militia troops arrived to defend the landholders, the tide turned quickly. The *Gazette*'s correspondent gleefully recounted that the "rioters," led by their "Captain Cowardice," became "so intimidated that, after they were summoned to surrender . . . they agreed, many of them with Tears in their Eyes." Nothing capped off the conquest of cowards quite like seeing them cry.[18]

The popular equation of tears with cowardice seems to have resulted as much from real concern about the proper emotional carriage required for courageous action as from rhetorical strategies designed to dishonor opponents. A 1751 account of the conduct of sailors caught in a storm at sea attests to the perceived dangers of crying. One survivor recounted, "The Captain behaved with Fortitude and Presence of mind, far superior to what I could have expected under such fearful Circumstances. . . . [He] was willing to give Spirits to some of the Sailors who were in Tears, and hiding themselves from the Fury of the Storm." While tears rendered the sailors ineffective, the captain's fortitude kept him from breaking down and allowed him to attempt to bolster the spirits of his men. Many men regarded tearful emotions as a genuine added hazard in life-threatening situations.[19]

Yet tears did not belong to weak women and vanquished cowards alone; they could also be attributed to valiant warriors and virtuous men. A 1760 poem commemorating the Battle of Quebec and consecrating the final hours of the dying but victorious General James Wolfe said of him:

> The Chief, while various passions shook his Breast,
> Heart-Rendring Sighs and manly tears suppress'd.
> (Such splendid Weakness dignifies the Brave!
> Such FRED'RIC pour'd o'er KEITH's distinguish'd Grave!)
> Hard was the Strife to vanquish Nature's Flow,
> Or drown in public Joy the private Woe!

This poem dramatically demonstrates the ambivalent associations attached to tears. As we might expect, the poem claimed that the general strove hard to repress his private woe and to "vanquish Nature's Flow" from his eyes. At the very same time, the tears he suppressed were described as manly, his weakness as splendid, and both linked to bravery and dignity. Nor was this an isolated formulation. Several years later, another report in the *Gazette* described a "Scene of Woe" at which "the most manly Fortitude could not check the generous Tear, which fell from almost every Eye." Again, though this writer took care to point out that the men who cried made attempts to check their tears, such displays were ultimately regarded as marks of generosity, not cowardice. How could such contradictory conceptions of the meaning of tears be reconciled?[20]

For one thing, though ready recourse to tears was widely considered a feminine trait, it was not always counted a negative one. Indeed, emotional sensitivity could be cast as the hallmark of civility. When an English group of oceanfarers found their ship seized by the French in 1760, women's tears played a crucial positive part in the drama. Hoping to persuade their enemies to cease the attack, a party hiding below deck sent up a woman named Mrs. Bull to bargain with the attackers. According to the *Gazette*, "To excite their Compassion, if any Spark remained, the Women went up first, led by Mrs. Bull, exposing her tender Infant . . . bathed in the Tears of its Mother, a scene which might have moved the most obdurate." Though the French remained unwavering, the English took satisfaction in being able to discredit their success in warfare by critiquing their failures of feeling.[21]

Though displaying tears might be the preserve of women, responding to them in kind was very much the proper province of men. A contemporaneous poem published in the *Gazette* put the matter this way:

A *Wife*! a *Mother*! Pity's *softest* names:
The story of her *Woes* indulgent hear,
And grant your *Supplicant* all she begs, A TEAR.

Spontaneous tears might be expected mainly of women, but sympathetic tears were required from all. Again, like Elizabeth Graeme, whose feelings Richard Peters sought to soothe even as he reproved her for "indulging" in them, wives and mothers—the epitome of pity—required indulgence with their woes. What seems to have determined whether a man's tears were judged cowardly and effeminate or splendid and manly is whether they were shed for "private woes" or only in response to the tears of others, that is, whether they were selfish or selfless. In the emerging emotional division of labor, *both* men and women were encouraged to cultivate their capacity to feel. But, where women's role was to call, men's duty was to respond. Put another way, while either men or women could offer sympathy, only women could ask for it. This was, of course, exactly the attitude of proarmament agitators in Seven Years War Pennsylvania, who called for military action as an act of compassion toward the tearful suffering of their "innocent babes" and "pretty wives and sweethearts."[22]

Significantly, these emotional roles were not supposed to mean that women were allowed to implore for feeling on their own behalf; on the contrary, they were most often praised for acting as emotional surrogates who shed sympathy-provoking tears in service of others. Yet another summons to action published in the *Gazette* at the outset of the war captures this dynamic nicely. Taking women's greater ease with emotion as a given, the author exclaimed: "In this dreadful Situation. . . . Even the tender Sex may here be of Service . . . the Silent but perswasive, Oratory of your tears, may do more to awake a thoughtless Husband to a Sense of his Danger and his Duty, than all the gravest Arguments of Reason and Religion." Clearly this writer assumed tears had a particular association with women (whom he referred to appropriately enough as the "tender sex"). Evidently, he also expected that men would without question respond to the tears of their wives, perhaps even with tears of their own. For he concluded by demanding of the "gentlemen" to whom his piece was addressed, "Could we help dropping a Tear over such unhappy Creatures?"[23]

Both men and women sought to promote acceptance of this masculine brand of feeling for others. Young Joshua Howell, sending advice to a female friend of courting age in 1752, urged her to recognize and value men who achieved this cultural ideal:

> Ask not for riches, riches ne'er can bind,
> Native contentment to a thoughtful mind.
>
> . . .
>
> Choose him pitying the distressed,
> He'll make you happy and he'll make you blessed.

This original poem underscores an important point: facility with feeling provided a new kind of cultural capital not only for women but also for men. This could prove particularly important for young men who did not yet control material wealth but who could nonetheless flaunt their emotional riches. Once again linking emotional sensitivity with religious sensibility, another writer pined to a male friend in 1760: "My heart, my eyes [are] full. The spiritual Man tis said judgeth all things so that I hope thou will be able . . . to feel for me." To cite one final example, Samuel Allinson favored the following "maxim," which he copied into his commonplace book around 1761: "A fool can neither . . . laugh nor cry . . . like a man of sense." Called variously the spiritual man and the man of sense, the man of the new masculine cultural ideal was one who pitied the distressed.[24]

Nor did men confine their efforts at achieving fellow feeling simply to relations with women. On the contrary, they also sought to feel for one another. The correspondence of a young Philadelphia man named Thomas Bradford helps reveal how sympathetic standards applied to masculine friendships. The son of the newspaper publisher William Bradford, Thomas Bradford was a well-educated young man whose circle of friends included many fellow students from the College of New Jersey. This group, very likely well versed in moral philosophy, fell into an easy way of discussing feeling with one another. Thus one friend wrote to tell Bradford in 1767 that, though he had very much enjoyed getting a letter from him, the news that Bradford was sick had "spoiled the composition." "For," he informed him, "you know there is such a thing as sympathetic pain."[25]

Earlier, in 1762, young Jim Clark wrote to Bradford about his family's financial struggles and the illness of his mother; "When I turn my eyes to my father's house I see nothing but sorrow and despair, my dear the best of mothers lying in the greatest agonies and dying away with that cruel disease the consumption. Think, but my dear Tomy, how I must feel."

Here one young man freely asked for the feeling of another. Significantly, Clark did not ask Bradford to sympathize with *his own* feelings. Rather, he asked Bradford to imagine what he must feel for his mother when he gazed on his parents' house! We may speculate that Clark himself would have felt great sorrow at the prospect of losing his mother, but the crucial point is that he himself did not say so. Instead, he focused on recounting what *she* felt, describing *her* despair and agony at the cruel workings of death. Though men sought to feel for other men as well as for women, they usually stopped short of actually requesting feeling for themselves.[26]

This was the pattern within Elizabeth Graeme's family. Even in the depths of December 1762, when she declared that her daughter would have to learn to press down her passions, Ann Graeme nonetheless also relished the chance to display her own well-developed powers of feeling. She assured her daughter, "I am very sure that I can meet with nothing that will affect me like what I feel for you." She hastened to add that Elizabeth's father felt just as much for her. She explained that, after reading the note in which Elizabeth had set down her emotional situation, "I showed it to your Papa, who read it with tears running down his cheeks in streams." Thomas Graeme's later remark about his own anxiety regarding his daughter's mind confirms that the entire Graeme family wished to cultivate the capacity for sympathy that Dr. Graeme was so sure would compensate his daughter for her distress.[27]

Shortly after Richard Peters wrote to inquire about her absent "intermittents" and inveigh against her tendency to "indulge" in excessive low-spirited thoughts, Elizabeth took a dramatic turn for the better. Her time in England began to pass gaily: a round of cookery classes and theater outings, garden tours and invitations to dine at some of England's best country houses. Her wit and her polish were widely admired by everyone, from the celebrated author Laurence Sterne to the Pennsylvania proprietor's wife, Lady Juliana Penn. By January 1765, Richard Peters was so well pleased with the progress she had made and with the power of his own good example that he wrote her a New Year's letter congratulating them both. Describing their departure from England, he reminisced: "Parting sighs were silently indulged, and though strong neither hurt the delicacy of your frame nor the greater tenderness of your affectionate spirits. . . . [We owe] thanks to a good Providence in a better situation at the opening of the new year than our most sanguine expectations would [have] permit[ed] us to hope for." With the worst of Elizabeth's crisis behind them,

Richard Peters could afford to take a relaxed attitude toward the emotional "indulgence" he had warned about just one month before. He renewed his praise for that aspect of Elizabeth's emotionalism, her "tender and affectionate spirits," which, presumably, formed the foundation of her ability to feel for others.[28]

"Strong and Natural Feelings of the Soul": Tears, Humanity, and Civility

As Elizabeth's recovery became more certain in the winter and spring of 1765, her friendships among the English flourished. Among her many admirers was Mrs. Juliana Ritchie, an Englishwoman who called her "my favorite flower" and told her that friendship had drawn "your image on my heart." The two addressed each other in verse, exchanged tokens like decorative fans and linen aprons, and accompanied each other on boating parties and sightseeing visits to local palaces. In Juliana's company, Elizabeth's maladies of the previous years were recast, attributed now, not to passionate self-absorption, but rather to the taxing effects of frequent and generous shows of feeling for others. Writing to Elizabeth about the illness of a mutual friend, for example, Juliana warned her against "the fatigue of attending her, in your delicate state of health." She told Elizabeth, "No motives of humanity should induce you to trifle with a point so essential to your future happiness, experience having proved to you, the bad effects of too much exercise more than once." Where once Elizabeth's parents had admonished her excessive willfulness, her new friends now attributed her delicacy to the fatigue of caring for others. The cultivated sensibility that Elizabeth was learning to embrace in England credited feeling with being the very basis of humanity.[29]

"Motives of humanity" became so important in Anglo-American identity that people like Elizabeth Graeme had to be cautioned not to overdo it. Anxieties concerning civility that cropped up in the midst of colonial cultural encounters persuaded many Anglo-Americans to consider emotions in a new light. As links between feeling and humanity drew ever tighter, to the point that shared feeling became almost synonymous with civilization, Anglo-Americans sought to appropriate it exclusively for themselves. Concerned though they were about possible links between feelings and effeminacy, many men came to the conclusion that the very emotions long ascribed to moral weakness and social subordination actually held the key to strength and civilization—if only they could discover the secret to unlocking the latter traits while cordoning off the former.

A startling pair of stories concerning ceremonial public deaths—one presided over by Philadelphia magistrates, the other by native American warriors in the Pennsylvania hinterland—captures the tension between masculinity and humanity felt by many Anglo-American men and suggests some of the early ways they sought to resolve it. These accounts appeared within months of each other in 1730 in the *Pennsylvania Gazette*. Consider first the tale of two English servant men who were sentenced to be hanged for burglary, then the description of a native American prisoner subjected to a ritual death.

A large crowd gathered near the Philadelphia prison to watch the convicted burglars, James Prouse and James Mitchell, hang for their crimes. Few expected they had any chance for clemency. Still, Mitchell's conduct at the execution ground persuaded the crowd to favor the prisoners. Though Prouse "appear'd extremely dejected," Mitchell "seemed to support himself with a becoming manly Constancy." As the time approached for the formal pronouncement of their sentence, *"Prouse* cry'd immoderately; but *Mitchel* (who had himself all along behaved with unusual Fortitude) endeavored in a friendly tender manner to comfort him [saying] *'Do not cry Jemmy.'*" Then, just at the moment the sentence was read, Mitchell "swooned away." Had he at last betrayed his true weak and reprehensible criminal nature? Not precisely. In fact, Mitchell had broken down only when he "heard the Words PITY and MERCY" announcing a stay of their execution, calling out, *"God bless the Governor. . . . for his mercy,"* before passing out. The author recounted, "All the way back to the prison, *Mitchel . . .* shed Tears in abundance" and concluded with satisfaction that the "Concern which appeared in every Face" upon seeing Mitchell cry provided "no small Argument of the general laudable Humanity even of our common People."[30]

The account of this episode reads like a primer on the right and wrong way for men to display tearful emotions. Prouse lost the crowd's respect because of immoderate crying while Mitchell gained it for his manly fortitude in avoiding tears and his "tender Manner" in assuaging his comrade's. In other words, Mitchell came close to the early-eighteenth-century ideal of emotional manhood; refusing to cry for himself, he was equally quick to assist his fellow at containing his tears. Though this account lauded "Constancy," emotional *self*-control, it also recognized the need to respond to the emotions of others. It portrayed Mitchell as overcome at last, not by his own emotions, but by the show of mercy on the part of the governor. And, the report emphasized, the crowd responded in kind, as moved by Mitchell as Mitchell had been by the governor.

Even at this early date, emotion had come to be regarded as an indirect but increasingly important component of humanity. The author of the account underscored its importance in speaking of the "laudable Humanity even of our common People" in connection with their show of concern. The class conventions invoked here are striking. Perhaps even more significant is the possessive adjective "our." In employing it, the writer implied that English settlers were culturally unique; so prevalent was humanity among them that it touched all members of society, from the colonial governor to commoners on down to criminals. The ultimate evidence of this supposedly superior humanity lay in the people's ability to respond with concern to displays of emotion by others.

Existing in almost exact counterpoint to the tale of Mitchell and Prouse was another article in the paper a month later. The second story again revolved around demonstrations of concern by Anglo-American men, but this time they were contrasted directly with the reactions of Indians. The report relates the execution of a native American war captive from Virginia by some enemy *"Shawana* Indians," as recounted by some Pennsylvania traders who watched the event. According to the *Gazette's* correspondent, the victorious band of warriors heated six gun barrels in a fire, then "began to burn the Soals of the poor Wretches Feet until the Bones appeared, and continued burning him by slow Degrees up to his Privities, where they took much pains; then they proceeded to burn him up to his Arm-pits after the same Manner." The Anglo-Americans witnessing this ritual offered no interference, apart from "one of our Traders [who] ask'd if he might give [the prisoner] a Dram, which being granted, he brought him half a Pint of Rum, and the poor Creature drank it off greedily."[31]

What did Anglo-American witnesses make of this event? On the one hand, the account hints at a certain grudging admiration for the stoic composure exhibited by the dying man. "During all this exquisite Torment he did not so much as Groan, fetch a Sigh, or shed a Tear." Whether the prisoner's absence of tears indicated the superficiality of his humanity or the depth of his manhood is a question the author avoided addressing. Instead, he chose to focus on the actions of the victorious warriors. "This

Barbarity they continued about six Hours. . . . At last they ran two Gun Barrels, one after the other, red hot up his Fundament, upon which he expired." The Anglo-American witnesses professed to be shocked by the "barbarity" of the ritual and by the absolute unconcern betrayed by the native American executioners for the "poor creature" being put to death at their hands. They contrasted the painstaking and methodical pain inflicted by the Indians with their own impulse to offer the dying man a good slug of rum. In the end, this anecdote reads as an account of British-American mercy contrasted with native American hardness and cruelty—with all its attendant implications of inhumanity.[32]

Although both the native American war captive and the Anglo-American convict exhibited a much-admired stoicism even in the face of death, the similarities in the two accounts end there. The story of the two servants emphasized the timely intervention of leaders capable of mercy and concern, but the story of the war prisoner was offered as evidence of the unrelenting cruelty of native Americans. The crucial difference conveyed in these parallel accounts is that, while native Americans and Anglo-Americans alike strove to maintain manly composure, Anglo-Americans prided themselves particularly on their capacity to show concern for the physical or emotional suffering of others. While only the native Americans achieved the stoic ideal—in marked contrast to the weepy Prouse—only the Anglo-Americans attempted to alleviate another's distress. The ability to respond appropriately to such emotion was already becoming crucial to Anglo-American cultural identity. It would not be long before displays of feeling would compel fellow feeling, before tears would be reinvented, not as a mere weakness of the down and dejected, but as the splendid weakness of the manly and the brave.

Increasingly, Anglo-Americans sought to define humanity in terms of the capacity to express fellow feeling and to present themselves as by far the best exemplars of the same. Their attempted emotional cartel excluded Africans in the colony even more fully than Indians. One searches in vain for a black person described as sympathizing with a white person in any records, public or private, generated in eighteenth-century Pennsylvania. In a sense, this is wholly unsurprising; emotional exchanges were supposed to build bridges between people, whereas most whites turned to race to establish and entrench social divides. Given that slaveholders through midcentury relied on the idea that "natural" slaves felt few emotions, whereas early abolitionists used the issue of emotional suffering as a means of critiquing the practice of slavery, the overall preference for silence is easy to understand. More remarkable is the related fact that Anglo-Pennsylvanians themselves seldom bothered to reproach the Africans in their midst for this ascribed absence of feeling.[33]

As striking as widespread discussions of Indian cruelty was the dearth of parallel remarks castigating black Pennsylvanians. True, Africans and their descendants were occasionally derided as "merciless wretches" capable of "horrid cruelties" in newspapers like the *Pennsylvania Gazette*. Yet these critiques almost invariably originated outside the colony, appearing first in writings from Barbados, South Carolina, Jamaica, or Antigua and only then reprinted in Pennsylvania papers. To be in a position to inflict cruelty or offer mercy required a certain degree of autonomy, if not authority. In Caribbean colonies, population ratios were such that by sheer dint of numbers even enslaved Africans could exercise a degree of such power. In Pennsylvania, by contrast, Africans' opportunities for contestation were constricted enough to obviate even much emotional communication. The story of a "Spanish Negroe fellow, named John," described in a *Gazette* runaway ad in 1748, captures such realities. According to the man who advertised for him, John was "proud, and dislike[d] to be called a Negroe, ha[d] formerly been a privateering, and talk[ed] much (with a seeming pleasure) of the cruelties he then committed." This was the one and only time a Pennsylvanian writing in the *Gazette* described a "Negroe" as cruel. Clearly, the advertiser noted John's purported boasts of cruelty in an effort to indict him for inhumanity and to justify his subjection to slavery. For John, the emotional freedom to choose between mercy and cruelty might have mattered most as a mark of the liberty that went with life as a privateer; his descriptions of cruelty might have been a way of keeping alive the memory of himself as an autonomous actor. Alternatively, John might never have actually boasted of cruelty at all. The information that he was not just a "Negroe" but a "Spanish Negroe" and one who liked "to make game at the ceremonial part of all religious worship, except that of the Papists," suggests that the author had relied as much on conventional elements of Spanish black legends as on actual aspects of John's temperament in composing his description. In any case, the larger point stands: power imbalances within Pennsylvania were stark enough that Africans and their descendants in the colony were discussed in connection with shared feeling only in the most exceptional cases.[34]

Such exclusionary emotional attitudes extended to non-English Europeans as well. Consider the 1748 case of one *"Nicholas Weyrick, a German,"* a settler who murdered his infant daughter. The *Gazette* reported countless graphic details of the case, saying, "There was not a Thumb's Breadth, between the Crown of its Head, and the Soles of its Feet, but what was cut, bruised and mangled, in the most shocking Manner imaginable." One of the most shocking effects of this treatment, as far as the writer was concerned, was that "the poor little Innocent . . . had . . . its Spirits so much broken, that it would suffer (whatever he inflicted) without Cry or Tear; so far was it spent and decayed." Here the lack of tears from the infant child was the ultimate proof of the depredations of the father. Only a "spent and decayed" female European child could fail to shed tears when tortured. Seeking to find a way to explain the father's cruelty while dissociating himself and his culture from the horror of the crime, the writer declared, "I don't know any Word in the *English* Language to express this Cruelty by, and hope our Language will never admit a Word into it expressive of so much Inhumanity." Faced with the spectacle of the mangled infant body, the author retreated into ethnocentrism. Indians might be cruel and unfeeling; on occasion, even other Europeans might be. But the English language, like English culture and the English people, could never be guilty of such enormities.[35]

By the 1750s, with the coming of the Seven Years War, free-flowing tears and easy emotion were frequently claimed as essential components of Anglo-American culture—to the exclusion of the French as well as of Germans and others. A 1756 poem (memorializing an early Anglo-American defeat and the death of General Edward Braddock) declared, "Braddock, unhappy chief! expir'd, And claim'd a Nation's Tear," and helped create the idea of national tears. Another author, that same year, proclaimed: "The French, instead of the Humanity they so much boast of to the World, not only delight in Cruelty and Bloodshed themselves, but encourage their Indians to commit the most unheard of Barbarities." Meanwhile, a 1759 speech by General Wolfe reprinted in the *Gazette* decried the "unparalleled Barbarities exerted by the French" while declaring, "Britons breathe higher Sentiments of Humanity, and listen to the merciful Dictates of the Christian Religion." Time and again, such references reinforced the easy assumption that Anglo-Americans enjoyed a kind of cultural monopoly on humane and civilized feelings.[36]

Remarkably, Anglo-American colonists never did attempt to argue that Indians were inherently incapable of civilized emotions, contending merely that their more humane impulses to feel for others had been blunted by war and stunted by their association with the French. An account from 1760 praised a display of English "Tears . . . which might have moved the most obdurate Savage," implying that, if sensitivity to the emotions of others was not a hallmark of the "savage state," Indians were nevertheless innately capable of at least rudimentary sympathetic responses. Despite incessant references to native American cruelty, Anglo-Americans never seriously contemplated the conclusion that their native American opponents sprang from a different stock than they themselves did. Such racialized arguments were tactically impossible both because Britain's central opponents were fellow Europeans and because Anglo-American colonists did not scruple to accept the assistance of native Americans willing to fight against the French. Practical considerations demanded that purported variations in emotional sensitivity be explained on the basis of culture, not innate difference.[37]

The following wartime poem contains a powerful commentary on the Anglo-American belief that the supposed lack of refined feeling among native Americans resulted, not from moral degradation, but from cultural deprivation. Describing the imagined response of Indians to hearing European music, one poem rhapsodized,

Th' enchanting Sounds thro' their whole Fabric crept,
And *Savage* Mortals wonder'd why they wept.

Though they might not understand "why they wept," Indians *could* feel the sort of tender sympathies that characterized people of civility. Natural and untutored emotional responsiveness lay waiting to be cultivated. Meanwhile, the poem exhorted Anglo-Americans to prove their own virtue by showing their ability to be moved by music:

Britons attend, be [your] Worth . . . approv'd,
And show you have the Virtue to be moved.

Admitting that even "*Savage* Mortals" could be moved by music's power, these verses urged Anglo-Americans to set an example for native Americans to follow. At least implicitly, it warned Anglo-Americans not to let themselves be shown up by the spontaneous if uncomprehending flow of feeling from Indians.[38]

By war's end, Anglo-Americans allowed that native Americans might be able to learn to emulate civilized emotions. Indeed, Indian allies might well be applauded for their emotional capacities. Casting themselves as benevolent tutors and Indians as precocious pupils, these Anglo-Americans delighted in attempts to display both their own so-called mastery of civilized emotion and their supposed ability to share this expertise with their benighted but deserving former enemies. What had allowed this remarkable shift in the attributes ascribed to native Americans by the educated Anglo-American elite? In large part this change reflected and reinforced changes in perceptions of their strength. So long as native American manhood seemed indisputable and unassailable, Anglo-American men felt compelled to compensate in the only way they could, by questioning their humanity. But once, flushed with victory, Anglo-American men had gained confidence in their own manly military prowess, the way was opened for a reconceptualization of the nature of Indian emotion.

This point is underscored by one final example from the *Gazette*, a 1769 account of the tears of a Seneca leader referred to only as Seneca George. In 1769 Joseph Shippen and William Smith, among other representatives of the Pennsylvania government, headed a conference to offer condolences to Seneca George, whose only son, a young man about eighteen years old, had been shot to death by settlers on the Susquehanna. Seneca George told the assembled men, through the interpreter Conrad Weiser, that "he and all his Family had shed many Tears for the sad Affair." In front of them all, with "Tears visibly falling . . . he started up and delivered a short Speech in so noble and beautiful a manner that it . . . did not fail to draw Tears from several who were present." A smug note of Anglo-American self-congratulation comes through clearly in this account. His people "in a starving Condition owing to a bad Crop of corn," Seneca George was in no position to exact retribution. The colonists had little intention of enacting justice; they offered him only a "Present of Condolence" so paltry even they felt obliged to apologize "for the Smallness thereof." But they were more than willing to participate in an exchange of emotion. Here, at last, was life arranged exactly to their liking, with a native American shedding tears of weakness for his own private misfortune while they themselves displayed their splendid and manly nature by offering up sympathetic tears of their own. The pleasurable pathos of this display of feeling could only have been heightened for the Anglo-Americans by the news, reported three weeks later, that on the way home from this meeting Seneca George "fell out of a Canoe . . . and was drowned."[39]

Over the course of the eighteenth century, the emotional qualities attributed to native Americans underwent a stark turnabout, from being lambasted as powerful but cruel, uncivilized, and unfeeling, to being lauded for their remarkable emotional capacity. Once the Seven Years

War had been won, colonists began to trumpet a reversal of rhetoric, which argued that native Americans were, not less, but *more* feeling than Anglo-Americans. William Smith, who took minutes at the meeting with Seneca George, remarked, "I verily believe that never was there a more striking Example of true Oratory exhibited in the whole World, than in the Delivery of this Speech. . . . Every Thing corresponded to express the strong and natural Feelings of the Soul." Such appreciation of Indian oratory, such commiseration with Indian suffering cost Anglo-Americans precious little. As the period of native American power began to recede into the misty past, a path was paved for a new era that emphasized Indian eloquence. Anglo-Americans were prepared to accord Indians humanity and civility only at the expense of mastery and autonomy. Meanwhile, whether interacting with Africans, Indians, Germans, or Frenchmen, they sought to attribute *all* of these much-admired qualities to themselves.[40]

The empty emotionalism offered to Seneca George should hardly surprise us in light of Juliana Ritchie's advice to Elizabeth Graeme to balance her humanitarian impulses with self-protection. In 1762, Ann and Thomas Graeme had counseled their daughter to press down willful passion and seek to cultivate feelings for others as a counter to feelings for self. During her travels in England, Elizabeth tried to do just that. Yet she kept coming back to the idea that her own emotions should not be denied. By 1772, just ten years later, a Philadelphia friend of Elizabeth, Mary Redman, would write to praise her genteel comportment and to reassure her that any doubts she might feel about her own emotional capacities arose only because "persons of your delicate and tender sensibilities are the most severe critics on their own actions." The emotionalism Ann Graeme had dismissed as willful passion in 1762 would be praised as motives of humanity by Juliana Ritchie in 1765 and then recast by 1772 as a desirable, delicate sensibility.[41]

Elizabeth Graeme remained ever grateful for the attentions of Juliana Ritchie, who had been so quick to attribute her emotionalism to laudable motives and to reassure her that putting her own health above that of a friend's would not necessarily endanger her reputation for humanity. Even thirty years after her return to Philadelphia, Elizabeth continued to feel a need "To write my *julia* that I held her Dear." The two women had drawn especially close when Elizabeth learned of her mother's death in July 1765. Coming across a party invitation from Ritchie years after her return to Philadelphia, Elizabeth scribbled a brief explanation that she had received it "the day I heard of my dear parents death" and that Ritchie "was so good as to give up the pleasure proposed and spend [the day] in a dark room with me, a favor that I never shall forget." Though Elizabeth grieved much over her mother's death, Ann Graeme's passing also allowed her to embrace Ritchie's views on the importance of balancing the desires of the self with the demands of others and to gently lay aside the more conservative views of her parents. That Ritchie could counsel Elizabeth to focus on herself while also congratulating her on her humanity indicates just how compromised the project of feeling for others could become.[42]

"The Compassionate Class": Shared Feeling and Social Standing

The cult of sensibility that swept over the Anglo-American world in the late eighteenth century grew out of nearly a century of intense popular and philosophical preoccupation with the passion question, the problem of how best to incorporate human emotion into the development of moral life. But the movement soon blossomed in unanticipated ways. Interest in feeling matured into an emphasis on sensory perceptiveness of all kinds, with emotional sensitivity being assessed as a measure of aesthetic taste, as evidence of a genteel responsiveness to beauty. By the time she left England near the end of the summer of 1765, Elizabeth Graeme had begun to draw on these emerging ideas in addressing her own emotional and social needs.

She wrote to her good friend, Eliza Stedman, "Upon leaving England," and advised her, "o! my Friend, keep yr. Heart open to be pleased with Nature." She concluded with some lines from Edward Young, adapted to her own taste:

> Give me indulgent God with Mind serene
> A guiltless Heart, to range the sylvan Scene,
> Where rural Objects, useful Thoughts suggest
> The Soul is ravish'd and Senses blest,
> In every Bush some pleasing Lesson grows
> In every Brook some soft Instruction flows.

Aesthetic appreciation, whether of nature or of feeling, could be "indulged" in guiltlessly in the certain knowledge that all that pleased the senses would inform the mind, that sensual enjoyment would bring useful moral instruction. Reflecting anew on her hopes for life, Elizabeth linked her aesthetic principles directly to her social aspirations. Though she insisted to Eliza that she did "not wish for a Fortune that would not require oeconomy," she also admitted that "fortune must be favorable to furnish a warm good House in the Winter, and airy pretty Gardens in the Summer." Confessing that having "Command of our Time . . . depends so much on the Station we are placed in," she acknowledged implicitly that a certain level of leisure and degree of wealth were required to ensure access to the kinds of sylvan scenes that ravished the soul and thus established emotional sensibility.[43]

During the middle third of the eighteenth century, many began to draw explicit connections between social class and emotional sensitivity. As the remark made back in 1730 about the humanity "even of our common people" suggests, social class and the capacity to feel concern for others had long been loosely linked in the Anglo-American cultural imagination. Another anecdote recorded in the *Gazette* helps illustrate this early association. A reader wrote in to the paper in January 1733 to complain that not only were the snowy winter streets so badly maintained that he had "caught two terrible Falls" but that witnesses to his accident had all "made themselves wonderful merry with my Misfortune." Cold, sore, and a laughingstock besides, he sought redress in the pages of the *Gazette:*

> I intend, the next slippery Time to make a Tour throughout the
> Town, and take a general List of all the Housekeepers, whom I will
> divide into three Classes. The humane, kind, compassionate, benevo-
> lent Class, I shall easily distinguish by the Ashes at their Doors. . . .
> The malicious and ill-natured Class I shall know by their Mirth at
> every Fall or accidental Slip. . . . The indifferent, thoughtless Class,
> are the rest.

He swore that he would "not so much as civilly salute" members of the latter classes and would make a point of directing his business and that of his associates away from their shops whenever possible. The author's explicit linkage of compassion and social class is remarkable enough. But even more intriguing is the apparent possibility that some members of society could enhance their social status by displaying feeling for others.[44]

Indeed, by the 1750s—by which time the concept of compassion had taken on great political weight—emotional sensitivity took on an impor-tant element of social cachet. When one gentleman wrote a letter of introduction on behalf of another, he was apt to recommend his friend's emotional capacities along with his other skills. In one particularly neat example of the social and professional importance of feeling, Joseph Shippen wrote to his brother-in-law, James Burd, "If you . . . can show any favour to that poor good natured and distressed man Capt. Eastburn it will give me a sensible pleasure." With this one line Shippen vouched for Eastburn's socially correct, good-natured emotions, invited Burd to show-case his own status by responding with concern to Eastburn's distress, and touted his own emotional capacity by affirming that seeing the other two men negotiate such an exchange of sentiment would give *him* a "sensible pleasure." Clearly, Shippen and Burd had the preferred parts in this social circle; it was they who could offer consolation, Eastburn who experienced distress. By confirming that Eastburn, too, was the right sort of man to receive Burd's favor, Shippen included them all in the warm glow of social inclusion through shared sentiment. Likewise, Francis Hopkinson echoed the assumption that gentility, masculinity, and sensibility went together when he described an English aristocrat a decade later by saying, "His lordship is a very sedate sensible gentleman." The genteel sensitivity on which women of Elizabeth Graeme's social circle prided themselves was equally important to their male counterparts.[45]

Nothing marked a gentleman like an easy sensibility, nor was the allure of emotion applicable only to men moving in the polite culture of ball-room and drawing room. On the contrary, emotional sensitivity was valued even in military camps. Given the desire to distinguish their brand of martial violence from the supposedly less civilized kind engaged in by Indians, military officers were especially likely to emphasize their capacity for refined feeling. In another letter written in the same year as his introduction for Eastburn, Shippen reconfirmed the significance of culti-vated emotion for social success in remarks to his father: "I have been very happy in the good company of Col. Bouquet and Mr. Glen. . . . They are both sensible pretty gentlemen and agreeable companions. The for-mer is much beloved and indefatigable in the business of the army." In fact (as will be seen in detail in Chapter 8), Bouquet's private reputation for civil sensibility was to become a facet of his public persona.[46]

Frontier folk too, though often objects of urban scorn, tried to boost their status with claims to refined feeling. Fur trader and some time slave trader George Morgan provides a useful case in point. A man who boasted openly and often about his exploits in drinking and betting and brawling, Morgan nevertheless took equal care to claim his esteem for the sensibility that marked men of standing, as in the missive he sent from Fort Pitt to his business partners back in Philadelphia in 1768. In one paragraph he boasted of his quick retaliation when a man called him a "little rascal." "The words were scarcely out of his mouth," Morgan chortled, "before my fist was against his nose from which such a fountain of matter immediately issued as to defile the linen of several of the standers by." Then, just two paragraphs later, Morgan promoted the social advancement of a friend who had come to his aid in the fight: "He is a person of as much sentiment and generosity as any man living and if ever it should lay in your way to oblige him or show him any civilities, I make a point of it that you do so on my account." Trader though he was, Morgan liked to style himself a merchant and considered himself the peer of military officers of the highest rank. His open admiration of brute force posed no contradiction at all in his mind to his appreciation of fine feeling. Strength marked a man to be reckoned with, and sentiment stamped a man of standing.[47]

Not surprisingly, emotional fluency came to be regarded as crucial social currency in the world of commercial transactions. The prominent role of patronage and personal relationships in the eighteenth-century marketplace has been well established. Successful business exchanges were conducted, at least ideally, on the basis of mutual affection and respect. The language of fellow feeling played an increasingly important part in such interactions. Thus one merchant thanked an investment partner in 1746, who had agreed to be "concerned in a wheat cargo": he was "sensible of [the] good opinion and intentions [thus] rendered" and assured him this show of confidence would "not be ungratefully noticed." Another man announced his desire to close out an account in 1747 by telling his correspondent he would be "ready at all times to receive your direction and settle it agreeable to your sentiments." And a third apologized for disappointing sales in 1751: "I am sensible thou and the owner of the wines must have expected they would have done better." The pages of Philadelphia merchants' correspondence are peppered with assertions that they were capable of the sort of emotional sensitivity expected from a high-ranking man and a desirable trade partner. Such claims are counterbalanced in the record by equally frequent calls for the display of feeling. Frustrated by the stinginess of some potential investors, Joseph Swift, dealer in cloth and clothing, remarked in 1757: "Their money is locked up in iron chests and as inaccessible as the most in[mo]st recesses of their hearts." Sensibility to sentiment became a key mark of commercial acumen.[48]

The idea that there existed such a thing as a "compassionate class," peopled by "sensible pretty gentlemen" and women of "refined tender sensibilities," developed slowly over the middle third of the eighteenth century and then rapidly gathered steam. Of course, within Pennsylvania, Quakers never entirely shifted from their core belief that all people had similar potential for communal feelings—and equal obligation to resist personal passions. Ultimately, as we will see, radical revolutionary commentators would argue not only that all people had the same propensity for both feeling and passion but also that each kind of emotion could prove laudable. Yet in the years surrounding the Revolution, the exaltation of a refined kind of emotional sensitivity gained great influence with would-be members of the upper orders. With shared feeling proving to be a decisive factor in everything from backwoods altercations to transatlantic business negotiations, it is small wonder that the era of the passion question gave way so completely to the age of sensibility.

No greater demonstration of the strength of this shift could be given than the sea change in the emotions attributed to the servant classes. Recall the many runaway ads of midcentury, which relied on formulaic descriptions of servants so subject to passion they could easily be recognized for what they were. Now contrast them with the following runaway ad in verse, which appeared in 1776. The owner and self-styled Sybil declared:

> This present instant, on the fourteenth day
> My apprentice boy did run away;
>
> . . .
>
> He has always been a vexatious lad,
> One reason why he is so meanly clad
>
> . . .
>
> Believe him not if you be wise,
> He is very artful in telling lies.
> He is also guilty of another crime,
> Of taking cloth from time to time
>
> . . .
>
> For which I whipped him, I thought severe,
> But did not make him shed one tear.

Where once servants were derided for their emotional excess, by the close of the colonial period they could be held in contempt for their failures of feeling. So soon as proof of social class was tied to shows of sentiment, servants who tried simply to restrain their emotions found themselves "meanly clad" in the outdated fashions of an older season.[49]

Still, contests over compassion among those striving for elite status left them open to manipulation by those of lesser social status. The disadvantaged person in any given social negotiation had an oblique means of directing the conduct of the supposed superior. For women, especially, the importance of tears as a source of leverage was widely understood. Two surviving examples, far separated in time, share some striking similarities that help illuminate how requests for compassion could convey real, if limited, advantage to the otherwise disadvantaged. In both cases mothers used calls for feeling in order to persuade intermediaries to intervene on behalf of their children.

In the first case, the Philadelphian Thomas Chase wrote to his friend Jasper Yeates about the fate of an illegitimate child Yeates had fathered. Yeates had evidently asked Thomas Chase to inform the mother of his legally unacknowledged infant daughter that, as he did not intend to help support them, he thought she should bind the girl out to be a servant. Chase reported back that, when he told the mother of this plan, "she burst into tears and said she could not bear the thoughts of binding it in the country to be made a slave." How Yeates responded to this burst of tears, the record unfortunately does not tell us. But Chase, for one, was swayed by the mother's display. He told Yeates that his daughter was "a neat pretty creature" and concluded, "I'm well assured was you to see it, you never would let her be bound out to suffer; was it mine it never should." Significantly, this mother shed tears not for herself but for her child. Her emotional display was itself a show of feeling for others, one that Chase felt compelled to equal. Together they challenged Yeates to prevent the child from suffering and prove that he himself did not fall short of the standards of compassion espoused by a fellow gentleman and adhered to by this simple woman as well.[50]

In the second case, an unnamed free black woman living in Philadelphia feared that her indentured son (identified in the *Gazette* only as Frank) was in fact going to be illegally enslaved. She sought the support of a well-to-do white man who just happened to be Samuel Allinson, the Quaker commonplace keeper who aspired to be a man of "Sense." This mother's dilemma provided Allinson with an excellent occasion to exercise his powers of feeling in the service of the antislavery cause. He explained in a letter reprinted in the *Gazette* in 1774, "I gave my Opinion and Advice, in order to obtain the *freedom* of the Negroe, whose *Liberty* is the present Subject . . . [as] his Mother (who appears to be a sober Woman) [came] with a Letter from a Person of Repute where she lives, accompanied by her Tears, [and] besought my Help to procure Justice for her Son." What makes this brief account so telling is Allinson's inclusion of Frank's mother's tears. By the last quarter of the century, antislavery activists began to invoke the emotional suffering of the enslaved as a means of countering traditional claims that Africans' "natural" emotional insensitivity fitted them for enslavement. As a man of position, Allinson was desirous to display his ability to feel for others and to respond with compassion to the tears of a subordinate. Frank's mother seems to have understood just what social forces were at work. Certainly, she presented herself as a sober person and came armed with the written support of a "person of repute." But she also understood that an appeal accompanied by tears was more—not less—persuasive than one backed by paperwork alone.[51]

The ability to bestow compassion was considered one of the most important forms of cultural capital accruing to those with power, and the importance of this conventional obligation was well understood by members of the elite. Thus an army officer asking a Pennsylvania governor to send him more men in 1756 prefaced his request by saying, "I am sure you are always deeply affected on hearing accounts of the people's being every now and then cut off on our frontiers." Likewise, when the New York governor's council sent a request for aid to the governor of Pennsylvania, they told him, "We send enclosed [a war report] by which you will perceive how distressed we are on our frontiers and desire your honor's will immediately render what assistance you can." In these situations, well-placed men put the onus on others in even higher positions of power to prove that they could indeed feel so well as to "perceive the distress" of others and be "deeply affected" by it.[52]

The reflections Elizabeth Graeme shared with her friend, Eliza Stedman, on the links between open hearts and favorable fortunes, were delivered with unanticipated and unintended irony. Just about a year after Elizabeth left England, her friend's father suffered a serious and irremediable reversal of fortune. When their mutual friend, Francis Hopkinson, heard the news that the Stedman family had lost all its holdings, he exclaimed: "This world is full of vicissitudes. How much I am grieved for Mr. A Stedman and his family. I see all his estate advertised in one of the Philadelphia papers." By this time Francis himself was in England, trying out his emotional fluency on the potential English patrons he hoped to impress. His show of concern for the Stedman family comported exactly with the requirements for genteel displays of fellow feeling expected in the social and business circles he desired to establish his place in. At the same time, his remarks reveal just how hollow the elite emphasis on feeling had become, for, no sooner did he declare the depth of his feeling, than he dismissed the subject altogether. He closed his letter to Elizabeth: "Poor Mrs. Stedman! I cannot sufficiently express my concern for her and her children. But these are very melancholy subjects and as I have neither time nor inclination to dwell on them now, I will put an end to this short letter." Though shared feeling was supposed to build bridges between people, it too often heralded the building of boundaries instead.[53]

Power and the "Principle of Action": The Changing Social Signals of Shared Feeling

The fall of the Stedman fortune sent shock waves throughout the Philadelphia elite. It was just the sort of catastrophe so dreaded by all participants in the volatile merchant economy that had poured such wealth into the city. With their worldly goods auctioned off, the Stedmans' last remaining token of their former status was their genteel comportment, their participation in the culture of feeling. Never had they greater cause to call for fellow feeling than in the face of financial disgrace, and, by and large, their fellows did offer such feeling. But just what brand of feeling their former peers were willing to proffer became crucial. The Stedmans could reap scant comfort and less profit from the sort of fleeting grief offered by the likes of Francis Hopkinson.

Such tepid offers of feeling were all too frequent. The flirtatious young Quaker, Peggy Emlen, for example, who kept up a constant correspondence with her cousin, Sally Logan, reported: "Peggy Stedman staid last evening with us. Oh how I pity her and can feel for her, I think it is our duty to take more notice of persons in affliction than those in prosperity; the one is too commonly neglected and forgot, whilst the others are sought after by everyone." Voicing pity for the Stedmans and vowing to continue to "take notice of them," Peggy Emlen's offer of fellow feeling did seem to carry the promise of social support. Yet, in another letter, Emlen all but argued that Peggy Stedman deserved her misfortune and was only getting her just deserts. Stedman was "really a sensible girl, much more serious than when I first knew her. . . . The misfortune of her parents perhaps may be an advantage to her, as giving her a more just and good way of thinking." Such an attitude would come as no surprise to Elizabeth Graeme, who had pithily, and presciently, remarked to Eliza Stedman while still in England: "We are but too apt to look on our own Misfortunes as Tryals and [those of] our Neighbours as judgments—Self-love leads us to this unkind Distinction."[54]

A key question arises out of all these discussions of the importance of feeling for others: just what did this cultural ideal reveal about the terms of the social relationships that were created and communicated through shared feeling? Taking note of the social cachet attached to the ability to feel for others—and how various groups were accorded or denied recognition of their capacity to do so—provides some answers. But another essential aspect of the exchange of feeling remains: the actual language of shared feeling. For, if the expression of so-called personal feelings played an important part in the assertion and negotiation of status, then exchanges of fellow feeling were all the more socially significant. Understanding the social signals sent when feeling was shared requires a close look at the vocabulary used to define such interactions. How did people select the best word to describe the capacity to feel for others, be it mercy, pity, compassion, or sympathy? What social meanings were implied by the use of a particular word to describe a given interaction?[55]

Scholarship has hesitated to differentiate between words for shared feeling at least in part because the connotations of any given word could vary so much according to who used it and when. It is important to remember, when distinguishing the shades of meaning and social messages associated with various words for shared feeling, that language was and is a living thing; delineating broad trends in usage cannot account for all the idiosyncrasies that emerge in the actual use of language. Still, that caveat understood, remarkable differences remain in the social signals conveyed by various assertions of feeling for others. Even a cursory consultation with the *Oxford English Dictionary* hints that the different words used to indicate varieties of fellow feeling were not exactly equivalent. When these standard definitions are placed in cultural context and then compared over time, significant distinctions emerge in the kinds of hierarchical relationships implied and the types of promises intended with offers of shared feeling. Understanding that the vocabulary of shared feeling could as easily help to shore up social distinctions as to break down social barriers is crucial to evaluating the ultimate influence of the eighteenth-century cult of feeling on the development of individualism and the maintenance of communal ties.[56]

Begin by considering the word *mercy.*" The *Oxford English Dictionary* defines it as: "forbearance and compassion shown by one person to another who is in his power . . . in a case where severity is merited or expected. . . . God's pitiful forbearance towards His creatures." Intrinsic to the definition of *mercy* is the designation of relative status. To offer *mercy* was to assert power, and to accept it was to submit to another's authority. Thus mercy was the favored form of feeling offered to others in situations where the lines of authority were well established and needed only to be upheld. Judges, for example, meted out mercy to those they deemed deserving, as when a justice declared of a negligent soldier in 1758, "The court recommends him for mercy as he bears a good character." When the governor commuted the death sentence of the prisoners Mitchell and Prouse, "mercy" was the trait for which Mitchell praised him. Likewise, God's most salient emotional attribute (apart from anger) was mercy. From Quakers like James Kenny, who praised the "Lord's great mercy," to Anglicans like Ann Graeme, who promised that God's "mercy extends to all," Anglo-Americans of all denominations attributed this most authoritative type of other-directed feeling to accepted masters, earthly and heavenly alike.[57]

The accepted association between mercy and power meant that discussions of mercy in everyday exchanges carried implications about the terms of social relations. When a debtor apologizing to a creditor for a botched business transaction admitted that he "deserved a punishment" and concluded, "This I must [leave] to your mercy and justice," he made an important show of subservience before one who could affect his financial fortunes. And, finally (as already noted in Chapter 5), when Anglo-Americans at midcentury upbraided their native American adversaries for their lack of mercy, their choice of words implicitly acknowledged the strength of their opponents. At first glance, the fact that the word *mercy* is defined by the use of related words like *pity* and *compassion* would seem to eliminate the possibility of distinguishing any one of these words from the others. However, the word *mercy* carried extreme power connotations and implied an ability to exercise immediate control over another person's fate; these aspects of its meaning did distinguish it from other terms.[58]

Take the term *pity* next. The *OED* defines *pity,* from the thirteenth century through the present day, simply as "a feeling or emotion of tenderness aroused by the suffering, distress, or misfortune of another and prompting a desire for its relief; compassion, sympathy." Here again it is tempting to conclude that *pity* is simply the linguistic equivalent of the interchangeable part, ready to be inserted as needed in the manufacture of feelings for others. But this word, too, carries certain noteworthy particularities that set it off from synonyms like *sympathy* and *compassion*. For one obsolete meaning of *pity* is "grief for one's own wrong-doing; remorse, repentance." Though the last citation for this use of the word is from 1591, attention to eighteenth-century usages among Pennsylvanians indicates that something of this sense of the word did carry over into later times.[59]

In fact, pity often contained a blend of censure and sympathy that allowed people to imagine the feelings of others without going so far as to identify with them. When Peggy Emlen said she pitied Peggy Stedman, she also intimated that Peggy's prior lack of seriousness in some way determined her present misfortune. Emlen's use of this word to convey not just feeling for but judgment of the objects of her pity comes through even more clearly in several other examples. In one letter to her cousin she remarked: "There is almost daily poor people begging. How I pity them, some starving with cold and hunger and tormented with a bad conscience which is wretchedness indeed." Though she sorrowed for their starving condition, she also blamed them for having bad consciences, and the word *pity* conveyed both these ideas. In another instance Emlen recounted how she had "happened to look out the window" and saw passing below a man who "was once a merchant in this city and reckoned a gentleman." She continued: "But now the poor man is a vagabond. It is a pity but had he had virtue enough to bear up amidst his misfortunes . . . [he would] not have so miserably sunk beneath them. I fancy the poor man took to drinking to drown sorrow and thereby made himself wretched indeed." Again, Emlen used the word *pity* to suggest that, while she felt something for these unfortunate people, her emotions fell far short of fellow feeling. As evidenced by her repeated use of the phrase "wretched indeed," such declarations of pity reinforced rather than reduced social distance.[60]

Emlen was far from unique in her use of the word pity to mete out sentiment and blame in equal measure. Quaker elder Sophia Hume argued that young people should be "taught to condemn and pity those under our name who walk inconsistently with the nature of the principles they make profession of." Likewise, a writer in the *Gazette* aimed a slur at a rival by saying, "We do pity that unhappy Temper, which renders him almost incapable of a solid thought, and useless to human Society." The same considerations influenced a wartime writer who defended the character of some French neutrals by declaring, "What appears to be obstinacy in them arises rather from a steadfastness of heart which . . . though it requires pity when . . . it is fixed on the wrong object, yet as it is noble in itself, so it strongly calls for forbearance." In all these cases, *pity* was the brand of feeling offered to those considered blameworthy and deserving of condemnation. Such feeble forms of feeling for others limited the obligations of those who expressed them and underscored the very distance between people that an emphasis on fellow feeling should ostensibly have undermined. To be sure, there were cases where the meaning of *pity* was more nearly neutral, as, for example, in the poem where a mother was called "pity's softest name." The important point is that pity very often was *not* "soft"; where *mercy* implied judgment tempered by clemency, *pity* often offered a verdict accompanied by moral censure.[61]

Now consider the case of *compassion*. The present definition of *compassion*, according to the *OED*, stretches back to the fourteenth century and looks at first glance remarkably like that of *pity*: "the feeling or emotion, when a person is moved by the suffering or distress of another, and by the desire to relieve it." But a note following this definition makes clear that the status implications of compassion were quite close to the surface: while initial uses of the word *compassion*, until the early seventeenth century, emphasized the idea of "suffering together with another," that is, a compassion "between equals or fellow-sufferers," later uses stressed that *compassion* was a brand of feeling "shown towards a person in distress by one who is free from it, who is, in this respect, his superior." So *compassion*, too, reinforced the social borders it supposedly should have bridged.[62]

For one thing, *compassion*, like *mercy*, was a recognized attribute of God. Thus one Quaker woman declared her reliance on "the throne of infinite compassion," and another called God "He who had compassion on me from the days of my infancy." When it came to earthly affairs, *compassion* was a form of feeling bestowed on the less fortunate by those in superior social positions. Nothing makes this point so well as a look at the celebrations of fellow feeling often offered in obituaries. In 1763 one Mrs. Ann Franklin (no apparent relation to Benjamin or William) passed away and was praised as "a faithful Friend, and a compassionate Benefactor to the poor . . . [who] often relieved them in the Extremity of Winter." In 1765, Quaker Rachel Pemberton (mother to Israel, "King of the

Quakers") won laurels for being "judicious and sincere in her Friendship, and kind and compassionate to the Poor and Afflicted." When Presbyterian John Mease died in 1768, his obituary noted that he had long been "a compassionate and liberal Helper of the Poor and Distressed of every Denomination." Finally, mourners remembered Quaker Joseph Stretch as "a kind Husband, a tender Parent, a good Master, compassionate to the Poor and Distressed." In every one of these cases, compassion was an emotional quality directed at the poor. Appropriate objects of compassion always came from inferior circumstances, and never once was compassion noted in connection with friends or family. Instead, the dead were praised as "faithful friends," "sincere friends," or "tender parents." Clearly, the connection between the demonstration of compassion and social subordination was well understood by the Pennsylvanians who employed the term.[63]

In fact, the only word available to describe a feeling for others that did convey a sense of shared feeling among social equals was *sympathy*. Though, according to the *OED*, this word, too, can be defined by reference to its synonyms as "the quality or state of being . . . affected by the suffering or sorrow of another; a feeling of compassion or commiseration," it also carries the distinctive sense of "conformity of feelings . . . which makes persons agreeable to each other; community of feeling; harmony of disposition" or "fellow-feeling." So the pattern of applying *compassion* exclusively to the poor could not have come about accidentally. When feeling for friends *was* at issue, obituaries turned directly to sympathy, as in the case of Catherine Carmichael, wife of a Presbyterian minister, who was described as having been "of a tender and sympathizing spirit, [with] a deep sense both of the comforts and afflictions of her friends." Alone on the well-ordered spectrum of feeling for others stood *sympathy*, a word that seemed to signal true parity between people.[64]

So clear was the connection between the exchange of feeling and the assumption of social equality that unspoken codes governing the proper social parameters for exchanges of feeling were seldom broken. Significantly, God, though called upon often for mercy, compassion, and sometimes pity, was never once described as "sympathetic," for never could a worshipper consider God as a peer. Likewise, while a high-ranking person might momentarily deign to put himself in the place of a commoner, offering mercy, pity, or compassion as the situation warranted, "sympathy" itself was seldom proffered, as this could undercut the social order. Conversely, though sympathy might be passed between people of all ranks so long as both were of the same rank, such an offer from a low-status person to someone higher in the social hierarchy would have been considered inappropriate, if not insubordinate. Doing so would involve the lower-ranking person's seeking to put himself in the place of the person of higher rank.[65]

One interesting example of the careful negotiation of such subtle signals comes in the following interchange between a newly appointed colonial governor and a delegation of ministers writing to welcome him. As was customary when one governor died and another was sent to replace him, the new governor and his subjects mutually declared their grief at the event. Such ritual exchanges established and tested the boundaries of the new relationship. In this case, which appeared in the *Gazette* in 1753, a group of ministers—themselves respected and recognized leaders among the *local* elite—wrote, "May it please your *Honour*, We . . . do beg Leave to express our tender Sympathy, in the general Grief of this Province, on Account of the sudden Death of his late Excellency." The ministers' task here was delicate; they wished to impress upon the governor both their own status as local leaders and their recognition of his own still higher status. They hoped that the governor would pay them the compliment of accepting their sympathy. But they had to tread carefully lest they presume too much; thus they "begged leave" to offer sympathy before they gave it and directed it at the people generally, rather than at the governor specifically. The governor, on the other hand, as the highest-ranking member of colonial society, was under no such constraints. He responded forthrightly: "Gentlemen, I Sympathize with you in the general Grief occasioned by the Death of his late Excellency." No need for the governor to engage in any begging of leave. He was free to offer sympathy to the ministers directly. Yet his reciprocation of sympathy, like his use of the polite address "Gentlemen," constituted an acknowledgment of the ministers' elevated rank. Though such statements of sympathy did not certify exact equality, they did define relations on terms of mutual respect.[66]

The subtle but sure social leveling implied in exchanges of sympathy charged this brand of fellow feeling with special significance. Sympathy could act as a kind of buffer, softening the most extreme effects of wild swings of fortune. If, for example, a man who was once "reckoned a gentleman" fell on hard times and found himself the object of general pity, he would know that he was done for. A man in such a position had lost all social capital along with his commercial credit. By contrast, Jonathan Scurth, a merchant, fell into debt and was met with "sincere sympathizing with . . . this unhappy accident . . . the void of that affluence you have been accustomed to." If a man was offered sympathy, he knew he could, at least, count on the continued "notice" of those he had always regarded as peers. In *sympathy* alone, then, do we finally find a word describing feeling for others that, by its very definition, promises, not to buttress, but to break down social barriers.[67]

Once the distinctions between various words for other-directed emotions have been uncovered, determining their relative importance in Anglo-American culture becomes an intriguing question. Keyword searches in the digitized version of the *Pennsylvania Gazette* reveal striking patterns in usage preferences. From 1728 (when the paper began) to 1800, *mercy* appeared more frequently than any other synonym for shared feeling. In 538 cases (in many of which power divisions were so explicit as to be indisputable) *mercy* was the word of choice. *Pity,* meanwhile, proved next most popular, occurring 304 times. It would have been the obvious word choice in any instance where people found it useful to overcome their desire to provide relief by simultaneously asserting a belief that the misfortune was deserved. *Sympathy* and *compassion* appeared somewhat less frequently; in three-quarters of a century, the two words occurred almost exactly the same number of times (*sympathy* 203, *compassion* 204). Though less common than some of the other words for shared feeling, as we will soon see, *sympathy* and *compassion* remain the most fascinating. Breaking down these aggregate numbers and comparing changes in the relative frequency of various words for shared feeling over the course of the eighteenth century reveals some remarkable trends in usage that hint at underlying shifts in social values (see Table 1).

Mercy, the most common word in overall numbers, was also the most frequently used in each of the periods studied (Table 1). Given the unambiguous signals this word sent about dominance and dependence, it was unlikely to be swapped for possible synonyms. Because it referred to power relations in their rawest and most immediate form, everyone capable of seizing physical power could grant or deny *mercy* irrespective of the usual status accorded one by society. In that sense, *mercy* existed almost outside the bounds of class considerations and so holds less potential to reveal the status calculations that underlay offers of shared feeling in more ambiguous social situations. Still, it is worth noting that *mercy* declined nearly ten percentage points over the century.[68]

The time-course for *pity* is still less remarkable than for *mercy.* With

TABLE 1. Frequency of Words for Shared Feeling in the
Pennsylvania Gazette

Term	Number, *Percent*				
	1728–1750	1751–1765	1766–1783	1784–1800	1728–1800
Mercy	74	104	195	165	538
	44.3	*47.1*	*39.6*	*35.3*	*40.0*
Pity	36	44	128	96	304
	21.6	*19.9*	*26.0*	*20.6*	*22.5*
Compassion	39	43	68	54	204
	23.4	*19.5*	*13.8*	*11.6*	*15.1*
Sympathy	5	10	68	120	203
	3.0	*4.5*	*13.8*	*25.7*	*15.1*
Commiseration	6	7	16	19	48
	3.6	*3.2*	*3.3*	*4.1*	*3.6*
Condolence	7	13	17	13	50
	4.2	*5.9*	*3.5*	*2.8*	*3.7*
Total	167	221	492	467	1,347
	100.1	*100.1*	*100.0*	*100.1*	*100.0*

Note: Deviations from 100.0% are due to rounding.

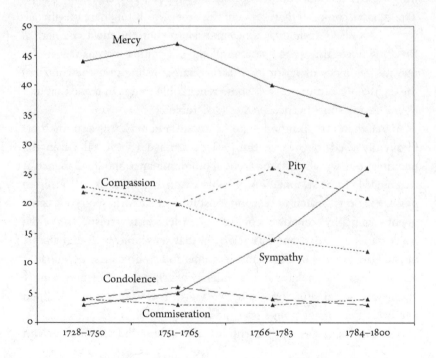

minor variations, *pity* comprised about 20 percent of all mentions of shared feeling to appear in the *Gazette* over the span. *Pity* was closely tied to assertions of status; offers of *pity* could put in their place those unfortunate people who had supposedly rendered themselves undeserving of finer forms of shared feeling. Still, like *mercy, pity* was generally employed in very particular situations and was unlikely to be interchanged with other words for shared feeling. By way of comparison, two other terms—*commiseration* and *condolence*—are of such minor importance they scarcely bear mention; each comprised a steady 3–4 percent of the total over the century. But their very constancy heightens the drama of the fluctuations in usage of other more important words.

The real interest in this exercise lies in comparing the relative frequency of *compassion* versus *sympathy*. These two words were closely related, and choosing between them involved a subtle negotiation of social signals. A dramatic shift in emphasis occurred between these two words during the century. In the period 1728–1750, *compassion* was, after *mercy*, the single most common word used to describe shared feeling, garnering about 23 percent of all mentions of fellow feeling. *Compassion* then began to lose proportional share in every subsequent period, dropping down to about 12 percent in the period 1784–1800. Over the same span, *sympathy* underwent exactly the opposite transition. Appearing only about 3 percent of the time in 1728–1750, it began as the least common word of all for shared feeling but rose dramatically to about 26 percent in the last period. Over the century, then, there was a precipitous drop in the use of the word *compassion* and a corresponding meteoric rise in the use of the word *sympathy*, which ultimately managed to steal share from *mercy* as well.

What these figures help establish is that, over time, the explicitly hierarchical messages conveyed by *compassion* began to lose favor to the more egalitarian ethos associated with exchanges of *sympathy*. Begun during the era of the passion question, from the 1730s through the mid-1760s when the nature of passion was heavily debated, the shift became decisive with the coming of the age of sensibility in the late 1760s. The two words met briefly as *sympathy* continued its upward arc and *compassion* traveled downward in the Revolutionary period from 1766 to 1783. What these figures make clear is that, although colonial Pennsylvania continued to be a vertically oriented society, right up through the Revolution, such stratified social organization was becoming ever more contested. Just as after the Seven Years War elites began to accept the universality of the passions even as they continued to seek ways to use anger to differentiate themselves from those they wished to subordinate (Chapter 4), the statistics on shared feeling indicate that hierarchy was gradually giving way to equality, at least as a cultural ideal.[69]

How did these trends affect the balance between communal and individual models of the self? Did the spread of sympathy, the one form of shared feeling that truly implied fellow feeling, at last help to build the kinds of social connections always hoped for by the advocates of feelings for others? In other words, was sympathy the ultimate antidote to the scourge of self encouraged by the embrace of passion? Much as proponents of sympathy might wish this were so, in the end, this form of fellow feeling proved the least effective of all in countermanding assertions of self. To understand why the one form of feeling that appears to have held the greatest potential for forging communal bonds should in the end prove the most isolating of all, we need to take stock of another as-yet-unmentioned feature that distinguishes various concepts of fellow feeling. The key consideration is whether the feeling in question elicited an active or passive response in those who expressed it.

A quick look back at the definitions offered by the *Oxford English Dictionary* readily reveals that the so-called synonyms for feelings for others are not all alike with respect to the key issue of action. *Mercy*, by its very definition, guarantees deliberate intervention. Tied most explicitly to the raw show of power, *mercy* also implies the most immediate action. *Mercy* has not been expressed until severe treatment has been forsworn and just assistance offered. Likewise, *pity* and *compassion*, even as they assert social dominance, each in its own way, promise that the person expressing such emotion not only feels moved by the suffering of another but also, crucially, that he or she feels a "desire to relieve it." While expressions of *mercy* guarantee action on behalf of recipients, *pity* and *compassion* both convey a somewhat more limited *wish* or *intention* to take action. With *sympathy*, by contrast, no impulse to action is implied. Though *sympathy* offered social parity, it promised no more than passivity, an inactive appreciation of the feelings of a fellow. In other words, there was an inverse relationship between how much social distance was closed and how much practical assistance was provided by offers of shared feeling.[70]

As the wartime rhetoricians (Chapter 5) had been quick to point out, compassion relied on passion for its qualities of action. If passion was the motivating force behind the will to act, it was a necessary component of active efforts to alleviate distress. In many cases, passion could be just another word for action. When Joseph Shippen considered the philosophical question of what distinguished material beings from empty space, he quoted Isaac Watts: "Every being has a capacity of action or passion." Likewise, the *Gazette* poem paraphrasing Alexander Pope declared, "Reason we bear and coolly may approve; / But all's inactive till the passions move." Elizabeth Graeme herself remarked, "Where [we speak] without Passion or Affection, we move but very slowly on to anything which requires activity." Those answering the passion question in the affirmative did so at least in part out of the conviction that only passion could guarantee active compassion.[71]

Indeed, a review of the wartime debates analyzed earlier (Chapter 5) reveals that, when prowar pamphleteers issued calls to arms during the Seven Years War, they never called for sympathy but always for compassion. They both appealed to men to assert their masculine mastery by showing compassion to the weak women and children being murdered by their enemies and announced that only active assistance would suffice. When pacifist Quakers—under fire for their feeble feelings for others—at last declared they did feel real concern for their countrymen, they were careful to couch their feelings in terms of sympathy, *not* compassion, both because they wished to showcase their disdain for social distinctions and because they could indicate thereby that concerns for suffering need not necessarily result in a commitment to military action.

The contest between sympathy and compassion thus reflected divergent ideas about the right role of the passions and the self in the ordering of social life. Compassion's linguistic link to passion mattered in practical ways. As we have seen, many argued that the embrace of passion, of individual willful emotion, led inevitably to an undesirable emphasis on the self. Yet, those who favored compassion tried to counter this trend by arguing that sympathy's innate passivity was itself inherently selfish. An essayist writing in the *Gazette* in 1744 concluded that only compassion fully met the demand for feeling for others. Seeking to define what characterized true compassion, he proclaimed, "One of the principle Duties in moral, and . . . in social Life, is certainly . . . a desire of relieving . . . Distress . . . and a Willingness to employ our Labour, our Money, and our Credit for those Purposes. . . . by Acts of Tenderness, Compassion and Generosity." This writer praised compassion as the truest form of fellow feeling, one that prompted people to put their money where their mouths were and *act* on the desire to relieve distress. Of sympathy, on the other hand, he had only this to say: "Fools may indeed have that Kind of good Nature that arises from weak Nerves and sympathizing Sensations, which is no more than . . . an Effect of Self-Love: But they can never have that which proceeds from Sentiment and Reflection." Twenty years later passive feeling was still portrayed as problematic. In 1764 another essayist deplored a decline in the true practice of compassion: "Compassion is, by some reasoners . . . resolved into an Affection merely selfish, an involuntary Perception of Pain, at the involuntary Sight of a being like ourselves languishing in Misery. But this sensation . . . will never settle into a Principle of Action." Yet even in the midst of objections that only genuine compassion could foster selfless action, sympathy slowly and inexorably began to gather steam.[72]

Comparing casual uses of the words *sympathy* and *compassion* confirms that the distinctions between them, and all their attendant moral implications, were well understood by eighteenth-century Anglo-Americans. A pair of reports that appeared in the *Gazette,* concerning the public response to two different calamitous fires, highlights the significance of such linguistic discriminations. In the first case, concerning a "most terrible Fire" that swept through Boston in 1760, the *Gazette* reported, "The distressed Inhabitants of those Buildings wrapped in Fire . . . Numbers [of whom] who were confined to Beds of Sickness and Pain, as well as the Aged and the Infant, demanded a compassionate Attention [and] they were removed from House to House." Here compassion for lesser members of society—infants and the indisposed—demanded and received an immediate, active response. Compare that report with another *Gazette* account of a Montreal fire of 1765 (following the commencement of British rule in Quebec). According to the *Gazette,* the New York legislature informed their governor in the wake of the fire: "You are pleased to solicit our Aid for the Relief of our Fellow Subjects at Montreal. But though we sympathize with them in their Affliction, such is the low state of our Commerce that . . . we find at present we dare not to make the least Addition [to aid efforts]." In the second case feeling alone was offered to those acknowledged as fellows; no active assistance accompanied it.[73]

The *Gazette* figures allow us to plot numerically the rise of the cult of sympathy, the bloom of the culture of sensibility. Sympathy simply was not a primary concern during most of the mid-eighteenth century this study has focused on. In the era of the passion question, compassion, though contested, continued to reign supreme. Over time, its prominence became more and more problematic, until it at last gave way to a new emphasis on sympathy. Sympathy's potential to promote both social parity and a return to communalism seduced those who fought the rise of selfishness yet could no longer openly countenance the rigid social divides imposed by compassion. As the fundamental tenets of natural rights philosophy gained currency in the years surrounding the American Revolution, compassion began to look ever more like a musty concept left over from an earlier era. The irony is that, for all its promise, sympathy itself did nothing to check the continued growth of the self. Achieving fellow feeling without personal feeling proved to be an impossible ideal. And so long as such social affections went unaccompanied by social action, the social bonds promised by sympathy proved no more than a shimmering mirage. Furthermore, the very capacity to feel that was supposed to have a leveling influence in society soon acquired all the trappings of genteel affectation. The more sympathy was emphasized, the more profound the collective inward turn became. Equality of opportunity came at the cost of real parity and community alike.[74]

Troubled as she was by the problem of self in life and in social relations, Elizabeth Graeme ultimately concluded that, like the illusion of ships that always appeared at the center of the horizon's circle, love of the self was an unavoidable natural principle. In fact, she came to believe that people should cease trying to denigrate the self and strive instead to incorporate it into moral life. If most forms of fellow feeling originated in selfish feeling, then the self should not be stifled. When she returned to Philadelphia from England, "overwhelmed with grief for the recent death" of her "ever dear mother," Elizabeth refused to comply with those who urged her to moderate her emotions. Instead she plunged into mourning, musing in an epitaph she wrote for her mother:

> Forgive great God this one last filial tear,
> Indulge my sorrow on a theme so near
>
> . . .
>
> Though Truth remonstrates, Self-love will prevail,
> And sink the beam in Nature's feeble scale.

Truth might well remonstrate against self-love and self-indulgent emotions, but Elizabeth was now convinced that this was simply the natural order of things. The self would always overbalance any counterweight placed on nature's scale.[75]

Not long after her mother's death, a second loss added to Elizabeth's sadness. Her beloved sister Ann, who had married Eliza Stedman's brother, Charles, also passed away. Defending her lengthy mourning for them both to Richard Peters in 1769, Elizabeth explained that she felt "deeply" sensations of "loss" and "regret," then conceded, "But I will not revive a theme which I know must be painful to you as I know you have blamed me in that respect." While giving due regard to Peters's views on overindulgence in emotion, Elizabeth still asserted her right to grieve. In fact, grieving for her departed mother and sister motivated Elizabeth to begin a verse edition of the Book of Psalms, a work that would help seal her reputation not only as a woman of feeling but also as a writer of genuine artistic merit.[76]

The string of losses suffered by Elizabeth Graeme and her friend, Eliza Stedman, in the years surrounding Elizabeth's return home shaped their lives forever after. The one had lost a mother and a sister, the other her family fortune and with it any chance for finding a socially desirable marriage match. The solution must have seemed simple to both. Elizabeth took Eliza in, and Eliza remained her devoted companion for the rest of their days. Though Elizabeth Graeme herself did eventually marry a man named Henry Fergusson in 1772, husband and wife lived together for only two years of their marriage. Initially separated by the wartime exigencies of the American Revolution, they seem to have soon settled into the conventional pattern of wealthy marriages of convenience. Richard Peters, whom Elizabeth ever regarded as "a second parent," had once joked to her during one of their long separations in England, "We are like your Modish Man and Wife, very complaisant at a distance, but never seen together." So the Fergussons might simply have enjoyed such a modish marriage. In any case, this state of affairs allowed Elizabeth's relationship with her old friend Eliza to thrive unchecked. She referred to her in a 1779 letter as "Miss Stedman, my Constant friend," and added, "Much I owe in my troubles to her Society and Steady friendship, and I do everything I can to render her Retirement easy." Perhaps, then, we should take all of Elizabeth Graeme's musings on the weight of the self with a grain of salt. We might conclude both that she allowed herself far fewer personal feelings than she might once have dreamed of in the first heady days of her courtship with William Franklin, and that her particular brand of fellow feeling, as evidenced by her support of Eliza, was more active and less selfish than all of her self-criticism would lead us to believe.[77]

The Complex Effects of the "Selfish Principle"

Without access to the nature's scale of Elizabeth Graeme Fergusson's imagination, it can be hard to arrive at an assessment of the sum of her life. She stands out in the historical record as one woman who spent an unusual amount of time reflecting directly not only on the great philosophical questions of her time but also on the practical problem of how to apply the lofty ideals of moral philosophy to the mundane concerns of her own life. Like many of her fellow Anglo-Americans, Elizabeth spent the remaining days of her life after her return to Pennsylvania trying to measure the weight and worth of the self. In the end, any easy redemption from the charge of selfishness runs contrary to the argument that Elizabeth herself wished to construct and artificially flattens the contours of a far more complicated process.

In evaluating the compromises Elizabeth Graeme Fergusson made in navigating between feeling and fellow feeling, we must weigh several key considerations. On the one hand, the sophisticated and celebrated poetry she produced showcased the finest possibilities of feeling. Unafraid to embrace the self and all its emotions, Elizabeth demonstrated the dazzling potential of unfettered individualism for people in general and for women in particular. Furthermore, she also succeeded in offering her impoverished friend Eliza Stedman a rare blend of sympathy *and* compassion, both reaffirming Eliza's social standing and actively providing her with material assistance. With this act, Elizabeth seems to have actually arrived at the sympathetic ideal so seldom achieved in the culture at large. Yet the emptiness of her marriage to Hugh Fergusson belies any attempt to advance the sweeping conclusion that, almost alone among her contemporaries, Elizabeth understood how to build reliable bridges of feeling. Nor was her hollow alliance with Fergusson her only or even her most serious failure of feeling. More significant, in a larger sense, is the fact that she never attempted to span the social distance between herself and the many members of the lower orders whose work went to support her style of life. She would have regarded such a suggestion as ridiculous. She once remarked to Eliza while describing her wishes for life, "As for the pleasure of relieving the distressed, and all that—People as frequently lose the Pleasure, as they obtain the Means, so that I shall say nothing on that Score." Indeed, when, following her father's death, Elizabeth discovered that his estate, too, was riddled with debt, she only reluctantly respected his wishes to provide small legacies for the family "servants," some of whom were, in all probability, enslaved.[78]

In this, as in so many other respects, Elizabeth's attitude reflected her society. For the subject of slavery—much less the emotions of the enslaved—almost never entered the private correspondence of elite Pennsylvanians. Grapple as they might with the question of passion, such people resisted extending the ideal of feeling for others to the cultural "others" whose lives were intimately intertwined with their own. By the eve of the Revolution, a select few in Pennsylvania would begin the crucial work of exposing the social and political significance of the cultural fallacy of the spiritless slave, unworthy of sympathy. For example, one remarkable antislavery essay appearing in the *Gazette* in 1774 began by urging, "The Heart, that bleeds for others Woes, / Shall feel each selfish Sorrow less," then proclaiming, "NOTHING has exposed Man to the Ridicule of his Fellow-men, or lessens his Character and Usefulness more, than a partial Conduct, which confines itself to the narrow Circle of Self-love." For any who might miss the larger significance of such ruminations, the writer explained, "I am led into this Train of Thought, on viewing the hard Lot of the poor tawny Africans, whom we have been so unhappy as to deprive and restrain of that *Liberty*, which they once enjoyed under the Gift of Providence." There can be no doubt that the culture of sympathy advanced by people like Samuel Allinson (and even more fundamentally by authors like Anthony Benezet and John Woolman) did represent an important first step in the history of abolition.[79]

However, cultural consensus on the importance of shared feeling by no means implied agreement over which people and groups were most deserving of emotional attention. For every person like Samuel Allinson, who lauded the tender tears of the black woman anxious over the fate of her freeborn son Frank, others—including Frank's attempted enslaver—continued to refer freely to blacks as unfeeling "brute beasts." Even Allinson, apparently so full of appreciation for Frank's mother's grief, conceded that Frank himself might be "vicious . . . foolish and weak in his understanding." As the ensuing discussion of grief will detail, common commitment to sympathy did not imply unvaried validation of sorrow, much less unquestioned acceptance of egalitarian attitudes. Though sympathy, to flourish, required some originating suffering for inspiration, the legitimacy accorded to any particular person's grief depended on the differential status of mourners and the mourned. As the changing vocabulary of shared feeling itself shows, emotional proximity could easily attenuate into social and political passivity. Ultimately, commendations of selflessness paled in comparison to the relentless pull of self.[80]

Reflective as she was, Elizabeth herself came close to acknowledging this. Writing to an old friend in 1779, just two years before her death, she decided: "I have sometimes been ashamed of this selfish principle but upon a more mature Survey of the Order of Man: Considered in his moral capacity I believe it is intended; that those troubles within our own Sphere; should affect us most, because they are of a Nature in our power often to relieve by our Sympathy." In the end, then, Elizabeth Graeme Fergusson emerges as a woman of her times, exemplifying both the promise and the perils of the rising self. In the years surrounding the Revolution, Americans as a people traded the sharp social distinctions conveyed by compassion for the insidious social apathy engendered by sympathy and associated with individualism.[81]

7

"Allowed to Mourn, but . . . Bound to Submit"

Grief, Grievance, and the Negotiation of Authority

When fifteen-year-old Thomas Bradford left home to attend the College of New Jersey in 1760, he and his favorite sister, thirteen-year-old Tace, found the separation hard to bear. As Tace put matters to Tommy in letters in August of that year, "Nothing can give me more pleasure than for you to be at home . . . your not liking it [college] makes me want you to come home so much the more." Nevertheless, their father, the successful Philadelphia printer William Bradford, had little patience with their pleadings for Tommy's return. "Consider, my dear, to leave college, or while at it you get but half your learning, you will be laughed at and you will repent it yourself in a few years. . . . I must therefore beg of you to put on the man." He would not hear of allowing the boy to come back home before his course of study was complete. Tace tried to make the best of things, promising, in the meantime, to be Tommy's "loving sister till death." The two continued to share many friends and were both especially fond of a young man named Jesse Leech, of whom Tace wrote teasingly in one letter, "Mr. Leech remembers his love to you. . . . But remember that . . . you are . . . at liberty to tell him if you please your own secrets but not the secrets of your friends." Little did any of them realize how quickly their promises of secrets kept and friendships maintained till death would be tested.[1]

In January 1761, their carefree correspondence was ruptured by the sudden death of Jesse Leech. William Bradford reported the news rather matter-of-factly to his son: "I informed you of the death of poor Jesse Leech; but I have not a line from you since at which I much wonder." Tace cried in contrast: "How shall I acquaint you with the afflicting news, that is your dear friend and mine is gone to an eternal rest? O my dear brother pity me and condole with me. . . . I can write no more for my heart is almost broke." Once again, Tommy received sharply contrasting messages from his father and sister, the one taciturn, the other tearful in the face of death. Both seemed to expect some response from Tommy: William wondered at his silence, and Tace wished him to condole with her. Yet they themselves displayed very different degrees of grief.[2]

On one level, the distinctive responses of father and daughter are quite unremarkable, easily explained by the fact that the younger Bradford had been closely connected with Jesse Leech while the elder had not. Behind the differing emotional displays of William and Tace Bradford lies a complex set of constraints and conventions surrounding eighteenth-century expressions of grief. Far from being simple and straightforward expressions of personal sadness, statements of grief conveyed critical social commentary in the eighteenth century. Just as William and Tace Bradford had divergent attitudes toward Tommy's homesickness, so they played different parts in reacting to the death of Jesse Leech.

The signals that were sent through the expression, suppression, or omission of grief were highly varied and complex, yet it is clear that social communication was an integral element of declarations made in the face of death. In a world in which personal identity and social standing alike were molded through complicated processes of social interaction, death created a crisis, tore a hole in the web of communal relations that defined subjectivity and social position. A major part of the work of mourning was to stop that rip from running through the social fabric, to measure and limit the loss. Statements of grief provided the thread with which to reweave the rent social web.

By the very nature of the situation they addressed, expressions of sorrow necessitated the negotiation of status. Such interactions required not merely the establishment of relations between two people but rather the triangulation of status between a minimum of three: the speaker, the listener, and the deceased person of whom they spoke. In considering the reactions of William and Tace Bradford to the death of Jesse Leech, one must assess not only the relation of each to Jesse but also the attitude of each toward Tommy. Tace wanted most of all for Tommy to come home, William for his son to become a man. As each sought to reach out to Tommy, these concerns counted at least as much as whatever feelings they had for Jesse.

What, then, did it mean to express grief at death? On the one hand, mourning the passing of the departed was an obvious act of respect. To lament over death was to pay tribute to the life of the person lost, to affirm the value of that vacant place in the social order. For that reason, tracing patterns in which people were deemed worthy of such recognition can help us to understand some of the nuances of social status in eighteenth-century British America. Tace's exuberant friend was William's unformed boy, and each grieved accordingly. On the other hand, even as the act of mourning could be interpreted as a show of respect, expressions of grief could also be interpreted as a sign of rebellion. Although grief could simply depict "mental pain, distress, or sorrow . . . for mishaps to oneself or others," *grief* might also signal *grievance,* that is, "a wrong or injury which is the subject of formal complaint or demand for redress." Indeed, *grief* and *grievance* stem from the same root. Though this sense of *grief* as synonymous with *grievance* is now considered obsolete, it continued through the nineteenth century. Any eighteenth-century statement of grief thus held the potential to challenge the standing social order at the very moment it was in its most exposed and fragile state. As we will see, Tace, for one, would not hesitate to try to leverage her tears into an excuse for at last bringing Tommy back home again.[3]

Who was being rebelled against in cases where grief turned to grievance? Any and all figures in positions of authority were potentially fair game. The most obvious target, of course, was God, by whose will the death had been allowed. But, because earthly power was so often founded on claims of divine sanction, the repercussions of rebellious grief could ultimately reach anyone whose claim to legitimate authority rested on his status as a proxy of God. In other words, while the highest-ranking men in society had the most at stake in the social accolades associated with expressions of grief, they also stood to suffer the most from grief gone awry and turned toward social resistance.[4]

Understanding why William and Tace Bradford reacted so differently to the death of Jesse Leech requires analysis of these ambivalent eighteenth-century attitudes toward grief, grievers, and the grieved. We shall see how differential standards governing displays of mourning can provide inadvertent information on a wide array of status distinctions, from gender divisions to cultural divides. By tracing the correspondence of Tommy and Tace Bradford, from the first letters Tommy received at school in the spring of 1760 to the last letters sent home to him by college chums in the summer of 1763; by stopping along the way to consider concurrent conversations about grief conducted across midcentury Pennsylvania; and by the diplomatic exchange of condolences between British-American negotiators and native American leaders—we can discover how debates about grief and mourning spanned divisions between the domestic and the public, linking men and women of many nations and stations in a series of continuing, connected conversations about status. Ultimately, the social messages sent by mourning could be heard from the British royal kingdom to Delaware Indian camps, from the corridors of the College of New Jersey to Tace's corner of the Bradford house. Indeed, the paradoxical implications of grief assured that it would be one of the most highly fraught and fiercely fought of all eighteenth-century brands of emotional expression.

Strange Vicissitudes of Emotion: The Alternate Celebration and Suppression of Grief

For Tace, the immediate effect of the death of Jesse Leech was exactly the opposite of what she would have hoped for. Instead of prompting her father to permit Tommy to return home, his loss led Tace herself to be bundled off, sent away from home for a change of scene. Writing to Tommy from the house of a family friend in February 1761, she declared, "I am at Mrs. Treat's with a broken heart and a merry countenance," then exclaimed, "O Tommy think on me with pity and think what I must suffer, but I know you do pity and excuse the distraction of [my] mind." Not only had her father refrained from making any great statement of grief at the death of Jesse Leech, but someone had obviously instructed her to try to do likewise. Though privately she continued to describe her grief to her brother in dramatic terms, publicly she tried to restrain it.[5]

Tace's February letter poses a series of puzzles. Why should she have bent her will to her father's and agreed to don the mask of a merry countenance, yet continued to insist to her brother on the depth of her feeling? The difference between this letter about Leech's death and the first one she wrote is dramatic and important. If her first inclination was to declare openly that her heart was almost broken by the "afflicting news," she was soon asking to have that same emotion excused. What function was served by such efforts at self-restraint, and what advantage could she have seen in continuing to declare her sorrow covertly?

As frequently as death occurred in colonial British America—and hardly a letter survives from Pennsylvania that does not mention some loss—it is entirely unsurprising that grief should have been such a focal emotion. Whether promoted or deplored, grief was never inconsequential. Despite the fact that grief carried the potential to convey resentment and even rebellion, the ability to feel mournful emotions was also counted among the basic requirements for participation in the emerging eighteenth-century culture of feeling. In a period when the capacity for sentiment was tied equally closely to religious salvation, civilized cultivation, and social elevation, death provided an ideal occasion for pious and genteel exchanges of feeling. Yet, ultimately, grief was greeted with ambivalence by those in positions of power. We cannot begin to assess the place of grief on the spectrum of socially significant emotions except against the backdrop of these highly conflicted attitudes.

Consider first the importance of grief for the practice of piety. In "heart religions" from evangelical Protestantism to Quakerism, grieving and mourning claimed first place among the "religious affections." Writing in 1756, Philadelphia New Light minister Gilbert Tennent admonished, "If we will not mourn over our own Sins, and the Sins of our Nation and Land, and reform our Ways, no human Measures, how apt soever, will protect us from . . . the Ruin and Destruction our Impieties deserve." Of all emotions basic to evangelical conversion, grief and mourning held the key to opening a sinner's heart to God. Tennent put the matter even more succinctly a few years later in his discussion of "the right use of the passions in religion" when he declared, "True Zeal is a compound of Anger and Grief, both [of] which proceed from *love* to God and Man."[6]

Likewise, members of the Society of Friends, from traveling ministers to individual believers, commented often on the importance of grief in the conduct of religion. The well-respected English Quaker Sophia Hume remarked in a 1752 letter (later copied into a Pennsylvania commonplace book): "Oh! that my head were waters and mine eyes a fountain of tears. That I might weep day and night. . . . I would just say that . . . the members of Christ's body often mourn together." Hume had traveled widely in the middle colonies, often staying in the homes of prominent Pennsylvania Quakers like her friends the Pembertons; her teachings reached even a poor Quaker woman in rural New Jersey named Ann Cooper Whitall, who confided to her diary a decade after Hume's letter: "I think to say with Sophia Hume, sorrow as she [did], weep and howl for your miseries that shall come upon you. . . . Our Lord pronounces a woe against them that laugh now, for they shall weep and mourn; but blessed are ye that weep now, for ye shall rejoice hereafter." Though Quakers and evangelicals maintained numerous doctrinal differences, grief was clearly central to many varieties of heart religion.[7]

Yet, in seeking to understand how grief emerged as a central emotion in British-American culture, the rise of heart religions provides only one important piece of the puzzle. Interactions with native Americans specifically must also factor in as a key part of the explanation for why grief enjoyed such importance. Ironically, in light of the prevalence of wartime propaganda proclaiming that Indians could neither feel for others nor shed tears for themselves, British-American negotiators regularly reported participating in Indian condolence ceremonies, exchanges in which ritual displays of grief and mourning were important to negotiations between rival groups. As early as 1750, for example, the Pennsylvania Assembly sent a message to its governor that was published in the *Gazette:* "We believ[e] it may be proper to send them a Message of Condolence on the Death of their Sachems. . . . which . . . may . . . afford us a greater opportunity of improving the good Disposition they have lately manifested towards us."[8]

The go-between, Conrad Weiser, wrote back to Philadelphia with accounts of British-American efforts to "signify to them [the native Americans] that the government [of Pennsylvania] do condole with them for the[ir] losses . . . according to the custom of that people." Or Indian agent William Trent might note that he had taken care to "condole with them . . . agreeable to an ancient custom of theirs," or that the British Americans and native Americans together had "condoled agreeable to their own custom." Remarkable in each of these examples is how forthrightly the authors credited native Americans with the custom of condolence, admitting that such exchanges of emotion were integral to native American culture, to which British Americans themselves had to learn to adapt. Significantly, Indian rituals clearly connected the display, discernment, and disarmament of grief with the smooth negotiation of social relations. Only those who had mutually acknowledged their grievances could effectively treat together. To be deemed a worthy partner for negotiations required a demonstration that one could and would share grief along with gains.[9]

Streams of grief could be as much a basis for negotiating status among British Americans as between them and Indians. Indeed, mourning came to be as much an avenue to social advancement as a means of access to God. Quaker, Anglican, or Presbyterian, male or female, eighteenth-century Pennsylvanians eagerly embraced the chance to proclaim their emotional agility and claim their share of grief. Eliza Stedman exclaimed, "I pity him from my heart the shock . . . on finding his mother dead." Peggy Emlen declared, "I pity her poor amiable sister who is left filled with unutterable grief." Quaker merchant William Logan assured a correspondent he was "daily in our remembrance with sympathy and sorrow." Prosperous planter Edward Tilghman was "too sensible" of his brother-in-law's misfortune and "sincerely condol[ed] with him [on] the loss of his wife." Eighteenth-century Pennsylvanians avidly exploited opportunities to showcase their ready sympathy with grief.[10]

Similarly, those positioned at the center of a circle of mourning often found their shows of grief interpreted as signs of their highly developed ability to feel. Reflecting on the nature of a young man who had recently lost his mother, an observer noted that he always "appeared to be very affectionate"; as he had "proposed much pleasure in seeing his mother . . . , to be so disappointed was very hard." In the same vein, writing to inform a friend about the demise of a mutual acquaintance, William Logan described the exchange of feeling surrounding "the death of poor Daniel Brown's wife": "I often sympathize with poor Daniel. As I believe him to be a man of [a] tender affectionate disposition . . . his loss must be great." Of course, it is only logical that the more affection felt during life, the greater the sorrow would be during death. The interesting point here is that Brown's grief for his wife, like the young man's for his mother, was offered up less as evidence of his particular feelings for the deceased than as evidence of his general disposition. Likewise, a young woman remarked about a friend who had lost both her parents: "How vastly changed is the gay and lovely Cleone. She seems to be left in the world entirely to herself. She is sensible and . . . now her spirits seem wholly depressed." Once again, extremes of grief were here interpreted as proof of profound emotional sensitivity. The grief of those known to be especially sensible was particularly poignant.[11]

Even the most open approbation of grief was seldom entirely unequivocal. Of course, for sympathy to flourish, there had to be some initial pathos to identify with. People could not possibly seek to share in others' feelings if there were none there to share, so certain cultural practices encouraged grief insofar as it provided fodder for sympathy. Still, there was also real societal reluctance to foster grief if it took the guise of selfish feeling. Though dictionary definitions might lump them together, "sorrow for mishaps to oneself" would prove to be far more problematic than "sorrow for mishaps to others." Consider the man who boasted of his wife,

"Although her natural affections to her relations . . . appears rather in the extreme, yet when it pleases the Lord to remove any . . . her resignation is Christian, and her behavior discreet." Isaac Norris wrote this letter on the occasion of the death of their son, and he clearly intended to praise his wife for the strength of her family feeling. Yet, much as he obviously approved of the extremity of his wife's affections, he also took care to add a caveat: her great inward grief did not compromise her discreet outward expressions of emotion.[12]

Though mourning for sin was essential to religious conversion in many denominations, mourning for personal losses was a sin in itself, a failure of obedience to the will of God. Widespread belief in God's living presence helps explain why *all* expressions of grief involved triangulations of status. Even where the griever confined his or her expression to the pages of a putatively private diary, the need remained to negotiate with God. The importance of avoiding immoderate grief was widely understood by men and women alike, and letters expressing grief were rife with references to such efforts. The widower David Cooper thus declared:

> My eyes and tongue put on dissembling forms
> I shew a calmness in the midst of storms;
>
> . . .
>
> And almost dead with grief discover none
> So smooth a face my Sorrow wears.

Ironically, a society that set great store on the value of sincerity approved of and even demanded self-censure in the expression of grief. Like Tace Bradford, with her broken heart and merry countenance, Cooper prided himself that, though he was "almost dead with grief," none could be discovered in his face. To feel grief yet tamp down its expression was an accomplishment worthy of recording.[13]

Indeed, in the contest to display emotional sensitivity without betraying socially and religiously unacceptable selfishness, elaborate evidence of efforts to overcome overwhelming grief was far preferable to either the utter absence of grief or its open expression. Almost humorous in its attempts to define the ideal of properly modulated grief is an earnest letter written by a woman on the efforts of some mourning friends. She reported approvingly to her sister: "I think I never saw a state of mourning that appeared more plainly to be seasoned with good throughout than this has. There was lively grief without murmuring. It might be called, as my God well observed, the sorrow of resignation." Mourning seasoned with good, grief without murmuring, the sorrow of resignation: implicit in this list is the cultural importance—and the practical difficulty—of defining acceptable bounds for grief. Ideally, grief vented sorrow yet neither incurred imputations of selfishness nor impugned the will of God. Most desirable of all was the figure of the deeply moved mourner who demonstrated willingness to submerge feelings of grief. Of course, the very act of commenting on the containment of grief could be itself a kind of expression, a paradox to which we will eventually return. The point here is simply to note how widespread was the expectation and acceptance of the dual imperatives of sensibility and self-restraint.[14]

Generalized grief for the presence of sin in the world might draw believers nearer to God; silent tears might suggest deep sensitivity. But open expressions of grief or pining over personal losses could signal a subversive focus on the self. Thus, confronted with her culture's conflicting messages concerning the propriety of grief, Tace simply hedged her bets, smiling publicly and pouring her grief into her letters. Not even to Tommy did she risk entirely flouting the rules of restraint. Eager to avoid any accusation of self-absorption, she justified her desire to express her grief by telling him, "My dear, my sorrows teaches me to feel for you . . . in the midst of my grief I have a piting and painful thought for you." Thus, Tace Bradford attempted to justify her expressions of sadness by identifying them as laudable marks of sympathy rather than lamentable evidence of selfishness. The question remains, however: how great a stake did dominant members of society really have in whether subordinate people like young Tace submitted to commands to maintain a cheerful countenance?[15]

Resignation or Rebellion:
Grief and the Negotiation of Gendered Authority

In actuality, Tace's emphasis on her own grief rather outweighed her expressions of sympathy or her efforts at repression. Her protestations that she sought to give vent to grief chiefly in order to deepen her ability to feel for her brother were belied by the frequent opportunities she took to express herself. As she told Tommy: "My grief sinks deeper and deeper every day. I find the merrier a countenance I put on, the greater my grief is in private." Safely returned from exile at Mrs. Treat's, Tace remained unrepentant in her strategizing to get her brother back to the Bradford's as well. She confided, "I came home last Monday and here everything I see renews my grief." Nothing, it seemed, could really stanch her sadness, save, perhaps, reunion with her brother. "I want to see you very much and want to talk to you and we may condole with each other." Thus, she marshaled unremitting grief in the service of a rebellious campaign to bring her brother home.[16]

Ironically, it appears that the very feelings of grief that were so highly sought after could both fatally strain the bonds of faith and challenge the bounds of status. Linked as grief was to grievance, those who mourned and cried in the face of death could be readily accused of rebelling against divine authority. Again and again, Pennsylvanians warned each other to beware slipping from the first surprise of grief into the snares of religious rebellion. Sounding such an alarm, an obituary in the *Gazette* publicly cautioned the mourners of one Mary Biddle to "dry up their tears and yield a perfect resignation to the Divine Will." So common and unquestioned was the importance of resignation that it became just one formulaic element in conventional notices of death.[17]

What social significance did religious rebellion hold? Why should tests of divine authority have socially subversive implications? In eighteenth-century British America, God was widely held to provide a model for earthly governors. We have already seen the impact of this analogy on wartime Pennsylvania politics; it proved equally powerful in the interpersonal realm. Because men were the self-styled masters, women the expected subordinates, each brought a different investment to any discussion of grief's expression or suppression. Whenever men and women addressed themselves to issues of sin and submission, they inevitably engaged in a continuing debate about the most desirable models of authority. Yet, contesting the terms of earthly dominance and dependence through the language of religious resignation or rebellion allowed men and women alike to seek safety in abstraction. Indeed, this alone may explain why the regulation of grief maintained such a grip on the eighteenth-century imagination.

Theoretically, eighteenth-century British-American Christians—Quakers, Anglicans, and Presbyterians, men and women alike—all viewed the infinite capacity for mercy and compassion as the defining element of God's governance. This heavenly trait became especially important during times of grief, when mourners turned to God as a primary source of solace. Ideally, mourners who freely resigned themselves to the will of God hoped to receive divine support in return. While God was in no way obliged to his believers, the faithful trusted that he would bestow such gifts with some regularity. This most commonly accepted model of relations between God and his believers was thus a reciprocal one that—much like affectionate relations between rulers and the ruled—relied on the habit of obedience by believers and the tradition of mercy from God.

Expectations about the proper attitude of mourners acting under this system are well summed up in a few lines by a locally celebrated Quaker poet, whose verses were widely quoted and copied in commonplace books. "Fidelia" issued advice to some mourning companions that applied as well to the culture at large:

> And you surviving friends, who bear the stroke
> Which thus your dear connection broke
>
> . . .
>
> Strive to submit beneath the hand divine
> And Heaven will heal if nature will resign.

According to this basic formulation, consolation came as a direct reward for resignation. God offered healing to those who had faith and who swore obedience to his holy will.[18]

A second poem, this one written by a woman herself in the midst of mourning, touches on similar themes. One Katherine Smith declared at the death of her sister:

> Borne down with grief and deep oppress'd with woe
> To find relief, where must I, can I go?
>
> . . .
>
> 'Tis Heaven alone that true support can give,
> To Heaven alone then, let me ever live.

According to these lines, the only sure means of lifting the oppression of woe was to seek relief from God. The healing power of faith was the grieving mourner's only sure recourse.[19]

This traditional model of authority was frequently abandoned in the breach. Many times, men and women each strayed from the standard in ways that signaled the divergent interests they brought to the negotiation of earthly social relations. When men made proclamations concerning the right relationship between God and his believers, they were in some way also commenting on their hopes and expectations for their own exercise of power. Meanwhile, women who rebelled against God called into question the earthly social system as closely as they did the divine order itself.

In any discussion of resignation or rebellion, then, men's stake in the discussion was subtly but significantly different from women's.[20]

Consider, in this light, a pair of testimonials offered by a dying man and a dying woman, statements of faith made on the eve of death, eagerly recorded, then read and circulated by mourners in the days immediately after their passing. Ellis Hugh reportedly lay ill for eleven days before his death, "during which he was mostly in extreme Pain, yet bore it with Patience and Resignation to the Divine Will." On his next to last day, he reportedly exclaimed, "Lord give me ease if it be thy Blessed Will." Then, shortly before he drew his last breath, he rose from his pallet to declare, " 'Fear God and serve him, and his Regard will be unto you, but if you neglect to Worship him, he will cast you off forever,' or words nearly to this Import." According to this formulation, God's inclination to offer relief or to impose suffering was entirely his own, made irrespective of the importuning of his believers. Hugh did not encourage his listeners to have faith in hopes of receiving some kind of divine recompense, but rather warned them that, if they did not have faith, an all-powerful God would forever cast them aside. In other words, Hugh urged faith, not as a way to attain a reward, but as a means to avoid punishment.[21]

To say, "Have faith or God will damn you," is a far stricter and harder requirement than the traditional exhortation: have faith and God will heal your hurts. Ellis Hugh's vision of God's authority was absolute, based on the undeniable superiority of divine power. His view of God proved so attractive that the male elders of the Quaker monthly meeting to which Hugh belonged published his words for the benefit of the community.

By contrast, the ailing Alice Griffith articulated a much different vision of God's authority, one far softer and more reciprocal than traditional models of God's power. As she lay dying, Griffith grew fearful and full of doubts about faith. According to those who kept company around her sick bed, she implored God, "I should be willing to Suffer whilst in this body any thing thou mayest Require, be the Exercise what kind soever if thou wilt give me strength and ability and favor me with thy living presence, then dear Lord shall not anything be too near or too dear to Part with for thy name." Here Griffith attempted to engage in a mutual exchange with God, asserting that she would accept divine dispensation, even if it meant bodily suffering, *if* God would personally appear to her and favor her with his living presence. In sharp contrast to Hugh, who claimed that God would cast off those who lacked faith, Griffith asserted that God had first to show himself and comfort her before she would accede to his will. According to the account, "some time after this she called her daughters one morning and said:

> I have to tell you of a glorious Visitation the Lord was pleased to favour me with as I was making my application to him for Deliverance and Redemption from my Sore Exercise . . . The Lord was graciously pleased to relieve me from my long Distress and renew my strength that my whole trust and confidence might ever abide in him which so filled my heart with Joy . . . that all my pain and grief and trouble vanished away.

Tellingly, Griffith maintained that God provided her with relief from her suffering *so that* her confidence might ever abide in him. In this version of God's authority, Alice Griffith submitted to the divine will, not out of a sense of tradition, nor in awe and fear of limitless divine power, but because of her belief that she had successfully negotiated a relationship with God based on mutual exchange.[22]

Griffith, like Hugh, expected that there would be some relationship between faith, rewards, and punishment. But where Hugh chose to emphasize the absolute aspect of divine authority, Griffith stressed the theme of reciprocity. God offered Griffith refreshment, she then gave him her faith, he in turn made her pain and grief entirely vanish, and she, finally, admitted herself ready to give her soul to God, to accept her own death without repining. It seems more than accidental that, while Hugh's testimony received official recording and publishing by the male leaders of his monthly meeting, Griffith's views were expressed to her daughters and then simply hand-transcribed for the benefit of another Quaker woman named Deborah Morris. Not only did this man and this woman articulate two very different visions of authority, but their views were also enunciated before two distinctly gendered audiences.[23]

In this vein are the musings of a new mother who gave thanks to God for the safe delivery of her child, even as she contemplated the distinct possibility that the sickly infant was on the verge of death. She declared in her diary: "I have to praise the glorious name [of God] for my safe delivery in childbirth. . . . Thy arm was stretched out . . . when my unbelieving heart was ready to say, Is he a God that hears prayer? If he is, why am I deny'd relief? But gracious God, thou suffered me not long to remain in doubt for thy arm assisted and I was delivered." Here again, a woman viewed her relationship with God in terms of mutual obligation. Her faith, wavering in the extremity of travail, was renewed, not through her own efforts to cast off sin in the fear of divine retribution, but by the timely provision of relief by a responsive God. In the wake of this event and still fearing she would yet lose her small son, she exclaimed: "Blessed God! Be pleased, I pray thee, still to continue to favour me with resignation. I dare not wish his life or death. Thy will be done." Significantly, this woman affirmed the need to submit to God's will and asked God to give her resignation but made no promises to achieve it unassisted.[24]

For women, then, grieving provided opportunities for ritualized rebellion, covertly qualifying the character of men's authority while not overtly contesting their subordinate social position. Both men and women were in basic agreement about the traditions on which heavenly and earthly authority alike were based, but men sometimes stressed an absolute model of divine power (and thus tried to strengthen their own position), and women on occasion used their struggles with faith to assert a more contingent conception of heavenly (and earthly) authority. Emotional control and social control could never be wholly seamless. Even in a world where *expressions* of emotion remained tightly constrained, all remained acutely aware that the underlying *experience* of emotion could never be wholly contained. True of every emotion, this fact became especially salient in relation to grief. For grief to signal submission, it had to be moderated. Yet, for the restraint to be effectively demonstrated, the grief had to be first displayed. Becoming present by its absence, restrained grief allowed lower-ranking members of society to contest the terms while accepting the fact of their subordination.

Thus, while women were perhaps most conspicuous in their rebellious navigation of grief, all members of society who were subordinated on whatever basis—race, class, age, or other factors—could engage in much the same kind of implicit debate. Consider the reaction of the young John Pemberton upon the death of his brother Charles: "The sense of the great loss I sustained by his death will ever live with me while it shall please Providence to favor me with the faculties of thinking and understanding." Describing Charles as "a very loving brother," he admitted, "I thought I could not have survived the loss of him." Still, determined as he was to declare his loss, John also recognized the expectation that he should display resignation. Reflecting on his struggle to submit to God's will, John declared that God "has cautioned me not to grieve too much, lest I should displease Him," but concluded that the "Lord was mercifully pleased to assist and help wherefore let my soul bless His name and may I be faithful to surrender body, soul, and spirit to his requirings." In this example, as with the women above, John Pemberton acknowledged the links between grief and rebellion and openly admitted the necessity of submission. Like them, he asserted that he had achieved this ideal only after God bestowed mercy upon him.[25]

While John's impulse to negotiate with God may at first glance appear as a gender aberration, it actually fits the larger pattern of subordinates' seeking to temper authority, for John's father Israel was on hand to insist on the importance of mortal obedience. Describing his attitude in a letter to a family friend (and referring to himself and his wife in the third person), he said, "His parents' affections were great toward him yet as to all appearance it was the Lord's pleasure to take him from us ... it was our duty to submit to divine will for he knew what was best for us." As far as Israel was concerned, the importance of deferring to divine power easily overcame the urge to express his own feelings. His dependent son John, on the other hand, called on the Lord to come to his comfort, showing clearly that the grieving had power to make claims on those toward whom they directed their tears.[26]

Grief-based protestations could even be injected into relations between slaveholders and the enslaved. As we have seen, whites were reluctant to recognize much in the way of emotion from blacks they held in bondage. The eighteenth-century stereotype of the down and dispirited —yet simultaneously largely insensate—slave served important symbolic functions in proslavery rationales. Exactly because of this fact, shows of tears by African-American women (such as those shed by the mother allied with antislavery activist Samuel Allinson) could help erode the ideology of slavery. The social submission conveyed by grief—as opposed to the implied social violence that accompanied anger—made African-American resistance to slavery more palatable for the few eighteenth-century British Americans willing to entertain ideas of abolition. Significantly, in Pennsylvania sources, only black *women* were ever mentioned in connection with mourning; black men never were. For blacks and whites alike, tears signaled weakness and subservience even as they also laid claim to the mercy of reigning masters.

Thus, the potential of grief as an instrument of rebellion can easily be overstated. Even many whites supportive of slavery simply accepted that "even to slaves it is permitted to rejoice and grieve at their own pleasure, and they who hold their bodies in subjection, cannot pretend to controul their affections." If this statement affirms that emotional freedom was the last bastion of liberty for those held in bondage, it also conveys a marked lack of concern about any threats conveyed by slave grief. Indeed, as historian Orlando Patterson and others have emphasized, given slavery's deep associations with death (actual and social), mourning might have been the consummate emotion of enslavement. In a world where dispiritedness was taken to be the usual condition of the "natural" slave, the leverage to be gained by displays of grief was inherently limited. Whites' studied indifference to sadness among the enslaved comes across clearly in both the overall lack of references to black grief in Pennsylvania sources and the very casual ways it was mentioned when noted. It is hard to know what to conclude, for example, about a May 1751 news item that read in its entirety: "The Negroe Girl now under Sentence of Death here, is to be executed the 16th of May next. Her Mother died with Grief about ten Days ago." At first this looks like nothing more than an objective observation of maternal grief. Yet, coming on top of a previous notice, made the week before, that "Phillis, the Negroe Girl, who pleaded guilty of murdering her Master's Child, by Poison . . . received a Sentence of Death," the report that Phillis's mother died of grief takes on a triumphalist note, confirming the emotional subjection of the rightfully enslaved. Gazette readers could dismiss the enslaved mother's excessive and deadly grief as evidence of natural depravity, not innate sensitivity.[27]

Perhaps not surprisingly, given the gendered issues of authority involved, it appears that men monopolized the right to serve as critical advisers on the conduct of mourners, whereas women were likely to remain more supportive observers. Male oversight of female grief usually involved efforts to reinforce resignation. Consider the counsel of a man named Nicholas Waln who informed his aunt in 1764:

> I am sensible thou hast undergone a great deal of affliction, and been wounded with the most piercing sorrow. . . . But as the dispensations of providence are always founded in the highest wisdom, it is undoubtedly our duty to submit to them with patience and resignation, and to say "thy will be done, O Father" without murmuring.

Such paternalistic references to God as father are rampant. The equation of divinity and paternity could not but bolster the status of earthly fathers, whose position was thus endowed with associations of divine power. Men like this one emphasized that, in subduing their grief, women could perform an act of submission as pleasing to those who styled themselves earthly masters as to God himself.[28]

Calls for resignation on the part of women frequently accompanied all kinds of deaths, from the loss of mothers to the passing of sons. In 1752, one Richard Hill urged restraint on his daughter Hannah at the death of her mother:

> Nothing under present circumstances would contribute so much to my consolation, as to know that thou my dear child hast with the resignation becoming a Christian, got over the first transports of surprise and grief. . . . Oh! my dear child address thyself in humility to the Divine Author of all the mercies we enjoy and submit to his will with entire confidence that he will protect and afford us whatever is best for us and do not repine or murmur at his dispensations.

In this instance, as in so many prior examples, the author placed a premium on the problem of murmuring. People appeared far less concerned with mitigating the experience of grief than with minimizing its expression.[29]

Again and again, when a man and a woman might be expected to have an equal interest in an occasion of grief, men targeted their advice directly to women. Thus, John Smith, learning of the death of one couple's child, declared that he felt "great sympathy with the afflicted parents of the surviving Lad on this melancholy scene," then added: "And oh! that his anxious mother may be supported by a divine power at a time when nothing human could do any good, to act with calm steadiness to the credit of religion." Men both appropriated the task of dispensing advice and focused their lopsided directives on the grief of women.[30]

The foregoing discussion could create the impression that there was an unending contest between men and women centered on issues of grief and grievance, in which men unrelentingly imposed resignation on women, focusing all their efforts on reining in women's grief. However, there was one crucial and widespread variation in this pattern. When men lost their wives, they imposed on themselves and one another the same standard of mourning with submission to which women were held. From Charles Inglis's description of the "anguish which penetrates my Heart under the Loss of one of the best and most Amiable of Women" to his pledge to accept "the will of heaven," and from David Cooper's "moaning" in multiple letters over the "corroding bitters of separation" from his wife to his effort to "cease to weep at all" and instead "seek seraphic hymns to sing . . . to Heaven's high and holy King," widowers often faced the loss of their wives with great grief and with a renewed sense of their own dependence on the divine. Meanwhile, other men were quick to advise them that their grief was acceptable only so long as it was accompanied by the customary submission. As one man told a friend, "Thy loss . . . may very justly be ranked among the greatest of all temporal ones." While "sensible" of what a "tender husband [must] feel," he went on to warn his friend "to bear it in a proper manner . . . believ[ing] all things may be made easy . . . by divine aid." It is, perhaps, a testament to the crucial part women played in sustaining the illusion of men's divinely ordained superiority that, only once they were gone, did men begin to recognize how hollow their supposedly absolute authority actually was.[31]

The regulation of grief took on great importance at least in part because of the widespread recognition that resignation and rebellion had important implications for the understanding of authority, divine and mundane alike. Adult men had the most at stake and were active both in advising mourners not to murmur against God and in painting, at times, the most absolute possible portraits of heavenly authority. Women (and to a certain extent subordinate members of society generally) attempted in quiet ways to use expressions of grief to counter men's masterly versions of divine power. Whether monitoring efforts at resignation or manipulating processes of negotiation, women could use the rituals of grief and restraint to promote more reciprocal models of authority relations.

In the midst of Tace's grief regarding Jesse Leech, another death befell the Bradfords. This time Samuel Davies, evangelical minister and president of the College of New Jersey, passed away. With the death of President Davies, the Bradfords engaged in an entirely new dynamic of grief. This time father and daughter united in the belief that grief was appropriate, and each told Tommy that they expected he would grieve greatly. Tace speculated: "I believe you are greatly distressed by the loss of such a president and such a friend. [It] must needs go very near your heart indeed." William's advice was equally strong. In contrast to his clipped report of the bare fact of Jesse Leech's death, he wrote Tommy that he was "extremely sorry to hear of dear Mr. Davies' death," adding, "It is a heavy stroke and ought to be laid at heart." Where William did not deign to express grief for the passing of a young friend of his children—and admonished Tace for her too open expressions of sadness on the occasion—he took an entirely different view of expressing grief for the death of a man of public prominence.[32]

Tributary Tears: Grief and Public Payments of Respect

The death of Samuel Davies provides one of those intriguing instances when the private lives of particular Pennsylvanians echoed in the larger culture. Many voices louder than Tace's chimed in to tell Tommy, and the people at large, how and how much they ought to grieve over the demise of this well-known figure. Unlike Jesse Leech, whose death and life alike would have remained unknown and unremarked by history if not for the friendship of the Bradford children, the passing of Samuel Davies was widely mourned. The death of a man of Davies's prominence—a man whose sermons had touched many hearers and whose printed essays had reached even more readers—created not simply an individual loss for his family and friends but also a public void that had to be addressed. So when Davies's fellow minister David Bostwick preached a eulogy for him, William Bradford published it.

For Thomas Bradford, then, Bostwick's words carried the authority not just of a church father but of his own father as well. Bostwick, like William, warmly recommended public grief for a public man, proclaiming Davies to have been "peculiarly dear in all the relative Characters of social Life, whether as a Husband, a Father,—a Tutor, or a Friend." He added, "Alas ... ! HE IS GONE!—He has quitted this inferior World, amidst the unfeigned Tears, and fervent Prayers, of his Family, his Friends,—the College, and the Country." Bostwick's eulogy argued that men who had played prominent social roles should be entitled to a measure of grateful grief.[33]

If mourning for private losses implied, at best, a weak and selfish inability to overcome emotion and lose one's will in God's will and, at worst, a sinful rebellion against heavenly authority with subversive implications for earthly social relations, grief for great men posed none of these problems. By definition, mourning for an important public figure precluded collapse into sinful and antisocial selfishness. The simplest justification for grief was that the sadness was shown for the loss of one essential to the common good. A 1772 poem on the death of several Quaker elders, including Samuel Fothergill and John Woolman, captures just this kind of justification. Titled "Reflections Arising from Well-Known Events," the poem asked:

> Whence O my friend that sadly pensive sigh?
> Whence those descending sympathetic tears?

Has thy firm Bosom met the adverse shock?
Or dost thou feel another's secret woe?
No, 'tis general universal grief
That swells thy bosom with augmenting pangs.

Clearly, the author believed that pensive sighs for secret woes were blameworthy. On the other hand, "general universal grief" for leaders of the
faith was acceptable and even desirable. The poem continued by affirming, "Thou . . . mourns the churches loss," asking who could see "pillars" of
the church fall "and not unite in tributary tears." The concluding line of
the poem erases any lingering doubts that, while rebellious grief was
dangerous, tears for a leader lost were a desirable form of recognition. In
striking contrast to the many instances when those faced with private
losses aimed and were urged to strive first and foremost for resignation,
this poem said nothing at all about the need for restraint.[34]

The very concept of paying tribute contained within it an implication
of submission. It was this that helped to assure that in instances of public
loss the display of grief could be socially and religiously unproblematic.
The definition of *tribute* is "something paid or contributed as by a subordinate to a superior . . . an acknowledgement of affection or esteem." Few,
if any, ever made the daring leap to the direct argument that paying
respect to departed public figures in some way enhanced the authority of
God. But neither did people ever voice any worry that this particular kind
of mourning would cause God to judge mourners to be in a sinful state of
rebellion. Indeed, when dealing with authority figures directly—without
the intervening fiction of God as proxy—people seemed utterly uncon-
cerned about questions of divine authority. They wasted no time whatsoever wondering whether exclamations of grief for public men in some
way expressed opposition to the divine will.[35]

On the contrary, the death of a prominent man provoked a flurry of
efforts to be sure that his social importance would be properly reflected in
pools of public grief. Such outpourings were supposed to be spontaneous
rather than contrived, an unstoppable collective overflow of loss and
longing. Consider, in this light, a poem written by "Fidelia" in memory of
Daniel Stanton:

I need invoke no Fabled Muse to mourn
Or pour feign'd Sorrow o'er our Prophets Urn,
For oh! too deep my Soul partakes the Woe.

Our Zion feels on such a piercing Blow.
Since in this Stroke (a common stroke) is found,
A public Loss as painful bleeding Wound.

Once again, this poem stressed emphatically that the grief expressed was for a "public Loss" rather than for any personal woe. Significantly, it also reiterates another recurring theme: the importance of affirming that the grief expressed for public losses was entirely genuine.[36]

Given the evidence of utter unconcern over those who went about with broken hearts and merry countenances or whose dissembling eyes and tongues smoothed the face of sorrow, this emphatic interest in asserting the authenticity of grief for public figures is all the more striking. From this poet's denial that "feign'd Sorrow" had been poured over the dead man's urn to Bostwick's emphasis on the importance of "unfeigned Tears," those who countenanced grieving countenances at the deaths of public figures tripped over themselves in efforts to authenticate such expressions. This is, of course, only what we would expect. While insincere submission did harbor certain dangers for those in positions of dominance, they were generally less severe than the risks of outright rebellion. On the other hand, sham shows of respect could act as a cancer on the social body, undermining the very authority it purported to uphold.

Such anxiety to affirm the authenticity of grief came up not only with relative unknowns like Quaker Daniel Stanton but also with kings. Indeed, when Britain's George II died in 1760, sincere grief made up a central part of the public spectacle of power. A poem by Fidelia published in the *Gazette* exulted:

See public sorrow unaffected flow,
O'er GEORGE the brave, compassionate and just.
 . . .
Ev'n on *Sylvania*'s Shore the humble maid,
Far from th' influence of her Prince's Eye;
Tho' not in public Pomp of woe Arrayed
Drops the soft Tear, and joins *Britannia*'s Sigh.

Going further than a simple mention of unfeigned grief, this poem went to great lengths to establish that this "public sorrow" was "unaffected." Even those far from the watchful eye of the prince, who could presumably have avoided shows of grief without attracting unfavorable attention, did sigh and cry over the loss of the king. In a culture deeply concerned about the rebellious potential of unregulated grief, this new insistence on the importance of allowing and authenticating unfettered grief is hard to ignore.[37]

Ostensibly, the relevant distinction was between public and private grief. While mourning over personal sorrows betrayed a lack of self-mastery and submission to God, grief expressed for public figures constituted a permissible exception to the general prohibition on grief. Because those mourned had acted in the public interest, such sorrow did not threaten the common good. Perhaps unsurprisingly, it emerged that many men had in fact performed some public service or other over the course of their lives. Thus, the seemingly strict injunction against rebellious grief evaporated easily at the deaths of most adult men. Sometimes the nature and extent of the public service of the deceased could be exceedingly obscure, as in the case of a Quaker man who wrote to another of the death of a mutual friend in 1771:

> The intelligence I rec'd of the departure of my worthy friend and kinsman . . . proves very affecting, being one of the oldest of my youthful companions. . . . I can feelingly condole with his family for their immediate loss and lament for the community on the removal of so serviceable a member.

The author of this letter was one James Pemberton, brother to the John Pemberton who had striven so mightily to achieve resignation upon the death of their brother Charles back in 1748. Now, twenty-three years later, the adult James felt no compunction of any kind at expressing open grief for the loss of a youthful companion. His young friend had grown into an authority figure, a "serviceable member" of the community. Pemberton never so much as bothered to explain what his friend's public contribution had been; the simple invocation of a public presence was enough to authorize an unrestrained expression of grief. He closed by assuring his correspondent, "I am affectionately condoling with you on the sorrowful occasion," without ever urging resignation on himself or his friend.[38]

If the definitions of public life and public interest could be stretched to justify, and even sanctify, unrestrained displays of grief for any man cast as a key member of the community, they proved far less elastic where women's deaths were concerned. If Fidelia was eager to pour unfeigned sorrow on the urns of male prophets, she took exactly the opposite attitude when it came to memorializing her female friends. She wrote a poem in 1775 upon the death of a woman named Sarah Morris that paints in stark relief the gendered distinctions that governed grieving:

> Ah! Shall the Tear of sorrowing Nature shed
> Our human weakness o'er the favour'd dead,
> What shall we mourn that exiled souls are free?
> In Life divine and Heaven's own liberty
>
> . . .
>
> No Dear Departed Friend, we will not mourn
> Or with our tears defile thy Peaceful urn
>
> . . .
>
> May we again the dear lost friend rejoin
> And while but Pilgrims in this desert road
> Patient submit to every stroke of God.

With the death of a woman at issue, Fidelia retired promptly and forcefully to the position that the chief duty of the survivors was to display submission to every stroke of God. Far from paying tribute to the life of her female friend, she declared, tears would actually "defile" the urn of a pious woman.[39]

It seems that, by basic definition, most women could not qualify as objects of tribute. If men's authority and God's authority were in some implicit way connected, women seldom found a chink through which to enter this chain of command. To note this is not to suggest for a moment that women were neither missed nor mourned. It is merely to observe the remarkable fact that people generally assumed that open expressions of grief for lower-ranking members of society, be they boys like Jesse Leech or Charlie Pemberton or women like Sarah Morris, would be unacceptable in the eyes of man and God alike. The desideratum of resignation took precedence over any personal inclination to give vent to sorrow. While a Jesse or a Charlie might not be worthy of mourning, a young man who survived long enough to become counted a "useful member of the community," as did the "youthful companion" of James Pemberton, could expect to be publicly mourned at death. Meanwhile, in most situations, no such avenues were open for females, no matter how long their journey from cradle to grave.

Given these facts, the question becomes, Were women *ever* presented as approved objects of grief? Insofar as women lived their lives in private capacities and the only ordinary occasion for open grief was the death of a public figure, we might well expect the answer to be no. In fact, there were certain intriguing aberrations from the general pattern against grieving for women. In some instances, Quaker women who became religious leaders did win recognition as public figures, and, on rare occasions, the deaths of these women could be greeted with "general universal grief" in the form of published praise or widely circulated manuscript memorials.

One example of this comes from the correspondence of Joyce Benezet, wife of Anthony Benezet, the social activist, abolitionist, and animal rights advocate remarkable then and now for the radical egalitarianism of his beliefs. She declared upon the death of a female friend: "Her death was matter of joy to herself, tho' of much grief and loss to the church. About the same time we lost our esteemed friend Stephen Comfort, who died during the time of the meeting, also much lamented on the same account." Here Joyce Benezet observed an exact parity in her commentary on the deaths of this man and this woman. Both of them had served as "public friends" within the Society of Friends, and the passing of each deserved to be lamented as a loss to the church. Benezet concluded, "Indeed there is great cause of mourning, for the removal of these and many others, who have been bright Instruments in the Lord's hand." On the one hand, such a letter lends credence to the contention that distinctions between who might and who might not be grieved had less to do with innate worth than with the realms in which they lived and worked. On the other hand, Quaker women were unique in being publicly recognized as religious leaders in the first place. The very fact that one of the few such examples to survive comes from a woman on the cutting edge of eighteenth-century social thought indicates just how unusual expressions of grief for women actually were.[40]

Consider in this vein the comments of one Benjamin Mason on the death of Alice Jackson, who died early, at the age of thirty-two for reasons left unexplained in the memorial that Mason wrote. He felt her death was premature: "I verily believe that . . . if it had pleased the Allwise disposer to have lengthened her days, that she would in His hand have become a Valiant in Our Israel. In that respect, I feel great disappointment and a loss that I cannot express." Here Mason gave himself permission to mourn a woman on the grounds that she *could have* become an important public figure in the Society of Friends. His decision to do so is rather remarkable, as is his explicitly defining his mourning with respect to her public functions. Indeed, he hastened to add, "As he who is omniscient has seen meet in his wisdom to call her from works to rewards, and accept of her tribute in the bloom of life, it becometh us finite creatures to be resigned to his righteous decrees, knowing that he is all sufficient." Even as he took the unusual step of paying public tribute to a woman, Mason was quick to reaffirm the resignation due from finite mortals and the tribute that death itself offered to the power of God. This example shows the complexities involved in mourning for women—and the potential destabilization of the social order created when the masculine authority of God was in any way associated with one whose customary position was as a model of submissive dependence.[41]

If the potential of unrestrained grief to signal rebellion made it generally sinful and seldom permissible, its function as a form of tribute also made it highly desirable. In negotiating conflicting imperatives for resignation and respect and in defining the parameters of acceptable grief, eighteenth-century British Americans relied primarily on the distinction between public and private persons. Those who had served as leaders had acted as earthly models of the power of God even as they had tried to mold and uphold their own authority through the divine image. To mourn the death of such people was to affirm the enduring importance of their social position while also confirming the imperative of submission—to earthly and heavenly authority alike. Only among Quakers, and only on rare occasions, were the boundaries of gender-based dominance and submission ever relaxed enough to allow a woman to become an object of "general universal grief," the recipient of public tears of tribute.

If men and women had to learn the nuances of mourning and the niceties of acceptable grief, the doors of the school of death stood ever open. For children like Tommy and Tace Bradford, losing a childhood friend and then losing a college president would hardly have been an unusual occurrence, for death was ever ready, taking high and low alike with grim regularity. If the Bradford children sat down and compared advice to muffle grief with a merry countenance with urgent exhortations to mourn public men, they could not long have remained uncertain about the relative social importance that distinguished the dead. Nor could they have been in doubt that, while sincerity was a virtue, selfless submission was an overriding imperative.

The eulogy for college president the Reverend Samuel Davies, written by David Bostwick and printed by Tommy and Tace's father, William Bradford, was actually added as a preface to the last sermon preached by Davies, delivered in memory of the late George II. Praising both the sermon and its author in his introduction, Bostwick proclaimed, "As the following Discourse naturally causes Tears of unfeigned Loyalty to flow from our Eyes, and open Springs of undissembled Sorrow [to flow] in every generous Heart, so the unexpected Death of the worthy Author must add new Weight to our Affliction, and give a double *Emphasis* to all our Expressions of Grief." For Bostwick, the unbroken lines of authority were clear as could be. Whether head of college or country, men in positions of power deserved torrents of public tears. In that situation, official censure came, not from shedding tears, but from shamming them. Indeed, elites had so great an investment in fostering such tears that they were prepared to defend their worth against any and all charges that they might be feigned.[42]

"Filial Tears" and Father Figures: Channeling Grief in the Interest of Authority

Bostwick's eulogy for Samuel Davies detailed the ideal response to the death of a public man with an exacting degree of precision. Of course, he spent a good deal of time encouraging his audience to let their sorrow flow. "LAMENT with sympathizing Tears, ye Men of Learning, Genius or Piety," he said, "HE who shone with every amiable Accomplishment of Nature and Grace." Then, suddenly, eight pages into his address, Bostwick sounded a note of caution: "BUT while we indulge the swelling Tide of Grief and suffer the rolling Tears to fall; let us beware of arraigning the divine Conduct, or cherishing an impious murmering Thought." All at once, Bostwick shifted his emphasis from the need to pay tribute to Davies to the importance of maintaining a stance of submission before God. Once Bostwick took off on this new tack, he grew ever more emphatic, exclaiming: "We are indeed allowed to Mourn—but are bound to submit. *It is the Lord, let him do what seemeth to him Good.*" What could account for this sudden rhetorical turn? After all, in the many examples above, those who grieved for public men seemed to have an exemption from the general requirement for resignation. The answer may well lie with the members of Bostwick's audience. It turns out they included not only the men of the college, students and tutors, alike, but at least one woman as well. In his very next line, Bostwick turned to address her, saying, "May the dear surviving partner who is PRINCIPAL in this tremendous Scene of Sorrow, be kindly supported from above and made to bear this heavy chastising ROD, with submissive Patience and christian

Fortitude!" Bostwick's sudden interest in Christian submission seems to have been aimed directly at Davies's widow.[43]

If mourning for public figures constituted a permissible and even desirable show of support for authority, while grief over private losses signaled a selfish capitulation to sin and potential social rebellion, a logical dilemma arose in instances where a public actor was also a private man. If the dead were divided into two distinct camps, public figures and private persons, then simple male heads of household were decidedly liminal figures. How could this ambiguity be effectively dealt with? Household heads straddled the line between public and private, occupying leadership positions in both the family and the society at large. Ordinarily, these dual roles were supposed to be mutually reinforcing: a man's home his kingdom, a king the father of his people. But in cases of death, when this role was left vacant, a passage between these worlds was left open. The very grief that would usually be seen as a sign of submissive respect could have the reverse effect of allowing formerly subordinate members of the household to openly flout the authority that usually governed their grief. In the end, the artificial unity of men's public and private power, the imposed equivalence of earthly and heavenly authority, inevitably unraveled.

What was to be done? A situation this fraught with complexity and contradiction could not but create different dilemmas for different people and admit of many solutions. Perhaps inevitably, men and women arrived at rather different conclusions, many of them quite surprising. It simply was not possible to identify one appropriate and culturally agreed-upon response to the abrupt interruption of men's many different roles.

Begin by considering the demise of men as husbands. As Bostwick's equivocation indicates—"We are indeed allowed to Mourn—but are bound to submit"—the grief of widows was simultaneously desirable and dangerous. To some extent, a widow's grief could be interpreted as a tribute to the husband and master she had lost, a respectful stance that strengthened men's overall social authority. But a widow who mourned was also in a state of potential defiance against the divine. Given that she no longer had any supervisory male with direct authority over her, a widow's grief carried particular potential to be socially subversive.

The men who considered a deceased husband to have been their equal and peer were especially anxious to ensure that, while widows displayed due respect for the departed, they did not overstep the bounds of propriety that governed the grieving of subordinates. Widows' correspondence with male relatives underscores the importance of a posture of respectful submission. Thus, when Margaret Morris lost her husband in 1766, her brother-in-law, George Dillwyn, advised her to strive for the "establishment [of] a perfect Resignation to the Dispensations of eternal Wisdom." Likewise, when Sarah Logan wrote to a brother at the death of her husband, James, in 1752, she began by telling him, "The death of my dear spouse . . . has been so great a shock to my nature that all things in Life have lost their Relish," but then hastened to add, "We had lived near 37 years together [and] I have now the pleasure to reflect that I never knowingly disobeyed him all that time, which together with a steady endeavour to trust in that kind Providence which has attended me all my Life is my greatest comfort." The link between obedience in life and resignation at death could hardly be made more compelling.[44]

An even more dramatic example of a widow's efforts to edit her grief in just such a way as to pay tribute to her deceased husband, while not openly appearing to strive for a new and improved social position, can be seen in a letter by Elizabeth Allinson. Following her husband's death, she evidently received word from his brother that, while he was aware of the event, he would like to hear of it in the widow's own words. Elizabeth's surviving rough draft tells him, "I understand that thee hath not . . . rec'd a letter relating the sorrowful and affecting news of my Husband's Death . . . who died after a very short illness of but a week." The surviving Allinson knew the news, but he wanted to hear the particulars from the widow, and he wanted some tribute to be paid to his brother. Though Elizabeth doubtless understood the complex cultural expectations she faced, her omission of the expected letter of condolence appears not to have been entirely accidental.[45]

When Elizabeth Allinson finally sat down and wrote to her husband's brother, she began: "The loss of a companion and the trouble which after his death I saw myself involved in gave me a very melancholy prospect of life. Before his death he had very much encumbered himself, much more than I had knowledge of his having been." These lines started out smoothly enough, paying tribute to the deceased by speaking of melancholy over his loss. But they soon veered off into a dangerous direction, as Elizabeth explained that her melancholy stemmed at least as much from the discovery of her late husband's debts as from his death itself. What is more, Elizabeth had entirely neglected to make any reference to the

"Allowed to Mourn, but . . . Bound to Submit"

importance of resignation or the rectitude of God's will. We can only imagine how Allinson's brother might have reacted to such a brazen display of disrespect.[46]

In actuality, however, he never saw *that* letter. Elizabeth must have read it over and realized it would never pass muster, for she edited the lines, scribbling in strategic additions and deletions that altered her words just enough to make them conform to the attitude expected of a respectful widow. When all the caret insertions and crossed-out lines are taken into account, the final version of her draft reads, "The loss of a companion and the trouble which after his death I saw myself involved in gave me a very melancholy prospect of life but blessed be the Lord who helped me in the time of trouble and distress." When she finally did bring up the subject of her husband's debts several lines later, she simply provided his brother with the relevant figure (three hundred pounds for cash loans "besides his other debts") as matter-of-factly as possible, leaving him to come to his own conclusions and read between the lines if he could. For a final flourish, she crossed out the salutation "Affectionate Brother" and substituted the phrase "Respected Brother."[47]

If the public version of Elizabeth Allinson's letter achieved exactly the balance of mourning and submission a widow was supposed to strive for, the uncut edition makes clear how much more complicated women's actual attitudes might have been. Men had every interest in insisting that mourners use the occasion of death to recommit themselves to a male-dominated system of authority. Widows who felt forced to pay lip service to such pronouncements might have paid very little actual attention to them. However much they might have felt for their husbands in life, widows betrayed a certain reluctance to reinforce male models of authority on the occasion of their death.

The very fact that expressions of grief could be alternately interpreted as signs of rebellion and tokens of tribute made arriving at a consensus on the proper response to the death of husbands inherently problematic. Eager as men were to offer advice and regulate a widow's remarks, it was somewhat difficult to know just what to ask for. The compromise solution of encouraging mourning *with* resignation was better than nothing, but hardly had the makings of a seamless system. Even a widow's most diligent attempts to achieve the correct balance could expose deep cracks in the system; and, among those with an ax to grind, the fissure could be pried wide-open. If some light is shed on this point by the small but significant discrepancies between men's advice and widows' actual remarks upon the deaths of husbands, attitudes toward fathers will illuminate matters more brightly still. Gendered patterns of advice as well as gendered patterns of expression diverge quite sharply in the case of fathers.

For men, focusing on grief for fathers presented a perfect solution to the foregoing dilemma. Fatherless children who were yet minors either had mothers or guardians or became wards of the state. Whatever the event, the gap left by the absent father was sure to be speedily filled. Unlike widows, who might remain masterless for months or for life, children were certain to be quickly returned to a subordinate position, if, indeed, they ever left it at all. While the risks associated with rebellion were low, the need to reaffirm the propriety of authority was especially high. Whoever stepped in to fill the father's place needed the legitimacy such respect for authority could confer. Men therefore proved to be unrelenting enthusiasts when it came to recommending unreserved grief for fathers lost.

John Pemberton had struggled greatly for resignation upon the death of his beloved brother. At the time, opinion was unanimous that excessive grief on his part would displease his earthly and heavenly fathers alike. When his father himself finally passed away several years later, the situation was entirely reversed. When Israel Pemberton, Sr., died, the prominent Quaker elder John Churchman wrote to John only to commiserate with "the sorrowful and deeply affecting news of the death of thy father." Making no mention at all of the need to accept God's will, this minister took time to imagine in great detail the extensive grief of the Pemberton family. Knowing that John had been in the middle of a transatlantic passage at the time of his father's death, Churchman "sympathetically felt" for him in advance, "in order to ballast thy vessel for such a storm which [the news] thereof would occasion." Finally, imagining the family scene that would ensue when John finally learned what had happened, Churchman envisioned that the "mutual tears of a tender mother and children would be mingled together," and concluded, "Methinks I measurably feel and saw the affecting scene." At no point was there any suggestion that any expression of grief on John's part could be ridiculed as rebellious.[48]

Likewise, when Quaker John Smith died, a cousin of his wrote to his daughter Hannah to tell her that, "having experienced afflicting dispensations of the same kind," he could "feelingly sympathize" with her. Adding, "I sincerely condole with you on this sorrowful occasion," he assured her that he appreciated how "piercing beyond description [was] the loss [she had] sustained." Having granted Hannah unrestricted encouragement to grieve, her cousin then went on to praise her "worthy father" as one of his "most valuable and oldest acquaintances." If the subversive element of grieving lay in its implicit protest against prevailing social conditions, then the one occasion for grief that carried little risk of insurgency involved mourning the death of a man of authority. Those who lamented the loss of a person of power, while themselves retaining a subordinate position, could hardly be suspected of covertly opposing the very authority their grief helped authenticate. The most socially stabilizing of all forms of mourning, then, was grief for the father.[49]

Nor was this exemption from resignation in any way a general one, applicable to parents of either sex. On the contrary, men and women who lost their mothers were typically cautioned to season their grief with submission to God. Thus the advice of John Morgan to a lady friend of his who lost her mother: "I am so sensibly affected with the irretrievable loss you have suffered in the death of one of the most valuable of Women and dearest of Mothers that I cannot refrain from joining my condolence with yours." Yet he immediately cautioned, "You have not only philosophy, but religion however to support you under the pressure of so great an affliction." No matter how worthy the woman, grief for mothers had always to be tempered by religious reflection. Only for fathers were the strictures governing grief lifted to allow the free flow tears untrammeled by resignation.[50]

Not surprisingly, sons took quite readily to advice to grieve for fathers without restraint. However young he was, every son stood poised to one day inherit his father's mantle. Meanwhile, sons who had already reached adulthood themselves were perfectly placed to reap immediate benefit from the accompanying affirmation of their own newfound authority. When Samuel Stokes lost his father, he immediately gained his father's old place. One of his father's business correspondents, Thomas Lawrence, wrote to Samuel: "I have received your letter . . . with the unwelcome tydings of the death of your good father. I partake of your sorrow on so melancholy an occasion to you and a sensible affliction to myself for the loss of a truly valuable correspondent." Sharing in Stokes's grief while offering nary a word concerning resignation, Lawrence offered powerful proof that both Stokeses were worthy men. He followed up this expression of emotion with a promise that he would take "especial care to continue the remembrance of the fathers in the sons." He then invited

FIGURE 12. Thomas Bradford. Simpson Portraits, Historical Society of Pennsylvania. *Permission The Historical Society of Pennsylvania*

Stokes to continue doing business with him: he was "well satisfied that the son of so worthy a father will follow his steps." As the traditional British phrase, "The king is dead, long live the king," should remind us, men who already occupied, or else aspired to assume, positions of mastery had every reason to underscore the general legitimacy of authority by mourning the passing of power.[51]

So universally accepted was grief for fathers—as opposed to more problematic brands of sorrow for mothers, daughters, sisters, sons, brothers, or friends—that it became the standard for all expressions of lamentation for the loss of leaders. When an English archbishop died in 1768, a Pennsylvania member of the Anglican Church declared, "Every true son of the *Church,* every lover of primitive integrity, piety, and unaffected simplicity of manners, must drop a tear, as for a father lost." If grief that expressed grievance potentially imperiled the standing social order, grief directed toward those who directed society could provide an important countervailing force. Placing fathers at the nexus between familial authority and public power, men saw the death of a father as one occasion when unchecked private grief was not only permissible but also completely desirable. In calling for flexibility for filial grief, men sought to show that fathers were the exception that proved the rule, that men's authority in their households and their power in the public domain all sprang from the same legitimate title to mastery.[52]

However, a startling fact emerges when one begins to scrutinize the gendered patterns of paternal grief. While men eagerly dispensed advice urging unfeigned and unfettered grief for fathers and while sons proved equally anxious to comply, women were far less sure of the propriety of such grief. When Margaret Morris lost her father, Richard Hill, she greeted the news with a great deal of grief: "It pleased the Lord to bring heavy affliction upon us, by sending the awful messenger of death to summon our dear parent to the grave." However much she mourned her father, Margaret was determined to meet his death with resignation. Foreshadowing the attitude she would soon take toward the death of her husband, she hastened to add to her statement of affliction a prayer of submission: "Sanctify Eternal Father, I pray thee, this cup unto us and as Thou who gave the dear blessing to us had a right to recall it in thy own time, suffer us not to murmur at thy allwise dispensations." No matter the earthly position of the man, as husband or father, Margaret Morris, for one, saw no occasion to omit a proper resignation to God.[53]

Note the range of reaction to the death of Isaac Norris, Sr., in which male and female observers took markedly different stances on the matter of mourning. We have already seen that Norris himself was a firm believer in the importance of resignation, having praised his wife's Christian discretion when they lost a son in 1727. However, when Norris himself passed on several years later in 1735, the situation was entirely different. Then, a published obituary urged survivors to mourn his loss, in language that made explicit the significance of grief for fathers as governors. The piece, which appeared in the *American Weekly Mercury*, declared with confidence: "In him the Publick lament the loss of a Man of Merit and Ability, and his Family, all that endear to them a Husband, Parent, and Master." Meanwhile, Isaac Norris, Jr., took possession of his father's name and his father's position with just the kind of elaborate grief we would by now expect. Writing to a business associate, Norris felt full freedom, if not obligation, to declare:

Tears flow sincere, prayers from the heart are heard
And groans in bitterness of soul preferr'd
How shall our bark securely reach the shore,
When thou the careful pilot art no more?

Interpreting these verses for his correspondent, Norris explained: "My circumstances have now placed me in a station difficult and new. . . . That parent who was a companion and friend is now removed too far for to reach his hand, when I miss my step. He has left only the brightness of his virtues to add infamy to his successors when they fall." His lament for the loss of his father's leadership left little room for the suspicion that his grief could threaten the structure of authority. On the contrary, it could only serve to strengthen his own as his father's "successor."[54]

While men from newspaper editors to trading partners agreed that Norris was indeed a man worthy of untrammeled tribute, a Norris family friend and well-traveled Quaker elder by the name of Susannah Wright was not so sure this proceeding was proper. A month after Norris penned the poem above, Wright gently chided him: although the "melancholy occasion the death of [his] good and affectionate father [wa]s yet a subject almost too tender to be mentioned," she could not forbear sending him a note. Wright did express sympathy for the grief of Norris and his family, but she also stepped in to warn Norris, " 'Tis in vain to repine at the eternal order of nature." Brief as that lone line of restraint is, it stands out in the great sea of free-flowing grief for fathers evidenced in the writing of so many men.[55]

Meanwhile, when Wright's own father died fully fifteen years later, she wrote to Norris once again to tell him the news and to muse on the difficult necessity of resignation to the divine will. "I well knew whenever it pleased God to call him it would very sensibly affect me." These opening lines clearly express respect and affection for her father as well as some reluctance to fully accept his death. Nevertheless, Wright felt certain that resignation was what was required. Struggling to achieve the ideal she set for herself, an endeavor all the more remarkable given that men in her society would have encouraged her *not* to make the effort, she observed:

> To be called into being without any will or act of our own, and taken out of it again, in the manner the greater part of mankind are, to human reason has an appearance of severity but there we must leave it and as well as we can rest satisfied in concluding that all that is, is right, tho we yet know not in what manner it is so.

While men advised grief for earthly fathers and father figures as if, in this one instance, God's authority could be questioned because man's was thereby affirmed, women more often insisted that resignation was as much a requirement at the death of fathers as of anyone else.[56]

The conflicting attitudes and assumptions of Isaac Norris and Susannah Wright are similarly evidenced in a pair of anonymous poems that addressed filial grief directly. They were copied into the 1775 commonplace book of a Quaker woman, Catherine Haines. The first poem was titled "By a Young Man on the Death of His Father, An Epistle to a Female Friend," the second called simply "Her Answer." In the first a son declares:

I feel the stroke! the last, the fatal blow,
For which my never ceasing tears shall flow.

. . .

Heart rending sighs declare my pondering woe,
And filial tears my darkening eyes o'erflow.

Such an unabashed declaration of grief would have been all but impossible without the justification that the unchecked tears were filial and therefore represented an affirmation, not a protest, of paternal power. This son betrayed no compunction whatsoever about the propriety of his grief.[57]

"Her Answer," on the other hand, cast grave doubts on the appropriateness of the young man's mourning. Like Susannah Wright, the young man's female friend did understand the impulse to mourn for a lost father. She told the young man, "My secret soul approves thy pious sighs / and loves the tears [that] flow from filial eyes." But she immediately cautioned him not to allow his grief to expand out of bounds: " 'Tis sacred grief, 'tis beautiful distress / yet think my friend, there's error in excess." Not only did these two poems showcase distinctly different gendered attitudes toward the death of a father: they did so deliberately. It is impossible to know the identity of the author(s) of this pair of poems, but it is clear that the dramatic juxtaposition of male and female attitudes toward filial grief showcased in them was intended. While men had every interest in paying tribute to the passing of fathers, women sometimes insisted on reminding them of the supremacy of God.[58]

Significantly, women made no objections to unguarded grief when it came to mourning public figures, those who had rendered service to country or church. But at least some women refused to acquiesce in the easy equation of public and paternal power. Even as men implicitly argued that the authority of household heads constituted a direct extension of the authority of God, women quietly but consistently challenged that exact equivalence. By insisting on consistency and observing a prohibition on paternal grief, such women countered the idea that earthly and heavenly power were one. They reminded men that God's authority was ultimate—that the requirement to subordinate the self and submit to the divine will could not be omitted simply because the lesser authority of a father was at stake.[59]

No doubt Samuel Davies himself would have highly approved William Bradford's apparent discrimination between inadvisable grief for an insignificant schoolboy and appropriate mourning for an important public figure. For, in his eulogy for King George, Davies declared, "Even the recluse Sons of NASSAU HALL, feel immense Bereavement, with all the Sensibility of a filial Heart; and must mourn with their Country, with *Britain,* with *Europe,* with all the World [for] GEORGE was *our* Father too." Davies proclaimed that nothing could be more natural or desirable than displays of grief for a father. Grief exhibited for the passing of authority could hardly be construed as subversive of that authority. Most tellingly of all, Davies concluded, "Let our tears flow down. . . . It will give Relief to our bursting Hearts, impatient of the Suppression of our Sorrows." In a culture in which people were continually admonished to restrain the self by reigning in grief, men argued that mourning for fathers should mark an important exception to this rule. They sought to channel the force of pent-up tears into a torrent of tribute for leading men, thereby deepening and strengthening the streams of male authority, making more absolute the model of male power. If grief that expressed grievance potentially imperiled the standing social order, grief directed toward those who guided society could provide an important countervailing force.[60]

No efforts to channel grief in sanctioned streams could ensure the purity of the current. The glitch was that women were not always prepared to follow the male model of grief. Tace Bradford, for one, was more than happy to allow all her griefs to flow together, streaming toward her ultimate goal of getting her brother home. By not mentioning either their friend or the college leader by name, Tace became free to express elaborate unspecified grief. In a March 1761 letter to Tommy she did so. "My dear my troubles is more than I am able to bear . . . if my grief does not grow less, I must fall under it." She signed herself, "your loving tho heart broken sister." In the days after Davies's death, as fear of fevers and contagion swept the college, it finally seemed that Tommy might be allowed home at last. Tace noted tartly, "O dear brother, it seems to moderate my grief to think I shall see you so soon." A break in their correspondence indicates that Tommy did arrive home for an extended visit; by the following August, a year after their struggle began, he at last arrived home for good.[61]

The Compliments of Condolence: Cross-Cultural Contests of Authority

The chorus of voices calling for the public outpouring of colonial mourning at the death of George II reached all the way up to Governor James Hamilton. In a rousing speech before the Pennsylvania Assembly, Hamilton expounded on the importance of paying tribute, warning, "It would argue the Greatest Insensibility as well as Ingratitude were we not most deeply affected with sorrow at so deplorable a Loss." The Assembly in turn proclaimed that it was "fully sensible of the Great Loss," declaring that it was its "indispensable Duty to present His Majesty an address of Condolence, on this affecting Occasion." Affirmation of George III required acclamation for George II. Membership not only in polite society but also in the American British Empire itself was defined by participating in shared displays of grief. To omit them would be to call into question all capacity for sensibility, along with any claims to moral and social rectitude.[62]

Given the great emphasis that Governor Hamilton and the Pennsylvania Assembly placed on sending their condolences back to Britain, Hamilton's omission of such expressions of grief on another solemn public occasion, less than twelve months before, becomes all the more striking. At a meeting held in Philadelphia in March 1760, the Delaware king, Teedyuscung, gravely informed Hamilton of some deaths among members of the Delaware nation: "Something has happened whereby our union is struck and wounded." While Hamilton would eagerly pronounce himself ready and willing to honor the "glorious memory" of his fallen king, he resolutely refused to offer the native American leader the same show of feeling. Hamilton promised simply that his government would "join with you in removing these and all the other dead Bodies that lye on the Earth between us uncovered, out of our sight." Moving to obliterate— rather than to celebrate—memory of the Indians, Hamilton metaphorically buried the dead "deep in the Ground, that it should not be in anyone's power to dig them up again and expose them to view."[63]

Did the governor's curious neglect of the "indispensable Duty . . . of condolence" and flirtation with the dangers of "Insensibility" simply reflect cross-cultural differences in the expected emotional attitude toward death? Not at all. On the contrary, Teedyuscung had journeyed to Philadelphia on his own initiative with the explicit purpose of informing the governor that, between Pennsylvania colonists and the Delaware nation, there lay "some dead bodies between us, uncovered on the ground, which fill our hearts with Grief and our Eyes with Tears." Indeed, for long centuries, members of the Iroquois League and affiliated nations like the Delawares had traditionally placed a great premium on the expression of grief and the exchange of condolences upon the occasion of death. Governor Hamilton was well aware of this practice and took great care to tell Teedyuscung of his intention to "wipe the Tears from your Eyes and remove all Grief from your heart." Despite all this, the governor did not personally profess any feelings of loss. He did not himself give voice to the slightest sensation of sorrow.[64]

Northeastern native American condolence ceremonies and British-American rituals of public mourning shared similarities too numerous to be ignored. Most important, all concerned understood the vital link between public avowals of grief and the acknowledgment of social place. Records of treaty negotiations frequently noted that "compliments of condolence for the deaths of persons of distinction [were] exchanged." Attitudes toward grief, grieving, and public tribute overlapped enough that they could and often did form the widest available channel for the emotional exchanges that could foster diplomatic relations. This semblance of similitude masked deep undercurrents of difference. If conventions concerning grief were mutually comprehensible between members of these cultures, they were also fiercely contested. At least in colonial Pennsylvania, the very streams in which British-American and native American emotional culture would seem to flow most closely together were more often dammed and divided.[65]

Of course, some British Americans approached the tasks of documenting and participating in native American condolence rituals more fully and more enthusiastically than others. If Hamilton represents one end of the diplomatic spectrum, Sir William Johnson (the royal Indian agent renowned then and since for the depth of his ties to the Iroquois) embodies the other. Johnson's records and those of his subordinates probably provide the best evidence of what native Americans considered essential to ritual grief and condolence. The notes recorded by Johnson's deputy George Croghan at a key meeting with the Iroquois are illustrative. Treating with representatives of the Six Nations in 1757 at a pivotal diplomatic moment (British prospects in the Seven Years War then looked bleak, and cementing their Iroquoian alliance was crucial), Croghan had his work cut out for him. Rising to the occasion, he offered, on behalf of Johnson and the government of Pennsylvania, what appears to have been a perfect enactment of traditional Indian condolence ceremonies, worthy of inclusion in a cross-cultural conduct manual (had such a thing existed).[66]

As host of the meeting, Croghan opened the proceedings with the expression of condolence. He began by wrapping a thin shawl of sensibility around them all, telling the assembled native Americans that both Johnson and the leaders of Pennsylvania were "truly sensible" of the Indians' "Affections, occasioned by the Deaths of many of your Counsellors and Warriors." According to his account, he emphasized that "they mix their Tears with Your's, and have desired me to condole with you, agreeable to the antient Custom of our Forefathers." Croghan made several notable moves in this opening statement, offering shared feeling to his native American listeners in terms that encompassed British- and native American traditions alike. Even as he invoked the value of sensibility, he explicitly claimed joint devotion to a ritual that was native American in origin. Further, he made a particular point of emphasizing the mixing of tears and the sharing of grief.[67]

Such expressions of mutuality were a key factor in native American condolence rituals. As a native American leader known as the Old Belt reportedly explained matters in 1756, "kind Expressions of Condolence" indicated that Indians and English had experienced "a common Loss [that] affected you as well as us, thereby signifying that we were one People and our Cause the same." Just as British Americans sought unity through sympathy, so native Americans expected condolence exchanges to serve similar bridging functions.[68]

Next in Croghan's minutes came a material offering. "I with these Strouds wrap up the Bodies of Your deceased Friends and bury them decently; covering their Graves with these Blankets and half Thicks." He added in his notes that he then "gave the goods." Native American protocol invariably called for the offering of "condolence presents" to those engulfed in grief. For example, when Conrad Weiser, Pennsylvania's official Indian translator, met to condole with the brother-in-law and successor of the deceased chief Lawachkamicky, he brought "some goods . . . to wipe off the Tears from Lawachkamicky's Friends and Family, and to cover his Grave according to Indian Fashion." For native Americans, condolences unaccompanied by presents were little more than empty words. The metaphorical action of wiping tears could be made concrete only by the offering of gifts. Conversely, British Americans considered death to be an occasion when emotion was everything and action availed nothing. Indeed, the insistence that, to be complete, condolences had to include both the sharing of feeling and the offering of assets sets native American understandings of sympathy and grief quite apart from British-American ones, much as they are couched in similar terms.[69]

Croghan ended the opening proceedings with a final symbolic gesture invariably included in native American condolence ceremonies: the removal of the mourner's grief. He told those assembled that with "the Dead decently buried, and their Graves covered, I with this Belt of Wampum wipe the Tears from your Eyes, and desire you may mourn no more." Again, the metaphoric removal of tears was made concrete by the offer of a belt of wampum, an action that set the seal on the offer of condolence. Unlike British Americans, who imposed on mourners the moral obligation to stanch their own tears and stem their grief themselves, native Americans counted the active ablation of grief among the most crucial duties of those offering condolences.[70]

If Croghan's desire that his hearers would mourn no more sounds slightly ambiguous on this removal, abundant evidence from similar sources makes the point more clearly. At the Albany Congress held in 1754, the English, under Johnson's guidance, told their Iroquois audience, "We condole You. . . . We wipe away all Tears from your Eyes and take away Sorrow from your Hearts." Along with the wiping of tears and taking of sorrow, the unusual use of "condole" in the transitive underscores the crucial element of action expected from those offering sympathy. To cite another instance, Scarroyady, a chief of the Oneida nation, brought the condolences of the Pennsylvania government to members of the Six Nations by promising to "remove sorrow and grief from their hearts, and wipe away the Tears from their Eyes." Clearly, the onus was on those offering condolence to put a stop to grief and end the period of mourning. Croghan's desire was not so much that his audience would impose an end to grief of their own accord as that his own efforts to eliminate it would meet with success.[71]

When British Americans sympathized with one another's grief, they invariably advised mourners to make strenuous efforts to master their own emotions, to submit their will to God's and to check their tears themselves. With the sole exception of public men and father figures, self-restraint in the face of grief was an overriding imperative for British-American mourners. Among native Americans, the opposite was true.

Mourners freely displayed their tears and forthrightly declared their grief in the expectation that those who condoled with them would take on the burden of taking their grief away. Far from being regarded as in any way sinful or indicating a failure of self-mastery, native Americans regarded the expression of grief as wholly acceptable and even desirable. Despite the pain of grief, native Americans valued its expression without qualification, precisely because of the occasion for social unity afforded by condolence exchanges.

Though they recognized the potential for diplomatic alliance that inhered in condolence exchanges, British Americans sought to avoid any implication that their participation in native American ceremonies involved capitulation to Indian imperatives. The key features of native American condolence ceremonies enacted by Croghan in 1757—the desire to honor the dead, the direct expressions of sadness and mingling of grief, provision of concrete material comfort to mourners, and active measures to remove the sorrow of mourners—were widely understood among members of the Pennsylvania government. Nevertheless, they were often only partially and imperfectly performed. Despite the real need to reinforce their Indian alliances during the Seven Years War, British Americans remained determined to keep the upper hand in their diplomatic relations. They expected native Americans to regard the British king as their metaphoric father and ultimate sovereign and sought to force them to defer to the king's colonial representatives as much as possible. Perhaps precisely because the social signals sent in the course of condoling with grief were so mutually intelligible, British Americans like Governor Hamilton often proved reluctant to pay tribute to native Americans as fully as the latter might have liked.[72]

Colonial governors and their representatives resisted complying with native American protocols whenever and however they could. One frequent tactic was to ridicule condolence rituals as insignificant, even ludicrous preambles to the conduct of serious business. On one occasion, Conrad Weiser complained that the Indians he had been sent to treat with had claimed that the British "had murdered above one hundred of their people without making Satisfaction for Them. . . . [and] made a long and tedious Relation using all the Indian Ceremonies and Phrases." Colonists routinely complained about wasting time on such condolences and were amused by the strange ways of an alien culture. Yet, their very reluctance to engage in such ceremonies is ample evidence that they fully understood the ceremony's significance and, indeed, that their understanding was augmented by the great importance that British Americans themselves attached to declarations of grief.[73]

Further telltale signs that British Americans critiqued native American condolence ceremonies largely to alleviate their discomfort at having to pay honor and tribute to those whom they wished to dominate can be seen in the ways they tried to cut corners in the performance of alliance rituals. Whenever they thought they could, they simply eliminated condolence exchanges from the opening ceremonies of diplomatic meetings. Thus Pennsylvania's governor in 1758, William Denny, opened a treaty at Easton, Pennsylvania, by declaring: "I wipe the Sweat and Dust out of your Eyes that you may see your Bretheren's Faces and look Chearful. With this String, I take all Bitterness out of your Breast." The decision to wipe dust and sweat, rather than tears, out of the eyes of his guests was significant. Denny's remarks carried the semblance of compliance with native American traditions; strings of wampum were offered and negative emotions removed from the breast. But it was far different to demand compliant cheerfulness from his negotiating partners rather than to offer them the fellowship of shared feeling and the tribute of condolence.[74]

Native Americans were quick to take note and find fault when British Americans attempted to wriggle out of participating in condolence ceremonies. Thus, one chief complained that, when "Nine Men were killed, he went, with three Belts and Tears in his Eyes . . . in order to have the matter made up, but he never received an Answer." Pennsylvanians quickly found that they ignored such rebukes at their own peril, as grief unassuaged and tribute unpaid cost dearly in the number of colonists captured or killed. On the other hand, native Americans promptly praised colonists who offered proper condolences, as did the Oneida chief who told an Indian agent, "You . . . wisely considered the antient Custom of our Forefathers in condoling with us, and mixing your Grief with Ours."[75]

Still, if condolence ceremonies could not be avoided outright, British Americans often sought subtle ways to abbreviate them so as to omit the elements with greatest symbolic resonance in British-American culture. Consider, Governor Hamilton's failure to express grief at his 1760 meeting with Teedyuscung. Hamilton was willing to wipe the tears from Teedyuscung's eyes and remove all grief from his heart, perhaps because such actions, while respecting native American protocols, also implied, according to British-American understandings, that the Indian lacked self-restraint and thus might be appropriately subjected to British-American mastery. He was even willing to provide "black Strouds, Handkerchiefs, and Stockings" to Teedyuscung, since these grave goods also placed the two in what Hamilton considered desirable positions of dominant patron and dependent client. What Hamilton would not do was express any sorrow for Teedyuscung's fallen fellows. That, and that alone, spelled deference and tribute to British Americans, and these the governor was determined to withhold.[76]

Furthermore, while British Americans sought military alliances with native Americans, they were by and large unwilling to accept the notion that the two groups might form one people. Comparing two sets of records made at a condolence ceremony held in Pennsylvania in 1756 reveals the reluctance many Pennsylvanians felt to entertain the idea of actual union with neighboring native Americans. In the official government minutes of the treaty, a Shawnee chief named Paxinosa was recorded saying, "Our Eyes are now running with Tears because of the Melancholy Sight; seeing our Country covered with Blood (we mean yours and ours)." Reading this, it appears that Paxinosa was simply declaring his grief on the occasion of both British-American and native American deaths.[77]

On the other hand, informal notes kept by the Quaker group known as the Friendly Association contain a minor variation in wording with implications of some magnitude. According to the Quakers, Paxinosa actually said: "Our Eyes are now running with Tears because of the Melancholy Sight. Seeing our Country covered with *our own* blood (we mean yours and ours)." The omission in the government record of those two little words, "our own," modifying "blood" greatly altered the intended meaning of Paxinosa's statement, shifting it from a statement uniting British Americans and native Americans as one people joined through grief, to one in which Paxinosa simply declared grief for the deaths of Pennsylvanians as well as for those of his own people.[78]

Calling attention to such subtleties may seem like hairsplitting. Certainly the British Americans who left them out attempted to argue as much. But when omissions and elisions all fall into the same general pattern and just happen to augment the status of those who orchestrate them, a healthy skepticism becomes warranted. For their part, native Americans were ever alert to such stratagems and demanded full compliance in condolence whenever they could.

Careful attention to the records of treaty negotiations can reveal the subterranean struggles involved as British-American colonists resisted following native American protocols for grief and native Americans insisted that they do so. In one dramatic example from Pennsylvania, the task is made easier by the possibility of comparing the notes taken by members of the Friendly Association with those provided in the official minutes of the Provincial Council: the meeting between the Pennsylvania governor William Denny and the Delaware leader Teedyuscung in November 1756.

The first mention of this meeting in the government minutes makes clear that Governor Denny was deeply preoccupied with how to establish dominance and compel deference in his dealings with Teedyuscung. Upon hearing from Conrad Weiser that Teedyuscung and his delegation sat ready at Easton, Pennsylvania, waiting to receive him, "the Governor expressed great dissatisfaction at [the thought of] this Journey, thought it rediculous to humour the Indians in such a manner, and that no Treaty should be held with them out of this City [Philadelphia]." Anxious to guard his own dignity, Denny loathed the idea of allowing Teedyuscung to dictate the place of their meeting. Nevertheless, five days later, he found himself face-to-face with Teedyuscung at Easton.[79]

It appears from the official record that, at their first meeting, Denny omitted the convention of offering condolence from his opening message. Was this a deliberate effort at retaliation? That Teedyuscung seized the initiative and himself offered condolences a couple of days later supports this inference. The Delaware leader declared: "The times are now [full of] . . . War and Distress. I am sorry for what has happened, and I now take and wipe the Tears from your Eyes, as there is great reason for Mourning." The governor felt forced to respond, yet he did not answer exactly in kind. Of Teedyuscung's expression of condolence, he said only, "I heartily thank you for it," then added, "I do likewise wipe your Eyes." Denny avoided any discussion of tears, speaking instead only of the wiping of eyes, and omitted any expression of sorrow, despite Teedyuscung's mentioning tears explicitly and saying directly that he was sorry.[80]

Then, suddenly, two days later, the Pennsylvania council minutes mention a ceremony of "condolance made on Captain Newcastle's Death," in which the governor provided "a String of Wampum, [and] eleven Black Strouds with some Handkerchiefs." Had the Delaware leader Newcastle died during the course of the conference? No. On the contrary, he and several of his associates had died in Philadelphia of smallpox nearly two weeks earlier. (Small wonder that Teedyuscung had refused to risk smallpox and travel all the way to the city!) Why, then, nine days into the treaty, was the governor abruptly moved to express his condolences and to declare, "I wipe away your Tears; I take the Grief from your Harts; I cover the Graves; eternal rest by with their Spirits"? The official record notes only that, following the governor's remarks, the Indians "spoke an Exortation, in the nature of a funeral Oration, after which Teedyuscung expressed to the Governor the great satisfaction given him at his condoling the Death of Captain Newcastle."[81]

Fortunately, notes made by the Friendly Association make clear that a power struggle lay at the heart of the governor's halting concessions and increasingly elaborate offers of condolence. On the final day of the conference

> the Governor . . . condoled with them on the Deaths of several of their People by the small Pox at Philadelphia and particularly of Capt. Newcastle . . . (they had in private remarked this being so long omitted, which according to their usual Concern for their deceased Friends would have been a very early part of their business if any of our People had dyed among them).

Far from resulting from a cross-cultural misunderstanding, the governor's failure to express his condolences arose from the fact that the social implications of grief were very much mutually comprehensible. While Denny bridled at the thought of being forced to show respect by "paying his respects," Teedyuscung defended his sense of prerogative and upbraided the governor for delaying the discussion of grief. Because the central issue at the negotiation was the cessation of Delaware attacks and the return of Pennsylvania prisoners, Denny could hardly afford to offend his diplomatic adversary, much as he wished to assert his own dignity. Indeed, in a letter accompanying a copy of treaty minutes sent to royal agent William Johnson, Denny fumed, "I now sit down to . . . acquaint you that I have, to my great Mortification, been obliged to go to one of the Frontier Counties, and there hold Conferences with the Delaware Chief Teedyuscung, which I would have been very glad to have been excused from."[82]

Such struggles continued throughout the war, the timing and content of condolence ceremonies often serving as coded signals of fluctuations in the relative strengths of the negotiating parties. At times, British Americans voluntarily followed Indian protocol to the letter; at some points they omitted key elements of condolence without any obvious opposition from native Americans. Most often, members of each group maintained a continuous tug-of-war, of which only tenuous evidence now remains.

Reading of another treaty held at Easton in 1758, this time between Governor Denny and the Cayuga chief Tokaaio, one can't help wondering whether Denny was up to his old tricks when he failed to include condolences in his opening ceremonies. The dry notation five days into the conference—"The Governors were charged by Tokaaio with having omitted some things"—was followed immediately by the transcript of a new speech in which Denny asserted, "With this String of Wampum we condole with you for the loss of your Wise Men."[83]

British Americans were not alone in regarding the withholding of grief as a failure to pay tribute. In both cultures, expressions of condolence conveyed a key kind of respect, their omission a sure sign of social division. Pennsylvania's leading figures were no more eager to engage in the performance of tribute for native Americans they sought to define as lesser subjects of their own king than they were to tolerate tears for lower-ranking members of their own society. When forced by their own strategic aims to participate in condolence rituals, they fudged the details wherever they could and focused on performing those aspects of Indian practices that could be read in ironic ways before British-American audiences. Oftentimes, they believed they had got away with such underhanded efforts to undermine native American claims to authority. Following his contretemps with Tokaaio, Denny crowed: "I flatter myself every thing [was] done on my part to their Satisfaction. They solemnly promise, immediately . . . to restore to us all the Captives they have taken from us." This was empty flattery indeed. Delayed condolences were reciprocated with a diplomatic stalemate, followed by the renewal of open hostilities. Pennsylvanians would be forced to wait seven years more before all those captives that native Americans had adopted to replace their own dead would be repatriated and reincarnated once more as colonial British Americans.[84]

Of course, most Pennsylvania colonists would have had little occasion to engage in Indian condolence ceremonies themselves. However, the issues of war and peace that such ceremonies helped resolve touched all members of society, from frontier settlers to city dwellers. Tommy Bradford, released at last from the College of New Jersey in 1761, was one such person. As he settled into work at his father's Philadelphia print shop, Tommy received a letter from an old school chum, John Lathrop, explaining that he had embarked on missionary work among the Indians and commenting on affairs in Pennsylvania. Lathrop began by telling Tommy, "My chief business at present is to teach the poor ignorant savages." As far

"Allowed to Mourn, but . . . Bound to Submit"

as these two educated young colonists were concerned, savage ignorance was the presumptive state of any Indian. Continuing his critique, Lathrop asked, "Altho Indian cruelty appears in so shocking a light in your parts, ought we not to endeavour to Christianize those who will receive it, especially those who have always been true and faithful Friends to the crown of Great Britain?"[85]

Reluctant to school their own emotional expression according to native American rules for ceremonial social exchange, British Americans preferred to see themselves as the only ones who could usefully impart cultural knowledge. Like Lathrop and Bradford, they focused on opposing Indian cruelty rather than on acknowledging the elements of Indian culture that spoke to sensibility. They could thus avoid recognizing the legitimacy of native American demands for condolence. Though, logically, condolence ceremonies could have provided an important point of convergence between Indians and colonists, most British Americans sought, rather, to distinguish between savage traditions and civilized customs. They attempted, thereby, to avoid bowing to Indian authority and to bolster instead their own claims to cultural superiority.

Grief, the Self, and Social Worth

Expressions of grief drew extensive comment in both British-American and native American cultures as a direct result of the manifold messages the emotion could send. Both groups saw opportunities for the formation of social bonds in the exchange of grief and condolence. Because open statements of grief could be offered as tokens of tribute, they were highly sought after by all of Pennsylvania's inhabitants. However, with the exception of the Society of Friends, most British-American men strove to reserve such public recognition for European male heads of household and leading public men. In all other cases, they sought to restrain displays of grief, on the several grounds that unchecked sorrow was a sign of willful selfishness, of sinful rebellion against God, of social subversion, and/or of an uncouth inability to properly marshal one's own emotions. In the case of native Americans, they often feigned failures of comprehension and simply declined to engage in those "savage" practices that corresponded to their own forms of respect. British and native Americans alike well understood the transgressive and even aggressive potential of grief. If proper tribute was not offered the dead, then the only way to repair their loss was through the taking of war prisoners. This is just what the Oneida

Scarroyady meant when he explained, "The French joked with Us on the Death of [our] King, and laughed, but We shall make them cry before We have done with them." For Indians, tears ignored could quickly turn to anger and a cause for action.[86]

The same nexus of anger and grief applied to Pennsylvania women, black and white, though their options were rather less ample than Indians'. As we have seen earlier, female expressions of anger were extremely rare. Unable to lay claim to the social honor conveyed by resentment, women were more apt to rely on mourning when seeking to have their grievances redressed, just the tactic employed by Tace Bradford, with at least some outward semblance of success. In a society in which women had few options but to accept the authority of men, women had need of forms of resistance that challenged specific social conditions while acknowledging their general submission. Meanwhile, in order to defend their own authority, British-American men had to keep a close eye out for potentially subversive assertions of sorrow on the part of all those whom they wished to subordinate.[87]

Yet, for all these points of commonality, the negotiations of authority implicit in the regulation of grief were decidedly different between British Americans and native Americans. Where the former saw sympathy as passive, the latter insisted that condolences be active. These differing expectations reflected crucial distinctions in native American and British-American understandings of the self. While British Americans emphasized self-mastery and submission in the face of grief, native Americans saw less need to submerge the self. Troubled by neither Protestant notions of sin and submission nor by a rising interest in individualism, native Americans readily accepted expressions of grief and placed emphasis on active offers of comfort rather than passive encouragement of self-restraint.

In the dominant British-American view, a lost individual was irreplaceable, grief at death largely irremediable. Though sympathy offered some solace, a mourner's only sure recourse was to trust in God and turn from grief. The sole exception came when the death of a father (figure) was in question, a person whose public role could and should be refilled. In this one instance, grief was permissible—precisely because it could be counted on to abate in due course. On the death of George II, Governor Hamilton made this point explicit when he stated that nothing "could alleviate the Grief which every good Subject must have felt upon this Mournful Occasion but the Consideration, that the Scepter hath devolved to a Prince" worthy to succeed him. Open grief at the death of a British-American man was allowable because, before long, the need to mourn would be obviated by the appearance of a new authority figure, ready to fill the vacancy created by death.[88]

One might argue that Indians, in their belief that the dead could be replaced (whether ritually through condolence presents or actually through adoption), set less store on the value of people as individuals. However, colonists' belief in the self as unique did not necessarily impart greater value to any particular life, a point that must be appreciated if we are to understand the true impact of Indians' and colonists' contrasting attitudes. In fact, Indians viewed the social roles played by *all* members of society as important and found it critical that each and every opening in the social order be filled. Not only did Indians enjoy greater latitude for self-expression on the occasion of death; they assumed that every member of society was worth such unrestrained grief. When Indians offered shared grief with colonists, they were sure to include that they were "sorry, from the Bottom of our Hearts, for the Death of your Men, Women, and Children," not restricting their words to those leading men that British Americans would have deemed worthy of such public tribute. They expected a similar capaciousness in the condolences offered them by British Americans, and they got it, as when members of the Pennsylvania council told them, "We condole with you for the loss of your Wise Men, and for the warriors . . . and likewise for your Women and Children; and we cover their Graves decently."[89]

In important ways, then, the native American approach to grief and condolence allowed for the relative dilution of authority. Indian condolence ceremonies reflected a worldview in which a relative diminution of the unique worth of any individual person allowed for an enhanced appreciation of the social importance of the roles filled by each. At the same time, the permittance of unrestrained mourning by and for all allowed for a measure of individual valuation and a degree of unfettered expression not possible under the British-American system.

Colonial men, by contrast, envisioned themselves as the administrators of absolute divine power and, as such, held themselves largely exempt from its strictures, whereas women promoted a view of God as a flexible figure responsive to the needs of his believers and willing to negotiate the terms of his authority—terms that were to apply equally to all. Men and women each had a great deal invested in adhering to distinctly different models of divine authority. For, if God could complete the triangle of grief, he never spoke directly to mourners and therefore could safely serve as proxy while men and women argued their own interests. Grief provided an arena in which British Americans could address tensions over earthly authority with the security of abstraction.

The need for subordinates like Tace Bradford to find a way to meet expectations for emotional sensitivity while avoiding accusations of selfishness, to negotiate the terms while accepting the fact of their submission, left them little room in which to maneuver. Only by generalizing her grief to include the death of a much-admired public figure was Tace able to give free reign to her sorrow over the loss of her friend Jesse Leech. By insisting that her main end in having the brother she called "my comforter, my all" return home was to alleviate the sympathetic sadness she felt on his behalf, she was able to pursue her aim of arranging his return. She told Tommy in August 1760, "Mr. Rush says you intend to try to stay at home for good and all when you come I shall use all my interest with Dady and Mamy to let you . . . for believe me my brother I would rather be miserable my whole life than you should be so one day." The problem was that, ultimately, the influence that Tace's grief gained her was slight indeed.[90]

By the following summer, of course, Tommy was home for good. Yet Tommy himself seems to have found his homecoming to be but a pyrrhic victory. No sooner was he once again settled under the family roof than he found himself sent out to work in his father's shop. Apparently in response to a new set of complaints from Tommy, a school friend wrote in 1762:

> In your last you informed me how often you covit the sweet repose that we enjoy . . . I am determined never more to open my mouth by way of complaint again, for my judgment is fully convinced a college life is the happyest part of time I shall ever spend. I'll assure you I have put a double price upon it since I read your letter.

In the end, William Bradford's eventual acquiescence to the desires of his children in no way deviated from the lines of his own original plans to educate his son to assist in the family print business. No doubt he remained satisfied that he had effectively exercised his authority for the greater good. Ultimately, the social conventions surrounding grief in British America were heavily stacked in favor of those with the strongest original claims to authority. But, as we shall see, the grievers who profited the most from shows of sadness also drew, alternatively, on anger.[91]

8

Ruling Passions

Surveying the Borders of Humanity
on the Pennsylvania Frontier

News of a massacre on the frontier flared through the Pennsylvania Provincial Council on December 19, 1763, just weeks after Governor
John Penn had been sworn into office. Spreading the tale to the colonial
Assembly, Penn described the "wicked and inhuman action" thus: a "Number of people well armed and mounted" had galloped into the Christian-
ized settlement of Conestoga, where a small group of peaceful Indians
lived, and "in cool blood, barbarously killed Six of the Indians settled
there . . . burning all their Houses." He urged the Assembly to join him in
taking measures to combat the "Fury" of that "lawless Party." Nevertheless,
days later, the same frontiersmen managed to finish off the few Indians
who had escaped their initial attack, tracking the Indians to a workhouse
where the government had hidden them for their protection, and slaying
them where they found them. Condemnation from the Assembly came
quickly. It declared that it was with "an Abhorrence altogether inexpressible" that it considered the fate of " 'these poor Creatures' . . . barbarously
butchered by a sett of Ruffians, whose audacious cruelty is checked by no
sentiment of Humanity." Elite Philadelphians agreed that events had exposed the frontier settlers as beings beneath the level of humanity.[1]

The Paxton Boys, as the instigators from Lancaster County came to be
called, were quick to counter such charges. Two of their representatives,
Matthew Smith and James Gibson, retorted that the Indians had been
killed out of necessity, in retaliation for "barbarous Cruelties" they had
inflicted on frontier settlers, cruelties that were themselves "shocking to

human Nature" and enough to "pierce every Heart, but that of the hardened perpetrators or their Abbettors." They argued that the Indians, not they themselves, should be depicted as being something less than human. Indeed, they declared, "We cannot but be filled with Indignation to hear this action of ours painted in the most odious and detestable Colors, as if we had inhumanly murdered," when they had "only killed . . . known enemies." So far as Smith and Gibson were concerned, accusations of inhumanity aimed at suffering frontiersmen fell far wide of their legitimate Indian mark. A decade of imperial warfare, culminating in a British victory over the French, had left many Pennsylvania war captives remaining among native Americans; meanwhile, a renewed Indian war in the backcountry was creating new captives and casualties daily. Yet the eastern elite did little to address the situation.[2]

Nor did backcountry settlers stop short at defending their own humanity and denigrating that of native Americans. They confronted their elite critics with the counteraccusation that it was the city dwellers who lacked "any Sentiments of humanity or any Bowels of Compassion for the miserable." Frontier families denounced the comfortable and complacent urban elite who seemed to greet tidings of torture, captivity, and death among their own countrymen with callous indifference. Indeed, those who made apologies for the Paxton Boys' conduct asserted that "those very Persons who are so hardened and destitute of the common Feeling of Humanity" as to ignore conditions in the backcountry "would, We doubt not, be softened, had they but shared with us in the lightest Parts of our Sufferings." Elite leaders who slung accusations of inhumanity at the people had to expect that such criticisms would be flung right back.[3]

To complicate matters further still, many elite government leaders actually agreed that at least some Indians were inhuman. Even Benjamin Franklin, the newspaper publisher and Assembly member who declared that he was appalled by "the cruel and inhuman . . . Act committed in the Heart of this Province on . . . *Indians,* who have lived peaceably and inoffensively among us," added that he was "far from desiring to lessen the laudable Spirit of Resentment in my Countrymen against those [Indians] now at War with us, so far as it is justified by their Perfidy and Inhumanity." In the wake of the massacres, aspersions of inhumanity and insensibility, allegations that one group or another lacked the basic emotional capacities that defined what it meant to be human, flew among all the colony's inhabitants.[4]

The Paxton uprising let loose anxieties that had long haunted colonial

Pennsylvania, augmenting widespread arguments about the nature of humanity that had mounted ever since the onset of the Seven Years War in 1754. Of particular interest was the question whether emotional capacities were constant across cultures. Should emotion be regarded as innate and basic to all human beings, thus potentially equal in all? Or might emotional capacities naturally occur with greater or lesser frequency among different ethnic or national groups? Alternatively, if emotions were largely a product of culture, might they actually be manifested more fully in the few who learned to cultivate them than in the masses who were unaware of the desirability of doing so? What role did and should different religions play in the promotion and regulation of emotion? Ever simmering in the colonial milieu, such concerns came to a boil in crises.

Pennsylvanians, from assemblymen to Paxton settlers, effectively embraced a universal model of emotion every time they launched arguments based on the "sentiments of humanity." On the face of it, this model of emotion promoted an optimistic and egalitarian view of human nature. Implicit in invocations of the "common feelings of humanity" was the acknowledgment that all human beings had the capacity for feelings recognized as humane. Yet, as these records of insult and invective show, Pennsylvanians often acknowledged the universal nature of emotion only in the breach. Indeed, they argued that, if the emotions essential to humane action could be cultivated and controlled, then some groups could make higher claims to humanity than others. These were more than abstract issues. During the controversy that ensued after the Conestoga Indian killings, the definition of humanity made all the difference between those who could claim to have taken revenge as innocent victims and those who would be condemned as the perpetrators of unwarranted aggression. In an age when emotion was widely accepted as the best barometer of morality, humanity gained cultural and conceptual importance as the embodiment of moral emotion in action.

Broadly speaking, eighteenth-century Pennsylvanians' discussions of the emotions necessary for humanity were shaped by three major issues: gentility, civility, and masculinity. When Assembly members denounced the Paxton insurgents not merely as cruel but as "audaciously cruel," they defined their merciless attack as a violent failure of moral feeling that was also a presumptuous defiance of decorum. At the same time, elites kept up their critiques on other fronts as well. When printer Benjamin Franklin deplored the lack of "Sense, Spirit and Humanity" among those who attacked the Conestoga Indians, he went so far as to brand them as

"CHRISTIAN WHITE SAVAGES." He derided them explicitly for acting to "the eternal Disgrace of their Country and Colour" and demanded, "Do we come to *America* to learn and practice the Manners of *Barbarians?*" Not content with critiques that cast aspersions on the Paxton Boys' gentility and civility, he concluded with an extra gibe at their masculinity, denouncing those "Unmanly Men! . . . who have already given . . . bloody Proofs of their Inhumanity and Cruelty."[5]

Elite leaders attempted to lay claim to exalted humanity on the basis of their emotive performance of class, racial or ethnic, and gender superiority. Yet their efforts were resisted, contested, and co-opted at every turn. Political pamphlets generated on all sides of the Paxton controversy, alongside official records of government correspondence and diplomatic exchanges, reveal the degree to which emotional language defined all people's understandings of events. At a time when colonial Pennsylvania was approaching its peak of social and political instability—with the aftershocks of the Seven Years War reverberating against the first tremors of Revolutionary resistance—questions about the universality of human emotions had the potential to shatter society irrevocably or, alternatively, to cement it solidly together on the strength of a new foundation.[6]

Discerning Gentility: The Senseless Banditti versus the Gentle and Easy

From the first, the violent attack at Conestoga was regarded in Philadelphia as being at least as much an assault on provincial power as a violation of Indian persons. Discussing the situation with the Assembly, Governor Penn ran the two things together when he described the action as a "horrid Scene of Barbarity, and [an] insolent and daring violation of the Laws." The adjective "insolent" underscored how much the frontiersmen's impertinent disrespect for authority rankled. The Assembly eagerly agreed with the governor's assessment and stressed the importance of "repressing the dangerous insolence of tumultuous Insurgents, who, guided by a blind rage, undertake by open force to controul the conduct of the Administration." Immediate efforts to discredit the legitimacy of the Paxton Boys' action included denigration of their emotional comportment. In the quest to shore up their own right to rule, elite leaders relied heavily on their knowledge of proper conventions of emotional expression and control.[7]

Because of the struggles surrounding the Seven Years War, Pennsylvanians had already expended a great deal of thought and spilled a great deal of ink defining the kinds of emotions that characterized gentility. William Smith—the provost of the College of Philadelphia who sat ever ready to wet his quill and opine on any public issue—summed up the consensus view in 1755 when he urged his fellow colonists to strive for emotional moderation in the pursuit of genteel advancement. "We either grovel beneath the true spirit of *Freedom;* or, if we aim at Spirit, we are borne by a sullen Ferocity to the other Extreme. We are yet too much Strangers to that rational Medium, which is founded on a more enlarged and refined Turn of Sentiment." If those of refined sentiments avoided emotional extremes, then the perpetrators of the Paxton uprising could more easily be ridiculed for inadequate emotional regulation.[8]

As Governor Penn and members of the Assembly chattered among themselves about the emotional transgressions of the insurgents, they careened between criticisms of the killers as excessively and uncontrollably passionate and characterizations of them as utterly emotionless. Thus, Penn's initial description of the attack had both decried the "Fury" of the "lawless Party" (that is, their fierce and frenzied anger) and included the claim that the Paxton men had killed "in cool blood" (without any emotion at all). Benjamin Franklin echoed this language in his own account, asserting that the attackers had "entered with the utmost Fury in their Countenances" and gone straight to work with their hatchets, so that all of the Indians present, "Men, Women, and little Children—were every one inhumanly murdered!—in cold Blood!" Franklin's exclamations were repeated in turn by another pamphleteer who affirmed, "An enraged Body of People . . . came to the Indian Town and killed and scalped six of them, in cool Blood." Genteel critics saw no inconsistency in such contradictory charges of fiery hot anger and icy cold blood, since each made the same point, that the Paxton Boys were incapable of achieving desirable emotional moderation.[9]

Critiques of the extremes of frontiersmen's anger constituted the most crucial element of elite efforts to discredit their emotions and discount their concerns. Charles Read, a New Jersey justice with Philadelphia connections, summed up neatly the attitude of the upper sort when he claimed, "Weak Minds are apt to be in extraordinary manner inflamed, and get into violent Ferments, on reading an Article in the Gazette of a few Persons being destroyed by *Indians;* yet these very Persons will with little or no Emotion, run over an Article of a Battle between two Armies, where Thousands fell on a Side." Unpredictable, irrational, and immoderate anger was the mark of weak-minded commoners. Elaborating on this theme, the author of another pamphlet declared, "In your Anger you have slain Man. . . . Cursed be your Anger, for it was fierce; and your Wrath for it was cruel." Anger itself was not the issue: only intemperate anger was at fault. Or, as Franklin put it, the problem was that the Paxton Boys had retained "a brutal undistinguishing Resentment against *all Indians*."[10]

According to elite rhetoric, it was the responsibility of those of a "refined Turn of Sentiment," those able to distinguish between different varieties of anger and make nice distinctions in its expression, to attempt to rein in the rage and fury of those one writer dismissed as "angry, giddy, violent and revengeful People." As another particularly confident and condescending member of the putative elite explained matters:

> The Lower Sort of People are very imitative of their Superiors.—They watch their Motions, Looks and Eyes:—If therefore the more sensible Part of you would openly avow your Disapprobation of these Measures, you will find this Rage and Clamour will soon subside; These People will disperse; they will crumble like the Dust, and disappear (at least in a hostile Manner) like the Snow that melted yesterday.

Transparently self-serving as such wishful thinking was, elites did not hesitate to assure and reassure themselves that events at Paxton arose, not from any legitimate concerns on the part of backcountry folk facing renewed Indian threats after years of frontier warfare, but rather from the uncontrolled anger of lower sorts in need of a firm hand and clear instruction in matters of anger management. This writer's easy equation of superiority and sensibility highlights how important emotion had become as a mark of elite status.[11]

Those presumptive elites asserted that their superiority was moral as well as social. Their gentility supposedly assured the moderation of their anger, and the careful control of their anger had a refining effect on their status. Such was the clear assumption of the writer who asked, "Will not the good Inhabitants of this Province, and all well-disposed People, awaken to Resentment, and put themselves in Readiness to repel" "the Fury and Rage of an incensed, riotous and lawless Mob"? "Resentment," the refined word for the restrained anger of the good sort, could best counter the rage and fury of the base, the undisciplined anger of the mob.[12]

Defenders of the Paxton Boys attempted to expose their detractors' emotional rhetoric as nothing more than empty tactical flourishes. Referring explicitly to Franklin's "cold Blood" and "utmost Fury" passage, a pamphlet attributed to Thomas Barton (himself a tested veteran of earlier pamphlet skirmishes during the Seven Years War) mocked such critiques. After observing that Franklin's *"Narrative* proceeds with all the *Pathos* of Language and Expression" in describing the attack, Barton commented caustically, "I would be glad to know who could give this Gentlemen so very particular an Account," given that the only eyewitnesses to the event were the slain Indians and the killers themselves. Still, the colony's leaders were undeterred by such objections. If the threat to their authority was to be met, they could not afford to neglect their exclusive claim to genteel comprehension of the nuances of emotional control.[13]

Faced with such widespread assumptions about their proper social place and the dangers of daring to step out of it, the Paxton rebels demonstrated a remarkable facility with elite emotional codes, giving lie to elite claims at a monopoly on such cultural knowledge. They understood completely that, as much mileage as eastern leaders got from condemning the immorality and inhumanity of the Indian massacre, the real issue at hand was the threat of social upheaval and the implied challenge to elite power created by the attack. Determined to salvage the situation, the insurgents decided to march to Philadelphia to press their case in person. The first written representation of events prepared by the Paxton rebels and presented at Philadelphia in February 1764 (some seven weeks after the initial attack) displayed a remarkable savvy concerning issues of sentiment as well as of status.[14]

In "The Declaration of the Injured Frontier Inhabitants" the two Paxton spokesmen who signed it, Matthew Smith and James Gibson, sought to disarm critics who claimed they were intent on subverting the government and to dispel worries that they were bent on defying the standing social order. Thus, they began their declaration with the "confess[ion]" that "nothing but necessity itself could induce . . . or justify" conduct such as theirs, "as it bears an Appearance of flying in the Face of Authority." They hastened to affirm that, all appearances to the contrary, they were, "to a Man . . . loyal subjects to the best of Kings, our rightful Sovereign King George the third." Even as they moved to confront their elite antagonists directly, they insisted that they did so without desire for social disruption.[15]

At the same time, frontier folk sought to defend the limited status they did enjoy as British subjects. Significantly, their assurances of loyalty and respect for authority were followed in short order by repeated assertions that measured resentment (*not* more violent varieties of anger) was the actuating force behind their actions. The Paxton rebels understood that restrained anger could command respect. They explained that grievances had "enflamed with resentment the Breasts of a number, and urged them to the disagreeable Evidence of it they ha[d] been constrained to give" and demanded, "Can it be thought strange" that repeated attacks by Indians "should awaken the resentment of a people grossly abused . . . ?" While the Paxton Boys understood the danger of open rebellion, they also appreciated the subtle social signals encoded in the vocabulary of anger.[16]

This comprehension is confirmed by the fact that the only other synonym for anger they used in their first declaration was "indignation," which implies the anger of one treated to unmerited contempt. Thus, they complained that Indians they regarded as "embittered Enemies" they "saw with indignation, cherished and caressed as dearest Friends." By invoking the language of resentment and indignation, and avoiding more inflammatory terms for anger, like "fury" or "rage," they displayed their determination to affirm the dignity of their discontent.[17]

With the arrival of the Paxton rebels on the outskirts of Philadelphia, defenders of their position were quick to point out their calm deportment and praise their emotional moderation. One sympathetically disposed city resident noted, "Instead of finding them a senseless rude and lawless Banditti, they found them a well behav'd and orderly People." According to this observer, the insurgents were neither cold-blooded nor weak-minded, neither lacking in emotional sensitivity nor subject to uncouth anger. Another favorable commentator broached the issue of gentility even more directly: "They were found a selected Band of Gentlemen . . . Their Demands were too reasonable to be rejected . . . [and] they were Gentle and easy." Such impressions were important. For in the days and weeks following the initial outbreak of violence, the governor, the Assembly, and assorted elite critics had gone further than simply penning elaborate denunciations of the Paxton rebels' deeds; they had also called for their arrest and prosecution on charges of murder. If the frontiersmen were to escape punishment and obtain redress for their complaints, they needed to position themselves as both respectful and respectable.[18]

To employ emotions coded as refined, the Paxton rebels had to assert not only that they had not given way to any anger more extreme than resentment but also to avow that they had turned to anger of any kind only as a rational last resort. Before resentment came grief; backcountry settlers and their defenders claimed that they had long suffered in silence and then begged sympathy in the most suppliant manner, before their anger finally burst forth. In the formal declaration made in February 1764, they said that they might even have continued to grieve "in silence for our abandoned and enslaved Brethren among the Heathens" and never mentioned their distress at all, had not continued Indians raids—along with the apparent indifference of the colony's urban elite—provided "still more flagrant Reasons of Complaint." Such claims were intended to undercut the idea that their statements and actions were either precipitous or presumptuous.[19]

Such a switch, from anger to grief, demonstrated a sophisticated emotional and social agility. By stressing their great grief and their reasoned efforts to refrain from expressing it, frontiersmen tried to shift the moral burden of proof over to the elite, to the leaders who had failed in their responsibility to show compassion for the plight of their suffering subjects. Portraying themselves as a "distressed, bereft, injured Frontier" allowed them to fault government officials for their failure to respond. These claims were quickly taken up by busy pamphlet writers, as eager to gain political advantage from the Paxton controversy as to defend the lives and reputations of the rioters. One Paxton apologist demanded in the voice of the frontiersmen themselves:

> Who could suspect that the Men in Power refused to believe the Sufferings of their fellow Subjects[?] Unnatural as this appears, yet many of us were but too well convinced of it and constrained to believe it and mourn in Silence over our hard Fate. When we applied to the Government for Relief, the far greater part of our Assembly . . . made light of our Sufferings.

Here again, backcountry settlers were depicted as virtuous and self-denying folk. Swamped with grief, not anger, they strived against their own tears while their so-called superiors betrayed the very lack of sentiment they so often ascribed to the lower sorts.[20]

As time went by, without any further outbreaks of violent unrest, political unity among competing elites in Philadelphia began to splinter. Some political wags began to see greater and greater advantage in using the short-lived Paxton crisis as a pretext for questioning the continuing dominance of the Quakers, who had so long and so decisively influenced the conduct of the Assembly. So attractive was the rhetorical pose of silent grief that it was adopted by yet another pamphleteer, writing months after the Paxton Boys first wrote their declaration:

It has long been my unhappy Lot to be a Spectator of the Distresses and Sufferings of my Fellow Subjects; my heart has often bled for them;—and I should still have continued a secret Mourner for what I had not Power to redress, had not the unaccountable Conduct of your City Quakers provoked me to speak my Sentiments.

Significantly, this writer again set the moral turpitude of urban dwellers against the virtuous example of the frontier folk, who would rather suffer silently than express emotions out of turn. The intended conclusion clearly was that only when the powerful failed to live up to their end of the social compact by offering compassion would the ordinary sort even think of giving voice to their grief, much less allowing it to mount into anger.[21]

If elite leaders greeted the news of Indian massacres with an iron determination to assert their dominance and to reinforce their exclusive claims to refinement, the Paxton rebels equally well understood the stakes of the contest and the rules of play. In essence, the rules allowed commoners to play a kind of double game, overtly expressing their deference even as their deft manipulations of the nuances of emotional expression covertly asserted their right to have their position respected and their concerns addressed. It should come as no surprise then, that, in the event, the governor's published comments on the Paxton Boys avoided referring to any brand of anger whatsoever. While he readily referred to the "fury of the rioters" in his private letters and conversations, Penn's published proclamation remarked only that the killings had occurred "without the least Reason or Provocation, in cool blood." Among themselves, elites might bandy about descriptions of anger that made clear the frontiersmen were guilty of the worst kind of passionate excess. Rather than argue the fine points in public, the governor simply implied that the rebels could lay claim to no feelings at all. Far easier to paint an all-or-nothing picture than to stoop to direct debates with commoners about the details of elite emotion codes.[22]

Defining Civility: Christian Indians, Christian White Savages, and the Sentiments of Humanity

Still, so stark was the picture elites wished to paint of the depravity of the murderous band of backcountry rebels that a simple emphasis on issues of refinement would not suffice. Instead, they used critiques of the frontiersmen's lack of feeling not only to scorn their lack of gentility but also to deny their very civility. As Charles Read argued:

> Such an inhuman murder as that at *Lancaster,* can only serve to convince the World, that there are among us Persons more savage than *Indians* themselves. To be cruel in War, and while the Blood is in a high, Ferment is frequent; but to assemble at a Distance, to march many Miles with Intent, in cool Blood, to butcher defenceless People . . . was an amazing Depravation of every Sense of Virtue and Humanity.

Indictments like this went beyond the simple assertion that the Paxton Boys were uncultivated and uncouth; they made the harsher argument that they were ungovernable and undeserving of recognition among moral men. To be branded as "CHRISTIAN WHITE SAVAGES," in Franklin's phrase, or as people "more savage than the Indians themselves," in Read's, was to be denied the right to participate in the essential workings of the colonial world.[23]

Philosophical discussions about the hallmarks of civilized versus savage emotion could have direct political repercussions: backcountry protesters marched on Philadelphia specifically to demand greater inclusion in the colonial government and a greater say in frontier policy. Since representation in the Assembly was disproportionately weighted toward the three eastern counties the Quakers controlled, frontier folk were vastly underrepresented. Their demands to be recognized as people of civility carried with them a strong desire for fuller participation in the polity. Meanwhile, the denial of their civility, by the governor as well as by assemblymen and their allies, carried with it a corresponding refusal to consider their political demands.

Many Pennsylvanians took for granted that the line between savagery and civility was drawn by Christian feeling. This assumption fueled much of the criticism eastern leaders aimed at the frontier settlers, leading one anti-Paxton pamphleteer to proclaim, for example, that no "Christian can here tell of so horrid a Crime as that committed at *Lancaster* without the deepest Sorrow mixt with Resentment." According to this school of thought, true Christianity fostered the kinds of feelings that supported humanity and civility, whereas lesser religions, or the utter absence of religion, led to inhumanity and incivility. Elites claimed that one central problem with the Paxton rebels was their "either not knowing or not distinguishing between Savage Indians, Heathen Indians, or Christian

Indians." They supposedly did not understand that different degrees of religion went along with varied levels of civility, rendering Christian Indians far from savage—and making settlers judged to be bad Christians potentially beyond the bounds of the civil.[24]

The backcountry and the city were divided not only along broad lines of class but also by ethnicity and by religious denomination. The majority of city inhabitants, English in origin, claimed membership in the Society of Friends or the Anglican Church, whereas the substantial contingent of Philadelphia Presbyterians had been divided for decades between Old Side and New Side adherents. The disgruntled frontiersmen, by contrast, were predominantly Scots-Irish Presbyterians with New Light leanings along with Germans of diverse denominations. Backcountry folk were acutely aware of efforts to deny them membership in the civilized Anglo-Christian community, even as native American converts were being offered easy entry. The Paxton rebels argued strenuously that, in conducting colonial policy, "Quakers ha[d] been partial, and shewn more real Affection for Enemy Savages than for their fellow Subjects, of certain Denominations." If the Paxton uprising was a social revolt, it was, in some sense, a religious upheaval as well.[25]

There *was* something in the charge that Quakers and their supporters reserved special contempt for frontier Presbyterians, spurning their brand of feeling and refusing to acknowledge them as true Christians. Some writers argued, essentially, that, while all people had the seeds of civility within them, humane emotions had to be carefully nurtured with the waters of pure Christianity. In this vision, Presbyterianism was a potential source of pollution. As one writer of an anti-Paxton pamphlet explained matters, it was only *"Pathos,* that w[ould] rouse the Christian in the Reader, and excite in him an endeavour to prevent the effusion of human Blood." According to this line of argument, Christianity and humanity connected fundamentally to sensibility. This writer went on to praise Franklin, the author who invoked the phrase "CHRISTIAN WHITE SAVAGES," as a "Gentleman of Integrity, of impartial Judgment, and of Sentiments untainted by infectious P——y." Few would have had any trouble decoding this claim that the emotions taught in the Presbytery were different from, and inferior to, the feelings that characterized other forms of Christianity. It was just such insulting attitudes that led pro-Paxton writers to assert, "To talk against Presbyterians as such . . . is the Effect either of Malice and Party Spirit, or Nonsense."[26]

Faced with such attitudes, the Paxton rebels elaborated their anti-

Indian rhetoric. The best way to counter accusations of savagery was to highlight the depravity of the "real" savages. Thus one writer declared that the massacred Indians were nothing more than "members of a Savage Nation, who Wolf-like for these many Years have been Murdering and Destroying Poor defenceless People." Still, Assembly-allied authors took forceful stances against blanket denunciations of all Indians as savages. They argued that the practice of reflexively including all Euro-Americans within the bounds of civility, while automatically excluding all native Americans, flew in the face of available evidence. Responding to pro-Paxton rhetoric that argued that native Americans were more like beasts than like men, one pamphlet writer went so far as to "conclude that the spiritual instinct, which the animal part hath [is] a Sympathy which binds the whole Creature to act for the Safety of his Neighbor as that of himself." This author argued, in essence, that the sympathetic emotions that formed the basis of religious spirituality were so intrinsic to all God's creatures as to be found even in animals. Not even the Paxtonites' accusations that Indians were wolflike murderers could induce critics of the Paxton Boys to doubt either native Americans' basic capacity for humanity or the right of Christian Indian converts to claim a place in civilized society.[27]

On the contrary, the author of this pamphlet asserted that the Paxton rebels alone, by dint of their violent actions, placed themselves beyond the pale. Anyone who would "murder [his] Neighbours in cool Blood" "omits that, which is the most assential part of his Duty in civil Society, viz. The Safety or Preservation of his Fellow Creatures Life." Again and again backcountry folk were denied not merely the lace of gentility but the very cloth of civility.[28]

Meanwhile, avid interest in the possibility of Christian emotions among Indians had a long history in colonial Pennsylvania. From the time of William Penn, Quakers had maintained an enduring curiosity concerning Indians' potential to feel the kinds of emotions that might ultimately allow them entrance into civilized society. During the war that immediately preceded the outbreak of violence at Paxton, members of the Friendly Association (the Quaker organization dedicated to establishing and preserving friendship with Indian nations) scrutinized the emotions of the native Americans they came into contact with. In one revealing incident, they reported with astonishment and delight on an emotional display by the Indian leader Teedyuscung. When the Delaware chief dissolved in tears at the end of a treaty council, members of the Friendly Association reported his outburst as an almost miraculous occurrence. In the official Association minutes they explained that

> in the Course of his Business He had endeavoured to turn his mind and look up to God for direction, that when he was alone in the woods and destitute of any other Counselor, he found by doing so he had the best direction, that he hoped God would Bless our Endeavours and desired to be remembered by his Friends. He followed us to the boat and was . . . much affected . . . [with] Tears . . . which as it appeared to be the effect of a divine Visitation to a savage Barbarian was a humbling scene and excited reverent and Thankful Sentiments in the minds of those immediately observing it.

Remarkably, this group of Quakers regarded the display of strong emotion in a native American as evidence of religious affection in an otherwise insensate savage. This only underscores how thoroughly all colonial Pennsylvanians discounted any emotion that was not culturally defined as civilized. At the same time, it shows how highly they valued the kind of emotion believed to be conducive to Protestant Christian conversion.[29]

By the time of the Paxton crisis, the idea that Indians could develop the kinds of Christian emotions required for conversion had become common among those writing in opposition to the frontier settlers' actions. Thus one pamphleteer explained that when God, "before whose Eye the Colour of Skin is nothing, hath been pleased in his boundless Compassion, to send Gospel Ministers amongst them," Indians were quick to convert. The "Proof . . . of their being rooted and grounded in the Living Power and Faith of the Gospel" lay in "their serene Looks and quiet Deportment, [which] plainly indicated an upright Heart, and a Mind at ease." Again and again, Indians were lauded for their ability to learn the emotions associated with cultivated Christian people, but backcounty settlers were derided with comments that made clear that their emotions were unlikely to ever measure up to the standards of civility.[30]

Elites had every reason to emphasize civility and argue for culturally based definitions of humanity. For, if the emotions that bounded civilized life could be learned, then Indian converts to Christianity could be said to have earned entry into the exclusive club of civilized society. The crime of killing them then became that much more morally abhorrent. Conversely, and conveniently, if true humanity arose from an accumulation of cultural knowledge, then the stigma of ignorance could be used to exclude the lower sort from membership in the civilized community. Even as frontiersmen tried to expose and discredit the development of social divides among members of different Christian denominations, city elites castigated backcountry commoners for their failures to recognize either humanity or civility in Indians.

As one author allied with the Quakers smugly claimed, "To confine virtue or vice to any particular sect or set of men, shews little knowledge in human nature and a most uncharitable narrowness of spirit; human nature being all formed out of the same essence, and only dispersed in different degrees to different men." The complexities of this position are quite striking. The author insisted simultaneously that all humans—regardless of "sect or set"—were of the same essence, yet that some men could lay claim to greater degrees of humanity than others. In other words, at the same time that the upper sort lectured the lower against drawing what amounted to racial divides between Euro-Americans and native Americans, they imposed barriers of class and religious culture between themselves and their political antagonists, those dismissed as men of different (and lesser) degree.[31]

The underlying intent of these convoluted constructions of civilized emotion was to allow elites the insidious ability to reproach frontier folk no matter what they did, dismissing them as insensate savages when they did not display emotion, yet lambasting them for their lack of civility when they did. Metropolitan admiration for Indian Christianity drove backcountry dwellers to distraction, as can be seen in the following bit of doggerel. Calling his piece "The Cloven Foot Discovered" and accusing the Quakers themselves of being in league with the devil, the author declared:

'Tis Sin, your Conscience too will say,
In Tongue unknown to preach or pray;
Yet, you can hear an Indian bellow,
And praise him for a pious Fellow,
Though what he means you cannot tell,
Nor if he talks of Heaven or Hell.

Starting off with a dig at Quaker reliance on religious conscience over revealed Scripture, this poem asked why prayers offered in an unknown tongue (as in a Scots-Irish brogue or, for that matter, in German or Swedish) should be assumed to be unacceptable to God, whereas ones bellowed out by an Indian could receive easy approbation. If British subjects (regardless of religious denomination or ethnic origin) agreed that Christianity was open to all and that in Christianity lay the essence of civility, then how could the fervor of Presbyterian devotion be disregarded in favor of the efforts of recent Indian converts? Impatience with such tactics led one pro-Paxton pamphleteer to insist, in defense of the work of Matthew Smith and James Gibson, that "the Sense or Sentiments of Nature alone, not of Presbyterianism or any other Denomination, breath[e] in their . . . Petition." If the "Sentiments of Nature" were truly universal, as available to Indians as to Englishmen, then how could one group of European Christians presume to dismiss the religious affections and moral positions of another?[32]

If Presbyterians were to successfully press the case that urban elites were at greater fault for dismissing their civility than they themselves were for denying that of native Americans, they would have to find a way to redefine the meaning of humane emotion. Not surprisingly then, Paxton apologists sprang to the task of uncovering Quaker hypocrisy on the question of humanity. They derided "meek, merciful, compassionate Quakers (who would seem to monopolize Christian Charity and all the Tenderness of human Nature amongst themselves)," exposing the hollowness of the Quaker version of Universalism that insisted that all human nature was "formed of the same essence" and yet that humanity could be "dispersed in different degrees to different men."[33]

Essentially, backcountry folk set out to show that they and their fellow subjects in Philadelphia were all the same kind of men, accidents of geography and circumstances of birth notwithstanding. They could then expose the contradiction enacted by Quakers who, though "easily affected with Pity for Indians, would not grant a single Farthing (as a Society) for the Relief of their Fellow Subjects." Such statements turned city logic back against itself, questioning the conduct of the self-declared elite who denied any sympathy or succor to their fellow Christians. Interestingly, frontier folk never went so far as to try to deny civility to the elite. Not even the most venomous defenses of the Indian massacres ever went so far as to insist or even imply that Quakers or members of the Assembly were guilty of savagery. Instead, the Paxton Boys and their allies decided that the key to countering elite claims to a monopoly on humane emotion lay in exposing the artful way their antagonists tried to gerrymander the boundaries of civility, drawing native Americans within them, while declaring backcountry folk to be beyond the line.[34]

A satiric print criticizing the Quaker position nicely captures the attitudes that so vexed frontier inhabitants (Figure 13). The cartoon pictures a tableful of dour Quakers lamenting the conduct of "those wicked Presbyterians" even as one of their number busily hands out tomahawks to Indians from a barrel labeled "I.P." (as in Israel Pemberton). The Quaker tells the Indian warriors in feather headdresses, "Exercise those on the Scotch Irish and Dutch and I'll support you while I can." Meanwhile, one Quaker seated at the table worries that "the Paxton spirit grows stronger," while another frets, "Verily I'm afraid Friend B——'s cool thoughts won't have the Warmth to prevail with them." The satire thus worked to lampoon Quaker claims that excessive spirit and warmth—that is, angry passions—made frontier folk particularly prone to violence, while also pillorying Benjamin Franklin's presumption in setting himself up as a model of cool moderation. The cartoon invited readers to agree that Paxton critics simply made themselves ridiculous when they assumed that backcountry commoners could be reached only with overheated emotion, not cool thoughts. Meanwhile, the cartoon implicitly critiqued stony-faced Quakers not only for their apparent alliance with enemy Indians but more especially for their utter lack of feeling for fellow colonists subject to Indian attacks.

Perhaps no one capitalized on this strategy more forcefully than Thomas Barton, who exclaimed in his pamphlet, *The Conduct of the Paxton-Men, Impartially Represented,* "What good Man is there, whose Heart does not bleed, when he sees a Set of Men amongst us embracing BARBARIANS, with more Tenderness and Hospitality than ever they shew'd to their distressed Countrymen and Fellow subjects?" Such rhetoric faulted the Quaker-led elite not simply for their failure of compassionate feeling but especially for their perverse bestowal of fellow feeling on so-called barbarians. It extended the critique of elite feeling beyond the issue of compassion (which the Quakers themselves had successfully sought to capitalize on) to the more charged question of how those with the proven capacity for feeling chose to share it.[35]

James Gibson and Matthew Smith, presenters of the Paxton rebels' first written declaration, well understood these fine distinctions and worked to capitalize upon them. Their strategic discussions of grief and grievance included not only the claim that, through years of Indian attacks, they had mourned silently and dutifully in the absence of any offer of sympathies but also the complaint that no one had deigned to grieve along with them. Neither city elites nor any Indians had taken the time to pay their respects to the settlers' dead. On the contrary, backcountry folk asserted that they had been forced to watch passively as government

FIGURE 13. *Franklin and the Quakers.* By James Claypoole.
Philadelphia, 1764. *Permission The Library Company of Philadelphia.*
  Even as this print lampoons the idea that frontier inhabitants were especially

prone to warm and angry passions, the inclusion of a Quaker man fondling an Indian
woman suggests that the Quakers' defense of Conestoga Indians had been motivated
by another kind of passion.

leaders shamelessly inverted traditional conventions surrounding the regulation of grief.

As noted earlier (Chapter 7), British-American diplomats engaged in Indian negotiations frequently found themselves forced to participate in condolence ceremonies, wherein offers of shared feeling had served as key signs of respect, and acceptance of the omission of such emotional offerings signaled submission. In a smooth interaction, each side involved in a treaty negotiation would offer condolences to the other. But, on occasion, British Americans deliberately avoided offering condolences to native Americans as a means of denying them deference. Not surprisingly, then, grieving frontier folk regarded it as adding insult to injury when their leaders not only neglected to express grief for slain settlers but also failed to extract such expressions from native Americans.

This was just the charge leveled by Smith and Gibson. A key passage from their opening declaration asserted:

> Exorbitant presents and great Servility . . . paid to Indians, have long
> been oppressive Grievances we have groaned under . . . At the last
> treaty, not only was the Blood of our many murdered Brethren tamely
> covered, but our poor unhappy captivated Friends abandoned to
> Slavery.

To observe death and misfortune without any expression of sorrow insulted mourners. The Paxton Boys charged that by covering over the issue of colonial deaths and failing to make mention of missing captives, Pennsylvania's leaders had servilely failed to call the Indians to account. By implication, Pennsylvania diplomats had not only diminished the importance of their countrymen's demise but actually debased the status of all Pennsylvania colonists.[36]

With these comments, the Paxton rebels attempted to make clear their determination not to be excluded from the emotional rituals of civility, as well as their resolve to have a greater voice in the conduct of war and diplomacy. They concluded, "How general Dissatisfaction those Measures gave, the Murmurs of all good People (loud as they dare to utter them) to this day declare." Here again, Gibson and Smith implied that elites ignored commoners' murmurs of discontent at their own peril. Though traditional conduct required lower-class complaints not rise above a murmur, their murderous action (followed by the march itself) showed what those who turned a deaf ear to discontent could ultimately expect.[37]

As it turns out, a great deal of truth lay beneath the Paxton Boy's charges that elite leaders had neglected the rituals of grief. In one of his first acts as the new governor of Pennsylvania, in early December 1763, John Penn had convened a treaty conference with representatives of the Delaware nation that utterly ignored the conventions of condolence by neither expressing nor soliciting grief. Perhaps Penn was so new on the scene that he did not himself understand the social niceties of condolence rituals. More probably he understood them but decided to forgo them in favor of exacting practical concessions from native Americans. With the European element of the Seven Years War at an end, Penn's priority was to try to resolve lingering Indian issues and move on to pressing domestic policy concerns.

Penn had inherited an entrenched set of conflicts that must have initially appeared to him to require far more attention than either Indian diplomacy or capital-backcountry relations. Throughout the Seven Years War, the colony had not only been deeply divided over whether to arm for frontier defense, the matter so pressing to the Paxton Rebels, but also over debates concerning how armament should be funded, if it was in fact allowed. Though pacifist-leaning Quakers (who exercised an enduring influence in the Assembly) might have stood against arming the colony, they saved their strongest objections for money matters. More than militarization itself, they opposed the idea that the colony should be armed entirely at the expense of its subjects while its aristocratic proprietors enjoyed the profits of vast estates entirely free from taxation. Year after year, throughout the course of the war and whether pacifists were in or out of power, assemblies sent up supply bills to a succession of governors that included proposals to tax proprietary family land. The governors, appointed by the Penn family but salaried by the Assembly, each wrestled in turn over how to find the funds to defend the colony yet not offend the family that hired them. Despite some support from aspiring elites antagonistic to Quakers, most notably from leading members of Philadelphia Anglican and Presbyterian churches, governors found their jobs an unending struggle. By 1763, with the war at an end, the Penn family had decided that the best way to eliminate the divided loyalties of the colony's governors and squelch talk of proprietary taxation was to send one of their own into service. This was the reason for John Penn's abrupt arrival in Pennsylvania and the most likely explanation for his distracted uninterest in the niceties of Indian diplomacy.[38]

Official government minutes recording December 1763 treaty transactions between Governor John Penn and Papounan, a "Mohickon" allied with the Delawares and Nanticokes, reveal the accuracy of Smith and Gibson's assertions concerning the governor's lack of ceremony. At first, Penn began with just the kind of strict condemnation of Indian inhumanity that frontier folk would have wished for, telling the assembled Indians, "Were we to enter into the particular Cruelties and the number of barbarous Murders committed against our Inhabitants, at a time when they thought all was ended, it would astonish you." But the governor then abruptly changed course and adopted a far more conciliatory tone: "But [as] you have expressed yourselves determined to forget every thing of that Nature, and we see by your good speeches, you have good Dispositions, we shall not on our part mention any of these disagreeable matters, but, so far as you are concerned, pass them by without any further Notice." This omission of any mention of the frontier murders amounted, in some sense, to a subservient avoidance of murmuring.[39]

Even worse, the governor neither demanded nor received any expressions of condolence from the assembled native Americans. Instead, he explained to the Assembly that he would take the dead bodies of the slain settlers and "by this String . . . bury them and cover them out of sight." Of course, such a statement made sense in diplomatic terms; if statements of grief constituted calls for action, then the decision to omit them underscored the governor's desire to dampen the Indian conflicts then crackling across the backcountry in favor of a quick and uncomplicated peace. Yet, as far as the Paxton folk were concerned, the governor's breach of traditional decorum only further demonstrated his disregard for his own subjects.[40]

Far from agreeing that the bodies of their dead were best covered over and buried out of sight, backcountry folk insisted both that their suffering should be made visible and that elites should make efforts to assuage it. So deep was their wish for recognition from eastern leaders that some time earlier, according to Thomas Barton, they had brought a "Waggon-Load of the scalped and mangled Bodies of their Countrymen . . . to *Philadelphia* and laid [them] at the *State-House Door.*" A more graphic demonstration of the desire to be seen, actually and socially, can scarcely be imagined. Tellingly, Barton claimed that, even after this grisly exhibition, the Philadelphia elite continued to ignore the settlers' grief. His pamphlet demanded, when the wagonload was brought: "Did we hear any of those Lamentations that are now so plentifully poured forth for the *Conestogoe Indians?*—O my dear Friends! must I answer—No? The *Dutch* and the *Irish* are murder'd without Pity." Again and again, frontier folk complained that city leaders' emotional comportment conveyed more respect for Indians than for their fellow Europeans and that the elite's omission of the expression of grief at the deaths of their countrymen amounted to an unbearable insult to the dignity and value of their lives.[41]

Such protests over the lack of mourning mounted for frontier dwellers grew out of long years of grievance. Throughout the Seven Years War just ended, as pacifist Quakers and proarmament Anglicans and Presbyterians had debated participating in the continental conflict, cries from the backcountry had emphasized the indignity of settlers' deaths almost as much as the tragedy of their demise. When Lutheran preacher and proarmament propagandist John Lidenius had wanted to dramatize the need for defensive war back in 1756, the lack of proper funerary rites was a dramatic element of his plea for frontier rights. Painting an elaborately detailed vision of violence and desecration, he had exclaimed: "See the flames! Smell the smoak! Look and behold the dear submissive wives, the delight of their husbands, forced away from the funerals of their husbands, now almost dead, and fetching their last sighs in their running blood!" Remarkably similar language had also showed up in a lament included in the private correspondence of a Pennsylvania man written in that same year. The letter began by declaring, "We are now in a grievous distressed condition [with the] barbarous inhuman ungrateful natives weekly murdering our back inhabitants." After devoting several paragraphs to elaborate and bloody scenes of death and destruction, the letter ended by proclaiming that colonial bodies were simply left to litter the ground "until by chance they are found by our companies who commits them to a private grave without winding sheet or coffin or surrounding weeping relations." Truncated rituals of death dishonored frontiersmen. Without the benefit of the traditional tributary tears of "submissive wives" and "weeping relations," backcountry men were undermined not only in the eyes of Indians and easterners but also before the family members whose customary dependence gave meaning to their claims of masculine mastery.[42]

Matthew Smith, James Gibson, and their fellows accepted that a certain measure of social subordination was inevitable, given their leaders' pretensions to gentility. They had, of course, signaled as much by acknowledging the importance of keeping their own expressions of grief down to a murmur. At the same time, frontier folk rejected all attempts at subjection on the basis of issues of Christian civility. They refused to keep their grief entirely quiet. And they expected elites to respond with prompt compassion to their softest intonations of sadness, not to rush instead to address the sorrows of "savages." Meanwhile, as will become quite clear, they were ever determined to defend and promote their own masculinity. The depth of the Paxton band's provocation is suggested by the very timing of their attack. Just four short days after Governor Penn proposed simply covering over the bodies of the backcountry dead without either demanding or expressing condolences, frontiersmen fell on the Christian Indians at Conestoga.

Delimiting Masculinity: Of Sensible Men and Spiritless Women

Governor Penn did not know it, but the early conduct of his administration had destabilized a very finely balanced social equilibrium. While the newly arrived governor and members of the Assembly had initially closed ranks to present a united upper-class front in opposition to the disorder of the lower orders, they did so only with difficulty. They had linked arms across a wide chasm of long-standing mutual antagonism in the effort to respond to an acute moment of crisis. In fact, the colony's elite had long been divided along denominational lines, with Anglican governors and their allies opposed to the Quaker-dominated Assembly. Quakers maintained their standing (despite being a numerical minority) by cultivating their relationship with German settlers of compatible pietistic persuasions. This left Anglican governors and proprietary supporters in Philadelphia to attempt to forge a competing coalition with disgruntled frontier Presbyterians. In trying to realign these hardened ranks, the governor found himself opposing entrenched interests in a manner not necessarily advantageous to himself.

The Paxton rebels and their propagandists tried every possible tack in attempting to take advantage of these facts. After their initial outburst of aggression and their threatening march on the city, frontiersmen had pulled back from the vanguard of violence to reassert their respectability and civility. Smarting from elite rhetorical attacks, from the governor's pronouncement urging their capture and punishment to Franklin's *Narrative* condemning their actions, the frontiersmen had engaged in a renewed effort to play by the rules. To do so, they had presented their version of events in the kind of emotional language best calculated to permit their smooth reintegration into colonial society on favorable terms.

In their first explanation to Governor Penn, Matthew Smith and James

Gibson made every effort to justify the attack at Conestoga, the subsequent murders, and finally their decision to descend on Philadelphia. Their declaration sought to assert their people's respectability while yet deferring to Philadelphians' gentility and to affirm their own civility while still appealing for cross-colony unity. Their rhetoric showed a clear understanding of the emotional conventions associated with gentility and civility, from their nuanced use of the vocabulary of anger, to their twofold reliance on grief (as a conduit for expressing grievance *and* as a channel for demanding tribute), to their insistence that they too shared in "the sentiments of nature." Their initial attempt failed on all counts.

Governor Penn tried to bury their declaration out of sight along with their dead. Faced with a document that navigated delicately between murmuring grief and resounding resentment, between calls for condolence and strong words against servility, Penn opted for discretion. He simply shelved the marchers' declaration and declined to share it with other members of the government. When assemblymen learned of the document's existence, they had to send representatives to request "the Governor would be pleased to lay before the House the Declaration of the Rioters." Only when they insisted did the governor finally relinquish the declaration. Yet the assemblymen themselves did not work up an interest in the declaration until the arrival of a second and more forceful statement made them wish to examine the first.[43]

For Smith and Gibson responded to the governor's inaction and inattention with a swift shift of tactics. They quickly sent in a second letter on February 13, 1764, this one not a declaration, but a "Remonstrance." While their declaration had used expressions of grief to add pathos to an apparently submissive petition to have grievances redressed, their remonstrance was couched in far more forceful terms of reproach. Instead of seeking to explain and excuse their own behavior, they focused on demanding specific measures from the government. They sought to convince urban leaders of the need to provide for frontier defense, to curb the government's determination to prosecute the perpetrators of the Conestoga killings, and, finally, to compel the Assembly to recognize the legitimacy of their demands for greater representation.[44]

Significantly, the second letter employed an entirely different emotional idiom than the first had. Gone were descriptions of themselves as murmuring mourners slowly moved to resentment. Gloves off, they now offered the ominous pronouncement "[Neglect] by the Public, is sufficient to make us mad with rage, and tempt us to do what nothing but the most violent necessity can vindicate." If extreme anger could connote uncouth incivility, it could also convey masculine strength and power.[45]

In place of the notion that restrained resentment was the only acceptable variety of anger, backcountry spokesmen now embraced the idea that extreme varieties of anger had laudable elements. They explained that, because city leaders had failed to provide the protection they owed to frontier folk, the settlers had been forced to seize the initiative themselves. And they warned one and all that they remained determined to wreak vengeance upon any Indian suspected of settler attacks, none of whom should hope "to elude the Fury of the brave Relatives of the murdered." Thus, they recast rage and fury as elements of bravery, not of depravity. Finding that their efforts to follow elite emotional forms went disregarded and unrewarded, they reverted to another set of standards, which argued that the model of emotion associated with their elite critics was not the only, much less the ideal, set of emotional conventions.[46]

Ultimately, though city leaders met only limited opposition to their exclusive claims of gentility and were never forced to directly defend their own civility, they discovered that they could not expect automatic respect for their masculinity. For example, one pro-Paxton pamphlet extended Smith and Gibson's complaints about servile diplomacy by claiming, "Indians . . . look with Contempt upon us as a pusillanimous Pack of *old Women,* divided among ourselves, without SPIRIT or RESOLUTION to call them to an Account." Frequently derided for their so-called savage ferocity, the Paxton rebels decided to counter those accusations with their logical counterpoint, deriding their elite antagonists as spiritless and emasculated men incapable of exercising invigorating anger.[47]

Indeed, the best evidence that masculinity was as much at issue as gentility or civility in the Paxton crisis comes from the name given to the rebellious settlers from Paxton by their critics: The Paxton Boys. Beginning with Benjamin Franklin—"Unmanly Men! who are not ashamed to come with weapons against the Unarmed, to use the Sword against Women and the Bayonet against Children"—anti-Paxton pamphleteers attempted to undercut any suggestion that the Indian attacks were manly acts and to underscore the assertion that the Paxton rebels were boys, not men. Those who spoke in favor of the backcountry folk did not describe them as boys. On the contrary, defenders made a point of calling them men, as in the case of Thomas Barton, who titled his pamphlet *The Conduct of the Paxton-Men, Impartially Represented.* Where violent action contrasted sharply with passive ineffectiveness, the burden of proof of masculinity fell far more heavily on the Paxton rebels' antagonists than on the settlers or their advocates.[48]

Critiques of elite manhood, especially of Quakers and allied Assembly members, had a long history. Throughout the Seven Years War just ended, debates about masculinity had framed discussions about the implications of pacifism and the moral legitimacy of frontier defense. Even as widespread agreement emerged concerning the links between Christianity and civility, debates continued over the relationship of each to masculinity. As one wartime sermonizer, the New Side Presbyterian Samuel Finley, had demanded of his fellow Pennsylvanians, "When we become *Christians,* must we cease to be *Men?*" This vexed question dogged Pennsylvania debates.[49]

Not surprisingly, Finley, an unswerving proarmament author, posed the question in order to be able to offer an emphatic denial that masculinity, civility, and sensibility were in any way incompatible:

> Could our *pious* and *valiant Forefathers* . . . see the . . . Dispositions of many of their *Offspring;* their *Effeminacy,* Luxury, false Notions . . . and absolute *Want of public Spirit,* what would they think? . . . When . . . our honour and safety are at *Stake* . . . shall we refuse to exert ourselves? . . . Will nothing but *destruction* itself make us *sensible?*

According to Finley, those who "refused to exert" themselves in defense of their colony did not understand the true mandate conferred by Christian emotion. Real sensibility encompassed masculinity and civility alike, employing emotion in the service of public spirit. Only those who had deeply misunderstood the meaning of Christian emotion could think that civil feeling and manly action were each at odds with the other.[50]

Another observer eager to assist militarist arguments had gone still further, turning to the Bible for examples of sensible men with martial spirits. In a sermon preached in Delaware colony but published in Philadelphia, the Anglican minister Matthias Harris chose to meditate on the lines from 2 Samuel, "Be of good courage . . . and let us play the Men for our people." What did it mean to "play the Men"? Praising the biblical character Joab, a general in King David's army, Harris declared:

> *Joab* . . . from a deep sense of the critical circumstances . . . to which he saw his country exposed, made a speech to his soldiers, full of a manly, martial and concise eloquence, animated with the noblest sentiments, . . . and strongest persuasives to a vigourous defence of their

country, their religion, their laws, and liberties, against a cruel, a perfidious and potent enemy; and concludes . . . "Be of good courage . . .
and let us play the Men for our people."

The feelings arising from a "deep sense" motivated a speech of manly and
martial eloquence. Those animated by noble sentiments would provide
the most spirited protection for their people. Here, as elsewhere, a people
of noble sentiments was presented in stark contrast to a cruel and perfidious one. In this model, the passions were essential for both the promotion of manly courage and the prosecution of war. What elites cast as
emotional refinement, the Paxton rebels would come to redefine as spiritless effeminacy.[51]

Adding to the stakes of this debate was that representatives of many
Indian nations were themselves scornful of Anglo-American masculinity.
In the midst of the earliest rumblings of war in 1754, Hendrick, a speaker
for Mohawk members of the Six Nations confederacy, chided the English
at the Albany Congress: "Look at the French, they are Men; they are
fortifying every where. But We are ashamed to say it, You are all like
Women, bare and open without any Fortifications." Hawkish Pennsylvanians took care to record this remark in official Provincial Council minutes of the conference. Much as the criticism must have smarted, it also
made potent propaganda for use against pacifists. Such negative assessments of Anglo-American manhood were not unusual.[52]

In another crucial instance a couple of years later, Scarroyady, an
Oneida Indian who often acted as a go-between for the Pennsylvania
government, urged Pennsylvanians: "Awake, shake off your Lethargy;
Stand up with your Hatchet in your Hand, and use it manfully. Your
Enemies have great advantage by your Inactivity; Show them you are
Men." Again, this mixture of advice and contempt survives in the rec-
ord probably only because it helped provide a pretext for proarmament
activities. Still, this account of native American contempt for Anglo-
American masculinity indicates how deeply rooted the Paxton rebels'
accusations actually were.[53]

Meanwhile, many British Americans remained in thrall to the idea
of Indian martial prowess and, by extension, Indian manhood. Writing
back to Pennsylvania's proprietors in England following a sweeping early
defeat of the British General Edward Braddock in 1755, for example,
one governor complained, "The General despised an Enemy of whose
strength and situation he was not sufficiently informed, and contemn'd

the Indian manner of fighting in a Country where it has infinite advantages." A Pennsylvania war captive named Robert Eastburn observed of his Indian captors, "They are strong hardy Men." He added, critically, "I wish there was more of this *Hardness,* so necessary for *War,* in our Nation, which would open a more encouraging scene than at present!" Anglo-American admiration for Indian strength and hardiness—emotional and physical alike—arose amid Indian contempt for colonial masculinity.[54]

Recall now William Smith's assertion, in 1755, that achieving a "rational Medium" of refined sentiment required avoiding *both* "sullen Ferocity" and the tendency to "grovel beneath the True Spirit of *Freedom.*" The central thrust of the Paxton rebels' critique was that, while their elite opponents might deride them for going to emotional extremes, and especially for veering toward ferocity, their leaders were vulnerable in turn to the charge that they lacked true spirit. Smith, for one, had pushed his argument to its logical conclusion, by claiming, "LIBERTY never deigns to dwell but with a prudent, a sensible and a manly People." Much as British Americans worried about their claims to civility, they were equally vulnerable to critiques of their masculinity.[55]

Pacifist influence notwithstanding, Pennsylvania's legislators themselves remained quite concerned about questions of masculinity and sensibility. Indeed, the Quaker speaker of the Assembly, Isaac Norris, had taken care to characterize the members of his chamber as "sensible manly people" from the outset of the Seven Years War. Such widespread agreement on the outlines of the British-American ideal would have made accusations that Assembly members lacked masculinity sting all the more smartly. Thus, in homing in on this issue, the pro-Paxton camp succeeded in finding and exploiting an important point of weakness in the seemingly solid flank of the elite.[56]

What emboldened the rebels to make assertions concerning anger and masculinity? Did their embrace of anger not play into the hands of their critics and undermine everything they had previously sought to achieve? As we have already seen, in the first days of the crisis, Philadelphia leaders never took note of any emotions but rage and fury in those they viewed as backcountry "barbarians." While acknowledging the dyadic nature of anger and grief, elites insisted that frontier folk lacked the genteel virtue needed to alternate easily between the two. They asserted, essentially, that the Paxton Boys' propensity for violence proved they did not deserve to be regarded as a people in mourning. By focusing on the Paxton Boys' anger (and refusing to credit them with the capacity for measured resentment), elites obviated the need to meet grief with compassion (that is, with the aid demanded by noblesse oblige), much less with condolence (that is, with sympathetic offers of respectful tribute). What made the frontiersmen's new stand viable was that the damning tale told by the Paxton critics was far from the full story.

All understood that popular rage could often prove useful and that elites frequently turned to the power of popular anger when push came to shove. John Penn's immediate predecessor, Governor James Hamilton, was a past master at marshaling the fury of ordinary frontier folk when it suited his needs. Pushed to the point of desperation in his power struggles with the Assembly and growing ever more anxious at reports of Indian encroachments, Hamilton began to wonder "to how small a distance from the Capitol our Frontier may be reduced." Though he implored the Assembly to "protect our people . . . [and] take a severe Revenge on our perfidious Foes," his recommendations went unheeded. Determined to press on in spite of the Assembly's intransigence, he then turned for sustenance to the wellspring of the people's anger.[57]

In one of his last acts as governor, a mere week before John Penn arrived in office, Hamilton all but authorized the murderous rage of the Paxton rebels. He told a group of British-allied Indians that the "renewal of Hostilities . . . without the least Provocation" had "enraged and provoked [his] people greatly . . . in revenge." Apparently well aware of the plans already brewing, he warned the assembled Indians, "Some of them have gone into the Indian Country to take their Satisfaction, and . . . in their great anger, they will not be able to distinguish between those who are our Friends and Those who are our Enemies." Hamilton was not merely presciently predicting the tragedy to follow; he was offering his own endorsement of the slaughter of innocent Indians.[58]

Hamilton asserted, "If any such thing should happen, you must blame those Indians who have so unjustly struck us, as People who have been so much hurt cannot be restrained from taking Revenge." On a final portentous note, he declared, "We cannot answer for those enraged, ungovernable people in their attempts to revenge the blood of their Fathers, Brothers, and Children . . . tho' we should do all in our power to prevent it." Here threats to British-American masculinity—the "blood of their Fathers"—could be avenged only with the weapon of backcountry rage. Not fool enough to avow unqualified approval for his subjects' murderous anger, Hamilton nevertheless spoke as openly as he dared. Perhaps emboldened by his impending departure from office, he seems to have deliberately incited a backcountry rebellion as his parting shot at the Assembly. In the event, his barely muted blast rang loud and clear through to the frontiersmen massing on the far edge of Penn's woods.[59]

Thus, three months later, when the Paxton rebels resorted to using the language of rage and fury in their second public comment on the crisis, the new governor, John Penn, snapped to attention. Rather than seek to reinforce his alliance with the assemblymen, with whom he was already increasingly at odds, Penn himself took his first tentative steps toward reconsidering his disapproval of popular anger. On February 17, four days after the remonstrance was delivered and the same day he finally handed over the Paxton Boy's written complaints to the Assembly, Penn sent a nervous letter to the royal superintendent of Indian affairs, Sir William Johnson, apprising him of the situation. He was deeply concerned "lest their Rage may not be restrained by any measures in the power of the Government" and urgently requested Johnson to allow him to transfer Pennsylvania's surviving Indian converts to the colony of New York "in order to put a stop to the present disturbances of the People." These were stark words and strange actions from a man who had promised, exactly two weeks before, a "speedy and effectual punish[ment] [for] the Rioters."[60]

Perhaps even more suggestive is that, while contemporaries believed the Paxton rebels prepared their first missive themselves, before their arrival on the outskirts of Philadelphia, popular opinion held that they received high-level assistance in writing their second piece. That is, while Smith and Gibson sought to showcase the restraint of frontier resentment in their "Declaration," they might well have been encouraged by elite allies to sound a more strident note of rage in their "Remonstrance." Ironically, then, the supposedly uncouth commoners seem to have succeeded in producing a statement written to the standards of refinement on their own, only to be counseled to take a coarser yet also more forceful approach by elite editors. The reasons for these strange inversions were to become increasingly clear.[61]

An association as strained as that between the governor and the Assembly was highly vulnerable to continued assaults. Every time Paxton apologists leveled their complaints about the conduct of frontier policy specifically at pacifist Quakers, they invited the governor to come around to their point of view. In such a situation, it was entirely possible that John Penn might come to identify more closely with the Paxton rebels than his initial denunciations of their actions would ever have led one to expect. In fact, three days after the arrival of the Paxton remonstrance, in response to a call for renewed cooperation by the Assembly, the governor reasserted the obvious point that "the legislative, and executive Powers of Government are independent of one another and are lodged in different hands." Meanwhile, just a month after that, with the notion of elite unity already in tatters, legislators would accuse the governor of taking steps to "enflame the Minds of unthinking people and excite Tumults against the Assembly . . . with a view to awe us into Proprietary Measures." Try as they might not to heed the Paxton Boy's claims, elites could not afford to entirely discount the force associated with backcountry anger. As Assembly members became ever more nervous about the possibility that Penn would try to inflame frontier settlers' anger against them, the governor himself came to admire the strength their anger imparted. In that important symbolic sense, the Paxton rebels accomplished their ends.[62]

For loud as their condemnation of "the Fury and Rage of an incensed, riotous and lawless Mob" had been, the governing elite found it impossible to maintain a united front. The rebels were neither punished nor rewarded for their violence, but simply sent home again to nurse their wounds. Meanwhile, Assembly members focused their efforts on wrangling with the Penns, loading military supply bills with the requirement for "fair and equal Taxation of the Proprietary with other Estates." When Governor Penn rejected three such bills in a row, the Assembly upped the ante by calling on the king to revoke the Penn charter and to reinvent Pennsylvania as a royal colony. Still, the Assembly could not ignore evidence of a continually mounting crisis on the frontier. Indian attacks carried on, as native Americans (inspired by the example of the Ottawa leader Pontiac) pressed hostilities down through the Ohio Valley and across the Pennsylvania hinterland. Finally, then, after months of dispute, the Assembly temporarily suspended its insistence on proprietary taxation and proposed a new fifty-five-thousand-pound military supply bill that did *not* tax the Penn family's estate. Governor Penn signed the bill at the end of May 1764; by August, Pennsylvania raised a regiment of one thousand men charged to fight enemy Indians under the command of the British officer, Colonel Henry Bouquet.[63]

Dramatic expressions of frontier anger must have played a key part in these developments. Indeed, the governor's efforts to "enflame the minds of the People" culminated with a July 7 decision to "declare and promise that, there shall be paid . . . to all and every Person . . . premiums and Bounties for the prisoners and Scalps of the Enemy Indians that shall be taken or killed within the Bounds of this Province." In so doing, Penn struck a strategic alliance with his rebellious subjects, the crowning moment in a concerted effort to placate the backcountry while maintaining a precarious balance of power within the Pennsylvania government.[64]

Together, the actions of governor and Assembly represented a wholesale retreat from the expansive definitions of humanity and civility they had once proposed to extend to Indians. Yet this capitulation was less a victory for frontiersmen than a setback for Indians. Loud as their condemnation of frontier violence had been, elite leaders' abhorrence of the Paxton rebels' actions paled beside their reluctance to allow them a greater voice in governance. Intricate as their description of the possibility of Indian civility had been, the governing class found it far easier to provide bounties for scalps than to take any other concrete action to end the agitation of the lower orders. Instead, elite Pennsylvanians invoked the language of emotion in ever more elaborate ways as they sought to entrench—yet obscure—divides of rank and race.

Denouement: Profiting from the Paxton Crisis

So began the last chapter in the story of "barbarous cruelties" that capped the pre-Revolutionary history of colonial Pennsylvania. The key test of the government's new political direction was whether the colony could secure the return of captured settlers that frontier folk had so long hoped for. Colonel Henry Bouquet was thus the man of the hour. A career military man with close ties to the anti-Quaker proprietary party, Bouquet's colonial reputation was built on Indian fighting. He had already made an important stand at Bushy Run the year before; in the autumn of 1764, he again delivered. With little bloodshed but great pomp, he succeeded in bringing the Shawnees and Delawares to terms and the captured settlers back to the colony. Making the most of this success, politically, required stamping it with the emotional ceremonies of superiority that backcountry inhabitants had come to demand as marks of respect. Fluent in the cross-cultural implications of emotion, Bouquet did not disappoint. Yet even before the curtain could fall on his commanding emotive performance, the stage would be set for an altogether new play, one in which affirmations of the universality of humanity would once more claim the spotlight.[65]

Throughout his negotiations, Bouquet sent back to Philadelphia detailed descriptions of his diplomatic efforts to communicate British-American dominance through practiced use of the language of feeling.

Bouquet's "Journal and Conferences with the Western Indians," addressed to the governor and his council and incorporated into the colony's official minutes, reported protracted talks with members of the Seneca, Delaware, and Shawnee nations from September 20 to November 14, 1764. He paid the utmost attention to the niceties of emotional expression that John Penn had omitted the year before; he also inadvertently reveals Indian skepticism about British Americans' exclusionary claims to civilized sensibility.[66]

Colonel Bouquet, by his own account, arrived in the Ohio Valley determined to conquer any Indians who dared to offer resistance. In his first public speech, on September 20, 1764, he took the rigid stance that he would "shew no mercy for the future to any one of your Nations that shall fall into my hands." Curiously, he backtracked almost immediately from the severity of this stance. Later in the same speech he clarified: "Though I have had it in my power to put you all to death . . . you have yet a door open to mercy." His quick revision is revealing, for, according to his understanding of elite forms, his communications with the Indians needed to convey both civility and strength. Proffering mercy while yet threatening to withdraw it offered one way to walk this line.[67]

Still, masterful as Bouquet intended this message to sound, it fell rather flat with his Indian audience. The irony of the fact that this high-ranking representative of the civilized world had arrived in Indian country and declared that he would not show mercy was not lost on the native Americans sent to treat with him. Perhaps aware that British Americans were in the habit of defining savagery explicitly as a lack of mercy—as when a British general referred to "Savages, who shew no Mercy in their Depredations," or when then-governor Hamilton deplored the "Savage cruelty of a merciless Enemy"—the assembled Indians wryly reminded Bouquet of his own investment in civility. Their first response to his proclamation, offered by "an Onondago and an Oneida Indian" on October 2, warned, "We still see you keep some evil designs in your minds." According to Bouquet's journal, they added that they hoped that the English would "remove all this from your hearts, and . . . receive them civilly . . . and they will treat you in the same manner." To underscore their point, the assembled Indians declined further substantive talks on prisoner exchange for another two weeks.[68]

Much as Bouquet wished to project manly strength, he had nothing to gain from relinquishing British-American claims to civility. Rather than continue alternately offering and withdrawing mercy, Bouquet shifted to fortifying mercy with anger, attempting thereby to create the perfect amalgam of sensibility and masculinity. At an October 20 meeting, he began by declaring to the Seneca, Delaware, and Shawnee representatives, "You must be sensible that you deserve the severest Chastisement, but the English are a merciful and generous people, averse to shed the blood even of their most cruel Enemies." Having laid claim to civility for himself and his people, Bouquet turned to the question of anger. Here he threw in a twist certain to play well with frontier audiences. Like Governor Hamilton before him when faced with recalcitrant Indians, Bouquet brandished the anger of backcountry commoners. He told the Indians that the month-long delay in negotiations over prisoner returns had to end because he had come accompanied by "the relations of those people you have massacred or taken prisoners . . . and it is with the greatest difficulty that I can protect you against their just resentment."[69]

Interestingly, Bouquet never attributed anger directly to himself; it was too important to retain an appearance of cool control, in view of his own immersion in the violence of war. Yet, while he kept his own hands clean (crucial in an official account intended for an elite audience), Bouquet also whitewashed the settlers' crimes (critical to making the greatest appeal to popular concerns). His choice to label settler anger "just resentment" provided a final generous flourish. The Paxton rebels could not have asked for a more effective means of social rehabilitation than Bouquet's reprise of Hamilton's solicitous attitude toward their anger. Still, what this episode really reveals is how complicit elites were in encouraging the very anger they at other times decried. Such an emotional division of labor not only allowed members of the putative elite to lay exclusive claim to gentility but also allowed them the convenience of imposing class divisions in definitions of civility. Ever anxious lest the rage of the lower orders should be redirected against the elite, precisely the problem in the aftermath of the Conestoga killings, the colony's leaders nevertheless turned with relief to the strength of popular anger when it suited their strategic needs. This system not only left commoners to do the bloody work of battle but also allowed elites to redirect lower-class demands away from the issue they held to be of greatest importance: control of the political process.[70]

If invocations of anger were important for the symbolic reduction of Pennsylvania's social tensions, Bouquet's account of the next steps in the negotiations was even more critical. Rather than engaged in the traditional rituals of native American diplomacy, Bouquet presented the assembled Indians with a detailed outline of the "numberless murders, Depredations and breaches of Faith" they were charged with. He followed this list with a warning that the army would not leave until the Indians had "fully complied with every Condition that is to precede any treaty." His speech omitted any of the traditional politeness conventionally expected at Indian conferences. Not only did he ignore the usual expectation of condolences, he avoided every symbolic gesture of welcome, even going so far as to explain that, "as they had expressed some uneasiness in our not shaking hands with them," they should know that "the English took [only] their friends by the hands and that they could not expect to be treated as such till a peace was concluded with them." Every item of this performance was calculated to convey to a backcountry audience that he would not give conquered Indians the kind of "Tenderness and Hospitality" Quakers had been ridiculed for readily bestowing on the enemy.[71]

For their part, the assembled Indians perfectly well understood the import of Bouquet's deportment, as shown by their uneasiness at his refusal to shake their hands. Declarations of anger were a key component of native American war preparations, and expressions of condolence were essential to the resumption of friendly relations. In light of Bouquet's aggressive stance, Indians eager to think no more of war hastened to initiate conciliatory measures. In the weeks after Bouquet's speech, waves of returning war captives were presented to the colonel, in a concrete show of goodwill designed to answer his declaration, "We shall judge of your Sincerity not from your Words but from your Actions." That accomplished, the Indians then moved to return to the familiar rituals of condolence. When peace negotiations recommenced in earnest on November 9, the first remarks made by the Seneca chief Keyashuta, on behalf of his nation as well as the Delawares, addressed the question of condolences. Concerned that a random murder threatened to undo the good effects of their work, he hastened to assure Bouquet, "The misfortune . . . gives us the Same Sorrow it gives you," adding, "By this String of Wampum we wipe the tears from your eyes and remove from your heart the resentment which this murder has raised against us." In moving to substitute their own sorrow for the grief and resentment of British Americans, the Indians signaled the seriousness of their desire for strategic rapprochement.[72]

Still, it seems that Bouquet would not rest until Indians paid full tribute in tears to all of the fallen British Americans killed in the late conflict. In this, his attitude conformed closely to the demands of backcountry settlers who had regarded earlier failures to demand condolences as unbearable examples of servility. He recorded no response of his own to Keyashuta's offer of condolences over the murder but did mention that, when he met the Indians again three days later on November 12, a Shawanee chief known as Red Hawk noted, "As we discover something in your Eyes which shews you are not satisfied with us, We now wipe away every thing bad between us." Making absolutely clear his intention to augment the condolences already offered, Red Hawk then said, "Many of our Young men on both sides have been killed by this War, occasioned by the Ottowas, but I now bury their bones, so that they shall be no more seen." In burying the bones of the British-American dead along with their own while also stating their sorrow and offering to wipe away all tears, these native American chiefs aimed collectively to mollify British Americans with elaborate displays of respect. At the same time, Red Hawk's mention that he was covering his own dead along with those of the colonists implicitly invited Bouquet to respond in kind.[73]

This was an invitation Bouquet was in no hurry to accept. Preferring to draw out the drama of victory, he still refrained from offering the reciprocal remarks of condolence demanded by traditional Indian protocol. He allowed them only the slenderest acknowledgment of their efforts: "I have heard your Speaker and have seen the papers you have laid before me; I shall take them into Consideration." More days of tough talk followed in which Bouquet continued to insist that not until every last British-American prisoner had been returned would he be willing to come to terms with his erstwhile antagonists. Finally, on November 14, 1764, Bouquet at last relented and told the assembled Indians:

> I came here determined to strike you with a Tomahawk in my hand, but since you have submitted, it shall not fall upon your heads, I will let it drop and it shall no more be seen. I bury the bones of all the people who have fallen [in] this War, and cover the place with leaves, so that the place shall no more be perceived. . . . Having now buried the dead, and seen that you have removed every thing bad from your hearts, I will again treat you as Brothers and speak to you as such.

Bouquet's long withholding of condolence became just one more way to mark British-American mastery. While Indians had begun offering condolences days before, as a cap to confidence-building measures and as a signal of the start of serious peace talks, Bouquet deliberately refused to respond until the closing moments of the ceremonies. Even when he did bury the bones of the dead, he made no move to wipe away the Indians' tears or to offer up sorrow of his own. His final omission of the full compliments of condolence reinforced his performance of dominance before native American and British-American audiences alike.[74]

Everything about Bouquet's self-described behavior was calculated to convey pan-British unity and to uphold British-American dignity at the expense of native Americans'. Whether invoking resentment or mercy, demanding condolences or withholding sympathy, he consistently sought to modulate his own emotional expression to convey the best possible mix of gentility, civility, and masculinity. Despite the elite's strident early stance against "ruffian" rage and their lofty assertions that human nature was all "formed out of the same essence," Pennsylvania's leaders eventually capitulated to the worst demands of backcountry commoners. Faced with funding frontier violence or empowering western settlers to vote for it themselves, elites chose the course they found less personally costly.

Indeed, elites did rather worse than simply capitulate to the worst demands of commoners. They deliberately listened selectively, harkening only to the most stridently anti-Indian aspects of frontier fury. Not only did members of the upper orders discourage the Paxton rebels from using genteel forms of anger expression; they also ignored evidence that western settlers understood the nuances of native American enmities and alliances. In fact, many frontier folk were more discriminating in their judgments of Indians than elite criticism of their "undistinguishing Resentment" would lead one to believe. For example, "The Apology of the Paxton Volunteers" included the allusion to "the Five Nations, that have ever retained some Reputation for Honour and Fidelity." The remark received no general recognition whatsoever. Not only did elites prefer to portray commoners as muddle-headed rubes; they actually depended upon them to play this part. Leaders benefited twofold from the anti-Indian element in the rhetoric of the lower orders: it provided an important political distraction while allowing elites to claim for themselves a unique moral elevation. Repeated expression of elite outrage at the depravity of the lower orders served to obscure their own contributions to anti-Indian policies.[75]

Thus, when the Paxton rebels reasserted their right to defend the Indian lands they seized, by reminding all of the power of popular rage and by reigniting anti-Indian fervor, they lost as much as they achieved. True, they gained the reassurance of a heightened military presence on the frontier. But, in place of gaining greater representation, the Paxton rebels won only the empty respect of modified emotional rhetoric. Those who lost the most, of course, were the Indians—massacred if they did convert to Christianity, warred upon if they did not, and subjected to aggressive landgrabs either way. As elites sought to defend their masculinity and commoners their respectability, both found it only too easy to shift their critiques to native American civility.[76]

The pro-proprietary faction in Pennsylvania immediately appreciated the propaganda value of Bouquet's efforts and sought to immortalize his actions. That ever-busy political operative William Smith rushed to prepare an expanded and edited narrative version of the journal, to be published under the title *An Historical Account of Colonel Bouquet's Expedition against the Ohio Indians in the Year 1764.* This account should have been the crowning offering in the Paxton crisis pamphlet wars.

Even before Smith's adaptation of Bouquet's record could be prepared, printed, and sold, new events overtook old concerns. The British Parliament had proposed the Stamp Act in its 1764 session, thereby kindling the spark that would ignite a revolution. This novel combination of circumstances irrevocably altered the issues shaping Pennsylvania politics. If Bouquet's journal had reflected the stresses of a colonial society beset by social, religious, and ethnic divides, Smith's recounting of the colonel's work marked the first stirrings of an emerging nation still at the dawn of self-definition. Suddenly, capitalizing on all that Henry Bouquet had accomplished had less to do with containing internal unrest or controlling Indian threats and more to do with encouraging a colonial self-confidence conducive to Revolutionary resistance.

Much of the intended appeal of Bouquet's journal had stemmed from the way he deliberately drew distinctions between the "English" (broadly defined to include all British subjects without regard to ethnic origin, class, or creed) and the Indians, continually chastising the latter with the emotional rhetoric of British-American power. William Smith, in turn, proved eager to celebrate both the man and his mission, offering praise for Bouquet's "firm and determined conduct." Yet Smith's commentary on the enduring implications of the peace councils departed dramatically from the ideas imparted by Bouquet's journal. Rather than consolidated the ideal of exclusive *European* civility, Smith aimed to incorporate "savage" passion into a new *American* brand of ideal feeling.[77]

Smith's account of Bouquet's final treaty session offers an especially dramatic example of this transformation. Far from consolidating Bouquet's claims to a monopoly on tender mercy, Smith instead dwelled at length on evidence of Indian sensibility. He portrayed that last meeting as one that "language indeed can but weakly describe; and to which the Poet or Painter might have repaired to enrich their highest colorings of the variety of human passions." Bracing his readers to prepare "to exercise all the tender and sympathetic feelings of the soul," he proceeded to depict the return of the British-American war captives who had been adopted into native American families. While Bouquet had confined himself to a simple numerical tally of the numbers of returning British Americans, Smith delved into an intricate description of the spectacle of separation and reunion. After recounting the emotions of the colonists, he went on to explain:

> The Indians too, as if wholly forgetting their usual savageness, bore a capital part in heightening this most affecting scene. They delivered up their beloved captives with . . . torrents of tears . . . and . . . bestowed on them . . . all the marks of the most sincere and tender affection.

While Smith's casual reference to the Indians' "usual savageness" acknowledged the prejudiced expectations of many of his readers, his own argument emphasized how laudable were the emotions displayed by the Indians.[78]

The vivid picture of this "affecting scene" was complemented by an actual engraving by noted painter Benjamin West. Titled *The Indians Delivering up the English Captives to Colonel Bouquet,* West's illustration focused on the careful representation of facial expressions of "tender affection" among Indian and colonists alike, with special emphasis on the sincere tears of Indians. Smith and West had long been enthralled with the possibilities of Indian emotion. According to an early West biographer, John Galt (who claimed to have written his account in direct consultation with the artist), Smith served as one of West's first teachers, and the two had set out together to counter "the peculiar manners of the quakers," who insisted that "the passions are the source of all evil." Striving to improve "the faculties of taste," spur "works of imagination," and ensure the development of "the fine arts" in Pennsylvania, Smith and West sought ways to combine the undisciplined authenticity of Indian passions with the cultured reserve of European feeling. Symbolic of this emotional and aesthetic balancing act is the fanciful claim of Galt that, as a young boy, the self-taught artist spontaneously combined red and yellow pigments supplied to him by Indians with indigo dye given to him by

The Indians delivering up the English Captives to Colonel Bouquet near his Camp at the Forks of Muskingum in North America in Nov. 1764.

FIGURE 14. *The Indians Delivering up the English Captives to Colonel Bouquet.* By Benjamin West. In [William Smith], *An Historical Account of Colonel Bouquet's Expedition against the Ohio Indians in the Year 1764* (Philadelphia, 1765). *Permission The Library Company of Philadelphia.*

his mother to create a full-spectrum painter's palate. In this vision, savage resources blended with civilized ones in the hands of an unschooled colonist to produce the most vigorous and sophisticated possible culture.[79]

Smith's efforts to define an emotional protocol for the anti-Quaker colonial elite led him to counter Quaker antipassion teachings with idealized images of Indian feeling, even as he simultaneously argued that civilized emotions would always be far more restrained and refined than those of so-called savages. Rejecting once and for all the notion that Indian savagery was irredeemable, his *Narrative* asserted that the appearance of affectionate tears "in savages challenge our just esteem." He concluded:

> Those qualities . . . should make us charitably consider their barbarities as the effects of wrong education . . . while we should look on their virtues as sure marks that nature has made them fit subjects of cultivation as well as us. . . . Cruel and unmerciful as they are, by habit and long example, in war, yet whenever they come to give way to the native dictates of humanity, they exercise virtues which Christians need not blush to imitate.

Of course, there was nothing new in this discussion of the "native dictates of humanity." Pacifist Quakers and Assembly allies had long insisted on the validity of this very concept. Coming from a self-appointed frontier spokesman and Quaker adversary, this argument was altogether unprecedented. Despite the predictable reference to Indians as cruel barbarians, Smith did not contemplate the conclusion that native Americans sprang from a different stock than did British-American colonists. He shrank from making racialized arguments about absolute difference, instead stressing the role of habit and culture in shaping universal human emotions.[80]

This dramatic difference in emphasis becomes explicable only when we recognize that the trope of the cruel savage (incapable of feeling) coexisted uncomfortably with the equally prevalent image of the noble savage (exceptionally well endowed with emotion). Throughout the war years preceding the Paxton crisis, British Americans had repeatedly remarked on Indians' skillful and subtle emotional expression. None other than George Washington, who fired one of the first shots of the Seven Years War, urged the Pennsylvania governor in a 1754 meeting with representatives of the Six Nations to "take proper Notice of their moving Speech." Equally impressed with the pathos and emotional eloquence of the Mohawk leader Hendrick, the Pennsylvania diplomat and interpreter

Conrad Weiser offered praise that same year for "a pathetic Speech, in which he set forth the constant good Usage of the Province of Pennsylvania and their affectionate and generous usage of the Indians." Meanwhile, in 1756, a group of Quaker pacifists marveled at the emotional skill of the Delaware leader Teedyuscung who "in a full and pathetic manner, expressed his concern for the Mischief which had been done" on the Pennsylvania frontier and who thereby "raised tenderness towards the Indians in most that was present." Not only were Indians regularly credited with feeling affection and fidelity themselves; they were recognized for their ability to stir similar feelings in their British-American audiences.[81]

Especially striking in this regard is a second engraving created by Benjamin West to accompany William Smith's *Narrative*. This scene shows an unidentified Indian in the midst of delivering what appears to be an impassioned speech. Gathered around him before a council fire is an audience of treaty participants, colonists on the left, Indians on the right, all deeply absorbed in the performance. Most remarkable of all are the deliberate parallels in the expressions of individual British and Indian audience members. Each of the five British-American listeners has a counterpoint Indian spectator whose facial expression mirrors, yet amplifies, the colonists' more measured display. Thus, every time British Americans claimed that native Americans were insensate savages incapable of feeling humane sentiments, they contradicted another, more positive stereotype: that because they were closer to an unspoiled state of nature, Indian emotions were closer to the "native dictates of humanity" than were Europeans'.

Such contradictory attitudes of admiration and condemnation shaped Smith's account of Indian emotion as a whole, but his narrative contained another extremely important element: grudging acknowledgment of the Indian tradition of oratorical eloquence. Describing the Indian reaction to Bouquet's speech demanding surrender, he bragged that the colonel had been able to "bend the haughty temper of the savages to the lowest degree of abasement; so that even their speeches seem to exhibit but few specimens of that strong and ferocious eloquence which their inflexible spirit of independence has on former occasions inspired." Smith concluded, finally, "Happy will it be for them and for us if . . . [this] shall make as lasting impressions on their savage dispositions." Here Smith claimed that schooling savage dispositions involved stripping Indians of their eloquence, that is, of their well-honed ability to make emotionally moving speeches. Coming on the heels of years of speculation and debate about

The Indians giving a Talk to Colonel Bouquet in a Conference at a Council Fire, near his Camp on the Banks of Muskingum in North America, in Octr 1764.

FIGURE 15. *The Indians Giving a Talk to Colonel Bouquet at a Council Fire.* By Benjamin West. In [William Smith], *An Historical Account of Colonel Bouquet's Expedition against the Ohio Indians in the Year 1764* (Philadelphia, 1765). Permission The Library Company of Philadelphia.

Indian and European facial expressions coordinate in a deliberate mirror effect.

whether Indians were even capable of the degree of sensibility required of civilized Christians, such a statement could not be more ironic. Yet it perfectly captures Smith's commitment to setting up martial British Americans as the ultimate arbiters of emotion, capable of seizing on the strong and manly spirits usually ascribed to Indians but laying equal claim to virtuous Christian affections.[82]

Smith's stance directly countered the conceptions of European theorists, who were more apt to assume that masculinity and sensibility were inherently antithetical, the former the advantage of "savages" and the latter the preserve of the "civil." Scottish moral philosopher Adam Smith in 1759, for example, explained in his *Theory of Moral Sentiments,* "The hardiness demanded of savages diminishes their humanity; and, perhaps, the delicate sensibility required in civilized nations sometimes destroys the masculine firmness of the character." Here Smith laid claim to emotional sensibility for Europeans while crediting superior masculine hardiness to Indians, and he put his finger on a source of considerable cultural anxiety: the belief that humanity, sensibility, and civility were somehow at odds with both savagery *and* masculinity. This presented British-American men with a perplexing dilemma: how to balance the passions between masculinity, which they certainly did wish to cultivate, and savagery, which they most assuredly did not.[83]

American-based writers like William Smith, observing Indians at close range, were much less likely to construe humane sensibility and hardy masculinity as being invariably at odds. Unlike Adam Smith, who simply set the civilized against the savage and then argued his positions from there, British-American colonists came to embrace a version of emotional Universalism that placed all cultural groups on the same human continuum. Colonists were willing to make greater allowance for the admissibility of civilized anger and give greater credence to the plausibility of Indian sympathy. Thus, divisions between the savage and the civilized that seemed so clear and so immutable in a Scottish lecture hall grew far more flexible in America.[84]

By British Americans' own descriptions, we could conclude that Indians came closer to achieving the idealized mix of emotion best suited to linking masculinity and sensibility, powerful strength and civilized refinement, than any British-American group. Indians alone were able to draw with equal facility on fierce anger and deep grief, to rage against antagonists and yet later condole with those same erstwhile adversaries as allies. According to the rhetoric of British-American men, only such a combination allowed for virtuous independence. In 1755, few had understood that, when William Smith declared liberty to be the exclusive right of the sensible and manly, he was articulating a uniquely American view of emotions. Yet he staked his claim: "We either grovel beneath the true Spirit of *freedom*; or, if we aim at spirit, we are borne by a sullen Ferocity to the other Extreme. We are yet too much Strangers to that rational Medium, which is founded on a more enlarged and refined turn of sentiment." He thereby advanced assumptions rather different from those commonly accepted on the other side of the Atlantic. His 1755 call for colonists to prove themselves both sensible and manly announced radically new possibilities of emotional—and social—organization.[85]

The Rational Medium of Sentiment

A decade later, as he reflected on Henry Bouquet's successful campaign, William Smith was finally willing to admit the superior claim Indians could make on these cultural traits. In the concluding section of his 1765 *Narrative,* in which he discussed "the temper and genius of the Indians," Smith at last came out and openly declared, "The love of liberty is innate in the savage: and seems the ruling passion of the state of nature." Taken directly from Alexander Pope's *Essay on Man,* the notion of "ruling passion" was complex in its implications. Pope had called such engulfing passions "the Mind's disease," saying that they "warm[ed] the heart" and "fill[ed] the head," and warning finally, "The ruling passion, be it what it will / The ruling Passion conquers Reason still." Developing his theme, he declared that all persons who became the "wretched Subjects" of a governing passion in effect offered obedience to a "weak queen," whose reign would teach humankind to "mourn our Nature." With his typical penchant for ellipsis, Pope added a few lines later that people should nevertheless respect passion's throne:

. . . Nature's Road must ever be prefer'd;
Reason is here no guide, but still a guard:
'Tis hers to rectify, not overthrow,
And treat this passion more as friend than foe.
    —Epistle II, 161–164

In other words, Pope once more reaffirmed the conviction that passion's predominance over reason was natural and even to be "preferr'd," though reason could always offer some guard over passion. When William Smith proclaimed that "love of liberty" was Indians' ruling passion, he portrayed them as paragons of nature whose example should be imitated.[86]

William Smith left room for those colonists who cultivated reason as a check on natural passion to claim ultimate superiority over the supposedly unmediated emotions of Indians. The fact remains that Smith's startling acknowledgment, indeed idealization, of the Indian passion for liberty came right alongside divisive language that echoed the most virulent extremes of anti-Indian rhetoric. Just a few paragraphs after his comment on Indians' "ruling Passion," he reasserted the old argument that Indians, "like beasts of prey . . . are rendered by habit almost insensible to the common feelings of humanity." In other words, William Smith's goals had nothing to do with rehabilitating the image of Indians and everything to do with inventing a new American version of virtuous feeling that would draw on the best of both European and Indian cultural traditions.[87]

Even as Smith made this statement, the eruption of new transatlantic political conflicts cast his decade-long meditation on the emotions of liberty in a whole new light. His account of the outcome of the Paxton crisis asserted a uniquely American identity with great appeal to a people determined to offer manful resistance to unpopular British policies while still defending their claims to civilized sensibility. Of course, he himself would almost certainly not have said or even thought as much back when his piece on Bouquet was published in the spring of 1765. First of all, Smith was not at all an antimonarchist; the highest public acclaim he could give Bouquet was to mention in print that the king in his "royal goodness" had seen fit to acknowledge the "Colonel's merit." Second, his ardent advocacy of natural liberty did not make him in any sense a social leveler. Of tearful British-American adoptees sorrowful at being separated from their native American families, he sneered, "For the honor of humanity, we would suppose those persons to have been of the lowest rank . . . bred up in ignorance and distressing penury." When British-American women and children showed reluctance to be repatriated, they undermined British-American men's patriarchal authority. Such an insult to colonial masculinity could be mitigated only by dismissing such people as ignorant and lowly. Smith's convictions on the commonality of human passions never stood in the way of his continuing desire to use emotion as a basis for inscribing social distinctions. Ultimately, however, he would be able neither to direct nor to stem the contributions of the propassion position to the rising patriot fervor.[88]

Scholars have long debated the relationship between the Paxton crisis and the American Revolution, seeking to understand to what degree democratic impulses shaped the conduct of the Paxton rebels. Analysis of the rhetoric of emotion suggests that the Paxton crisis *did* presage the Revolution, but not in the ways many modern readers would hope. While backcountry commoners were concerned about their influence in the polity, they were equally interested in masculinity, civility, and social respectability. They wanted their anger to be regarded as a source of masculine strength, rather than as a source of servile shame, their dead to be accorded the respect of condolence, and their grief to be met with compassionate action. Where these things were granted, when their land claims were allowed, and when their basic needs for physical security were met, frontier settlers might settle, at least provisionally, for scalp bounties in place of Assembly seats.[89]

As for elite attitudes, analysis of the language of emotion shows that, while leaders eagerly embraced florid rhetoric about the universality of humanity and freedom, they did so largely in an effort to maintain their own social standing. They readily abandoned such ideals in a pinch. The same assemblymen who railed against the Paxton Boys as "audaciously cruel" later came to allow scalp bounties. Meanwhile, exacting and then advertising condolences from Indians fell short of offering real respect in the form of expressions of elite grief for either slain Indians or injured frontier folk. This restricted emotional expression mirrored the elite's limited political actions; rather than respond to the Paxton rebels' demands for political representation, assemblymen dropped the decades-old demand for proprietary taxation and agreed at last to raise money and men for frontier defense. Likewise, the proprietary faction's strategic use of the anger of commoners did not necessarily involve offering them an alliance as equals.[90]

When the Paxton crisis began, the ability to carefully rule one's passions constituted the refined ideal. Yet, as the ensuing controversy proved, British Americans valued masculinity at least as much as gentility, and no group was willing to relinquish claim to civility. All efforts to define who truly possessed these desirable traits were subject to complaints that no one could neatly rule between good and bad passions, judging some admirable and others unacceptable. On the contrary, a judiciously tempered mix of emotions came to be seen as the ideal expression of humanity. By balancing anger and mercy, passion and compassion, Pennsylvania colonists embraced a fragile new emotional equilibrium, a "rational medium" between masculine firmness and civilized sensibility. To the extent that this emotional balance was open to all, it did represent a radically new and egalitarian understanding of human nature. William Smith called this ruling American passion a "love of liberty," and many colonists would soon rally to this call. But, as analysis of Revolutionary rhetoric will further confirm, close attention to the language of emotion indicates just how carefully this liberty was defined and constrained.

9

A Passion for Liberty—The Spirit of Freedom

The Rhetoric of Emotion in the Age of Revolution

In October 1775, with Independence still a year distant but military confrontations already under way, General George Washington sought to explain the American position to the world at large. To justify the American right to rebellion, he declared that, far from suffering "poverty of soul, and baseness of spirit," the "freeborn sons of America, animated by the genuine principles of liberty and love of their country" were well "capable of distinguishing between the blessings of liberty, and the wretchedness of slavery." Washington's conviction that moral emotions—virtuous spirits—motivated love of country, devotion to freedom, and despisement of slavery grew out of eighteenth-century versions of classical theories. His assertions followed the Aristotelian teaching that *thumos,* or spirit, distinguished those with natural claims to liberty from those who were inherently slavish. We are now so accustomed to speaking of the "spirit of freedom" and, perhaps, even more commonly of the "spirit of '76" that we have forgotten to query the curious connection such phrases assert between exalted feelings and legal freedom. Yet the language of rebellion demonstrates that eighteenth-century Anglo-Americans regarded emotional capacities as the linchpin of liberty.[1]

Washington's claims might easily have been based in part on ideas disseminated at the College of Philadelphia. In May 1775, shortly after Washington had arrived in the city to take up the post of commander in chief of the American Revolutionary forces, the college had conducted a very public commencement, in which ancient theories of slavery and freedom received prominent attention. On May 17, some two decades after

Francis Hopkinson had participated in the first-ever commencement exercises of the College and Academy of Philadelphia, the Reverend William Smith welcomed "the honorable members of the Continental Congress" to a graduation ceremony that offered a tutorial on the emotional comportment that accorded with liberty. Student speakers assured the "Gentlemen Delegates" and other members of the audience that "in these American regions" "liberty is in full vigour" thanks to "the native efforts" of those "fired with the love of justice." Lest the classical origins of the animating spirit of freedom be lost on listeners, graduate Thomas Ennals explained, in an address entitled, "On *ancient Eloquence*," that, among Americans, "the sense of liberty is deeply implanted in every bosom." "We have not yet departed far from that simplicity of life and purity of manners, which distinguished ancient republics." For American Revolutionaries, connections between emotional sensitivity and natural liberty could not have been clearer. Those whose hearts and "bosoms" harbored strong feelings and sensations, of "love of their country" and "love of justice," could lay easy claim to the "blessings of liberty," for spirit fostered the civic virtue that in turn validated claims to free citizenship. Meanwhile, those of "base spirits" could be rightly regarded as slavish by nature.[2]

The significance that Revolutionaries attached to links between *thumos* and liberty, feeling and freedom, has long been overlooked. Historians confronting apparent logical contradictions in the rhetoric of patriots who fought a revolution in the name of liberty—even as they held hundreds of thousands in slavery—have long focused on what Bernard Bailyn referred to as "slavery as a political concept." They have tried to explain conflicts between liberty and slavery by arguing that, while patriots opposed slavery on political terms, they were simply unable to do without it in economic terms. Revolutionaries thus launched vociferous arguments against slavery, "without making the connection between politics and social institutions." However, attention to the rhetoric of emotion reveals another side to the story. Following Aristotle, many whites preferred to regard slavery, not as any kind of man-made institution, but rather as the inborn condition of those whose innate lack of emotional spirit made them inherently slavish. For Revolutionaries, to display "spirit" was both to claim and explain one's right to freedom. For historians, then, the study of competing assumptions about the prevalence of emotion—from insistence on its deep cross-group variance to belief in its universal natural occurrence—provides the key to understanding evolving social attitudes in the Revolutionary era.[3]

In the earliest days of colonial protests, when new British fiscal policies in the wake of the financially draining Seven Years War had just begun to provoke opposition, many Anglo-Americans assumed that display of emotions, like manners, served well as status markers, parting the rude from the refined. Colonial protesters seeking allies among the English elite thus worked to establish their own emotional credentials as skilled performers of genteel feeling. Drawing on the transatlantic culture of sensibility, they tried to renegotiate yet reaffirm alliances with their British brethren. Stressing above all the well-modulated nature of their tender emotions, protest leaders emphasized that their carefully considered sentiments bore no relation to the alternately inadequate and excessive passions of the lower sort (be they enslaved blacks or white workers). But, when the British responded to American emotional overtures of protest with nothing but scorn, colonists began brandishing the stronger passions of the people. Though local American elites had no desire to cede social or political control to the masses, they found that they could not advance in the cause of revolution without the aid of that immoderate emotion they had so recently eschewed in their communications with Britain. They thus began seeking ways to combine the civility and respectability attributed to refined feelings with the force and might believed to stem from popular passions.[4]

Patriot leaders found their solution in the notion of *spirit*, a vehement brand of emotion that burnished the power of passion with the luster of classical virtue. As protest efforts gathered steam, from early petitions against the Stamp Act through to the Declaration of Independence, Revolutionaries shifted their tactics, away from simple attempts to affirm membership in a British-dominated cult of sensibility and toward complex assertions of the superior worth of American emotions. When William Smith had complimented Indians on "their strong and ferocious eloquence" and their "inflexible spirit of independence," back in 1765, he had pursued the very themes that would preoccupy his students and members of Congress another decade later. Unlike enslaved Africans, so often denigrated as spiritless, native Americans were alternately castigated and celebrated for their supposedly extreme degree of spirit. Euro-American colonists sought to appropriate laudable elements of Indian spirit even as they also made claim to the best of European sensibility.[5]

Indeed, in emphasizing Indian eloquence, William Smith credited Indians with just the kind of emotional expressiveness needed for the furtherance of classical values. And when he declared the "love of liberty" to be the "ruling passion of the state of nature," he invited the colonial inhabitants of North America to be defined by American nature, even as he also invoked ancient virtue. Here again, attention to the language of emotion pays unexpected dividends. It allows us to perceive the hidden strength of Revolutionaries' classical devotion, despite their frequent lack of direct exposure to ancient texts. Meanwhile, it also allows us to appreciate the ways in which they viewed their own emotional cultivation as a defining American attribute, not simply a derivation of British cultural forms and social formations.[6]

An amalgam of patriotic love, just anger, communal sympathy, and political grief, American spirit was to distinguish those worthy of natural liberty from those deserving enslavement. Indeed, white colonists would ultimately argue that patriot spirit should be distinguished not only from Indians' excessive ferocity and Africans' emotional stupor but also from the emotional torpor that they began claiming had suddenly beset the British. They insisted that superior American emotion alone could bind colonists together in the creation of a new nation. Only in this context can we truly appreciate the meaning of Washington's promise that the "freeborn sons of America" were so "animated by the genuine principles of liberty" as never to betray "baseness of spirit."

The quest to forge an independence movement, to nurture incipient nationalism and the common identity on which it would rest, required a new set of social precepts and social connections that forced changes in society. Revolutionaries' search for the common foundations of humanity in shared emotionality led them to collapse some social divisions. Even as emotion contributed to racialized theories of natural difference between free whites, Indians, and enslaved blacks, it provided a new basis for cross-class unity among American whites. A dawning belief in emotional parity among patriots provided important underpinning for emerging ideas about natural equality. The intention here is to trace the rapid development of an American emotional vernacular in the decade before the Declaration of Independence, the better to understand the unlimited potential, yet tragically limited application, of the principles of natural rights.[7]

"Soft Emotions" and "Sensible Men":
The Use of Sentiment in Early Attempts at Protest and Rapprochement

Emotional rhetoric rose to prominence almost as soon as George III's chief minister, George Grenville, proposed new colonial taxes on all printed materials, in the form of the Stamp Act of 1764. Colonists instantly challenged the plan and declared that the threat of "general Penury . . . and impending Ruin" "must doubtless affect every tender Breast." Determined to demonstrate their opposition to the act, they warned one another, "Deaf . . . must we be to the Voice . . . of Reason and Virtue and totally callous to every softer Emotion, if without sufficient Cause, we refuse to join our fellow Citizens in so indispensable a Work." But the members of Parliament were not to be swayed. In March 1765 they passed the tax and told the king:

> Being thoroughly sensible of your Majesty's paternal Concern for the Relief and Welfare of your People, in recommending to us the Improvement of the public Revenue. . . . we assure your Majesty that, animated with these Sentiments, we will endeavour to . . . pursu[e] every Plan which shall appear to us to be calculated for the public Advantage.

The language of feeling was widely spoken in the Atlantic world confronted by colonists opposed to the Stamp Act. Delicacy of sentiment was acknowledged to be a sure mark of taste and status, from colonial parlors to royal courts. So, from the very beginning, this imperial conflict was argued with emotional rhetoric, as colonial protesters who felt "soft emotions" in tender breasts called across the Atlantic to members of Parliament who claimed to be "sensible" men.[8]

What was the immediate appeal of emotion in the midst of imperial upheavals? Consider the set of problems faced by colonists who wished to oppose the Stamp Act. First, they had to find a mode of protest that could be couched in terms of loyal opposition. In 1765 there was no colonial consensus in favor of independence, yet there was a concerted desire for increased recognition from Britain. Without abandoning a stance of deference, many colonists wanted to affirm their dignity. They needed to find a means of protest that would signal dissent without disrespect, resistance without rebellion. Second, the propertied classes leading the charge against the new policy needed to find a way to respond to popular opposition, to ensure it remained directed against the king's ministers and not the local elite. And, finally, colonists had to find a way to react to a new direction in British policy: the imposition of intracolonial policies that would standardize imperial relations across British America. They needed to forge a united response that could transcend both the traditional rivalries that existed across colonies and the social divisions that existed within each. The new language of sentiment seemed to offer a solution to all of these problems.[9]

When word of the possibility of new taxes first arrived in 1764, a number of colonies decided to send written petitions to Parliament, presenting the case against the new policies in the most pressing terms they could pen. Mounting such petitions was regarded as a traditional right of Englishmen. But colonists introduced a distinctive eighteenth-century element by grafting the new language of feeling onto the old form of complaint. In the following missive sent from Massachusetts to Britain (so popular as to be reprinted in a South Carolina newspaper and again in one from Rhode Island) the writers explained: "There have been communicated to your petitioners sundry resolutions of the house of commons in their last session, for imposing stamp duties or taxes upon the inhabitants of the colonies, the consideration whereof" "must create a very sensible concern and grief." Though this brief mention of "grief" and "sensib[ility]" may not appear to the modern reader to be an especially dramatic example of emotional language, the colonists themselves counted this one of the most important aspects of the petition. The accompanying newspaper article emphasized, "The petitions and representations of New-York, Rhode-Island, etc. are much to the same effect with the above, most of them exceeding it in length and pathos." Colonists regarded pathos as the essential element of effective persuasion.[10]

In sending this first set of petitions to Parliament, colonists believed they were protesting the new imperial policies in the most respectable *and* the most respectful possible terms. Their intention was to use the emotional conventions of politesse to press their case in terms that asserted their own status and rights as Englishmen while offering no insult to members of Parliament. As one writer in the *Providence Gazette* explained matters, "Presenting a petition . . . is an act that carries in itself all the marks of submission." Yet members of Parliament did not respond to colonial objections in at all the way they had hoped. On the contrary, they approved the proposed new taxes and passed the Stamp Act in March 1765, declaring that they *were* sensible men but that the sentiments that actuated *them* pointed to the necessity of enhancing royal revenues, not the need to heed colonial concerns.[11]

Meanwhile, metropolitan observers judged the colonists' carefully phrased petitions to be coarse, uncouth, and unworthy of notice. A report from Rhode Island, irksome enough to be reprinted in New York, claimed that Londoners had found the colonial petitions to have been written "with such warm and unbecoming Expressions, that it would have been dangerous to have presented them to the parliament." Even the colonists' erstwhile allies "expressed much Concern" and "requested they would proceed with Coolness and Moderation." Far from recognizing the colonists' refined command of the culture of feeling and appreciating their petitions' carefully painted pathos, leaders in Britain derided the colonists for the kind of overheated passions usually attributed to the lower sort.[12]

The colonists found this state of affairs utterly untenable. Not only had they failed in their efforts to prevent passage of the revenue act, but their efforts to participate in the genteel culture of sensibility had also been laughed off in a most humiliating way. The Stamp Act was due to go into effect on November 1, 1765, and, in the months leading up to this deadline, colonists grew ever more restive. In the summer of 1765, they launched a series of protests that grafted elite and popular emotional culture in various experimental combinations, each an effort to craft a workable response to Britain's unwelcome new assertions of power.

Since Parliament had dismissed the colonists' first set of petitions as simply too heated to be taken seriously, one possible remedy was to emphasize calmer, cooler emotions while still trying to communicate colonial objections to the Stamp Act. This was the tack taken by freemen in Newport, Rhode Island, who sent instructions to their representatives in the assembly: "We expect that you will give your utmost Attention to . . . the Act for levying Stamp Duties: That while you express the greatest Affection and Loyalty to our SOVEREIGN, and all proper Regard to that august Assembly, the British PARLIAMENT, you assert our Rights with a becoming Firmness." To speak of their affection for the king did help to guarantee continued colonial fealty, but such expressions of affection did little to articulate their central bone of contention. Just what emotional statement would combine fidelity with strength and "firmness"?[13]

Another possible avenue for protest was offered by assertions of anger. Associated closely with strength and resolve, expressions of anger could more effectively help to convey the depth of colonial determination not to acquiesce in new tax measures. Such tactics were tried. According to an account from Boston reprinted in the *New-York Mercury,* "Friends of the Stampman for New Hampshire" warned the recently appointed stamp collector that, unless he resigned voluntarily from his new post, they would "leave him to the consequences of the popular Resentment."[14]

The "consequences of the popular resentment" were becoming ever more dire as mobs from Rhode Island, Massachusetts, and Connecticut marched through the streets in August and early September 1765, looting and burning the homes and offices of those designated as collectors of the dreaded tax and even going so far as to hang the collectors in effigy. An account from Connecticut, published in the *Pennsylvania Gazette*, well captures this phase of colonial resistance. In an elaborate protest conducted that August, the "VIRTUAL representative" of the tax collector was first tried, then hanged, and then finally burned in effigy. Meanwhile, an allegorical figure representing the injured mother country begged the tax collector not to "enslave your Country." When the tax collector refused her, "indignant Wrath swelled the Bosom of [that] venerable Matron," an anger equaled only by "the Rage of the Populace." Far from cooling down their emotional rhetoric, these colonists shifted from pouring forth "pathos" to announcing their anger. Sensibility alone was insufficient to resist "enslavement."[15]

Yet colonists also believed that, left unchecked, anger could easily veer out of control. Though popular rage directed against Britain could prove to be a potent source of strength for patriot leaders, that same anger aimed against members of the local elite could prove far more problematic. Propertied men became extremely alarmed at the possibility that such violence could easily increase and even be turned against members of the local elite. Throughout the colonies people were demanding to know—as a writer in the *New-York Mercury* put it—how Stamp Act supporters could "hold up their heads, amidst the reproaches and execrations of a justly enraged people." The *Mercury* essay noted with pointed irony: "N.B. This Piece was wrote several Days before the late Stirs in Boston." The ramifications of the "justly enraged people" were beginning to be all too apparent. If the propertied classes might have initially tolerated or even encouraged muscular mass protests, they began to literally fear for their necks.[16]

Upon consideration, colonial leaders decided to draw back from unqualified endorsements of popular anger. If, as classical theory maintained and as many colonists had come to believe, civic stability depended on emotional civility, then successful states needed the emotional involvement of all freemen. In the colonies, where the lack of a titled aristocracy combined with assertive legislatures and strong traditions of local governance to magnify the importance of ordinary people's involvement in government, members of the presumptive elite finally found themselves with little incentive for making exclusive claims to upright emotion. Instead, colonial leaders began to endorse the idea that emotions were a natural and universal human attribute. Elites allowed that even commoners, if carefully schooled, could contribute to public virtue. Noting that "our government is . . . in the strictest sense of the word, a *democratical government*," a *Providence Gazette* essayist theorized, "Now since there are, and can be none in office, but by the suffrages of the people . . . these constituents ought to be qualified with sentiments so far refined, as to be capable of distinguishing between right and wrong." Even the lower sort, he explained, "ought to have so true a sense of humanity, as utterly to abandon that rancorous rage and violence of proceeding, which are the distinguishing principles they [too often] adopt." Ordinary colonists were being told they could indeed be qualified with the refined sentiments that would allow them to "abandon rancorous rage" in favor of more measured emotions.[17]

Colonists concluded that the main reason the petitions of the previous year had not produced the desired results was, not that they themselves were inept at expressing genteel sensibilities, but that Parliament was incapable of responding suitably. They began to argue that the only proper recipient of colonial petitions was the king himself, not his ministers or minions in Parliament. Colonists who had not supported the earlier petition drives now claimed that they had refrained from doing so only because they had realized all along that Parliament would not respond with feeling and should not be allowed to exercise authority over the colonies. An open letter from colonists in New Jersey, printed in the *New-York Mercury* in September, affirmed, "The inhabitants of th[is] colony are sensible of the imposition [of the Stamp Act] and spurn at it . . . [yet] the fate of the petitions which were sent, is quite sufficient to show our brethren of the other colonies, that they, in the form they were sent, might better have been spared." What, then, were colonists to do? "I hope all the provinces will unite in sending their several humble petitions to his majesty, without delay; whose royal heart, I doubt not, will be touched with the reasonable complaint of so great a body of his faithful subjects." This writer was all for returning to the tactic of petitioning but advised his fellow colonists to aim their efforts at the king, not at Parliament, confident that the "royal heart" would be "touched" by the complaints of "sensible" subjects.[18]

At the same time, reports began to surface reminding colonists of the ways in which the rules of petition were supposed to work. An opinion piece in the *New-York Mercury* harkened back to a political conflict from earlier in the century, in which Queen Anne responded appropriately to a petition from her New York subjects. The queen, "well judging how to set an intrinsic value on the affections of her American subjects return'd them this most gracious answer (which ought to have been wrote in letters of GOLD, and preserved to the latest posterity, for the worthy imitation of her successors) 'She had heard the CRIES of her injured subjects.' " The question was just how the colonists could be sure their cries would be heard by the current king. Clearly something more moving than the unsuccessful petitions to Parliament of 1764 was called for, yet patriot leaders had to take care not to overstep their bounds and do insult to the crown. Though they wanted to send a forceful signal of discontent, they hoped to find a more controlled means than the violent crowd actions that had recently rocked many colonies.[19]

Hoisting Their Colours Half Mast High: Mourning as a New Mode of Protest

Was there, in fact, any way to address all the patriot leaders' problems at once, to contain popular unrest, maintain a stance of loyalty to the king, and yet retain a message of opposition? The solution, which had been temporarily submerged by affectionate addresses and angry actions alike, appeared to involve an emphasis on grief. For, in the midst of colonists' renewed interest in petitioning for the redress of their grievances, another of their early initiatives began to bear fruit. From the beginning, even as they had tried to sway Parliament with sentiment, they had also launched a boycott program designed to reduce their overall economic dependence on Britain. Beginning in 1764, many of the colonies entered into nonimportation agreements with one another, pledging not to purchase a variety of English goods including, significantly, such traditional mourning goods as black cloth, scarves, gloves, and rings. Dozens of notices to this effect appeared throughout colonial newspapers. The *New-York Mercury* reported that the colony's "principle Merchants" had "come into a Resolution to curtail many superfluities in Dress" and that "the usual manner of expressing . . . Regard and Sorrow for a deceased Friend or Relative, by covering [oneself] in Black, is . . . in the List of Superfluities." Historians have generally treated this development as nothing more than an economic measure, and it must be noted that mourning goods could at times eat up as much as 40 percent of a person's estate. But, when we consider that these restrictions on private mourning were made in the context of very purposeful public declarations of feeling, we have to suspect that these actions had additional symbolic significance.[20]

According to a late-August report, by 1765 colonial grievances had begun to cause the British textile industry grief; the colonists' nonimportation policies had left "Multitudes of Manufacturers . . . almost wholly out of Employ." In response, "40,000 Weavers, Glove-makers, and other Manufacturers, appeared in the City of London with black Flags" of mourning, determined to make the king address their difficulties. This action was counted a great success, for, according to the report, the "Groans and Lamentations of the Subject[s] having reached the Royal Ear, an Alteration of Men and Measures would soon take Place." In effect, the British protesters had literalized the language of grief, marching on London with the very funeral symbols they could no longer market in the colonies.[21]

The writer was quick to grasp the potential this kind of protest held to further the aims of American colonists, for he declared: "All America is in Commotion, and the People very exactly copy the Example set Them by their Brethren at Home. GOD grant that our Groans, though uttered at so great a Distance, may also reach the Royal Ear." If colonists could really "copy the Example" of the British and couch their declarations of grief and grievance in terms of actual mourning, they might at last have found an effective means of obstructing the Stamp Act while still preserving order at home and obedience to the crown.[22]

The promise these possibilities held for colonial protesters was first put to the test in Pennsylvania, where recent events, from the Seven Years War to the Paxton Crisis, had primed people to appreciate the political effectiveness of calls for compassion. Throughout late summer and early fall, shipments of stamped paper, intended for the production of all printed material after November 1, began to arrive in colonial harbors. The October 3 issue of the *Pennsylvania Gazette* reported tensely that the *Captain Holland* had arrived from London carrying "the Stamped Paper on board for this Province." Pennsylvanians braced for the ship's entrance into the Philadelphia harbor itself. Then, according to the next *Gazette*, as the ship carrying the papers sailed into Philadelphia on October 5, "all the Vessels in the Harbour hoisted their Colours half Mast high, the Bells began to ring, being first muffled, and continued so until the Evening, and every Countenance added to the Appearance of sincere Mourning, for the approaching Loss of Liberty." Not content to simply hang their stamp distributor in effigy nor to deliver closely reasoned instructions to members of the provincial Assembly, Pennsylvania protesters instead mounted a massive show of mourning. After months of avoiding elaborate funeral rites in private life, the people of Pennsylvania channeled their opposition into a massive pageantry of public grief.[23]

Unlike the formal early petitions sent to Parliament, which made mention of grief but failed to sway the members, engaging in actual mourning advanced the interests of colonial leaders opposed to the Stamp Act in several important ways. At the most basic level, this tolling of the bells linked the demonstration of grief to the declaration of grievance in dramatic fashion. At the same time, it created a new means of protest that demanded a response without revealing disrespect. On both sides of the Atlantic, compassion had become a key emotion for those who wished to assert the right to rule. To grieve and mourn was to express one's own feelings, thus indicating a failure of self-control and a subordinate status, while to respond to such grief, to put another's feelings ahead of one's own, demonstrated the kind of self-mastery that could justify social mastery. So, by displaying grief, colonists could simultaneously reaffirm their subsidiary status with respect to Britain and make an irresistible claim on the king's compassion. The king and his ministers could not appear to remain unmoved by compelling representations of colonial grief/grievance without calling into serious question their fitness to reign.[24]

The one major drawback to displays of grief as declarations of grievance was the possibility that colonists might come across not merely as properly subordinate but as hopelessly subservient. For grief, unlike anger, had certain feminine associations that left colonists open to aspersion. They had a fine line to walk between humility and humiliation. They wanted to succeed in being, as a committee from Massachusetts put it, "open and unreserved, but decent and respectful." Thus, notwithstanding their many protestations, elite men themselves could not resist recurring on occasion to angry passion with its implicit assertions of strength.[25]

The report on protest in Pennsylvania tried to forestall detrimental interpretations of public grieving by emphasizing that colonists were not merely saddened but also angered by the arrival of the stamps. The article in the *Gazette* explained that the Pennsylvania stamp distributor had been spared, not out of cowardice, but out of compassion for his very ill health. The protesters were "transported with Resentment, and it is impossible to say what lengths their Rage might have carried them, had not . . . his Situation raised their Compassion." Only a move to safeguard the "Stamp Papers on board His Majesty's Ship, prevents them from being exposed to

A Passion for Liberty—The Spirit of Freedom

the Resentment of an injured and enraged People." Thus, protest leaders continued to invoke the threat of mob violence even as they experimented with another, more conciliatory means of protest. Combining "transports of resentment" with torrents of tears allowed elite leaders of the Stamp Act opposition to threaten violence to officials abroad even as they strove to contain it at home. They could tap the wild "passions" of the masses while continuing to make status claims on the basis of genteel finer "feelings."[26]

This complicated balance of rage and mourning, of calls for and demonstrations of sympathy and compassion, grew naturally out of the internal contests and compromises that had so recently roiled Pennsylvania. Of course, the Paxton rebels and their Philadelphia supporters had turned to just such an amalgam of anger and grief in their efforts to forge a "happy medium" between masculinity and civility. Despite their apparent consonance with the transatlantic culture of sensibility, grief-based protests took an important departure by the inclusion of popular anger.[27]

For the very first time, protesting colonists began to describe their emotions explicitly in terms of the issue of *spirit,* that trope tied by classical theory to the natural right to freedom. As a September statement (originating in Rhode Island) explained in the *Gazette,* "The Inhabitants of the . . . Colonies, affected with their present Distresses, and animated with the noble Spirit of Liberty, have proposed . . . [to] assert our Rights with a becoming Firmness." Where once moderate claims of being "sensibly affected" were all that resisters cared to make in their public statements, they now turned to invocations of "noble spirit" in order to better display "becoming firmness," flaunting virtuous vigor alongside civilized refinement. From the intersection of classical theory, eighteenth-century sensibility, and Revolutionary emotional upheaval a new political ideal was emerging, which would unite colonists across class even as it divided them in new ways from their brethren in Britain. Once introduced, "spirit" would soon be embraced as the watchword of revolution.[28]

Philadelphia's angry mourners reported with satisfaction, "The cool thinking People among us, congratulate themselves, and their Country, on finding Spirit enough exerted, to put us on the same Footing with the rest of the Continent; and that this was done by Men who had Moderation not to proceed to any unnecessary Acts of Violence." On the one hand, displays of mourning helped contain the protests; they allowed the local elite to channel popular resentment into grief and thus to keep dissatisfaction focused on England and not on leaders at closer hand. Yet an emphasis on "spirit" also expanded the stakes of protests, asserting that colonists (and perhaps colonists alone) could lay claim to the emotions of liberty. While the Philadelphia account still assumed that "the cool thinking People" could be distinguished from those with overheated passions, it would not be long before the "spirit of liberty" would come to be cast as the common birthright of *all* "Inhabitants of the . . . colonies."[29]

Pennsylvania's experimental protest soon inspired wider interest, occurring as it did just two days before the gathering of the Stamp Act Congress in New York City. Reports of events in Philadelphia soon spread there to the patriot leaders from across the colonies who had agreed to meet to coordinate colonial resistance. On October 7, the first day the congress was in session, the *New-York Mercury* carried a piece written in Philadelphia describing how "rage, resentment and grief appeared painted in every countenance," adding, "The mournful language of one and all our inhabitants seems to be farewell liberty!" The writer ended: "I cannot proceed—tears of vexation and sorrow stop my pen—O my country, my country!" Colonists were coming to appreciate the many positive results of melding "vexation and sorrow." Grief backed up by anger could convey resistance in respectful terms while heading off any imputations of weakness. Meanwhile, channeling popular rage into public mourning could help dilute the danger of mob violence, instead opening new avenues for cross-class unity.[30]

At the very same time, British representatives began sending signals that, if the colonists could successfully portray the depth of their grievances while yet conveying their continued loyalty and subservience to Britain, the crisis might yet find a satisfactory conclusion. According to the October 7 issue of the *Mercury,* Massachusetts governor Francis Bernard had lectured the Massachusetts assembly in late September, criticizing mob violence and warning it that the British would "require a Submission to their Authority as a Preliminary to their granting you any Relief." Similar admonishments arrived straight from Britain. One in the *Pennsylvania Gazette* later that month "from a gentleman in London" offered the advice: "Now is your Time to represent your Grievances, in moving Manner, and I flatter myself you will be attended unto." What better way to represent grievances in a moving manner than by conducting mass exhibitions of public grief?[31]

So widespread was the appeal of mourning as a mode of protest that the November 1, 1765, deadline for imposition of the act was met with nearly universal tears and lamentations. In Philadelphia, none other than

William Bradford, printer and parent to Tommy and Tace, put out a funeral edition of his paper, the *Pennsylvania Journal* (Figure 16). Bradford fashioned his masthead into a tombstone and closed out the issue with a black coffin signaling the death of the press at the hands of the Stamp Act. On November 7 the *Pennsylvania Gazette* further reported, "On Friday and Saturday last, the dreadful first and second days of November, our bells were rung muffled, and other demonstrations of grief shewn." In Boston, they declared, "When our sacred rights are infringed, we feel the grievance," and New York asserted, "As soon as this shocking Act was known, it filled all British America, from one End to the other, with Astonishment and Grief." In Boston, Newport, Rhode Island, and Portsmouth, New Hampshire, the bells were rung "in token of mourning" on that day, and South Carolina soon followed suit. At last colonists seemed to have found an effective formula for protesting the Stamp Act. The rhetoric of grief allowed them to criticize Parliament even as they maintained their allegiance to Britain.[32]

Excellent evidence of the deliberateness with which colonists turned to this tactic comes in the form of a satirical print produced and distributed on November 1 to showcase the grief of "America who is in deep distress," as the *Pennsylvania Gazette* explained it. The etching was closely modeled on a British cartoon *The Deplorable State of America; or, Sc—h Government* (Figures 17, 18). Comparing the English and American versions of the print reveals the lengths to which colonists were willing to go in their efforts to represent their grievances in a diffident yet "moving manner."[33]

The basic scene in both cartoons presents Britain, figured as a mature matron, attempting to hand the Stamp Act, labeled Pandora's Box, to her reluctant children, Liberty and America. Various classical figures circle around and try to prevent the transfer. In both versions a female figure, Minerva or Wisdom, counsels against accepting the box, and Loyalty, another female figure, leans against a liberty tree threatening to faint if the tree falls; a male figure, Mercury or Commerce, flees the scene. But key alterations in the American version subtly change the meaning of the print and amplify its emotional content.

The most obvious difference between the two prints is artistic assurance. An early collector scribbled in the margin of a surviving copy of the Philadelphia version (now in the holdings of the Library Company of Philadelphia) that it was "the wretched copy done in Philadelphia," and modern critics have been quick to echo the judgment. Comparatively

FIGURE 16. "Expiring: In Hopes of a Resurrection to Life Again." William Bradford, *Pennsylvania Journal, and Weekly Advertiser*, Oct. 31, 1765. Permission The Library Company of Philadelphia.

Numerous details signify death and mourning: the tombstone masthead; the skull and crossbones (front page, bottom right); the coffin (back page, bottom right);

the motto "Adieu, Adieu to the LIBERTY of the PRESS" (margin, front page); the heavy black leading separating columns. The text included the exclamation, "How melancholly to pine and die while no kind physician is allowed to explore the Cause," but also reasserted colonial claims to being "loyal Subjects and free Born Britons."

FIGURE 17. *The Deplorable State of America; or, Sc——h Government.* Anonymous. England, ca. 1765. *Permission The Library Company of Philadelphia*

FIGURE 18. *The Deplorable State of America.* By Robert Wilkinson.
Philadelphia, 1765. *Permission The Library Company of Philadelphia*

coarse as the American etching was, however, in an important sense its wretchedness was deliberate, designed to forefront American suffering, play up American obedience, and elicit a compassionate response in Britain.[34]

As so often when American copyists transferred British engravings, the Philadelphia version reversed the direction of the English original. Britannia, seated on the lower right in the English version with her arm outstretched to the left, hovers on the left side of the Philadelphia version with her arm outstretched to the right. But the more significant flip was analytical; American artists switched not just the physical location but also the gender positions of America and Liberty. In the English version, America, portrayed as a muscular Indian man wearing a blanket and carrying a quiver of arrows, pushes away the box and calls to Minerva, "Secure Me, O Goddess, by thy Wisdom for I abhor it as Death," while Liberty, figured as a long-locked young woman reclining on a rock, exclaims, "It is all over with Me." But in the American version, America, now portrayed as a weeping maiden (distinguished from the classical European figures only by the feather ornament in her hair), issues her plea while tending to Liberty, now a dying man partially draped in classical robes, who implores, "and canst thou mother! O have pity this horrid Box." While the British version of the print rendered America as a threatening warrior who aggressively shoves back the arm of the British matron offering Pandora's box even as Liberty languishes without hope, in the American version, America sheds refined feminine tears over the imminent demise of a virtuous public man while Liberty, near death, explicitly calls on British feeling—pity.

Such shifts underscored colonists' steadfast claims that their resistance to the Stamp Act arose from loyal opposition. Far from portraying themselves as fierce warriors, ready for action, Americans still preferred to figure themselves as respectful supplicants. The American alterations to the English print reinforced the message that colonists protested out of concern for the preservation of *British* liberty and remained ever mindful of their rightfully subordinate position within the empire.

Yet the American version of the print not only retained a tiny image of a scaffold off to one side labeled "Fit Entertainment for St——p M——n" but also added the further detail of a man with a dripping tar brush demanding, "Will you resign?" and of another figure who responds, "Yes, yes, I will." The angry aggression of the mob thus remained to reinforce the passive resistance of grief. If, at this point, uncertainty continued about how elite feeling and popular passion could best be balanced, the careful retention of rage along with the elaboration of grief nonetheless reinforced the emergent belief that each benefited from the other. Ultimately, of course, colonists would shift their sights from clamoring for British liberty to claiming natural rights. When they did, they would view the twined impetus of anger and sympathy as fundamental to a supremely *American* spirit of freedom.[35]

The "Concourse of Manners" Consisted of "Persons of All Races": Coordinating Protests across Colony and Class

For the time being, however, internal cross-class tensions remained a paramount concern among colonists. Stemming the most aggressive impulses of the common people greatly preoccupied members of the self-styled local elite. Indeed, in eschewing the imagery of furious Indians in this still-early stage of protest, colonial leaders not only signaled their own obedience to Britain but also attempted to discourage violent assertions on the part of their own subordinates. For the moment, leading colonists preferred to privilege grief over anger.

In Boston, for example, elite relief at the prevention of violence on November 1 was palpable. Though once again officials were hanged in effigy and then torn limb from limb, the protests remained symbolic, and no property was destroyed. The *Pennsylvania Gazette*'s summary of the November protests in Boston highlights the critical part played by the controlled display of emotion:

Last Friday, being the Day the Stamp-Act was to take Place, the Publick were not much alarmed or displeased at the Morning's being ushered in by Tolling of Bells in several Parts of the Town, and the Vessels in the Harbour displaying their Colours half-mast-high, in token of Mourning. . . . The Evening was more remarkable for Peace and Quietness than common; a Circumstance that would at any Time redound to the Honour of the Town, but was still more agreeable, as the Fears of many were great lest it should prove another 26th of August; for the horrid Violences of which Night, we hope the good Order of this [one] will in some Measure atone, as it is a Proof such Conduct was not agreeable to the Sentiments of the Town, but was

only the lawless Ravages of some foreign Villains, who took advantage
of the over heated Temper of a very few People of this Place, and
drew them in to commit such Violences and Disorders, as they shud-
dered at with Horror in their cooler Hours.

The Boston elite regarded the ability to tamp down overheated popular
passions and control mob violence as crucial to the containment of
protest and the prevention of chaos. Had tempers been allowed to rage
unchecked, they feared the protest results would likely have been far more
radical. By channeling anger into grief, elite leaders were able to articulate the "Sentiments of the Town" on terms that advanced their own
interests.[36]

Still, the social attitudes conveyed in this account contained the seeds
of a new, more egalitarian outlook. Where the seemingly similar Philadelphia description definitively distinguished "the cool thinking people" from
the hotheaded masses, this article instead portrayed even those of overheated tempers as capable of enjoying "cooler hours." Implicitly, then, this
account posited that *all* colonists—unlike foreigners—could experience a
range of emotions, rather than insisted that different classes of people
could be grouped according to definitive emotional characteristics.

On November 1, colonists from Rhode Island took the new tactics to
the logical extreme and held an actual funeral for Liberty. As reported in
the *Pennsylvania Gazette* of November 7, "The Sons of Freedom sunk
beneath the horrid Gloom, and everone was struck with the Melancholy,
at the approaching Funeral of their departed, beloved Friend, LIBERTY!"
As was true in the colonial version of *The Deplorable State of America*
cartoon, the personification of the abstract concept of liberty was a crucial step; it allowed colonists to shed their tears in public tribute to an old
English virtue, not in selfish distress for petty pecuniary concerns. Civic
grief was to be read as a sign of deep feeling, one that demonstrated the
refinement of the person in mourning as well as the respect in which the
deceased was held. Colonists' tears showed they held liberty in the highest esteem, higher even than did the king's ministers and members of
Parliament. This stance allowed them to insist that their protests were not
rebellions at all but merely the honorable display of an honorary emotion,
a move that left the British obliged to prove in turn their own refinement
and devotion to liberty. Indeed, grief for liberty's loss could be cast as the
ultimate manifestation of the very classical emotions supposed to mark
and motivate the naturally free.[37]

A Passion for Liberty—The Spirit of Freedom

The Rhode Island demonstrations of devotion to liberty capture the complexity of colonial approaches to slavery, feeling, and freedom. Consider, now, the full description of their funeral procession:

> Summoned by Death's cankling Knell, the Funeral began to move at 12 o'clock, from the Crown Coffee House, towards the Burying Ground. The Concourse of Mourners and Spectators was prodigious, consisting of Persons of all Ranks, from the highest, even down to the Blacks, who seemed, from a sense of their Masters Sufferings to join the Mourning Course. The Procession was solemn; and with sullen Tread and heavy Hearts, at length arrived at the Place of Interment, where the mourners were about taking their LAST FAREWELL of their old friend LIBERTY—"Oh!—Liberty!—Oh! FREEDOM—where art thou going?—Oh! my ruined Country!" The mournful Aspiration was scarcely uttered, when a Son of LIBERTY, emerging from the horrid Gloom of Despair, addressed himself thus:—"O LIBERTY! the Darling of my Soul!—Glorious LIBERTY! admir'd, ador'd by all true Britons! LIBERTY dead! it cannot be!" A Groan was then heard, as if coming from the Coffin; and upon closer Attention, it proved to be a Trance, for Old FREEDOM was not dead.—The Goddess Britannia had ordered a Guardian Angel to snatch Old FREEDOM from the Jaws of frozen Death. . . . The Afternoon was spent in Rejoicing, and Bell-ringing—The Court House was ornamented with the Ensigns of Loyalty.

There are a number of points of interest in this account. First of all, the mourners consisted of "Persons of all Ranks," which underscores the effectiveness of displays of mourning at creating cross-class alliances. If emotional sensibility was a sign of gentility while immoral violence arose from the force of rage, then members of the mob who mourned could claim higher status than those who brawled. Thus the funerals furthered colonial social cohesion even as they advanced transatlantic political protests. Second, the funeral made the challenge to Parliament quite clear: all "true Britons" adored liberty and would mourn her passing. If members of Parliament did not demonstrate their fellow feeling with the colonists by repealing the Stamp Act, their very claim to Britishness, their natural devotion to liberty and freedom, could be called into question. Meanwhile, both messages were heightened by the inclusion of the information that "Blacks" too participated in this idealized protest.[38]

The brief mention that all colonists attended the protests "even down to the Blacks" provides one of the only references to African Americans in reporting on Stamp Act protests. Whatever the actual intent of the enslaved blacks' show of mourning for liberty (surely they had more than their masters' taxes in mind), it is fair to assume that the protest organizers saw the African colonists' participation as evidence that ritualized mourning was an effective mechanism of social control at all levels. As we have seen repeatedly earlier, British Americans in northern colonies did all they could to ignore the emotions of African Americans in their midst, claiming that they were downcast and spiritless yet refusing to acknowledge their ever-accumulating grief. African Americans' open grief for liberty thus offered further shame to the British, who could defend their own claims to classical virtue only by engaging in a corresponding display of feeling. Any further failures of sympathy risked making the British appear more debased than even the "naturally slavish."[39]

If modern readers find irony in triumphal colonial accounts of patriotic public mourning by the enslaved, contemporaries perceived no contradiction. Concerned primarily to assert their own claims to the virtuous feelings of natural liberty, most colonists saw in the spectacle of black grief only an opportunity to emphasize Parliament's comparative emotional and political degeneracy, not an obligation to acknowledge black humanity, much less a requirement to allow their freedom. Indeed, this Rhode Island account's concluding verses underscored the growing claim that white colonists were the true heirs of the classical virtues that ought to distinguish the British from all others:

> The Birthright of Britons is FREEDOM,
> The contrary is worse than Death's Pangs.
> HUZZA for GEORGE the Third,
> CHORUS. Britannia's Sons despise Slavery,
> And dare to be nobly free.

Far from questioning slavery as an *institution*, such rhetoric affirmed the naturalness of slavery as the innate *condition* of all those who, lacking a love for liberty, failed to "despise Slavery." Patriots' primary concern was, not to critique slavery per se, but rather to assert that they themselves had inherited the emotional spirit that distinguished those who could claim freedom as a "Birthright."[40]

Similar concerns shaped demonstrations in Portsmouth, New Hampshire, where grieving protesters also snatched Liberty from the grave. Friday, November 1, began in that town with "tolling all the Bells" and public "Notice given to the Friends of LIBERTY to attend her Funeral . . . a Coffin having been previously prepared, and neatly ornamented, on the Lid of which was wrote LIBERTY, aged 145, STAMPED." Significantly, while Liberty was explicitly gendered female in this account (in contrast to Newport, where Old Freedom might well have been male), she was noted as having reached the incredible, venerable age of 145 and therefore being worthy of public tribute. In other respects, the account of the New Hampshire funeral stressed the same essential themes the Rhode Island one had: the unity across social classes of the mourners, the great grief expressed by spectators at the funeral, the nonviolent nature of the protest, and the cathartic effects of grief transformed into gladness by the revival of liberty. The *Gazette* reported:

> The procession began from the State-House, attended by a great concourse of people of all ranks, with unbraced drums, and after marching through the principal Streets, it passed the Parade, on which Minute Guns were fired, and continued till the Corpse arrived at the Place of Interment, which was about half a Mile out of Town, when after much Sorrow expressed for our *expired Liberty,* a Funeral *Oration* was pronounced, greatly in Favour of the Deceased, which was hardly ended before the Corpse was taken up, it having been perceived that some Remains of Life were left, at which the inscription was immediately altered, and then appeared to be *Liberty Revived*—and the Stamp-Act was thrown into the grave, and buried,—at which the Bells immediately altered their Melancholy to a more joyful [note which] diffused into every Countenance. The whole was conducted with the utmost Decency.

New Hampshire protesters extended the funeral metaphor as far as it would go by not only setting out to bury Liberty but by successfully interring the Stamp Act. Significantly, they displayed joy, not melancholy, while burying the act they hoped to make a dead letter. Only Liberty merited the tribute of tears.[41]

This article too described protest participants as "*people* of all ranks," echoing the Rhode Island description of "*persons* of all ranks." Such appellations were doubtless intended to include women as well as men. In a world where emotional expression provided the basis for coding and contesting rank, women had long occupied the sort of position now being espoused for colonists at large. Often documented in tears but seldom recorded as enraged, women were already exemplars of the transmutation of anger into grief and the subsequent transcendence of grief through cheerfulness. Just as wives could negotiate but never repudiate the authority of their husbands, so colonists cast themselves, through mourning and gladness, as loyal subjects seeking redress. Thus, the resurrection of liberty mattered because it conserved loyalty through emotional catharsis. As in Rhode Island, where colonists who began the day with "sullen Tread and heavy Hearts" ended with an afternoon spent "rejoicing," New Hampshire demonstrators "altered their melancholy" to joy. The use of sentiment allowed colonists to reaffirm their essential virtue and display "Ensigns of Loyalty," all the while refining their claims to liberty.

So appealing was this new interpretation of sadness that it spread even to Connecticut, the colony that, back in August, had personified liberty, using anger alone. By November 1, protesters in Connecticut weighed in on the importance of sympathy and fellow feeling between Parliament and the colonists by declaring, "We . . . find ourselves distressed with the most alarming Apprehensions, when we observe that grand Legislature to entertain Sentiments so different from ours, respecting what we ever reckoned amongst our most important and essential Rights as Englishmen." At the same time, they affirmed their attachment to Britain and capacity for elevated mourning when they claimed, "Inspired with the warmest Sentiments of affectionate Loyalty and Duty . . . we are therefore filled with the most sensible Grief and Concern, and think it a Duty we owe to His Majesty, to the Nation, to ourselves, and to Posterity, to express and declare the Sense we have respecting the Rights and Privileges which we may justly claim, and humbly hope to enjoy, under his Majesty's gracious Protection and Government." Though this statement contains echoes of the colonists' earliest attempts to link grief and grievance, it was uttered in an entirely new and more highly charged context. In a sense, these protesters brought the use of sentiment full circle by incorporating the language of grief from the petitions of 1764 into far more forceful public demonstrations. Again, the niceties of sentiment were redeployed for political ends.[42]

The colonists' mass demonstrations of mourning combined with the forced resignations of the stamp distributors and the confiscation of the stamped papers to convince Parliament that enforcement of the Stamp Act was not only impossible but undesirable. When backed by anger, explicit or implicit, such shows of grief allowed protesters to reaffirm their cultured refinement and natural love of freedom even as they challenged members of Parliament to confirm theirs. Grieving for liberty became a widespread means of popular protest because it tapped into widely prevalent ideas about emotional sensibility recognized on both sides of the Atlantic. It was effective because it avoided so many potential pitfalls of the resistance movement. The mourning for the death of Liberty allowed colonists to show dissent without disrespect: they could cloak their statements of grievance in expressions of grief while declaring that their tears were shed in tribute to British virtue. Perhaps most important of all, displays of mourning elevated the political importance of compassion, making it the standard by which leaders should be judged. In March 1766, Parliament formally repealed the Stamp Act. Not surprisingly, the repeal was widely celebrated in both England and America as the death of the stamp tax.[43]

Reaction to the news in Pennsylvania underscores just how important compassion had become as a measure of mastery as well as how crucial the language of sentiment had been to the successful colonial strategy. The introductory issue of the *American Monitor* asserted that the news that the Stamp Act had been repealed and that "our . . . Grievances . . . redressed . . . cannot but fill every breast in *America,* with the deepest Sentiments of loyalty and gratitude to our Most Gracious SOVEREIGN, who has lent so indulgent an Ear to our just Complaints; as well as evince to us the Justice and Tenderness of the *British* Parliament and Nation in general." This writer praised the king in very particular terms; the price of colonial loyalty was the proffering of an indulgent ear. Had the king not responded to colonial cries for relief and granted their grievances redress, their breasts might well have been filled with other, more ominous sentiments.[44]

At the same time, the writer was anxious to place colonial cries for feeling in the best possible light, far from the shadow of rebellion. Of the colonists' opponents he wrote, "I hope [they] have formed no wrong Judgment of our Temper." Once more affirming that colonial feelings were calculated not only to demand but also to demonstrate respect, he affirmed, "We may give all due Applause to the Justice, the Tenderness, and the *patriotism* of our Friends, who have relieved us from Burdens which we thought grievous and injurious to our essential Liberties, without proclaiming any insolent Exultation over those who laboured to subject us to such Burdens." Once good relations with Britain had been restored, colonists sought to avoid at all costs any imputations of insolence. They claimed that their protests had never meant to convey a hierarchical challenge of any kind. On the contrary, they insisted that their protests had simply stemmed from feelings deeply felt, which, once assuaged, would simply melt away.[45]

The *Monitor* author insisted it had been obvious all along that "our Discontents only flowed from a Sense of our Oppression; and that a Restoration of our Quiet would infallibly attend a Redress of our Wrongs." The essay avowed that only enemies of the colonies had ever harbored any doubts about the hidden content of colonial protests: "Our real friends will . . . rejoice that they had not formed wrong Notions of our Dispositions. . . . They insisted that we had shewn a Spirit of liberty, not of sedition; that we had not the most distant Thought of assuming an Independency on our Parent Country." The social messages intended by colonial expressions of sentiment could not have been more plainly summarized. The colonies, it seemed, had never been rebellious at all, merely grieved by their sufferings and galled by Britain's threatened fall from classical virtue. By reinvigorating the "spirit of liberty," colonists reconfirmed an essential element of Englishness. Sadness and sedition were two totally separate things, or at least so they could claim.[46]

The beauty of sentiment as a rhetorical strategy is that it both conveyed and cloaked the true colonial position. The forced resignations of the stamp distributors, the looting of the houses of royal officials, and the impounding of the stamped papers left little room for the British to doubt that violent opposition underlay colonial declarations of grief. Yet, an emphasis on mourning allowed colonists to disavow the very messages they dispatched. Likewise, in repealing the Stamp Act, members of Parliament did not have to concede that they had been swayed by colonial violence or intimidated by the logic of their reasoning—indeed, they were careful to reassert their power to pass laws for the colonies by issuing the Declaratory Act. They simply had to prove that they could respond with compassion to the suffering of their subordinates. In the end, both sides relied on the subtle yet substantial social signals sent by expressions of emotion. Still, no amount of emotional finesse could obscure the fundamental fact that the Stamp Act Crisis had brought tensions to the brink. Even if not strictly seditious, the "spirit of liberty" advanced far more radical aims than did simple claims of sensibility.

So eagerly awaited had the repeal been, London printers had prepared celebratory satiric engravings commemorating the rescission long before it actually occurred. Having been imported to the colonies in advance and reprinted in places like Philadelphia, such prints were handed around by colonists and posted at taverns and coffee houses as soon as the news of the repeal arrived. One especially significant print pictured *The Repeal; or, The Funeral of Miss Ame—Stamp* (Figure 19). The scene, set on a London wharf with merchant ships at anchor in the background, portrayed Lord Grenville mired in deepest grief walking toward a tomb while cradling a tiny infant-sized coffin labeled "Miss Ame Stamp, B. 1765 *died* 1766" in his arms. A train of mourners followed Grenville, hands on hearts, crying copiously. Numerous details in the print invited observers to laugh rather than sorrow at the death of the tax, starting with the inclusion of a small dog that lifted its leg to relieve itself on the robe of the minister preaching the funeral sermon.[47]

The most telling elements of the Stamp Act funeral print relate to emotional comportment. First, and most important, the men assembled to mourn for the Stamp Act engaged in the socially inappropriate act of mourning publicly for an infant child. As discussed before (Chapter 7), stoic resignation was regarded as a far more exemplary fatherly response to the loss of a child than was unguarded emotionalism. In grieving for an infant—and a female at that—Grenville was made to unman himself. Accentuating the idea that Grenville's was an embarrassing private lapse, rather than a fitting example of public tribute, was the fact that the ships in the harbor flew their flags at full mast. In marked contrast to the scene in Philadelphia a year earlier, when "all the Vessels in the Harbour hoisted their Colours half Mast high," these flags flew freely, demonstrating that the general public did not join in the unseemly grief displayed by Grenville and company (and showing how glad merchants and traders would be to see boycotts cease and trade resume). Adding to the imputations heaped on the mourners was the man crying most conspicuously into a long white handkerchief: he had extraordinarily skinny legs. In a world where full muscular calves were the mark of a gentleman, signaling both virility and gentility, this effeminate weeping figure underscored the weakness of those who had supported the Stamp Act.[48]

Though they drew on the same set of conventions surrounding grief and sympathy, popular portrayals of Stamp Act funerals sent distinctly different political signals than did services held for the loss of liberty. Unlike patriots who mourned in public-minded tribute to British liberty, British magistrates supposedly indulged in selfish private grief for the failure of their own misbegotten plans. Unlike colonists who backed the refined restraint of grief with the strength of anger, Grenville and his fellows were reduced to effeminate ineptitude by their unfettered weeping. In a final visual flourish that underscored the intended inversions

FIGURE 19. *The Repeal or the Funeral of Miss Ame——Stamp.* By Benjamin Wilson. England, ca. 1765. *Permission The Library Company of Philadelphia*

The Sheffield and Birmingham Warehouse

Goods NOW shipd for America

Leeds

Liverpool

Archbp
of M[?]

Black Cloth
from America

Stamps
from America

H-ll x S-nd-ch   Bᵖ of Sᵗ Davids
Bᵖ of Gloster.

created by depictions of the Stamp Act funerals, Grenville and his phalanx of grievers stood on a wharf scattered with packing crates labeled "Black Cloth from America" and "Stamps from America." As the Stamp Act's opponents rejoiced in their political success, they left the king's magistrates to put on mourning.

"The Animated Spirit of Liberty": Mounting Praise for Patriot Emotion

Despite the way the immediate crisis was resolved through the smooth exchange of colonial grief and British compassion, emotional rhetoric ultimately retained the power to communicate dissent and even sow division. When the restoration of good relations between the colonies and the mother country proved fleeting, the new strain of colonial resistance germinated by the November 1765 mourning protests would come to be critical. Though the importance of sentiment remained decisive over the following decade, the significance and usage of shared feeling would be elaborated in previously unanticipated ways, uniting colonists with one another and dividing them from Britain.

No sooner did tensions wane over the defeated Stamp Act than royal minister of the moment, Charles Townshend, in 1767 pushed through a new revenue measure that leveled import duties on the colonies, and began enforcement of the Quartering Act (1765), which required colonists to supply the king's army in the colonies. Faced with the Townshend Acts, colonists responded by deepening their commitment to the feelings of freedom. As a Rhode Island observer put it in remarks reprinted in Philadelphia in December 1767, "That noble spirit of liberty, which procured the repeal of the Stamp Act, seems to be bursting forth with fresh vigour." Up and down the American coast, protesters geared up for a new round of resistance, buoyed by the growing conviction that they themselves were the truest stewards of the virtuous classical emotions to which "true Britons" ought to lay claim. Yet, in American mouths, emotional ideals were shifting subtly but substantially. Gone was the early emphasis on sensitivity to "every softer emotion," replaced by a new insistence that the key to spirit was manly "vigour."[49]

With delicacy losing appeal to strength, Pennsylvania lawyer John Dickinson won widespread approval for his exhortation to colonists: "All mankind must with unceasing applauses confess, that YOU indeed DESERVE liberty, who so *well understand* it, so *passionately love* it, so *temperately enjoy* it, and so *wisely, bravely,* and *virtuously assert, maintain,* and *defend* it." Here Dickinson called, not for refined feeling, but rather for wise understanding of and passionate love for liberty, for *thumos* to be marshaled in the service of public virtue.[50]

Dickinson's contemporaries found in his comments a rousing cry for action, a direct and deliberate spur to "spirit." The *Gazette* reported admiration from across the colonies for Dickinson's approach. Bostonians declared that, "at a Time when public Liberty is in Danger," anyone who could show the threat that British policies posed to "the Rights and Privileges of a free People" was engaged in "an Employment worthy the ablest Head, and the most benevolent Heart"—exclaiming, "This has been lately done in a masterly Manner, by the worthy and patriotic Writer of the Farmer's Letters." They urged their fellow colonists to prove likewise that they were "not destitute of the noblest Passion by which the human Breast is animated." The "Head" and the "Heart": here again patriots emphasized their devotion to the strong yet reasonable passions that could animate virtuous action. They made no mention of tender feelings. A writer from Rhode Island chimed in: "The FARMER's Letters are the *best pieces* which have been published. . . . All which I have read breathe the same *temperate,* but *animated* spirit of liberty." For this writer, as for so many others, Dickinson appealed precisely because the model of passionate virtue he espoused seemed to promise colonists both respectability and virility.[51]

The bravery called for in Dickinson's vision of passionate love for liberty left no room for servile pleading. Far from advocating a return to the simple tactics of petition, Dickinson painted a dire picture of what would happen to colonists who took the advice to patiently wait for the appearance of parliamentary compassion. Warning that "there may be some on this continent *against whom you ought to be upon your guard,*" he wrote: "From *them* we shall learn how *pleasant* and *profitable* a thing it is, to be for our SUBMISSIVE behaviour well spoken of at *St. James's* or *St. Stephen's;* at *Guildhall,* or the *Royal Exchange.*" He predicted that, should colonists adopt a submissive tone, Parliament's response would bring nothing more than empty conciliation: "It will be insinuated to us . . . how *prudent* it is to please the *powerful*—how dangerous to provoke them . . . the perpetual incantation that freezes up every generous purpose of the soul in cold, inactive expectation." Though Dickinson was still advocating a moderate stance by colonists in 1768, he proposed that they do much more than simply describe their afflictions and await Parliament's "affectation of concern." In place of "inactive" anticipation, colonists should band together in sympathetic participation with one another. He was less concerned with venerating Parliament or ministers of the crown and then awaiting their compassion than with generating sympathy among the colonists themselves.[52]

Dickinson's belief that liberty belonged to those who passionately loved it was radical in another way as well. He explicitly advanced the idea that *all* Americans were capable of experiencing and expressing the same natural feelings and passions. Far from complying with the convention that accorded refined feelings to the elite and strong passions to the masses, he called forth:

> Let us, with a truly wise *generosity* and *charity,* banish and discourage all *illiberal dictinctions,* which may arise from differences in *situation,* forms of *government,* or modes of *religion.* . . . BENEVOLENCE *of temper towards each other,* and UNANIMITY of *counsels,* are essential to the welfare of the whole. . . . You will be a *"band of brothers,"* ce-mented by the dearest ties,—and strengthened with inconceivable supplies of force and constancy, by that sympathetic ardor, which ani-mates good men, confederated in a good cause.

With these words, the role of shared feeling was transformed altogether; no longer was it expected to motivate Parliament to redress colonial grievances. Instead, it was expected to mitigate colonists' social, political, and cultural differences and help draw them together. With *"illiberal distinctions"* disavowed, *"benevolence of temper"* and *"sympathetic ardor"* were to join colonists in unanimity as a " '*band of brothers*' cemented by the dearest ties."[53]

From the moment that colonists had first sent petitions to Britain, they had been laying claim to the language of sensibility and asserting their own right to the culture of feeling. Now they made new claims to "ardor," to the kind of spirited emotion that "animates good men." With these essays, Dickinson began to lay the groundwork for claims that true classi-cal spirit was a uniquely American emotion, and not a British one at all. Rather than incite Parliament to action, "sympathetic ardor" would acti-vate the colonists, "good men, confederated in a good cause."

Indeed, at the same time that he urged colonists not to indulge in *"illiberal distinctions"* in their emotional interactions with one another, Dickinson contended that they could make "PROPER DISTINCTIONS" in their dealings with Britain. They could remain respectful to the home country, yet continue to engage in spirited resistance to any encroachment on liberty. He urged: "You have nothing to do, but to call forth into use the *good sense* and *spirit* of which you are possessed. . . . By *these means* you will support the character of *freemen*, without losing that of *faithful subjects*." He expounded on the finer points of his proposed emotional and political stance: "You will *prove*, that *Americans* have that true *magnanimity* of soul, that can resent injuries, without falling into rage; and that tho' your devotion to *Great-Britain* is the most affectionate, yet you can make PROPER DISTINCTIONS, and know what you owe *to yourselves*, as well as *to her*." Dickinson's words represent the logical evolution of the rhetoric of emotion used just a few years earlier at the height of the Stamp Act Crisis. Colonists had the ability to "resent without rage." For Americans with "true *magnanimity* of soul," anger could be controlled and directed toward useful ends. Once they had claimed sympathy as their own, colonists knew they could always call on compassion to direct their passions. Meanwhile, protesters well versed in culture of feeling should seek unity through sympathy with one another and not with the crown.[54]

According to Dickinson, colonial men universally possessed the "spirit" needed to "support the character of freemen." (It is worth noting here the emphasis on white manhood encoded in Dickinson's calls to *free men*.) In trading sensibility for spirit, American Revolutionaries tightened lines of gender and race even as they relied on "sympathetic ardor" to breach the social boundaries that had once divided white men from one another. For, if anger was closed to women, then they could lay little claim to either public spirit or political action. So long as grief was called for, those subordinated by race and gender could yet contribute. But anger honed down to "resentment" remained, as always, open only to men, and love and sympathy were attributed only to whites. Spirited ardor—that meld of anger, sympathetic grief, and love of liberty that bound good men together in a good cause—was thus attributed uniquely to patriotic white men.

Where they had once stood vulnerable to British critiques that their emotional comportment was too coarse for polite consideration, Revolutionaries now assured themselves that their spirited brand of emotion was better evidence of civic virtue. As an essayist from Pennsylvania triumphed in the pages of the *Gazette*, Americans "warm'd with the love of *freedom*" would leave the world *"dazzled* with the *splendor* of so *sublime* a character as that of *a son of liberty*." The writer explained, "The *Farmer* has long since sounded the alarm . . . examples of public spirit are crowding in upon us." Any who failed to heed Dickinson's call were "to be ranked among the callous slaves of Turkey or Japan!—*servum pecus!* a servile herd!" Again, and again, the message was clear: the warmth of strong love and anger were the fuel of public spirit that animated the white men who called themselves *"sons of liberty."* Shows of such virtuous emotion authenticated freedom and invalidated slavery.[55]

For patriots, the ideal spirit of liberty steeled the genteel values of sensibility with the vigorous assertion of masculinity. Consider, for example, this reprint from a Virginia political pamphlet, *Monitor,* No. 5, which appeared in the *Gazette* just a month after Dickinson's piece did. *Monitor* began with the dire prediction that, if Britain began by seizing America's money to pay imperial debts, before long it would seize America's young men as well, to fight imperial wars. Cautioning against "the very probable consequences of a peaceable acquiescence under the late assumed authority of the *British* parliament," it declared: "I see already men torn from their weeping and distressed families . . . by an unrelenting, lawless crew . . . wantonly cruel in their execution of despotic power. I see every endearing tie of father, husband, son and brother, torn asunder, unrespited, unpitied, unreprieved." Such rhetoric repeated the growing colonial conviction that grief and tears were "unavailing" forms of protest, given the dulled sensitivities of members of Parliament. The British were "wantonly cruel" and absolutely impervious to the "weeping and distressed." Equally important, if colonists could only cry in the face of British injustice, they would themselves quickly become unmanned. It intoned: "I see my weeping country, worn down with reiterated sorrows and alarms. . . . Alas! . . . Her youthful sons are now no more . . . nothing but feeble age remains to mix his unavailing tears with hers." Grief without anger was a recipe for impotence, something no self-respecting son of liberty would ever agree to endure.[56]

What were colonists to do? The answer in *Monitor* did not involve "peaceable acquiescence" or passive pleas for redress:

> Oh, God! are we men, and shall we suffer the foundation to be laid
> for miseries like these; shall we look tamely on while the yoke is fixed
> upon us, under which we must forever groan?—We and our posterity
> forever. . . . Our property, our liberty, our happiness given up to ministers, who . . . shall contrive for us new hardships, new oppressions,
> and tyrannize without measure, without fear, without mercy?

With pleas that echoed back to the proarmament arguments of Pennsylvania's militant faction in the Seven Years War, *Monitor* urged patriots to prove their manliness by springing to action. Since neither Parliament nor the king's ministers could be depended on to show mercy, then feeling colonists must oppose slavery's "yoke" and eliminate misery before it occurred. Where a few years earlier colonists had counted dramatic displays of grievance as a successful tactic to demonstrate loyal opposition, they no longer believed that Parliament could be depended on to respond appropriately to displays of emotional distress. It was left to patriots to demonstrate spirited manhood, the classical virtue of a Cicero, by standing for liberty.[57]

Members of Parliament were slow to perceive this shift in colonial assessments of the functions of feeling. The British, after all, had been fairly satisfied with the peaceful denouement of the Stamp Act Crisis. Though the response had resulted in repeal of the act, it had also brought a reassertion of parliamentary power and position. When colonists struck a stance of supplication, they allowed the British both to save face and to congratulate themselves on their own benevolence. The subsequent crisis in New York over enforcement of the Quartering Act looked at the time like another victory for the British. But it actually further unraveled the system of supplication and held ominous portents for the British.

The *Gazette* published two letters from England in May 1769 that underscored the growing divide between Britain and America in their respective understandings of the role emotional expression might play in mediating their interactions. One letter, purportedly received in Boston from a member of Parliament, lectured: "The colonies stand, at present, in a strange point of light here, especially since the late resolves of the assembly of New-York. . . . They want some instances of temper and moderation, whereon to found an application for the repeal of the late acts of regulations." Here Parliament tried to castigate the colonists for being unable to regulate their passions, to exercise temper and moderation. The writer condescended to explain the proper rules of emotional deportment: "Would the Colonies petition with temper, and with full acknowledgment of the supreme right of this country to regulate the general commercial system, I have little doubt, that the unhappy idea of taxation, would long, even for ever, be laid aside." As Anglos on both sides of the Atlantic recognized mastery of emotion as a key sign of the right to membership in the master class, the clear implication of this letter was that the colonies were inferior in status to Britain and must make proper shows of subservience before their concerns could be addressed. The writer was oblivious to the fact that, while similar advice had proved effective in 1765, colonists were no longer willing to cede the power of sympathy to the British. On the contrary, colonists had done much to popularize images of themselves as uniquely spirited people, guardians of classical virtue whose chief sympathies lay with one another.[58]

A companion letter in the same issue of the *Gazette* offered a colonial alternative of how feeling might come into play. This second letter, not from a member of Parliament, but "from a gentleman in England to his friend in Connecticut," offered a more prescient view of colonial affairs. Remonstrating colonists to "let nothing provoke you to have a recourse in arms," this anxious Englishman was nonetheless far from urging more moderate petitions to Parliament. "You must . . . let nothing move you from your resolutions." He stressed, "The merchants . . . must agree to submit to any difficulty . . . for a firm adherence to their resolutions will so affect our manufacturers . . . excite compassion, and raise up a party to espouse their interest, that for our own sakes we shall be obliged to comply." While this correspondent had not lost all hope that Britain's compassion could be revived, neither did he think colonists should elicit it through simple statements of sadness. Rather, he recommended that they use economic pressure to induce Britain to return to sentiment.[59]

Patriots, meanwhile, remained far more focused on trumpeting their own spirit than on futilely trying to elicit British compassion. As a Williamsburg pamphleteer declared, "The eyes of all Europe are now turned upon America, and the friends to freedom expect such a conduct from you, as becomes a people animated with the sacred spirit of liberty." The air filled with calls for colonists to demonstrate that they and they alone could serve as stewards of the virtuous emotions the British themselves were supposed to have preserved from the classical world. So loud were the protests that at least some in Britain began to take heed. According to a letter circulated in Boston and reprinted in the *Gazette,* credited to yet another anonymous "Gentleman in London," even some British observers admitted that "Asiatic Despotism" did "not present a Picture more odious in the Eye of Humanity" than did British policies in America. This letter concluded by counseling colonists to maintain "at the same Time your own Dignity, and the true Spirit of Liberty," a commission that colonists were eager to accept. So, while members of Parliament congratulated themselves that protesters in New York had been put in their place, their lack of savvy in the arts of sensibility exposed, colonists themselves espoused a markedly different interpretation. The fact that Parliament succeeded in imposing its will only confirmed for colonists that, since the British were devoid of mercy, they themselves should focus on the cultivation of spirit.[60]

Such a conclusion freed colonists to pursue the increasingly radical actions that were to amplify protests over the ensuing years, transforming loyal resistance into a movement for Independence. As a Merchant in Philadelphia presciently observed in a letter to London reprinted in the *London Chronicle* and then again in the *Gazette:* "The Spirit of Liberty will be kept awake, and the Love of Freedom deeply rooted. And when Strength and Liberty combine, it is easy to foresee, that a People will not long submit to arbitrary Sway." As this writer spelled out, love of freedom defined the spirit of liberty. Virtuous emotion in the classical vein imparted the "strength" needed to resist slavery's "Sway." Where once colonists had cringed at being labeled passionate hotheads, they now affirmed that emotional power, moral strength, and political determination marched together, the regiment of revolution.[61]

By the time of the Boston Massacre in March 1770, colonists had already fully committed to the notion that their emotional energies were best expended on one another and not on efforts to reach British policymakers. Defying the British to impose slavery on American colonists, a writer in New York proclaimed, "What in Britain no Man dare attempt, let none expect to see accomplished in America." Voicing confidence in the protective armor of American virtue, the writer challenged, "Though there be among us . . . Miscreants, actuated by slavish principles . . . still of Men of Spirit . . . of avowed, determined, inflexible Friends of Liberty, there is a numerous Multitude." The colonial majority, "actuated" by "Spirit," would preserve liberty from the machinations of "slavish" "Miscreants" on both sides of the Atlantic. It should come as no surprise, then, that Paul Revere's *Bloody Massacre* (the print that most shaped public understandings of that conflict) cast the altercation between colonial protesters and British regulars in just such morally laden emotional terms (Figure 20).[62]

Eyes wide, Revere's respectably dressed colonists in waistcoats and buckled shoes confront grim-faced British regulars brandishing smoking muskets against the backdrop of Butcher's Hall. The poem that accompanied declared:

FIGURE 20. *The Bloody Massacre Perpetrated in King Street Boston on March 5th 1770 by a Party of the 29th Reg.t.* By Paul Revere. Boston, 1770. Facsimile, republished in Boston, 1832. *Permission The Library Company of Philadelphia*

If scalding drops from Rage from Anguish Wrung
If speechless Sorrows lab'ring for a Tongue,
Or if a weeping World can ought appease
The plaintive Ghosts of Victims such as these;
The Patriot's copious Tears for each are shed,
A glorious Tribute which embalms the Dead.

In the complicated emotional cadence of this poem, colonists veered between anger and sorrow before settling into grief. Scalding rage, that most forceful, yet least civil and refined, kind of feeling, alternated with speechless sorrow, that most restrained and respectful mode of emotional protest. Neither kind of feeling moved the British, portrayed as "fierce Barbarians grinning oe'r their Prey / [who] Approve the Carnage and enjoy the Day." Therefore, according to the poem, the only option left to patriots was to withdraw their feelings entirely from the British, neither threatening with rage nor appealing with sorrow, but instead pouring their grief into tributary tears for their fellows.

No longer willing to shed their tears for British liberty, they saved their sentiments as "glorious Tribute" for their compatriots. With the coming of the massacre, the metaphoric use of grief came full circle and gave way once more to actual acts of mourning. Having restrained their funerary practices in the name of British liberty back in 1764, colonists at last lifted mourning restrictions, but only in honor of American patriots.

Liberty, Unity, and American Feeling

When the final break with Britain became imminent, colonists invoked spirit more loudly than ever before to rally their fellows and justify their position to the world. With the June 1, 1774, implementation of the Boston Port Act (to seal the Boston port until colonists provided compensation for tea destroyed in protest), colonists across North America were fully ready to bind themselves together with the strands of sympathy. As a circular letter sent by the Philadelphia Committee of Safety formally declared, "All the Colonies, from South-Carolina to New-Hampshire, seem animated with one spirit in the common cause." At last the spirit of liberty could fully be put to its intended use, spurring action and ending faction, animating colonists as "one" across both social and geographic boundaries. The time had arrived to have "our liberties fixed upon a permanent foundation." "This desirable end can only be accomplished by a free communion of sentiments, and a sincere fervent regard to the interests of our common country."[63]

Throughout the colonies, people joined in protest against the strictures placed on Massachusetts. Philadelphians declared, "[Since] our Brethren and Fellow-Subjects, suffering in the common Cause of Liberty, are to have their Port . . . shut up . . . many of the inhabitants of this City . . . propose to express their Sympathy and Concern for their distressed Brethren, by suspending Business." Protest organizers relied on the language of feeling to incite their fellow citizens to join the protest action. Drawing on the by-then-widespread acceptance of the importance of public spirit, Philadelphians attempted to achieve unity through sympathy.[64]

A certain letter "To the Inhabitants of the British Colonies in America," which appeared two weeks later in the *Gazette*, underscored how accepted spirit had become as the standard by which virtue and status would be judged. More than ever before, European sensibility gave way to a new American emotional culture, in which passion served as a source of strength and compassion alone could indicate fitness to rule. Defending colonists in Massachusetts against renewed charges of unbecoming comportment, the author claimed they had little choice but to privilege the stronger passions, given the British incapacity for compassion. "What could they do?" he demanded. "Their *humble petitions* were haughtily and contemptuously rejected." When repeated lamentations did not arouse merciful action, more drastic measures became essential.

> The more they *supplicated*, the more they were *abused*. By their tears, and Heaven knows how many they have shed, their persecutions flourished, as trees by water poured on their roots. Their very virtue and passionate fondness for . . . their Mother country occasioned this objected error.

Virtuous colonists had been unable to move unfeeling Britons; supplication was useless where sympathy was wanting. Thus the rhetorical use of tears and displays of grief had been revolutionized. No longer would colonists' tears stand as symbols of their dependence on the just and compassionate leaders of Britain. Instead, colonial tears would showcase the colonists' capacity for elevated feeling in contrast to the debased insensibility of a people no longer fit to rule.[65]

A passionate love of liberty was the pride of an emerging American people, indulged in the pursuit of freedom. Lest there be any doubt that colonial tears were now offered, not as a show of subservience, but as evidence of colonists' virtuous spirit, the author explained: "Great clamour has been raised at home against *Massachusetts-Bay*. . . . The truth is— that people, animated by an ardent and generous love of liberty, saw, and peculiarly felt the projects against the freedom and happiness of America[ns]." It was colonists who "peculiarly felt." (*Peculiar* here was clearly used, not in the sense of "odd" or "strange," but in its strict sense of "distinctive.") Colonists were a peculiar people, exalted over those in the "Mother country" because of their ability to feel the emotions conducive to classical virtue and natural freedom.[66]

Finally, the author exhorted colonists across North America to join the strength of their passions to the civility of their sentiments in pursuit of public unity and public spirit. "Let us cherish and cultivate sentiments of brotherly love and tenderness amongst us," he told them. "To whom under the cope of Heaven can we look for help in these days of 'darkness and trouble,' but one to another. O my countrymen! Have pity one on another—Have pity on yourselves and your children. Let us . . . wisely and kindly unite in one firm band, in one common cause." Colonists' insistence that they, not the British, were the true bearers of ancient emotional spirit had assumed both strategic value and social significance. "Brotherly" love—an emotion of equals—would allow colonists to bridge divides of rank and region to meet the British threat as "one firm band."[67]

Historians have perennially queried what causes allowed colonists to unify across classes and across the continent, despite the social and regional differences. Modern scholars have been particularly interested in the role of communal action in transforming disparate colonists into a concerted anti-British faction. Some historians have stressed street politics, seeing participation in public parades and protests as pivotal for the forging of civic consciousness, and others have emphasized market transactions, claiming that collective nonconsumption pacts were pivotal to building "trust" across the colonies. Still, colonists themselves believed that the passions preceded, indeed produced, action. For colonial patriots, emotion was elemental.[68]

Because civic commitment was believed to spring from public spirit, sympathetic identification among colonists was a necessary precursor to any attempt at developing a national identity. Time and again, the capacity for sympathy remained the symbol that distinguished the righteous from the wrong. In August 1774, Bostonians reported that those who came to the aid of their blockaded port city (from South Carolinians far to the south who gave "the benefaction of rice," to Marblehead residents nearby who sent "twelve cart loads of good salt fish, also a quantity of oil") were motivated by fellow feeling. The goods aided the colonial cause, "being the generous donation of our sympathizing brethren." Salt fish and sentiment: in crucial practical and symbolic ways, sympathy unified colonists as Americans.[69]

Revived interest in the role of emotion in the production of republican virtue gave colonists new justification for flaunting their feelings as the basis of freedom. Elite patriots became less invested in maintaining the notion that their refined feelings were distinct from the strong passions of the masses, and all were intent on sustaining their common devotion to the spirit of liberty. As members of the Continental Congress put matters at a gala dinner held in Philadelphia: "May every American hand down to Posterity pure and untainted the Liberty he has derived from his Ancestors. . . . May no Man enjoy Freedom, who has not Spirit to defend it." Echoing John Dickinson before them, they toasted American spirit with American manhood; "untainted liberty," founded in the feelings of natural freedom, was the birthright that *every* American man should bequeath to his sons. Spirit bound white men together as brothers across all divides.[70]

Patriots' careful emotional calibrations derived from a deliberate political calculus. Where once they had prided themselves on crafting petitions that bore "all the marks of submission," they now asserted that submission itself equated with slavery. In a special issue of the *Gazette*, coinciding with the report of the congressional banquet, committeemen from Massachusetts demanded, "The question now is, Whether, by a submission to some late acts of the Parliament of Great Britain, we are contented to be the most abject slaves, and entail that slavery on posterity after us, or, by a manly, joint and virtuous opposition, assert and support our freedom." The formula for such manly virtue was becoming increasingly clear: it required nothing less than devotion to the spirit of liberty. Offering an explicit definition of the term, the Massachusetts statement explained, "There is a mode of conduct, which . . . we would wish to adopt; a conduct, on the one hand, never tamely submissive to tyranny and oppression—on the other, never degenerating into rage, passion and confusion." Here again, Americans announced their determination to achieve a balance between insensate submission and excessive passion. "This is a spirit," they asserted, that was "exhibited in former ages, and will command applause to latest posterity." Claiming pride of membership in liberty's lineage, they insisted that *their* sentiments, unlike those of the "naturally slavish," "are founded in truth and justice, and therefore [are] sentiments we are determined to abide by."[71]

Indeed, widespread belief in the idea of a lineal right to liberty, begun in the ancient republics and passed down through generations of free-spirited Britons, helps to explain the long-lingering loyalties of even the most rebellious colonists. As one polemicist proclaimed in the pages of the *Gazette* in March 1775, "It is hard to divest a *real* Englishman of his love of liberty." Of even the British soldiers, whose presence had caused such contention, he said: "There may be some mongrels among them as well as among ourselves; yet . . . they are not divested of feeling, and far from becoming ministerial butchers. If things should come to extremities, it is not to be doubted but they will discover further signs of a *true English spirit.*" Love, feeling, spirit: emotion defined the essence of Englishness, the core of virtue. In contrasting "real Englishmen" with "mongrels" this writer alluded clearly to racialized boundaries of freedom; only those pure of blood and clean of heart had the right to liberty. While colonists saw little difficulty in excluding Africans from freedom's circle, they were much slower to condemn their English "brethren." As late as 1775, many protesters still insisted that, while the king's ministers represented a dead branch in freedom's family tree, all other Englishmen could still make valid claims to the spirit of liberty.[72]

By May of that year, however, colonists ratcheted up declarations that their capacity for natural spirit—as evidenced by displays of mutual love and sympathy—formed a bulwark against spreading British tendencies toward unnatural oppression. As a writer in the *Gazette* said, "One general spirit of union and brotherly affection animate all Americans, as all of them must equally share in the event of this contest, be it freedom or slavery." The assertion that each American had an *equal* share in the stakes of liberty was founded in the claim that "one general spirit" animated all. Eschewing distinctions between the rarefied and the rude, patriots instead emphasized once again "brotherly affection," that emotion exchanged only among free men of equal standing. Meanwhile, the General Committee of Association in New York promised, "America is grown so irritable by Oppression, that the least Shock in any Part is, by the most powerful and sympathetic Affection, instantaneously felt through the whole Continent." Americans were "one man in the cause of liberty." By this rhetoric, the heightened spirit of the colonists allowed them to feel one another's grief and come to one another's aid, even as members of Parliament, dead to sympathy, pursued a dark "Design to erect in this Land of Liberty, a Despotism scarcely to be paralleled in the Pages of Antiquity." Colonists were still not openly or unanimously in favor of separating from Britain. New York's letter professed that protests were yet restrained by "Loyalty to our Prince, and the Love we bear to all our Fellow-Subjects in his Majesty's Realm and Dominions." But patience with British governance was clearly running out as colonists came to see themselves keepers of the flame of the classical spirit of liberty against debased members of Parliament.[73]

As open rebellion against Britain evolved from unthinkable sedition to undoubted patriotism, whether the British people as a whole had become as insensible as their representatives in Parliament became a serious issue for American colonists. Just a few months after New York's boast that powerful sympathy bound the entire North American continent, members of the Continental Congress issued a challenge to the British people to demonstrate that they at least had retained the feelings that their leaders lacked. On July 8, 1775, they issued a letter from the "Twelve United Colonies by Their Delegates in Congress, to the Inhabitants of Great Britain" and proclaimed, "If you still retain those sentiments of compassion, by which Britons have ever been distinguished—If the humanity which tempered the valour of our common ancestors has not degenerated into cruelty, you will lament the miseries of their descendants." With these words, colonists claimed that the British people themselves were responsible for the growing transatlantic rift, the result of their declension from ancient ideals of virtue. They, not their American counterparts, had broken from British tradition, and colonists claimed that a final rupture was all but inevitable, demanding: "When the pride of ancestry becomes our reproach, and we are no otherwise allied than as tyrants and slaves . . . can we hesitate about the choice? Let the spirit of Britons determine." Reiterating once more the key connection between feeling and freedom, colonists claimed that they alone stood as standard-bearers for the true spirit of liberty.[74]

Thus, the central aim of colonists' claims to superior spirit was to shift the responsibility for a transatlantic split away from the Americans and onto the British. Only by demonstrating that they could still feel compassion (that is, by caving in to colonial demands) could the British exonerate themselves from the charge that *they*, and not the colonists, had forced a separation. After all the urging from "gentlemen in England" for colonists to "petition with temper" and strive to "excite compassion," colonists reproached the British with the charge that *they*, not the Americans, had failed in the proper modulation of feeling. The letter from the Continental Congress closed by chiding the British: "If justice and humanity have lost their influence on your hearts; still motives are not wanting to excite your indignation at the measures now pursued: your wealth, your honour, your liberty are at stake." According to this rhetoric, the British lack of humanity was not merely a source of tension with the colonists; it was actually destructive to their own self-interest. The colonial indictment continued: "Notwithstanding the distress to which we are reduced, we sometimes forget our own afflictions, to anticipate and sympathize in yours. We grieve that rash and inconsiderate councils should precipitate the destruction of an empire, which has been the envy and admiration of ages." Like the Romans before them, the British were suffering fatal failures of feeling; loss of empire would be the inevitable result. Virtuous colonists, on the other hand, were so proficient at feeling that they had sympathy to spare; unlike in the days of the Stamp Act Crisis, they now grieved not for themselves nor even for their liberty but for the fact that justice and humanity had lost their influence on British hearts. What is more, their claim to sympathize with the British put them on par with the British, ending forever their stance as subordinates asking for the compassion of their masters.[75]

A letter printed in the *Gazette* the following month, "To the People of Ireland from the Delegates Appointed by the United Colonies . . . in General Congress at Philadelphia," took accusations of dispirited insensibility to the next and final level. When the Stamp Act Crisis began, the sympathies of members of Parliament first had been played to, then deplored. Next, the king's compassion had been questioned, though ultimately affirmed. Later colonists appealed directly to British citizens, demanding to know whether they yet retained a capacity for sympathy and clearly implying that perhaps they did not. Only on the very eve of Independence did colonists decry the king himself as insensible and question his fitness to rule. Proclaiming their position publicly in the letter to Ireland, colonists summarized recent events:

A Congress, consisting of Deputies from Twelve United Colonies, assembled. They in the most respectful terms laid their grievances at the foot of the throne; and implored his Majesty's interposition in their behalf. . . . Flattered by a pleasing expectation, that the justice and humanity which has so long characterized the English nation would on proper application afford us relief, they represented their grievances in an affectionate address to their brethren in Britain, and entreated their aid and interposition in behalf of these colonies. . . . With anxious expectation did all America wait the event of their petition.—All America laments its fate.—Their Prince was deaf to their complaints: And vain were all attempts to impress him with a sense of the sufferings of his American subjects. . . . Instead of directions for a candid enquiry into our grievances, insult was added to oppression, and our long forbearance rewarded with the imputation of cowardice.

As far back as 1766, "Loyalty and Gratitude to our Most Gracious Sovereign" had been predicated on the king's proffering "an indulgent Ear to our just Complaints." A decade later, colonists held the king to the same standard and found him wanting. Both "brethren in Britain" and the king himself were "deaf to their complaints." As the endgame approached, patriots began using the language of feeling to appeal to international observers and to justify their growing inclination to break with Britain. The fact that their "long forbearance [was] rewarded with the imputation of cowardice" served only to make them more determined to prove their courage. As the letter to Ireland went on to say, they were "determined to behave like men." Indeed, protesters invariably viewed superior masculinity as a key constituent of American spirit.[76]

A final example of the invocation of American spirit will establish once and for all the key characteristics of that crucial kind of emotion: an address delivered to Massachusetts soldiers, then published in the *Gazette* in November 1775 under the byline A Soldier. Once more casting the Revolution as a struggle for manhood itself, the speech began with the by-then-almost-conventional demand, "Let us ask ourselves whether we will see our wives and children, with every thing that is dear to us, subjected to the merciless rage of uncontrouled despotism?" Only a firewall of manly spirit could shield the country. Turning once more to tradition for guidance, the author advised, "Let us repair to the graves of our sleeping forefathers," warning colonists that, unless they stood ready to fight, their fathers would "with . . . noble indignation upbraid us with ingratitude to *them*, and want of spirit and manly resolution." He urged, "Let us . . . swear to those venerable shades, that their sons will never disgrace *their* unsullied manes with the execrable epithet of slave." Those who lacked true spirit could justly be called slaves, but those who could feel the love of freedom deserved to have their liberty defended and preserved. Merciless rage was the stuff of savagery; but noble indignation, love of country, and sympathetic feeling converged to create the very spirit of virtue exemplified in the first republics.[77]

If patriots often omitted direct mention of the classical inspiration for liberty's spirit, emphasizing instead its British heritage, their debt to the ancient world was nevertheless implicit in frequent references to "ancestors," "birthrights," and the like. A Soldier spelled out this point when he demanded: "What rendered the Spartan army the glory of Grecian empire? . . . What, but an unreserved confidence of the Roman soldiers . . . procured them the empire of the world, by wresting it from the hands of the *Grecian warriors*? What, but a neglect of *this*, rendered them an easy prey to their savage neighbours?" Casting Americans in the role of classical heroes, the British in the place of barbarian hordes, A Soldier explained that uncontrolled British rage was leading them into the error of savage passionate surfeit. Meanwhile, he charged that those few Englishmen who avoided excess did so only because they careered to the opposite extreme of insensate slavishness. A Soldier charged his fellow colonists to demonstrate the optimal emotional blend of sensitized civilized restraint and spirited manly strength: "Let *Americans* catch that beautiful regularity, and hardy form of discipline, which *Britons*, through debauchery and effeminacy, are losing." He drove his point home: "A few more spirited struggles, and we secure our liberties; a few more successful battles, and we are a free and happy people." The emotional emphasis that had at first promoted colonial claims to a respectable place in the British Empire now served an entirely new purpose. Classical spirit was to galvanize united military action by freedom-loving Americans drawn together in the cause of liberty.[78]

Liberty's Probate

George Washington's October 1775 assertion that the "freeborn sons of America" were "animated by the genuine principles of liberty and love of their country" drew on the by-then-widespread conviction of the social significance and martial advantage of American spirit. Though some leaders might be slow to relinquish exclusionary claims that genteel feeling differed in degree and kind from popular passions, visionaries like Washington saw the value in declaring that "the cause of America, and of

Liberty, is the cause of every virtuous American citizen; whatever may be his religion or his descent." So long as patriots cleaved to virtue and shied from what Washington called "poverty of soul, and baseness of spirit," there could be no cause for social discrimination. Indeed, Washington affirmed, "the united colonies know no distinction but such as slavery, corruption and arbitrary domination may create." Emotion thus proved essential for both the abstract elaboration and the daily application of the new philosophies of natural equality destined to be among the most renowned elements of Revolutionary doctrine.[79]

Celebrations of spirit articulated a rousing new worldview, stimulating European colonists' efforts to renegotiate their relations with Britain as well as with one another. Emotional exchanges helped to define and redefine relative status, between peripheral provincials and imperial magistrates, between the upper and lower sorts within particular colonies as well as between northern colonists and southern. If the earliest opponents of the Stamp Act sought to use the vocabulary of sensibility to reaffirm their kinship with the British ruling class, their right to be respected as partners in a transatlantic empire, later protesters would invoke emotion in markedly different ways. When the British rebuffed colonial efforts to exhibit refined feeling, patriots began to emphasize instead the power of popular passions. Protesters soon ceased calling on Parliament to respond in kind to colonial shows of sensibility, and they turned instead to muscular assertions of mass rage and grief.

Some colonial leaders—William Smith provides an obvious example— doubtless would have preferred to stop there, to utilize genteel feelings and popular passions in separate but coordinated attacks on British policies. Such a strategy insisted on the endurance of emotional differences between classes, even while conceding the mutually beneficial advantages of each emotive style. Yet many patriots took a more radical stance and argued that *all* Americans could lay claim to roughly the same set of universal emotions. In this view, *natural* spirit could bind all Americans together far more closely than *cultivated* sensibility had ever linked provincial elites with metropolitan aristocrats. The dawning conviction that Americans shared a unique emotional legacy that derived originally from classical virtue became the foundation of Revolutionary organizing efforts and the basis for new theories of natural equality.

By 1776, colonists would be ready to cease all emotional overtures to Britain. Instead of appealing to British sensibility, Revolutionaries would then emphasize the importance of united American spirit. The final step in this progression, and one that colonists hesitated long before taking, would require declaring an end to emotional bonds with the king. Only after arriving at the conviction, voiced in June 1776, that "the iron hand that is lifted up against us" belonged to the king himself would colonists conclude they could no longer "contentedly continue the subjects of such a Prince, who is deaf to our . . . grievances, but, on the contrary, seems to take pleasure in our destruction." Only then would colonists claim that no kind of emotional communication could save strained transatlantic connections. Making this position a matter of common sense would require the efforts of Thomas Paine, whose motivational call on the "passions and feelings" of "all mankind" is the subject of the Postlude.[80]

For the moment, it is enough to note that by the end of 1775 Revolutionaries placed American spirit atop a pinnacle; drawn from many traditions, American emotion supposedly transcended all. The spirit of liberty arose from the careful blend of genteel feeling and popular passion. Consisting of a heady blend of civic love, mighty anger, and communal sympathy and public grief, it was to mediate between the debased insensibility imputed to the enslaved and the excessive spirit ascribed to Indians while also avoiding the ineffectual effeminacy attributed to English civility. According to eighteenth-century understandings, love was unknown among "natural slaves," mercy and sympathy were absent in "savages," and anger was admirable only in men. So, while an emphasis on spirit opened a rhetorical door to equality for free white men, it effectively closed it to Africans, Indians, and women. Even Washington specified that liberty belonged to all American *citizens*, that is, to those recognized as having the right to membership in the polity, not more broadly to all American inhabitants. Although patriot leaders declared the spirit of liberty to be the universal birthright of all Americans "without distinction," in actuality they took care to ensure that this emotional inheritance would be closely entailed.[81]

Postlude

The Passions and Feelings of Mankind

In the waning days of George III's American reign, Thomas Paine issued a clarion call to "examine the passions and feelings of mankind," confident that emotional scrutiny would lead to the acknowledgment of natural rights and, consequently, to support for American Independence. In the introductory pages of *Common Sense*, he declared:

> The Cause of America is in a great Measure the Cause of all Mankind. . . . The laying a Country desolate with Fire and Sword, declaring War against the natural Rights of all Mankind, and extirpating the Defenders thereof from the Face of the Earth, is the Concern of every Man to whom Nature hath given the Power of feeling of which Class, regardless of Party Censure, is the
>
> AUTHOR.

With these words, Paine claimed once more the "power of feeling" for the patriot movement and made emotion, a gift of nature, the common trait of all mankind. In so doing, he furthered the concept of innate equality basic to the theory of natural rights, for in one fell strike he defied the use of sentiment for any sort of social division. The only social class Paine cared to acknowledge was the universal one defined by the common feelings of all humanity. No more would the better sort be able to claim exclusive control over the power of feeling; feeling was not the special defining attribute of the few, but rather a gift of nature open to all. His evident belief that all mankind shared the same passions and feelings foreshadowed the position soon to become famous as the rallying point

439

of a revolution, that all men were created equal. Indeed, in addressing himself to *all* mankind, Paine announced a progressive agenda that surpassed that of even the most ardent proponents of patriotic "spirit."[1]

Uncompromising emotional universalism lay at the heart of Paine's politics. He insisted that in emotion lay the essence of shared humanity. Critiquing the very notion of hierarchy, and with it all inflexible social divisions, "MANKIND being originally equals in the order of creation," he declared, "How a race of Men came into the World so exalted above the rest, and distinguished like some new species, is worth enquiring into." For Paine, invoking the biological absurdity of assigning human beings to different species exposed the corresponding farcicality of social divisions. Emotion was the distinctive characteristic of humanity as a whole: "The Almighty hath implanted in us these unextinguishable feelings for good and wise purposes. . . . They distinguish us from the herd of common animals." In asking his readers to be emotionally moved, Paine thus invited them to fully embrace the radical egalitarianism with which he hoped to imbue the Revolutionary movement.[2]

From contemporary critics to modern scholars, readers have long noted Paine's emotional tone, "the 'daring impudence,' the 'uncommon frenzy,' which gave *Common Sense* its unique power." Yet too often historians have dismissed the emotional element of Paine's work simply as a matter of style, of persuasion, overlooking the fact that the language of emotion was necessary to the very substance of Paine's thought. Paine's brand of revolutionary rhetoric achieved widespread influence, not because (as has so often been held) it appealed successfully to the passions of ordinary people, but rather because it rendered passion itself ordinary. Paine cast passions and feelings alike as the common trait of all people, the basis of natural equality.[3]

Paine believed it to be simple common sense to regard "the passions and feelings of mankind" as "the touchstone of nature," the best basis on which to form judgments on any matter, even the vexed choice between reconciliation and Revolutionary rebellion that faced Americans in 1776. When Paine claimed that "the passions and feelings of mankind" were granted by nature equally to all and were intended to provide a moral touchstone accessible to all, he argued implicitly for the natural right to political participation. Since moral standing could be better measured by emotional sensitivity than by social status, all with "the power of feeling" should have an equal share in the organization of governance.[4]

In Paine's work, the medium was the message. His audience in Revolutionary America well understood the full implications of his emotionalism. Indeed, loyalist writers like Pennsylvanian James Chalmers countered that in "plain truth"—as Chalmers titled his published rebuttal—the "purpose[s] of nations" should be decided apart from "the passions of men" and "should have no connections to human nature." Paine offered such a clear case for viewing emotion as the source of moral conscience and the universal birthright of all humanity that his opponents felt forced to try to derail his argument by deriding his rhetoric. Chalmers took time to denounce "the passions of men" who favored Independence precisely because he believed that by so doing he could discredit Paine's progressive politics as being too base for serious engagement.[5]

In ways that have previously been insufficiently appreciated, *Common Sense* reflects the uniquely fertile environment that Pennsylvania provided for debating questions of sentiment, self, and society. Written and published in Philadelphia, *Common Sense* commented and capitalized on decades of local debates about the passions. Although Thomas Paine, a recent arrival to the city in late 1774, has often been cast primarily as a transatlantic figure—an Englishman who stopped off for a time in America on his way to revolutionary France—he should also be recognized as a Quaker-born writer who composed *Common Sense* in Pennsylvania at the close of a decades-long pamphlet war that had pitted Quakers, Anglicans, and Presbyterians against one another in a pitched battle for social and political control. In years of conflict over Assembly versus proprietary family prerogatives and disputes over military policy, a religiously inspired emotional rhetoric had played a key part in the definition of political positions. With twelve months' involvement in the Philadelphia print trade before penning *Common Sense,* Paine had more than enough time to absorb the local political lingo and to integrate it into his own emotional style. Doing so would have required little special effort; for, faced with the gathering crisis, Pennsylvanians used the year 1775 to reprint highlights from the previous decades of pamphleteering. Furthermore, Paine's efforts in *Common Sense* were edited and augmented by none other than Benjamin Franklin, seasoned veteran of Pennsylvania's satiric skirmishes.[6]

Selling 120,000–150,000 copies, or one for every five adults in colonial British America, Paine's pamphlet broadcast the Pennsylvania consensus in favor of a balanced approach to feeling and passion. At the same time, it spoke to patriots across the continent who were already primed to cleave to links between feeling and freedom. If members of the Library Company of Philadelphia had hoped back in the 1730s to situate their city as a point of dissemination for the best of British literature and philosophy while positioning themselves to fill "the most important offices of life," they had not imagined their colony's emergence, by the 1770s, at the forefront of a new American understanding of emotion. With the publication of *Common Sense*, Pennsylvania saw its transatlantic role transformed; it shifted from being a key center of reception to serving as a major site of production for a new brand of emotional culture, one that would promote an egalitarian ethos based on the language of universal emotion.[7]

"The Hour of Passion": Emotional Rhetoric in Cross-Class Appeals for Revolution

Perhaps no single individual better exemplifies the democratization of emotional culture than the Philadelphia printer William Bradford. He began by encouraging positive views of popular passions with the printing of the first-ever accessible and affordable American edition of Pope's *Essay on Man* in 1747, then spearheaded public opposition to the stamp tax and promoted patriot grief by publishing a funeral edition of the *Pennsylvania Mercury* in 1765, and finally ended by putting out the first full edition of Paine's *Common Sense* in the spring of 1776. By then, Bradford was firmly established as a patriot printer. When Pennsylvania Revolutionary leaders created a Committee of Safety to coordinate the activities of those working for the American cause, they turned to Bradford to print their pronouncements. Immediately after its organization in July 1775, the committee requested "that the Rules and Regulations for, and the Recommendations to the Associators, be published by William Bradford, and that he print two thousand of each on good paper, for the use of the Association."[8]

William's son Thomas joined eagerly in this Revolutionary work. Firmly established as his father's business partner by 1775, Thomas was mentioned by name in the committee's print request, which resolved that "William and Thomas Bradford be directed to Print in the English language 1000" additional copies. Only a few years before, Thomas and his sister Tace (herself now grown up and married to a Colonel Joshua Wallace of the Continental army) had used the language of grief to express their own grievance at William's decision to send Thomas from home and school him in Princeton. Now, however, Thomas willingly positioned himself by his father's side at the press and applied his old passionate tactics to politics. Evidence of Thomas's evolution comes in a letter from his old school friend John Lathrop in September 1775 thanking "Tommy" for his "friendly expressions with respect to the poor sufferers at Boston." No doubt Thomas seconded Lathrop's declaration: "When I think of my poor friends yet confined in Boston by that perfidious villain General Gage, my soul is overwhelmed with grief." In following his father's schooldays advice to "put on the man," Thomas had come to understand the value of using emotional symbolism in civic affairs.[9]

Thus, when Thomas Paine issued a common sense call to his imagined reader to "suffer his reason and his feelings to determine for themselves: that he will put *on* or rather that he will not put *off* the true character of a man," he neatly summed up an understanding that had long been building in Pennsylvania. His statements simply gave an important added boost to established arguments that true men were sensible men and that truly sensible men could not help supporting Independence. As Paine himself put it, "As a man sensible of injuries, I could never relish the doctrine of reconciliation. . . . I mean not to exhibit horror for the purpose of provoking revenge, but to awaken us from fatal and unmanly slumbers." For those who could feel, freedom was the only aim.[10]

The capacity to experience, express, and exchange emotions became a key factor in colonial resistance and, by 1776, *the* crucial component of Revolutionary rhetoric. Those who supported Paine's views on emotion and egalitarianism quickly reiterated them. One Paine defender, who published under the pseudonym Rusticus (positioning himself as a commoner), declared: "The benefits we have derived from Great-Britain are far from being innumerable. The evils we this day derive from her oppressive demands on us we very sensibly feel." Here, exalted sensibility was expressed by one claiming to be utterly ordinary. At the other end of the social spectrum, leading patriot and president of the College of New Jersey (Princeton) John Witherspoon described in May of 1776 "how deeply affecting" the prospect of "civil war" was; he had only praise for the "universal ardour that has prevailed among all ranks of men, and the spirited exertions in the most distant colonies." Again and again pamphleteers identified emotion as the impetus behind the Revolutionary movement and as the common trait that bound together elites and commoners alike as patriots.[11]

Those who opposed Paine's viewpoint were left with little means to counter the power of feeling other than to deny it altogether, a position that led to some awkward contortions. William Smith (so well known for his penchant for injecting emotion into politics that back in 1765 one wag had dubbed him the "Rev. *Sentiment-dresser-General*") criticized "the author of *Common Sense*" for offering "insults to his country in distress" by "addressing the inflamed passions rather than the sober reason" of colonists. Indeed, Smith spent the better part of March and April 1776, following the publication of Paine's pamphlet, penning and anonymously publishing under the pseudonym Cato a series of eight letters "To the People of Pennsylvania," in which he attempted to refute Paine point by point. In the urge to confront Paine, the onetime Sentiment-dresser-General seemed prepared to abandon all invocations of emotion and instead focus exclusively on the use of reason.[12]

Loyalist critics characterized emotions as essentially dangerous. James Chalmers hit this note again and again, warning: "Nations, like individuals, in the hour of passion attend to no mediation. But when heartily drubbed, and tired of war, are very readily reconciled." According to Chalmers, uncontrolled passion, not considered political commitment, was the driving force behind the movement for Independence. Appalled, he urged colonists to decide their stand, "not in the hour of passion, riot, and confusion, but in the day of peace and tranquil reflection." Smith so appreciated Chalmers's line about "passion, riot, and confusion" that he repeated it verbatim in his third "Letter to the People of Pennsylvania": "These words I borrow from a pamphlet just published under the title of *Plain Truth*; which I would recommend to your perusal, as containing many judicious remarks upon the mischevious tenets and palpable absurdities held forth in the pamphlet so falsely called *Common Sense*."[13]

William Smith's newfound antipathy toward passions in politics seemed to know no bounds. The same man who had not hesitated to declare, "Surely no Warmth can be unseasonable at a Time when all that we account dear or sacred is threatened with one indiscriminate Ruin," back when he wished to support Pennsylvania's entry into the Seven Years War in 1755, warned piously against allowing the passions to spur men to war twenty years later. He intoned in a 1776 sermon: "Men having their minds inflamed and the weapons of defence in their hands, seldom know the just point where to stop." He went on to claim that even General Richard Montgomery, who had died leading an unsuccessful American charge on Quebec, "desire[d] rather to soften than enflame violent humors, wishing that America, in all her actions, might stand justified in the sight of God." The more time that passed, the more adamant Smith grew on this point.

And he laid the blame for the patriots' increasing emotional heat squarely at Paine's door. In his fourth "Letter," in March 1776, he complained with a barely veiled pun: "Who would endure this Pain, This foul discharge of wrath[?] . . . Common Sense . . . can be tolerated by none but those who are so far inflamed or interested, that separation from Great-Britain at any risque is their choice, rather than reconciliation, upon whatever terms." How quickly seasonable warmth could be recast as foul inflammation![14]

Yet the problem for Smith, Chalmers, and other Paine antagonists was that his pamphlet had already largely anticipated their likely objections. In true Popian fashion, Paine had denied any conflict between the rational and the emotional, calling on his imagined reader to let "his reason and his feelings . . . determine" his attitude toward Independence. Aware of the arguments that advocates of last-minute reconciliation might probably advance, Paine had declared: "An independent constitution . . . at any price will be cheap. But to expend millions for the sake of getting a few vile acts repealed . . . is unworthy the charge. . . . Such a thought is unworthy a man of honour, and is the true characteristic of a narrow heart and a pedling politician." Whether or not Paine was deliberately invoking the 1757 commencement address in which Smith had charged Pennsylvanians to "disdain a narrow unfeeling heart," his remarks must have smarted with Smith all the same. With Paine's claim of feeling *and* passion for patriots, the onetime Sentiment-dresser-General stood denounced as a narrow-hearted peddling politician.[15]

So prevalent had approval of the passions become, not even Smith and Chalmers could afford to disavow them altogether. Chalmers, for example, seemingly oblivious to his own inconsistency, declared in the very same pamphlet that denounced "riot, passion, and confusion" that he was "passionately devoted to true Liberty" (presumably the British kind) and that he "glow[ed] with the purest flame of Patriotism." Better proof of the importance of emotion in the language of politics can scarcely be imagined.[16]

Meanwhile, Smith asserted in his fifth "Letter," with rather more candor than perhaps was strictly prudent, that he too had the ability to stir emotion, "had [he] been disposed to work upon the passions, rather than address the reason of . . . readers." Unsurprisingly, he tried to contrive a solution to his dilemma a few letters later. Beginning with the assertion that "the author of Common Sense" was "labouring to fill the hearts of [his] fellow-mortals with irreconcileable hatred; and the *feelings of the Devil*," he then explained, "As for my *feelings* on this occasion, I trust they are founded on the doctrines of the SAVIOUR OF MANKIND." Where Paine favored a naturalistic, universalist view of emotion, Smith fell back on the claim—long familiar in Pennsylvania—that cultivated Christian feelings were superior to any other kind. In so doing, he only mired himself deeper in contradiction. First of all, he again discountenanced his own prior pronouncements on the passions common to the state of nature. Second, in stepping away from his short-lived vow to address only the "sober reason" of colonists, Smith further strengthened Paine's position that in the definition of popular passion versus refined feeling lay a distinction without a difference.[17]

Despite these erratic attempts to seize the power of feeling for the loyalist cause, the language of emotion still remained strongly associated with the Independence movement. A dramatic case in point comes with the activities of the Philadelphia printer Robert Bell, who opened a shop in 1774 just three blocks from where the Continental Congress gathered. Though eager as any printer to accept whatever business there was to be had, Bell made a special point of trying to identify himself with that emotional primer for patriots, *Common Sense.* Claiming a share of Paine's glory, Bell asserted, "When the work was at a stand for the want of a courageous Typographer, I was then recommended by a gentleman nearly in the following words, 'There is Bell, he is a Republican Printer, give it to him, and I will answer for his courage to PRINT IT.'" Further touting his own work, he had exclaimed, "The judicious and discerning have perception sufficient to observe" that "the Provedore to the sentimentalists doth . . . PRINT decent EDITIONS." Heralding himself simultaneously as a "Republican Printer" *and* as a "Provedore [purveyor] to the sentimentalists," Bell made clear how deeply entwined patriotism, republicanism, and sentimentalism had quickly become.[18]

Of course, not everyone who supported Independence agreed without reservation that sentiments and passions would necessarily improve public life. Still, the trend was too overwhelming to be easily opposed. John Witherspoon, a Presbyterian minister as well as a college president, offered his support for the patriot cause and his approval of ardor, only in the context of a sermon, *The Dominion of Providence over the Passions of Men.* Having helped to preside over the recent end of the Presbyterian schism that had seen Old Side and New Side Presbyterians divided in their attitudes toward emotion, Witherspoon remained skeptical that God could really approve of willful passions. He maintained a certain old-school distaste for excesses of enthusiasm. Nevertheless, he could recognize which way the wind was blowing. Taking issue with the tone, though not the general substance, of "a well known pamphlet, *Common Sense*," Witherspoon demanded wryly:

> Was it *modest* or *candid* for a person without name or character, to talk in this supercilious manner . . . ? I thought the grand modern plea had been freedom of sentiment, and charitable thoughts of one another. Are so many of us, then, beyond the reach of this gentleman's charity? I do assure him that such presumption and self-confidence are no recommendation to me either of his character or sentiments.

Though a committed Revolutionary who would sign the Declaration of Independence just six weeks after delivering this sermon, Witherspoon remained mired in the idea that acceptable sentiments were most likely to stem from those who could already claim a respected name. Not even firsthand knowledge that virtuous ardor could be exhibited by "all ranks of men" could inhibit Witherspoon's reflexive belief that some ranks had a higher right to sentiment than others. Paine, a newcomer and a commoner both, irked the well-established Witherspoon with his "supercilious manner."[19]

Witherspoon's remarks make clear just how radical Paine's views on the common passions of humanity actually were. As an intellectual and religious leader privileged to head up an elite center of higher learning, Witherspoon did not altogether appreciate the efforts of a presumptuous upstart like Paine. At the same time, he could not deny how important emotion had become as a marker of American modernity in the minds of all those who participated in the Revolutionary movement. Like it or not, the "grand modern plea" for sentiment was widely recognized as *the* Revolutionary rallying cry.[20]

For this, Paine refused to apologize. Too much was at stake. He insisted, in essence, that the common "passions and feelings of mankind" provided the basis for commitment to the "natural Rights of all Mankind." Presciently forestalling the protestations of those like William Smith, who contended that only the "interested or inflamed" could tolerate *Common Sense*, Paine declared that he was "not inflaming or exaggerating matters, but trying them by those feelings and affections which nature justifies, and without which we should be incapable of discharging the social duties of life." In other words, emotional language did more than simply stir people up with an especially effective form of rhetoric: expressions of emotion communicated a special set of social ideals.[21]

Paine claimed that, far from being divisible into refined and base, God-sent or devil-driven, as Smith would have it, the feelings of all people could play a positive part in society. Nothing could better foster the development of a just social order than the cultivation of feeling. Precisely because they revealed the common basis of human nature, emotions formed the very basis of ideal society. He declared in the opening lines of the body of *Common Sense:*

> Society is produced by our wants, and government by our wickedness; the former promotes our happiness *positively* by uniting our affections, the latter negatively by retraining our vices. The one encourages intercourse, the other creates distinctions. . . .
>
> Society in every state is a blessing, but Government even in its best state is but a necessary evil.

In other words, affections could unite people as members of a common society, facilitate social interactions, and mitigate social divisions. While emotion alone might not be enough to inhibit vice (this was the right role for government), it provided the surest source of social virtue. Departing from the class-bound views that continued to inform the thinking of elitist loyalists and patriots alike—from James Chalmers to John Witherspoon—Paine opened new vistas by celebrating the socially leveling implications of bonds based on feeling. In asserting that united affections could trample social distinctions, he enunciated truly revolutionary hopes.[22]

Doctrines Propagated Long before the Present Day: The Pennsylvania Context of Common Sense

As the editor of the *Pennsylvania Magazine,* Paine published the work of many Philadelphians who had long been steeped in debates about the nature of emotion. Prominent among these was Francis Hopkinson. After years of quiet campaigning, Hopkinson had at last obtained a royal sinecure as a custom's collector in 1772, only to resign the post almost immediately in light of the Revolutionary crisis. Switching gears, he then began writing political satires illuminating colonial concerns. As a onetime student of William Smith's, Francis must have remained conscious of Smith's teachings. Yet, where Smith shied away from applying the rhetoric of emotion to the patriot cause, Hopkinson stepped in eagerly to do so. He felt sure, as he wrote in the summer of 1776, that emotion would give force to patriot plans, that colonists were "hearty and eager for action and full of spirits, animated . . . by the spirit of patriotism." Like Witherspoon's praise of the "universal ardor" of "all ranks of men," Hopkinson's praise for the "spirit of patriotism" might have been less than a full acceptance of personal passion. Indeed, Hopkinson's very desire for social prominence obviated full concurrence with Paine's egalitarianism. (No doubt he would have been pleased to know that the aristocratic-leaning John Adams, who "met Mr. Francis Hopkinson" during his time in Philadelphia, had judged him to be "genteel and well-bred.") Nevertheless, Hopkinson ended his long musings on emotion by openly advocating spirit, and with it the social mobility necessary to the full achievement of his own ambitions. He capped his Revolutionary career by signing the Declaration of Independence with a flourish and jumping at the chance for leadership in the new nation by supervising the Navy Board of the Continental Congress.[23]

Thomas Paine's radical philosophy cannot be properly understood apart from the Pennsylvania context that helped to produce it. For *Common Sense* was, in a very real sense, the culminating production of the eighteenth-century Pennsylvania pamphlet wars. Supporters of both the Assembly party and the proprietary party had spent the preceding decades debating which side was in danger of doing the greatest damage to Penn's holy experiment: Assembly party members willing to risk the rights guaranteed in the colony's original charter in order to seek assistance from the crown in curtailing the aristocratic proprietors and their allies, or proprietary party supporters who (like the Anglican converts of the proprietary family) were willing to squander the colony's pacifist Quaker traditions in pursuit of their own advancement. Suddenly, with the coming of revolution, partisans on both sides faced a crisis that threatened to end decisively the era each had been stridently vowing to defend. For Pennsylvanians across the political spectrum, the possibility of revolution created something of a referendum on the colony's history as well as on its potential legacy. In consequence, colonists rushed all at once to reprint, reprise, and in some cases recast many of the most important tracts and speeches produced over the previous several decades.

Understanding the controversies to which *Common Sense* responded first requires consideration of the pamphlets that immediately preceded it. In 1775—Paine's first year in Pennsylvania, the one that, as he so aptly put it, saw a shift "from argument to arms"—Pennsylvania politicos gave the old disputes one last airing. Pacifist Quakers restated their philosophical objections to all wars in different "testimonies," "epistles," and "advices" published that year. Pro-Revolution advocates dusted off Anglican convert Samuel Chew's 1741 disquisition *On the Lawfulness of Defense against an Armed Enemy* and sent it off to be reprinted. The patriotic Presbyterian minister John Carmichael played with the title of John Lidenius's 1756 sermon *The Lawfulness of Defensive War* in order to offer his own reflections: *A Self-Defensive War Lawful, Proved in a Sermon*. Meanwhile, William Smith trotted out his 1757 address for the first-ever commencement of the College and Academy of Philadelphia one more time for the 1775 commencement, explaining that it was from "the charge given at the first commencement, viz. 1757" that "a considerable part of this [his 1775 address] is quoted" and boasting proudly to the members of the Continental Congress present that he "wish[ed] all America to know" that "doctrines propagated" at the college "long before the present day" were "not, however, unsuitable" to the concerns of the current crisis. These reprints from Pennsylvania's decades of pamphlet wars set the tone for the new social and political doctrines Paine was soon to propagate.[24]

This recapitulation of the emotional rhetoric of Pennsylvania's longtime political debates would lead to reinventing the role of emotion in politics. The British elite had long insisted that refined feeling differed from popular passion: the role of the former was to restrain the latter. Pennsylvania Quakers, on the other hand, persistently held to the opinion that all humankind had the same set of emotions. Yet they too believed that passion (tainted by selfishness) should be subordinated to feeling (inspired by the Christ within); only feeling could underpin consensus and advance the common good. By the 1740s, an alternative position, well articulated by Alexander Pope, had begun to prevail: though all people could claim both sociable feeling and personal passion, passion should be allowed to predominate, since it best motivated man's "actions" and furthered his "aims." This stance was then revised in the minds of some members of the elite to mean that, though refined feeling and mass passion remained distinct, popular passion could sometimes, with elite oversight, serve as a useful political stimulus. Paine's position was to supersede all those that came before it; his perspective melded a Quakerly insistence that social and emotional parity made virtuous feeling open to all with a Popian commitment to passion and action. Meanwhile, as Paine's views began to take hold in Revolutionary Pennsylvania, both Quaker pacifists and social elitists became increasingly alarmed. From markedly different philosophical starting points, each in turn arrived at the conviction that, in the midst of such complexities, emotion was often better avoided altogether. It was in this context that Paine's pamphlet achieved its impact.

The process of review and refutation began with a subtle but significant shifting of position by Quaker leaders. At first, members of the Society of Friends responded to the mounting Revolutionary crisis exactly according to form. On January 5, 1775, the Quarterly Meeting renewed its traditional antiwar agenda by publishing a warning *Epistle* urging members to be on guard against the stormy passions of war: "We tenderly salute you, desiring that we may all press after, and seek for an establishment on that rock, against which the gates of hell shall never prevail, that we may be supported stedfast when storms and tempests . . . are permitted." While such reference to storms and tempests may seem at best a buried reference to emotion, this was in fact a classic eighteenth-century metaphor for emotion, made famous in Pennsylvania by Alexander Pope's oft-quoted epigram, "Passion is the gale." The *Epistle*'s reminder to believers always to seek a rock in a storm summed up the pacifist position on the relation between passion and action, anger and war. And it clearly recalled the unequivocal declaration made twenty years before, in 1755, in which Quakers had denounced violent emotion and action at once: "With Respect to the Commotions and Stirrings of the powers of the Earth at this Time . . . we are desirous that none of us may be moved thereat. 'But repose ourselves in the Munition of that Rock that all these Shakings shall not move.'" In invoking these lines, society members vowed not to be moved either martially or emotionally by the Revolutionary struggle.[25]

Just as the writers of this epistle sought to reiterate Quakers' traditional negative stance on the passions of war, so too they sought to reaffirm the basic social vision that underlay Quakerism: an egalitarian belief that all people shared equally in the light of Christ within, the source of the finest selfless feelings. Even when remonstrating wayward members for contributing to Revolutionary unrest by participating in nonimportation agreements, the *Epistle* took care to couch its reproach in terms that conveyed their basic commitment to treat all people with the same respect:

As some public resolves have been lately entered into, with the concurrence and approbation of some members of our religious society . . . our minds have been deeply affected with affliction and sorrow, and we have in much affection and brotherly love, been engaged . . . to convince these brethren of their deviation.

Alternating between affliction and affection, these lines in praise of peace stuck to conventional Quaker ground, issuing advice without asserting authority. Both the implied request to have sorrow redressed and the explicit assertion of "affection and brotherly love" spoke of "friendly" advice exchanged among equals. Meeting elders thus couched their counsel in terms of persuasion and disavowed the possibility of coercion. Finally, they deliberately heightened this effect by signing off, "in a degree of that divine love which unites in christian Communion and fellowship."[26]

Yet, if Quakers began 1775 determined to resist the onset of revolution by drawing on the largely successful legacy of the 1750s, they soon shifted both the style and the substance of their remarks. In a brief *Testimony of the People Called Quakers* offered on January 24—just nineteen days after issuance of the *Epistle*—they slid from proclaiming fellowship and dispensing advice to dictating a pacifist course of action and denouncing those that did not follow the official meeting position. Though they spoke in their opening lines of their "real sorrow" at the "unhappy contest between the legislature of Great-Britain and the people of these colonies," that was the extent of the emotional language employed in the testimony's four clipped paragraphs. Gone were references to brotherly love, affection, and Christian fellowship. In their place came stern warnings that Revolutionary protests were "destructive of the peace and harmony of civil society." More striking still, the authors decided to "publicly declare against every usurpation of power and authority . . . and against all combinations, insurrections, conspiracies, and illegal assemblies." Coming from a group who had long argued in favor of liberty of conscience and the right to free assembly, these were markedly reactionary remarks. This appeal to power and authority represented a real withdrawal from Quakers' traditional emphasis on egalitarian fellowship.[27]

Quaker leaders simply could not accept the turn events had taken. They had watched with alarm as the tenor of Revolutionary protests had shifted from cries of grief and pleas for redress to increasingly militant action, expressions of anger, and assertions of spirit. By 1775, though an actual declaration of independence still lay eighteen months away, they could already sense that the tide was turning. Thus, the central recommendation of their January 24 *Testimony:*

We have grounds to hope and believe, that decent and respectful addresses from those who are vested with legal authority . . . would avail towards obtaining relief . . . and we deeply lament that contrary modes of proceeding have been pursued.

Yearning for a return to the call and response of colonial grief and royal compassion that had successfully ended the Stamp Act Crisis, the authors of this statement bandied about a language of rank and class that was at odds with basic Quaker teachings. Appeals to respect authority took primacy over any effort to express fellow feeling. This attitude stood in contrast to the development of a far more successful Quaker rhetoric during the Seven Years War. Recall, for example, how in their 1757 tract *An Apology for the People Called Quakers* Society members had declared themselves "affectionately concerned in true sympathy" for their suffering fellow subjects and vowed to "freely contribute towards their relief," even as they opposed the war itself. Nothing of the kind was proposed in 1775. Instead, in the face of Revolutionary crisis, leading Quaker commentators came surprisingly close to adopting the very attitudes they had long deplored.[28]

Such slippage did not go unnoticed. An anonymous piece called *An Earnest Address to Such of the People Called Quakers as Are Sincerely Desirous of Supporting and Maintaining the Christian Testimony of Their Ancestors, Occasioned by a Piece, Intituled "The Testimony of the People Called Quakers"* explicitly criticized Quaker meeting members for forsaking the "testimony of their ancestors" in their 1775 *Testimony*. In *An Earnest Address*, the author (now believed to be Anthony Benezet) demanded that readers "remember, that what the colonies contend for, *is their right,* and by Friends acknowledged to be so, and then tell me whether our last Yearly Meeting Epistle is not a most striking and shameful deviation from the honest boldness and plainness of speech which distinguished our ancestors." Not only did Benezet believe in the justice of the patriot cause; he contended that support for protests represented the truest reflection of founding Quaker ideals. One of Benezet's central objections, in fact, was that, where Quakers had once eschewed honorific titles and insisted on addressing one and all as friends, they now resorted to demanding respect for authority. He challenged his fellow meeting members, "Ask the Prophets of old in what language they spoke to the men in power when they acted unjustly."[29]

Indeed, for Benezet, the question of "what language they spoke" was key, and he eagerly revived the use of emotion:

These things have pained my heart, and filled my mind with sorrow and affliction. . . . When I beheld a People, whose religious standard is truth and sincerity, incautiously drawn in by those, who call themselves their representatives, to assert that, "From their past experience of the clemency of the King . . . they have grounds to hope and believe, that decent and respectful addresses, from those who are vested with legal authority . . . would avail towards obtaining relief . . ." I felt an involuntary sigh arise within me and I could not repress the emotions of my spirit.

Here Benezet both rejected Quakers' newfound servile dedication to "respect" and reasserted emotion's importance in animating patriotism. Thus stirred, he went on to detail how "sensible were [some] friends, as well as all ranks of people . . . of the absolute necessity of either submitting to slavery or exerting themselves in some other way for our relief." In so doing he reclaimed the egalitarian implications of the concept of common sensibilities reaching across ranks and embraced the appropriation of emotional language for the patriot cause. At the same time, he castigated mainstream pacifist-loyalist Quakers for turning away from their own social, political, and cultural—that is, emotional—birthright.[30]

Many others who jumped into the fray to criticize the Quaker pacifists also couched their support for the Revolutionary movement in emotional language that bore the clear stamp of previous decades of debate. An especially fine example comes in the Reverend John Carmichael's June 4 sermon, *A Self-Defensive War Lawful*, in which he bemoaned the fact that "there are some Christian people in the world . . . who . . . do maintain it as a sacred conscientious tenet . . . *not to go to war, or take up arms on any occasion whatsoever.*" While Carmichael concurred with Quaker teachings on the link between passion and war, he disagreed as to the consequences of this connection. On the one hand, he "bewail[ed] . . . how many evil passions and appetites rage in the world!" stating that from "envy, wrath, malice . . . arise those crushing woes and calamities of war." Here, he recognized that *some* passions could be evil, a concession to the standard Quaker critique. Yet, he also argued, "Where our Lord enjoins us to love our enemies—he can't possibly mean we should love them better than ourselves." Carmichael thus reaffirmed that avoiding evil passions meant neither denouncing all passion nor altogether denying the self. On the contrary, God approved of the defense of self, home, and family and blessed those who, because they could feel for the suffering of their countrymen, took measures to alleviate it. Casting his eye up to Boston—whose port was stopped by a British blockade and whence news had just come of the April 19 casualties at Lexington and Concord—he lectured Pennsylvanians fortunate enough to live "far from any scene of either blood or slaughter—in the heart of a rich province," chiding them, "You hear of distress, but you do not yet feel it." The emerging position linking emotion and patriot action was quite consistent.[31]

This fact was to prove increasingly inconvenient for William Smith, the colony's onetime Sentiment-dresser-General. Smith's longtime efforts at careful emotional calibration—his advice to elite young men to "get the Dominion of your own Passions" jibing uneasily with his admiration for those with "the passion for liberty"—became ever more difficult to sustain. The heated emotion that he had found so salutary in debates about the Seven Years War became far more threatening once independence was at issue. A longtime proponent of the notion that the elite could use their refined feelings to channel the power of popular passions for political action, Smith hardly knew what to do once he found himself in the unfamiliar position of arguing against action. For all of his efforts to help define a "true spirit of freedom," to find a "rational medium . . . founded on a . . . refined turn of sentiment," Smith had never envisioned Americans' breaking with the British; he seems to have encouraged Americans to prove their facility with the feelings of freedom only in order to enable them to earn a more respected place within the empire. Unwavering in his elitism and in his loyalism, he was as baffled by the progressive uses to which the emotions could be put as he was startled by the Revolutionary turn that events seemed to be taking.

In the spring of 1775, then, even as Smith prided himself on becoming a leader before the Continental Congress, no task seemed as pressing as finding a way to contain the popular passions that he himself had once been pleased to unleash. Recognition of Smith's dilemma helps to explain the otherwise inexplicable: the rendition of his 1757 commencement address that he provided to members of Congress. Despite his deliberate claim to be sharing wisdom developed at the academy long before the Revolutionary crisis, upon actual examination, Smith's 1775 version of his 1757 "Charge Delivered . . . in the College and Academy in Philadelphia" bears little more than a glancing resemblance to the original. Leaving his students to declare themselves "fired with love of justice" even as their "bosoms" swelled with the spirit of liberty, Smith himself wholly cast aside the language of feeling and emphasized instead the importance of reason. Far from warning his audience, as he actually had done in 1757, to beware the dangers of the "unfeeling Heart, coiled up in its own scanty Orb," Smith instead focused exclusively on problematic aspects of the passions, cautioning his listeners, "Strength of passion, will be apt to bear down that sober reason and cool reflexion, which are your best guides." Perhaps the most striking aspect of this performance was Smith's pointed insistence that he was reiterating a long-held position. Though he was actually disavowing decades of positive teachings on emotions, he falsely led his audience to believe that he had always emphasized "sober reason and cool reflexion" above all else. Where once he had distinguished between the necessary regulation and the undesirable elimination of emotion, Smith now dismissed it out of hand.[32]

Nominally still in the patriot camp but increasingly tentative, Smith spent 1775 trying to downplay the very emotions he had once so stridently championed. Indeed, in a June sermon, *On the Present Situation of American Affairs,* he offered the following previously uncharacteristic equivocation:

> The tempers of men are cast in various moulds. Some are quick and *feelingly alive* in all their mental operations, especially those which relate to their country's weal, and are therefore ready to burst out into flame upon every alarm. Others again, with intentions alike pure, and a clear unquenchable love of their country, too stedfast to be damped by mists of prejudice, or worked up into conflagration by the rude blasts of passion, think it their duty to weigh consequences, and to deliberate fully upon the probable means of obtaining public ends. Both these kinds of men should bear with each other; for both are friends to their country.

In these lines, Smith sounded for all the world like the Reverend Francis Alison at the 1758 Presbyterian synod, scolding those "MEN of warmth and zeal, [who] can hardly bear with their fellow Christians of equal goodness, who are naturally more calm and moderate; who are not so easily, nor so vehemently, moved against the errors and iniquities of the times, as they themselves are." The irony, of course, is that when Alison's sermon was delivered—in the midst of the Seven Years War—Smith himself had been acting as exactly the kind of man of intolerant zeal that the

Presbyterian sought to rebuke. Now, however, Smith found himself pleading for recognition as a friend to his country, despite his refusal to endorse Independence and give way to "rude blasts of passion."[33]

Ironically, then, William Smith and loyalists like him—including men like Joseph Shippen, Jr., and Benjamin Chew, to name but a few—ultimately took up an impassively antipassion position much like that of pacifist Quakers—among them James Pemberton, signer of the infamous 1775 *Testimony of the People Called Quakers* as well as his brothers John and Israel. Patriots might have reprinted the prowar speech that Samuel Chew had made in 1741 in breaking with the Quaker faith, but Benjamin Chew, Samuel's loyalist son, ultimately found himself on the same side of the British-American conflict as his erstwhile nemesis Israel Pemberton. Given the political rivalry and personal enmity that had long divided these men, it is quite telling that they should all have arrived at the same distrust of and disgust for so-called popular passions, the same socially conservative position in opposition to the coming of revolution.[34]

Quaker influence on the Independence movement has long been overlooked, not only because their pacifism prevented them from active military resistance but also because many of their leaders slipped into accidental alliance with the loyalist elite, their language and politics converging in ways unimaginable even a decade before. Still, these facts should not blind us to the pivotal role that Quakers played through decades of Pennsylvania debate as well as through the continuing efforts of men like Anthony Benezet, who sought to apply the fundamentals of Quaker principles to a revolutionary age. In fact, Quaker arguments played a key role in the development of a social philosophy and an emotional rhetoric that would fundamentally shape the thought of Thomas Paine—and with it the ideas and ideals of his hundreds of thousands of Revolutionary readers.

Degrees of Tenderness: Paine in Dialogue with Pennsylvania

For the Quakers Elizabeth Sandwith Drinker, her husband Henry, and his brother John, the onset of revolution created a predicament that threatened their basic livelihood as well as their deepest beliefs. The crisis came when John, a merchant, refused to recognize bills of credit issued by the Continental Congress as legal tender, on the grounds that doing so would amount to supporting the war and subverting the spirit of pacifism. In 1776, Elizabeth noted in her diary with characteristic terseness: "Janry.

30. JD. call'd before the Committee." Her scant entry complements a lengthier broadside published on February 5 by the Pennsylvania Committee of Safety. The committee, charged with maintaining order and enforcing the dictates of the Continental Congress, responded to Drinker by issuing a public declaration to "hold up to the world, the said JOHN DRINKER," along with two other Quaker merchants, "as ENEMIES to their Country." The committee then ordered that they be *"precluded* from all *trade* or *intercourse* with the inhabitants of these Colonies." Four days later, Henry fled for safety along with John, leaving his devoted wife Elizabeth to remark, "1776 Febry 9. HD. JD. left home about noon for King-Wood—Paper out from the Committee." Only ten days later, after the Drinker store had been, in Elizabeth's words, "shet up by the Committee," did the two return, believing the worst was over. Though the Drinkers' difficulties continued throughout the war, their troubles did not force them to leave their Philadelphia home, nor ultimately prevent them from enjoying a long and prosperous residence as citizens of the new United States.[35]

As Elizabeth's brother-in-law John had remarked a few years before, "Properly speaking, no real evil can befall us that we do not perversely and willfully bring upon ourselves; I say no real evil, for generally speaking, . . . 'tis no uncommon thing . . . to mistake good for evil." John Drinker's remarks were philosophical and general yet are also quite apropos to the problem of assessing the impact of the Quaker legacy on the philosophy of the American Revolution. The fact that the language and politics of the Quaker and the proprietary parties largely converged at the point of revolution might have allowed history to "mistake good for evil." In actuality, however, traditional Quaker emphasis on egalitarian fellow feeling made important contributions to the Revolutionary movement that long went underappreciated. While easily dismissing Drinker as a public enemy because of his pacifist stance, patriot leaders overlooked the positive impact that Quakers' long emphasis on shared feeling had had on public life.[36]

If Thomas Paine's pamphlet calling on the "passions and feelings of mankind" now looks much like an effort to have the last word in a long-running argument, this may also be exactly how eighteenth-century Pennsylvanians understood it. Paine first introduced *Common Sense* on January 9, 1776, in the midst of the charged atmosphere that would shortly lead to the Drinkers' arrest. From the beginning, his pamphlet cast implicit criticism on Quakers; no doubt his pronouncements helped embolden the Committee of Safety that called Drinker to account exactly three weeks after his essay appeared. For example, responding directly to the Quakers' 1775 calls for reliance on the king's "clemency" and a return to the tactic of "respectful addresses" petitioning for relief, Paine asserted:

> Every quiet method for peace hath been ineffectual. Our prayers have been rejected with disdain; and hath tended to convince us that nothing flatters vanity or confirms obstinacy in Kings more than repeated petitioning. . . .
>
> To be always running three or four thousand miles with a tale or a petition . . . will in a few years be looked upon as folly and childishness—There was a time when it was proper, and there is a proper time for it to cease.

As far as Paine was concerned, the king's disdain demonstrated an abject failure of feeling that, when paired with patriots' credible claims to the same, justified the cessation of petitions and the beginning of action. He gave short shrift to passionless passivity and pacifism alike.[37]

So important had feeling become as a measure of virtue, patriots could hardly conceive of justifying their political position without this moral measuring stick. For a decade, protesters had charged members of Parliament with being unfeeling, yet always before they had stopped short of laying such a critique at the feet of the king. Suddenly, Paine changed all that. As he himself explained:

> No man was a warmer wisher for reconciliation than myself, before the fatal 19th of April 1775, but the moment the event of that day was made known, I rejected the hardened, sullen tempered Pharoah of England for ever; and disdain the wretch, that with the pretended title of FATHER OF HIS PEOPLE can unfeelingly hear of their slaughter, and composedly sleep with their blood upon his soul.

For the first time, it was stated outright that the king, like his ministers and his minions in Parliament, was "hardened," "unfeeling," and therefore unfit to rule.[38]

This rhetorical move could hardly have come as a surprise to Pennsylvanians with memories long enough to remember when times had been different and people had tried to oust, not George III, but Quaker assemblymen with claims they could not feel. Once Nicholas Scull had rhymed:

George by force, we must confess,
Has freed his neighbors from distress;
Has sav'd their Lives and Liberties,
And set their aching hearts at ease.

Critiquing Quaker legislators who he claimed were unfeeling and unable to respond to their fellow colonists' heartache, he added of those who could not take action:

. . . I think they shou'd,
Have left their Seats to those that wou'd.
. . .
And to be short, the Fact is plain,
Their love of Pow'r, has been our Bane.

The confidence colonists like Nicholas Scull had casually expressed in George II's capacity to respond to the suffering of his people back in 1755 had all but evaporated by the reign of George III in 1776. The connection between the capacity to feel and the right to rule remained stronger than ever, but faith in the feelings of the king had weakened beyond repair. The rhetoric Paine used against the king descended directly from that contrived in the 1750s to counter exclusive Quaker claims to virtuous feeling.[39]

Meanwhile, following closely the prescriptions of John Carmichael, who had lectured those who "hear of distress" but "do not yet feel it," Paine urged all Pennsylvanians to let their own emotions prod them to show solidarity with their compatriots in Boston and lend their support to the Revolutionary cause. He began by reminding Pennsylvanians, "It is the good fortune of many to live distant from the scene of present sorrow; the evil is not sufficiently brought to *their* doors to make *them* feel the precariousness with which all American property is possessed." Such distance could, according to Paine, be quickly closed through a moment of sympathetic identification. "Let our imaginations transport us for a few moments to Boston," he urged readers, explaining: "Those men have other feelings than [do those of] us who have nothing suffered. All they *now* possess is liberty, what they before enjoyed is sacrificed to its service, and having nothing more to lose, they disdain submission." Paine's central purpose in writing *Common Sense* was to promote unity of feeling across the colonies, to stir a passion for liberty that would prepare one and all to disdain submission.[40]

Finally, Paine's decision to include an extended "Address to the People Called Quakers on Their Testimony" in an enlarged edition of *Common Sense* published on February 14 provides the best evidence of all that his pamphlet was fundamentally—not merely coincidentally—a product of Pennsylvania. He wrote it in direct response to Quaker efforts to articulate a persuasive antiwar position. Immediately after the initial publication of Paine's pamphlet on January 9, Quakers had countered on January 20 with a new pamphlet of their own: *The Ancient Testimony and Principles of the People Called Quakers, Renewed . . . Touching the Commotions Now Prevailing in These and Other Parts of America*. Central to their critique of the patriot position was the statement, "We cannot but with distressed minds, beseech all . . . to consider that . . . by their acting and persisting in a proud, selfish spirit" they are pursuing "such measures . . . as tend to the shedding of innocent blood." This represented not only a close reformulation of the classic Quaker critique that war resulted from selfish passions but also an almost verbatim rendition of an argument made by Anthony Benezet back in 1759. In *Thoughts on the Nature of War*, Benezet had criticized "selfish, sensual, proud spirits" and concluded, "Selfish and wrathful passions . . . issues in war." In fact, Quakers set such store by the arguments Benezet advanced there that they brought it to press again sometime in 1776, adding it to the long list of works from the Seven Years War era reprised and reprinted in the age of revolution. Still, given that Benezet—following his own radically egalitarian philosophy—had apparently already thrown himself behind the patriot cause with his 1775 *Earnest Address,* this thrust ultimately lacked much force.[41]

For his part, Paine refused to remain silent in the face of this critical Quaker appraisal. Seeking to undermine Quaker objections to Independence and armament, Paine fell back on a long-standing Pennsylvania rhetorical tradition. Justifying the Independence movement, he directed his remarks squarely at the Quakers' *Ancient Testimony:*

> Perhaps we feel for the ruined and insulted sufferers in all and every part of the continent, with a degree of tenderness which hath not yet made it's way into some of your bosoms. But be ye sure that ye mistake not the cause and ground of your Testimony. Call not coldness of soul, religion.

As proprietary party supporters had done so many times before him, Paine used the rhetoric of emotion to charge Quakers with a fatal lack of feeling. Denying any moral viability to the pacifist position, he tarred Quakers with the same brush already being used to smear American loyalists and British Tories: those who could not feel tenderness should not wield influence.[42]

The conventional Quaker view held that "passions," unlike Christian "feelings," stemmed from mortal sin, a stance well summed up by Benezet's 1759/1776 declaration in *Some Thoughts on the Nature of War* that good Christians bore an obligation to seek "the death of the will and of all the appetites and passions of fallen animal nature." From the 1740s through the 1760s, such emotional schemas had been strongly countered by the Popian position that passions were "the elements of Life," an essential aspect of human nature ordained by God. But, with Independence imminent, even many previous proponents of Pope, startled by the Revolutionary ramifications of his views, came to embrace the argument (advanced by William Smith in his 1775 commencement address) that, "to keep animal joy alive, till the pall'd sense recoils and refuses the hated load—will be found at last 'a bed shorter than a man can lie himself upon.'" Never mind that Smith himself had done much to make this bed. As we have already seen, faced with the full implications of stretching out on passion's pallet, he simply refused to lay himself down.[43]

Paine, of course, did not accept the idea that the emotions of American patriots were sinful or animalistic. By insisting that feelings "distinguish us from the herd of common animals," he had declared—in a decidedly Quakerly vein—that the "unextinguishable feelings" that "the Almighty has implanted in us" were "the Guardians of his Image in our hearts." For him, emotion was fundamental to the operation of a just social order: "The social compact would dissolve, and justice be extirpated from the earth, or have only a casual existence were we callous to the touches of affection." The attraction of passion lay in its connections to action; by no means did Paine intend to endorse promotion of the self at the expense of the public good.[44]

Thus, when faced with Quakers' January 1776 critique that patriots betrayed a "proud and selfish spirit," Paine did adopt a defensive crouch, suddenly proclaiming, "We fight neither for revenge nor conquest; neither from pride nor passion." In the original edition of *Common Sense* Paine had called for his readers to examine *both* the "passions and feelings of mankind," as a means of invalidating emotion-based social distinctions while motivating patriot actions. When, in his "Address to the People

Called Quakers," he backed down and declared that patriots did *not* fight from passion, he did so only in order to answer Quakers on their own terms, to deny their central claim that the brand of emotion implicated in war was inherently sinful and selfish, the trait of "fallen animal nature."[45]

Throughout, Paine's goal remained the same: to awaken "those of passive tempers" from potentially "fatal slumbers" and hoist the flag of Revolution on the staff of the "passions and feelings of mankind." For this he was branded, even by fellow patriots of a socially conservative bent like John Carmichael, as a man whose promotion of "self-love" deserved "no recommendation." Still, much like Alexander Pope, who had long ago argued that "SELF-LOVE and SOCIAL are the same," Paine continued to believe that only self and society working cooperatively could possibly create an effective affective social compact.[46]

Popguns and Heavy Cannon: Emotional Expression as Political Communication in Common Sense *Debates*

Elizabeth Graeme Fergusson, celebrated poet and forsaken wife, owed much of her unhappy history to the very challenges Paine described. She well understood the links between passion and action that Paine promoted, remarking in a 1779 letter, "Sympathy . . . would flow but coldly, was there not Some Stimulative more active to push us on than bare reason." Yet she also understood that, even spurred by passion, sympathy might not be enough to ensure people's devotion to society over self. She remarked in the same missive, "Alas so strongly are we formed, that the trouble we feel for an individual that is dear to us is of a more heart piercing nature than the greatest Scene of Afliction that can be exhibited from a Sufering Nation." Elizabeth had good reason to make this reflection. Following her 1772 marriage to Henry Hugh Fergusson, she herself had put family before country and suffered markedly as a result.[47]

Her desire to support her new husband, an Englishman born and bred, resulted in her emotional and financial near destruction. As a consequence of performing a seemingly minor favor for him in October 1777, Elizabeth found herself charged by General George Washington with participating in a "ridiculous" and "illiberal performance" that bordered on treason. Her crime lay in passing over the American lines, at Henry's behest, a letter from Jacob Duché to General Washington that urged ending the fight for Independence. Washington scorned the letter and told Elizabeth he "highly disapproved of the intercourse she seemed to have been carrying on, and expected it would be discontinued." Soon after, Henry fled back to Britain, never to live with his wife again. Meanwhile, the new American government threatened to retaliate against Elizabeth by confiscating Graeme Park, her family's farm, her sole support in her effectively single state.[48]

Elizabeth Graeme Fergusson maintained ever after that her own loyalty to her "much loved Country" had never wavered, despite the misadventures in which marriage had involved her and Henry Fergusson. As she would later lament to a friend, "My Husband . . . is now on Earth without Home or Habitation: so much has this Coming of the British done for Him: As for me I have no right to Complain of them; because from first to last, I have Sincerely been their Enemy as far as Christianity will admit of Enmity." Despite the staunch support of local friends, she faced a difficult task in convincing the Pennsylvania Assembly of her loyalty.[49]

In the end, her most effective tactic turned out to be the invocation of sentiment. In 1781, she sent in a petition appealing to the legislators' sense of "Humanity" and asking them to "benevolently relinquish the publick Claims of her Estate," assuring them in the final lines of her letter that "she flatter[ed] herself their own Feelings w[ould] never reproach them for the Act." At the last, her appeal to humane feeling succeeded, and she was allowed to retain the Graeme family farm. As a friend of hers explained matters, it was "a favourable Circumstance for Mrs. Ferguson that the Powers which c[ould] contribute most to her Relief" were lodged with men who valued their reputations as "Gentlemen of Tenderness and Consideration" and took pains to "shew a proper Liberality of Sentiment." Even as she mused privately and perceptively on the limitations that feeling held as a foundation for nations, Elizabeth drew on the conventions of sentiment to salvage what she could of her own situation. Fortunately for her, at the height of the Revolution, patriots remained committed to the promotion of unity through shared emotion.[50]

Just what were the particular emotions that patriots hoped could bind them together? Looking beyond abstractions about feelings, passions, and so forth, how did Paine and his fellow pamphleteers utilize the language of emotion in the effort to define, refine, and even reassign allegiances in the Revolutionary arena? The same core emotions—love, anger, sympathy, and grief—that helped shape social negotiations in myriad realms across colonial Pennsylvania also played key roles in Revolutionary political rhetoric. Because many on both sides of the Atlantic imagined the diplomatic links between Britain and America as a series of family ties, modern ideas concerning divisions between the domestic and the politic had only limited eighteenth-century applicability. Instead, the popular vision of politics as interpersonal relationships writ large meant that "private" emotion played a key part in Revolutionary public life.

Love claimed pride of place in the emotions deemed central to describing the transatlantic relationship. Just as in eighteenth-century courtship, where declarations of love helped to veil negotiations of power, so the language of love had long played a similar cloaking function in the imperial realm. Bonds of love and affection supposedly drew together colonial "children" with "mother" country and "father" king. Indeed, appeals to the paternal affection of George III endured long after calls for fellow feeling from "brothers" in Parliament had ceased. So long as the king's American subjects related to him in terms of filial love and affection, they could claim not to be violating the political loyalty symbolized by emotional fealty. Yet, as early as 1774, some polemicists would contend that colonists had begun "to see that their Father's Affections were alienated from them." While intraimperial relations had traditionally been imagined as the connection of parent to child or brother to brother, this convention would soon undergo an important transformation in *Common Sense*. Thomas Paine would recast the transatlantic relationship as a failed one between unfaithful lovers.[51]

Some especially fine Pennsylvania examples of traditional uses of love in transatlantic politics can be found in the writings of William Smith. In one typical example, from a sermon in 1775, Smith declared, "Cemented by mutual love and mutual benefits, we trod the path of glory with our brethren for an hundred years and more. . . . esteeming our relation to them our greatest felicity; adoring the providence that gave us the same progenitors." Here Smith justified metaphoric descriptions of the British as brothers on the basis of actual familial and genetic links between peoples. Describing British and American brethren as treading the "path of glory" together, he conjured up an image of brothers walking shoulder to shoulder, equal in stature and bound only by love. In another, still stronger statement of this position, Smith exclaimed again in February 1776, "We considered ourselves as co-operating with our brethren for the glory of the empire . . . to become strong in our strength . . . and to derive *that* from our affection, which no force can extort from a *free* people; and which the miserable and oppressed cannot give!" A clearer statement on the presumptive connection between love and power could scarcely be asked for. Asserting that love could never be coerced, but only freely given, Smith claimed that, therefore, the political use of expressions of love and affection signaled full concord between governors and the governed. He argued, in essence, that, where love was exchanged, arbitrary power could not reign.[52]

Likewise, William Franklin, comfortably ensconced as the governor of New Jersey, drew on his decades-long practice with the language of love to declare in May 1775 that all colonists should maintain "a sense of *duty* to our Sovereign, and of *esteem* for our mother country" as a way to show they had "experienced the pleasures of *gratitude* and *love,* as well as *advantages* from that connexion." When it came to expressing allegiance to the "mother country," Franklin maintained the stance of a loving and dutiful child and remained a loyalist to the last. Ironically, of course, he did so in opposition to the Revolutionary activism of his actual father, Benjamin Franklin.[53]

William Smith too clung to such constructions to the end. As late as April 3, 1776, a mere three months before the decisive Declaration of Independence, he insisted, "The whole family of Britons, on both sides of the Atlantic, may yet be bound together, by fresh ties of mutual love and interest." Smith was badly out of step with his own brethren in America, who believed the path to glory led away from Britain, and who had long since shifted their so-called brotherly allegiances from their British connections to their fellow colonists. Still, it is important to understand that colonial claims of love for the king lasted up to the final hour precisely because withdrawal of affection would have been widely understood as tantamount to political defection.[54]

In spite of loyalist rhetoric of affection, patriots would soon lay out a powerful case for withdrawing love from the monarch. Revolutionary writers began by disparaging king and kingdom as bad parents who were undeserving of the continued love of colonial children. A classic example of this kind of protest rhetoric comes in the June 1775 sermon of John Carmichael, in which he declared of British leaders, "We would love them if they would suffer us—we would be peaceable, obedient, loving subjects if they would let us; but it would seem as if the present ministry were determined to cram disloyalty and disobedience down our throats." Since the king's ministers had colluded to "butcher their own children in America, that have been so obedient, useful and affectionate," colonists should not now hesitate to take up arms to defend themselves. Where affection failed, arms might prevail.[55]

The publication of Paine's *Common Sense* soon took this argument to its logical conclusion. Paine swiftly upended all conventional understandings of the metaphoric relations between rulers and the ruled by denying outright that the monarch could legitimately be regarded as the "FATHER OF HIS PEOPLE." Instead, he dismissed the king as a "wretch" worthy only of "disdain," one who fraudulently took a "pretended title" in claiming to be a father-king. Part of Paine's objection was factual. Unlike William Smith, who lingered over the idea that colonists had literal familial connections to the British, Paine forthrightly declared, "Europe and not England is the parent country of America. . . . We claim brotherhood with every European Christian, and triumph in the generosity of the sentiment." But his symbolic critique was still more fundamental.[56]

In a Revolutionary assertion with far-reaching implications, Paine insisted that the bonds of love that once tied colonist to home country had all along been romantic, not filial. In calling for an end to love and affection for the king, Paine declared, "As well can the lover forgive the ravisher of his mistress, as the [American] Continent forgive the murders of Britain." Denying that the king could legitimately claim the part of father, Paine recast the British nation in the role of faithless woman, the king in the part of her seducer. Like an anxious young suitor criticizing his intended's lack of love in order to lay the blame for the failure of courtship squarely with her, Paine accused the British of lacking the capacity for love. Drawing on the popular eighteenth-century metaphor for marriage as a silken chain or cord, he complained, "The last cord is now broken, the people of England are presenting addresses against us." He thus faulted the British while forgiving Americans for the end of their long transatlantic partnership. Still more explicitly, he argued (as had so many disappointed young men before) that Americans should have realized all along that Britain's "motive" for maintaining ties with the colonies had been *"interest* not *attachment,"* money rather than love.[57]

Paine actually cast Britain not exactly as an unsuitable love object for a rising young suitor eager to establish as his own domain, but rather as a sinful and adulterous woman who had betrayed her already-existing marriage vows. Claiming that America's "affections" had been "wounded thro' a thousand pores," he demanded: "Can ye give to prostitution its former innocence? Neither can ye reconcile Britain and America." Arguing as if for a transatlantic divorce, Paine told his American audience, "Your future connection with Britain whom you can neither love nor honour, will be forced and unnatural, and being formed only on the plan of present convenience, will in a little time, fall into a relapse more wretched than the first." With his use of the phrase "love and honour" (already then a conventional phrase in marriage ceremonies) Paine redefined the love lost between America and Britain as that between husband and wife, not parent and child. In so doing, he recalibrated the gendered roles and the presumptive balance of power between the two.[58]

In a few phrases, Paine transformed Britain's masculine paternal position into a stance of sinful feminine submission. At the same time, he reinvented America's relative status, trading the figure of the wayward child for that of an adult man, a master of his own domain roused to set his house in order. Crucial to the success of this maneuver was the invocation of love; this allowed Paine to gloss over the questionable desirability of casting America as a cuckold and to focus instead on reproaching Britain for lacking love, for being "callous to the touches of affection" that supported social justice. While it is easy to assume that emotion is always automatically emasculating, this rhetoric should make clear that the opposite was actually the case. An ability to express love was integral to the refined eighteenth-century masculine ideal. Because of this, Britain became more—not less—feminine as the result of "her" failures of feeling.[59]

The best measure of the effectiveness of Paine's reformulation of British-American relations is the effort William Smith immediately expended to counter it. In his third "Letter to the People of Pennsylvania," March 26, 1776, Smith claimed, "Among people naturally friends, and connected by every dearer tie, who knows not that their quarrels (as those of *lovers*) are often but a stronger renewal of *love?*" Trying to salvage the possibility of last-minute reconciliation, Smith concluded, "In such cases, the tide of affection reverting to its course is like that of water long pent back." Unfortunately for Smith, it was he, not Paine, who was swimming against the tide. As Paine put it, "To talk of friendship with those in whom our reason forbids us to have faith, and our affections wounded thro' a thousand pores instruct us to detest, is madness and folly. . . . Can there be any reason to hope, that as the relationship expires, the affection will encrease . . . ?"[60]

Other patriot pamphleteers soon stepped in to build on Paine's portrayal of Britain as a fallen woman empty of feeling. The pseudonymous author Rusticus claimed that Americans ought to break with Britain, since nothing could "prove the justice of her conduct towards us." With words that paralleled the judgment of Eliza Moode (who had once warned the courting Elizabeth Sandwith, "[Do] not take pleasure in shewing thy power, neither stretch it to the limit, for thou knows these things are weakened when carried too far"), Rusticus said of Britain: "Had she not indeed the absolute possession of our hearts and affections? And yet . . . she sought for still more—sought to subjugate us so entirely to her power as to leave us nothing we could call our own, independent of her arbitrary will and pleasure." By the spring of 1776, colonists were depicting themselves as disgusted suitors and disillusioned husbands, exasperated with the loveless and self-interested ambitions of their erstwhile British consorts and impatient to prove their manly resolve. This public withdrawal of affection essentially amounted to an admission of treason, a coded but quite comprehensible declaration of the desire for full political separation.[61]

Meanwhile, the same assumptions that shaped considerations of transatlantic love also applied to discussions of imperial anger. For each emotion, pamphlet writers posited almost literal parallels between interpersonal relations and political negotiations. Anthony Benezet well anticipated the attitudes prevalent on the eve of the Revolution when in *Thoughts on the Nature of War* he assailed "the selfish and wrathful passions, that between individuals, engender envy, hatred, injury, resentment, and revenge; and between nations, a peculiar kind of enmity and wrong, that issues in war." Benezet, of course, was a Quaker and could hardly be expected to take a favorable view of anger. Yet his words captured to a surprising degree the majority view that would emerge among social leaders across the political spectrum by 1776.[62]

On the one hand, Pennsylvania colonists had enjoyed many opportunities to observe the efficacy of anger in the two-plus decades from the start of the Seven Years War through the coming of Independence. Many had gloried in righteous wrath with the British triumph over the French at Quebec. Meanwhile, from the march of the Paxton Boys to the drama of early Stamp Act protests, popular rage had proved a potent source of grassroots power. Yet, enraged crowds also provided proof on a dramatic scale of the social instability that invocations of anger could foment. The violence of the Paxton riots in Pennsylvania and the Stamp Act protests across the colonies ultimately convinced many in power that anger brought danger above all else. By 1776, few spokesmen on either side of the Independence debate cared to draw on unalloyed anger in advancing their positions.

This shift left even committed patriots, especially those of the elite, remarkably uncertain on the subject of anger. The Reverend John Witherspoon's May 1776 sermon provides an excellent opening example of this conflicted attitude. He derided George III for giving way to the "resentment of a haughty monarch"; deplored the fact that British and American soldiers who were "the same in blood, in language, and in religion, should, notwithstanding, butcher one another with unrelenting rage"; yet also boasted that patriot pride was so strong that "the ineffable disdain expressed by o[ne] fellow subject, in saying, 'That he would not hearken to America, till she was at his feet,' has armed more men, and inspired more deadly rage, than could have been done by laying waste a whole province with fire and sword." Witherspoon's rapid shifts from denigrating to celebrating rage typify the prevalent attitude of ambivalence. While patriot leaders recognized that they probably could not do without anger altogether, they did their best to contain its influence and downplay its importance.[63]

Thomas Paine, for one, took a pragmatic yet critical view of anger in his *Common Sense* commentaries. To be sure, he did clearly recognize that anger had lent strength to the patriot movement. Still, anger's potential dangers alarmed him, as seen in his comments on the need to plan for effective governance in the coming post-Independence era. He chided, "Even the Tories (if such beings yet remain among us) should, of all men, be the most solicitous to promote" "a wise and well established government," for "the appointment of committees at first protected them from popular rage." Cleverly playing both sides of the fence, Paine proved his appreciation for the leverage provided by popular rage even as he argued in favor of finding ways to contain it.[64]

Elsewhere in the pamphlet, Paine took even closer aim at anger's negative aspects. In commenting on the plight of Bostonians subject to the British blockade, he warned that they might continue to suffer even if a rescue effort was undertaken, since "in a general attack for their relief, they would be exposed to the fury of both armies." Such emphasis on the devastation wrought by martial fury made clear Paine's basic distaste for anger. Most telling of all, however, were Paine's efforts to personally disassociate himself from such emotion. Perhaps betraying his own Quaker background, he twice denied that he had been in any way motivated by anger in writing *Common Sense.* In the first edition, he asserted, "I am not induced by motives of pride, party, or resentment to espouse the doctrine of Separation and independance; I am clearly, positively, and conscientiously persuaded that 'tis the true interest of this continent to be so." With that statement he disavowed anger altogether, even in the attenuated and "refined" form of resentment. So important did Paine find this point, he took special care to repeat it in the "Address to the People called Quakers," appended to the second edition. At the close of that piece, he reaffirmed, "Here without anger or resentment, I bid you farewell." While invocations of anger had done much to advance the patriot movement, they had also alarmed many with the specter of anarchy. Not even a relative radical like Paine conflated the desire to disrupt the standing social order with the total embrace of disorder. For Paine, anger had little positive role to play in the social compact. On the contrary, good government had to do as much to restrain rage as to advance the affections.[65]

Despite the efforts he made to distance himself from anger, Paine remained subject to attack on exactly that ground. Writing under the sobriquet Candidus, James Chalmers mocked him in *Plain Truth:* "The town has lately been amused with a new political pamphlet, entitled Common Sense," whose author could not keep himself from "venting his spleen against the English form of government." Likewise, William Smith declared that "the *authors,* or if I must say *author,* of what is called Common Sense" (a sly reference to the fact that Paine was widely known to have had local assistance in preparing his pamphlet) had let fly "foul discharge[s] of wrath from . . . Their Pop-guns here, and there their heavy Cannon." Smith kept up this attack down to his next-to-last "Letter to the People of Pennsylvania," saying, "The author of Common Sense stands singular in his rage for condemning the English constitution." Still, such comments could do only limited damage, given that loyalist pamphleteers were themselves vulnerable to similar aspersions. For example, the author signing himself Rusticus issued a warning in his pamphlet, *Remarks on the Late Pamphlet Entitled Plain Truth,* urging readers of *Plain Truth* to beware of "Candidus foaming with rage and hurling vengeance around him—Let us therefore not dare approach him in his wrath." The renewed use of accusations of anger as a form of insult represented a return to early-eighteenth-century attitudes and a retreat from the more open embrace of anger prevalent at midcentury.[66]

Still, on the eve of Independence, no patriot wanted to link himself to the fearful weakness associated with expressions of sorrow and grief. As the Reverend President Witherspoon warned, "Abhorred scene[s] of civil war" were "apt to overcome a weak mind with fear or overwhelm it with sorrow." Thus, one key reason why patriot commentators could not utterly abjure anger was its continued association with action and strength. Witherspoon promised that the same scenes apt to inspire fear in the weak were "in the greatest number . . . apt to excite the highest indignation, and kindle up a spirit of revenge." Defending his decision to endorse indignation over sorrow, Witherspoon reinforced his remarks: "If this last [indignation] has no other tendency than to direct and invigorate the measures of self-defence, I do not take upon me to blame it, on the contrary, I call it necessary and laudable." As Samuel Chew had observed more than thirty years before in his speech on "Lawful Defence" (which was reissued in 1775), "I know of no alternative, but the relying upon prayers and tears, or resisting by force." Presented with the choice to cry or fight, patriots chose the latter.[67]

In fact, by the eve of Independence, the only pamphleteers still invoking grief and sorrow were pacifist Quakers and loyalist polemicists. For all his richly evocative emotional language, Tom Paine, for one, made only rare and glancing references to grief in Common Sense. Consider, for example, his comment, "The good People of this Country are grievously oppressed," hardly a stirring expression of sorrow. By contrast, Quakers repeatedly invoked emotions of sadness and grief. In January 1775 Friends stated that, though they had "considered with real sorrow, the unhappy contest between the legislatures of Great-Britain and the people of these colonies," they believed, "from [thei]r past experience of the clemency of the king," that petitions could still "avail towards obtaining relief." They "deeply lament[ed] that contrary modes of proceeding ha[d] been pursued." In two further statements in October of that year, Quakers reiterated that "the sorrowful Alteration in the State of this once peaceful Province" had caused them "deep Concern and Affliction" and concluded, "We cannot therefore but sorrowfully lament, that any should now forget the Equity and Justice of their Laws and Government . . . by preferring their own Schemes." Finally, in response to Paine's arguments for Independence issued in Common Sense, Quakers repeated in January 1776 that they deplored the "animosities, and unhappy contentions which now sorrowfully abound." All the Quakers' lamentations were aimed at diverting attention from calls for armed action.[68]

Likewise, William Smith placed heavy emphasis on tearful sentiments, as when he urged an audience in June 1775, "I am sure you will indulge the passing tear," since there was "Great and deep distress about to pervade every corner of our land!" He warned his hearers, "Even Victory itself [would] only [yield] an occasion to weep over friends and relatives slain!" Smith hoped to convince listeners that, even if Independence could be achieved, it would bring with it only further suffering. "These are melancholy prospects; and therefore you will feel with me the difficulties I now labor under . . . left to lament alone." Smith was indeed left nearly alone in his sorrowful stance. Ironically, his only company came from pacifist Quakers, his longtime antagonists—a fact that must have afforded cold comfort. Among patriots primed for action, the passive remonstrations of lamentation advocated by pacifist and loyalist pamphleteers held very little attraction.[69]

As grief lost ground, expressions of sympathy and other forms of fellow feeling continued, conversely, to gain in importance. One final example comes in the words of Presbyterian minister John Carmichael, who charged a Pennsylvania audience in 1775, "Sympathize with your distressed suffering brethren in Boston, both with your prayers and your purses." Sympathy remained the best guarantor of patriot unity as well as the strongest symbol of natural equality. Still, the qualifications Carmichael took care to include in his invocation of sympathy hint that the emotion did not have infinite symbolic utility. Colonists who wished to unite on the basis of sympathy remained subject to the same dilemmas that had always plagued the promotion of shared feeling: the inverse relation between the social distance bridged and the active assistance provided by emotional exchange. Carmichael tried to skirt the issue by reminding his audience to open its purses along with its hearts and prayer books. He prodded his listeners to back sympathy with action, to offer material as well as emotional and spiritual aid, but edging around the problem solved much less than confronting it head on. Recognizing this fact, Paine was soon to take a different path.[70]

Nations Not Apt to Think Until They Feel

Perhaps no single tale better exemplifies the pitfalls of relying on feeling to advance the cause of social progress than the story of the Benjamin Chews. One might logically expect that Benjamin Chew, Sr., and Benjamin Chew, Jr., father and son, would have been firm adherents of the Revolutionary cause. After all, the father of Benjamin, Sr., Samuel Chew, had authored a 1741 pamphlet in support of defensive war so stirring that proponents of the patriot cause saw fit to reprint it in 1775. Its words anticipated the Declaration of Independence:

> In a state of nature. . . . life and liberty, the immediate gifts of God, were common to all men, and every man had a natural title . . . a right to preserve and defend them from the injuries and attempts of others, as they concerned his happiness. . . . The natural desire then of happiness, and that principle of self-preservation, common to all men, must first have inspired them . . . with notions of compacts, of laws, and of governments.

Clearly, these lines resonate closely with Thomas Jefferson's pithier and far more famous explanation of "the Laws of Nature," which declared that all men "are endowed by their Creator with certain unalienable Rights, that among these are Life, Liberty, and the Pursuit of Happiness—That to secure these Rights, Governments are instituted among Men." Chew, in opposing Pennsylvania Quaker pacifists and breaking with the faith of his birth, had blended local emotional idiom and Lockean political philosophy several decades before Jefferson arrived at the same combination in the declaration he composed in Philadelphia in 1776.[71]

Yet, when Benjamin Chew, Sr., had followed his father out of the Quaker Meeting and into a life of lucrative proprietary posts, he set forth on a path that led to loyalism. He embraced every important aspect of Philadelphia Anglicanism, including a brand of social conservatism inimical to doctrines of natural equality. Not only did he become a communicant at Christ Church, but he also sent his son and namesake, Benjamin Chew, Jr., to be educated at the College and Academy of Philadelphia under the careful supervision of the college's provost, the Reverend William Smith. Young Benjamin flourished at the college. He eagerly steeped himself in fashionable literature and eventually emerged at the 1775 commencement exercises as his class's valedictorian. On that May day, before the audience that included members of the Continental Congress, he had declared:

> I know, my dear Fellow Graduates, that your hearts join me, and all the soul of the PATRIOT exults within you, while I now step forward and PLEDGE myself . . . that we who have this day been so highly distinguished in their sight, will make our country's good . . . the grand

object of all our pursuits. We will consider LIBERTY as the choicest gift of heaven . . . exalting human nature, and inspiring every nobler sentiment.

In circulating a printed version of Chew's remarks, William Smith had gushed, "The speaker, through the whole [of his performance], and particularly in his pathetic conclusion" (which comprised the lines quoted above) showed "he FELT, and was thoroughly POSSESSSED with, his subject." Despite his much-remarked-upon depth of feeling, the junior Benjamin Chew, like the senior, ultimately declined to support the Revolution. When shells fell on Cliveden, the Chews' grand country estate, they shot from the guns of patriot opponents. Still, like their friend and ally William Smith, the Chews weathered the crisis surprisingly well. Adhering to a steady but unobtrusive brand of loyalism, they hedged their bets and reemerged in the postwar period with their fortunes and reputations largely intact.[72]

The Chews' determination to retain their advantageous social position provides the best explanation for their refusal to embrace the Declaration of Independence. Despite that document's remarkable similarity to Samuel's 1741 essay, which had largely shaped the Benjamin Chews' lives up to 1775, the two works did differ in crucial ways. Nowhere did Samuel Chew ever advocate or even consider the concept of natural equality. On the contrary, where Jefferson prefaced his discussion of unalienable rights with the assertion that "all men are created equal," Chew emphasized the importance of men of property. Indeed, in defining just what he meant in invoking happiness, Samuel Chew explained that in the state of nature, "what is called estate or property, was . . . absolutely essential to human happiness." Despite the devotion of Benjamin Chew, Jr., to sentiment and rhetorical embrace of liberty, Samuel's descendants saw little appeal in a revolution predicated on equality.[73]

The attitudes of men like the Chews reveal the vulnerabilities of Thomas Paine's vision of universal human emotion. Despite the soaring rhetoric of *Common Sense,* Paine's egalitarian philosophy ultimately ran aground on social realities. By their very nature, personal passions (which motivated action yet promoted the self) and sociable feelings (which engendered apathy even as they advanced the common good) could coexist only in unstable equilibrium. Meanwhile, maintaining balance between self and society presented formidable challenges in a milieu in which many, from Declaration author Thomas Jefferson to Declaration signer Francis Hopkinson, chafed against fixed social divisions the better to enable their own preferment.

Of course, in making feeling the basis of social compacts while asserting that passions could be a source of virtue, Paine may seem to have simply staked a decisive position on the winning side of a waning debate. If colonial Pennsylvanians, along with eighteenth-century commentators at large, had long debated the virtues of emotion in all its many forms, by the last quarter of the century a new consensus was emerging. From tying passion to servility and feeling to gentility, as Pennsylvania writers had done frequently up through the 1730s and 1740s, to connecting feeling to civility and passion to virility as they had in the 1750s and into the 1760s, through at last to defining all emotion as the basic attribute of humanity in the later 1760s and the 1770s—Pennsylvanians had undergone an utter transformation in their attitudes. Far from seeing emotions as the source of sin, Pennsylvanians, with their fondness for Pope, had come to view all emotions, including willful passions, as potential fonts of virtue. Thus, Pennsylvania's long debates about the passions helped to shape *Common Sense,* one of the fullest-ever articulations of American arguments for natural equality.

Central to this shift was a growing acceptance of the proposition that, whether laudatory or derogatory, emotion-based social categorizations were fundamentally unsound. Paine did not so much pander to the passions of the masses as oppose the very idea of using emotional traits for social differentiation. Confronted with the accusations of Quakers and other critics that he and the Revolutionaries acted from unreasoning anger, Paine explicitly affirmed that they led the fight for Independence neither "from pride nor passion." At the same time, he refused to recognize distinctions between emotion and reason, claiming that a man should make use of *both* "his reason and his feelings to determine" a position on Independence. And, most important of all, he easily ablated the lines between refined feelings and popular passions, blurring them together as "the passions and feelings of mankind." Paine used the notion of universal emotion to make the case for embracing social equality on the basis of common humanity—a position considerably farther-reaching than the carefully circumscribed notion of the "spirit of liberty."[74]

Paine himself understood the limitations of emotion as a guarantor of social justice. It is crucial to remember that at the very outset of *Common Sense,* as he asked his readers to imagine a primordial society, he had warned them, "Nothing but Heaven is impregnable to vice." Though, in an imagined state of nature, people could be expected to naturally draw together, Paine cautioned that cooperation based on shared feeling was invariably temporary. "It will unavoidably happen that in proportion as they surmount the[ir] first difficulties . . . they will begin to relax in their duty and attachment to each other: and this remissness will point out the necessity of establishing some form of government to supply the defect of moral virtue." In other words, while emotional attachment might band people together, it could not hold them fast forever.[75]

A society founded on emotional ideals nonetheless needed government to foster ethical interactions. Paine well grasped that the shift from disparagement to praise of passion actually signaled its growing social and political inadequacy. He dismissed the idea that human beings could be counted on to act invariably according to the dictates of virtue. While he fully believed that emotion was necessary for morality, he did not think for a moment that it was sufficient. For those who might have missed this point in the first edition of *Common Sense*, Paine repeated and reinforced it a month later:

> The present state of America is truly alarming to every man who is capable of reflexion. Without law, without government, without any other mode of power than what is founded on, and granted by courtesy. [It is] held together by an unexampled concurrence of sentiment, which is nevertheless subject to change, and which, every secret enemy is endeavouring to dissolve.

In Paine's portrayal, patriots could justly take pride in the virtue and feeling they displayed. Their emotional unity, their "concurrence of sentiment," had allowed them to forge firm sympathetic bonds. The key word here was "unexampled." Paine predicted that such unprecedented harmony would not last, and he begged his readers to prepare for a stronger system of association. Where feeling might fail, government must be made to prevail.[76]

Paine's conception of the relation between emotion and virtue was truly revolutionary precisely because he fully understood the limitations of their link. If Paine took a universal view of human nature, it was *not* a universally positive one. On the contrary, he repeatedly spoke in *Common Sense* of the problem of vice as an unwelcome but ever-present companion of virtue. While Alexander Pope had declared that passions could promote the work of virtue, and many Pennsylvanians, following his lead, had eventually roused their passions in virtue's cause, Paine's work reminded people that Pope's advice had always been two-sided. When Paine declared that "defects of moral virtue" must "inevitably happen," no matter the strength of feeling, he echoed Pope's contention that only fools failed to understand the enduring influence of vice. Paine's pivotal contribution, then, came not just in appreciating passion's potential but also in emphasizing the forces restricting its promise.[77]

Indeed, beneath the soaring optimism of the patriot movement, undercutting rousing rhetoric on liberty and freedom and bracing statements on equality and natural rights, ran an anxious countercurrent. Like Paine, many Revolutionary writers believed that, while the passions might foster virtue, they could not put an end to vice; while individual advancement might lead to collective improvement, personal sacrifice was unlikely to provide a steady source of social amelioration. In this vein, Thomas Jefferson—transcribing lines from Pope's *Essay on Man* into a commonplace book in his youth—had paired the seemingly sanguine assessment, "For more Perfection than this State can bear / In vain we sigh; Heaven made us as we are" with the far darker observation, "Fools . . . from hence into the Notion fall / That Vice or Virtue there is none at all." Such consciousness of the problem of selfish vice shadowed even the most celebratory assessments of American promise.[78]

Ultimately, then, the tension between self and society that Pope had tried to dispel with a few simple couplets continued to plague Revolutionary writers. Pope had promised

That REASON, PASSION, answer one great aim;
That true SELF-LOVE and SOCIAL are the same;
That VIRTUE only makes our Bliss below;
And all our Knowledge is, OURSELVES TO KNOW.
—Epistle IV (395–398)

Yet, on the eve of Independence, Thomas Paine denied that even the most virtuous feelings could ever ensure bliss "below," since "nothing but Heaven is impregnable to vice." The dilemmas between self and society, so poignantly perceived and so eloquently articulated by a host of Pennsylvanians across the eighteenth century, ultimately played a pivotal role in the emergence of a new nation.

Paine's charge to frame a government capable of safeguarding communal values while accommodating individual ambition would usher in a new era. We can hear the echoes of his ideas in Jefferson's more famous assertion that, when people exercise the right to "institute new Government," they should be sure of "laying its Foundation on such Principles and organizing its Powers in such Form, as to them shall seem most likely to effect their Safety and Happiness." Still, neither *Common Sense* nor the Declaration itself could bring an end to a distinctively American dilemma, one that haunts us to this day. As a people, we have never agreed how best to sit astride that awkward balance between personal advancement and community enhancement, between the pursuit of selfish passion and the promotion of social feeling.[79]

Appendix

Toward a Lexicon of Eighteenth-Century Emotion

Like the proverbial Eskimo vocabulary for *snow,* terms for emotion abounded in colonial British America, and they evidence both people's intense interest in emotion and their disagreements as to its functions and foundations. According to eighteenth-century understandings, emotions could be sorted into markedly different categories—affections, feelings, sensibilities, sentiments, passions—each with its particular characteristics and implications. Though often melded in today's usage, various words for emotion carried distinct connotations in eighteenth-century English. Pausing to sort out the subtleties of a few of the most common emotion terms will greatly aid analytic precision.[1]

The word *emotion* itself was employed only infrequently in the eighteenth century, one reason why I have chosen it to encompass the various other terms under discussion. According to the *Oxford English Dictionary, emotion* in the sense of "agitation or disturbance of mind, feeling, passion; any vehement or excited mental state" is first cited about 1660. However, the word seldom appears in Pennsylvania sources. Meanwhile, the modern definition of *emotion* as "a mental feeling or affection as distinguished from cognitive or volitional states of consciousness" is not even cited until sometime about 1808. The absence of such a concept from eighteenth-century vocabulary is significant. While present definitions of the word regard *emotion* as separate from the mind and from the will, "from cognitive or volitional states," people of the eighteenth century made no such assumptions. Indeed, as abundantly evidenced in this book, it was exactly emotion's presumptive possible connections to volition and cognition that made it the focus of much attention.[2]

Consider, then, the term *affection*. *Affection* today is popularly associated with positive emotion felt toward another, what the *OED* refers to as "goodwill" or "kind feeling." And such feelings of liking were often expressed with the word *affection* in the eighteenth century. However, this is a secondary definition for *affection;* the literal meaning, dating back to 1660, is the "act of being affected," or acted upon. As a broad category of emotion, affection means "an affecting or moving of the mind in any way; a mental state brought about by any influence." So *affection* carries with it the connotation of an outside influence that has an impact on a mental state. In eighteenth-century British America, such influences were very often thought to be godly. Evangelical itinerant George Whitefield used the word in just this way, in a spiritual autobiography published in Philadelphia in 1740, when he described his conversion experience by saying, "My Understanding was enlightened, my Will broke, and my Affections more and more enlivened with a Zeal for CHRIST." Figuring himself as the receptive object of God's influence, Whitefield described religious conversion as a transformation that involved simultaneous interconnected shifts in cognition ("understanding"), volition ("will"), *and* emotion ("affections"). This is the sense in which *affection* was commonly used by eighteenth-century Pennsylvanians, most often with the connotation of being positively affected, whence the word's more specific association with liking.[3]

The related term *feeling* placed particular emphasis on the sensory experience of emotion. Indeed, the word *feeling* could denote not just emotion but sensory perception of any kind. In the *OED*, the earliest definition of *feeling* is "the faculty or power by which one feels." A secondary definition is "the condition of being emotionally affected . . . an emotion." A final definition of *feeling* emerged about 1739: "an intuitive cognition or belief neither requiring nor admitting of proof." In eighteenth-century British America, then, emotions experienced as feelings might have arisen either from within or without; in any case, *feeling* implied an active seeking after information and experience absent from the more passive notion of affections. Thus, when the Reverend Gilbert Tennent, a New Light Presbyterian preacher in colonial Pennsylvania, said, in 1743, "We should beware of resting satisfy'd with the Doctrinal Knowledge of Truth, without feeling the efficacious Influence thereof upon Heart and Life," he encouraged his followers to seek just this kind of intentional yet intuitive sensory engagement. In a similar vein, when the traveling Quaker minister Rachel Wilson described participating in a gathering of the Philadelphia Monthly Meeting of the Society of Friends in 1768, she relied on her feelings to further her sense of communion with fellow Quakers. On that occasion, believers were so "unsettled [in] mind" that even a few "sweet" words offered by one worshipper "made no great alteration in General feeling." So Wilson herself "stood up [to speak] having as [she] thought a sense of the state of the meeting." Here Wilson actively searched her senses to take an intuitive reading of the feelings of the Quakers gathered with her for worship.[4]

Despite subtle differences in meaning, then, in eighteenth-century Pennsylvania affections and feelings were both associated with moments of social, and often religious, connection. Because either could further the reception of signals from without, they each played important roles in the conceptualization of moral and spiritual development. Quakers believed that feelings could be one important manifestation of the light of Christ within, while New Light evangelicals believed—in tandem with Jonathan Edwards—in the importance of religious feelings and affections in the work of religious conversion. Both kinds of emotion facilitated believers' relations with God as well as with being in general. Both assumed the submission of human will to God's will, the submission of self to a greater good.[5]

Another variant on terms emphasizing emotion as sensory perception was *sensibility*, which placed special stress on the strength and discernment of a person's sensitivity. According to the *OED*, eighteenth-century *sensibility* was associated particularly with delicacy of taste, with a "readiness to feel compassion for suffering, and to be moved by the pathetic in literature or art." Because *sensibility* was so closely associated with literary culture, colonial booksellers frequently invoked it in their advertisements, as when Pennsylvania merchant John Rivington advertised for sale "a new and excellent Novel that cannot fail of affecting every Reader of Sensibility." As this quotation implies, evaluations of *sensibility* imposed moral and aesthetic judgments on a person's emotions; a reputation for *sensibility* conferred status. When young Becky Owen passed away in Philadelphia in 1755, she earned praise for having "the nicest Sensibility of Heart, [which] justly regulated a fine Understanding and consummate Virtue." Ironically, then, although *sensibility* putatively emphasized receptivity to the emotions of others, a primary intent and effect of its cultivation was the elevation of self.[6]

Sentiment, meanwhile, is described in the *OED* as denoting both "a mental attitude (of approval, disapproval, etc.), an opinion or view as to what is right or agreeable," and "a mental feeling, an emotion." That is, *sentiment* is linked to opinion. In eighteenth-century British America, *sentiment* was tied explicitly to the capacity to make moral judgments and lay somewhere between the realms of thought and feeling. Despite the fact that reason and emotion often appeared as opposing forces in eighteenth-century thought, the two were also frequently combined in the now-nearly-forgotten category of sentiment. When Adam Smith published his *Theory of Moral Sentiments* in 1759, following on the heels of philosophers like David Hume and Francis Hutcheson, he sought to solidify the idea that emotion could be a force for social good, the source of sympathetic identification between separate social actors. His particular usage of the word *sentiment* had widespread resonance in Pennsylvania. Not only could colonial book buyers find "Smith's Sentiments" advertised for sale in Philadelphia by 1760, but by 1761 even a bookseller's advertisement for a "New Collection of Fairy Tales" for children promised that the stories included "contain[ed] many useful lessons [and] moral sentiments." According to conventional colonial views then, though *sentiment* differed in emphasis from affections or feelings, it too was supposed to privilege society over self.[7]

By century's end, *sentiment* would begin to take on another sense as "refined and tender emotion . . . a manifestation of 'sensibility,' an emotional reflection or meditation, an appeal to the tender emotions in literature or art." But it is important to note that the *OED* does not find this definition of *sentiment* until 1768, and its negative connotations of excessive emotion of sentimentality did not develop until later still. For the period under discussion, *sentiment* is best understood as a brand of emotion that owed something to the head as well as the heart and that had the potential to influence moral judgments but was unrelated to the kind of concern with refinement of feeling or nervous theories of emotion that came to characterize the culture of sensibility. Although the broad interest in emotion that this study documents can help us to understand the emergence of what scholars refer to as the "culture of sensibility," it is important to recognize that *sensibility* was but one late-developing manifestation of a rising concern with emotion whose roots stretched back at least to the Great Awakening, if not before.[8]

In marked contrast to other emotional referents, *passion* came closely associated with self and with will, qualities often, though not necessarily, regarded as negative. Because the *passions* had so many definitions and connotations, it is best to consider them one by one. Then as now, the word *passion* was often linked to two specific emotions: anger and lust. In the eighteenth century, such associations could taint any emotion labeled a *passion* as debased and dangerous to reason and morality—or could simply emphasize the strength of the emotion. For *passion* was also widely used as an umbrella term for any strong emotion, being defined in this sense, according to the *OED*, as "the fact or condition of being acted upon or affected by an external agency; subjection to external force; affection; an effect or impression produced by action from without." Though the *OED*'s final citation for this definition is from 1690, it must be kept in mind when considering debates about the passions that occurred in Pennsylvania in the 1730s–1770s. For the sense of *passion* as being produced from without also spills over into the basic modern definition provided by the *OED*: "affection of the mind . . . any kind of feeling by which the mind is powerfully affected or moved; a vehement, command-ing, or overpowering emotion." And from the perspective of eighteenth-century British America, the sense of the *passions* as an overpowering force was the crucial element of any definition.[9]

The notion of commanding passions led colonial British Americans to make deep associations between passion and servility, often regarding persons subject to passion as fit subjects for mastery. Meanwhile, colo-nists who wished to exert social control believed they had first to demon-strate self-control. So contended the Pennsylvania commentator who claimed in 1756 that only the man who would "divest himself in particular of all . . . Passion, Revenge, and other selfish Views, and have no other Emulation than to prove himself a worthy Member of the Community" could hope to be counted among those "worthy, fit, and capable Per-sons . . . solicited to accept Offices in Government." According to those who understood passion to be the source of willfulness, reining in one's own will—the better to serve "the community"—was a necessary first step in establishing the right to rule over others. In direct contrast to feelings, affections, and sentiments, all thought to aid the advancement of selfless-ness, *passion* was traditionally regarded as an obstacle to effective social engagement.[10]

The *OED* further equates *passion* with excess as "a fit or mood marked by stress of feeling or abandonment to emotion; a transport of excited feel-ing." This sense of abandonment was especially important to eighteenth-century understandings of the *passions,* as it again carried with it the idea that *passions* involved capitulation to the will. Surrendering to *passion* involved the flouting of self-restraint, submersion in selfishness and sin. Thus, warnings against what one writer in the *Gazette* in 1769 called devotion to the "momentary Gratification of . . . selfish and sordid Passions" were rife in colonial Pennsylvania. All in all, then, according to conventional eighteenth-century critics, those mastered by their own *passions* lacked the capacity for religious convictions, reasoned decisions, or social commitments.[11]

Still, as the *OED* also notes, *passion* can be associated with positive qualities, with "action," with "movement," and with "transport"; therein lay its dormant attraction for colonial British Americans. Over the course of the eighteenth century, many eventually became enamored of the idea that, because of its organic connection to human will, *passion* alone, of all varieties of emotion, could confer the power of action. Such was clearly the view maintained by the poet featured in the *Gazette* in 1744 who explained, "Not him I praise, who, from the world retir'd, / By no enlivening, generous passion fir'd, / On flow'ry couches slumbers life away, / And gently lets his active powers decay." Paradoxically, for all its dangerous associations with sin and servility, *passion* could also be seen as a key source of power and virility. These basic definitions can greatly enhance our understanding of eighteenth-century debates about emotion.[12]

Acknowledgments

I will always remember the first piece of advice Kathleen M. Brown gave me in 1997 when agreeing to supervise my dissertation: "Be sure to choose a topic you really love and believe in. You'll be working on it for the next decade." At that point, a decade seemed an impossibly long time to devote to thinking about any one thing. But in this, as in many things, her counsel proved exactly right. This project has been a "ruling passion" of mine for a good ten years, and I feel deeply grateful to the many teachers, students, colleagues, family, and friends who have shared my enthusiasm.

At New York University I am fortunate to belong to a wonderfully vital community of scholars working on the history of the Atlantic world. I especially thank my colleagues in the Atlantic History Workshop: Thomas Bender, Lauren Benton, Michael Gomez, Martha Hodes, Walter Johnson, Karen Kupperman, John Shovelin, Sinclair Thomson, and Joanna Whaley-Cohen. Greatest thanks are due to Karen (workshop founder and guiding spirit), Laurie (also my highly supportive department chair), and Martha (historical storyteller par excellence), who each read the manuscript draft in full and offered much-valued suggestions. I also deeply thank my colleagues in the History of Women and Gender Program, especially Linda Gordon, Fiona Griffiths, Martha Hodes, Barbara Krauthamer, and Molly Nolan, who provided critical help in framing this book's Introduction. Thanks also to good friends and colleagues in the wider NYU community, including, especially, Pat Bonomi, Robert Dimit, Marion Katz, Sharon Street, Gabrielle Starr, and Bryan Waterman. In my first position, at Rutgers University, Camden, I enjoyed the stimulating company of many fine colleagues, especially Laurie Bernstein, Howard

Gillette, Janet Golden, Margaret Marsh, Philip Scranton, Jacob Soll, and Chair Andrew Lees.

Before I had colleagues, I had teachers, though in their generosity they would all probably prefer to be described as friends. At the University of Pennsylvania, I benefited greatly from the unflagging dedication of Kathleen Brown, who supervised my dissertation, and of Richard Dunn and Michael Zuckerman, who served as members of my committee. They each in their unique ways set a high standard for scholarship and for sheer humanity. It has been a privilege to continue to work with them over the years. Key advisers at Penn also included Drew Faust, Lynn Hunt, and Daniel Richter. As an undergraduate at Yale University, I was first initiated into the delights of early American history by John Demos, who contributed insights to portions of the dissertation and to whom I remain gratefully indebted.

Becoming part of far-flung knowledge networks is one of the true pleasures of academic life. I owe a very great deal to Jan Lewis, who read the dissertation in full and has remained a key resource for me in the years since. Many thanks as well to Andrew R. L. Cayton, who read the manuscript for the Omohundro Institute of Early American History and Culture, made crucial interventions, and has offered continued guidance and support as my scholarship develops in new directions. Informal teachers have taught me as much as the formal ones. Special thanks to G. J. Barker-Benfield, Stephen Bullock, Elaine Crane, Laura Edwards, Edward Larkin, Michael Meranze, Richard Sher, David Shields, Eric Slauter, and Peter Stearns. I owe an extra debt to Michael Meranze, who not only closely critiqued Chapter 9 but also suggested the book's ultimate subtitle!

I have been fortunate in receiving institutional and financial assistance throughout the development of this project. I thank the University of Pennsylvania for support (including key fifth-year funding made possible by the Andrew W. Mellon Foundation). In my last two years of graduate work, I benefited from a Charlotte W. Newcombe Doctoral Dissertation Fellowship from the Woodrow Wilson National Fellowship Foundation and from a Marguerite Bartlett Hamer Dissertation Fellowship from the McNeil Center for Early American Studies. I treasured my time in residence at the McNeil Center and am grateful for many exchanges formal, informal, and, above all, fun with Wayne Bodle, Julia Boss, Joan Bristol, Seth Cotlar, Carolyn Eastman, Matt Hale, Dallett Hemphill, Rodney Hessinger, Brooke Hunter, Susan Klepp, Kon Dierks, Sally Gordon, Nikki Gothelf, Ann Kirshner, Sarah Knott, Trish Loughran, Brendan McConville, Roderick McDonald, Beth Pardoe, Marti Rojas, Peter Silver, John Smolenski, John Wood Sweet, Kirk Swinehart, Randolph Scully, Colleen Terrell, Karim Tiro, Mark Thompson, Rachel Wheeler, Stevie Wolf, Kirsten Wood, and Kariann Yokota as well as, of course, with founding director Richard Dunn, current director Dan Richter, Kathy Brown, and Mike Zuckerman. Crucial financial and intellectual support also came in the form of summer fellowships and research grants from the Pew Program in Religion and American History (where I gained by the comments of directors Jon Butler and Harry Stout and my fellow participants); the Haverford College Quaker Collection (where curator Emma Lapsansky-Werner and archivist Diana Franzusoff Peterson provided much-appreciated research help); and the David Library of the American Revolution. I also wish to thank the research staff at the Historical Society of Pennsylvania and the Library Company of Philadelphia (including most especially Librarian James Green and Reference Chief Phillip Lapsansky).

As I worked to transform the completed dissertation into a finished book, I profited enormously from an Andrew W. Mellon Postdoctoral Research Fellowship from the Omohundro Institute of Early American History and Culture. Ronald Hoffman, director, and Fredrika J. Teute, editor of publications, both provided invaluable encouragement in critical moments. Their willingness to create a flexible definition of "residency requirements" should provide a progressive model for other research institutes seeking to accommodate scholars with families. My one-week-a-month consultations with Fredrika created an ideal alternating rhythm of solitary writing and convivial collaboration. I am hugely grateful for her searching questions and suggestions as well as for the keen insights and ready assistance of the many devoted faculty, fellows, and staff also in residence in my time at the Institute, including James Axtell of the College of William and Mary, Wendy Bellion, Kimberly Foley, Chris Grasso, Paul Mapp, Sally Mason, Beverly Smith, and Karin Wulf. Finally, a timely sabbatical leave provided by New York University's Goddard Junior Faculty Fellowship allowed me to fully realize the plans for revision laid at the Institute.

I am grateful to have had opportunities to discuss this project with the conveners and audiences of many conferences and colloquia, including the American Historical Association, the American Society for Eighteenth-Century Studies, the Boston Area Early American History Seminar, the German Historical Institute Conference on Early Modern

Emotion, the Library Company of Philadelphia–McNeil Center for Early American Studies Conference "The Atlantic World of Print in the Age of Franklin," the New York University Atlantic History Workshop, the New York University History of Women and Gender Group, the Newberry Library Seminar in Early American History and Culture, the Organization of American Historians, the Princeton University Eighteenth-Century Society, and the University of North Carolina at Greensboro conference "Creating Identity and Empire in the Atlantic World, 1492–1888." Particular thanks to the Columbia University Early American History Seminar, especially to Richard Bushman, Ira Cohen, Elaine Crane, Ann Fabian, Sara Gronim, Evan Haefeli, David Jaffee, Ned Landsman, John Murrin, Herb Sloan, and Kathleen Wilson.

I also owe appreciation to editors and readers at journals and presses. First, I thank Drew Cayton and an anonymous reader for the Institute, who commented on the entire manuscript. Some of the contents appear in different form elsewhere. I thank Peter Stearns and Jan Lewis, who worked with me on the article " 'The Cornerstone of a Copious Work": Love and Power in Eighteenth-Century Courtship" (*Journal of Social History*, XXXIV [2000–2001]), which appears here as part of Chapter 3; Dan Richter and George Boudreau who edited "Vehement Movements: Debates on Emotion, Self, and Society during the Seven Years' War in Pennsylvania" (*Explorations in Early American Culture*, V [2001]), which appears here as part of Chapter 5; Chris Grasso, Laura Edwards, and three anonymous readers who assisted me with "The Sentimental Paradox: Humanity and Violence on the Pennsylvania Frontier" (*William and Mary Quarterly*, 3d Ser., LXV [2008]), which appears here as part of Chapter 8; and Richard Sher, Jim Green, and Ros Remer, who commented on the paper "Self-Love and Social Be the Same: Alexander Pope and Anglo-American Debates on the Passions" (at the Library Company of Philadelphia–McNeil Center for Early American Studies Conference "The Atlantic World of Print in the Age of Benjamin Franklin"), which here forms part of Chapter 1 and is to appear in a conference volume.

As my work on this project has drawn to a close, I have been immensely aided by the professionalism of the Institute's publications staff, including Mendy Gladden and many hardworking anonymous editorial apprentices. Gil Kelly has been witty and wise as a copy editor. His generous remark that my manuscript was one of the "cleanest" he has encountered is a tribute, not to me, but to the many who helped me, most particularly to Colleen Terrell, who copyedited my entire dissertation in exchange for nothing more than my enduring gratitude, as well as to Elizabeth Wulf, who helped prepare the footnotes for the final manuscript.

The culmination of this project coincided with the climax of another one, the struggle to have a child. I want to comment publicly on the need for universities to maintain leave and tenure-clock-stoppage policies that support parents and to thank New York University for doing both.

On that note, I would like to thank my family, loyal supporters through thick and thin. My parents, Thomas and Cecilia O'Donnell Eustace, encouraged my love of words from early on. They bought me a blank book for my half-birthday when I was seven and encouraged me to fill it. Little did they know how much the idea would catch on! I count my brother Ned Eustace as one of my closest friends and thank him for many great conversations as I was writing this book. My dear Nana, Florence Cruess Eustace, who passed away just as this book went into copyediting, would have been certain that this was the world's "best" book. I'm so grateful she lived long enough to enjoy the fruit of my other long project. Would that I could say the same of Grandfather Louis Klancnik, who passed away just two weeks after his first great-grandchild was born. The rest of my extended family, including Dorothy Klancnik, Jim Klancnik, Maggie Klancnik, Gordon P. W. Klancnik and Michelle L. K. Walters, Will Klancnik, and Elizabeth Paddock Klancnik, along with numerous aunts and uncles and cousins, asked many interested questions about the manuscript over the years but kindly avoided inquiring just when it would be finished! Special thanks to two staunch friends, Jenna Saidel Lebowich and Rachel George Hartnett; had we not spent countless hours playing "Laura Ingalls" together starting in second grade, I doubt whether I would ever have become a historian. Finally, a warm thank you to Jaitrie Paul, the most loving, caring, and giving caregiver our family could have hoped to find.

I think I may at last be out of words. This book is about the power of emotion, the strength of language. But it remains beyond my skill to capture what my husband Jay and our son Jem mean to me. This book is for them.

Notes

Introduction

1 The classic statement on the importance of Enlightenment rationalism in the American Revolution (along with English common law, country politics, and other schools of British political thought) is in Bernard Bailyn, *The Ideological Origins of the American Revolution*, rev. ed. (Cambridge, Mass., 1992), 26–27. On the Scottish influence, see Garry Wills, *Inventing America: Jefferson's Declaration of Independence* (Garden City, N.Y., 1978).

   Foundational work on emotional life in early America from the standpoint of social history includes Carol Zisowitz Stearns and Peter N. Stearns, *Anger: The Struggle for Emotional Control in America's History* (Chicago, 1986); Stearns and Stearns, eds., *Emotion and Social Change: Toward a New Psychohistory* (New York, 1988); Peter N. Stearns and Jan Lewis, eds., *An Emotional History of the United States* (New York, 1998).

2 [Thomas Paine], *Common Sense: Addressed to the Inhabitants of America . . .* (Philadelphia: R. Bell, [1776]), [iii], 41.

3 "Of True Happiness," *Pennsylvania Gazette,* Nov. 20, 1735 (hereafter cited as *PG*).

4 Alexander Pope, *An Essay on Man,* II, ll. 97–98, 101–108, quoted in Joseph Shippen Commonplace Book, 1750, Shippen Family Papers, Historical Society of Pennsylvania (HSP), Philadelphia (hereafter cited as Shippen Papers).

5 On philosophical approaches to emotion, see especially John Corrigan, Eric Crump, and John Kloos, *Emotion and Religion: A Critical Assessment and Annotated Bibliography* (Westport, Conn., 2000); Corrigan, " 'Habits from the Heart': The American Enlightenment and Religious Ideas about Emotion and Habit," *Journal of Religion,* LXXIII (1993), 183–199; Nicholas Capaldi, *Hume's Place in Moral Philosophy* (New York, 1989); V. M. Hope, *Virtue by Consensus: The Moral Philosophy of Hutcheson, Hume, and Adam Smith* (New York, 1989); Albert O. Hirschman, *The Passions and the Interests: Political Arguments for Capitalism before Its Triumph* (Princeton, N.J., 1977); Henning Jensen, *Motivation and the Moral Sense in Francis Hutcheson's Ethical Theory* (The Hague, 1971).

   For literary studies, see Julie Ellison, *Cato's Tears and the Making of Anglo-American Emotion* (Chicago, 1999); Elizabeth Barnes, *States of Sympathy:*

Seduction and Democracy in the American Novel (New York, 1997); Barnes, "Affecting Relations: Pedagogy, Patriarchy, and the Politics of Sympathy," *American Literary History,* VIII (1996), 597–614; Julia A. Stern, *The Plight of Feeling: Sympathy and Dissent in the Early American Novel* (Chicago, 1997); Adela Pinch, *Strange Fits of Passion: Epistemologies of Emotion, Hume to Austen* (Stanford, Calif., 1996); Pinch, "Emotion and History: A Review Article," *Comparative Studies in Society and History,* XXXVII (1995), 100–109; Ann Jessie Van Sant, *Eighteenth-Century Sensibility and the Novel: The Senses in Social Context* (New York, 1993); G. J. Barker-Benfield, *The Culture of Sensibility: Sex and Society in Eighteenth-Century Britain* (Chicago, 1992); Alan T. McKenzie, *Certain Lively Episodes: The Articulation of Passion in Eighteenth-Century Prose* (Athens, Ga., 1990); Janet Todd, *Sensibility: An Introduction* (New York, 1986).

Studies of American emotion that have made considerable use of conduct books are Stearns and Stearns, *Anger;* Jacquelyn C. Miller, "An 'Uncommon Tranquility of Mind': Emotional Self-Control and the Construction of a Middle-Class Identity in Eighteenth-Century Philadelphia," *Journal of Social History,* XXX (1996–1997), 129–149; Christina Dallett Hemphill, "Class, Gender, and the Regulation of Emotional Expression in Revolutionary-Era Conduct Literature," in Stearns and Lewis, eds., *An Emotional History.*

6 Joseph Shippen, Jr., to Edward Shippen, Dec. 18, 1752, Shippen Papers.

7 Henry Jamison, *PG,* July 8, 1762.

8 William Smith, "Preface," in Thomas Barton, *Unanimity and Public Spirit: A Sermon Preached at Carlisle* . . . (Philadelphia, 1755), xi.

On issues of civility and gentility, see, for example, C. Dallett Hemphill, *Bowing to Necessities: A History of Manners in America, 1620–1860* (New York, 1999); David S. Shields, *Civil Tongues and Polite Letters in British America* (Chapel Hill, N.C., 1997); Richard L. Bushman, *The Refinement of America: Persons, Houses, Cities* (New York, 1992); John F. Kasson, *Rudeness and Civility: Manners in Nineteenth-Century Urban America* (New York, 1990); Bernard W. Sheehan, *Savagism and Civility: Indians and Englishmen in Colonial Virginia* (New York, 1980); Roy Harvey Pearce, *The Savages of America: A Study of the Indian and the Idea of Civilization,* rev. ed. (Baltimore, 1965).

9 See, for example, Stephen Saunders Webb, " 'The Peaceable Kingdom': Quaker Pennsylvania in the Stuart Empire," in Richard S. Dunn and Mary Maples Dunn, eds., *The World of William Penn* (Philadelphia, 1986), 173–194. On Pennsylvania's political history and religious rivalries, see Alan Tully, *Forming American Politics: Ideals, Interests, and Institutions in Colonial New York and Pennsylvania* (Baltimore, 1994); Sally Schwartz, *"A Mixed Multi-*

tude": The Struggle for Toleration in Colonial Pennsylvania (New York, 1988). Clare A. Lyons has cast eighteenth-century Philadelphia as a place beset by "a cascading series of problems and possibilities for the organization of society and the fulfillment of the individual," in *Sex among the Rabble: An Intimate History of Gender and Power in the Age of Revolution, Philadelphia, 1730–1830* (Chapel Hill, N.C., 2006), 2.

10 On Pennsylvania's formative relations with neighboring Indian nations (and especially the status anxieties such interactions laid bare), see Jane T. Merritt, *At the Crossroads: Indians and Empires on a Mid-Atlantic Frontier, 1700–1763* (Chapel Hill, N.C., 2003); Gregory Evans Dowd, *War under Heaven: Pontiac, the Indian Nations, and the British Empire* (Baltimore, 2002); Richard Slotkin, *Regeneration through Violence: The Mythology of the American Frontier, 1600–1860* (Middletown, Conn., 1973), 230. See also Fred Anderson and Andrew Cayton, *The Dominion of War: Empire and Liberty in North America, 1500–2000* (New York, 2005), 103.

On Pennsylvania's mid-eighteenth-century emergence as a slave society, see Ira Berlin, *Many Thousands Gone: The First Two Centuries of Slavery in North America* (Cambridge, Mass., 1998), esp. 179, 181; and see Gary B. Nash, *Forging Freedom: The Formation of Philadelphia's Free Black Community, 1720–1840* (Cambridge, Mass., 1988).

11 For the "universalist" school, see, for example, Silvan S. Tomkins, *Affect, Imagery, Consciousness,* 4 vols. (New York, 1962–1992); Paul Ekman and Richard J. Davidson, eds., *The Nature of Emotion: Fundamental Questions* (New York, 1994). Their perspective has been taken up recently by such scholars as Zoltán Kövecses, *Metaphor and Emotion: Language, Culture, and Body in Human Feeling* (Cambridge, 2000).

For the constructionist school, see Catherine A. Lutz, *Unnatural Emotions: Everyday Sentiments on a Micronesian Atoll and Their Challenge to Western Theory* (Chicago, 1988), and see Lutz and Lila Abu-Lughod, eds., *Language and the Politics of Emotion* (New York, 1990).

12 William M. Reddy, "Against Constructionism: The Historical Ethnography of Emotion," *Current Anthropology,* XXXVIII (1997), 327–351, esp. 335. For a complementary perspective, see also Anna Wierzbicka, *Emotions across Languages and Cultures: Diversity and Universals* (Cambridge, 1999).

Reddy stresses the important point that statements of emotion (which he dubbed "emotives") reshape the inner experience of emotion even as they attempt to represent it. Significantly, his theory of a "gap" between language and subjectivity meshes well with findings from neuropsychology. These stress that, while the facial expressions and changes in voice tone used to convey emotion are both produced and interpreted in the right hemisphere of the brain, the language used to describe what is felt or perceived is processed in the left hemisphere. As Bryan Kolb and Ian Wishaw report, "Although the right hemisphere may be dominant for the processing of faces and facial expression, . . . the left hemisphere assigns verbal tags to expressions" (*Fundamentals of Human Neuropsychology* [New York, 1990], 624–625).

13 Within the field of history, two basic approaches to Western emotions have predominated. One, pioneered by Phillipe Ariès and then famously pursued by Lawrence Stone, proposed a model of fundamental difference between early modern and modern people and argued that strong affective ties within the family developed only with the emergence of individualism. The other school, promoted by people like Steven Ozment in European history and Daniel Blake Smith in colonial American history, argued the opposite, that there was no sound reason to believe that early modern men and women felt less for one another than people do today. Essentially, the historical study of emotion had reached an impasse, with neither side giving ground to the other. The theoretical distinction between the subjective experience and the linguistic definition/expression of emotion that Reddy's thinking helps formulate thus offers an important intervention in long-standing debates about emotion and historical change. See Philippe Ariès, *Centuries of Childhood: A Social History of Family Life,* trans. Robert Baldick (New York, 1962); Lawrence Stone, *The Family, Sex, and Marriage in England, 1500–1800* (New York, 1977); Steven Ozment, *When Fathers Ruled: Family Life in Reformation Europe* (Cambridge, Mass., 1983); and Daniel Blake Smith, *Inside the Great House: Planter Family Life in Eighteenth-Century Chesapeake Society* (Ithaca, N.Y., 1980).

14 William M. Reddy argues that emotional expression plays a central role in the creation of subjectivity and is therefore concerned to analyze the ability of dominant members of society to curtail the expression and thus constrain the identities of subordinate members of society; see "Emotional Liberty: Politics and History in the Anthropology of Emotions," *Cultural Anthropology,* XIV (1999), 256–288, esp. 260; and Reddy, *The Navigation of Feeling: A Framework for the History of Emotions* (Cambridge, 2001), 104–109. Suggesting a focus on the body as the site of emotional experience, the place where "the self shapes and reshapes itself," Michael Meranze observes that "experience proceeds through a continual spiral of internalization and externalization"; see "Materializing Conscience: Embodiment, Speech, and the Experience of Sympathetic Identification," *Early American Literature,* XXXVI (2002), 71–88, esp. 73. See also Michael Roper, "Slipping out of View: Sub-

jectivity and Emotion in Gender History," *History Workshop Journal,* LIX (2005), 57–72.

By contrast, my own investigations of emotion in eighteenth-century Anglo-America have considered emotional expression less as an articulation of individual subjectivity than as an act of social communication. Because eighteenth-century conceptions of the self combined individual and communal elements, writers could not imagine acts of self-expression that were not also simultaneously social declarations. On this point, see "Introduction," in Gail Kern Paster, Katherine Rowe, and Mary-Floyd Wilson, eds., *Reading the Early Modern Passions: Essays in the Cultural History of Emotion* (Philadelphia, 2004), 12, 13; Ian Burkitt, "Social Relationships and Emotions," *Sociology,* XXXI (1997), 37–55, esp. 40; Ralph B. Hupka, Alison P. Lenton, and Keith A. Hutchinson, "Universal Development of Emotion Categories in Natural Language," *Journal of Personality and Social Psychology,* LXXVII (1999), 247–278, esp. 259–260; and Elizabeth Heckendorn Cook, *Epistolary Bodies: Gender and Genre in the Eighteenth-Century Republic of Letters* (Stanford, Calif., 1996).

On the eighteenth-century emergence of the distinctive modern notion of the individual self, see Dror Wahrman, *The Making of the Modern Self: Identity and Culture in Eighteenth-Century England* (New Haven, Conn., 2004); and see Charles Taylor, *Sources of the Self: The Making of Modern Identity* (Cambridge, 1989).

On changing early American views of the self, see Richard White, " 'Although I Am Dead, I Am Not Entirely Dead; I Have Left a Second of Myself': Constructing Self and Persons on the Middle Ground of Early America," in Ronald Hoffman, Mechal Sobel, and Fredrika J. Teute, eds., *Through a Glass Darkly: Reflections on Personal Identity in Early America* (Chapel Hill, N.C., 1997); Philip Cushman, *Constructing the Self, Constructing America: A Cultural History of Psychotherapy* (Boston, 1995); Louis P. Masur, " 'Age of the First Person Singular': The Vocabulary of the Self in New England, 1780–1850," *Journal of American Studies,* XXV (1991), 189–211; Joanne Cutting-Grey, "Franklin's Autobiography: Politics of the Public Self," *Prospects,* XIV (1989), 31–43; Michael Zuckerman, "The Fabrication of Identity in Early America," *WMQ,* 3d Ser., XXXIV (1977), 183–214.

On the history of speech and power in colonial America, see Jane Kamensky, *Governing the Tongue: The Politics of Speech in Early New England* (New York, 1997); and Robert St. George, " 'Heated' Speech and Literacy in Seventeenth-Century New England," in *Seventeenth-Century New England,* Colonial Society of Massachusetts, Publications, LXIII, Collections (Boston, 1984), 275–322.

15 T. H. Breen has recently revamped arguments in favor of analyzing material displays as marks of social status. See T. H. Breen, *The Marketplace of Revolution: How Consumer Politics Shaped American Independence* (Oxford, 2004). See also Cary Carson, Ronald Hoffman, and Peter J. Albert, eds., *Of Consuming Interests: The Style of Life in the Eighteenth Century* (Charlottesville, Va., 1994).

On the concept of microhierarchies, see sociologist Candace Clark, *Misery and Company: Sympathy in Everyday Life* (Chicago, 1997).

On the use of semantic techniques in the interpretation of emotion, see Cliff Goddard, "Anger in the Western Desert: A Case-Study in the Cross-Cultural Semantics of Emotion," *Man*, XXVI (1991), 265–279, esp. 269.

Chapter One

1 This information is taken from the official minutes of the Library Company. See Directors of the Library Company of Pennsylvania to the Honourable Thomas Penn, Esquire, May 24, 1733, in "A Book of Minutes, containing An Account of the Proceedings of the Directors of the Library Company of Philadelphia. Beginning November 8th 1731 taken by the Secretary to the Company. Volume 1st. Collected, Copied, and Continued by Fra. Hopkinson, 1759," 27, MS, the collections of the Library Company of Philadelphia (hereafter cited as LCP Minutes). On the publication of Pope's essay, see Reginald Harvey Griffith, *Alexander Pope: A Bibliography*, I, *Pope's Own Writings, 1709– 1734* (London, 1968), 211.

2 Alexander Pope, "The Design," and Epistle III, l. 318, in *The Poems of Alexander Pope*, I, i, *An Essay on Man*, ed. Maynard Mack (New Haven, Conn., 1950). Unless otherwise noted, all further citations from the *Essay* will refer to the epistle and line numbers in the Mack edition.

3 The estimate of 26 advertisements in Pennsylvania is based on an informal, and by no means exhaustive, survey of advertisements printed in the *Pennsylvania Gazette* (hereafter cited as *PG*) (accessed on line) and the lists provided in Philadelphia booksellers' catalogs available in the Evans Early American Imprints Digital Edition. Miscellaneous other citations were added as they happened to surface, for a total of 33 advertisements offering 66 different editions of Pope, 26 of them either his collected works or *An Essay on Man*. No doubt my method has underestimated the total number of times that editions of Pope's works were advertised for sale in Pennsylvania; still, even this presumed undercount results in an impressive number.

The three editions of Pope published in Philadelphia seem to have been the only ones published anywhere in British America between 1700 and 1776. It appears that only the work of Isaac Watts exceeded Pope in popularity, with various sermons, treatises, and psalm collections having gone through a staggering twenty-six separate American editions in this period. (Not surprisingly, Watts's views on the passions were compatible with Pope's; see below.) By comparison, three editions of the work of John Locke were published in the colonies in this period and one of Addison's *Cato* (to which Pope himself contributed a preface). There were also at least two American reprints of Steele, one of Hume, and one of Swift. For other popular authors whose work was frequently advertised by importers alongside Pope's, including Dryden, Fielding, Hutcheson, Milton, Richardson, Shaftsbury, Smith, and Spencer, there were no American editions. Again, my numbers should be regarded as no more than suggestive. Keyword searches in the online version of Evans miss some editions.

For these web resources, see *Evans Digital Edition: Early American Imprints, Series I, Evans (1689–1800);* and see *Pennsylvania Gazette.*

Philadelphia editions of Pope: Alexander Pope, *An Essay on Man: In Four Epistles: Enlarged and Improved by the Author, to Which Is Added the Universal Prayer* (Philadelphia: Bradford, 1747); Alexander Pope, *An Essay on Man: Enlarged and Improved by the Author, with Notes by William Warberton [sic], M.A.* (Philadelphia: W. Dunlap, 1760); Alexander Pope, *An Essay on Man: Enlarged and Improved by the Author, with Notes by William Warberton, M.A.* (Philadelphia: Re-printed by W. Dunlap for G. Noel, Bookseller, in New York, 1760), all at LCP.

Pope's colonial popularity, once common knowledge, has faded from view in recent years; the present chapter on the reception of *An Essay on Man* in Pennsylvania is one of the first sustained scholarly assessments of Pope's impact in British America in nearly a century. No doubt this is due in no small part to the traditional geographic divisions of historical and literary scholarship, which made British authors like Pope the subject of English literature and history, rather than American. An important new initiative to introduce transatlantic perspectives comes from Julie Ellison, who focuses on the influence of Joseph Addison's *Cato* in creating and sustaining an Anglo-American culture of emotion over the long eighteenth century (*Cato's Tears and the Making of Anglo-American Emotion* [Chicago, 1999]).

Despite the current disregard for Pope among scholars of colonial British America, one old but still highly useful work by Elizabeth Cook confirms Pope's influence throughout the colonies, finding him quoted widely in colonial newspapers. See Elizabeth Christine Cook, *Literary Influences in Colonial*

Newspapers, 1704–1750 (New York, 1912), 246; and see also Michael Warner, *The Letters of the Republic: Publication and the Public Sphere in Eighteenth-Century America* (Cambridge, 1990), 133.

4 In this blanket description of Stoicism as requiring complete suppression of the passions, I follow common eighteenth-century usage. On this point, see Douglas H. White, *Pope and the Context of Controversy: The Manipulation of Ideas in "An Essay on Man"* (Chicago, 1970), 127.

5 May 24, 1733, LCP Minutes.

6 "Passion," 6c, *Oxford English Dictionary Online*, 2d ed. (2001) (cited hereafter as *OED*). Note that the *OED Online* has been undergoing continual revision. Most of the definitions one reads here appear in the print second edition of 1989 (which can still be accessed online). A fuller discussion of the eighteenth-century meanings of *passion* in comparison to other terms for emotion, including many examples from colonial Pennsylvania, is to be found in the Appendix.

7 Literary critic Harry M. Solomon similarly calls for a reassessment of the importance of Pope; see *The Rape of the Text: Reading and Misreading Pope's "Essay on Man"* (Tuscaloosa, Ala., 1993), 1, 5.

8 Benjamin Franklin to William Strahan, Philadelphia, Feb. 12, 1745, in Leonard W. Labaree et al., eds., *The Papers of Benjamin Franklin*, III (New Haven, Conn., 1961), 13. Many thanks to James Greene of the present-day Library Company of Philadelphia for providing me with this citation, for recommending many other valuable sources, and for giving guidance to the eighteenth-century Philadelphia book trade.

9 J[ames] L[ogan], "On Reading Pope's Essay on Man, by J. L. 1735," James Logan Papers, G. M. Howland Collection, Haverford College Quaker Collection, Haverford, Pennsylvania (hereafter cited as HCQC). Logan does not appear to have joined the Library Company formally, but members were eager to secure his approval, and he does seem to have made use of their holdings. The Company secretary noted in the official minutes for 1733, for example, that he had taken "to Mr. Logan a Catalogue of all the Books in the Library and of those sent for—He having lately mentioned to me his regard for the Library" (LCP Minutes, 33).

10 For an excellent discussion of the unmatched singularity of Pope's philosophical position on self-love (in comparison to Shaftesbury, among others) see White, *Pope and the Context of Controversy*, 128–132.

11 The appeal of such a position among colonial Americans and Pope's central role in advocating it has long been underestimated by historians. Gordon S. Wood, for example, attributed such views only to Mandeville. More recently,

Colin Wells has positioned Pope's *Essay on Man* in opposition to both Hobbes and Mandeville. Pope himself left ample room for such an interpretation of his work (as will become evident below). However, as eighteenth-century Pennsylvanians read him, Pope's positive comments on self-love had far more in common with Mandeville than prior scholars have suggested. See Wood, *The Creation of the American Republic, 1776–1787* (Chapel Hill, N.C., 1969), 69; Colin Wells, *The Devil and Doctor Dwight: Satire and Theology in the Early American Republic* (Chapel Hill, N.C., 2002), 43.

12 L[ogan], "On Reading Pope's Essay on Man."

13 Benjamin Franklin [Richard Saunders, pseud.], Poor Richard, 1736, *An Almanack for the Year of Christ 1736 . . .* (Philadelphia, [1735]), 4, quoting *Essay on Man,* Epistle I, 35–42. Wells rightly places Pope squarely within the Augustinian tradition, which stresses humankind's inherently limited knowledge of the divine, but he acknowledges that eighteenth-century philosophers did not necessarily draw explicit links between man's truncated understanding of the divine will and the commission of sin. See Wells, *The Devil and Doctor Dwight,* 42, 87–88.

14 Logan approved of the Library Company to the extent that he left it his extensive personal collection of books (reputed to be the largest personal library in the colony) upon his death. Franklin, meanwhile, remained a close Quaker ally throughout the colonial period, championing Quaker causes through his press as well as through his numerous public activities, including service in the Pennsylvania Assembly.

15 "Mr. Franklin . . . ," *PG,* Aug. 7, 1736. On Franklin's desire to print in his paper "private letters" from "gentlemen" as a means of demonstrating gentility and claiming a place in a transatlantic information network, see David D. Hall, "The Politics of Writing and Reading in Eighteenth-Century America," in Hall, *Cultures of Print: Essays in the History of the Book* (Amherst, Mass., 1996), 155. Likewise, on colonists' engagement with British literature as a kind of "imitative commerce with the imperial capital," see Warner, *Letters of the Republic,* 133.

16 "Tobacco, in Imitation of Mr. Pope," *PG,* Aug. 7, 1736. Elizabeth Cook identifies the true author of this poem as Isaac Brown, who first published the poem in the *London Magazine* of November-December 1735, and suggests that the letter that appeared in the *Gazette* might well have been a fabrication of Franklin's. (If Franklin did write the so-called letter to the editor, the letter's jokes about the ambiguities of authorship take on yet another twist in meaning!) See Cook, *Colonial Newspapers,* 104, 107, 134.

17 For records of booksellers' stocking copies of *An Essay on Man,* see the

advertisement "Books Just Imported in the Mary, Captain Stevenson, from London, and to be Sold by James Read . . . ," *PG*, Nov. 24, 1743, which includes "Pope's Essay on Man." See also the listing of "Pope's Ethic Epistles" in the advertisement "Books, Sold By B. Franklin," *PG*, May 19, 1743.

The first edition of Pope to be published in the colonies was *An Essay on Man* (Philadelphia, 1747).

18 For the copy described here, see Pope, *An Essay on Man* (Philadelphia, 1747) in the collections of the Historical Society of Pennsylvania (hereafter cited as HSP) held on deposit at LCP.

19 John Smith, *The Doctrine of Christianity, as Held by the People Called Quakers, Vindicated: In Answer to Gilbert Tennent's Sermon on the Lawfulness of War* (Philadelphia, 1748), 34.

20 Bradford also included a brief introduction composed by Pope titled "The Design" (in which he announced his "not *imperfect* system of Ethics"). See Pope, *An Essay on Man* (Philadelphia, 1747), iii–vi, 49–51.

21 For comparison, see, for example, Alexander Pope, *An Essay on Man, Enlarged and Improved by the Author, with Notes by Mr. Warburton* (London: J. and P. Knapton on Ludgate Street, 1748), in the collections of the New York Public Library.

22 [William Warburton], "An Advertisement," in Pope, *An Essay on Man* (Philadelphia, 1747), iii, iv.

23 So important was this question in Christian theology that Jonathan Edwards was soon to write a treatise with this very title, his 1754 essay "Freedom of the Will" (*A Careful and Strict Enquiry into the Modern Prevailing Notions of . . . Freedom of the Will* . . . [Boston, 1754]). The piece was drafted just four years before Edwards assumed the presidency of the College of New Jersey (now Princeton), where many Pennsylvania Presbyterians, including William Bradford's son Thomas, attended. For an excellent synopsis of this Edwards essay, see George M. Marsden, *Jonathan Edwards: A Life* (New Haven, Conn., 2003), 436–446. For another account of Pope's position on freedom of the will in relation to the "Universal Prayer," see A. D. Nuttall, *Pope's "Essay on Man"* (London, 1984), 186.

24 The affirmation of free will of the "Universal Prayer" spoke to broad colonial concerns. On the colonial preoccupation with free will and free grace (and the role of literature in helping to address such questions), see Lawrence C. Wroth, *An American Bookshelf, 1755* (New York, 1969), 109–111.

25 The surviving copy of the 1747 Bradford edition of the *Essay on Man* has damage to pages 49–51 containing "The Universal Prayer." This citation and punctuation are therefore from a 1780 edition printed in Massachusetts.

(Mack does not include the prayer in his edition.) Enough survives of the torn Bradford pages to indicate that the lines quoted here from the 1780 edition were all present in the 1747 Philadelphia edition. See Alexander Pope, *An Essay on Man in Four Epistles: Together with the Notes by Alexander Pope, Esq.* (Newbury, Mass., 1780), 49.

It should be noted that modern scholars believe that Pope might have written "The Universal Prayer" as early as 1703, decades before composing the *Essay on Man*. It is entirely possible that his thought had shifted over that period and that he resurrected "The Universal Prayer" only in a defensive attempt to defuse the criticism that his *Essay* had provoked. On the timing of the writing of "The Universal Prayer," see Howard Erskine-Hill, "Alexander Pope: The Political Poet in His Time," *Eighteenth-Century Studies*, XV (1981–1982), 123–148, 136. For an account of contemporary criticism of Pope's poem, see Michael Srigley, *The Mighty Maze: A Study of Pope's "An Essay on Man"* (Stockholm, 1994), 11–20.

James McLaverty presents convincing evidence that Pope deliberately obfuscated whether his poem should be read within a Christian framework. See McLaverty, *Pope, Print, and Meaning* (Oxford, 2001), 107, 112; James Noggle, *The Skeptical Sublime: Aesthetic Ideology in Pope and the Tory Satirists* (New York, 2001), 109. On Franklin and religion, see Douglas Anderson, *The Radical Enlightenments of Benjamin Franklin* (Baltimore, 1997), esp. chap. 2.

26 Pope, *An Essay on Man* (Newbury, Mass., 1780), 50.

27 Society of Friends, *An Epistle from Our Yearly-Meeting, Held at Burlington . . . Seventh Month . . . 1746* [Philadelphia, 1746], 1; "Wilfulness," 1, *OED*. Evans's *Early American Imprints* originally identified Franklin as the publisher of the Friends' *Epistle*. However, the American Antiquarian Society and NewsBank, Inc., the creators of *Evans Digital Edition (1639–1800)* have concluded that publication should be attributed to William Bradford, Jr.

28 Friends, *Epistle, 1746*, 3; Isaac Norris to S[usannah] Wright, July 22, 1746, Norris Papers, HSP. Norris's reference to "Pope's Letters" all but certainly referred to the *Essay on Man*, which was commonly abbreviated as Pope's *Epistles* (the terminology used by the Library Company in ordering its copy of the *Essay*).

29 Friends, *Epistle, 1746*, 2.

30 Smith, *The Doctrine of Christianity*, 1, 2.

31 Gilbert Tennent, *The Late Association for Defense, Encourag'd; or, The Lawfulness of Defensive War, Represented in a Sermon Preach'd at Philadelphia December 24, 1747* (Philadelphia, 1748), 30; Gilbert Tennent, *The Late Association for Defence Farther Encouraged: or, Defensive War Defended . . . in a Reply to . . .*

The Doctrine of Christianity, as Held by the People Called Quakers, Vindicated (Philadelphia, 1748).

32 [Benjamin Franklin], *Plain Truth; or, Serious Considerations on the Present State of the City of Philadelphia, and Province of Pennsylvania*, 2d ed. ([Philadelphia], 1747), [iv]. The translation was also featured in *PG*, Nov. 19, 1747. Franklin himself, despite his oft-demonstrated appreciation of Pope, did not here offer an unequivocal endorsement of the passions. Though he did bemoan those who were "insensible" of "publick Danger," he also warned that those who held no pacifist scruples, yet did not support armament just because Quakers would not share the costs, demonstrated that "our Passions, when violent, often are too hard for the united force of *Reason, Duty* and *Religion*" (A2, 18). William Bradford joined the militia in time to fight in the American Revolution.

33 See Joseph Shippen, "Joseph Shippen Commonplace Book 1750," Shippen Family Papers, HSP. On Pope's distinctive theories of the connections between emotion and motivation, that is, between passion and action, see White, *Pope and the Context of Controversy*, 133.

34 Shippen, Dec. 15, 1750, "Commonplace Book 1750," 1. The lines Shippen quoted correspond to Epistle II, 97–110, in standard editions.

35 *PG*, Apr. 25, 1754.

36 See John Woolman, *Some Considerations on the Keeping of Negroes, Recommended to the Professors of Christianity of Every Denomination* (Philadelphia, 1754); Society of Friends, *An Epistle of Caution and Advice, concerning the Buying and Keeping of Slaves* (Philadelphia, 1754); [Anthony Benezet], *Observations on the Inslaving, Importing, and Purchasing of Negroes, with Some Advice thereon Extracted f[ro]m the Yearly Meeting Epistle of London . . .* (Germantown, Pa., 1759); John Woolman, *Considerations on Keeping Negroes; Recommended to the Professors of Christianity, of Every Denomination, Part Second* (Philadelphia, 1762). On the rise of slavery in colonial Pennsylvania, see Gary B. Nash, *Forging Freedom: The Formation of Philadelphia's Black Community, 1720–1840* (Cambridge, Mass., 1988).

37 [Benezet], *Observations on the Inslaving, Importing, and Purchasing of Negroes*, 3, 12, 13. Rates of slave ownership first rose in 1729–1732 when import duties on Pennsylvania slaves were first reduced, then eliminated. A new upswing began with the onset of the Seven Years War. The Pennsylvania slave trade then fell off again in the later 1760s, following the end of the war. On chronological trends in slave ownership, see Gary B. Nash, "Slaves and Slaveowners in Colonial Philadelphia," *William and Mary Quarterly*, 3d Ser., XXX (1973), 223–256, esp. 229–232.

38 Woolman, *Some Considerations,* 8.

39 Ibid., A2, A3, emphasis in original.

40 Ibid., A3, A4, emphasis in original.

41 Woolman, *Considerations on Keeping Negroes,* 23, 31. On Philadelphia patterns of slaveholding, see Nash, "Slaves and Slaveowners in Colonial Philadephia," *WMQ,* 3d Ser., XXX (1973), 223–256, esp. 248.

42 Staking a strong position on such debates, John Morillo writes, "Malleable notions of emotions hovering between self and other helped to produce . . . class politics." Of Pope specifically, he says that the "*Essay on Man* reveals as many of the costs as the benefits of benevolence." Morillo confines his commentary to the question of social class, whereas (as can clearly be seen here), in eighteenth-century Pennsylvania, Pope's ideas applied to far broader questions of rank, including issues of race and gender as well as what we would now call class. See Morillo, *Uneasy Feelings: Literature, the Passions, and Class from Neoclassicism to Romanticism* (New York, 2001), 10, 102, 110.

43 Adam Smith, *The Theory of Moral Sentiments* (Indianapolis, Ind., 1976), 71, 283.

44 Anthony, earl of Shaftesbury, *Characteristics of Men, Manners, Opinions, Times,* II, *An Inquiry concerning Virtue and Merit* (1714; rpt., Hampshire, Eng., 1968), 22, 23, emphasis in original.

   Rebecca Fergusson emphasizes that a key to Pope's " 'departure from the benevolists' " was his refusal to acknowledge "a dichotomy in the nature of good and ill passions." See *The Unbalanced Mind: Pope and the Rule of Passion* (Philadelphia, 1986), 75, 86.

   While White and Fergusson explicitly contrast Pope's thinking with Shaftesbury's, Morillo lumps them together. In fact, however, given Pope's exceptional popularity, it is significant (and, incidentally still consonant with Morillo's argument) that Pope's philosophy could be interpreted in ways that were far more socially conservative than could Shaftesbury's. See Morillo, *Uneasy Feelings,* 108, 102; White, *Pope and the Context of Controversy,* 128–132.

45 Friends, *An Epistle of Caution and Advice,* 3, 4.

46 [Franklin], *Plain Truth,* 13–14.

47 General Assembly to Robert Hunter Morris, Feb. 11, 1756, in *Minutes of the Provincial Council of Pennsylvania, from the Organization to the Termination of the Proprietary Government,* VIII (Harrisburg, Pa., 1851), 38.

48 Of course, some mentions of the emotions of the enslaved have survived; such evidence is analyzed and amplified as much as possible throughout this study. However, the simple fact that eighteenth-century Pennsylvania slaveholders avoided contemplating the emotions of those held in bondage de-

serves to be explored and explained. For a related discussion of the role of emotional appeals in building antislavery agendas, see John Wood Sweet, " 'More than Tears': The Ordeal of Abolition in Revolutionary New England," *Explorations in Early American Culture,* V (2001), 118–172.

To be sure, sympathy for the enslaved, though perhaps necessary for abolitionism, was not in itself sufficient. See, for example, Joyce E. Chaplin, *An Anxious Pursuit: Agricultural Innovation and Modernity in the Lower South, 1730–1815* (Chapel Hill, N.C., 1993), 56.

49 [Benezet], *Observations on the Inslaving, Importing, and Purchasing of Negroes,* 2. In fact, though he owned slaves through the 1760s, Franklin eventually became president of the Pennsylvania Abolition Society. For an account of the evolution of Franklin's attitudes (which emphasizes that Franklin continued to hold racist views, despite his eventual adoption of an antislavery position), see David Waldstreicher, *Runaway America: Benjamin Franklin, Slavery, and the American Revolution* (New York, 2004), xii, xiii. And see Willam E. Juhnke, "Benjamin Franklin's View of the Negro and Slavery," *Pennsylvania History,* XLI (1974), 374–388.

50 For population figures, see Nash, *Forging Freedom,* 33. Importantly, this silence on the matter of African-American emotion was part of a broader reluctance to so much as admit the actual presence of enslaved Africans in Philadelphia. See Nash, "Slaves and Slaveowners in Colonial Philadelphia," *WMQ,* 3d Ser., XXX (1973), 224.

51 On William Dunlap and John Dunlap (the nephew who succeeded him in the printing business in 1766), see Isaiah Thomas, *The History of Printing in America . . .* (1810; New York, 1970), 386–387, 393.

52 Thomas Barton, *Unanimity and Public Spirit: A Sermon Preached at Carlisle . . .* (Philadelphia, Lancaster, 1755).

53 [William Dunlap], *Books and Stationary, Just Imported from London, and to Be Sold by W. Dunlap, at the Newest-Printing-Office on the South-Side of the Jersey-Market, Philadelphia* (Philadelphia, [1760]), 1; Dunlap, *Pettey's Island Lottery for Effects to the Full Value of 10,000 Dollars, or £3750, without Any Deduction* [Philadelphia, 1761], 1.

54 See Pope, *An Essay on Man* (Philadelphia: Dunlap, 1760); Pope, *An Essay on Man* (Philadelphia: Dunlap, for G. Noel, Book-Seller, in New York, 1760), both at LCP. The two editions are identical, except for the addition of the phrase "for G. Noel, Bookseller, in New York" in the New York edition.

55 [Dunlap], *Lottery,* 1. The creator of the engraving in the Dunlap edition of the *Essay* remains unknown; Dunlap likely commissioned someone else to pro-

duce it. The inference that it was home-produced rather than imported is based on the stylistic oddities discussed below.

For more on the history of the importation and local production of engravings in the colonies, see Sinclair Hamilton, *Early American Book Illustrators and Wood Engravers, 1670–1870* (Princeton, N.J., 1968), I, xxvi–xxvii.

56 My account of the engraving's publication history is based on Warburton's explanation of the image (see below) as well as examination of a 1751 edition of the *Essay* that contained the note "Published by J. and P. Knapton Feb. 6th 1744" beneath the engraving. See Pope, *An Essay on Man* (London: J. and P. Knapton, 1751). On Pope's state of mind just prior to his death, see Mack, ed., *An Essay on Man,* 131 n. 34.

57 Just whether or not Pope's poem *should* be read in a Christian context, and if so what this says about its social implications, has been the subject of sustained modern debate. See Nuttall, *Pope's "Essay on Man,"* 150–151; Morillo, *Uneasy Feelings,* 116; Solomon, *The Rape of the Text,* 90–91, 95; and also see Srigley, *The Mighty Maze,* 8, 133.

58 Many of Pope's contemporaries, as already noted, found fault with the *Essay's* myriad philosophical inconsistencies. For Voltaire's objections, see Richard Gilbert Knapp, *The Fortunes of Pope's "Essay on Man" in Eighteenth Century France,* Studies on Voltaire and the Eighteenth Century, LXXXII (Geneva, 1971), 79.

59 On creating engravings, see Arthur M. Hind, *A History of Engraving and Etching, from the Fifteenth Century to the Year 1914* (New York, 1963), 1–17.

60 On the revolutionary political significance of how "Americans' view of antiquity was highly selective, focusing on decline and decadence," see Wood, *The Creation of the American Republic,* 51.

61 Elaine Forman Crane, ed., *The Diary of Elizabeth Drinker* (Boston, 1991), Oct. 23, 1803, III, 1698; Eliza Stedman to Elizabeth Graeme, Aug. 7, 1762, Elizabeth Graeme Fergusson Correspondence, 1757–95, HSP.

Betsy Moode married Samuel Emlen in 1761. For an example of an edition of Pope's collected works featuring the *Essay on Man* in vol. III, see Alexander Pope, *The Works of Alexander Pope, Esq. in 9 Volumes* (London: J. and P. Knapton, 1753), in the collections of the Library Company of Philadelphia and on deposit at Cliveden of the National Trust, Germantown, Pa.

62 [Dunlap], *Lottery,* 1. Interestingly, Pope has often been noted for a strong misogynistic strain running through his work. His decision to place wives in the same category with dogs and drink in the couplets just quoted certainly hints as much. Yet, overall, the *Essay on Man* contains remarkably

little commentary of any kind specifically on women. Meanwhile, it uses the words "man" and "mankind" interchangeably throughout. This left eighteenth-century female readers free to assume that his musings concerned human nature as a whole without respect to sex.

63 One of the primary reasons for Pope's power is that his poem could, with equal legitimacy, be interpreted in ways that were simultaneously socially progressive *and* conservative. On this point, see Solomon, *The Rape of the Text*, 61; Helen Deutsch, *Resemblance and Disgrace: Alexander Pope and the Deformation of Culture* (Cambridge, Mass., 1996), 4.

64 Perhaps because, as Harry Solomon notes, *An Essay on Man* has so often been "dismissed as bad philosophy or bad poetry or both," the singularity and radicalism of Pope's position on the passions, his unique place in the development of moral philosophy, has seldom been noted. One important exception comes in the evaluation of literary scholar A. D. Nuttall, who explains that Pope's "tense review of the relations between reason and passion, especially" is "distinctive." See Solomon, *The Rape of the Text*, 3; Nuttall, *Pope's "Essay on Man*," 191–193.

65 For other examples of English prints that, compared to their derivative American versions, were "better drawn, ha[d] fewer figures, fewer symbols, and ma[de] [their] point more clearly and with less ado," see William Murrell, *A History of American Graphic Humor*, I, *1747–1865* (New York, 1933), esp. 22. Rebecca Fergusson discusses Pope's use of the sun's rays as a symbol of reason in *The Unbalanced Mind*, 80.

66 The information on Francis Bacon is taken from Mack, ed., *An Essay on Man*, 72 n. 148.

67 Benjamin Swett to Rachel Wilson, 3 Eleventh Month 1771, Benjamin Swett Letterbook 1765–1806, HCQC.

68 William Percy, "Commonplace Book," 3, Journal and Commonplace Book of William Percy (1774–1776), HSP. Please note that this book was written in from front to back (journal half) and back to front (commonplace book half).

69 LCP Minutes, 1. The Hopkinson volumes are now on deposit at the Library Company. See Alexander Pope, *The Works of Alexander Pope, Esq.* (London: J. and P. Knapton, 1754). Intriguingly, the Hopkinson volume that contained *The Essay on Man* is missing from the holdings, while the Company has many miscellaneous copies of collected editions containing *only* the *Essay*. Together, these facts suggest that, when Pennsylvanians bought Pope's collected works, it was *The Essay on Man* that traded hands most often, sometimes winding up isolated from the rest of the volumes in surviving collections. I thank current librarian Jim Green for this useful insight.

Chapter Two

1 This brief account of Hopkinson's early life is based on material in the Hopkinson Family Papers, Letters, 1736–1800, the Historical Society of Pennsylvania (HSP), Philadelphia (hereafter cited as Hopkinson Papers). This research is supplemented by Charles R. Hildeburn, "Francis Hopkinson," *Pennsylvania Magazine of History and Biography,* II (1878), 314–324. Modest silent clarifications of spelling and punctuation have been made in some quotations.

2 On the founding of the college, see William Smith, "Account of the College, Academy, and Charitable School of Philadelphia in Pennsylvania," *Pennsylvania Gazette,* Aug. 12, 1756 (hereafter cited as *PG*); [Benjamin Franklin], *Proposals Relating to the Education of Youth in Pennsylvania* (Philadelphia, 1749); Benjamin Franklin, *Proposals Relating to the Education of Youth in Pensilvania* (Philadelphia, 1931). The standard institutional account of the founding is Edward Potts Cheyney, *History of the University of Pennsylvania, 1740–1940* (Philadelphia, 1940). On connections between colonial status anxieties and the founding of the college, see Jack P. Greene, "Search for Identity: An Interpretation of the Meaning of Selected Patterns of Social Response in Eighteenth-Century America," in Greene, *Imperatives, Behaviors, and Identities: Essays in Early American Cultural History* (Charlottesville, Va., 1992), 167; Stephen C. Bullock, *Revolutionary Brotherhood: Freemasonry and the Transformation of American Social Order, 1730–1840* (Chapel Hill, N.C., 1996), 68, 334n; George W. Boudreau, "The Surest Foundation of Happiness: Education and Society in Franklin's Philadelphia" (Ph.D. diss., Indiana University, 1998).

3 William Smith, "A Charge Delivered May 17, 1757, at the First Anniversary Commencement in the College and Academy of Philadelphia, by the Reverend Mr. Smith, Provost of the Same . . . ," *PG*, Aug. 11, 1757 (hereafter cited as Smith, "Charge").

4 Smith, "Charge." Benjamin Franklin, in laying the groundwork for the creation of the college in 1749, had recommended explicitly that Alexander Pope be incorporated into the curriculum, including the author along with Joseph Addison and Richard Steele in a brief list of "some of our best Writers" whose works ought to be held up as examples for imitation by young "gentlemen." See [Franklin], *Proposals* (1749), 13, 14.

5 Smith, "Charge."

6 Like the opening scene, this sketch of Hopkinson's biography is based on material in the Hopkinson Papers, supplemented by the information provided in Hildeburn, "Francis Hopkinson," *PMHB*, II (1878), 314–324.

7 Francis Hopkinson to Mary Hopkinson, June 26, 1766, July 4, 1767, Hopkinson Papers.

8 "Disposition," 6, and "Personality," 2a, *Oxford English Dictionary Online*, 2d ed. (2001) (cited hereafter as *OED*).

Because *disposition* is by far the older word, any current thesaurus will list *disposition* as a synonym for *personality*; but no thesaurus does the reverse. See, for example, *Roget's Superthesaurus* (Cincinnati, Ohio, 1995), 384; *Webster's College Thesaurus* (New York, 1997), 510; or *Chamber's English Thesaurus* (Edinburgh, 1991), 465.

9 "Personality," 2a, and "Disposition," 1a, *OED*. In thinking about the way the self was viewed in British America in the mid-eighteenth century, I have found the modern poststructuralist concept of the "subject-position" to be very helpful. This concept combines in a single term the creation of self and the distribution of power, making it clear that each is inextricably linked to the other, thus explaining why the expression of emotion was not merely a private description of internal feelings but a public comment on—and creation of—external social relations. For an explication of the term "subject-position," see Linda Alcoff, "The Problem of Speaking for Others," *Cultural Critique*, no. 20 (1991–1992), 5–32.

Dror Wahrman has also noted the consonance between premodern and postmodern approaches to the self, but without highlighting an important difference: this time we seek to expose rather than impose interconnections between identity formation and power relations. See *The Making of the Modern Self: Identity and Culture in Eighteenth-Century England* (New Haven, Conn., 2004), xviii.

10 Smith, "Charge."

11 "On Happiness," in Mary Flower's Commonplace Book, 1757, Haverford College Quaker Collection (HCQC), Haverford, Pa. (hereafter cited as Flower Commonplace Book).

12 "Dear Clemy since the single state, you've left and chose yourself a mate . . . ," anonymous poem, Dec. 8, 1768, Plumstead Papers, HSP.

13 Joseph Shippen, Jr., to Edward Shippen, Dec. 18, 1752, Shippen Family Papers, 1701–1856, HSP (hereafter cited as Shippen Papers); Governor William Denny to Major Burd, July 6, 1757, Shippen Papers.

14 John Van Elten, "A Journal of Capt. John Van Elten Station'd at Fort Hyndshaw in the Penselvany forces," John Van Elten Journal, 1757, HSP.

15 Aristotle, *Politics*, as quoted in Russell Bentley, "Loving Freedom: Aristotle on Slavery and the Good Life," *Political Studies*, XLVII (1999), 100–113, esp. 109. Bentley asserts persuasively that "thymotic deficiency" is central to Aristotle's

conception of natural slavery, while "the absence of a deliberative faculty may be secondary" (109).

16 White unwillingness to acknowledge black emotion can actually be quantified using the records of the *Pennsylvania Gazette*. Key-word searching in the digitized version of the *Gazette* can identify every article that mentioned the word *Negro* between 1728, the year Franklin began publishing, and 1776. From a total of approximately 60,000 items, I found 3,469 pieces making reference to "Negro." I then read each of these. Amazingly, a mere 130 (3.75 percent) made any mention, positive or negative, of African-American emotion. Meanwhile, references to Anglo-American emotion in the same period are literally countless. For this web resource, see the *Pennsylvania Gazette* online.

See "Wretch," 2, 3, 2d, *OED*; "Extract of a Private Letter from a Gentleman at Cape-Fear . . . ," Sept. 17, 1741; and "Sottish," 1, *OED*. Now obsolete, the final *OED* citation for this definition of *sottish* is from 1737.

17 *PG*, July 19, 1759.

18 Of the 130 mentions of black emotion in the *Gazette* between 1728 and 1776 (of 3,469 articles containing the word *Negro*), only 2 mention "cheerfulness" (*PG*, Aug. 21, 1735, Mar. 7, 1765).

On ads for runaway slaves, see also David Waldstreicher, "Reading the Runaways: Self-Fashioning, Print Culture, and Confidence in Slavery in the Eighteenth-Century Mid-Atlantic," *William and Mary Quarterly*, 3d Ser., LVI (1999), 243–272. For an argument that the phrase "down-look" reflected the "polite conviction that plebeian types should neither stand erect nor stare back," see Jonathan Prude, "To Look upon the 'Lower Sort': Runaway Ads and the Appearance of Unfree Laborers in America, 1750–1800," *Journal of American History*, LXXVIII (1991–1992), 124–159, esp. 140–141. I thank Professor Woody Holton for encouraging me to explore the emotional component of "down-looks."

19 *PG*, Nov. 7, 1743, Nov. 26, 1761, Sept. 15, 1763.

20 *PG*, Mar. 17, 1737. See "Conspire," 1, 4, *OED*. Definition 4, "to concur or agree in spirit, sentiment . . . etc.," is now considered obsolete but was still current as late as 1737.

21 *PG*, Nov. 5, 1741.

22 *PG*, Feb. 15, 1738.

23 For an excellent theoretical discussion of such issues, see James C. Scott, *Domination and the Arts of Resistance: Hidden Transcripts* (New Haven, Conn., 1990).

24 Francis Hopkinson to Mary Hopkinson, May 25, 1766, and Francis to Mary, Dublin, July 12, 1766, Hopkinson Papers.

25 Francis Hopkinson to Mary Hopkinson, Hartlebury, Aug. 10, 12, 1766, Hopkinson Papers.

26 Ibid. Of course, the regulation of emotional expression was but one of the many aspects of genteel self-presentation Francis and others like him had to master.

27 A few modern authors are exploring the role of emotion in refinement, or the importance of emotion for the construction of genteel culture. I am more concerned here with studying the related issue of the part emotion played in the practice of power, that is, the way that emotional expression could send signals of domination and subordination in social interactions. Displays of status and negotiations of power, though clearly closely linked, are not in fact the same. See Jacquelyn C. Miller, "An 'Uncommon Tranquility of Mind': Emotional Self-Control and the Construction of a Middle-Class Identity in Eighteenth-Century Philadelphia," *Journal of Social History*, XXX (1996–1997), 129–148, esp. 131. See also Miller, "The Body Politic: Passions, Pestilence, and Political Culture in the Age of the American Revolution" (Ph.D. diss., Rutgers University, 1995). And see Christina Dallett Hemphill, "Class, Gender, and the Regulation of Emotional Expression in Revolutionary-Era Conduct Literature," in Peter Stearns and Jan Lewis, eds., *An Emotional History of the United States* (New York, 1998).

28 Mary Peasely to William Brown, 16 Third Month 1752, William Brown Letterbook, Brown Family Papers, HSP (hereafter cited as Brown Papers).

29 John Swift to "Uncle," Sept. 24, 1750, John Swift Papers, 1740–1789, Swift Family Papers, HSP (hereafter cited as Swift Papers). The complete text of the surviving letter is as follows. The phrases in parentheses are the draft versions that Swift crossed out: ". . . I am very sorry that anything (should have) that has slipped from my pen should give you (the least reason) cause to be offended at me (so much as to cause you to write to me in such a severe manner as you have done) as you seem to be when you wrote this letter. I assure you that I had no intention to give offense, nor did I imagine that anything I said in that letter could have had that effect, but I shall [for the] future endeavor to be more upon my guard." Of particular note is Smith's decision to omit criticism of his uncle's "severe manner," which would have revealed yet more of Swift's emotions.

30 George Morgan to ——, Apr. 5, 1768, George Morgan Journal and Letterbook, 1767–68, HSP.

31 For more on Conrad Weiser and his relation to the Philadelphia elite, see Elizabeth Lewis Pardoe, "The Many Worlds of Conrad Weiser: Mystic Diplo-

mat," *Explorations in Early American Culture,* a supplemental issue of *Pennsylvania History* (2001).

32 Richard Peters to Conrad Weiser, Jan. 24, 1751, Correspondence, 1741–1766, Conrad Weiser Papers, HSP (hereafter cited as Weiser Papers).

33 *PG,* July 8, 1742, July 26, 1753.

34 *PG,* May 11, 1749.

35 For more on the "manners double-bind," see C. Dallett Hemphill, *Bowing to Necessities: A History of Manners in America, 1620–1860* (New York, 1999), esp. part 1.

36 *PG,* Feb. 7, 1738. There can be no doubt that the servant's aspirations to join the Freemasons signaled a desire to enhance his social standing. On the social meanings of Freemasonry, see Steven C. Bullock, "The Revolutionary Transformation of American Freemasonry, 1752–1792," *WMQ,* 3d Ser., XLVII (1990), 347–370, and Bullock, *Revolutionary Brotherhood,* 50–51, 66–67.

37 *PG,* Feb. 7, 1738.

38 For information on sumptuary laws and social status, see Karin Calvert, "The Function of Fashion in Eighteenth-Century America," in Cary Carson, Ronald Hoffman, and Peter J. Albert, eds., *Of Consuming Interests: The Style of Life in the Eighteenth Century* (Charlottesville, Va., 1994), 252–283.

39 Joseph Worrell to Thomas Lawrence, Mar. 9, 1754, Thomas Lawrence Papers, 1689–1754, Lawrence Collection, HSP; William Franklin to Elizabeth Graeme, Apr. 25, 1757, Elizabeth Graeme Fergusson Correspondence, 1757–95, Fergusson Family Papers, HSP (hereafter cited as EGF Correspondence); John Bartram to Peter, Sept. 25, 1757, John Bartram Letterbook, Bartram Papers, HSP (hereafter cited as Bartram Papers); unattributed letter, Philadelphia, May 1760, Brown Papers.

40 Elizabeth Chew to Benjamin Chew, Sept. 11, 1768, Correspondence and General Papers, 1743–1777, Chew Family Papers, HSP (hereafter cited as Chew Papers).

41 Francis Hopkinson to Mary Hopkinson, Sept. 23, 1766, Hopkinson Papers.

42 Ibid.

43 Anxieties about sincerity and authenticity were endemic to modern Western culture since at least the Reformation and always carried with them concerns about relative social status and stability—whether that status stemmed from meetinghouse or marketplace. For an argument that sincerity was invented by Martin Luther and other early reformers (but one that analyzes sincerity only insofar as it affects the development of the autonomous self and without regard to the impact of issues of sincerity on social relations), see John

Martin, "Inventing Sincerity, Refashioning Prudence: The Discovery of the Individual in Renaissance Europe," *American Historical Review,* CII (1997), 1309–1342, esp. 1326, 1327. For further work on the tight link between the exigencies of religion and anxieties about sincerity and authenticity, see Judith Shklar, "Let Us Not Be Hypocritical," *Daedalus: Journal of the American Academy of Arts and Sciences,* CVIII, no. 3 (Summer 1979), 1–26, esp. 3. For emphasis on issues of performance and the influence of Elizabethan theater, see Jean-Christophe Agnew, *Worlds Apart: The Market and the Theater in Anglo-American Thought, 1550–1750* (New York, 1986), xi. Turning to colonial British America, see Stephen C. Bullock, "A Mumper among the Gentle: Tom Bell, Colonial Confidence Man," *WMQ,* 3d Ser., LV (1998), 231–258, esp. 235; Toby L. Ditz, "Shipwrecked; or, Masculinity Imperiled: Mercantile Representations of Failure and the Gendered Self in Eighteenth-Century Philadelphia," *JAH,* LXXXI (1994–1995), 51–80. For Revolutionary America, see Gordon S. Wood, "Conspiracy and the Paranoid Style: Causality and Deceit in the Eighteenth Century," *WMQ,* 3d Ser., XXXIX (1982), 401–441; Jay Fliegelman, *Declaring Independence: Jefferson, Natural Language, and the Culture of Performance* (Stanford, Calif., 1993), 2–3. For issues of sincerity in the early national and antebellum United States, respectively, see Larzer Ziff, *Writing in the New Nation: Prose, Print, and Politics in the Early United States* (New Haven, Conn., 1991); Karen Halttunen, *Confidence Men and Painted Women: A Study of Middle-Class Culture in America, 1830–1870* (New Haven, Conn., 1982), 52–54.

44 Lionel Trilling, *Sincerity and Authenticity* (Cambridge, Mass., 1972), 115.

45 John Smith to James Pemberton, 28 First Month 1742, Pemberton Family Papers, 1740–1780, HSP; Mary Peasely to William Brown, 13 Second Month 1752, Brown Papers; John Swift to John White, May 24, 1751, Swift Papers.

46 John Smith to Dr. William Logan, June 2, 1750, Letterbooks of John Smith (1722–1771), HCQC (hereafter cited as Smith Letterbooks); "A Short Account of the Travels, Services, and Labours in Love in the Work of the Ministry of the Dear and Faithful Servant of Jesus Christ, William Hunt, deceased . . . ," anonymous essay appended to William Hunt, "The Journal of William Hunt's Travels in the Service of Truth 1748–72," William Hunt's Journal (1733–1772), HCQC.

47 James Read to Edward Shippen Esq., Sept. 4, 1757, Shippen Papers.

48 Deborah Hill to Richard Hill, July 26, 1737, Hill Family Papers, HCQC (hereafter cited as Hill Papers); Samuel Chew to Richard Peters, Oct. 2, 1743, Chew Papers; Charles Norris to William Griffitts, Apr. 23, 1746, Norris Papers; Joseph Swift to John Swift, Aug. 13, 1773, Swift Papers.

49 Adam Thomson to Benjamin Chew, Nov. 1, 1755, Chew Papers. Scholars who

have considered the role of sincerity in social control have viewed this problem in similar terms. On the alternate insistence on sincerity and toleration of hypocrisy all in the service of domination and coercion, see Shklar, "Let Us Not Be Hypocritical," *Daedalus*, CVIII, no. 3 (Summer 1979), 1, 4, 9. On the perils of insincerity for princes, see Martin, "Inventing Sincerity," *AHR*, CII (1997), 1340.

50 *PG*, Sept. 1, 1737, Sept. 4, 1746, July 28, 1748, Sept. 4, 1760.

51 *PG*, Aug. 1, 1745, Mar. 8, 1775.

52 Benjamin Mifflin, "Journal of a Journey from Philadelphia to the Cedar Swamps and Back, 1764," June 24, 1764, Benjamin Mifflin Journal, HSP.

53 Stephen Bullock has written ably on this aspect of elite preoccupations with issues of sincerity—concern that their own hypocrisy could be exposed, as opposed to worries about falling victim to the insincerity of others. See Bullock, "A Mumper among the Gentle," *WMQ*, 3d Ser., LV (1988), 234, 247.

54 John Swift to Arbam [Taylor], Sept. 29, 1750, Swift Papers; John Smith to Isaac Walker, Jr., 3 Fourth Month 1751, Smith Letterbooks.

55 Stephen Bayard to Thomas Bradford, Nov. 29, 1766, Bradford Collection Correspondence, 1747–1795, HSP (hereafter cited as Bradford Correspondence); P[eggy] E[mlen] to Sally Logan, n.d., Margaret Emlen Letters, 1768–71, Marjorie Brown Collection 1763–1871, HSP; Charles Norris to Mary Parker, Jan. 5, 1759, Maria Dickenson Logan Family Papers, HSP; Richard Peters to Elizabeth Graeme, July 9, 1765, EGF Correspondence.

56 Francis Hopkinson to Mary Hopkinson, Sept. 23, 1766, Hopkinson Papers.

57 Ibid. Toby Ditz concluded in her study of eighteenth-century Philadelphia merchants that merchants scrambling for influence and connection developed heightened concerns about reputation. See Ditz, "Shipwrecked," *JAH*, LXXXI (1994–1995), 57.

58 Francis Hopkinson to Mary Hopkinson, Apr. 20, 1767, Hopkinson Papers.

59 Conrad Weiser to Richard Peters, Mar. 8, 1755, Andrew Monture to Conrad Weiser, Apr. 15, 1755, Weiser Papers. This difficulty came in part because Anglo-Americans were so intent on delineating differences between the emotions felt by native Americans and those they felt themselves. Richard White has recently argued that Europeans regarded Indian emotion as aberrant because they lacked the kinds of feelings appropriate to ranked persons. See " 'Although I Am Dead, I Am Not Entirely Dead: I Have Left A Second of Myself': Constructing Self and Persons on the Middle Ground of Early America," in Ronald Hoffman, Mechal Sobel, and Fredrika J. Teute, eds., *Through a Glass Darkly: Reflections on Personal Identity in Early America* (Chapel Hill, N.C., 1997), 404–413, esp. 413.

60 James Kenny, "A Journal to the Westward," James Kenny Journal (1758–1761), HSP (hereafter cited as Kenny Journal). Quotations are from June 3–July 3, 1759, 35–41. Jane T. Merritt notes that, while fighting in Pennsylvania had largely come to an end by 1758, "the peace was an uneasy one" until a final treaty was signed in 1763. See *At the Crossroads: Indians and Empires on a Mid-Atlantic Frontier, 1700–1763* (Chapel Hill, N.C., 2003), 235.

61 John Bartram to Peter, Feb. 4, 1756, Bartram Papers; Conrad Weiser to Richard Peters, Sept. 27, 1746, Weiser Papers.

62 "Sincerity," 2, 2b, *OED*.

63 *Minutes of the Provincial Council of Pennsylvania, from the Organization to the Termination of the Proprietary Government* (Philadelphia, Harrisburg, 1851–1852), VIII, 212, 615 (hereafter cited as *MPCP*).

64 Conrad Weiser to Richard Peters, n.d. 1754, Mar. 15, 1754, Weiser Papers.

65 *MPCP*, VI, 315.

66 William Trent, William Trent Journal, 1759–1763, HSP, 6, 8, 12. Irregular dating in Trent's journal makes it possible to cite entries by page number but not by date.

67 Ibid., 34, 51; *MPCP*, IX, 217.

68 Thomas Lloyd to James Burd, Oct. 7, 19, 1757, Shippen Papers.

69 James Young to Major James Burd, Nov. 1, 1757, Shippen Papers.

70 Thomas Lloyd to Colonel Burd, Apr. 14, 1759, Shippen Papers.

71 Thomas Fisher to "Father" [Joshua Fisher], 21 First Month 1764, Letters of Thomas Fisher, Cadwalader Collection, HSP. The literature on the role of the figure of the "other" in constructions of identity is vast and complex. The work of Stephen Greenblatt has been particularly influential: see *Renaissance Self-Fashioning: From More to Shakespeare* (Chicago, 1980). Edward Gray analyzes Anglo-American attempts to define a genteel identity for themselves in opposition to the "savagery" of native American language, though he stops short of discussing *emotional* language specifically; see *New World Babel: Languages and Nations in Early America* (Princeton, N.J., 1999). And see also Matthew Lauzon, "Savage Eloquence in America and the Linguistic Construction of a British Identity in the Eighteenth Century," *Historiographia Linguistica*, XXIII (1996), 123–158.

72 Smith, "Charge."

73 Francis Hopkinson to Mary Hopkinson, Apr. 20, July 4, 1767, Hopkinson Papers.

74 Ibid., Apr. 20, 1767.

75 Ann Graeme to Elizabeth Graeme, Dec. 3, 1762, EGF Correspondence.

76 Tace Bradford to Thomas Bradford, Aug. 20, 1760, Bradford Correspon-

dence; Mary Hill to her brother [Richard Hill?], Apr. 25, 1741, Hill Papers; Mary Peasely to William Brown, 16 Third Month 1752, Brown Papers; Kenny Journal, 13 Tenth Month 1761. On the relation of emotions to bodily sickness, see Miller, "An 'Uncommon Tranquility of Mind,'" *Journal of Social History,* XXX (1996–1997), 131; Miller, "The Body Politic."

77 The complexities of Quaker conventions concerning speaking and silence have been very ably elucidated by Richard Bauman in two excellent ethnographic studies on the subject, but Bauman does not address the specific importance of *emotional* expression in Quaker theology. See Richard Bauman, "Speaking in the Light: The Role of the Quaker Minister," in Bauman and Joel Sherzer, eds., *Explorations in the Ethnography of Speaking* (New York, 1989); Bauman, *Let Your Words Be Few: Symbolism of Speaking and Silence among Seventeenth-Century Quakers* (New York, 1983).

78 William Logan to John Churchman, 19 Fifth Month 1750, Logan Papers; John Churchman to John Pemberton, 30 Third Month 1754, Brown Papers.

79 James Sproat Journal, 1753–1786, HSP, Aug. 12, 1753; Joseph Swift to John Swift, Feb. 12, 1757, Swift Papers; Smith, "Charge." The particular emphasis on emotional *expression,* as distinguished from a more generalized preoccupation with the motivating role of emotions in moral and social life, was initially an interest specific to Quakerism. This heightened focus on the expression of emotion seems to have been an outgrowth of the broader Quaker concern with speech and divine communication documented by Richard Bauman (see note 75, above).

80 Joseph Norris to Isaac Norris, May 18, 1731, Norris Papers.

81 "A Remarkable Dream," Flower Commonplace Book, 1757, 30 Tenth Month 1762. Flower's entry, "A Remarkable Dream," also appears in other Quaker manuscripts and publications, including the Mrs. E. W. Smith collection at Haverford, *The Irish Friend,* and *The Friend.* My thanks to Ann Kirschner for bringing these additional citations to my attention.

82 Flower, Commonplace Book, 30 Tenth Month 1762.

83 Ibid.

84 Ibid.

85 *PG,* Dec. 5, 1766, Nov. 25, 1772.

86 Smith, "Charge."

87 See Adam Smith, *The Theory of Moral Sentiments* (Indianapolis, Ind., 1976), 25. A number of writers who have considered the problem of the self have remarked the irony that self-control inevitably requires enhanced self-focus, a wholly unintended outcome. See Louis P. Masur, "'Age of the First Person Singular': The Vocabulary of Self in New England, 1780–1850," *Journal of*

American Studies, XXV (1991), 202; White, " 'Although I Am Dead,' " in Hoffman, Sobel, and Teute, eds., *Through a Glass Darkly,* 409.

88 Trilling, *Sincerity and Authenticity,* 2.

89 Trilling notes the second half of Shakespeare's advice, but does not incorporate it into his analysis. Ibid., 5–6.

90 Smith, "Charge."

Chapter Three

1 Henry Drinker to Mary Sandwith, Bristol, England, Jan. 1, 1760, Drinker and Sandwith Family Papers, Historical Society of Pennsylvania (HSP), Philadelphia (hereafter cited as Sandwith Papers). Modest silent clarifications of spelling and punctuation have been made in some quotations.

Even more than in other areas of social life, the documentary record of courtship brings us remarkably close to direct observation of actual eighteenth-century interactions, since letters could often comprise the entire relationship. See Ellen Rothman, *Hands and Hearts: A History of Courtship in America* (New York, 1984), 9–11.

In advancing the argument that public declarations of love were a distinctive aspect of eighteenth-century courtship that had social as well as personal implications, I follow the thinking of David Cressy and Jan Lewis. See Cressy, *Birth, Marriage, and Death: Ritual, Religion, and the Life-Cycle in Tudor and Stuart England* (New York, 1997), esp. 260–261; Lewis, " 'Those Scenes for Which Alone My Heart Was Made': Affection and Politics in the Age of Jefferson and Hamilton," in Peter Stearns and Jan Lewis, eds., *An Emotional History of the United States* (New York, 1998), 57.

2 William Franklin to Madam, London, Oct. 24, 1758, Elizabeth Graeme Fergusson Correspondence, HSP (hereafter cited as EGF Correspondence); Margaret Abercrombie to Ann Graeme, Apr. 4, 1759, EGF Correspondence.

On the shifting emphasis from social and economic factors to romantic ones and declining public involvement in courtship from the seventeenth to the nineteenth century, see Daniel Scott Smith, "Parental Power and Marriage Patterns: An Analysis of Historical Trends in Hingham, Massachusetts," *Journal of Marriage and the Family,* XXXV (1973), 426. For eighteenth-century Philadelphia specifically, see Robert J. Gough, "Close-Kin Marriage and Upper-Class Formation in Late-Eighteenth-Century Philadelphia," *Journal of Family History,* XIV (1989), 119–136.

Authors like Lawrence Stone, John Gillis, and Alan Macfarlane have made similar arguments for Europe, though these authors do disagree on whether the appearance of romantic language in the eighteenth century was merely a difference of emphasis and ideals (Macfarlane) or of actual feeling (Stone). See Stone, *The Family, Sex, and Marriage in England, 1500–1800* (New York, 1977); Gillis, *For Better, for Worse: British Marriages, 1600 to the Present* (New York, 1985); and Macfarlane, *Marriage and Love in England: Modes of Reproduction, 1300–1840* (New York, 1986).

3 Politics were as emotionally laden as the domestic realm, and power was as endemic to marriage relationships as to political ones. See Toby L. Ditz, "What's Love Got to Do with It? The History of Men, the History of Gender in the 1990s," *Reviews in American History,* XXVIII (2000), 167–180, esp. 170. Ann Laura Stoler has noted the importance of affect for the advancement of colonial projects; see Stoler, "Tense and Tender Ties: The Politics of Comparison in North American History and (Post) Colonial Studies," *Journal of American History,* LXXXVIII (2001–2002), 832.

4 On wavering devotion to the ideal of a communal society as well as on the social and political instability of eighteenth-century Pennsylvania (and British America more broadly), see Gary B. Nash, *The Urban Crucible: The Northern Seaports and the Origins of the American Revolution,* abr. ed. (Cambridge, Mass., 1986), 97, 135.

5 On "affective individualism," see Stone, *Family, Sex, and Marriage,* 22; Karen Lystra, *Searching the Heart: Women, Men, and Romantic Love in Nineteenth-Century America* (New York, 1989), 3–4. For a critique of this idea, see Ruth H. Bloch, "Changing Conceptions of Sexuality and Romance in Eighteenth-Century America," *William and Mary Quarterly,* 3d Ser., LX (2003), 20, 41.

6 On "emotional or affectional authoritarianism," see Jay Fliegelman, *Prodigals and Pilgrims: The American Revolution against Patriarchal Authority, 1750–1800* (New York, 1982), 260.

7 A pervasive sense of social and political uncertainty arose in eighteenth-century British America not only as a result of transatlantic Enlightenment upheavals in moral philosophy and political theory but also as a result of British Americans' precarious place on the edge of empire, simultaneously colonizers and colonized. See Michael Warner, "What's Colonial about Colonial America?" in Robert Blair St. George, ed., *Possible Pasts: Becoming Colonial in Early America* (Ithaca, N.Y., 2000), 49–70.

On the declining utility of traditional status markers in eighteenth-century British America (particularly genteel displays of material culture) and on the anxiety generated thereby, see T. H. Breen, *The Marketplace of Revolution: How Consumer Politics Shaped American Independence* (New York, 2004), 153–158.

8 "The Humble Address of the Mayor, Recorder, Aldermen, and Commonalty of the City of New Brunswick," *Pennsylvania Gazette,* Mar. 10, 1763 (hereafter cited as *PG*).

9 Numerous historians have begun to emphasize youth and life-cycle as an important analytical category. As Cressy so succinctly puts it, "Courtship prefigured marriage, and marriage was the business of adults" (*Birth, Marriage, and Death,* 234). C. Dallett Hemphill used age (along with rank, class, and gender) as one of the key categories of analysis in her 1987 dissertation as well as her book; see *Bowing to Necessities: A History of Manners in America* (New York, 1999). And see also Martha Tomhave Blauvelt, *The Work of the Heart: Young Women and Emotion, 1780–1830* (Charlottesville, Va., 2007).

10 Edward Tilghman to Benjamin Chew, Wye, Oct. 20, 1743, Correspondence and General Papers, 1743–1777, Chew Family Papers, HSP (hereafter cited as Chew Papers). Writing on women, marriage, and status, Karin Anne Wulf has urged that marital status should be seen as a key category of historical analysis, calling it an "experiential frontier"; see "A Marginal Independence: Unmarried Women in Colonial Philadelphia" (Ph.D. diss., Johns Hopkins University, 1993), 19; *Not All Wives: Women of Colonial Philadelphia* (Ithaca, N.Y., 2000). Daniel Scott Smith has also written on the importance of "householding" in determining status for men and women alike; see "Female Householding in Late Eighteenth-Century America and the Problem of Poverty," *Journal of Social History,* XXVIII (1994–1995), 83.

11 Samuel Allinson, "A Miscellaneous Commonplace: Samuel Allinson's, 1761," Manuscript 975b in the Haverford College Quaker Collection (HCQC), 26. On the connections between men's household roles and civic standing, see Toby L. Ditz, "Shipwrecked; or, Masculinity Imperiled: Mercantile Representations of Failure and the Gendered Self in Eighteenth-Century Philadelphia," *JAH,* LXXXI (1994–1995), 65. For another good discussion of men's role as household master, see Carole Shammas, "Anglo-American Household Government in Comparative Perspective," *WMQ,* 3d Ser., LII (1995), 104–144.

    The centrality of age markers for men's sense of themselves is also suggested by E. Anthony Rotundo's work on nineteenth-century masculinity, and courtship's particular resonance for young eighteenth-century men (and its potential to provoke rage and frustration) is documented in Kenneth A. Lockridge's work. J. A. Leo Lemay also discusses bitterness and rage among Virginia suitors. See Rotundo, *American Manhood: Transformations in Masculinity from the Revolution to the Modern Era* (New York, 1993); Lockridge, *On the Sources of Patriarchal Rage: The Common Place Books of William Byrd and Thomas Jefferson and the Gendering of Power in the Eighteenth Century*

(New York, 1992); Lemay, ed., *Robert Bolling Woos Anne Miller: Love and Courtship in Colonial Virginia, 1760* (Charlottesville, Va., 1990).

12 "The Conduct and Doctrine of the Rev. Mr. Whitfield Vindicated," *PG,* Dec. 13, 1739; *PG,* Nov. 14, 1754. On connections between sentiment and subordination in marriage, see Ingrid H. Tague, "Love, Honor, and Obedience: Fashionable Women and the Discourse of Marriage in the Early Eighteenth Century," *Journal of British Studies,* XL (2001), 76–106, esp. 88.

13 "Extract from the Votes of the General Assembly of the Colony of New York," *PG,* Nov. 29, 1753.

Such an emphasis on the links between love and authority may at first glance seem anomalous when applied to colonial Pennsylvania. After all, William Penn founded Philadelphia as the city of "brotherly love." Yet, when all citations for the word *love* ever to appear in the *Gazette* between 1728 and 1765 are taken together (834 in all), a mere 15 citations (fewer than 2 percent) refer to "brotherly love." And 3 of those uses referred to the names of ships, not to actual expressions of affection between social actors! Meanwhile, the phrase "brotherly affection" occurred only a single time. While the existence of concepts like "brotherly" love and "brotherly" affection indicates that love and affection were *not* inherently or necessarily linked to the imposition of hierarchy, the very need for such fraternal modifiers indicates that—unless otherwise specified—love and affection could be assumed to signal ranked relations. On William Penn and the founding ideals of Pennsylvania, see Richard S. Dunn and Mary Maples Dunn, eds., *The World of William Penn* (Philadelphia, 1986).

14 John Swift to John White, Sept. 24, Oct. 12, 1750, Swift Family Papers, 1740–1790, HSP. On the importance of using the notion of friendship as a means of obfuscating the economic dependence of colonial debtors, see T. H. Breen, *Tobacco Culture: The Mentality of the Great Tidewater Planters on the Eve of Revolution* (Princeton, N.J., 1985), 102–103.

15 *PG,* Aug. 8, 1754, Jan. 17, 1760. The 1754 description of "a Negroe man, named Jack" included the information that he was "much pock marked, a lover of white women, and a great smoker." Such concerns clearly related to clichés about black passions and appetites (sexual and otherwise) and not to the type of love and affection rhetorically reserved for relations between people of closer rank. Public ridicule of cross-race relationships occurred regularly in colonial America. See Winthrop D. Jordan, *White over Black: American Attitudes toward the Negro, 1550–1812* (Chapel Hill, N.C., 1968), 136–178; and see Werner Sollors, *Neither Black nor White Yet Both: Thematic Explorations of Interracial Literatures* (New York, 1997), 286–335.

If "examples of true love" between Afro- and Anglo-Americans occurred in colonial Pennsylvania, as Graham Russell Hodges has documented for Afro-Lutheran society in colonial New York, they received little notice in the surviving record. As discussed below, love's primary role in the public record was to give the gloss of voluntarism to relations of dominance and dependence. In the case of the enslaved in particular, no such fiction could be sustained. The absence of love and affection in reference to African Americans therefore says nothing at all about blacks' actual emotional interactions with whites (much less with each other), but much about the meaning of the emotional terms with which whites chose to characterize power relations. See Hodges, "The Pastor and the Prostitute: Sexual Power among African Americans and Germans in Colonial New York," in Martha Hodes, ed., *Sex, Love, Race: Crossing Boundaries in North American History* (New York, 1999), 60–71, esp. 61.

16 *PG*, Oct. 24, 1734; "Speech . . . Made to the House by His Honor the Governor," *PG*, Mar. 29, 1733; George Clinton, "His Excellency's Speech to the General Assembly of the Colony of New York," *PG*, Nov. 24, 1743.

17 *PG*, Oct. 1, 1730, Nov. 27, 1731, Jan. 4, 1733. Findings on the vocabulary associated with *affection* come from analysis of the 520 entries generated by database searching. Words were counted as "associated" if they appeared in series with *affection* (that is, linked by the conjunctions *and* or *or*) or if they appeared as direct modifiers of *affection*. By this count, there were 130 pair words. Authority-associated meanings (including *duty, esteem,* and *respect*) accounted for 50 examples, or just more than one-third of the total (38.5 percent). Other submeanings were also significant; those of some prominence will be discussed in due course. Still, the aggregate appearance of status-related qualifying words far outstripped any other set of words.

18 *PG*, Oct. 29, 1730, Oct. 28, Nov. 27, 1731.

19 *PG*, Oct. 28, 1731.

20 *PG*, Feb. 13, 1740.

21 "Duty," 3c, *Oxford English Dictionary Online,* 2d ed. (2001) (cited hereafter as *OED*) (this definition includes supporting citations from 1536 to 1861); *PG*, Feb. 13, Mar. 12, Apr. 17, Sept. 25, 1740.

22 *PG*, May 27, 1756.

23 *PG*, Jan. 22, 1741.

24 These phrases were the titles of available books. See "New Books Just Imported This Day by Rivington and Brown, Booksellers," *PG*, Sept. 30, 1762; "Just Published and to Be Sold by the Printer . . . ," *PG*, Nov. 15, 1744.

25 "The Happy Man," *PG*, Feb. 28, 1749.

26 Blauvelt notes of a slightly later period that "one of the functions of ro-

mance is to divert women from their fears, even though those fears were well grounded in economic, legal, and political realities." See *The Work of the Heart,* 109.

27 Ann Swett to Betsy Sandwith, 1752, Elizabeth Moode to Elizabeth Sandwith, 11 Month 1755, Sandwith Papers. (All translations from letters originally written in French are my own.) On the evolution in women's attitudes from acceptance of hierarchical divisions within marriage to a new standard of difference without inferiority, see Nancy F. Cott in Linda K. Kerber et al., "Forum: Beyond Roles, beyond Spheres: Thinking about Gender in the Early Republic," *WMQ,* 3d Ser., XLVI (1989), 567.

28 Isaac Norris to Prudence Moore, Dec. 10, 1731, Norris Family Papers, Norris Family Notebooks, HSP (hereafter cited as Norris Papers). Both of these expansive assertions of the rights of women were articulated by Quaker women. Though it is clear that women of varied religious backgrounds shared concerns about women's roles in marriage, it does seem that Quaker doctrine —itself less restrictive for women than that of other Protestant sects—might have allowed Quaker women to voice broader concerns than non-Quakers. For an excellent discussion of differences between Quaker women and other Protestant women, see Mary Maples Dunn, "Saints and Sisters: Congregational and Quaker Women in the Early Colonial Period," *American Quarterly,* XXX (1978), 582–601.

29 Elizabeth Stedman to Elizabeth Graeme, Dec. 16, 1764, EGF Correspondence.

30 William Franklin to Elizabeth Graeme, New York, May 2, 1757, EGF Correspondence; Elizabeth Graeme to Nathaniel Evans, and "Laura's Answer," cited in David S. Shields, *Civil Tongues and Polite Letters in British America* (Chapel Hill, N.C., 1997), 139.

31 *PG,* Feb. 18, Mar. 4, 1735. As Linda K. Kerber has noted, "The fictive volition of the pair was always taken to be the same as the real will of the husband"; see *Women of the Republic: Intellect and Ideology in Revolutionary America* (Chapel Hill, N.C., 1980), 120.

32 *PG,* Mar. 4, 1735. Katherine A. Lynch points out that, historically, the fiction that men and women shared the same interests within families has been so entrenched that even many modern scholars fall into the trap of allowing such assumptions to frame their analysis. Ruth H. Bloch discusses the origins of such ideas. See Lynch, "The Family and the History of Public Life," *Journal of Interdisciplinary History,* XXIV (1993–1994), 665–684, esp. 667–668; and see Bloch, "Changing Conceptions of Sexuality and Romance," *WMQ,* 3d Ser., LX (2003), 28, 41.

33 *PG,* June 17, 1742.

34 *PG,* July 11, 1765. The language used in Philadelphia echoes that of English proponents of poor hospitals. See Gary Nash's discussion of the founding of Pennsylvania Hospital in *The Urban Crucible,* 160.

35 *PG,* Nov. 9, 1738, Nov. 19, 1741. Overall, the word *loyalty* appeared alongside *affection* in 18 instances, the word *fidelity* in another 4. Together, these 22 cases comprised 17 percent of all tandem terms accompanying *affection.*

36 Governor Robert Hunter Morris, "At a Council held at Philadelphia, Wednesday the 16th April, 1755," *Minutes of the Provincial Council of Pennsylvania, from the Organization to the Termination of the Proprietary Government* (Philadelphia, Harrisburg, 1851–1852), VI, 371 (hereafter cited as *MPCP*).

37 *PG,* July 5, 1733.

38 *PG,* Nov. 8, 1733.

39 *PG,* Mar. 12, 1754. On the Albany congress, see Timothy J. Shannon, *Indians and Colonists at the Crossroads of Empire* (Ithaca, N.Y., 2000).

40 *PG,* July 14, 1763. As Ann Marie Plane notes, Indian marriages did not "automatically subsume the wife's identity under that of her husband"; see *Colonial Intimacies: Indian Marriage in Early New England* (Ithaca, N.Y., 2000), 68; on distinctive elements of Indian marriage as compared to English forms, see 132, 141. Nancy Shoemaker describes the frequent use of body metaphors in colonial exchanges and argues for their general efficacy in "Body Language: The Body as a Source of Sameness and Difference in Eighteenth-Century American Indian Diplomacy East of the Mississippi," in Janet Moore Lindman and Michele Lise Tarter, eds., *A Centre of Wonders: The Body in Early America* (Ithaca, N.Y., 2001), 211–222. For a contrasting view (more in line with my own) that focuses on the ways in which Indians and English could wield parallel metaphors at cross-purposes, see Jane T. Merritt, "Metaphor, Meaning, and Misunderstanding: Language and Power on the Pennsylvania Frontier," in Andrew R. L. Cayton and Fredrika J. Teute, eds., *Contact Points: American Frontiers from the Mohawk Valley to the Mississippi, 1750–1830* (Chapel Hill, N.C., 1998), 60–87.

41 *PG,* Feb. 23, 1758.

42 *PG,* June 7, 1744, Aug. 3, 1758.

43 *PG,* June 4, 1747, Mar. 25, 1756.

44 *PG,* Oct. 5, 1738, Sept. 26, 1754.

45 *PG,* Sept. 13, 1753.

46 *PG,* May 26, 1743.

47 Isaac Watts, *Discourses on the Love of God, and Its Influence on All the Passions; With a Discovery of the Right Use and Abuse of Them in Matters of Religion; Also,*

a Devout Meditation Annexed to Each Discourse (Philadelphia, 1799), 31; Watts, "To His Excellency Jonathan Belcher, Esq.," *PG*, Aug. 13, 1730.

As noted, the source for the first quotation, from Watts's *Discourses,* comes from a 1799 edition, the first published in Pennsylvania. However, the 1729 edition was available in the colony by the 1740s, when imported editions were offered for sale by booksellers. Stephen Potts advertised "Berry Street Sermons, By Dr. Watts, Watt's Doctrine Of The Passions, Watt's Ruin And Recovery Of Mankind" in May 1743, while James Reed offered "Watt's Ruin and Recovery of Mankind, and Doctrine of the Passions" in November 1743. See *PG,* May 26, Nov. 24, 1743.

48 *PG,* Nov. 30, 1758.

49 *PG,* Aug. 26, 1756.

50 Elizabeth Graeme to William Franklin, "The Foregoing Song Answered by a Young Lady," cited in Shields, *Civil Tongues and Polite Letters,* 134. Shields discusses the Franklin-Graeme courtship in the context of its relation to Philadelphia's literary salon culture. I have relied on his analysis in explaining Graeme's standing in literary circles (130).

Elizabeth Sandwith's needlework inventory is published in Elaine Forman Crane, ed., *The Diary of Elizabeth Drinker* (Boston, 1991), 1–3. I have also consulted Elizabeth Sandwith Drinker Diary, HSP (cited hereafter as ESD Diary). For another discussion of gifts in courtship (in seventeenth-century England) see Cressy, *Birth, Marriage, and Death,* 263–266.

51 Eliza Moode to Babette, Friday Morning, 8 o'clock, Sandwith Papers; Elizabeth Graeme, "On the Preference of Friendship to Love," in Shields, *Civil Tongues and Polite Letters,* 130. P[eggy] E[mlen] to Sally Logan, Philadelphia, 4th day afternoon, Marjorie Brown Collection of Margaret Emlen Letters, 1768–71, HSP (hereafter cited as Emlen Letters). The pattern of men's effusiveness and women's reticence continued into the nineteenth-century period Rothman studies; see *Hands and Hearts,* 9–11.

52 Elizabeth Moode to Elizabeth Sandwith, June 30, 1754, Sandwith Papers (my translation from the French).

53 William Franklin to Madam, London, Oct. 24, 1758, EGF Correspondence. Combing William's letters for clues to explain their breakup suggests that Elizabeth might have been concerned about religious and political conflicts between their families—the Graemes supported Pennsylvania's proprietors against Benjamin Franklin's attempts to assert the power of the colonial Assembly and maintained ties to the Reverend William Smith, the politically meddlesome preacher Franklin began by promoting but ended by despising. William had his own theory, discussed at length below.

For the contrary argument that eighteenth-century "sentimental norms" expanded rather than diminished the risks to reputation that men ran during courtship, see Lisa Wilson, *Ye Heart of a Man: The Domestic Life of Men in Colonial New England* (New Haven, Conn., 1999), 38, 56–57.

54 William Franklin to Madam, London, Oct. 24, 1758, EGF Correspondence.

55 *PG*, Aug. 17, 1738. On the strategic political significance of newspaper publication of the proceedings of colonial assemblies in Pennsylvania, see Nash, *The Urban Crucible*, 62.

56 *PG*, Apr. 12, 1739.

57 *PG*, Aug. 7, 14, 1740.

58 *PG*, May 22, 1755.

59 *PG*, Aug. 14, 1755, July 7, 1757.

60 Women's ability to exercise indirect power in relationships "through the actual or threatened withholding of affection and through 'playing the coquette'" has long been recognized. However, the corollary proposition—that omitting declarations of affection in political rhetoric could signal lack of consent—has not been made. See Herman R. Lantz et al., "Pre-Industrial Patterns in the Colonial Family in America: A Content Analysis of Colonial Magazines," *American Sociological Review*, XXXIII (1968), 413–429, 418; and see Tague, "Love, Honor, and Obedience," *Journal of British Studies*, XL (2001), 96.

61 *PG*, Dec. 31, 1754.

62 *PG*, Jan. 17, 1755.

63 *PG*, June 23, 1763.

64 *PG*, June 12, 1746.

65 *PG*, Aug. 30, 1750.

66 *PG*, July 10, 1760. On the influence of extramarital liaisons on colonial divorce cases and the rising association of women's sexual and social transgressions, see Clare A. Lyons, *Sex among the Rabble: An Intimate History of Gender and Power in the Age of Revolution, Philadelphia, 1730–1830* (Chapel Hill, N.C., 2006), 54. On English attitudes toward cuckoldry, with probable implications for the British-American case, see David M. Turner, *Fashioning Adultery: Gender, Sex, and Civility in England, 1660–1740* (Cambridge, 2002), 85.

67 *PG*, Nov. 13, 1755.

68 *PG*, Nov. 13, 1755.

69 *OED*, "Alien, v.," 1, and "Alien, adj.," 1, 2a.

70 *PG*, Oct. 31, 1754.

71 *PG*, Dec. 28, 1758.

72 *PG*, July 24, 1755; "To the Honourable Robert Hunter Morris, Esquire, Lieu-

tenant Governor of the Province of Pennsylvania etc. . . . The Address of the . . . General Assembly," Feb. 11, 1756, *MPCP*, VIII, 38.

73 *PG*, Mar. 1, 1764.

74 William Franklin to Madam, London, Oct. 24, 1758, EGF Correspondence.

75 Historians researching courtship in other eras have also noted the rising importance of sincerity. See Rothman, *Hands and Hearts*, 43; and Lucia McMahon, "'While Our Souls Together Blend': Narrating a Romantic Readership in the Early Republic," in Stearns and Lewis, eds., *An Emotional History*, 81.

76 Eliza Moode to Betsy Sandwith, Mar. 11, 1755, Sandwith Papers. On temporary power reversals, see Bloch, "Changing Conceptions of Sexuality and Romance," *WMQ*, 3d Ser., LX (2003), 24–25. Of course, some women did wind up single by choice or by circumstance. The larger point is simply that women's options were highly constrained compared to men's. See Wulf, *Not All Wives*.

77 Eliza Moode to Betsy Sandwith, 14 Second Month 1760, Sandwith Papers.

78 P[eggy] E[mlen] to Sally Logan, Jan. 3, 1768, Emlen Letters.

79 Ingrid Tague notes that "obedience was women's part of the marriage contract, a vow made voluntarily that they could not break." Tague, "Love, Honor, and Obedience," *Journal of British Studies*, XL (2001), 86.

80 P[eggy] E[mlen] to Sally Logan, Jan. 3, 1768, Emlen Letters. The issues of women's disguise, present in Pennsylvania only metaphorically, was a literal matter in Europe and in European novels where masquerade balls allowed women ritual opportunities to act out the arts of concealment drawn on by women in Pennsylvania. Interestingly, scholars who have analyzed these actual masquerades have also emphasized that the so-called power they brought women was ephemeral if not an actual mirage. See Catherine Craft-Fairchild, *Masquerade and Gender: Disguise and Female Identity in Eighteenth-Century Fictions by Women* (University Park, Pa., 1993).

Other authors have also noted that women's penchant for disguise during courtship speaks as much to the limits of their power as to power itself. See Judith Norton, as quoted in Mary Anne Schofield, *Unmasking and Masking the Female Mind: Disguising Romances in Feminine Fiction, 1713–1799* (Newark, Del., 1990), 23.

81 ESD Diary, Nov. 28, 1760.

82 Henry Drinker to Elizabeth Sandwith, Bristol, Jan. 1, 1760, Sandwith Papers.

83 See John Locke, *Two Treatises of Government*, ed. Peter Laslett (Cambridge, 1988), First Treatise, par. 98, Second Treatise, pars. 78, 81, 82.

While scholars from Carole Pateman to Mary Beth Norton and Ruth Bloch have claimed that Locke severed all associations between family relations and state formation, I read his *Two Treatises on Government* quite differently. My argument is that Locke wrote in opposition to absolutism but not to the idea of authority itself. Acknowledging marriage's role as a model for contract means admitting that, while Locke's ideal of authority, his vision of government, was built in opposition to absolutism, it was never intended to entirely undermine social and political hierarchies. Feminist scholars are quite right to point out that Locke made little place for women in politics, but it is important to note that he did reserve a role there for affectionate relations. Indeed, the language of love, like the metaphor of marriage, achieved such resonance in the eighteenth century exactly because its built-in ambiguities helped temper the tensions let loose by attempts to oppose absolutism yet preserve authority. On these debates, see Pateman, *The Sexual Contract* (Stanford, Calif., 1988), 52–55, 91–94; Norton, *Founding Mothers and Fathers: Gendered Power and the Forming of American Society* (New York, 1996), 5; Bloch, "Changing Conceptions of Sexuality and Romance," *WMQ*, 3d Ser., LX (2003), 35–36; Kerber, *Women of the Republic*, 17.

Commentators on connections between family and the state in colonial British America and the new United States have once again begun to stress the connections between marriage and the state (though without explicitly reconceiving Locke). See Nancy F. Cott, *Public Vows: A History of Marriage and the Nation* (Cambridge, Mass., 2000), 14, 64; Plane, *Colonial Intimacies*, 17.

Chapter Four

1 Benjamin Chew, "The Diary of Benjamin Chew at Easton 1758," Oct. 7, 1758, Historical Society of Pennsylvania (HSP), Philadelphia. The diarist labeled his book "Journal of a Journey to Easton." All quotations from the Chew diary refer to this manuscript (hereafter cited as Chew Diary). Modest silent clarifications of spelling and punctuation have been made in some quotations.

2 Chew Diary, Oct. 7, 1758.

3 For attention to the political and legal issues underlying the Easton treaty, see Ralph L. Ketcham, "Conscience, War, and Politics in Pennsylvania, 1755–1757," *William and Mary Quarterly*, 3d Ser., XX (1963), 416–439.

4 "Indignation," 1, 2, *Oxford English Dictionary Online*, 2d ed. (2001) (cited hereafter as *OED*).

5 Anthropologist Cliff Goddard, in his work on the people of the Western Desert in Austalia, outlines the basic methodology that I employ in this

chapter. Because Goddard's case study dealt specifically with analyzing the language used to talk about anger (both one's own and other people's), I found his emphasis on lexicography and semantic analysis especially helpful. See Goddard, "Anger in the Western Desert: A Case-Study in the Cross-Cultural Semantics of Emotion," *Man*, n.s., XXVI (1991), 269.

6 Chew Diary, Oct. 7, 1758.

7 Chew Diary, Oct. 7, 1758.

8 *Pennsylvania Gazette*, Oct. 14, 1736 (hereafter cited as *PG*).

9 Patricia U. Bonomi notes that in the colonies "suspect officials were repeatedly depicted as . . . given to violent fits of rage"; see *The Lord Cornbury Scandal: The Politics of Reputation in British America* (Chapel Hill, N.C., 1998). Steven C. Bullock has also worked on this issue; see "The Rages of Governor Francis Nicholson: Anger, Politeness, and Politics in Provincial America," paper presented to the Columbia University Early American History Seminar, Mar. 8, 2005.

   On ancient philosophy and anger, see John M. Cooper, *Reason and Emotion: Essays on Ancient Moral Psychology and Ethical Theory* (Princeton, N.J., 1999). On anger in the Old Testament, see Kari Latvus, *God, Anger, and Ideology: The Anger of God in Joshua and Judges in Relation to Deuteronomy and the Priestly Writings* (Sheffield, 1998). Writing on medieval clerics, Richard E. Barton differentiates between lordly anger and the anger of deadly sin; see " 'Zealous Anger' and the Renegotiation of Aristocratic Relationships in Eleventh- and Twelfth-Century France," in Barbara H. Rosenwein, ed., *Anger's Past: The Social Uses of an Emotion in the Middle Ages* (Ithaca, N.Y., 1998), 155.

   There is another strain of historiography, which I believe is now on the wane, which argues that premodern and early modern people readily and uncritically accepted passionate emotion generally, and anger specifically. Johan Huizinga, Norbert Elias, and Marc Bloch all wrote in this tradition. Many later historians, including the majority of contributors to Rosenwein's excellent volume as well as the editor herself, are now intent on countering this notion. See Barbara H. Rosenwein, "Controlling Paradigms," in Rosenwein, ed., *Anger's Past*, 243.

10 Isaac Norris to Leon[ar]d Vassel, Pennsylvania, 8 Tenth Month 1722, Norris Family Papers, HSP (hereafter cited as Norris Papers).

11 Isaac Norris to John Askew, Pennsylvania, Eleventh Month 1724/5, and I. Norris to J. Dickinson, Pennsylvania, 23 Eighth Month 1727, Norris Papers.

12 As Stephen D. White argues, "representing another person's anger is never a neutrally descriptive or politically neutral act"; see "The Politics of Anger," in Rosenwein, ed., *Anger's Past*, 150.

13 *PG*, Apr. 22, 1731, Feb. 28, Dec. 30, 1733.

14 *PG*, Feb. 13, 1734, Oct. 7, 1742, Jan. 16, 1753. My analysis of the kinds of anger attributed to low-ranking members of society is drawn from my survey of anger word citations in the *Pennsylvania Gazette*. The actual number of entries about common people that concerned anger (or any emotion) was small.

15 *PG*, July 8, 1742.

16 [Benjamin Franklin], *Plain Truth; or, Serious Considerations on the Present State of the City of Philadelphia, and Province of Pennsylvania*, 2d ed. ([Philadelphia], 1747), 13–14.

17 *PG*, Oct. 26, 1738, Aug. 13, 1747. Such views of the passions as dangerous and antirational were by no means confined to the realm of informal "common knowledge" in this period, but actually figured importantly in the learned theories of moral philosophers. See Jeffrey Barnouw, "Passion as 'Confused' Perception or Thought in Descartes, Malebranche, and Hutcheson," *Journal of the History of Ideas*, LIII (1992), 397–424, esp. 401.

18 *PG*, Mar. 6, Nov. 29, 1753, May 3, 1759.

19 This attitude on the part of elites also had long roots stretching back at least to the Middle Ages. See Paul Freedman, "Peasant Anger in the Late Middle Ages," in Rosenwein, ed., *Anger's Past*, 171, 173.

20 Isaac Norris, Sr., to Isaac Norris, Jr., Oct. 3, 1733, Norris Papers.

21 George Thomas, *PG*, June 3, 1742. Modern theorists disagree sharply about the relationship between reason and anger (especially in its extreme forms, like rage). James R. Averill represents one extreme position in arguing that *all* anger necessarily involves reason. Claire Kahane's views are very nearly antithetical to Averill's; she regards rage as a somatic, not cognitive experience. See Averill, *Anger and Aggression: An Essay on Emotion* (New York, 1982), 95; Kahane, "The Aesthetic Politics of Rage," in Renée R. Curry and Terry L. Allison, eds., *States of Rage: Emotional Eruption, Violence, and Social Change* (New York, 1996), 126–146.

My own interest lies, not in attempting to present some objective or definite theory about the relationship of anger and rationality, but rather in documenting the views eighteenth-century Anglo-Americans held on the topic and in analyzing the social intent and implications of those ideas, following Goddard's insight that "the full cultural significance of a[n] [emotional] concept can only be appreciated in the light of how it figures in social action." See Goddard, "Anger in the Western Desert," *Man*, n.s., XXVI (1991), 276.

22 *PG*, Nov. 16, 1733. For an insightful discussion of the relation of anger to honor,

see William Ian Miller, *Humiliation and Other Essays on Honor, Social Discomfort, and Violence* (Ithaca, N.Y., 1993). See also Thomas J. Scheff, *Bloody Revenge: Emotions, Nationalism, and War* (Boulder, Colo., 1994), esp. 151.

23 *PG,* Oct. 9, 1760. On the relation of sexual continence and honor for men and women, see Elizabeth A. Foyster, *Manhood in Early Modern England: Honour, Sex, and Marriage* (London, 1999). For a discussion of the growing importance of economic success in the definition of eighteenth-century male honor, see Pieter Spierenburg, "Masculinity, Violence, and Honor: An Introduction," in Spierenburg, ed., *Men and Violence: Gender, Honor, and Rituals in Modern Europe and America* (Columbus, Ohio, 1998).

24 Henry Bouquet to Madame, July 2, 1765, Chew Family Papers, HSP (hereafter cited as Chew Papers). Restrictions on women's anger have a long history in Western culture. On this point, see Spierenburg, "Masculinity, Violence, and Honor," in Spierenburg, ed., *Men and Violence,* 2–3. For a discussion of the relation of such restrictions to the workings of patriarchy, see Scott Hendrix, "Masculinity and Patriarchy in Reformation Germany," *Journal of the History of Ideas,* LVI (1995), 177–193.

25 *PG,* Mar. 31, 1768, Dec. 28, 1774. On European discussions of African women's sexuality (and lack of sexual honor) from the beginning of the Atlantic slave trade to the antebellum United States, see Jennifer L. Morgan, *Laboring Women: Reproduction and Gender in New World Slavery* (Philadelphia, 2004), 29–36; Deborah Gray White, *Ar'n't I a Woman? Female Slaves in the Plantation South* (New York, 1985), 28–34. On slaveholders' inability to understand "the racial threat as gendered feminine," despite the prominent demographic presence of enslaved women in urban colonial households, see Morgan, "Accounting for the Women in Slavery: Demography and the Epistemology of Early American Slavery," paper presented to the Harvard University Conference "Transformations: The Atlantic World in the Seventeenth Century," Mar. 31, 2006, 7. On the increasing but still equivocal use of anger for feminine self-assertion, see Martha Thomhave Blauvelt, *The Work of the Heart: Young Women and Emotion, 1780–1830* (Charlottesville, Va., 2007), esp. 141–145.

26 Ebenezer Kinnersley, *PG,* July 15, 1740.

27 *PG,* Mar. 30, 1738.

28 *PG,* Dec. 19, 1749.

29 William Denny, *PG,* Jan. 26, 1758.

30 Chew Diary, Oct. 8, 1758.

31 Chew Diary, Oct. 8, 1758. According to the *OED, peevishness* describes the exhibition of "petty vexation" and implies that the person whose anger is so described is "silly . . . foolish . . . or childishly fretful" ("Peevishness," 1;

"Peevish," 1, 5, *OED*). There is little doubt that this would have been Chew's understanding of the word's meaning. A correspondent of his wrote mockingly in 1743 of his young son's problems teething, saying, "Dicky's teeth . . . have kept him low and peevish so that the title to gov[ernmen]t of the family seems disputable" (Edw[ar]d Tilghman to Benjamin Chew, Wye, Md., Oct. 20, 1743, Chew Papers).

32 This narrative of treaty events is based on the Chew Diary, Oct. 9, 10, 11, 1758.

33 Chew Diary, Oct. 11, 1758.

34 Chew Diary, Oct. 11, 1758.

35 Sophia Hume to William Brown, London, 19 Third Month 1752, William Brown's Letterbook, 1738–1761, Brown Family Papers, HSP. In her letter, Hume attributes these lines to another Quaker elder, Stephen Crisp.

36 Susannah Wright to Doct[o]r Reigher, n.d., ibid. This undated letter was written in response to published criticisms of Quaker policies with respect to war. Nominally a piece of private correspondence, it must have met with widespread approval in the Quaker community, for it was copied into William Brown's letterbook, where it is preserved to this day.

37 Susanna Wright, "To a Friend—On Some Misunderstanding by the Same," undated, in Catherine La Courreye Blecki and Karin A. Wulf, eds., *Milcah Martha Moore's Book: A Commonplace Book from Revolutionary America* (University Park, Pa., 1997), 141–142.

38 Benjamin Mifflin, "Journal of a Journey from Philadelphia to the Cedar Swamps and Back," 1764, Benjamin Mifflin Journal, HSP. The conceptual links Quakers made between anger, violence, and undue concern with honor and social status are now shared by many modern social theorists. For an example of work on such topics in the modern American context, see Richard E. Nisbett and Dov Cohen, *Culture of Honor: The Psychology of Violence in the South* (Boulder, Colo., 1996). Scheff speculates that the honor-anger-violence nexus might have gone unnoticed for much of the twentieth century because of the dominance of materialist explanations for conflict. See Scheff, *Bloody Revenge,* esp. 39–40.

39 Samuel Chew to Benjamin Chew, Oct. 12, 1743, Chew Papers.

40 Benjamin Chew to Samuel Chew, London, Dec. 7, 1743, Chew Papers.

41 Chew Diary, Oct. 11, 1758.

42 Chew Diary, Oct. 11, 1758.

43 Chew Diary, Oct. 12, 1758. For an account of Teedyuscung's demands, see Jane T. Merritt, "Metaphor, Meaning, and Misunderstanding: Language and Power on the Pennsylvania Frontier," in Andrew R. L. Cayton and Fredrika J.

Teute, eds., *Contact Points: American Frontiers from the Mohawk Valley to the Mississippi, 1750–1830* (Chapel Hill, N.C., 1998), 60–87.

44 *PG,* Apr. 28, May 26, Nov. 24, 1743, Oct. 29, Dec. 19, 1749, May 30, 1751. For information on the college curriculum, see William Smith, *Account of the College, Academy, and Charitable School of Philadelphia in Pennsylvania,* ed. Thomas R. Adams (Philadelphia, 1951).

45 Joseph Shippen, Joseph Shippen Commonplace Book, 1750, Papers of the Shippen Family, HSP (hereafter cited as Shippen Papers). It is worth noting in this context that Joseph Shippen's grandfather, Edward Shippen, had been a Quaker merchant in Philadelphia; so while Joseph himself had been raised an Anglican, he (like Benjamin Chew) might have had added lingering uncertainties on the subject of anger because of his family's Quaker origins.

46 *PG,* June 26, 1746.

47 The proportion of *Pennsylvania Gazette* articles (from 1751 through October 1758) discussing fury that related to native Americans was 16 of 25, or 64 percent.

The first two definitions for *fury* in the *Oxford English Dictionary* (both of which date back at least as far as the sixteenth century) include the following descriptions: "fierce passion, disorder or tumult of mind approaching madness; *esp.* wild anger, frenzied rage," and "fierce impetuosity or violence; *esp.* warlike rage, fierceness in conflict, attack, or the like" ("Fury," 1, 2, *OED*).

Bernard Sheehan in his now classic work, *Savagism and Civility,* comments on the fact that native Americans could be construed by Europeans as rageful or not depending on the political needs of the colonists. See Bernard W. Sheehan, *Savagism and Civility: Indians and Englishmen in Colonial Virginia* (New York, 1980), 37.

48 *PG,* June 6, 1751, Dec. 13, 1753, Oct. 31, 1754.

49 *PG,* Aug. 22, 1751.

50 *PG,* Oct. 30, 1755. This very incident at Shamokin is the subject of an article by James H. Merrell, who conjectures that colonists who tried to read Montour's countenance wanted to determine his ethnicity and thus the likelihood that Montour was "one of them." However, Merrell's insightful analysis overlooks an important aspect of European preoccupations with countenance: the emerging importance of emotion generally, and anger specifically, in defining and communicating relations of power. See " 'The Cast of His Countenance': Reading Andrew Montour," in Ronald Hoffman, Mechal Sobel, and Fredrika J. Teute, eds., *Through a Glass Darkly: Reflections on Personal Identity in Early America* (Chapel Hill, N.C., 1997), 13–39.

51 *PG*, Nov. 18, 1756. Richard Slotkin has already made much the same argument about the inspiration colonists drew from the military success of native Americans, albeit without any mention of the importance of anger. Significantly, Slotkin believes this process occurred to a greater extent in Pennsylvania than anywhere else. He speculates that this was due to Pennsylvania's central and cosmopolitan location, a position which allowed it to serve as a kind of cultural clearinghouse for new ideas. I would add that the competition for social dominance initiated by Quaker rivals must have made the existence of an alternate, non-Quaker standard of masculinity particularly appealing in Pennsylvania. See *Regeneration through Violence: The Mythology of the American Frontier, 1600–1860* (Middletown, Conn., 1973), 223, 230.

52 *PG*, May 17, 1759.

53 Chew Diary, Oct. 13, 1758.

54 Chew Diary, Oct. 13, 1758.

55 Chew Diary, Oct. 13, 1758.

56 Chew Diary, Oct. 17, 1758.

57 Tho[ma]s McKee to William West, Susquehannah, Dec. 14, 1755, Norris Papers.

58 Kirk Davis Swinehart's work on cultural interchange between native Americans and Anglo-Americans argues that Anglo-Americans felt particularly threatened by native appropriations of European material culture, including clothing. See Swinehart, "This Wild Place: Sir William Johnson among the Mowhawks, 1715–1783" (Ph.D. diss., Yale University, 2002).

For an interesting discussion on elevated levels of violence and increased concern with honor in frontier societies, see Christopher Waldrep, "The Making of a Border State Society: James McGready, the Great Revival, and the Prosecution of Profanity in Kentucky," *American Historical Review*, XCIX (1994), 767–784.

59 *PG*, Aug. 21, 1755.

60 *PG*, Apr. 25, 1754.

61 "A Parody on Pope's Prologue to Cato, Addressed to Mr. Henry Bridges, Constructor of That Elaborate Piece of Mechanism, the Microcosm," *PG*, Jan. 22, 1756.

62 James Burd to Sally Burd, Oct. 14, 1758, Shippen Papers.

63 Joseph Shippen, scrap dated May 12, 1752, and signed Joseph Shippen, Junr; James Burd to Sally Burd, Camp at Loyal Hannon, Oct. 14, 1758, Shippen Papers.

64 *PG*, May 3, 1759.

65 *PG*, Oct. 12, 1758, Oct. 25, Nov. 8, 1759.

66 *PG,* May 7, 1752, June 2, 1757, Nov. 16, 1758, Aug. 11, 1763.

67 Chew Diary, Oct. 20, 1758.

68 Chew Diary, Oct. 20, 1758.

69 Chew Diary, Oct. 20, 1758.

70 *PG,* Nov. 8, 1759.

71 *PG,* Mar. 20, 1760, May 27, 1762.

72 *PG,* Sept. 27, 1759.

73 William Smith, "A Charge Delivered May 17, 1757 at the First Anniversary Commencement in the College and Academy of Philadelphia, by the Reverend Mr. Smith, Provost of the Same," *PG,* Aug. 11, 1757.

74 *PG,* May 26, 1763.

75 George Morgan to Dear Partners, George Morgan Journal and Letterbook, 1767–68, 84, HSP.

76 *PG,* June 5, 1766.

77 Edward Tilghman to Benjamin Chew, Feb. 20, 1761, Chew Papers.

78 This argument appears prominently in the work of Carol Zisowitz Stearns and Peter N. Stearns, whose *Anger: The Struggle for Emotional Control in America's History* (Chicago, 1986) is the standard in the field. The Stearnses argue that anger was extremely prevalent in premodern and early modern eras, that people then had an accepting attitude toward anger, and that it was not generally viewed negatively until the close of the eighteenth century. They see a single trajectory from the time of the Greeks, who celebrated the pleasures of anger, to the twentieth century, by which time anger had become almost taboo (27). The Stearnses' original research pertains to the nineteenth and twentieth centuries; closer study of the colonial period reveals some zigzags in the overall path of emotional change so well charted by them.

    John Demos concludes that, while anger *was* extremely prevalent in seventeenth-century Plymouth, colonists "could find nothing at all to say in favor of anger." Robert St. George's work on "heated speech" in seventeenth-century New England concurs with this view. See Demos, *A Little Commonwealth: Family Life in Plymouth Colony* (New York, 1970), 137; St. George, " 'Heated' Speech and Literacy in Seventeenth-Century New England," in *Seventeenth-Century New England,* Colonial Society of Massachusetts, Publications, LXIII, Collections (Boston, 1984), 275–322.

79 "The Maiden's Best Adorning, or A Father's Advice to His Daughter," in Mary Flower's Commonplace Book, 1757, Haverford College Quaker Collection (HCQC), Haverford, Pa.

80 "Dear Clemy since the single state, you've left and chose yourself a mate . . . ," anonymous poem, Dec. 8, 1768, Plumstead Papers, HSP. Though these lines

may initially appear to present a revolutionary inversion of the traditional association of men with rationalism and women with emotionalism, such an interpretation offers at best a distorted oversimplification. These verses do imply that rage, like war, remained an appropriate element of masculine action. But the proper place of reason also remained in the heart of man. Though a good wife could help her husband recover his reason, she was nowhere encouraged to try to claim it for her own.

81 *PG*, June 9, 1773.

82 James Kenny, "A Journal Kept by James Kenny on his journey to Pittsburgh and notes or remarks of what he judged worth taking notice of while he remained there," 1761, HSP.

83 Ibid., 4 Seventh Month 1761, 18 Ninth Month 1761, and 4 Eleventh Month 1762.

84 Ibid., 4 Seventh Month 1761, 18 Sixth Month 1762.

85 Ibid., 20 Third Month 1763, 29 Fifth Month 1763.

86 Ibid., 27 Second Month 1763.

87 Chew Diary, Oct. 20, 1758.

88 Chew Diary, Oct. 20, 1758; "A Short Account of the Travels, Services, and Labours in Love in the Work of the Ministry of the Dear and Faithful Servant of Jesus Christ, William Hunt, deceased . . . ," in William Hunt's Journal (1733–1772), HCQC.

89 *PG*, Dec. 29, 1763.

90 *PG*, Aug. 21, 1755, Aug. 14, 1760.

91 *PG*, Sept. 12, 1754.

92 *PG*, Nov. 28, 1754. This is not, of course, to argue that social distinctions based on anger were ever eradicated entirely any more than one would argue that social distinctions themselves were completely eliminated. On continuing connections between anger expression and status, see John F. Kasson, *Rudeness and Civility: Manners in Nineteenth-Century Urban America* (New York, 1990), 159–160.

93 William Denny, "Run Away from the Subscriber," *PG*, Sept. 18, 1766.

Chapter Five

1 Modest silent clarifications of spelling and punctuation have been made in some quotations.

On Anglo-French debates about civility, savagery, and barbarism (with particular emphasis on Pennsylvania), see David A. Bell, "English Barbarians and French Martyrs," in Bell, *The Cult of Nation in France: Inventing National-*

ism, *1680–1800* (Cambridge, Mass., 2003), 78–106. See also Gordon M. Sayre, *Les Sauvages Américains: Representations of Native Americans in French and English Colonial Literature* (Chapel Hill, N.C., 1997), 251. On enduring connections between sentiment and civility, see Andrew R. L. Cayton, " 'Noble Actors' upon 'the Theater of Honor': Power and Civility in the Treaty of Grenville," in Cayton and Fredrika J. Teute, eds., *Contact Points: American Frontiers from the Mohawk Valley to the Mississippi, 1750–1830* (Chapel Hill, N.C., 1998), 240, 245.

For good basic accounts of the political contests between Quakers and their rivals in Pennsylvania during the Seven Years War period, see Joseph E. Illick, *Colonial Pennsylvania: A History* (New York, 1976); Joseph J. Kelley, Jr., *Pennsylvania: The Colonial Years, 1681–1776* (New York, 1980). For elucidation of the religious elements undergirding Quaker–non-Quaker social and political rivalries, see Sally Schwartz, *"A Mixed Multitude": The Struggle for Toleration in Colonial Pennsylvania* (New York, 1988).

For accounts of the Seven Years War as a whole, see Fred Anderson, *Crucible of War: The Seven Years' War and the Fate of Empire in British North America, 1754–1766* (New York, 2000); Francis Jennings, *Empire of Fortune: Crowns, Colonies, and Tribes in the Seven Years War in North America* (New York, 1988).

2 Alan Tully argues for the importance of studying the politics of colonial Pennsylvania, both as a means of extending our understanding the roots of American political philosophy in the pre-Revolutionary era and as a means of expanding the geographic scope of early American political history. See *Forming American Politics: Ideals, Interests, and Institutions in Colonial New York and Pennsylvania* (Baltimore, 1994), 2–3, 126.

3 Society of Friends, *An Epistle from Our General Spring Meeting . . . 1755 . . .* (Philadephia, 1755), 1; Francis Alison, *Peace and Union Recommended . . .* (Philadelphia, 1758), 24. "Move, v.," 1a, 7a, 8, 9b, *Oxford English Dictionary Online* (2001) (cited hereafter as *OED*).

4 On the enduring impact of war on the "American historical dialectic," see Fred Anderson and Andrew Cayton, *The Dominion of War: Empire and Liberty in North America, 1500–2000* (New York, 2005), xxiv.

5 The combined influence of "heart religions" and moral philosophy had a profound effect on the role of emotional language in political rhetoric. Even Jon Butler, who has cast the Great Awakening as an "interpretive fiction," concedes that "a significant number of New England ministers changed their preaching styles as a result of the 1740s revivals." In Pennsylvania, too, preachers in diverse denominations from Lutherans to Anglicans and Presbyterians

came to rely on the emotions. This new reliance on the rhetoric of emotion— far from being a superficial distraction from the real issues of the Awakening —had a profound influence on political debates. See Butler, "Enthusiasm Described and Decried: The Great Awakening as Interpretive Fiction," *Journal of American History*, LXIX (1982–1983), 305–325, esp. 314, 319, 320, 324; Alan Heimert, *Religion and the American Mind from the Great Awakening to the Revolution* (Cambridge, Mass., 1966), esp. chap. 6.

On the role of religious leaders in providing an important source of unity during the Seven Years War era, see Harry S. Stout, *The New England Soul: Preaching and Religious Culture in Colonial New England* (New York, 1986), 244, 248; Gary B. Nash, "The Transformation of Urban Politics, 1700–1765," *JAH*, LX (1973–1974), 606, 625.

On the role of ministers in transmitting the ideas of Scottish revival philosophy in the middle colonies, see Richard B. Sher and Jeffrey R. Smitten, eds., *Scotland and America in the Age of Enlightenment* (Princeton, N.J., 1990); Sher, "Making Scottish Books in America, 1770–1784," in Sher, *The Enlightenment and the Book: Scottish Authors and Their Publishers in Eighteenth-Century Britain, Ireland, and America* (Chicago, 2006). On New England, see Evan Radcliffe, "Revolutionary Writing, Moral Philosophy, and Universal Benevolence in the Eighteenth Century," *Journal of the History of Ideas*, LIV (1993), 221–240, esp. 221.

6 Benjamin Franklin began discussions of the need to provide for defense in 1747. His proposals, set out in the pamphlet *Plain Truth*, met with a mixed response from Quakers, who were themselves somewhat divided about the permissibility of defensive war. But his proposals were eagerly taken up, indeed taken over, by those who styled themselves Quaker rivals. See [Benjamin Franklin], *Plain Truth; or, Serious Considerations on the Present State of the City of Philadelphia, and Province of Pennsylvania* ([Philadelphia], 1747).

7 Society of Friends, *An Epistle from Our Yearly-Meeting, Held at Burlington . . . Seventh Month . . . 1746* ([Philadelphia, 1746]), 2.

8 Ibid., 1, 3. It is important to emphasize the distinction Quakers drew between passions, which they universally decried, and feelings, for which they had nothing but praise. Thus, one Quaker elder might remind another of the importance of "delivering innocent truths in such language as the spirit thereof feelingly dictates," and a second might lament "the want of solid skillful, vigilant elders, capable of feeling." See John Churchman to John Pemberton, 30 Third Month 1754, William Brown Letterbook, Brown Family Papers, Historical Society of Pennsylvania (HSP), Philadelphia, and Thomas Greer to William Brown, Dungannon, 26 Seventh Month 1761.

9 Gilbert Tennent, *The Late Association for Defence, Encourag'd; or, The Lawful-ness of Defensive War* . . . (Philadelphia, [1748]).

10 Ibid., 9, 34.

11 Ibid.

12 Ibid., 38.

13 John Smith, *The Doctrine of Christianity, as Held by the People Called Quakers, Vindicated: In Answer to Gilbert Tennent's Sermon on the Lawfulness of War* (Philadelphia, 1748), 2, 27, 54–56. For Smith's own account of writing and publishing this pamphlet, see John Smith, *The Diary of John Smith,* in Albert Cook Myers, *Hannah Logans Courtship . . . and Divers Other Matters . . . as Related in the Diary of . . . John Smith . . .* (Philadelphia, 1904).

14 Smith, *The Doctrine of Christianity,* 1, 36. To be sure, in quieter times, the Quaker faith left plenty of space for the development of the self, for the creation of personal connections between Christ and his followers. Yet, as the volume of their debates with Pennsylvania's prowar faction increased, they began to articulate a more extreme stance against the self. Overshadowed by misgivings about the social costs of selfishness, positive views of the self were seldom voiced by Quakers in this period.

15 Ibid., 4; Tennent, *Defence, Encourag'd,* 10.

16 Society of Friends, *An Epistle from Our General Spring Meeting, 1755,* 1–3. This characterization of Quakers as opposed to military actions of any kind re-quires qualification. In fact, some Quakers, Isaac Norris prominent among them, remained in the Assembly throughout the war and voted in favor of measures of defense. To some extent, then, charges that Quakers opposed even defensive wars were simply politically expedient accusations leveled by rivals determined to loosen Quaker control of the Assembly by any means possible. On Quaker divisions, see John J. Zimmerman, "Benjamin Franklin and the Quaker Party, 1755–1756," *William and Mary Quarterly,* 3d Ser., XVII (1960), 293.

17 Philip Reading, *The Protestant's Danger, and the Protestant's Duty: A Sermon on the Occasion of the Encroachments of the French . . .* (Philadelphia, 1755), 26.

18 William Smith, "Preface," in Thomas Barton, *Unanimity and Public Spirit: A Sermon Preached at Carlisle . . .* (Philadelphia, 1755). The pamphlet in ques-tion damned Quakers directly for the defenseless state of the colony and blamed their continued political power on the support of "insolent, sullen, and turbulent" Germans. See [William Smith], *A Brief State of the Province of Pennsylvania . . . in a Letter . . . to His Friend in London . . .* (London, 1755), 28. For a colorful account of the "incendiary impact" of this pamphlet in London and Philadelphia, see Tully, *Forming American Politics,* 111–116.

19 Smith, in Barton, *Unanimity and Public Spirit*, vi, xiii, xiv.

20 Barton, *Unanimity and Public Spirit*, 2.

21 Ibid., 4, 7–8.

22 Smith, in Barton, *Unanimity and Public Spirit*, xi. On the theoretical connec-
    tions between divine attributes and human benevolence, see Norman S.
    Fiering, "Irresistible Compassion: An Aspect of Eighteenth-Century Sympa-
    thy and Humanitarianism," *Journal of the History of Ideas,* XXXVII (1976),
    195–218, esp. 208.

23 Smith, in Barton, *Unanimity and Public Spirit*, xi.

24 Isaac Norris, Speaker, "A Message to the Governor from the Assembly," *Penn-
    sylvania Gazette,* Aug. 14, 1755 (hereafter cited as *PG*). In opposing executive
    power, the Pennsylvania legislature would have paralleled efforts in many
    other colonies to assert local control in opposition to transatlantic directives.
    On the prevalence and persistence of colonial localism, see Anderson and
    Cayton, *The Dominion of War,* 140.

25 "Copies of Several Public Papers Which Have Passed in the Province of
    Pennsylvania in the Month of November, 1755," HSP, in Library Company of
    Philadelphia.

26 Ibid.

27 For an alternative account of the elections, which stresses Quaker resiliency
    but concedes the loss of their legislative majority, see Tully, *Forming American
    Politics,* 151–156, esp. 156.

28 John Abr. Lidenius, *The Lawfulness of Defensive War . . .* (Philadelphia, 1756),
    13–16.

29 Ibid., 16.

30 John Bartram to Peter, Feb. 4, 1756, John Bartram Letterbook, Bartram Pa-
    pers, HSP.

31 Lidenius, *Defensive War,* 14.

32 Gilbert Tennent, *The Happiness of Rewarding the Enemies of Our Religion and
    Liberty . . .* (Philadelphia, 1756), 17, 32.

33 Ibid., 7.

34 [Nicholas Scull], *Kawanio Che Keeteru: A True Relation of a Bloody Battle
    Fought between George and Lewis, in the Year 1755* (Philadelphia, 1756), 9, 15.

35 *An Address to Those Quakers, Who Perversely Refused to Pay Any Regard to the
    Late Provincial Fast . . .* (Philadelphia, 1756), 1.

36 [Scull], *George and Lewis,* 16. On the image of the cuckold in eighteenth-
    century Philadelphia, see Toby L. Ditz, "Shipwrecked; or, Masculinity Im-
    periled: Mercantile Representations of Failure and the Gendered Self in

Eighteenth-Century Philadelphia," *Journal of Social History*, LXXXI (1994–1995), 51–80.

37 *To Quakers Who Refused*, 7, query 8.

38 Ibid., query 16.

39 William Smith, *The Christian Soldier's Duty* . . . (Philadelphia, 1757), 16, 24. Presumably Smith took the trouble to describe the enthusiasm he had in mind as "rational" to differentiate it from the "giddy enthusiasm" for which Quakers had been much criticized during the previous year.

40 Ibid., 6, 16, 27, 32.

41 Ibid., title page.

42 Matthias Harris, *A Sermon Preached in the Church of St. Peters* . . . (Philadelphia, 1757), 26.

43 Friendly Association, *To William Denny . . . The Address of the Trustees and Treasurer of the Friendly Association for Regaining and Preserving Peace with the Indians by Pacific Measures* (Philadelphia, 1757), 1.

44 Society of Friends, *An Apology for the People Called Quakers . . . 1756* (Philadelphia, 1757), 1.

45 Ibid., 3.

46 Samuel Finley, *The Curse of Meroz; or, The Danger of Neutrality* . . . (Philadelphia, 1757), 5, 6.

47 Ibid., 22, 28.

48 Ibid., 7, 22.

49 On the continued electoral success of the Quaker party, see Tully, *Forming American Politics*, 203–209, 272–274, esp. 305–309. Tully attributes this to the development of a Quaker party made up of pragmatic Quakers and their allies in various religious denominations who all adhered to what he has aptly termed an ideology of "civil Quakerism" (258).

50 On the role of the Quaker Friendly Association in peace negotiations, see Jennings, *Empire of Fortune*, 342–348, 396–403.

   Smith's public pronouncements in favor of war as well as passion had no doubt been a constant irritant to pacifist Quakers. For a comprehensive account of the Smith libel case, see Peter C. Hoffer, "Law and Liberty: In the Matter of Provost William Smith of Philadelphia, 1758," *WMQ*, 3d Ser., XXXVIII (1981), 681–701; and see Nash, "The Transformation of Urban Politics," *JAH*, LX (1973–1974), 626; Tully, *Forming American Politics*, 119–121.

51 Ebenezer Durham, *To the Inhabitants of the Province of Pennsylvania* (Philadelphia, [1758]), 1.

52 Alison, *Peace and Union Recommended*, 24.

53 "Warm, a.," 1, 10a, 10b, 11, 12a, *OED*.

54 Alison, *Peace and Union Recommended*, 24–25.

55 Gilbert Tennent, *Sermons on Important Subjects* . . . (Philadelphia, 1758), v, vi, 1. For a summary of Tennent's role in both the healing of the Presbyterian schism and the awakening at the College of New Jersey, see Milton J. Coalter, Jr., *Gilbert Tennent, Son of Thunder: A Case Study of Continental Pietism's Impact on the First Great Awakening in the Middle Colonies* (New York, 1986), 156. See also Stout, *The New England Soul;* and see Ned Landsman's discussion of enthusiasm in the context of middle colonies awakenings, "Revivalism and Nativism in the Middle Colonies: The Great Awakening and the Scots Community in East New Jersey," *American Quarterly*, XXXIV (1982), 149–164.

56 Humphrey Scourge [pseud.], *Tit for Tat; or, The Score Wip'd Off* (New York, 1758), 2. Authorship of this pamphlet has never been established, and it is unclear whether it was actually written by a Quaker or simply by a Quaker supporter. Ralph L. Ketcham, for one, speculates with some credibility that the author might even have been Benjamin Franklin: "Conscience, War, and Politics in Pennsylvania, 1755–1757," *WMQ*, 3d Ser., XX (1963), 416–439.

57 Scourge, *Tit for Tat*, 1, 2.

58 Philo-Pennsylvaniae [pseud.], *A Serious Address to the Freeholders and Other Inhabitants, of the Province of Pennsylvania* (New York, 1758), 8, 13.

59 Society of Friends, *From Our Yearly Meeting Held at Philadelphia . . . 1759* (Philadelphia, 1759), 2, 3.

60 Society of Friends, *The Epistle from Our Yearly-Meeting, for New-Jersey and Pennsylvania . . . 1760* (Philadelphia, 1760), 4.

61 Gilbert Tennent, *A Persuasive to the Right Use of the Passions in Religion . . .* (Philadelphia, 1760), 6, 8–13, 15.

62 Friends, *Epistle, 1760*, 3, 4; Tennent, *Passions in Religion*, 10.

63 Society of Friends, *The Address of the People Call'd Quakers, in the Province of Pennsylvania, to John Penn, Esq.* . . . (Philadelphia, 1764), 7, 8.

64 For an excellent analysis of broad Anglo-American philosophical debates on how to harness the emotions for moral ends, see Albert O. Hirschman, *The Passions and the Interests: Political Arguments for Capitalism before Its Triumph* (Princeton, N.J., 1982).

65 A close consideration of the rhetoric of emotion can help us to arrive at a fuller understanding of the nuances of a political philosophy that emphasized shared feeling. My argument is that those who embraced emotion did so out of a considered desire to balance the competing ideals of liberalism and republicanism, the exigencies of self and society. However, I have avoided using the terms "liberalism" and "republicanism" in the text, believing that it

is more fruitful to consider eighteenth-century politics on its own terms and according to its own vocabulary—to listen to the language of feeling—than to try to pigeonhole it according to what Daniel T. Rodgers has scathingly referred to as the "taxonomic tics of political theorists." See Rodgers, "Republicanism: The Career of a Concept," *JAH*, LXXIX (1992–1993), 11–38, esp. 36. On debates about the ethics of self-interest within colonial America, see Tully, *Forming American Politics*, 397; John M. Murrin, "Gordon S. Wood and the Search for Liberal America," *WMQ*, 3d Ser., XLIV (1987), 597–601, esp. 601. On the importance of sympathy in the formation of an American self-image, see Andrew Burstein, *A Sentimental Democracy: The Evolution of America's Romantic Self-Image* (New York, 1999).

Chapter Six

1 William Franklin to Dear Madame, London, Oct. 24, 1758, Elizabeth Graeme Fergusson Correspondence 1757–95, Historical Society of Pennsylvania (HSP), Philadelphia (hereafter cited as EGF Correspondence); Ann Graeme to Elizabeth Graeme, Dec. 3, 1762, EGF Correspondence. Modest silent clarifications of spelling and punctuation have been made in some quotations.

2 Dr. Thomas Graeme to Elizabeth Graeme, Jan. 8, 1763, EGF Correspondence.

3 Elizabeth Graeme Fergusson to Mrs. Campbell, May 9, 1779, cited in Simon Gratz, "Some Material for a Biography of Mrs. Elizabeth Fergusson, *née* Graeme," *Pennsylvania Magazine of History and Biography*, XLI (1917), 389; Eliza Stedman to Elizabeth Graeme, Aug. 7, 1762, EGF Correspondence.

4 *Pennsylvania Gazette*, May 27, 1756 (hereafter cited as *PG*).

5 Karen Halttunen discusses philosophical emphasis on sensibility as a "way to counteract the perils of rampant self-interest," in "Humanitarianism and the Pornography of Pain in Anglo-American Culture," *American Historical Review*, C (1995), 303–334, esp. 305. Literary scholar Elizabeth Barnes has also noted the oft-overlooked fact that the embrace of sympathetic emotions was initially intended to counter, not encourage, the growth of individualism; see *States of Sympathy: Seduction and Democracy in the American Novel* (New York, 1997), 14. For a similar view of the function of sympathy in contemporaneous *English* fiction, see Barbara M. Benedict, *Framing Feeling: Sentiment and Style in English Prose Fiction, 1745–1800* (New York, 1994), 6.

6 How the self, the passions, and society were interrelated formed the crux of eighteenth-century investigations in moral philosophy and influenced literature as well as everyday life. Barbara Benedict notes how "sentimental fictions represent the dialectic . . . between human isolation from the material world

and human interdependence" (*Framing Feeling*, 3). And see Janet Todd, *Sensibility: An Introduction* (London, 1986); Adela Pinch, *Strange Fits of Passion: Epistemologies of Emotion, Hume to Austen* (Stanford, Calif., 1996); Laura Wispé, *The Psychology of Sympathy* (New York, 1991). On the impact of the market economy on ideas about the self, see Jean-Christophe Agnew, *Worlds Apart: The Market and the Theater in Anglo-American Thought, 1550–1750* (New York, 1986). On the relationship between emotions, social relations, and economic relations, see John E. Crowley, "The Sensibility of Comfort," *AHR*, CIV (1999), 749–782, esp. 776. For analysis of how sentimentalism could constitute both "an appeal for the overcoming of hierarchy, and an indirect apology for hierarchy" (in the context of revolutionary France), see David J. Denby, *Sentimental Narrative and the Social Order in France, 1760–1820* (Cambridge, 1994), 243.

7 "A Few Extracts from E. G.'s Journal," 1764, cited in Catherine La Courreye Blecki and Karin A. Wulf, eds., *Milcah Martha Moore's Book: A Commonplace Book from Early America* (University Park, Pa., 1997), 202. Toby L. Ditz, too, notes the futility of the exercise of sympathy as a means of overcoming the ascendance of the self; see "Shipwrecked; or, Masculinity Imperiled: Mercantile Representations of Failure and the Gendered Self in Eighteenth-Century Philadelphia," *Journal of American History*, LXXXI (1994–1995), 51–79, esp. 74.

8 Richard Peters to Elizabeth Graeme, Liverpool, Nov. 20, 1764, EGF Correspondence.

9 W[illia]m Attkinson to Phoebe Radcliffe, 13 Third Month 1721, Oliver Hough Family Papers (1721–1857), HSP; T. Wiley to Samuel Neale, Cork, 21 First Month 1753, William Brown Letterbook, Brown Family Papers, HSP (hereafter cited as Brown Letterbook).

A very similar view of the relation between emotion and individualism is offered by French literary scholar Anne Vincent-Buffault. On the one hand, she posits that emotions initially gained favor in the eighteenth century as a means of forging bonds between people, yet she stresses that the subjective experience of emotion ultimately led to the discovery of self: see *History of Tears: Sensibility and Sentimentality in France*, trans. Teresa Bridgeman (New York, 1991), vii–ix, 38–39. However, other scholars probing the relationship between emotion and individualism have viewed the issue in decidedly different terms. Alan T. McKenzie, for example, argues that passions served just the purpose that eighteenth-century writers hoped they would, helping to forge social bonds at the expense of individual subjectivity. Responding explicitly to McKenzie, Adela Pinch questions whether emotions necessarily bore any direct relation (positive or negative) to the development of individualism. By contrast, I argue that the history of passions and the history of individuality were intimately intertwined, despite the fact that eighteenth-century actors were not themselves always clear on just how they were related. The key to containing these many contradictions is to recognize that in the eighteenth century there were two simultaneous, overlapping, and competing visions of the self. See Pinch, *Certain Lively Episodes: The Articulation of Passion in Eighteenth-Century Prose* (Athens, Ga., 1990), 20; Pinch, *Strange Fits of Passion,* 196.

10 Samuel Neale to ——, Dublin, 29 Twelfth Month 1753, Brown Letterbook.

11 "Some Account of the Convincement Christian Experiences and Travels of Jane Hoskins, 1760," cited in "Mary Brown, Her Book," Brown Family Papers, HSP (hereafter cited as Jane Hoskins in MBHB).

12 William Logan to John Churchman, 19 Eighth Month 1756, William Logan Letters, in the Maria Dickinson Logan Papers, HSP; Samuel Allinson, "Friendship," Samuel Allinson Common Place Book, 1761, 31, Haverford College Quaker Collection, Haverford, Pa. (HCQC).

13 Edward Shippen to Thomas Lawrence, Lancaster, Jan. 28, 1754, Thomas Lawrence Papers, 1689–1754, Lawrence Collection, HSP (hereafter cited as Lawrence Collection); Tace Bradford to Thomas Bradford, Aug. 18, 1760, Bradford Collection Correspondence 1747–1795, HSP (hereafter cited as Bradford Correspondence); John Swift to John White, 1761, John Swift Papers, 1740–1789, Swift Family Papers, HSP (hereafter cited as Swift Papers).

14 Elizabeth Graeme to Reverend Richard Peters, London, Jan. 18, 1765, in Gratz, "Some Material for a Biography," *PMHB,* XXXIX (1915), 386; Elizabeth Graeme, "Remarks on the Passage from Philadelphia to Liverpool," June 1764, in Blecki and Wulf, eds., *Milcah Martha Moore's Book,* 200, 201.

15 Richard Peters to Elizabeth Graeme, Liverpool, Dec. 14, 1764, EGF Correspondence; "A Few Extracts from E. G.'s Journal," Blecki and Wulf, eds., *Milcah Martha Moore's Book,* 203.

16 Scholars have taken a wide variety of positions on the gendering of sentiment. Some, picking up the topic of sensibility only in the late-eighteenth century, accept the assumption that sensibility arose out of a distinctively feminine culture. See, for example, Julia Stern, *The Plight of Feeling: Sympathy and Dissent in the Early American Novel* (Chicago, 1997), 2–3. Others argue only for a gradual feminization of sentiment over time: for example, Robert A. Erickson, *The Language of the Heart, 1600–1750* (Philadelphia, 1997), xi; Pinch, *Strange Fits of Passion,* 25. Still others insist that sensibility continued to play an important role in masculine culture through the nineteenth cen-

tury. For this view, see Mary Chapman and Glenn Hendler, eds., *Sentimental Men: Masculinity and the Politics of Affect in American Culture* (Berkeley, Calif., 1999), 8. Another approach has been to accept the association between femininity and sensibility but to ask what hegemonic purposes such an association served. On this point, see Claude Rawson, *Satire and Sentiment, 1660–1830* (Cambridge, 1994), 210; Laura Hinton, *The Perverse Gaze of Sympathy: Sadomasochistic Sentiments from "Clarissa" to "Rescue 911"* (Albany, N.Y., 1999), 3.

On balance, it seems clear that men were always deeply involved as writers, thinkers, and everyday actors in the production and construction of the culture of emotion. But there does seem to have been a reduction over time in how openly associated men were with such culture. More important, it is crucial not to speak as though there was *one* emotional culture that stretched, unvaried, over the eighteenth century and applied equally to men and women alike. On the contrary, even in eras when both men and women were urged to cultivate their capacity for feeling, distinct differences could remain in just which men and women deserved to receive such feeling.

17 *PG*, Oct. 9, 1760.

18 *PG*, Dec. 21, 1769.

19 *PG*, Jan. 1, 1751. That this description of the risks associated with crying predates the onset of the Seven Years War is almost certainly significant. See below.

20 *PG*, Mar. 13, 1760, "Pangyrical Verses on the Death of General Wolfe"; *PG*, June 9, 1773.

21 *PG*, Apr. 10, 1760.

22 *PG*, July 12, 1759. Just as women had earlier been viewed as more prone to bodily desires and willful passions than men, so they were now held more likely to give way to problematic tears for the private concerns of self. Anne Vincent-Buffault has also noticed this tendency to validate public over private tears in eighteenth-century French literature; see *The History of Tears*, 9.

23 *PG*, Sept. 5, 1754. On "dialectical structure that endorses yet edits the feelings" "in order to satisfy the [eighteenth-century] audience's taste for sentiment while preserving the rules of decorum and restraint," see Benedict, *Framing Feeling*, 1.

24 R. G. to Friend, Philadelphia, Fifth Month 1760, Brown Letterbook; JH (Joshua Howell) to Elizabeth Sandwith, Oct. 16, 1752, Drinker and Sandwith Family Papers, HSP.

25 M. Treat to Thomas Bradford, New York, Jan. 17, 1767, Bradford Correspondence.

26 Jim Clark to Thomas Bradford, New York, Nov. 9, 1762, Bradford Correspondence. Clark's phrase "I turn my eyes" is striking in light of eighteenth-century spectral theory, which posited that the visual perception of suffering was what prompted feelings of sympathy. That Clark made the explicit choice to cast himself as a spectator, as one who "gazed" on the misfortunes of others, reinforces the interpretation that he did not believe he was asking for sympathy for himself, but rather for those with whom he sympathized. For a study of sensibility that focuses on the importance of spectatorship, see Ann Jessie Van Sant, *Eighteenth-Century Sensibility and the Novel: The Senses in Social Context* (New York, 1993), xi.

27 Ann Graeme to Elizabeth Graeme, Dec. 3, 1762, EGF Correspondence. Noted at the end of the letter, in Elizabeth Graeme's handwriting, are the words "Letter Relative to my breaking with Mr. W. Franklin 1762." Vincent-Buffault claims that such episodes of fatherly feeling gained particularly important cultural resonance in the eighteenth century; see *The History of Tears*, 20–21.

28 Richard Peters to Elizabeth Graeme, Liverpool, Jan. 3, 1765, EGF Correspondence.

29 Juliana Ritchie to Elizabeth Graeme, Jan. 27, 1765, EGF Correspondence. The pastimes of Ritchie and Graeme are described in this letter. See also JR to EG, July 9, 1765, and EGF to JR, Philadelphia, 1795, cited in Gratz, "Some Material for a Biography," *PMHB*, XXXIX (1915), 408.

30 *PG*, Jan. 20, 1730.

31 *PG*, Feb. 24, 1730.

32 In his classic study of the Senecas Anthony F. C. Wallace discusses the ritual aspects of torture in native American religious life, noting that "tormentors" hoped not to inflict "emotional collapse," but rather to inspire "unconquerable self-control . . . defiance and self-respect"; see *The Death and Rebirth of the Seneca* (New York, 1972), 103–107. If evidence for the Senecas can be extrapolated for the Shawnees, it would seem that what these British-American observers reported as a lack of feeling could have been more accurately described as the successful control of its outward expression. For another thoughtful, corroborating interpretation of native American attitudes toward stoic suffering, see Gordon M. Sayre, *Les Sauvages Américains: Representations of Native Americans in French and English Colonial Literature* (Chapel Hill, N.C., 1997), 297. On European claims about the insensibility of "savages," see David B. Morris, *The Culture of Pain* (Berkeley, Calif., 1991), 39.

33 In the course of research for this project, all 3,469 articles containing any variant of the word "Negro" to appear in keyword searches of the digitized *Pennsylvania Gazette* from 1728 to 1776 were read, analyzed, and cataloged. In

no instance was a "Negro" ever mentioned in positive *or* negative association with the display of pity, compassion, or sympathy. As explained below, a "negro" was criticized on occasion for lack of "mercy," but only in articles written outside the colony. See *Pennsylvania Gazette* online. (All further keyword searches of the *Gazette* discussed in this chapter refer to this database.)

34 For the case of "Spanish John," see *PG*, June 23, 1748. For discussions of a "negro" as cruel or merciless that originated outside the colony but were printed in the *Gazette,* see, for example, *PG*, Dec. 13, 1753, July 19, 1759, Jan. 26, 1764, Oct. 12, 1769.

35 *PG*, Aug. 11, 1748.

36 *PG*, Sept. 30, Nov. 18, 1756, Dec. 27, 1759.

37 *PG*, Apr. 10, 1760. Whether Indians were regarded as racially versus culturally distinct from Europeans is discussed at length in Chapter 8.

38 "A Parody on Pope's Prologue to Cato, Addressed to Mr. Henry Bridges, Constructor of That Elaborate piece of Mechanism, the Microcosm," *PG*, Jan. 22, 1756.

39 *PG*, Aug. 17, 1769, Sept. 7, 28, 1769. On the dying Indian as "vehicle for sentiment," see Laura M. Stevens, *The Poor Indians: British Missionaries, Native Americans, and Colonial Sensibility* (Philadelphia, 2004), 160–194, esp. 194.

40 *PG*, Sept. 7, 1769. Andrew R. L. Cayton writes perceptively on native American understandings of sympathy and the ways they were capitalized on by Americans in "'Noble Actors' upon 'The Theater of Honor': Power and Civility in the Treaty of Grenville," in Cayton and Fredrika J. Teute, eds., *Contact Points: American Frontiers from the Mohawk Valley to the Mississippi, 1750–1830* (Chapel Hill, N.C., 1998), 235–269, esp. 258–259. For another view of the changing face of native American emotion, as painted in Anglo-American literature, see Michelle Burnham, *Captivity and Sentiment: Cultural Exchange in American Literature, 1682–1861* (Hanover, N.H., 1997).

41 Mary Redman to EGF, Oct. 2, 1722, in Gratz, "Some Material for a Biography," *PMHB*, XXXIX (1915), 283.

42 EGF to JR, Philadelphia, 1795, ibid., 408; Juliana Ritchie to Elizabeth Graeme, Jan. 27, 1765, EGF Correspondence.

43 Elizabeth Graeme, "A Few Extracts from E. G.'s Journal," in Blecki and Wulf, eds., *Milcah Martha Moore's Book,* 204–206.

44 *PG*, Jan. 11, 1733.

45 Edward Shippen to Col. James Burd, Lancaster, July 29, 1758, Papers of the Shippen Family, HSP (hereafter cited as Shippen Papers), and Francis Hopkinson to Mary Hopkinson, Hartlebury Castle, Aug. 10, 1766, Hopkinson Family Letters, 1736–1800, Hopkinson Papers, HSP (hereafter cited as Hop-

kinson Papers). Stephen C. Bullock has also noted the importance of shows of shared feeling in helping a man establish status as a gentleman: see "A Mumper among the Gentle: Tom Bell, Colonial Confidence Man," *WMQ*, 3d Ser., LV (1998), 231–258, esp. 247, 251.

46 Joseph Shippen to Edward Shippen, Camp at Rays Town, Aug. 15, 1758, Shippen Papers.

47 George Morgan, George Morgan Journal and Letterbook, 1767–68, HSP, 229.

48 Charles Norris to Messrs. Williams and Rockecliff and Capt Martin, Philadelphia, Apr. 25, 1746, C. Norris Letterbook, 1744–47, Norris Family Letters, Norris Family Papers, HSP (hereafter cited as Norris Papers); Thomas Lawrence to Messrs. Williams and Rockcliff, Philadelphia, Nov. 20, 1747, Lawrence Collection; John Smith to Isaac Walker, Jr., 3 Fourth Month 1751, the Letterbooks of John Smith (1722–1771), HCQC; Joseph Swift to John Swift, London, Feb. 12, 1757, Swift Papers. Evidently, Norris and Lawrence were corresponding with the same merchants. This is a sheer coincidence; their letters are in different collections at the HSP, and I have found no correspondence at all between Norris and Lawrence themselves. Norris was a Quaker; Lawrence was not. If anything, this coincidence indicates just how small merchant circles remained in mid-eighteenth-century Philadelphia and just how much need there would have been for bonds of feeling to supplement lines of credit.

49 *PG*, Mar. 6, 1776. Of course, the emotional fortitude this servant displayed while being whipped could well have been intended as a sign of manly strength, a display that might have irked his master as much as his original offense. But the master does not seem to have interpreted his servant's lack of tears in this favorable light. On the contrary, the servant's absence of tears, like that of the tortured Indian and German baby earlier, seems to have been offered as evidence of his lack of humanity and civility. Ultimately, whatever a servant did was bound to be interpreted as evidence of inferiority by members of the master class. The crucial point here is that this servant was derided for his dearth of feeling rather than for excessive passion. Elaine Forman Crane, writing on pain, has arrived at a similar analysis of portrayals of stoicism among native Americans and low-ranking members of Anglo-American society; see "'I Have Suffer'd Much Today': The Defining Force of Pain in Early America," in Ronald Hoffman, Mechal Sobel, and Fredrika J. Teute, eds., *Through a Glass Darkly: Reflections on Personal Identity in Early America* (Chapel Hill, N.C., 1997), 379.

50 Thomas Chase to John Yeates, July 27, 1733, Jasper Yeates Correspondence, Yeates Family Papers, HSP.

51 Samuel Allinson, *PG*, Nov. 16, 1774. David Denby notes that, in sentimentalism, tearful victims are nearly always credited with moral virtue. Such valorization of victimization adds pressure on those more empowered to match this goodness in turn. The observation and alleviation of suffering thus figured at the very center of philosophical theories of the development of the moral sense. See Denby, *Sentimental Narrative and the Social Order in France*, 2, 130.

52 Edward Shippen to Governor Morris, Lancaster, Aug. 4, 1756, Shippen Papers; Arch'd Kennedy to Richard Peters, New York, Aug. 12, 1757, Chew Family Papers, HSP.

53 Francis Hopkinson to Elizabeth Graeme, London, Feb. 21, 1767, Hopkinson Papers.

54 Peggy Emlen to Sally Logan, Philadelphia, July 9, 11, 1770, Margaret Emlen Letters 1768–71, Marjorie Brown Collection, HSP (hereafter cited as Emlen Letters); "A Few Extracts from E. G.'s Journal," in Blecki and Wulf, eds., *Milcah Martha Moore's Book*, 211.

55 To this list of words that describe feelings for others we might also add *commiseration, condolence,* and *empathy.* For various reasons, these words will not be considered in detail here (see below). *Commiseration,* defined simply as "a feeling or expression of pity or compassion," actually does seem to be simply a synonym, with few if any distinguishing nuances of meaning. In any case, it was used only rarely in the eighteenth century. *Condolence,* on the other hand, is of such specific denotation that its selection in a given situation is always easily explained. It is invariably used to describe "sympathetic grief." Used exclusively in the context of mourning, the choice of the word *condolence* seldom, in itself, carries significant social symbolism. Expressions of grief did of course carry important social consequences, which will be analyzed at length in Chapter 7. Finally, as for *empathy,* it is a twentieth-century coinage invented in the context of German psychological theory and altogether unknown in the eighteenth century. "Commiseration," 1b; "Condolence," 1, 2; "Empathy," *Oxford English Dictionary Online,* 2d ed., 2001. All subsequent citations from the *OED* are noted as such in the text and refer to this database.

56 Although numerous scholars, including Adela Pinch, Ann Jessie Van Sant, and Janet Todd, have offered thoughtful discussions of distinctions between the meanings of various words for emotion, they have seldom distinguished between words for feeling and the words for *fellow* feeling associated with the culture of sensibility, much less discriminated between the various synonyms for fellow feeling. Literary scholar Julie Ellison declares: "What these terms have in common is much more important than what differentiates them from

one another. . . . One of the reasons why it is difficult to stabilize the meanings of terms like 'sensibility,' 'sympathy,' and 'sentiment' is that they . . . vary according to their usage in distinct historical contexts." However, when we do consider the shades of meaning contained and the cultural changes reflected in the evolving emotional vocabulary of the eighteenth century, we can glean what, to historians, at least, is valuable information about "distinct historical contexts." See Ellison, *Cato's Tears and the Making of Anglo-American Emotion* (Chicago, 1999), 5.

57 "Mercy," 1a, b, *OED*. These definitions for *mercy* date back to the thirteenth century and are still current. "Proceedings of a Court Martial held in camp at Reas Town, the 30th August 1758, by order of the commanding officer, Capt. John Paine president," in Shippen Papers; James Kenny, "A Journal to the Westward" (1758–61), 48, HSP; Ann Graeme to Elizabeth Graeme, Dec. 3, 1762, EGF Correspondence.

58 John Swift to Capt Robinson, Mar. 23, 1761, Swift Family Papers.

59 "Pity," 2a, 5, *OED*.

60 Peggy Emlen to Sally Logan, "Philad[elphia] January 7th day night," and "Philadelphia March 4th day afternoon," Emlen Letters.

61 Sophia Hume to Israel and Rachel Pemberton, Manchester, 25 Fifth Month 1749, Pemberton Family Papers, 1740–1780, HSP; *PG*, Apr. 19, 1759, Aug. 18, 1763. There *was* a specialized situation when the word *pity* was often used without an accompanying sense of condemnation; in cases of death, pity was often invoked. Still, pity for the suffering caused by death remained a passive kind of feeling; since nothing could be done to reverse death, people offering pity put themselves under no obligation to offer substantial assistance to the mourner. For more on the significance of active versus passive feeling, see below.

62 "Compassion," 1, 2, *OED*.

63 Sarah Harris to "Dear and Much Esteemed friend," Long Compton Warwickshire, Eighth Month 1751, Brown Letterbook, and Jane Hoskins in MBHB; *PG*, May 5, 1763, Feb. 28, 1765, Jan. 21, 1768, Apr. 11, 1771.

64 "Sympathy," 3a, 3b, *OED*; *PG*, Aug. 17, 1774.

65 Sociologist Candace Clark has theorized at length about how the sharing of feeling helps establish the terms of social relations. On the "micropolitical consequences" of "a sympathy transaction in the socioemotional economy," see Clark, *Misery and Company: Sympathy in Everyday Life* (Chicago, 1997), 228, 245.

66 *PG*, Nov. 15, 1753.

67 Isaac Norris to Jonathan Scurth, 7 Ninth Month 1732, Norris Papers.

68 In preparing these descriptive statistics, I have relied on the chronological divisions established by the creators of the digital version of the *Gazette*. Included are the six most common words for shared feeling that I identified: *mercy, pity, compassion, sympathy, commiseration,* and *condolence*. In doing keyword searches, I looked for all grammatical variants of each given word (*mercy, merciful, mercifully,* and so forth). To create comparisons on word usage I then analyzed every use of these words in the *Gazette* from 1728 to 1776.

69 Just when the age of sensibility began or ended remains contested. Janet Todd emphasizes the period from the 1740s to the 1770s, as does Barbara Benedict. Adela Pinch calls for recognition that a cultural "investment in finding feelings out" began in the late seventeenth century and stretched through to the early nineteenth century. Julie Ellison argues that the age of sensibility should be expanded considerably from its traditional confines. I would advance the following timeline: philosophical interest in emotion developed in a sustained way in Britain from the end of the seventeenth century. The rise of Quakerism, with its distinctive emotional practices, indicates that emotion was already a point of religious and cultural focus by the 1680s. I regard the 1730s to 1760s a critical period in Anglo-America when the rise of evangelical religions set the stage for wider-spread discussions about emotion. Debates linking passion to willfulness or, alternatively, to compassion or simply to human nature were extremely prevalent in this period. With the coming of sensibility, the dominant model of emotion became, not passion, but feeling, and especially feeling for others. But this turn toward feeling could not end the ascendance of the individual self, and, by the end of the eighteenth century, sensibility was deteriorating into sentimentalism. See Todd, *Sensibility: An Introduction,* 4; Benedict, *Framing Feeling,* 1; Pinch, *Strange Fits of Passion,* 11; Ellison, *Cato's Tears,* 6, 16–17.

70 Scholars are taking up the issue of active versus passive feelings for others, yet, even those few who discuss passivity have not considered the degree of "active principle," to use the eighteenth-century phrase, that was actually encoded in the words for shared feeling themselves. See, for example, Wispé, *The Psychology of Sympathy,* 158.

71 "Watts Ph[ilosophical] Es[says]," Joseph Shippen Commonplace Book, Feb. 18, 1751, 28, Shippen Papers; *PG,* Apr. 25, 1754; Elizabeth Graeme Fergusson to Mrs. Campbell, May 9, 1779, in Gratz, "Some Material for a Biography," *PMHB,* XLI (1917), 387. Such associations between action and passion were basic to many eighteenth-century philosophical theories on emotion. See

Janet Todd's discussion of Hume in *Sensibility: An Introduction*, 25–27; Pinch's commentary on the work of Henry Home, Lord Kames, whose *Elements of Criticism*, which discusses such issues, was first published in 1762 (Pinch, *Strange Fits of Passion*, 16). For a seventeenth-century comparison, see Susan James, *Passion and Action: The Emotions in Seventeenth-Century Philosophy* (New York, 1997).

72 *PG*, Dec. 18, 1744, July 19, 1764.

73 *PG*, Apr. 3, 1760, Dec. 5, 1765.

74 Literary theorist Elizabeth Barnes offers a perceptive related critique of the inability of sympathy to truly bridge gaps between people; see *States of Sympathy*, 4–5, 7; see also Barnes, "Affecting Relations: Pedagogy, Patriarchy, and the Politics of Sympathy," *American Literary History*, VIII (1996), 597–614. Writing on sentimental novels, Barbara Benedict makes a similar point about the limits of sympathetic identification, discussing the fact that even sympathy came to be viewed as just one more mark of gentility; see *Framing Feeling*, 11, 13.

75 Elizabeth Graeme to Richard Peters, Mar. 25, 1769, Elizabeth Graeme Fergusson Commonplace Book, HSP.

76 Ibid. Though Elizabeth Graeme Fergusson never published her version of the Psalms, they, along with much other original poetry, circulated widely in literary circles and can be found in manuscript at HSP. See Elizabeth Graeme Fergusson Commonplace Book, HSP. On Fergusson's far-reaching reputation, see David S. Shields, *Civil Tongues and Polite Letters in British America* (Chapel Hill, N.C., 1997), 126–140; Anne M. Osterhout, *The Most Learned Woman in America: A Life of Elizabeth Graeme Fergusson* (University Park, Pa., 2004).

77 Richard Peters to Elizabeth Graeme, Sept. 22, 1765, in Gratz, "Some Material for a Biography," *PMHB*, XXXIX (1915), 283, and Elizabeth Fergusson to Mrs. Campbell, May 9, 1779, *PMHB*, XLI (1917), 389.

78 Milcah Martha Moore, "Upon Leaving England," May 31, 1765, in Blecki and Wulf, eds., *Milcah Martha Moore's Book*, 206. Writing to Richard Peters in 1773, Elizabeth griped, "Old Joseph I must take care of Papa desired he always might; Then there is Andrew Bodin who used to doe nothing But gardin 25£. John Jinny 30 £[,] Sam 10 £[,] two maids 20 £. . . . Every Thing is [apprised] high the personal Estate is swelld out much above its real Value." Joseph and Sam, referred to without last names, were probably enslaved. Faced with a possible reduction in her own genteel standard of living, Graeme begrudged her family's servants any share in her father's estate, chafing at the fact that

even a man who did nothing but garden could count on getting twenty-five pounds. See Elizabeth Graeme Fergusson to Richard Peters, Feb. 5, 1773, in Gratz, "Some Material for a Biography," *PMHB*, XXXIX (1915), 389–390.

79 *PG*, Feb. 2, 1774.

80 *PG*, Oct. 26, Dec. 7, 1774.

81 Elizabeth Fergusson to Mrs. Campbell, May 9, 1779, in Gratz, "Some Material for a Biography," *PMHB*, XLI (1917), 386–387. In a brilliant critique of the limits of the culture of feeling, Julia Stern faults the passivity of sympathy, making particular reference to slavery, pointing out that American emphasis on feeling for others did not necessarily prompt active efforts to end inequality. See Stern, *The Plight of Feeling*, 25.

Chapter Seven

1 Tace Bradford to Thomas Bradford, Aug. 18, 20, 1760, William Bradford to Thomas Bradford, May 29, 1760, Bradford Family Correspondence, Historical Society of Pennsylvania (HSP), Philadelphia (hereafter cited as Bradford Correspondence). Modest silent corrections of spelling and punctuation have been made in the quotations cited here and throughout.

2 Tace Bradford to Thomas Bradford, n.d., and William Bradford to Thomas Bradford, Jan. 23, 1761, Bradford Correspondence.

3 "Grief," 2b, 7a, and "Grievance," 3, *Oxford English Dictionary Online*, 2d ed. (2001) (cited hereafter as *OED*).

   To foreground the social management of grief is not to imply that statements of sorrow, when made, were merely mechanical or manipulative. Nor is it to argue that any absence of tears indicates a corresponding lack of feeling on the part of early modern people. As the many moving accounts cited below show, eighteenth-century people clearly felt a full spectrum of feelings in the face of loss. Far from making any argument concerning the actual degree of emotional pain experienced by mourners, then, this chapter analyzes instead the directives issued to those who mourned and the responses given by the grieving. It focuses exclusively on understanding what factors framed discussions of sorrow, seeking to elucidate the expression, not the experience, of grief.

4 My exploration of the links between earthly and heavenly authority has been informed by the work of Max Weber. See Max Weber, *The Protestant Ethic and the Spirit of Capitalism*, trans. Talcott Parsons (Los Angeles, 1996); Weber, *Economy and Society: An Outline of Interpretive Sociology*, ed. Guenther Roth and Claus Wittich, trans. Ephraim Fischoff et al., 3 vols. (New York, 1968).

5 Tace Bradford to Thomas Bradford, Aug. 18, 1760, and Abbington, February 1760 [1761], Bradford Correspondence. From the content, it is clear the second letter quoted was written in 1761, not 1760, as dated. Both this letter and another letter from Tace, clearly dated Mar. 5, 1761, refer to the death of Samuel Davies (on which see below) and use the phrase "merry countenance." Also, all of William Bradford's letters on the subject date from that year as well.

6 Gilbert Tennent, *The Happiness of Rewarding the Enemies of Our Religion and Liberty* . . . (Philadelphia, 1756), 26; Tennent, *A Persuasive to the Right Use of the Passions in Religion* . . . (Philadelphia, 1760), 15.

7 S[ophi]a Hume to W[illia]m Brown, London, 19 Third Month 1752, William Brown Letterbook, Brown Family Papers, HSP (hereafter cited as Brown Letterbook); Ann Cooper Whitall, Ann Cooper Whitall Diary, 1760–62, Haverford College Quaker Collection (HCQC), 106. Hume's extensive correspondence with the Pemberton family documents her ties to the Philadelphia Quaker elite. See Pemberton Family Papers, 1740–1780, HSP.

8 *Pennsylvania Gazette,* Nov. 1, 1750 (hereafter cited as *PG*).

9 Conrad Weiser to ——, Feb. 8, 1750/1, Conrad Weiser Correspondence, 1741–1766, Conrad Weiser Papers, HSP; William Trent, William Trent Journal, 1759–1763, 7, 75, HSP.

10 Eliza Stedman to Elizabeth Graeme, Aug. 7, 1762, Elizabeth Graeme Fergusson Correspondence, HSP (hereafter cited as EGF Correspondence); Peggy Emlen to Betsy, n.d., Margaret Emlen Letters, 1768–71, Marjorie Brown Collection, HSP (hereafter cited as Emlen Letters); William Logan to Sally Logan, "Philadelphia 7th day evening" 1769, William Logan Letters, Maria Dickenson Logan Papers, HSP (hereafter cited as Logan Papers); E[dward] Tilghman to B[enjamin] Chew, Dec. 22, 1771, Chew Family Papers, HSP (hereafter cited as Chew Papers).

11 Eliza Stedman to Elizabeth Graeme, Aug. 7, 1762, EGF Correspondence; William Logan to John Churchman, May 24, 1751, Logan Papers; Peggy Emlen to Sally Logan, Philadelphia, February, "1st day night 1770," Emlen Letters. On links between refinement and the restraint of grief, see Jacquelyn C. Miller, "An 'Uncommon Tranquility of Mind': Emotional Self-Control and the Construction of a Middle-Class Identity in Eighteenth-Century Philadelphia," *Journal of Social History,* XXX (1996–1997), 129–148.

12 Isaac Norris to Joseph Pike, 10 Third Month 1727, Norris Family Papers, Norris Family Notebooks, HSP (hereafter cited as Norris Papers).

13 David Cooper to Samuel Allinson, Second Month 1772, Samuel Allinson Letterbook, 1764, Allinson Family Papers, HCQC (hereafter cited as Allinson Papers).

14 Sarah Hill Dillwyn to Margaret Hill Morris, Apr. 25, 1769, Dillwyn Letters, Edward Wanton Smith Collection, HCQC (hereafter cited as Dillwyn Letters).

15 Tace Bradford to Thomas Bradford, Mar. 5, 1761, Bradford Correspondence.

16 Ibid.

17 *PG*, Feb. 10, 1773.

18 Fidelia, "To the Memory of My Valued Friend Margaret Mason," 1775, Collection #950, HCQC.

19 Katherine Smith, "On the death of Elizabeth Allinson, Wife of Samuel Allinson, by her sister Katherine Smith," ca. 1768, Elizabeth Smith Allinson Folder, Allinson Papers.

20 These three basic models of authority (traditional, charismatic-authoritarian, and rational-relational) were proposed by Max Weber. See Weber, *Economy and Society,* ed. Guenther and Wittich, trans. Fischoff et al. For a very helpful synopsis of Weber's categories of authority, see Donald McIntosh, "Weber and Freud: On the Nature and Sources of Authority," *American Sociological Review,* XXXV (1970), 901–911. See also Leonard Krieger, "The Idea of Authority in the West," *American Historical Review,* LXXXII (1977), 249–270.

21 "The Testimony of Friends belonging to Exeter Monthly Meeting Concerning Ellis Hugh/Hughes, deceased," 1764, Allinson Collection, Memorials, Allinson Papers (hereafter cited as Allinson Memorials).

22 "To Deborah Morris, These . . . Testimony Concerning Alice Griffith," ca. 1749, Allinson Memorials.

23 In a fascinating twist, both of these testimonials are preserved today in the same collection of Quaker family papers (Allinson Memorials), fitting evidence, perhaps, of the uncertainty that surrounded competing models of authority.

24 Margaret Morris, 1760, "Margaret Hill Morris, Journal, 1751–74," HCQC (hereafter cited as Morris Journal).

25 John Pemberton, "Testimony," Pemberton Family Papers. This is undated testimony by John Pemberton concerning the death of his brother, Charles Pemberton; internal evidence from this essay suggests it was written in May 1748.

26 Israel Pemberton to Thomas Gawthrop, 29 Fifth Month 1748, John Pemberton, "Testimony," Pemberton Family Papers.

27 *PG*, Dec. 20, 1748, Apr. 25, May 2, 1751. Orlando Patterson emphasizes that many rituals of enslavement force bound people to ceremonially enact their own deaths. See Patterson, *Slavery and Social Death: A Comparative Study* (Cambridge, Mass., 2005), 5.

28 Nicholas Waln, "Copy of a Letter written by Nicholas Waln to his Aunt,

London, the 22nd of the 1st mo, 1764," in Mary Flower's Commonplace Book, HCQC.

29 Richard Hill to Hannah Hill, Mar. 15, 1752, Hill Family Papers, HCQC.

30 Israel Pemberton to Edmund Peckover, 19 Eighth Month 1748, Pemberton Family Papers, 110, John Smith to "Dear Cousin," Burlington, 24 Ninth Month 1760, Pemberton Family Papers.

31 Charles Inglis to John Morgan, July 20, 1765, Ferdinand J. Dreer Autograph Collection, American Clergy, 99, HSP; David Cooper, "Moanings of D. C. on Losing his Wife," ca. 1759; David Cooper to Samuel Allinson, 4 Eleventh Month 1764; David Cooper, "On the Death of Sibyl Cooper, 1759," n.d., and John Cooper to Samuel Allinson, 18 Ninth Month 1768, Allinson Papers.

32 Tace Bradford to Thomas Bradford, Mar. 5, 1761, William Bradford to Thomas Bradford, Feb. 7, 1761, Bradford Correspondence.

33 David Bostwick, "A Preface," in Samuel Davies, *Sermon Delivered at Nassau-Hall, January 14, 1761: On the Death of His Late Majesty King George II . . .* (Philadelphia, 1761). The tactic of channeling grief in support of authority appears to have been a recurring practice in American history, although the exact terms of the process could change according to historical context. See Mitchell Robert Breitwieser, *American Puritanism and the Defense of Mourning: Religion, Grief, and Ethnology in Mary White Rowlandson's Captivity Narrative* (Madison, Wis., 1990), 9, 210; Julia A. Stern, *The Plight of Feeling: Sympathy and Dissent in the Early American Novel* (Chicago, 1997), 241; Robert E. Cray, Jr., "Commemorating the Prison Ship Dead: Revolutionary Memory and the Politics of Sepulture in the Early Republic, 1776–1808," *William and Mary Quarterly*, 3d Ser., LVI (1999), 565–590.

34 M[ary] Bernard, "M. Bernard on the Death of S. Fothergill, Wm Hunt and Jno Woolman Belonging to R. Jones . . . Reflections Arising from Well-Known Events," 25 Tenth Month 1772, Allinson Memorials.

35 "Tribute," 2a, *OED*. This, the current modern definition of *tribute*, goes back to 1585.

36 "To the Memory of Daniel Stanton," in Catherine La Courreye Blecki and Karin A. Wulf, eds., *Milcah Martha Moore's Book: A Commonplace Book from Revolutionary America* (University Park, Pa., 1977), 177. The MS poem circulated widely and can also be found in Allinson Papers.

37 *PG*, Philadelphia, Jan. 29, 1761. Fidelia, the pen name of Quaker Hannah Griffitts, apparently submitted this poem to the *Gazette* with payment to cover publication costs. However, the publishers refused payment, saying, "Fidelia is desired to send for the Money which accompanied the above Lines as we take no Gratuity for obliging the Public with such Performances." The

poetry of Fidelia is featured and discussed extensively in Blecki and Wulf, eds., *Milcah Martha Moore's Book*. The fact that grief long circumscribed could flow gratefully into approved channels, even if those channels strengthened the powers of those who restricted grief in the first place, is artfully described by Breitwieser as an "alluring oppression"; see Breitwieser, *American Puritanism and the Defense of Mourning*, 58, 69.

38 James Pemberton to William Dillwyn, 28 Third Month 1771, G. M. Howland Collection #1000, HCQC.

39 Fidelia, "To the Memory of my Respected Friend Sarah Morris, who died at Philadelphia the 24th of the 10th mo. 1775," 27 Tenth Month 1775, Allinson Memorials.

40 Joyce Benezet to Sarah and Deborah Morris, Philadelphia, 16 Tenth Month 1772, Collection #851, HCQC.

41 Benjamin Mason, "A few Expressions Inscribed to the Memory of our dear Deceased friend and fellow travellor Alice Jackson," 26 Eleventh Month 1778, Allinson Memorials.

42 Bostwick, "Preface," in Davies, *Sermon on the Death of King George*, i.

43 Ibid., viii.

44 G[eorge] Dillwyn to M[argaret] Morris, April 1766, Dillwyn Letters; Sarah Logan to "Dear Brother," 7 Twelfth Month 1752, G. M. Howland Collection #1000.

45 Elizabeth Allinson to "Respected Brother," 8 Ninth Month 1757, Allinson Papers.

46 Ibid.

47 Ibid.

48 John Churchman to John Pemberton, London, 30 Third Month 1754, Brown Letterbook. Johan Huizinga has also commented on the eighteenth-century association of weeping and veneration; see *The Autumn of the Middle Ages*, trans. Rodney J. Payton and Ulrich Mammitzsch (Chicago, 1996), esp. p. 8.

49 James Pemberton to Hannah Smith, Philadelphia, 28 Third Month 1770, G. M. Howland Collection #1000.

50 John Morgan to Elizabeth Graeme, Philadelphia, June 20, 1765, Richard Peters Papers, HSP. Intriguingly, Julia Stern documents an almost obsessive interest in the deaths of fathers occurring in the early American novels of the 1790s. She demonstrates convincingly that much of the melancholia that characterized the gothic sentimentality of the early Republic stemmed from the need to reconstitute, revise, resist, or simply reflect on the relations of authority and submission that had been so profoundly destabilized by the Revolution. See Stern, *The Plight of Feeling*, 9.

51 Thomas Lawrence to Samuel Stoke, Jan. 26, 1747, Thomas Lawrence Letter-book, Thomas Lawrence Papers, 1689–1754, Lawrence Collection, HSP.

52 *PG*, Oct. 20, 1768.

53 Margaret Morris, Jan. 29, 1762, Morris Journal.

54 *American Weekly Mercury* (Philadelphia), June 4, 1735; Isaac Norris, [Jr.], to Robert Jordan, July 1735, Norris Papers.

55 Susa[nnah] Wright to Isaac Norris, Aug. 8, 1735, Norris Papers.

56 Ibid., Nov. 14, 1749, Norris Papers.

57 Anonymous, "By a Young Man on the Death of His Father," "Catherine Haines Commonplace Book, 1775."

58 Anonymous, "Her Answer," ibid.

59 In the two pairs discussed above, both the man and the woman were Quaker. In light of the greater degree of gender parity prevalent in Quaker faith and practice (as compared with other Protestant denominations), it is interesting to observe both that Quaker men followed societal gender norms in these instances and that Quaker women were willing to challenge them.

60 Davies, *Sermon on the Death of King George*, 1, 2.

61 Tace Bradford to Thomas Bradford, Mar. 14, 1761, Bradford Correspondence. Patricia Meyer Spacks comments directly on emotional expression as a source of hidden power in her review of eighteenth-century female-authored senti-mental fiction; see "Oscillations of Sensibility," *New Literary History*, XXV (1994), 505–521, esp. 508.

62 James Hamilton, "A Message from the Governor to the Assembly," Jan. 27, 1761," in *Minutes of the Provincial Council of Pennsylvania, from the Organiza-tion to the Termination of the Proprietary Government* (Philadelphia, Har-risburg, 1851–1852), VIII, 521 (hereafter cited as *MPCP*), and "A Message from the Assembly to the Governor," Jan. 30, 1761," VIII, 560.

63 Governor James Hamilton to Teedyuscung, "At a Council Held at Phila-delphia, Saturday the 29th March, 1760," ibid., 465.

64 Ibid., 464.

65 Members of the Pennsylvania Council, "On Considering the Several Matters Set forth in the Former Minutes of Council . . . Dec. 24, 1754," ibid., VI, 274. On condolence ceremonies, see Richard White, *The Middle Ground: Indians, Empires, and Republics in the Great Lakes Region, 1650–1815* (Cambridge, 1991); Daniel K. Richter, *The Ordeal of the Longhouse: The Peoples of the Iroquois League in the Era of European Colonization* (Chapel Hill, N.C., 1992); Richter "War and Culture: The Iroquois Experience," *WMQ*, 3d Ser., XL (1983), 528–559; Timothy J. Shannon, *Indians and Colonists at the Crossroads of Empire: The Albany Congress of 1754* (Ithaca, N.Y., 2000); Sandra M. Gustafson, *Elo-*

quence Is Power: Oratory and Performance in Early America (Chapel Hill, N.C., 2000), esp. chaps. 2, 3; Gordon M. Sayre, *Les Sauvages Américains: Representations of Native Americans in French and English Colonial Literature* (Chapel Hill, N.C., 1997), esp. chap. 6.

66 On the influence of Sir William Johnson, see Shannon, *Indians and Colonists at the Crossroads of Empire*, 3–6.

67 George Croghan, "At a Meeting of the Six Nations and Their Allies, and George Croghan, Esqr., Deputy Agent to the Honble. Sir William Johnson . . . at John Harris', the 1st day of April, 1757," *MPCP*, VII, 507.

68 Speech by the Old Belt as reported by Governor James Hamilton, "At a Council Held at Carlisle, Thursday the 15th January, 1756," ibid., 1.

69 Croghan, "At a Meeting of the Six Nations," ibid., 508; Conrad Weiser, "Journal of the Proceedings of Conrad Weiser in His Way to and at Aucquick . . . in the Year 1754, in August and September," ibid., VI, 153.

70 Croghan, "At a Meeting of the Six Nations," ibid., 507.

71 New York Council and Commissioners, "Draught of the General Speech . . . at a Meeting in the Court House at Albany, June 27th, 1754," ibid., VI, 69, and Governor Robert Hunter Morris, "Instructions of the Honourable Robert Hunter Morris, Esquire . . . to Scarroyady, one of the Chiefs of the Oneido Nation . . . ," ibid., VI, 697.

72 Previous scholars commenting on Pennsylvania's participation in condolence ceremonies have not always identified colonial deviations from Indian forms as deliberate. See, for example, Nancy L. Hagedorn, " 'A Friend to Go between Them': The Interpreter as Cultural Broker during Anglo-Iroquois Councils, 1740–70," *Ethnohistory*, XXXV (1988), 60–80; see also Jane T. Merritt, "Metaphor, Meaning, and Misunderstanding: Language and Power on the Pennsylvania Frontier," in Andrew R. L. Cayton and Fredrika J. Teute, eds., *Contact Points: American Frontiers from the Mohawk Valley to the Mississippi, 1750–1830* (Chapel Hill, N.C., 1998), esp. 75–76.

73 Conrad Weiser, "Memorandum," Feb. 22, 1756, *MPCP*, VII, 53.

74 Governor William Denny, "At a Conference Held in the Town of Easton on the 8th of October, 1758," ibid., VIII, 175.

75 Teedyuscung, "At a Conference Held at Easton on the 18th of October, 1758," ibid., VII, 200, and Scarroyady, "At a Meeting with the Indians at John Harris', April 2nd, 1757," VII, 509.

76 "At a Council Held at Philadelphia," ibid., VIII, 466.

77 Paxinosa, "The Answer, 31st May, of 1756," ibid., VII, 140.

78 Paxinosa, n.d., as quoted in "Minutes of the Proceedings of the People called Quakers in Philadelphia towards regaining and preserving Peace with the

Indians by pacific Measures, 1755–1757," 26 [July 1756], MS, HSP (hereafter cited as "Friendly Minutes"). Please note that this group later took the official name The Friendly Association for Regaining and Preserving Peace with the Indians by Pacific Measures. The minutes for 1755–1757 are dated only sporadically, and no page numbers are provided. Citations here are by date when possible and represent a best guess in cases where dates given in the manuscript were incomplete.

79 William Denny, "At a Council Held at Philadelphia, Wednesday the 3rd November, 1756," *MPCP,* VII, 311.

80 Teedyuscung, "At a Conference Held on Saturday, the 13th November, 1756," Governor William Denny, "At a Conference Held on Monday, November 15, 1756," ibid., 321, 328. For an account of the opening ceremonies, see "At a Conference with the Indians, Held at Easton, on Monday the 8th November, 1756," ibid., VII, 308. The Friendly Association set itself up as an independent monitoring group dedicated to observing the Pennsylvania government's dealings with local Indians.

81 "At a Council Held at Easton, November 17th, 1756," ibid., 337, 338.

82 Society of Friends, "On the 17th the Conference Ended . . . ," [Nov.] 17 [1756], "Friendly Minutes," and Governor William Denny to Sir William Johnson, Philadelphia, Dec. 6, 1757, ibid., 351.

83 Members of The Pennsylvania Council, "At a Conference Held at Easton with the Indians, October the 26th, 1758," ibid., VIII, 219. For a description of the opening ceremonies, see "At a Private Conference with the Indians Held at Easton, October 21st, 1758," ibid., 211–212.

84 Governor William Denny to "Mr. Speaker and Gentlemen of the Assembly," Nov. 16, 1758, ibid., 228.

85 John Lathrop to Thomas Bradford, Aug. 27, 1761, Bradford Correspondence.

86 Scarroyady, "At a Council Held at Philadelphia, Monday, 31st March, 1755," *MPCP,* VI, 342.

87 Historian Stephen D. White has noted that in fact "in both Old French and Latin, anger and grief merge to form a single emotion—a kind of sad anger, angry sadness, or grief." That the two emotions are so linguistically separate in English may only attest to the defining power of gendered constructions of emotion, a topic where E. Anthony Rotundo has made initial explorations. See White, "The Politics of Anger," in Barbara H. Rosenwein, ed., *Anger's Past: The Uses of the Emotions in the Middle Ages* (Ithaca, N.Y., 1998), 135; Rotundo, "Exploring Cultures of Emotion, 1750–1850" (paper presented to Michael Zuckerman's Early American Discussion Group, Jan. 27, 2000). For another discussion of the dialectic relationship between anger and grief, see Paul

Freedman, "Peasant Anger in the Late Middle Ages," in Rosenwein, ed., *Anger's Past,* esp. 188.

88 James Hamilton, "A Message from the Governor to the Assembly," Jan. 27, 1761," *MPCP,* VIII, 521–523.

89 Seneca George, "At a Conference with the Indians at Easton, on Monday the 3rd August, 1761," and Pennsylvania Council, "At a Conference Held at Easton with the Indians, October the 26th, 1758," ibid., 220, 631. On native American condolence ceremonies, their cultural meanings, and their implications for selfhood, see Richard White, " 'Although I Am Dead, I Am Not Entirely Dead: I Have Left a Second of Myself': Constructing Self and Persons on the Middle Ground of Early America," in Ronald Hoffman, Mechal Sobel, and Fredrika J. Teute, eds., *Through a Glass Darkly: Reflections on Personal Identity in Early America* (Chapel Hill, N.C., 1997), 404–413.

90 Tace Bradford to Thomas Bradford, Mar. 14, Aug. 18, 1761, Bradford Correspondence.

91 Nemo to Thomas Bradford, Sept. 10, 1760, John Lathrop to Thomas Bradford, Aug. 11, 1762, Bradford Correspondence.

Chapter Eight

1 John Penn, "A Message from the Governor to the Assembly," Dec. 21, 1763, in *Minutes of the Provincial Council of Pennsylvania, from the Organization to the Termination of the Proprietary Government* (Philadelphia, Harrisburg, 1851–1852), IX, 94–95 (hereafter cited as *MPCP*), and "A Message from the Assembly to the Governor," Jan. 20, 1764, *MPCP,* IX, 124.

2 Mathew Smith and James Gibson to "the Honorable John Penn, Esquire, Governor," Feb. 13, 1764, *MPCP,* IX, 138–142 (hereafter cited as Smith and Gibson, "Remonstrance").

3 "The Apology of the Paxton Volunteers Addressed to the Candid and Impartial World," n.d., MS, Collections of the Historical Society of Pennsylvania (HSP), reprinted in John R. Dunbar, ed., *The Paxton Papers* (The Hague, 1957), 186–187 (hereafter cited as "Apology of the Paxton Volunteers").

4 [Benjamin Franklin], *A Narrative of the Late Massacres, in Lancaster County, of a Number of Indians, Friends of This Province, by Persons Unknown, with Some Observations on the Same* (Philadelphia, 1764), 23.

5 [Franklin], *Narrative,* 9, 25, 27, 29.

6 Alison Gilbert Olson estimates that enough copies of the various pamphlets were printed for "every adult male to own a copy of at least one." Familiarity with the emotional culture the pamphlets reflect would have been equally

widespread. See Olson, "Pennsylvania Satire before the Stamp Act," *Pennsylvania History*, LXVIII (2001), 507–532, esp. 526.

7 "A Message from the Governor to the Assembly," Jan. 3, 1764, and "A Message to the Governor from the Assembly," Jan. 20, 1764, *MPCP*, IX, 109, 124.

8 William Smith, "Preface," in Thomas Barton, *Unanimity and Public Spirit: A Sermon Preached at Carlisle* (Philadelphia, 1755), ix (hereafter cited as Smith, in Barton, *Unanimity and Public Spirit*).

9 Penn, "A Message from the Governor," Dec. 21, 1763, *MPCP*, IX, 95; [Franklin], *Narrative*, 8–9; *A Serious Address to Such of the Inhabitants of Pennsylvania, as Have Connived at, or Do Approve of, the Late Massacre of the Indians at Lancaster; or, The Design of Killing Those Who Are Now in the Barracks at Philadelphia* (Philadelphia, 1764), 6. *A Serious Address* proved so popular that it was quickly reprinted, reaching a fourth edition in a few days. See *A Serious Address . . . To Which Is Now Added, A Dialogue between Andrew Trueman and Thomas Zealot, about the Killing the Indians at Connestogoe and Lancaster)* (Philadelphia, 1764) (hereafter cited as *A Dialogue*).

On the practical or legal level, it might have seemed important to balance accusation of anger with charges of cold blood, since acting in "cold Blood" might have made the attackers more liable for the consequences of violence. As Barbara Donagan notes with regard to early modern England, "Actions that might be condoned if committed in hot blood became inexcusable in cold blood, a distinction that survives in law and war." See Donagan, "Atrocity, War Crime, and Treason in the English Civil War," *American Historical Review*, XCIX (1994), 1137–1166, esp. 1144.

10 Charles Read to John Ladd, Jan. 7, 1764, published as Charles Read, *Copy of a Letter from Charles Read, Esq; to the Hon: John Ladd, Esq; and His Associates, Justices of the Peace for the County of Gloucester* (Philadelphia, 1764), 4; *A Dialogue*, 8; [Franklin], *Narrative*, 30. The Read letter went through three Andrew Steuart editions in 1764. In another sign of the widespread readership for the Paxton pamphlets, Steuart advertised in his third edition of the *Letter from Charles Read* that he had available at his shop "all the pamphlets that have been publish'd on the same Subject." See *Copy of a Letter*, 3d ed. (Philadelphia, 1764); [Franklin], *Narrative*, 30.

11 *A Dialogue, Containing Some Reflections on the Late Declaration and Remonstrance, of the Back-Inhabitants of the Province of Pennsylvania* (Philadelphia, 1764), 7 (hereafter cited as *Reflections on the Late Declaration and Remonstrance*); *A Serious Address*, 12. For the sake of clarity, the order of the phrases in this excerpt has been reversed from their position in the original.

Alden T. Vaughan mentions that Benjamin Franklin employed class language in discussing the uprising, complaining that the Paxton rebels' "action was almost universally approved by the common people." Benjamin Franklin to John Fothergill, Mar. 14, 1764, as quoted in Vaughan, "Frontier Banditti and the Indians: The Paxton Boys' Legacy, 1763–1775," *Pennsylvania History*, LI (1984), 1–29, esp. 5. Alison Olson argues that social divides were evidenced even in which Pennsylvanians had access to which political pamphlets, with some elaborately argued and expensively bound pamphlets being aimed at the upper sort while cheaply printed tavern songs were intended to appeal to the lower. See Olson, "The Pamphlet War over the Paxton Boys," *Pennsylvania Magazine of History and Biography*, CXXIII (1999), 31–55, esp. 36.

12 *Reflections on the Late Declaration and Remonstrance*, 10.

13 [Thomas Barton], *The Conduct of the Paxton-Men, Impartially Represented, with Some Remarks on the Narrative* (Philadelphia, 1764], 21. On Barton's authorship of this pamphlet, see James P. Myers, Jr., "The Rev. Thomas Barton's Authorship of *The Conduct of the Paxton Men, Impartially Represented* (1764)," *Pennsylvania History*, LXI (1994), 155–184. For a biographical account of Barton's involvement in Paxton, see Marvin F. Russell, "Thomas Barton and Pennsylvania's Colonial Frontier," *Pennsylvania History*, XLVI (1979), 313–334.

14 Jane T. Merritt has emphasized the centrality of challenges to authority in shaping government reaction to the Conestoga killings as has John Justin Smolenski. See Merritt, *At the Crossroads: Indians and Empires on a Mid-Atlantic Frontier, 1700–1763* (Chapel Hill, N.C., 2003), 287; and see Smolenski, "Friends and Strangers: Religion, Diversity, and the Ordering of Public Life in Colonial Pennsylvania, 1681–1764" (Ph.D. diss., University of Pennsylvania, 2001), 403.

15 Matthew Smith and James Gibson, "The Declaration of the Injured Frontier Inhabitants," February 1764, *MPCP*, IX, 143.

16 Ibid., 143, 145.

17 Ibid., 143.

18 [David James Dove], *The Quaker Unmask'd; or, Plain Truth: Humbly Addressed to the Consideration of All the Freemen of Pennsylvania* (Philadelphia, 1764), 7; Well Wisher, *An Historical Account, of the Late Disturbance, between the Inhabitants of the Back Settlements of Pennsylvania, and the Philadelphians Etc.* (Philadelphia, [1764]), 5.

19 Smith and Gibson, "Declaration,," February 1764, *MPCP*, IX, 143.

20 "Apology of the Paxton Volunteers," 187.

21 [Barton], *Conduct of the Paxton-Men*, 3.

22 John Penn, "A Proclamation," Dec. 22, 1763, *MPCP*, IX, 95.

23 Read, *Letter from Charles Read,* 3.

24 Philanthropos, *The Quakers Assisting to Preserve the Lives of the Indians in the Barracks, Vindicated and Proved to Be Consistent with Reason, Agreeable to Our Law, [Which] Hath an Inseparable Connection with the Law of God, and Exactly Agreeable with the Principles of the People Call'd Quakers* (Philadelphia, 1764), 7; *Reflections on the Late Declaration and Remonstrance,* 8. Such attitudes were widespread; Laura M. Stevens documents that missionaries with the Society for the Propagation of the Gospel believed that "a capacity for feeling marked the difference between Christian and non-Christian." See Stevens, *The Poor Indians: British Missionaries, Native Americans, and Colonial Sensibility* (Philadelphia, 2004), 118.

25 [Dove], *The Quaker Unmask'd,* 8. Many frontier inhabitants were of German origin, from Lutherans to Moravians. However, despite the evident hopes of anti-Quaker political factions to use the Paxton controversy to undermine the traditional alliance between Quakers and German Pietists, *religious* rhetoric for and against the Paxton Boys focused almost exclusively on "Presbyterianism," with no mention of particular German sects.

26 Philadelphiensis, *Remarks on the Quaker Unmask'd; or, Plain Truth Found to Be Plain Falsehood, Humbly Addressed to the Candid* (Philadelphia, 1764), 4; [Dove], *The Quaker Unmask'd,* 15.

On the eighteenth-century rise in philosophical interest in the moral value, social efficacy, and civilizing function of the passions, see Norman S. Fiering, "Irresistible Compassion: An Aspect of Eighteenth-Century Sympathy and Humanitarianism," *Journal of the History of Ideas,* XXXVII (1976), 195–218, esp. 208. See also Evan Radcliffe, "Revolutionary Writing, Moral Philosophy, and Universal Benevolence in the Eighteenth Century," *Journal of the History of Ideas,* LIV (1993), 221–240, esp. 221.

27 Well Wisher, *Historical Account,* 6; Philanthropos, *The Quakers Assisting,* 8, 9. Nancy Shoemaker analyzes animalistic metaphors generally and wolf images particularly in terms of a trade-off between masculinity and civility: see "An Alliance between Men: Gender Metaphors in Eighteenth-Century American Indian Diplomacy East of the Mississippi," *Ethnohistory,* XLVI (1999), 239–263, esp. 249.

Writing on seventeenth-century discussions of savagery and civility, Bernard W. Sheehan notes: "The habit of attributing bestial qualities to native Americans sprang from the very substance of savage dogma. . . . Like animals, their grip on the world was sensate. They did not reason; they only felt and acted." By the eighteenth century, with emotion newly emerging as the very basis of European notions of civility, charges that Indians were animalistic could not carry the same opprobrium as before. See Sheehan, *Savagism and Civility: Indians and Englishmen in Colonial Virginia* (New York, 1980), 68.

For more on evolving eighteenth-century ideas about connections between feeling and civility, see Andrew R. L. Cayton, " 'Noble Actors' upon 'the Theater of Honor': Power and Civility in the Treaty of Grenville," in Cayton and Fredrika J. Teute, eds., *Contact Points: American Frontiers from the Mohawk Valley to the Mississippi, 1750–1830* (Chapel Hill, N.C., 1998), 240; Karen Halttunen, "Humanitarianism and the Pornography of Pain in Anglo-American Culture," *AHR*, C (1995), 303; John F. Kasson, *Rudeness and Civility: Manners in Nineteenth-Century Urban America* (New York, 1990), 4; David S. Shields, *Civil Tongues and Polite Letters in British America* (Chapel Hill, N.C., 1997), ix.

28 Philanthropos, *The Quakers Assisting*, 8, 9. The order of the phrases excerpted in this quotation has been reversed from their position in the original.

29 Society of Friends, "Minutes of the Proceedings of the People called Quakers in Philadelphia towards regaining and preserving Peace with the Indians by pacific Measures, 1755–1757," Nov. 17, 1756, MS, HSP (hereafter cited as Friendly Minutes). This group later took the official name The Friendly Association for Regaining and Preserving Peace with the Indians by Pacific Measures. The minutes for 1755 to 1757 are dated sporadically and without page numbers. Citations here represent a best guess in cases where manuscript dates were incomplete.

On Indian attitudes toward Christian conversion, including the case of Teedyuscung, see Jane T. Merritt, "Dreaming of the Savior's Blood: Moravians and the Indian Great Awakening in Pennsylvania," *William and Mary Quarterly*, 3d Ser., LIV (1997), 723–746, esp. 729–731.

30 *Reflections on the Late Declaration and Remonstrance*, 9.

31 Philalethes, *The Quaker Vindicated; or, Observations on a Late Pamphlet, Entituled, The Quaker Unmask'd, or Plain Truth* ([Philadelphia], 1764), 13. In laying bare intramural antagonisms between western and eastern colonists of British America, I echo the judgment of Ian K. Steele: "Neither Amerindians nor Europeans were ever racist enough before 1765 to put aside pre-existing enmities and unite against the strangers." See Steele, *Warpaths: Invasions of North America* (New York, 1994), vii. Nature versus culture debates surrounding issues of civility had a long history in colonial America, going back to the very year 1609. Only the emphasis on the role of emotion was new to the eighteenth century. See James Axtell, "The White Indians of Colonial America," *WMQ*, 3d Ser., XXXII (1975), 55–88.

32 "The Cloven Foot Discovered," in [John Shebbeare], *A Letter, from Batista*

Angeloni . . . Wherein the Quakers Are Politically and Religiously Considered . . .
(Philadelphia, [1764]), 8; [Dove], *The Quaker Unmask'd,* 15.

33 [Dove], *The Quaker Unmask'd,* 5.

34 [Dove], *The Quaker Unmask'd,* 5.

35 [Barton], *Conduct of the Paxton-Men,* 30.

36 Smith and Gibson, "A Declaration," February 1764, *MPCP,* IX, 143.

37 Ibid.

38 On Pennsylvania's history of political skirmishing, see Alan Tully, *Forming American Politics: Ideals, Interests, and Institutions in Colonial New York and Pennsylvania* (Baltimore, 1994); and see Sally Schwartz, *"A Mixed Multitude": The Struggle for Toleration in Colonial Pennsylvania* (New York, 1988).

39 John Penn, as quoted in notes taken "At a Council Held at Philadelphia on Saturday the 10th December, 1763," *MPCP,* IX, 86.

40 Ibid.

41 [Barton], *Conduct of the Paxton-Men,* 30.

42 John Abr. Lidenius, *The Lawfulness of Defensive War . . .* (Philadelphia, 1756), 15–16; John Bartram to Peter, Feb. 4, 1756, Bartram Papers, HSP.

43 Untitled notes for Friday, Feb. 17, 1764, *MPCP,* IX, 142.

44 The initial "Declaration" and the later "Remonstrance," originally delivered in the form of a letter to the governor dated Feb. 13, 1764, and entered into the colony's official minutes, were subsequently published as *A Declaration and Remonstrance of the Distressed and Bleeding Frontier Inhabitants of the Province of Pennsylvania, Presented by Them to the Honourable the Governor and Assembly of the Province, Shewing the Causes of Their Late Discontent and Uneasiness and the Grievances under Which They Have Laboured, and Which They Humbly Pray to Have Redress'd* ([Philadelphia: Bradford], 1764). Significantly, given the undercurrents of religious and ethnic tension that shaped the course of the Paxton controversy, the printer William Bradford was himself a Scots-Irish Presbyterian. Class tensions, religious splits, and ethnic conflicts were deeply entwined.

Meanwhile, Smith and Gibson's "Declaration and Remonstrance" was published in German as well as English, with Smith identified therein as "Matthäus Smith," rather than as Matthew Smith. See Matthäus Smith and James Gibson, *Eine dem hochedlen Herrn Guvernör und der Landesversammlung der Provinz Pennsylvanien übergebene Erklärung und Vorstellung von den bedrängten und in Todesgefahr stehenden Einwohnern an den Grenzen dieser Provinz . . .* ([Philadelphia], 1764).

45 Smith and Gibson, "Remonstrance," *MPCP,* IX, 140.

46 Ibid., 139.

47 [Barton], *Conduct of the Paxton-Men*, 7. Krista Camenzind argues persuasively that "the brutality of the Paxton Boys" was "integral in the development of the American frontier as a place where White men expressed their manhood through acts of violence against Native Americans." However, she does not take into account that admiration for Indian manhood accompanied colonial insecurities about masculinity. See Camenzind, "Violence, Race, and the Paxton Boys," in William A. Pencak and Daniel K. Richter, eds., *Friends and Enemies in Penn's Woods: Indians, Colonists, and the Racial Construction of Pennsylvania* (University Park, Pa., 2004), 204.

48 [Franklin], *Narrative*, 29–30; [Barton], *Conduct of the Paxton-Men*. While it may be that the term "boys" was not always used in a pejorative sense, it does seem to me that the conflict highlighted by Franklin's description of the Paxton Boys as "unmanly men" versus Barton's references to them as the "Paxton-Men" indicates that use of the term 'boy" was deliberately derogatory when used by critics of the Paxton settlers. On the role of age in the definition of masculinity, see E. Anthony Rotundo, *American Manhood: Transformations in Masculinity from the Revolution to the Modern Era* (New York, 1993).

On critical assessments of Quaker masculinity, see Smolenski, "Friends and Strangers," 416; Peter Rhoads Silver, "Indian-Hating and the Rise of Whiteness in Provincial Pennsylvania" (Ph.D. diss., Yale University, 2000), 350.

49 Samuel Finley, *The Curse of Meroz; or, The Danger of Neutrality* (Philadelphia, 1757), 26. Concerns about the possibility that Christianity and masculinity were somehow incompatible would continue to flare from time to time, as shown, for example, by Janet Moore Lindman's work on masculinity in Revolutionary Virginia. However, Lindman equates elite concern about emotion with a desire for stoicism, rather than, as I argue, with a desire for emotion with moderation. See Lindman, "Acting the Manly Christian: White Evangelical Masculinity in Revolutionary Virginia," *WMQ*, 3d Ser., LVII (2000), 393–416, esp. 398–400.

50 Finley, *The Curse of Meroz*, 28.

51 Matthias Harris, *A Sermon Preached in the Church of St. Peters* (Philadelphia, 1757), 11. The links drawn between warfare, masculinity, and emotional capacity in this sermon are all the more striking in light of the fact that calls to "play the men" (which quotes 2 Sam. 10:12) had often been used in the past to rally Christians to war without making any mention of emotion. See, for example, Jill Lepore's explication of Increase Mather's use of this same Bible verse in

1675 in Lepore, *The Name of War: King Philip's War and the Origins of American Identity* (New York, 1999), 89.

52 Hendrick, as quoted in notes taken "At a Meeting [at Albany] Tuesday the 2d July, 1754, P.M," *MPCP*, VI, 81. Indian critiques of European masculinity were widespread and have finally caught the attention of historians. See Jon William Parmenter, "Pontiac's War: Forging New Links in the Anglo-Iroquois Covenant Chain, 1758–1766," *Ethnohistory*, IV (1997), 617–654, esp. 623. And see Nancy Shoemaker's acute analysis of eighteenth-century Pennsylvania in "An Alliance between Men," *Ethnohistory*, XLVI (1999), 246–249. On deliberate Indian efforts to emasculate white men, see Merritt's compelling account, *At the Crossroads*, 179.

53 Scarroyady, as quoted in notes taken "At a Council Held in the State House at Philadelphia Saturday the 10th of April 1756," *MPCP*, VII, 79. On Indian assumptions about the physical inferiority of white men, see Axtell, "White Indians," *Ethnohistory*, XXXII (1975), 83.

54 Robert Hunter Morris, "A Letter from the Governor to the Honourable Thomas Penn, Esquire, Philadelphia, July 31st, 1755," *MPCP*, VI, 517; Robert Eastburn, *A Faithful Narrative of . . . His Late Captivity among the Indians* (Philadelphia, 1758), 11.

Many other authors have also noticed that the tendency to dramatize native American strength and ferocity could also valorize their masculinity, proving that the very traits Europeans most abhorred in native Americans were the ones they were most drawn to. Richard Slotkin notes that "the emergence of the Indian as the model for an American heroism" occurred most prominently in Pennsylvania during the Seven Years War: "Of all the colonies, Pennsylvania produced the most generally appealing assessment of the meaning of the war and the most viable image of the American hero." As shown here, competition for social dominance initiated by Quaker rivals made the existence of an alternate, non-Quaker standard of masculinity particularly appealing in Pennsylvania. See Slotkin, *Regeneration through Violence: The Mythology of the American Frontier, 1600–1860* (Middletown, Conn., 1973), 223; Gordon Sayre, *Les Sauvages Américains: Representations of Native Americans in French and English Colonial Literature* (Chapel Hill, N.C., 1997), 128; and see also Shoemaker, "An Alliance between Men," XLVI (1999), 254.

55 Smith, in Barton, *Unanimity and Public Spirit*, xi.

56 "A Message to the Governor from the Assembly," Aug. 8, 1755, *MPCP*, VI, 532.

57 James Hamilton, "A Message from the Governor to the Assembly," Oct. 15, 1763, *MPCP*, IX, 58. The depths of Hamilton's frustrations with the Assembly

were long ago noted by Brooke Hindle, though not Hamilton's consequent moves to encourage backcountry revolt. See Hindle, "The March of the Paxton Boys," *WMQ*, 3d Ser., III (1946), 461–486, esp. 465.

58 James Hamilton, as quoted in notes taken "At a Council Held at the State House on Saturday the 22nd October 1763," *MPCP*, IX, 68.

59 Ibid. While there is no direct evidence that frontier settlers knew of Hamilton's treaty speech on anger, the mere fact that the governor seems to have known something in advance about the coming attack at Connestoga would indicate that the backcountry and the governor's circle were communicating. This inference is further substantiated by the fact that frontiersmen clearly did know the content of Governor Penn's diplomatic exchanges, given that his failure to exact condolences in December 1763 became the subject of Smith and Gibson's complaints about bodies "tamely covered" at "the last treaty" in February of 1764. For an alternative interpretation of the October 22 exchange that glosses over the threatening elements of Hamilton's speech, see Merritt, *At the Crossroads*, 284.

60 John Penn to William Johnson, Feb. 17, 1764, *MPCP*, IX, 137. Penn signed a bill entitled An Act for Preventing Tumults and Riotous Assemblies, and for the More Speedy and Effectual Punishing the Rioters, on Feb. 3, 1764. See *MPCP*, IX, 131.

61 Brooke Hindle cites Quaker correspondence gossiping about the assistance Smith and Gibson received with writing their remonstrance. James E. Crowley suggests that differing authorship or editorship could account for shifts in tone between the "Declaration" and the "Remonstrance," probably written and presented separately. See Hindle, "The March of the Paxton Boys," *WMQ*, 3d Ser., III (1946), 482; Crowley, "The Paxton Disturbance and Ideas of Order in Pennsylvania Politics," *Pennsylvania History*, XXXVII (1970), 317–339, esp. 319–321.

62 James Hamilton, "The Governor's Answer to a proposal made to him by the Committee of Assembly . . . ," Feb. 20, 1764, *MPCP*, IX, 147; "A Message to the Governor from the Assembly," Mar. 24, 1764, *MPCP*, IX, 165.

63 *Reflections on the Late Declaration and Remonstrance*, 10; "A Message to the Governor from the Assembly," May 30, 1764, *MPCP*, IX, 188. On the supply bills and the eventual commissioning of Henry Bouquet, see notes for May 29, 30, 1764, in *MPCP*, IX, 182–184; [William Smith], *An Historical Account of Colonel Bouquet's Expedition against the Ohio Indians in the Year 1764* (Philadelphia, 1765), 3. Hindle notes that the decision to raise one thousand men was the "direct result of the Conestoga massacre": see "The March of the Paxton Boys," *WMQ*, 3d Ser., III (1946), 468.

64 John Penn, "A Proclamation," July 7, 1764, *MPCP,* IX, 191. Gregory Evans Dowd has noted that Pontiac's War "began in regions where land was not an immediate issue and where British and colonial officials, far more than frontier folk, brought it on. During the war, moreover, these officers urged, ordered, and approved the indiscriminate slaughter of Indians." Clearly, this observation applies quite well to Pennsylvania, despite the sole blame Paxton inhabitants have traditionally taken for the course of events. Yet many modern historians have ignored this charge in assessing the reasons for Penn's abrupt refusal to join forces with the assemblymen in February after acting in concert with them in December and January. See Dowd, *War under Heaven: Pontiac, the Indian Nations, and the British Empire* (Baltimore, 2002), 175; and see Crowley, "The Paxton Disturbance," *Pennsylvania History,* XXXVII (1970), 331, 337; Hindle, "The March of the Paxton Boys," *WMQ,* 3d Ser., III (1946), 483; Merritt, *At the Crossroads,* 287; Olson, "Pamphlet War over the Paxton Boys," *PMHB,* CXXIII (1999), 43.

Further evidence of Penn's acquiescence in the Paxton uprising comes from the research of James P. Myers, Jr., who shows that Thomas Barton, presumed author of the radically pro-Paxton pamphlet *The Conduct of the Paxton Men,* was later rewarded for his efforts by a grant of farmland from the governor, which was none other than Conestoga Manor, former home of the massacred Indians! See Myers, "The Rev. Thomas Barton's Authorship," *Pennsylvania History,* LXI (1994), 176, 178.

Finally, Alden T. Vaughan demonstrates that Indians, too, understood the Pennsylvania government's complicity in frontier atrocities. See Vaughan, "Frontier Banditti," *Pennsylvania History,* LI (1984), 18, 20.

65 Dowd notes that the 1764 campaign, like Bouquet's "victory" at Bushy Run, was "hardly the unqualified conquest it has too often been deemed." Attention to the language of emotion confirms the vulnerability just beneath the surface of British claims to mastery. See Dowd, *War under Heaven,* 163.

66 Henry Bouquet, "Colonel Bouquet's Journal and Conferences with the Western Indians," *MPCP,* IX, 208–233. Dowd emphasizes that historians have underplayed the significance of Indians' use of "words as other powers failed them"; see *War under Heaven,* 162–168, esp. 162.

67 Henry Bouquet, "Speech to . . . the Delaware Chiefs with Him at Fort Pitt," Sept 20, 1764, "Colonel Bouquet's Journal," *MPCP,* IX, 208–209. On the need for British shows of force during Pontiac's war, see Parmenter, "Pontiac's War," *Ethnohistory,* XLIV (1997), 630.

68 "General Amherst to the Governor," June 12, 1763, *MPCP,* IX, 34; James Hamilton, "A Message from the Governor to the Assembly," Oct. 15, 1763,

MPCP, IX, 59; "Speech of an Onondago and an Oneida Indian to Col. Bouquet, at Fort Pitt," Oct. 2, 1764, "Colonel Bouquet's Journal," *MPCP*, IX, 209.

Please note: while the two treaty speeches discussed in these paragraphs involved different native American groups, they appear consecutively in Bouquet's journal, and both occurred at Fort Pitt. It appears highly probable that, though different native American nations were addressed separately, they were privy to the contents of each other's deliberations with Bouquet. At the very least, the speeches' side-by-side placement in the journal suggests that Bouquet himself thought of them as related.

The use of emotion generally and compassion specifically to conjure up the best of Anglo-American culture was not perhaps unique, though it might have been pursued with particular determination by these eighteenth-century Pennsylvanians." See Felicity Nussbaum, "Introduction: The Politics of Difference," *Eighteenth-Century Studies*, XXIII (1990), 379. On connections between compassion and civility, see Elaine Forman Crane, " 'I Have Suffer'd Much Today': The Defining Force of Pain in Early America," in Ronald Hoffman, Mechal Sobel, and Fredrika J. Teute, eds., *Through a Glass Darkly: Reflections on Personal Identity in Early America* (Chapel Hill, N.C., 1997), 379; Sheehan, *Savagism and Civility*, 38; Sayre, *Les Sauvages Américains*, 251.

69 Henry Bouquet, "At a Conference Held with the Senecas and Chiefs living upon the Ohio, the Delawares and Shawanese," Oct. 20, 1764, "Colonel Bouquet's Journal," *MPCP*, IX, 218, 219.

70 The full dimensions of Bouquet's anti-Indian attitudes are captured in Ian Steele's account of his exploits, which notes that Bouquet referred to Indians as "vermin" in his personal correspondence and that he deliberately delivered smallpox-infested blankets to Indians on the Ohio. See Steele, *Warpaths*, 239.

71 Bouquet, "At a Conference Held with the Senecas and Chiefs Living upon the Ohio, the Delawares and Shawanese," Oct. 20, 1764, "Colonel Bouquet's Journal," *MPCP*, IX, 219–220.

72 Ibid., 217; Keyashuta, as quoted in notes taken "At a Conference . . . at the Camp upon Muskingham," Nov. 9, 1764, "Colonel Bouquet's Journal," *MPCP*, IX, 223.

73 Red Hawke, as quoted in "Minutes of a Conference Held with the Shawanese," Nov. 12, 1764, "Colonel Bouquet's Journal," *MPCP*, IX, 229, 230.

74 Henry Bouquet, "Colonel Bouquet's Answer," Nov. 12, 1764, and "Colonel Bouquet's Answer," Nov. 14, 1764, "Colonel Bouquet's Journal," *MPCP*, IX, 230, 232. Jane Merritt has also noted Bouquet's deliberate omission of condolence rituals; my analysis of the politics of emotional expression amplifies

her discussion of Bouquet's power plays and also brings to light the significance that Bouquet's omissions and the Indian's offerings had for frontier settlers. See Merritt, *At the Crossroads,* 302.

75 "Apology of the Paxton Volunteers," 193. Numerous scholars, including Peter Silver, have noted the intertwined nature of race and class tensions in the Paxton crisis that led to a more militant Indian policy. What the language of emotion shows is how very vexed this relationship was, how elites were implicated along with commoners, and how articulate members of both groups understood (and futilely sought to avoid) the extremes of race-based divides. Few historians have credited the Paxton rebels as well as credited easterners with being able to distinguish between friendly and enemy Indians. Nor have most dwelt on the fact that even the Quaker-influenced Assembly, with Quaker Isaac Norris as its speaker, turned toward far more militantly anti-Indian policies in the wake of the Paxton uprising. See Crowley, "The Paxton Disturbance," *Pennsylvania History,* XXXVII (1970), 333; Slaughter, "Crowds in Eighteenth-Century America," *PMHB,* CXV (1991), 20; Silver, "Indian-Hating and the Rise of Whiteness," 2, 13.

76 This assessment of the impact of British-American attitudes and policies on native Americans is intended to emphasize the repeated land encroachments and breaches of promises to which Indians dwelling in and around Pennsylvania were subjected. I am convinced by Alden Vaughan's argument that disgust with such treatment was what led many native Americans living on Pennsylvania's borders to side with the British with the onset of revolution. Still, this stance is not intended to contradict the equally persuasive argument of historians like Parmenter and Dowd that Indians did achieve some diplomatic and strategic successes in Pontiac's War. See Vaughan, "Frontier Banditti," *Pennsylvania History,* LI (1984), 21–22; Parmenter, "Pontiac's War," *Ethnohistory,* XLIV (1997), 617; Dowd, *War under Heaven,* 167.

77 [Smith], *Historical Account,* 6.

78 Ibid., 26, 27.

79 John Galt, *The Life and Studies of Benjamin West, Esq. . . . Compiled from Materials Furnished by Himself* (Philadelphia, 1816), 26, 28–29, 51–52.

80 [Smith], *Historical Account,* 27. This understanding of savagery and civility was shared by Smith's protégé Thomas Barton. See Russell, "Thomas Barton," *Pennsylvania History,* XLVI (1979), 320. My argument that Smith shrank from racialized characterizations of Indians is at odds with Slotkin's interpretation of Smith's *Historical Account.* Slotkin interprets that work as stating that Indians' " 'racial' lack of 'common feelings of humanity' renders them monstrous in war." While Slotkin is absolutely right to comment on the strong

strain of concern with the "monstrous" in Anglo-American anti-Indian rhetoric, I think the evidence shows that such differences were attributed to the
power of benighted culture to eclipse natural common humanity rather than
to innate difference. See Slotkin, *Regeneration through Violence*, 233.

I find the argument of Alden T. Vaughan far more persuasive. Without
specifically addressing emotional culture, he argues cogently: "Englishmen,
then, perceived Indians as essentially white"; and "early English writings
reflect a deep bias against Indian culture but not against Indian color, shape,
or features; the American native was socially deplorable but physically admirable"; and "a lingering reluctance to perceive the Indians in essentially racial terms . . . weakened, however, as the eighteenth century wore on." See
Vaughan, "From White Man to Redskin: Changing Anglo-American Perceptions of the American Indian," *AHR*, LXXXVII (1982), 927–934. For an
argument that the Paxton crisis represented a key turn toward racialized
hatred of Indians, see Camenzind, "Violence, Race, and the Paxton Boys," in
Pencak and Richter, eds., *Friends and Enemies*, 205, 216.

81 George Washington, "A Letter to Govenor James Hamilton, from Mr. Wash-
ington, received the 3d May 1754," *MPCP*, VI, 28; Notes taken "At a Meeting of
Seventy of the Six Nations at Mr. James Stevenson's, in Albany, Friday the
Fifth Day of July, 1754," *MPCP*, VI, 118; Friendly Minutes.

82 [Smith], *Historical Account*, 17. On the importance of ritual exchanges among
native Americans and the British, with special attention to the role of the
Iroquois in instructing the British in traditional ceremonial protocol, see
Sandra M. Gustafson, *Eloquence Is Power: Oratory and Performance in Early
America* (Chapel Hill, N.C., 2000), esp. chap. 3.

83 Adam Smith, *The Theory of Moral Sentiments* (Indianapolis, Ind., 1976), 341
(first delivered as a series of university lectures at Glasgow, then published in
1759 at the height of the Seven Years War). Adam Smith's belief in the incom-
patibility of civilized and savage virtues characterized many Euro-Indian interactions. Roy Harvey Pearce states, for example: "Through the first three-
quarters of the eighteenth century, the problem of the relation of the Indian
to American life came more and more often to be stated . . . [as] the problem
of the relation of savage to civilized life. . . . They might have a kind of good
life in that state; for there were specifically savage virtues, natural virtues, even
if there were not specifically noble savages. . . . [Yet] how relate that good to
the obviously greater good of civilized societies? How believe in two ideas of
order?" This piece discusses one distinctive solution to this dilemma arrived
at by Anglo-Americans. In the course of the Seven Years War, as they sought
to embrace simultaneously "two ideas of order," Anglo-Americans came to

espouse a new conception of emotion that encompassed both masculinity and civility. See Pearce, *The Savages of America: A Study of the Indian and the Idea of Civilization,* rev. ed. (Baltimore, 1965), 48.

84 Karen Ordahl Kupperman has emphasized that, from the first moments of colonial encounter in North America, the opinions and observations of those who interacted with native Americans directly were rather different from the ideas of Europeans free to consider them only in theory. My argument is that, by the mid-eighteenth century, Anglo-Americans were coming not only to conceive of native Americans in different terms than Europeans did but to conceive of themselves in distinct terms as well. See Kupperman, *Indians and English: Facing off in Early America* (Ithaca, N.Y., 2000).

85 Smith, in Barton, *Unanimity and Public Spirit,* xi.

86 [Smith], *Historical Account,* 38. Alexander Pope, Epistle II, 138, 141, 149, 150, 153, in *The Poems of Alexander Pope,* III, ii, *An Essay on Man,* ed. Maynard Mack (New Haven, Conn., 1950). The lines ending ". . . will" and ". . . still" appeared in the original 1734–1735 edition of the *Essay* (the copy owned by the Library Company of Philadelphia) between lines 148 and 149, but were dropped from subsequent editions and are not numbered by Mack.

87 [Smith], *Historical Account,* 38.

88 Ibid., 29, 33. On colonial women's reluctance to sever family ties with native American families, see John Demos, *The Unredeemed Captive: A Family Story from Early America* (New York, 1994). On the threat Indian warfare posed to "patriarchal identities," see Camenzind, "Violence, Race, and the Paxton Boys," in Pencak and Richter, eds., *Friends and Enemies,* 205.

89 As Gary B. Nash has noted in a related context, "It was not political power itself the laboring classes yearned for, but an equitable system in which they could pursue their modest goals." See Nash, *The Urban Crucible: The Northern Seaports and the Origins of the American Revolution,* abr. ed. (Cambridge, Mass., 1986), 148.

On Revolutionary connections, see David Sloan, "Protest in Pre-Revolutionary America: The Paxton Example," *Indiana Social Studies Quarterly,* XXVII (1974–1975), 29–37. Sloan argues, correctly in my view, that political motivations were not paramount at Paxton. James E. Crowley likewise argues that the Paxton rebels' "motivation involved social not political frustrations." Still, I do not share Crowley's view that social motivations made frontier folk unsophisticated. Rather, they reflect a widespread rank-focused mind-set in an era new to political action, an era when gentlemen also routinely disavowed interest in politics and officeholding in favor of the pursuits of private life. See Crowley, "The Paxton Disturbance," *Pennsylvania History,* XXXVII

(1970), 325. For contrary views, emphasizing the primacy of politics or figuring the Paxton uprising as a direct precursor of the Revolution, see John R. Dunbar, "Introduction," in Dunbar, ed., *The Paxton Papers;* and see Edwin Thomas Schock, Jr., "The 'Cloven Foot' Rediscovered: The History of the Conestoga Massacre through Three Generations of Scholarship," *Journal of the Lancaster County Historical Society,* XCVI (1994), 99–112. Frank J. Cavaioli's work is the most suggestive on this point, as he is able to show that the five men most centrally involved in the Paxton uprising, including Smith and Gibson, all fought on the patriot side in the Revolution. Still, at most, it seems to me that Paxton participants who initially emphasized social over political concerns might have become disillusioned with elite leadership in the years after the uprising, rather than in the weeks and months leading up to it. See Cavaioli, "A Profile of the Paxton Boys: Murderers of the Conestoga Indians," *Journal of the Lancaster County Historical Society,* LXXXVII (1983), 74–96. For a thorough analysis of the politics of scalp bounties, see James Axtell, "The Moral Dilemmas of Scalping," in Axtell, *Natives and Newcomers: The Cultural Origins of North America* (New York, 2001), esp. 272.

90 James Kirby Martin has considered similar questions. He concludes, rightly, that, though there probably was some sort of alliance between members of the proprietary faction and Scots-Irish Presbyterians, the political connection did not lead to unity through the Revolution. This point is amplified and made more explicable by analysis of the emotional language used to articulate the proprietary faction–Paxton relationship. Pennsylvania's governors and their supporters used popular rage only as leverage. Implicit in their choice of extreme labels for frontier anger was the idea that backcountry commoners were strong yet unrefined. They never intended to create a Revolutionary democratic partnership. See Martin, "The Return of the Paxton Boys and the Historical State of the Pennsylvania Frontier, 1764–1774," *Pennsylvania History,* XXXVIII (1971), 117–133, esp. 132.

Chapter Nine

1 George Washington, "To the Inhabitants of Canada," *Pennsylvania Gazette,* Oct. 11, 1775 (hereafter cited as *PG*). For discussion of Aristotle's theories on the relationship between emotional spirit *(thumos)* and natural slavery versus natural freedom, see Russell Bentley, "Loving Freedom: Aristotle on Slavery and the Good Life," *Political Studies,* XLVII, (1999), 100–113. For a more detailed discussion of the colonial application of Aristotelian ideas to enslaved African Americans, see Chapter 2.

2 *PG*, May 31, 1775.

3 Bailyn goes on to assert that connections between actual economic and symbolic political slavery were soon to be made and indeed that the battered logic of the proslavery argument "bore the marks ever after" of its encounter with Revolutionary rhetoric. Attention to the language of emotion suggests the more troubling view that racist debates about the very humanity of enslaved African Americans, about their ability to feel virtuous spirit, provided a key element of arguments for and against slavery in the eighteenth century. Ultimately, of course, in the hands of abolitionists who focused attention on the emotional sufferings of the enslaved, racial emotional distinctions would prove as vulnerable as social ones. (For extended discussion of the pivotal place of emotion in the development of slavery critiques among groundbreaking Quaker activists, see Chapter 1.) Yet nineteenth-century slaveholders would concede a degree of emotional capacity to the enslaved only to reemphasize their supposed rational shortfalls, claiming they were so foolish as to be happy with life under slavery. Attention to the issue of spirit requires acknowledging the deep roots and enduring power of American racism, rather than simply accommodating the comfortable confirmation of the inevitability of slavery's demise. See Bernard Bailyn, *The Ideological Origins of the American Revolution* (Cambridge, Mass., 1967), 232–246, esp. 233, 238, 246.

4 For work on the role of emotion in the demonstration of respectability in the eighteenth century, see Jacquelyn C. Miller, " 'An Uncommon Tranquility of Mind': Emotional Self-Control and the Construction of a Middle-Class Identity in Eighteenth-Century Philadelphia," *Journal of Social History*, XXX (1996–1997), 129–149; and C. Dallett Hemphill, "Middle Class Rising in Revolutionary America: The Evidence from Manners," *Journal of Social History*, XXX (1996–1997), 317–344. On connections between sensibility and virtue in the "man of feeling," see Karen Halttunen, "Humanitarianism and the Pornography of Pain in Anglo-American Culture," *American Historical Review*, C (1995), 303–334, esp. 303.

5 In colonial North America, Indians functioned vis-à-vis enslaved Africans much as Julie Ellison argues that North Africans functioned vis-à-vis sub-Saharan Africans in the Roman Empire depicted in Joseph Addison's *Cato*. Construed as emotionally savage when compared with Europeans, they nonetheless enjoy an enviable reputation when contrasted with sub-Saharan Africans. Their comparative emotional advantages thus became a kind of cultural resource that colonists felt free to draw on. Or, as Ellison puts it, their "liminal" status makes them "available for imaginative use" in the development of ideas

about the connections between "racial difference" and "emotional difference." See Ellison, *Cato's Tears and the Making of Anglo-American Emotion* (Chicago, 1999), 48–49, 59.

6 On the importance of emotional eloquence in the Revolutionary period, particularly its classical inspirations and Indian correlations, see Sandra M. Gustafson, *Eloquence Is Power: Oratory and Performance in Early America* (Chapel Hill, N.C., 2000), esp. 139, 147. On the synthesis of classical traditions and Enlightenment moral philosophy in Revolutionary oratory, see Christopher Grasso, *A Speaking Aristocracy: Transforming Public Discourse in Eighteenth-Century Connecticut* (Chapel Hill, N.C., 1999), esp. 395–398. On the American transmission of classical thought generally and Aristotelian influences specifically by Scottish-trained university professors (such as William Smith in Philadelphia and John Witherspoon at the College of New Jersey [Princeton]), see Thomas P. Miller, "Witherspoon, Blair, and the Rhetoric of Civic Humanism," in Richard B. Sher and Jeffrey R. Smitten, eds., *Scotland and America in the Age of Enlightenment* (Princeton, N.J., 1990), 102–103, 108.

My analysis grows from, yet also revises, two highly influential earlier accounts of Revolutionary culture offered by Bernard Bailyn and Julie Ellison. Bailyn famously argued that Americans' political inspiration originated less in classical sources (of which they had only superficial knowledge) or American experiences (of which Bailyn thought Puritanism to have been the more likely candidate) than from the English whig tradition. By contrast, Ellison's path-breaking work has done much to reinvigorate awareness of the importance of classical traditions in the eighteenth-century British Atlantic as well as to turn attention to the significance of connections between emotion and politics. However, her reliance on literary sources (in the pre-Revolutionary period, all of them derived from Britain) leads her too to an overemphasis on elements of continuity between Britain and America. In particular, her exclusive focus on sensibility precludes attention to other essential elements of Revolutionary emotion, such as anger. She thus does not differentiate between British sensibility and American *spirit*. See Bailyn, *Ideological Origins*, 26, 32; Ellison, *Cato's Tears*, esp. 4–6.

Insistence on the ultimately *American* nature of Revolutionary emotional rhetoric allows us to more fully appreciate the significance of cross-cultural interactions among Europeans, Africans, and Indians on the American continent. Appropriations and negations of competing emotional attributes led to the emergence of a composite American spirit, one that sought to draw on the advantages of gentility, civility, and virility simultaneously and thereby unite white men across America.

7 Bernard Bailyn has claimed that "the American Revolution was above all else an ideological, constitutional, [and] political struggle," not one that had been "undertaken to force changes in the organization of the society or the economy." Whatever the originating political intentions, the immediate social effects of the Revolutionary movement were significant. Bailyn's broader conclusion regarding the essentially political nature of the Revolution is possible only if one is willing to cordon off politics from society, to assume that the boundaries of the political and personal are unbreachable. Yet attention to the intrinsic links between emotion and power—to the connections between personal expression, social communication, and political negotiation—render such assumptions untenable. Bailyn, *Ideological Origins,* vi, and see also 47.

The tendency to view feeling as primarily important in the realm of family and fiction, femininity and faith endures. Even those scholars who have begun to link sentiment to politics have often continued to characterize feeling as feminine. See, for example, G. J. Barker-Benfield, *The Culture of Sensibility: Sex and Society in Eighteenth-Century Britain* (Chicago, 1992); Julia A. Stern, *The Plight of Feeling: Sympathy and Dissent in the Early American Novel* (Chicago, 1997), 2; Andrew Burstein and Catherine Mowbray, "Jefferson and Sterne," *Early American Literature,* XXIX (1994), 21, 31.

Newspapers are the logical place to investigate the role of emotional rhetoric in the creation of patriot unity, given that, as David Waldstreicher has observed, newspapers themselves functioned to transform "the local and present-oriented recent past" into an apparently "self-evident . . . extralocal future." The primacy given to the *Pennsylvania Gazette,* among a number of newspapers consulted, reflects both the emotional influence of Pennsylvania on the culture at large and the fact that the *Gazette* by printing and reprinting accounts originating in many other colonies functioned as a kind of journalistic clearinghouse for the colonies at large. See Waldstreicher, *In the Midst of Perpetual Fetes: The Making of American Nationalism, 1776–1820* (Chapel Hill, N.C., 1997), 33–34. And see Charles E. Clark and Charles Wetherell, "The Measure of Maturity: The *Pennsylvania Gazette,* 1728–1765," *William and Mary Quarterly,* 3d Ser., XLVI (1989), 279–303, esp. 277–278, 295–296.

8 *New-York Mercury,* Dec. 3, 1764, Apr. 8, 1765. The unparalleled standard account of the Stamp Act Crisis in the colonies is Edmund S. Morgan and Helen M. Morgan, *The Stamp Act Crisis: Prologue to Revolution* (Chapel Hill, N.C., 1953; 1995). I have relied extensively on the Morgans' work in constructing my own chronology of the Stamp Act Crisis.

9 Now-discredited evidence that protesters did favor Independence comes, not from the protesters themselves, but from the propaganda of English propo-

nents of the Stamp Act who used claims that colonists sought separation to discredit the colonial protest movement. On this point, see Michael D'Innocenzo and John J. Turner, Jr., "The Role of New York Newspapers in the Stamp Act Crisis, 1764–66," Part 1, *New-York Historical Society Quarterly,* LI (1967), 215–231, esp. 224.

On the issue of violence and potential class conflict, see Pauline Maier, "Popular Uprisings and Civil Authority in Eighteenth-Century America," *WMQ,* 3d Ser., XXVII (1970), 28–29.

10 *Providence Gazette; and Country Journal,* Mar. 16, 1765.

11 *Providence Gazette,* Mar. 9, 1765.

12 *New-York Mercury,* May 6, 1765.

13 *PG,* Sept. 19, 1765.

14 *New-York Mercury,* Sept. 16, 1765.

15 *PG,* Sept. 19, 1765.

16 *New-York Mercury,* Sept. 16, 1765.

17 *Providence Gazette,* Sept. 29, 1764.

18 *New-York Mercury,* Sept. 16, 1765.

19 *New-York Mercury,* Sept. 2, 1765.

20 *New-York Mercury,* Aug. 27, 1764.

21 *Providence Gazette,* Aug. 24, 1765.

22 *Providence Gazette,* Aug. 24, 1765.

23 *PG,* Oct. 3, 10, 1765. Scholarly assessments have typically accorded little importance to Pennsylvania in setting a model for colonial protests, instead bestowing historical favor on Massachusetts or Virginia. For claims about the influence of Massachusetts, see Benjamin H. Newcomb, "Effects of the Stamp Act on Colonial Pennsylvania Politics," *WMQ,* 3d Ser., XXIII (1966), 257–272; or Simon Newman, *Parades and the Politics of the Street: Festive Culture in the Early American Republic* (Philadelphia, 1997), 25. On Virginia, see, for example, J. A. Leo Lemay, "John Mercer and the Stamp Act in Virginia, 1764–1765," *Virginia Magazine of History and Biography,* XCI (1983), 19. In slighting contributions from Pennsylvania, historians have underplayed a significant aspect of Stamp Act resistance—mourning as a mode of protest.

24 On mourning and the communication of loyal opposition, see Waldstreicher, *In the Midst of Perpetual Fetes,* 25. On tearful protests, see also Elizabeth Barnes, "Affecting Relations: Pedagogy, Patriarchy, and the Politics of Sympathy," *American Literary History,* VIII (1996), 597–615.

25 *PG,* Oct. 3, 1765.

26 *PG,* Oct. 3, 10, 1765.

27 Close examination of the specific language of emotion provides key investiga-

tive opportunities: to understand the full spectrum of emotions expressed by actual historic actors, to identify the range of social and political strategies enabled by the invocation of different emotions, and to discern the developing differential character of American emotional ideals.

28 *PG*, Sept. 19, 1765. This statement, offered by the freemen of Newport, Rhode Island, on Sept. 9, 1765, is the first use of the phrase "Spirit of Liberty" to appear in the *Gazette* in connection with Revolutionary protests. While the phrase was not utterly unknown in prior years (it appeared in the *Gazette* on two earlier occasions: May 1, 1755, in a Seven Years War era speech against France; Feb. 28, 1765, in Pennsylvania debates on the royal colony movement), it had not previously been appropriated by American protesters. Its sudden appearance thus marks a clear turning point in the patriot movement.

29 *PG*, Oct. 10, 1765.

30 *New-York Mercury*, Oct. 7, 1765. Both contemporary commentators and modern scholars have noticed the distinctive pattern of control achieved in Pennsylvania. However, unlike contemporary leaders of the protest movement, scholars have been slow to recognize either the impact of strategic use of emotional expression or the influence of Pennsylvania on this process. See, for example, Newcomb, "Effects of the Stamp Act," *WMQ*, 3d Ser., XXIII (1966), 263, 269; Morgan and Morgan, *The Stamp Act Crisis*, 135, 137, 194; or Newman, *Parades*, 23.

31 *New-York Mercury*, Oct. 7, 1765; *PG*, Oct. 24, 1765. Other letters from England also urged protesting colonists to make emotional appeals and were published in colonial newspapers. For example, D'Innocenzo and Turner cite a letter from an Englishman republished in May 1765 in the New York paper the *Post-Boy* which encouraged colonists: "Cry aloud and spare not. If ever there was an occasion to do so, the present is a most alarming one." D'Innocenzo and Turner, "The Role of New York Newspapers," *NYHS Quarterly*, LI (1967), 221.

32 *Pennsylvania Journal, and Weekly Advertiser*, Oct. 31, 1765; *PG*, Nov. 7, 1765.

33 The English engraving was apparently first copied in Boston by John Singleton Copley, then further pirated in Pennsylvania (*PG*, Nov. 21, 1765, under the byline, "Boston, November 7th"). The Wilkinson copy of the engraving discussed here was printed with the notation, "For the Exp[lanation] see the Pennsya. Gazett No. 1926," which is the November 21 edition. For further discussion of the print's publication history as well as identification of all figures, see William Murrell, *A History of American Graphic Humor*, I, 1747–1865 (New York, 1933), 22–25; Ann Uhry Abrams, "Politics, Prints, and John Singleton Copley's Watson and the Shark," *Art Bulletin*, LXI (1979), 265–276,

esp. 269–271; Albert Boime, "Blacks in Shark-Infested Waters: Visual Encodings of Racism in Copley and Homer," *Smithsonian Studies in American Art*, III (1989), 18–47, esp. 28.

34 For an assessment that the English version is "much better drawn . . . and makes its point more clearly and with much less ado," see Murrell, *A History of American Graphic Humor*, I, 22.

35 Some scholars, including Abrams, have concluded that in the American version the ailing figure of Liberty is portrayed as a male *Indian*. While it would be quite interesting if Liberty's race as well as gender were transformed in the American versions, suggesting perhaps the idea that true liberty was no longer British but American, I am not persuaded on this point. There are no symbolic markers (such as feathers) that might indicate the artists intended to depict Liberty as an Indian, and I find the figure of Liberty to be all but indistinguishable from that of Mercury—apart from the latter's symbolic props such as a winged helmet. See Abrams, "Politics, Prints," *Art Bulletin*, LXI (1979), 272.

36 *PG*, Nov. 7, 1765.

37 *PG*, Nov. 7, 1765. The article is dated "Newport, November 4." On British liberty, see Bailyn, *Ideological Origins*, 69.

38 *PG*, Nov. 7, 1765.

39 *PG*, Nov. 7, 1765.

40 *PG*, Nov. 7, 1765.

41 *PG*, Nov. 21, 1765.

42 *PG*, Nov. 21, 1765.

43 The standard account of repeal in Britain is P. D. G. Thomas, *British Politics and the Stamp Act Crisis: The First Phase of the American Revolution, 1763–1767* (New York, 1975). For a later account, which includes a discussion of Parliament's need to save face in light of colonial rebellions, see John L. Bullion, "British Ministers and American Resistance to the Stamp Act, October–December 1765," *WMQ*, 3d Ser., XLIX (1992), 89–107. An extremely useful account of parliamentary debates about repeal, based on the coded diary of a participant, appeared in Lawrence Henry Gipson, "The Great Debate in the Committee of the Whole House of Commons on the Stamp Act, 1766, as Reported by Nathaniel Ryder," *Pennsylvania Magazine of History and Biography*, LXXXVI (1962), 10–41. Gipson's account makes clear that key figures in support of repeal, including Edmund Burke and William Pitt, were particularly preoccupied with the problem of how to show themselves responsive to colonial grievances yet assertive of parliamentary authority.

In assessing the impact of the rhetoric of sympathy and grief on Parliament's decision to repeal, I think it significant that the "star witness" from the colonies in parliamentary debate over repeal (so Benjamin Franklin has been repeatedly characterized by historians) was from Pennsylvania. Franklin took great pains to assure members of Parliament of the affection that colonists felt for Britain (Stephen E. Lucas, *Portents of Rebellion: Rhetoric and Revolution in Philadelphia, 1765–76* [Philadelphia, 1976], 126). This invocation of affection deserves notice because it underscores the importance of mourning as a mode of protest in Pennsylvania; it was the remarkably peaceful nature of protests mounted through mourning that allowed Franklin to credibly make claims of colonial affection even in the face of colonial resistance.

44 *PG,* May 8, 1766.

45 *PG,* May 8, 1766.

46 *PG,* May 8, 1766.

47 English artist Benjamin Wilson (who perhaps not coincidentally was a close friend of Benjamin Franklin) made *The Repeal; or, The Funeral of Miss Ame-Stamp.* The print was widely reproduced; E. P. Richardson concurs with R. T. Haines Halsey in calling it "probably the most popular satirical print ever issued" (E. P. Richardson, "Stamp Act Cartoons in the Colonies," *PMHB,* XCVI [1972], 291). Murrell states that it was reprinted in Philadelphia by May 26, 1766, when Wilkinson (the same printer that issued the *Deplorable State* cartoon) advertised it for sale in *Der wochentliche philadelphische Staatsbote* (see Murrell, *A History of American Graphic Humor,* I, 25). It can now be found in Bernard F. Reilly, Jr., *American Political Prints, 1766–1876: A Catalog of the Collections in the Library of Congress* (Boston, 1991).

48 For further symbolic analysis and political background, see Frederic George Stephens, *Catalogue of Prints and Drawings in the British Museum,* Division I, *Political and Personal Satires, IV, A.D. 1761 to c. A.D. 1770* (London, 1883), 368–373. Stephens notes that the figure weeping into a handkerchief was supposed to be Earl Temple, nicknamed "Lord Gawke . . . so called from his tall and slender figure" (370). While Temple's calves might have been portrayed as especially thin in reference to his actual physique, the artist's decision to portray the skinniest of the eleven men as the one wiping his eyes with a handkerchief surely played deliberately on gendered stereotypes of tearful grief. On the importance of fat calves for the performance of genteel virility, see Karin Calvert, "The Function of Fashion in Early America," in Cary Carson, Ronald Hoffman, and Peter J. Albert, eds., *Of Consuming Interests: The Style of Life in the Eighteenth Century* (Charlottesville, Va. 1994), 274.

49 *PG,* Dec. 31, 1767.

50 "Letters from a Farmer in Pennsylvania to the Inhabitants of the British

Colonies, Letter XII," *PG*, Feb. 18, 1768. Dickinson's series of essays protesting the Townshend Acts, known as "Letters from a Farmer in Pennsylvania," were published sequentially in Pennsylvania papers, including the *Gazette*, in 1768 and widely reprinted throughout the colonies. Too often, these letters have been regarded by modern commentators as a textbook case of ineffective temporizing. It is easy to isolate Dickinson's advice to "speak at the same time the language of affliction and moderation" to make the case that Dickinson's outlook was tepid, his impact comparatively inconsequential, as in George Brown Tindall and David E. Shi, *America: A Narrative History* (New York, 1992), 191. Such an interpretation misrepresents the true significance of Dickinson's influence. While Dickinson's essays did continue to counsel the careful regulation of emotional expression in order to bring about desired parliamentary concessions, they also signaled an important shift in emphasis in the way that spirit and sympathy were to be used. Bernard Bailyn has in fact called Dickinson's letters "the most influential pamphlet published in America before 1776" (*Ideological Origins*, 100).

51 *PG*, Mar. 31, Apr. 7, 1768.

52 *PG*, Feb. 18, 1768.

53 *PG*, Feb. 18, 1768.

54 *PG*, Feb. 18, 1768.

55 *PG*, May 12, 1768.

56 *PG*, Apr. 21, 1768.

57 *PG*, Apr. 21, 1768.

58 *PG*, May 11, 1769.

59 *PG*, May 11, 1769.

60 *PG*, June 22, July 6, 1769.

61 "Extract of a Letter from a Merchant in Philadelphia to His Friend in London, Dated November 26, 1769," *PG*, May 10, 1770.

62 *PG*, Feb. 22, 1770.

63 *PG*, July 6, 1774.

64 *PG*, June 1, 1774. Their invocation of fellow feeling was significant for a second reason as well; as during the Seven Years War, pacifist Quakers in Philadelphia opposed any and all actions that might lead to war. Though members of most denominations supported the work stoppage, influential Quakers opposed it and sent the *Gazette* their own public declaration: "If any of our Community have countenanced or encouraged this Proposal, they have manifested great Inattention to our religious Principles and Profession" (*PG*, June 1, 1774). Thus, the mention of sympathy by those in favor of the protest also represented an attempt to use a, by then, tried-and-true means to discredit

the Quakers—suggesting that only those insensible to feelings of sympathy would abstain from participation in protests.

65 *PG,* June 15, 1774.

66 *PG,* June 15, 1774.

67 *PG,* June 15, 1774.

68 The very notion of "trust," stressed repeatedly in T. H. Breen's work *The Marketplace of Revolution,* implies the importance of emotional considerations. Yet, for Breen, market exchanges seem to subsume emotional ones. Work on street politics and protest rituals has been more attentive to emotion but has not looked closely at the specific role of sympathy in signaling intercolonial bonds. See Breen, *The Marketplace of Revolution: How Consumer Politics Shaped American Independence* (Oxford, 2004), esp. 1, 9, 200, 254.

69 *PG,* Aug. 17, 1774.

70 *PG,* Sept. 21, 1774.

71 Supplement, *PG,* Sept. 21, 1774.

72 *PG,* Mar. 8, 1775.

73 *PG,* May 3, 17, 1775.

74 "The Twelve United Colonies, by Their Delegates in Congress, to the Inhabitants of Great Britain," *PG,* July 12, 1775.

75 Ibid.

76 *PG,* Aug. 9, 1775.

77 *PG,* Nov. 29, 1775.

78 *PG,* Nov. 29, 1775.

79 Washington, "To the Inhabitants of Canada," *PG,* Oct. 11, 1775.

80 "The Humble Address of the General Committee of Mechanics in Union, of the City and County of New-York . . . ," *PG,* June 12, 1776. Modern studies have begun to emphasize how late in the course of the protest movement sentimental bonds were broken. Barnes argues that only after the battles of Lexington and Concord did "a 'new era of politics' [arise] . . . that reconceive[d] the relationship between Britain and America as economically and not sentimentally based." Brendan McConville stresses the long duration of colonial affection for the king and how significance of the ultimate withdrawal of that affection was for the coming of revolution. While in broad agreement with McConville's analysis, I would suggest that colonial "affection" for the king should not be accepted as transparent and devoid of power implications. As detailed in Chapter 3, political affection was synonymous with political loyalty; declarations of affection for the king thus amounted to denials of treason as much as to expressions of emotion sincerely felt. See Barnes, "Affecting Relations," *American Literary History,* VIII (1996), 602; and

see McConville, *The King's Three Faces: The Rise and Fall of Royal America, 1688–1776* (Chapel Hill, N.C., 2006), esp. 251–252.

81 On the issue of citizenship and identity, see Caroll Smith-Rosenberg, "Dis-Covering the Subject of the 'Great Constitutional Discussion,' 1786–1789," *Journal of American History*, LXXIX (1992–1993), 841–873; on racial patri-archy in the United States, see Pauline Schloesser, *The Fair Sex: White Women and Racial Patriarchy in the Early American Republic* (New York, 2002).

My findings complement those of Holly Brewer, who notes that as reason, rather than birth, became a primary qualification for power, public roles and citizenship rights became increasingly closed to anyone other than adult white males. Coincidentally, my metaphoric use of the term "entailment" echoes Brewer's more literal discussion of the issue. The coincidence is tell-ing, for our findings, taken together, show once more the interrelation of reason and emotion and demonstrate that emphasis on either could work equally to tighten lines of authority. See Brewer, "Entailing Aristocracy in Colonial Virginia: 'Ancient Feudal Restraints' and Revolutionary Reform," *WMQ*, 3d Ser., LIV (1997), 307–346, esp. 346; Brewer, *By Birth or Consent: Children, Law, and the Anglo-American Revolution in Authority* (Chapel Hill, N.C., 2005).

Postlude

1 [Thomas Paine], *Common Sense; Addressed to the Inhabitants of America . . .* , 1st ed. (Philadelphia: Bell, 1776) (Evans 14954), [ii], 41. This first edition of *Common Sense,* published (without attribution) on Jan. 9, 1776, does not contain either the "Appendix" or the "Address to the People Called Quakers," both of which were published subsequently in a "New Edition" printed by William and Thomas Bradford on Feb. 14, 1776 (Evans 14959). *Common Sense,* like the majority of pamphlets discussed in this chapter, was originally published anonymously. In discussing these works, many of them now less well known than Paine's, I have relied on the commonly accepted attributions suggested by Charles Evans and his successors that are provided in *Evans Digital Edition: Early American Imprints, Series I: Evans (1689–1800)*.

2 [Paine], *Common Sense*, 1st ed., 12, 13, 60.

3 The importance of emotional rhetoric in eighteenth-century Pennsylvania politics—and the influence of this rhetoric on Paine's masterwork—has often gone unappreciated. Bernard Bailyn, for example, has argued that, taken as a whole, the pamphlet literature of the American Revolution is remarkable for its "absence of motivating power" and lack of a "'peculiar emotional in-

tensity.'" Of Paine specifically he claims, "The 'darling impudence,' the 'uncommon frenzy' which gave *Common Sense* its unique power, Paine brought with him from England in 1774; it had been nourished in another culture and was recognized at the time to be an alien quality in American writing." To the contrary, I argue that Paine's *Common Sense* grew directly out of the fertile soil of Pennsylvania's emotional culture and achieved the extraordinary popularity that it did precisely because it succeeded so well in marshaling the emotional language that was intrinsic to the articulation of Revolutionary political thought across America. See Bernard Bailyn, *The Ideological Origins of the American Revolution,* enl. ed. (Cambridge, Mass., 1992), 17–18. And see Eric Foner, *Tom Paine and Revolutionary America* (New York, 1976), 82.

4 [Paine], *Common Sense,* 1st ed., 41.

5 Candidus [James Chalmers], *Plain Truth: Addressed to the Inhabitants of America* (Philadelphia, 1776), 2. Chalmers credits these lines to Rousseau.

6 The assertion that Benjamin Franklin not only read but also "revised parts of the manuscript" before it went to print comes from Franklin's grandson, William Temple Franklin. On Franklin's claim, see John Keane, *Tom Paine: A Political Life* (Boston, 1995), 107, 555. For a critique of W. T. Franklin's general unreliability, see J. A. Leo Lemay, "Franklin and the *Autobiography:* An Essay on Recent Scholarship," *Eighteenth-Century Studies,* I (1967), 185–211, esp. 193–195. Other scholars have also emphasized the importance of Paine's connections to such Philadelphia figures as Benjamin Rush and David Rittenhouse. See Scott Liell, *Forty-six Pages: Thomas Paine, "Common Sense," and the Turning Point to American Independence* (Philadelphia, 2003), 66; Foner, *Tom Paine,* 73–75.

Of course, Paine *was* very much an international figure. Still, awareness of the length and breadth of Paine's legacy should not preclude consideration of the American inception and impact of *Common Sense.* On Paine's internationalism, see Seth Cotlar, "Radical Conceptions of Property Rights and Economic Equality in the Early Republic: The Trans-Atlantic Dimension," *Explorations in Early American Culture,* IV (2000), 191–219, esp. 197. On the significance of the Pennsylvania context of *Common Sense,* see Edward Larkin, "Inventing an American Revolutionary Public: Thomas Paine, the *Pennsylvania Magazine,* and American Revolutionary Political Discourse," *Early American Literature,* XXXIII (1998), 250–276, esp. 253.

7 I have followed Robert A. Ferguson's considered assessment that *Common Sense* likely went through 120,000–150,000 copies in its first year alone. Richard Gimbel provides a comprehensive bibliography of *Common Sense* editions; *Common Sense* went through sixteen Philadelphia print runs, plus

twenty more editions across the colonies, plus nearly that many again in Britain, all in 1776 alone. See Robert A. Ferguson's excellent essay, "The Commonalities of *Common Sense*," *William and Mary Quarterly*, 3d Ser., LVII (2000), 465–504, esp. 466; Richard Gimbel, *A Bibliographical Check List of "Common Sense," with an Account of Its Publication* (Port Washington, N.Y., 1956).

8 [Thomas Paine], *Common Sense; Addressed to the Inhabitants of America . . . A New Edition, with Several Additions in the Body of the Work, to Which Is Added an Appendix; Together with an Address to the People Called Quakers* (Philadelphia: Bradford, [1776]) (Evans 14959); "In Assembly . . . Resolved," June 30, 1775, *Minutes of the Provincial Council of Pennsylvania, from the Organization to the Termination of the Proprietary Government* (Philadelphia, Harrisburg, 1851–1852), X, 280 (hereafter cited as *MPCP*); "In Congress . . . Resolved," Aug. 26, 1775, *MPCP*, X, 292; "Rules for Establishing Rank or Precedence amongst the Pennsylvania Associators," Aug. 26, 1775, *MPCP*, X, 321.

9 "Rules for Establishing Rank or Precedence amongst the Pennsylvania Associators," Aug. 26, 1775, *MPCP*, X, 321; John Lathrop to Thomas Bradford, Providence, Sept. 6, 1775, Bradford Correspondence, Historical Society of Pennsylvania (HSP), Philadelphia, and William Bradford to Thomas Bradford, May 29, 1760. Information about Tace Bradford Wallace was gleaned from William Bradford, Jr., to Col. Joshua M. Wallace, Jan. 27, 1778, in "Selections from the Wallace Papers," *Pennsylvania Magazine of History and Biography*, XL (1916), 335–343, esp. 336–338.

As will become clear below, Lathrop's use of the language of grief in his personal correspondence echoed the Revolutionary rallying cries that had been in use among political pamphleteers for much of the last decade but were already fading in popularity among propagandists eager to turn from words to action. Indeed, Lathrop's declaration that his heart filled with grief *on behalf* of those in Boston was actually closer in intent to an expression of sympathy than of sorrow, a point that coincides with the shifting emphasis of pamphlet literature.

10 [Paine], *Common Sense*, 1st ed., 17, 29, 42, 52. The quotation here reverses Paine's original order.

11 Rusticus [pseud.], *Remarks on a Late Pamphlet Entitled Plain Truth* (Philadelphia, 1776), 21; John Witherspoon, *The Dominion of Providence over the Passions of Men . . .* (Philadelphia, 1776), 11, 30, 45.

12 William Smith, "A Charge Delivered May 17, 1757, at the First Anniversary Commencement in the College and Academy of Philadelphia, by the Reverend Mr. Smith, Provost of the Same . . . ," *Pennsylvania Gazette*, Aug. 11, 1757

(hereafter cited as Smith, "Charge," 1757); [Paine], *Common Sense*, 1st ed., 41; Jack Retort [Isaac Hunt], *A Humble Attempt at Scurrillity in Imitation of the Great Masters of That Art, the Rev. Dr. Sm——th . . .* ([Philadelphia], 1765), 10; Cato [William Smith], "To the People of Pennsylvania, Letter VIII," *Pennsylvania Gazette*, Apr. 24, 1776 (hereafter cited as *PG*). Smith's eight "Cato" letters were published in *PG* between Mar. 13 and Apr. 24, 1776.

13 Candidus [Chalmers], *Plain Truth*, 51, 53, 59–61; Cato [Smith], "To The People of Pennsylvania, Letter III," *PG*, Mar. 20, 1776.

14 William Smith, "Preface," in Thomas Barton, *Unanimity and Public Spirit: A Sermon Preached at Carlisle . . .* (Philadelphia, 1755), xiii; William Smith, *An Oration in Memory of General Montgomery . . .* (Philadelphia, 1776), 25; Cato [Smith], "To the People of Pennsylvania, Letter IV," *PG*, Mar. 27, 1776.

15 [Paine], *Common Sense*, 1st ed., 63. There is every reason to think Paine was provoking Smith deliberately. Not only would Smith take it upon himself to critique Paine at length in his guise as Cato, but Paine replied to Smith's Cato letters in kind with a series of "Foresters Letters" of his own, published in several Pennsylvania papers in the spring of 1776. Furthermore, this possible reference to Smith's own discussion of "narrow hearts" recalls a section of Smith's speech ("Charge," 1757) that he omitted when reissuing it in 1775, precisely because its inclusion was no longer politically convenient. For more on the 1775 version of Smith's "Charge," see below. On the "Foresters Letters," see Edward Larkin, "'Could the Wolf Bleat like the Lamb': Thomas Paine's Critique and the Early American Public Sphere," *Arizona Quarterly*, LV (1999), 1–37, esp. 11–13.

16 Candidus [Chalmers], "Introduction," *Plain Truth*, n.p.

17 Cato [Smith], "To the People of Pennsylvania, Letter V," *PG*, Apr. 3, 1776.

18 Robert Bell, "Robert Bell, Bookseller, To the Public," in [Thomas Paine], *Common Sense . . .*, 3d ed. (Philadelphia: Bell, 1776) (Evans 14966), [149].

Unfortunately for Bell, he and Paine soon had a falling out, leading Paine to turn to William and Thomas Bradford to publish the complete edition of *Common Sense*. Still, Bell's loss is our gain, since his effort to defend himself in print provides clear evidence of the way he viewed his Revolutionary role. Bell published the pamphlet quoted here to compete with Paine's expanded Bradford edition of *Common Sense*, adding his own selection of additional essays to a pirated version of the Bradford edition. For a fuller account of the Bell-Paine conflict, see James N. Green, "English Books and Printing in the Age of Franklin," in Hugh Amory and David D. Hall, eds. *A History of the Book in America*, I (Cambridge, 2000), 295–296.

Bell frequently referred to himself as the "Provedore to the Sentimental ists," doing so in the front matter to an edition of *Plain Truth* that also contained an advertisement for his edition of *Common Sense*. See Robert Bell, "The Printer to the Public: On the Freedom of the Press," in Candidus [Chalmers], *Plain Truth*. Jay Fliegelman has also noted Bell's use of the sobriquet "Provedore to the Sentimentalists," though without tying it to Bell's other favorite appellation, "republican printer." In fact, Flielgelman notes, when Bell opened up a circulating library in 1774, he placed in each book a bookplate bearing the claim that his library was a place "where SENTIMEN-TALISTS, whether LADIES or GENTLEMEN, may become READERS." See Fliegelman, *Declaring Independence: Jefferson, Natural Language, and the Culture of Performance* (Stanford, Calif., 1993), 60–61, 79.

19 Witherspoon, *The Dominion of Providence*, 14.

20 Witherspoon was not alone in his criticism of Paine as a man without established social standing. In order to appreciate the truly revolutionary nature of Paine's political and social philosophy, it is important to recognize just how entrenched class pretensions had become among the colonial Philadelphia elite by the second third of the eighteenth century. On these points, see Foner, *Tom Paine*, 72, 85. For another view of social tensions in Pennsylvania society, see Michael Zuckerman, "Authority in Early America: The Decay of Deference in the Provincial Periphery," *Early American Studies*, no. 2 (Fall 2003), 1–29.

21 [Paine], *Common Sense*, 1st ed., ii, 41, 42.

22 Ibid., i–ii, 3. Bernard Bailyn has identified "Paine's view of society and human nature" as being particularly reviled by his Tory attackers. See Bailyn, *Ideological Origins*, 287.

23 See Charles R. Hildeburn, "Francis Hopkinson," *PMHB*, II (1878), 314–324, esp. 319; John Adams to Abigail Adams, Aug. 21, 1776, as cited in George E. Hastings, "A Note on 'Miss Keys, a Famous New Jersey Beauty,' " *PMHB*, LVI (1932), 277–279; Paul M. Zall, ed., *Comical Spirit of Seventy-six: The Humor of Francis Hopkinson* (San Marino, Calif., 1976), 10, 11, and, on Hopkinson's biography, 58–59.

Adams's antidemocratic tendencies led him to abhor Paine's *Common Sense* on social grounds. Paine's pamphlet was "so democratical . . . that it must produce confusion and every Evil Work." See John Adams, *Thoughts on Government*, as quoted and discussed in Ferguson, "The Commonalities of *Common Sense*," *WMQ*, 3d Ser., LVII (2000), 488. For further discussion of Adams's social conservatism, see Bailyn, *Ideological Origins*, 289; Foner, *Tom Paine*, 122.

24 [Paine], *Common Sense,* 1st ed., 31; William Smith, "Charge," 1757; and Smith, "Charge to the Graduates," in *Account of the Commencement in the College of Philadelphia, May 17, 1775* (Philadelphia, 1775), 10–15. Paine arrived in Philadelphia on Nov. 30, 1774. Colonial Pennsylvania pamphlets reprinted or reprised on the eve of the Revolution include [Anthony Benezet], *Thoughts on the Nature of War . . .* (Philadelphia, [1766]), and *Thoughts on the Nature of War Etc.* ([Philadelphia, 1776]); Samuel Chew, *The Speech of Samuel Chew . . .* (Philadelphia, 1741), and *The Speech of Samuel Chew . . . Now Re-published by Desire of Several Gentlemen* (Philadelphia, 1775); Society of Friends, *An Apology for the People Called Quakers . . .* ([Philadelphia, 1757]), and *An Apology for the People Called Quakers . . . Re-published by the Direction of the Meeting for Sufferings . . .* (Philadelphia, 1776); John Abr. Lidenius, *The Lawfulness of Defensive War . . .* (Philadelphia, 1756), and John Carmichael, *A Self-Defensive War Lawful . . .* (Philadelphia, 1775).

25 Society of Friends, *An Epistle from the Meeting for Sufferings, Held in Philadelphia for Pennsylvania and New-Jersey, the Fifth Day of the First Month 1775* (Philadelphia, 1775), 3; Society of Friends, *An Epistle from Our General Spring Meeting . . .* (Philadephia, 1755).

26 Friends, *An Epistle from the Meeting for Sufferings,* 1, 3.

27 Society of Friends, *The Testimony of the People Called Quakers, Given Forth . . . the Twenty-fourth Day of the First Month, 1775* (Philadelphia, 1775).

28 Ibid.; Friends, *An Apology for the People Called Quakers* [1757], 1.

29 [Anthony Benezet], *An Earnest Address to Such of the People Called Quakers as Are Sincerely Desirous of Supporting and Maintaining the Christian Testimony of Their Ancestors, Occasioned by a Piece Intituled, "The Testimony of the People Called Quakers" . . .* (Philadelphia, 1775), 7.

30 Ibid., 9–11, 14. Benezet's quotation from *The Testimony* was verbatim. The ellipses here are mine, inserted for the sake of consistency with the brief passage of *The Testimony* excerpted above.

31 Carmichael, *A Self-Defensive War Lawful,* 9, 15, 24, 27–28.

32 Smith, "Charge," 1757, and "Charge to the Graduates," in *Account of the Commencement,* 1775, 13.

33 William Smith, *A Sermon on the Present Situation of American Affairs . . .* (Philadelphia, 1775), 28–29; Francis Alison, *Peace and Union Recommended . . .* (Philadelphia, 1758), 24.

34 Eric Foner discusses the unlikely alliance between " 'the two aristocracies' of the Quaker and Proprietary elites" that emerged in opposition to the Revolutionary movement in Pennsylvania. See Foner, *Tom Paine,* 60, 108.

35 Elizabeth Sandwith Drinker, in Elaine Forman Crane, ed., *The Diary of Elizabeth Drinker* (Boston, 1991), I, 214–215; Philadelphia Committee of Inspection, *In Committee, of Inspection and Observation, February 5th, 1776* (Philadelphia, 1776).

36 John Drinker to Samuel Allinson, 31 Twelfth Month 1771, Samuel Allinson Letterbook, 1764–, Allinson Family Papers, Haverford College Quaker Collection.

37 [Paine], *Common Sense,* 1st ed., 43, 52.

38 Ibid., 47.

39 [Nicholas Scull], *Kawanio Che Keeteru: A True Relation of a Bloody Battle Fought between George and Lewis, in the Year 1755* (Philadelphia, 1756), 9.

40 [Paine], *Common Sense,* 1st ed., 40.

41 Society of Friends, *The Ancient Testimony and Principles of the People Called Quakers, Renewed, with Respect to the King and Government; And Touching the Commotions Now Prevailing in These and Other Parts of America, Addressed to the People in General* ([Philadelphia, 1776]), 3; [Benezet], *Thoughts on War Etc.* [1776], 3, 8. Significantly, in republishing the former pamphlet, Quakers clearly hoped to revive their old pacifist alliance with Pennsylvania Germans, as an edition was also published in German (*Das alte Zeugniss und die Grund-Sätze des Volks so man Quäker nennet . . .* [Germantown, 1776]).

42 "Address to the People Called Quakers," in [Paine], *Common Sense* (Philadelphia: Bradford, [1776]) (Evans 14959), 46.

43 [Benezet], *Thoughts on War* [1776], 3; Smith, "Charge to the Graduates," in [Smith], *Account of the Commencement, 1775,* 13. For the line "Passions are the elements of Life," see Pope, *An Essay on Man,* Epistle I, 170, as quoted in Chapter 1.

44 [Paine], *Common Sense,* 1st ed., 60.

45 "Address to the People Called Quakers," in [Paine], *Common Sense* (Bradford, [1776]) (Evans 14959), 46.

46 [Paine], *Common Sense,* 1st ed., 60. For the line, "SELF-LOVE and SOCIAL are the same," see Pope, *An Essay on Man,* Epistle III, 318, as quoted in Chapter 1.

47 Elizabeth Fergusson to Mrs. Campbell, Graeme Park, May 9, 1779, in Simon Gratz, ed., "Some Material for a Biography of Mrs. Elizabeth Fergusson, *née* Graeme," *PMHB,* XLI (1917), 385–398, esp. 386, 387.

48 George Washington, "Extracts from a Letter of Washington to Congress," Oct. 16, 1777, in Simon Gratz, ed., "Some Material for a Biography of Mrs. Elizabeth Fergusson, *née* Graeme," *PMHB,* XXXIX (1915), 257–391, esp. 290.

49 Elizabeth Graeme Fergusson, "To the Honourable Representatives of the Freemen in General Assembly Met," Feb. 20, 1781, in Gratz, "Some Material for a Biography," *PMHB*, XXXIX (1915), 308, and Elizabeth Fergusson to Mrs. Campbell, Graeme Park, May 9, 1779, *PMHB*, XLI (1917), 388.

50 Elizabeth Graeme Fergusson, "To the Honourable Representatives of the Freemen in General Assembly Met," Feb. 20, 1781, in Gratz, "Some Material for a Biography," *PMHB*, XXXIX (1915), 308, and Joseph Reed to Mrs. Stockton, June 14, 1779, 297.

51 Peter Grievous, Esq, A.B.C.D.E. [Francis Hopkinson], *A Pretty Story Written in the Year of Our Lord, 2774* (Philadelphia, 1774), 16.

52 Smith, *Sermon on the Present Situation*, 11–13, and *An Oration in Memory of General Montgomery*, 21.

53 William Franklin, "Speech of His Excellency William Franklin . . . to the General Assembly," *PG*, May 24, 1775.

54 Cato [Smith], "To the People of Pennsylvania, Letter V," *PG*, Apr. 3, 1776.

55 Carmichael, *A Self-Defensive War Lawful*, 31, 32.

56 [Paine], *Common Sense*, 1st ed., 34, 47.

57 Ibid., 33, 60.

58 Ibid., 41, 60. On the use of the phrase "love and honor," see, for example, Samuel Richardson, who, in the 1748 novel *Clarissa* (widely read in Britain and British America alike) had his heroine use the phrase, "vowing love and honour at the altar." For this quotation, see "Violator," 1, *Oxford English Dictionary Online*, 2d ed. (2001).

59 See Ferguson, "The Commonalities of *Common Sense*," *WMQ*, 3d Ser., LVII (2000), 475; Larkin, "Inventing an American Revolutionary Public," *Early American Literature*, XXXIII (1998), 250–276, esp. 253; Jay Fliegelman, *Prodigals and Pilgrims: The American Revolution against Patriarchal Authority* (Cambridge, 1982), 124; and see Winthrop D. Jordan, "Familial Politics: Thomas Paine and the Killing of the King, 1776," *Journal of American History*, LX (1973–1974), 294–308, esp. 302–303.

   Masculinity as a Revolutionary preoccupation has attracted renewed scholarly attention. Edward Larkin notes that Paine frequently "stigmatized any opposing arguments as not only unthinking and/or reactionary, but also effeminate." See Larkin, "The Early American Public Sphere," *Arizona Quarterly*, LV (1999), 9. On revolutionary connections between masculinity and sensibility, see Sarah Knott, "Sensibility and the American War for Independence," *American Historical Review*, CIX (2004), 19–40.

60 Cato [Smith], "To the People of Pennsylvania, Letter III," *PG*, Mar. 20, 1776; [Paine], *Common Sense*, 1st ed., 59.

61 Rusticus, *Remarks on a Late Pamphlet,* 29, 30; Eliza Moode to Betsy Sandwith, 14 Second Month 1760, Drinker and Sandwith Family Papers, HSP.

Far from being transparent reflections of colonists' inner state, expressions of affection had concrete ramifications for the status of the state. Declarations of love for the king amounted to denials of treason, and claims of royal alienation equated with calls for Independence. For an argument that colonial claims of love for the king did evidence a deep-seated commitment to monarchism, see Brendan McConville, *The King's Three Faces: The Rise and Fall of Royal America, 1688–1776* (Chapel Hill, N.C., 2006), 10–11, 281–311.

62 [Benezet], *Thoughts on War Etc.* [1776], 3.

63 Witherspoon, *The Dominion of Providence,* 11, 32–33, 43.

64 "Appendix," in [Paine], *Common Sense* (Bradford, [1776]) (Evans 14959), 44. Robert Ferguson reads this same line on "popular rage" differently than I do, asserting that "Paine is vehemently part of that rage" and arguing that "anger provides the cohesive social force" behind *Common Sense.* Insofar as Ferguson's goal is to consider *Common Sense* as a "seminal text for thinking about 'the art of persuasion' in American life," his speculations on passages that could be interpreted as sounding angry may well be valid. However, in ignoring Paine's avoidance of the actual language of anger as well as in omitting discussion of Paine's own explicit disavowals of this emotion, Ferguson misses the chance to understand the full implications that expressions of anger held for social communication in eighteenth-century America as well as the peculiar Quaker-influenced Pennsylvania context that circumscribed Paine's ability to invoke anger openly. See Ferguson, "The Commonalities of *Common Sense,*" *WMQ,* 3d Ser., LVII (2474), 465, 492, 493, 497.

65 [Paine], *Common Sense,* 1st ed., 41, 45; "Address to the People Called Quakers," in [Paine], *Common Sense* (Bradford, [1776]) (Evans 14959), 50.

66 Candidus [Chalmers], *Plain Truth,* 71, 75, 80; Cato [Smith], "To The People of Pennsylvania, Letter IV," *PG,* Mar. 26, 1776, and "Letter VIII," *PG,* Apr. 10. 1776; Rusticus, *Remarks on a Late Pamphlet,* 14.

67 Witherspoon, *The Dominion of Providence,* 11; Chew, *The Speech of Samuel Chew* (1775), 3.

68 [Paine], *Common Sense,* 1st ed., [i], 1; Friends, *The Testimony of the People Called Quakers,* [i]; Society of Friends, *To the Representatives of the Freemen of the Province of Pennsylvania, in General Assembly Met: The Address of the People Called Quakers* ([Philadelphia, 1775]), [i, ii]; and Friends, *Ancient Testimony Renewed,* 3.

69 Smith, *Sermon on the Present Situation,* 17.

70 Carmichael, *A Self-Defensive War Lawful,* 29. In contradistinction to Fer-

guson's characterization of *Common Sense* as a work defined in large part by anger, Andrew Burstein has argued for appreciating the importance of sympathy. His portrayal of *Common Sense* comes closer to my own, stressing as it does the importance of feeling as a source of "communion." Burstein does not discuss these *limits* of feeling outlined in Paine's vision, my subject here. See Burstein, "The Political Character of Sympathy," *Journal of the Early Republic*, XXI (2001), 601–632, esp. 605.

71 Chew, *The Speech of Samuel Chew* (1775), 2–3; *In Congress, July 4, 1776, A Declaration by the Representatives of the United States of America, in General Congress Assembled* (Philadelphia: Dunlap, [1776]).

72 Benjamin Chew, as quoted in "An Account of the Valedictory Oration, *Spoken by* Benjamin Chew, B.A.," and William Smith, remarks, in *Account of the Commencement in the College of Philadelphia, May 17, 1775,* 10. On young Benjamin Chew's ownership of Pope, see Chapter 1.

73 Chew, *The Speech of Samuel Chew* (1775), 3. On the reluctance of Pennsylvania's old ruling elite to embrace the cause of Independence, see Foner, *Tom Paine,* 120.

74 In emphasizing Paine's effort to collapse the supposed boundaries between the emotions of elites and those of commoners I take a position that is subtly but significantly different from that of scholars like Robert Ferguson who, following Evelyn Hinz, argues that "the great master stroke in [Paine']s rhetorical plan" was his "uncanny ability to articulate the emotions of the mob." See Ferguson, "The Commonalities of *Common Sense*," *WMQ*, 3d Ser., LVII (2000), 493.

Importantly, Paine's position resonates nicely with the foundational assumptions of this study regarding modern debates on emotion, biological universalism, and social constructionism. Paine clearly recognized the possibility of social and cultural influences on the expression of emotion. He stated outright in the very first line of *Common Sense* that the "Sentiments contained" in his pamphlet might not have been "sufficiently fashionable to procure them general Favour." Feelings subject to fashion are clearly candidates for being labeled as what we would today call social constructions. Yet Paine had no difficulty squaring this common sense observation with the argument that God had "implanted" emotions—feelings and passions—in *all* mankind in order to distinguish men from animals. By denying the reality of cultural assumptions about divisions between the "passions" of commoners and the refined "feelings" of the elite, Paine, in postmodern terms, "denaturalized" an important marker of social divisions. Along with the numerous Pennsylvanians both renowned and obscure whose words have been analyzed in the course of this project, Paine provided a language and a theory through which to popularize Enlightenment ideas on natural equality. See William M. Reddy, "Against Constructionism: The Historical Ethnography of Emotion," *Current Anthropology*, XXXVIII (1997), 327–351. (Reddy's work is discussed extensively in the Introduction to this study.)

75 [Paine], *Common Sense*, 1st ed., 3–4. Prior scholars have sometimes provided a rather different portrayal of Paine and his philosophy. Colin Wells, for example, credits Paine with envisioning "an earthly utopia of reason and virtue." Taking a broad view of Paine's collected works (rather than of *Common Sense* specifically), Eric Foner came to similar conclusions about Paine's outlook. See Wells, *The Devil and Doctor Dwight: Satire and Theology in the Early American Republic* (Chapel Hill, N.C., 2002), 10, 18; Foner, *Tom Paine*, 89–91.

My assessment is in line with that of Gordon S. Wood, who argues that for Paine, as for Calvinist clergy, "the Enlightenment image of a virtuous society seemed extremely cloudy" (*The Creation of the American Republic, 1776–1787* [Chapel Hill, N.C., 1969], 114–115).

In emphasizing Paine's advocacy of formal government during the American Revolution, I follow Robert Ferguson as well as Michael Warner. See Ferguson, "The Commonalities of *Common Sense*," *WMQ*, 3d Ser., LVII (2000), 499, 503; Warner, *The Letters of the Republic: Publication and the Public Sphere in Eighteenth-Century America* (Cambridge, Mass., 1990), 106. On Paine's constitutionalism, see Alfred F. Young, "English Plebeian Culture and Eighteenth-Century American Radicalism," in Margaret Jacob and James Jacob, eds., *The Origins of Anglo-American Radicalism* (Boston, 1984), 200–201.

76 "Appendix," in [Paine], *Common Sense* (Bradford, [1776]) (Evans 14959), 41.

No doubt the culture of sensibility did help to encourage some social progressivism such as the development of antislavery arguments. However, the fact remains that the actual end to American slavery came not through moral suasion but by government decree—an outcome Paine might have foreseen a century in advance. Given Paine's own involvement in antislavery activities in Philadelphia, it seems fair to suggest that he might well have had this and other similar issues in mind (including the rights of propertyless men as well as, perhaps, women's rights) when he argued against turning only to emotion to try to shore up unsteady virtue and advocated instead reliance on the rule of law. Significantly, Paine published the essays "African Slavery in America" and "An Occasional Letter to the Female Sex" in the *Pennsylvania Journal; and the Weekly Advertiser* in 1775, shortly before beginning work on

Common Sense. He was also one of the first members of the Pennsylvania antislavery society organized in Philadelphia on April 14, 1775. See Philip S. Foner, ed., *The Complete Writings of Thomas Paine* (New York, 1969), 15–19, 34–38.

77 Paine's aim was *not* simply to contain what Ferguson labels the "emotionally driven mob" through the rule of law, but rather to persuade high and low alike that passions and feelings were the same across classes. Elites could no more shirk the rule of law on the assumption that their so-called refined feelings would always be virtuous than commoners could be allowed to run amok giving free rein to their supposedly angry passions. Significantly, when Paine raised the specter of the rage of the people, he did so chiefly in order to persuade elites to support a written constitution that would guarantee rights for all. See Ferguson, "The Commonalities of *Common Sense*," *WMQ,* 3d Ser., LVII (2000), 499, 503.

78 Thomas Jefferson, entries 204, 205, in Douglas L. Wilson, ed., *Jefferson's Literary Commonplace Book* (Princeton, N.J., 1989), 90; on the dating of those entries, see Appendix A, esp. 201–203. Many other members of the Revolutionary generation also quoted the *Essay on Man.* John Dickinson, for example, quotes Pope on vice in *Letters from a Farmer in Pennsylvania, to the Inhabitants of the British Colonies* (Philadelphia, 1768), 59.

79 *In Congress, July 4, 1776, A Declaration by the Representatives of the United States of America, in General Congress Assembled* (Philadelphia: Dunlap, [1776]).

Appendix

1 In the discussion that follows, definitions from the *Oxford English Dictionary* provide a starting point for discussion, not the last word on usage in eighteenth-century British America. Indeed, many of the fine distinctions I call close attention to are not highlighted in the *OED.* For each term of emotion under consideration, only those *OED* definitions deriving from the eighteenth century are mentioned, and supporting citations are drawn from my research in eighteenth-century Pennsylvania sources. While it is not practical to provide multiple supporting citations for each word defined here, interested readers will note many further supporting examples in material quoted throughout this book.

2 "Emotion," 4a, b, *Oxford English Dictionary Online,* 2d ed. (2001) (cited hereafter as *OED*).

It is important to note in this vein that the modern definition of emotion as a "mental feeling" denies a connection to the body and its processes, a further contradiction of eighteenth-century ways of considering the issue. In the eighteenth century, the relation of emotion to the will was central to religious ideas about emotion while the relations of emotions to the body, and specifically to humoural theory, were crucial to evaluations of the worth of emotions. My intention in employing the word *emotion* in my analysis is not to impose twenty-first-century, putatively "scientific," definitions on the eighteenth century, but rather to underscore that my interest in emotion encompasses a set of concerns that might or might not have been viewed as linked in the eyes of my eighteenth-century subjects.

3 "Affection," 1a, 2a, 6a, *OED*; George Whitefield, *A Brief and General Account of the First Part of the Life of the Reverend Mr. Geo. Whitefield, from His Birth, to His Entering into Holy Orders* (Philadelphia, 1740), 50.

4 "Feeling," 2a, 4a, 9d, *OED*; Gilbert Tennent, preface, *Twenty Three Sermons upon the Chief End of Man* . . . (Philadelphia, 1744); Rachel Wilson, "Religious Visit of Rachel Wilson of Kendal, England to The Meetings of Friends in the American Colonies (made chiefly on horeseback) from New England to Charleston, S.C. 1768–69," 79, MS, Haverford Colllege Quaker Collection. Significantly, as noted in the text, Wilson was among Philadelphia Quakers when she had this experience. Her manuscript journal circulated widely among Pennsylvania Quakers.

5 On Jonathan Edwards's *Treatise on Religious Affections,* see George Marsden, *Jonathan Edwards: A Life* (New Haven, Conn., 2003), 284–290, esp. 286–287. In discussing the role of emotion in Edwards's ministry, Catherine Brekus makes the useful point that "Edwards did not want ministers to move their listeners' *passions* (a negative term for him), but their *affections,* which he defined as involving not only the heart, but the understanding as well." Brekus's taxonomy of Edwardsian emotion fits well with the conclusions I've drawn regarding patterns of language usage in eighteenth-century Pennsylvania. As I argue, passion was a traditionally negative term not only for Edwards but also for most Anglo-Americans, making Pope's proclamations to the contrary revolutionary in impact. See Catherine A. Brekus, *Strangers and Pilgrims: Female Preaching in America, 1740–1845* (Chapel Hill, N.C., 1998), 34.

6 "Sensibility," 6, *OED*; *Pennsylvania Gazette,* Dec. 11, 1755, June 17, 1762 (hereafter cited as *PG*).

7 "Sentiment," 6a, 7a, 9a, *OED*; William Dunlap, *Books and Stationary, Just Imported from London, and to Be Sold by W. Dunlap, at the Newest-Printing-Office on the South-Side of the Jersey-Market, Philadelphia* ([Philadelphia], 1760), 1; David Hall, "Imported and to be Sold . . . at the New Printing Office

on Market Street," *PG*, Mar. 19, 1761; and see Adam Smith, *The Theory of Moral Sentiments* (Indianapolis, Ind., 1976).

8 "Sentiment," 9a, *OED*.

9 On passion as anger and lust, see "Passion," 7a, b, 8a, b, 9, *OED*; for quoted material, see "Passion," 5a, 6a; and see also 10a.

10 *PG*, May 27, 1756.

11 "Passion," 6c, *OED*; *PG*, May 25, 1769.

12 *PG*, Dec. 18, 1744. The fascination of early modern philosophers from Hobbes to Locke with uncovering links between passion and action has been described in Susan James, *Passion and Action: The Emotions in Seventeenth-Century Philosophy* (Oxford, 1997).

Index

An (Society of Friends), 222–223, 450, 452–453

Aristotle, 70, 386, 510–511n. 15

Athens: as Philadelphia model, 17, 51

Attkinson, William, 241, 243

Authenticity of emotion, 64, 82–85, 87–94, 97, 103–104, 228, 305, 374

Authority, 6, 15, 564n. 14; and love, 112–116, 119, 128–131, 140, 146–149; and anger, 163; and mercy, 268; gendered, and grief, 287, 294–320, 332; and Indian condolence ceremonies, 330–331; Indian versus Anglo-American models of, 332–334; in backcountry conflicts, 338, 341, 381; in revolutionary age, 393, 452–454

Backcountry: cultural characteristics of, 44, 51, 181, 192, 214, 336, 340–351, 355–358, 360, 363–372, 382

Barton, Thomas, 44, 209–210, 213–214, 226–227, 340–341, 351, 356, 360

Belcher, Jonathan, 115

Bell, Robert: as provedore to the sentimentalists, 446, 589–590n. 18

Benezet, Anthony: and critique of selfishness, 37; and antiwar stance, 37; and antislavery activism, 37, 43, 282; and Revolutionary activism, 453–454, 461–462, 469

Benezet, Joyce, 308

Boston Massacre, 425–427

Boston Port Act, 427–429

Bostwick, Rev. David, 303, 305, 309–311

Bouquet, Col. Henry, 93, 261, 366–381

Braddock, Gen. Edward: death and defeat of, 208–209, 255, 362

Bradford, Tace: on sociable sympathy, 243; on restraint, 293; and leverage, 334; marriage of, 442

Bradford, Thomas: and male sympathy, 248–249; and Indian affairs, 330–331; as Revolutionary printer, 442

Bradford, William: as publisher of Pope, 28–29, 31–32, 42–45; as Revolutionary printer, 399–400, 442

Bradford family: on death of Jesse Leech, 285–288; on death of Samuel Davies, 302–303; and comparison of deaths, 316

Brown, Daniel, 291

Brown, William, 538n. 8

Burd, James, 93–94, 183, 261

Burd, Sally (Shippen), 183

Captivity, 37, 196, 252–253, 330, 336, 354, 363, 370, 374–375

Carmichael, Rev. John, 450, 454, 460, 463, 466, 473

Chalmers, James, 441, 444–445, 448, 471

Chase, Thomas, 264

Cheerfulness: as acceptance of social place, 5–6, 68–69, 84–85, 94, 96, 105, 239; withholding of, as means of protest, 69–70, 75, 78, 293; and black emotion, 70–75; in Indian diplomacy, 326; and Revolutionary protests, 412

Chew, Benjamin, Sr.: as member of Library Company, 26; as mentor to Francis Hopkinson, 65; at Easton conference, 151–154, 164–167, 171–172, 177–179, 184–186, 194–195; loyalism of, during American Revolution, 457, 474–475

and Gibson), 341–343, 351, 354, 359, 365

Declaration of Independence, The, 387–388

Deference: emotional indicators of, 77–81, 99, 344; and affection, 115–116; anger as denial of, 160; in Indian diplomacy, 327–328, 354

Delaware Indians, 125, 140, 142, 166, 172, 177, 185, 198, 212, 221–222, 225, 288, 321–322, 328–329, 347, 355–356, 361, 367, 369–370, 377

Denny, William, 142, 151, 153–155, 164, 167, 198–199, 326, 328–330

Dickinson, John, 418–422, 430, 583–584n. 50, 597n. 78

Dillwyn, George, 312

Dinwiddie, Robert, 175

Disposition: defined, 66–67

Doctrine of Christianity, The (Smith), 206–207

Dominion of Providence, The (Witherspoon), 443, 446–449, 470, 472

Dove, James, 342, 346, 349–350

Down looks, 68, 72–73, 79, 410

Drinker, Elizabeth (Sandwith): as reader of Pope, 53; and courtship with Henry Drinker, 107, 111, 120–121, 131–132, 145–148; on women's roles, 120, 145; Revolutionary neutrality of, 457–459

Drinker, Henry, 107, 111, 131–132, 145–148, 457–459

Drinker, John, 457–458

Duché, Jacob, 463

Dunlap, William, 43, 49, 51; as printer of Pope, 43–45, 49, 51–55

Durham, Ebenezer, 226–227

Eastburn, Robert, 261, 363

Easton, Pa., treaty negotiations at, 151–199, 225, 326–328, 330

Edwards, Jonathan, 483, 502n. 23, 598n. 5

Emlen, Elizabeth (Moode), 53, 120, 131–132, 145–146, 469

Emlen, Margaret (Peggy), 131, 146, 266, 269, 291

Emotion: history of, 3, 11, 496n. 13; in daily life, 5–7; in politics, 5–7, 14; anthropological versus psychological study of, 11–12; definition of, 12, 481–482; academic theories of, 493n. 5, 495n. 12

—dilemmas of, 9, 13, 17–19, 61–105; and self versus social order, 65–75, 102–105; and expression versus control, 75–82; and social authenticity versus personal sincerity, 82–89; and Indian diplomacy, 89–95; and religious requirements, 96–102; and anger versus sympathy, 232–234; and feeling versus passion, 380–383

—distinctions in vocabulary of, 481–486, 550–551n. 56; affection, 482–483; feeling, 482–483; sensibility, 483; sentiment, 484; passion, 484–486

Emotives, 495n. 12

Epistles, Quaker: (1754), 37, 41; (1755), 202, 208, 451; (1759), 230; (1760), 231–232; (1775), 451–452

Essay on Man, An (Pope), 4, 13, 17–60, 173–174, 277, 380, 442, 451; Pennsylvania publication of, 18, 28–30, 43–45, 51–55, 498n. 3; importation of, 18, 59, 498n. 3, 501–502n. 17; Pope's commentary on, 29–32, 45–47, 49,

58; and women readers, 53, 237, 240, 507–508n. 62; in college curricula, 63; Revolutionary influence of, 462–463, 476–478, 597n. 78

Evangelical religions, 3, 14, 56–57, 118–119, 162, 203–207, 213–219, 226–228, 230–234, 241, 289, 482–484, 537n. 5, 552n. 69

False friends, 85–86, 93

Feelings: and social good, 8, 14, 41, 43, 54, 58, 63–64, 68, 76, 237, 475

Fergusson, Elizabeth (Graeme): as reader of Pope, 53, 240; and courtship with William Franklin, 107–108, 121–122, 130–133, 134, 144–145, 235–237, 280; reflections of, on self versus society, 240–241, 243–244, 249–250, 258–261, 265–267, 279–283; Revolutionary troubles of, 463–464

Fidelia (Hannah Griffitts), 295, 304–307, 557n. 37

Finley, Rev. Samuel, 223–225, 361

Flower, Mary, 68, 100–101, 190

Fothergill, Dr. John, 234

Fothergill, Samuel, 303

Franklin, Benjamin: and Library Company founding, 17; as reader of Pope, 21; as popularizer of Pope, 24–27; as author of *Plain Truth*, 34, 41, 158; as slaveholder, 39; and *Narrative*, 336–337, 341

Franklin, William: and courtship with Elizabeth Graeme, 107–108, 121–122, 130–133, 134, 144–145, 235–237, 280; as governor of New Jersey, 111, 143–144

Freedom of the will, 30–33, 77; Jonathan Edwards on, 502n. 23

Freemasons, 80

Friendly Association (Quakers), 165–166, 178, 222, 327–329, 347

Gentility, 48, 261, 337–340, 342, 345, 347, 359, 372, 382, 415; and colonial provincialism, 8–9; and claims of local elites, 45, 64, 339, 357, 360, 369; and civility, 64, 95, 152; and emotional modulation, 78, 82, 96, 152, 409, 476

George II (king of England), 113, 216, 305, 309, 321, 332

George III (king of England), 388, 439, 459–460, 465, 470

George and Lewis [Scull], 216–218, 460

Gibson, James: and Paxton controversy, 335–336, 341, 350–351, 354, 356–360, 375

God, emotions of, 35, 155, 167, 203–207, 268, 270–271, 294–298

Gordon, Patrick, 116–117

Graeme, Ann, 97, 235, 237–238, 249, 258–259, 268

Graeme, Elizabeth. *See* Fergusson, Elizabeth (Graeme)

Graeme, Thomas, 235, 237, 238, 249, 258

Great Awakening. *See* Evangelical religions

Greenville, George, 388, 415

Greer, Thomas, 538n. 8

Grief, 286–334; and expression of status distinctions, 286–288; defined, 287; standards for expression of, 288–293; religious, 289–290; civilized, 290; social, 291–293; and gendered authority, 294–302, 571n. 87; and ritualized rebellion, 298–300;

as tribute to public figures, 303–309; for paternal figures, 310–320, 558n. 50; and condolence in Indian diplomacy, 321–332; and conceptions of self, 331–334; versus experience, 554n. 3

Griffith, Alice, 296–297

Griffitts, Hannah. *See* Fidelia

Grimes, Moses, 102

Hall, David, 18

Hamilton, James, 139, 321, 364

Happiness, 47–48

Harris, Rev. Matthias, 221–222, 351

Hill, Hannah, 302

Hill, Richard, 301, 317

Hendrick (Mohawk speaker), 362, 376

Hopkinson, Francis: and Library Company, 36, 59; as reader of Pope, 59; biographical sketch of, 61–62; and social dilemmas, 65–68, 73–76; on cheerfulness, 75; on restraint, 82; on difficulties of emotional interpretation, 82–84; and sincerity, 88–90, 96–97; and friendship with Elizabeth Graeme, 237, 261; on male sensibility, 261; and feeling limits, 265–266; and Revolutionary spirit, 448–449; as signer of Declaration of Independence, 449

Hopkinson, Thomas, 61

Hoskins, Jane, 242

Howell, Joshua, 248

Hugh, Ellis, 296–297

Human nature, 4–5, 18, 40, 49, 54, 103, 168, 192, 198–199, 336–337, 349–350, 367, 372, 383, 441, 448, 462, 475–477

Hume, Sophia, 167, 269, 289

Hunt, Isaac, 444

Hunt, William, 85, 195

Illness: of body and emotion, 97–101, 235–237, 249, 597–598n. 2

Individualism, 8, 12, 14, 19, 39, 54, 57, 63–64, 66–67, 74, 105, 108–110, 118–119, 149, 203, 239–241, 268, 281, 283, 332–333, 478, 544n. 9

Inglis, Charles, 301

Inhumanity, 14, 214–215, 253–255, 335–336, 338–341, 345, 357

Iroquois, Six Nations of, 91, 126, 139–140, 142, 322, 324, 362, 376

Jackson, Alice, 308–309

Jefferson, Thomas, 474–475, 478

Johnson, Sir William, 92, 322, 329

Kawania Che Keeteru [Scull], 216–218, 459–460

Kenny, James, 90–91, 98, 192–196, 268

King George's War, 203–207

Kinsey, John, 84

Lathrop, John, 330–331, 443

Lawfulness of Defensive War, The (Lidenius), 213–215, 220, 257, 450

Lawrence, Thomas, 315, 549n. 48

Leech, Jesse, 285–288, 302–303, 307, 334

Liberalism, 542–543n. 65

Liberty: and passion, 8, 10; funerals for, 408–418

Library Company of Philadelphia, 17

Lidenius, Rev. John Abraham, 213–215, 220, 257, 450

Life cycle: as analytic category, 111–112, 520–521nn. 9–11

Lloyd, David, 242

Lloyd, Grace, 242

Locke, John (*Two Treatises of Government*), 18, 44, 474; and theories of marriage and political consent, 148–149, 527–528n. 83; and theories of passion and action, 599n. 12

Logan, James: on Pope and dangerous passions, 22–27, 30, 32, 33, 38; death of, 312; and Library Company, 500n. 9, 501n. 14

Logan, Sally, 131, 146, 266

Logan, Sarah, 312

Logan, William, 171–172, 242, 291

Love and affection, 107–150; Christian views of, 38–40; and union of interests, 109, 121–131; and social dominance, 111–121; vocabulary of, 115, 117, 124, 522n. 17; of country, 128, 206, 209, 385–386, 388, 435, 456, 465; role of, in consent, 129–131, 134, 137, 142, 147–149, 526n. 60, 527–528n. 83; and political alienation, 131–145, 593n. 61; and obfuscation of power, 145–150; and Lockean theories of marriage, 148–149, 527–528n. 83; in opposition to anger, 167–171; of liberty, 380–383, 387, 410, 412, 418–422, 428–429, 437; brotherly, 431, 452, 466, 521n. 13; and Revolutionary protests, 418–422, 428, 431–432, 435–437, 465–469

McKee, Thomas, 180

Masculinity, 9; and anger, 161, 179, 184, 190–191; and war, 213–215, 217–218, 220, 224–226, 232, 234, 337–338, 357–364, 369, 372, 379–384; and shared feeling, 244–249, 251–253,

260–265, 277, 545–546n. 16; and grief, 309; in Revolutionary rhetoric, 397, 422, 468, 593n. 59

Mason, Benjamin, 308–309

Microhierarchies, 13, 551n. 65

Mifflin, Benjamin, 87, 168

Mohawks, 177–179, 362, 376

Moode, Betsy. *See* Emlen, Elizabeth (Moode)

Moore, Milcah Martha, 168

Moral philosophy, 3, 14

Morgan, George, 77, 189, 261–262

Morgan, John, 315

Morris, Deborah, 297

Morris, Margaret (Hill), 312, 317

Morris, Robert Hunter, 86, 92, 136–138, 140–142, 212

Morris, Sarah, 307

Movement (emotional and martial): defined, 202

Music: and emotional regulation, 182–183, 256

Native Americans: captivity among, 37, as rhetorical figures, 49–50, 577–578n. 5; and emotion in diplomacy, 50; elite sympathy with, 51; and sincerity, 89–95; and affection, 125–127, 139–144; and anger, 174–179, 183; and masculinity, 203, 362–364; and sensibility, 251–258, 374–380; idealization of emotional eloquence of, 256–258; and condolence ceremonies, 290, 321–331, 354–358, 367–372; and the self, 331–334; and the spirit of liberty, 380–381, 387–388, 407, 437. *See also individual nations*

Natural equality, 3, 5, 13, 15, 48–51,

272–279, 288, 380–383, 436–440, 473, 478

385–388, 410, 412, 418–422, 425,
428–429, 431–432, 435, 437, 582–
583n. 43, 585–586n. 80; of slavery,
385–386, 388, 409–410, 422–425,
430–431, 436; of cross-class emotional unity, 386, 408, 420, 427–435,
579n. 7; of British sensibility, 388–
391, 423–424; of sympathy, 388, 397,
407, 410, 412, 415, 420–421, 424,
427–433, 437; of popular anger, 391,
396–397, 406–407, 427; of democratic emotion, 392–393; and social
control, 392, 394, 397, 407–408; of
grief, 394–407, 427; of compassion,
395–397, 406, 413–414, 418–421,
424, 428, 432–433; Pennsylvania
influence on, 395–407, 580n. 23,
581n. 30; and masculinity, 397, 418,
422–423, 430, 434–435, 579n. 7; and
funerals for liberty, 408–418; of
loyal opposition, 413–414
Ritchie, Juliana, 250, 258–259

Sandwith, Elizabeth. *See* Drinker, Elizabeth (Sandwith)
Scarroyady (Oneida leader), 324, 332,
362
Scull, Nicholas, 216–218, 459–460
Self: in tension with society, 8, 17, 19,
47, 54, 58–59, 63, 97, 103–105, 124,
203, 234, 237–239, 241, 279, 283,
478–479, 483–486, 543–544nn. 5–
6; eighteenth-century conceptions
of, 12, 14, 66–67, 74, 97, 103–105,
108, 497n. 14; submerged through
love, 111–121; versus native American
conceptions of, 332–333
Self-advancement, 15, 19, 23, 26, 32, 49,
102–103, 240, 478

Self-Defensive War Lawful, A (Carmichael), 450, 454–455, 466–467,
473
Self-love: philosophical praise of, 18–
20, 38, 40, 463, 478; popular appeal
of, 28, 45, 243, 279, 463; religious
defense of, 34, 205–206, 216, 223–
224, 454; criticism of, 37–40, 216–
219, 267, 278–279, 282, 478; and
social love, 48, 54–55, 203, 238, 243–
244
Semantics, 13, 529n. 5
Seneca George, 257–258
Senecas, 166, 257–258, 368–370
Sensibility, 211–214, 258–263, 278–279,
361–369, 379–383, 387, 436, 545–
546n. 16, 552n. 69; defined, 483
*Serious Address . . . of the Late Mas-
sacres, A,* 339–340
Serious Address to the Freeholders, A,
229–230
Sermon on the Death of King George
(Davies), 309–310
Sermon on the Present Situation, A
(Smith), 456, 466, 472–473
*Sermon Preached in the Church of
St. Peters, A* (Harris), 221–222, 351
Seven Years War: as emotional and
political turning point in Pennsylvania, 14, 35, 50, 95, 177, 195; anxieties
about slaveholding during, 37–38,
41–42, 143; and Indian emotion, 90,
126–129, 174–176, 258; and Quaker
Assembly conflicts, 135–136; and
Anglo-American identity, 183–184,
255; and politics of compassion, 277;
and emotion in diplomacy, 323–325;
definition of emotional gentility
during, 339; and urban-backcountry

532n. 38; and masculinity, 162, 179, 214; and war, 167–172, 369; and compassion, 210, 221; and civility, 261; and frontier culture, 351, 358, 363, 372; elite reliance on popular forms of, 366–367, 372, 397, 414; elite ambivalence on, 392–393, 398, 407–409

Virtue: and civic life, 17, 21, 201–202, 386–389, 393, 408–414, 419, 421; and passion, 23, 27, 36, 53, 62, 203; and classical models, 421–432, 435–436, 448, 459; limits of, 475–489, 596nn. 75–76

Warburton, William, 29–30, 45
Washington, George, 376, 385, 388, 435–437, 463

Watts, Isaac, 129, 172, 277, 499n. 3
Weiser, Conrad, 78, 91–92, 257, 290, 323–325, 328, 377
Wesley, Rev. John, 218
Whitall, Ann Cooper, 289
Whitefield, Rev. George, 112, 482; *Life*, 482
Wiley, Thomas, 251–252
Witherspoon, Rev. John, 443, 446–449, 470, 472
Wolfe, Gen. James, 183, 187, 246, 255
Women's emotional roles, 120, 121, 145–148, 161–162, 247–248, 299–301, 523n. 28, 535–536n. 80, 546n. 22
Woolman, John, 37–39, 53, 282, 303
Wright, Susannah, 33, 167, 318–319

Yeates, Jasper, 264